AFTER THE DIVORCE

A do-it-yourself guide to enforcing or modifying a divorce judgment in Michigan

By Michael Maran — Michigan Attorney

Grand River Press
P.O. Box 1342
E. Lansing, MI 48826

After the Divorce: A Do-It-Yourself Guide to Enforcing
or Modifying a Divorce Judgment in Michigan
by Michael Maran

Published by:
Grand River Press
P.O. Box 1342
E. Lansing, MI 48826

Printing history:
First edition: November 1999
Second edition: March 2005
ISBN 0-936343-15-X
Printed in the United States of America

Notice of Liability: The information in this book is provided on an "as
is" basis, without warranty. Neither the author nor the publisher shall
have any liability to any person or entity with regard to any liability,
loss, or damage caused or alleged to be caused directly or indirectly by
the information contained in this book.

Warning: This book contains information that may become outdated
when laws, court rules or court forms change.

■ **After the Divorce: A Do-It-Yourself Guide to Enforcing or Modifying a Divorce Judgment in Michigan** $29.95

    Update $1.00

ALSO AVAILABLE:

■ **The Michigan Divorce Book: A Guide to Doing an Uncontested Divorce without an Attorney (without minor children)** $24.95

■ **The Michigan Divorce Book: A Guide to Doing an Uncontested Divorce without an Attorney (with minor children)** $29.95

■ **The Michigan Estate Planning Book: A Complete Do-It Yourself Guide to Planning an Estate in Michigan** $29.95

TITLE	PRICE	QUANTITY	TOTAL

Subtotal	
Add 6% Sales Tax	
Postage	$2.50
TOTAL	

Method of Payment:

☐ Check or money order (payable to **Grand River Press**)
☐ Charge: ☐ Visa ☐ MasterCard
Account # ☐☐☐☐☐☐☐☐☐☐☐☐☐☐☐☐☐☐☐

Expiration Date   Signature

Name

Address

City   State   Zip

Please send form to: Grand River Press, P.O. Box 1342, East Lansing, Michigan 48826

Cover:
Patric Fourshe

Lettering and layout:
Altese Graphic Design

Editing:
Mark Woodbury

Contents

Chapter 1

A: Introduction

B: Questions and Answers

C: Legal Basics

Chapter 6   Alimony

Chapter 7   Name Change

Chapter 8   Tax Problems

Forms

Chapter 1

CHAPTER 1A:
Introduction

Whether your divorce was contested or uncontested, friendly or bitter, you could face problems in carrying out the divorce judgment. Lawyers call these "post-judgment" (after-judgment) matters.

Divorced people encounter all kinds of post-judgment problems, some as small as deciding who buys shoes for the children, others as important as changing the custody or residence of children. Big or small, all these problems really amount to just two things: *enforcement* of the judgment or *modification* of the judgment.

Enforcement

By far the most important document from your divorce is the judgment of divorce. Examining the divorce judgment, you'll see that the document contains a number of separate court orders, arranged by subject: end of marriage (the actual divorce), custody, parenting time (formerly known as visitation), residence (or domicile) of children, child support, alimony (also called spousal support), property division, etc. All these orders must be put into effect after your divorce.

If all goes well, you and your ex cooperate and carry out the judgment of divorce without much fuss. But if not, you must enforce the orders in the judgment against your ex, usually with the help of the court that granted the divorce.

Grounds for Enforcement

It's simple: Violation of a divorce judgment provides grounds for enforcement. The various orders inside the judgment tell the ex-spouses to do various things: take care of the children (custody order), spend time with them at specified intervals (parenting time order), maintain a residence for the children (residence-of-children order), pay child support (child support order), etc. If one of the parties disobeys any of these orders, the other party has grounds for enforcing the judgment.

To be enforceable, the orders of the judgment of divorce must be clear and forceful. Most divorce judgment orders are worded that way. But if the wording is fuzzy, it may be difficult to enforce the orders. In that case, you must have the divorce court clarify the judgment before you can enforce its orders, adding an extra step to enforcement.

Methods of Enforcement

You can sometimes enforce a divorce judgment yourself, without going to court. For example, a well-crafted judgment should authorize you to carry out the property division by recording the judgment with the register of deeds to transfer ownership of property.

You need the help of the courts for other kinds of enforcement. Your first stop is always the friend of the court when you have minor children and/or receive alimony. By law, the friend of the court is supposed to enforce all custody, parenting time, residence-of-children, child support and alimony orders. If your ex is violating any of these orders, notify the friend of the court, in writing, and it may take care of the problem for you.

These days, the friend of the court possesses a number of powerful enforcement remedies. It can enforce custody or parenting time orders by threatening the violator with a contempt of court. The friend of the court can collect child support or alimony by withholding money from the payer's income, threaten contempt or revocation of driver's, occupational or sporting/recreational licenses, reporting the nonpayment to consumer reporting agencies, such as credit bureaus, or adding surcharges to the debt. State agencies teamed with the friend of the court have other even more powerful remedies, which are described in the issue chapters in this book.

If the friend of the court won't intervene, you will have to seek enforcement yourself. Most of the friend of the court's enforcement remedies aren't available to you. But you can collect support by a contempt-of-court proceeding or normal debt collection methods, such as execution (seizure) against property or garnishment of money. It's also possible to enforce custody or parenting time orders through state, federal or international kidnapping laws, and child support and alimony orders by invoking state or federal criminal nonsupport laws.

Modification

A judgment of divorce remains in effect until the youngest child of the divorced parties reaches the age of 18. Thus, if you have young children when you divorce, your divorce judgment may govern your lives for many years to come.

During that time, the circumstances of you, your ex and children can change, requiring modification of the divorce judgment. Fortunately, divorce courts keep control of divorce cases and can modify their judgments during the post-judgment period.

As you recall from, a divorce is more than simply ending a marriage. In all, there are at least seven important issues:

- end of marriage
- custody
- parenting time
- residence of children
- child support
- alimony
- property division

Judgment orders for two of these issues—end of marriage and property division—are closed by a divorce and normally cannot be modified later. However, end of marriage and property division can be reopened after divorce if the divorce judgment is defective. See "When Is My Divorce Judgment Defective?" on page 13 for more about the things that make a judgment of divorce defective. The orders for the remaining five issues are modifiable by the divorce court, with proper grounds for modification.

New issues may also crop up after a divorce. For example, a divorce can leave lingering debt, credit or tax problems that have to be solved. Or the ex-wife may now want a name change for herself and/or the children. The divorce judgment might have to be modified, or other steps taken, to deal with these new issues.

Grounds for Modification

The customary grounds for modifying custody, parenting time, residence-of-children, child support and alimony orders have been a post-judgment change of circumstances. The person seeking modification must show a change of circumstances of the ex-spouses and/or children since divorce to obtain modification. Recently, some Michigan courts have edged away from change-of-circumstances grounds and said that modification is permissible for "proper cause" (sometimes phrased as "good cause").

Despite the different wording, the two modification grounds overlap quite a bit. The change-of-circumstances grounds are usually the bare facts for modification, while proper cause grounds are the same set of facts and a legal rule supporting modification.

Example: A father receives a cut in pay and moves for a decrease in child support, alleging the pay-cut as a change in circumstances. Proper cause for the decrease would be the reduced ability of the father to pay child support after the pay-cut (as explained in Chapter 5, the ability of parents to pay child support from their income is part of the legal basis for child support).

Both grounds are based on the same facts: the loss of pay. But the change of circumstances is just the fact of the pay-cut, while proper cause is the pay-cut and application of the legal rule of ability of the father to pay the support.

Several of the modification motion forms cite both change of circumstances and proper cause as grounds for the motion. If called for, include both grounds in your motion. Many judges are used to change of circumstances as the grounds for modification and may not allow modification for proper cause alone. By including both grounds in your motion, you cover all bases and boost your chances of winning the modification motion.

New Grounds for Child Support Modifications

Recently, new child support collection laws were passed altering the grounds for modification of child support. The new grounds, which only apply to divorces completed after June 30, 2005, are explained in detail in Chapter 5. Basically, "reasonable grounds" are necessary for friend of the court-filed modifications after a periodic review of child support by that office. Stricter "substantial change of circumstances" grounds are required for party-filed modification motions. For divorces completed before July 1, 2005, the old rules apply: A simple change of circumstances is all that's needed for either friend of the court- or party-filed modification motions.

Methods of Modification

A modification must be court-ordered to be binding legally. An informal modification where you and your ex informally agree to a change, outside of court, works while you abide by the agreement. But when there's a violation, courts will refuse to enforce your agreement, making an informal modification practically worthless.

Sometimes, you don't have to do anything for a modification, since the friend of the court does everything for you. The friend of the court is supposed to review child support periodically. It may decide that the amount ordered in your judgment needs adjustment and ask for an increase or decrease.

If you and your ex agree on the modification, you can stipulate to a modification order, without appearing in court. The court, which has the final say on all modifications, could reject your proposed modification, but will usually approve it.

No agreement? Then you must file a motion for modification. The court may refer the matter to the friend of the court for mediation or refereeing, and the issue may be settled there. If not, the motion must be heard by the judge during a court hearing. The judge decides the motion and signs an order either accepting or rejecting the proposed modification.

CHAPTER 1B: Questions and Answers

Post-judgment cases take all shapes and forms. But ex-spouses often have similar problems and ask the same questions about post-judgment procedures, such as the following topics.

Which Orders Can Be Enforced or Modified?

The focus of this book is on enforcement and modification of divorce judgments. But other family-related orders can be enforced or modified like divorce judgments. In all, these family orders can be enforced or modified with the instructions and forms in this book:

- judgment of divorce
- judgment of annulment
- judgment of separate maintenance (Michigan's version of legal separation)
- family support order
- filiation order (establishes fatherhood of out-of-wedlock children) from a paternity case

All these family orders may contain custody, parenting time, residence-of-children, child support or alimony provisions which must be enforced or can be modified. Nevertheless, the emphasis in this book is on divorce judgments and these alone will be discussed in the following chapters. But keep in mind that whatever is said about enforcement or modification of divorce judgments also applies to other kinds of family orders.

Where Do I Go to Enforce or Modify My Divorce Judgment?

For enforcement or modification of a divorce judgment, you normally return to the court and judge who granted your divorce. But in some cases you may have to go to a different court for post-judgment relief.

In January 1998, Michigan reorganized its court system and created family courts. These courts handle all family-related cases, including divorce and post-judgment cases. If you got divorced before January 1998, your case may have to be reassigned to a family court judge, unless it's already been reassigned. See "Court System" on page 21 for more about Michigan's new family court system.

Ordinarily, you go back to the judge who granted your divorce for post-judgment relief. But sometimes the judge may not be there because of death, disability, retirement, electoral defeat, reassignment to another court or some other reason. If your former judge has left the court, your divorce case will usually be assigned to the judge's successor and that's whom you go to for relief.

Sometimes, you can transfer your divorce case from the Michigan county where you were divorced to the Michigan county where you now live, and then seek post-judgment relief there. The transfer must be for the sake of convenience and in the best interests of your children. There are also strict county residence requirements. Appendix B on page 199 explains the case transfer rules and has forms to seek a transfer.

If you were divorced out of state and then moved to Michigan, you may be able to obtain post-judgment relief here. In the reverse situation—you divorced in Michigan and then moved out of state—you usually go back to the Michigan court that granted your divorce for relief. But sometimes it's possible, or necessary, to seek post-judgment relief outside Michigan. See "Can I Enforce or Modify My Divorce Judgment across State Lines?" on page 10 for more about this complicated topic.

How Soon after My Divorce Can Enforcement or Modification Begin?

After a divorce judgment is "entered" (filed with the clerk) at the end of a divorce, the judgment normally cannot be touched during the 21-day appeal period following entry of a judgment. This usually rules out enforcement or modification for 21 days after a divorce.

On the other hand, divorce judgments often specify immediate effectiveness at entry, so the judgment can be put into effect quickly after the divorce is final. There is some doubt about whether these acceleration provisions are legally permissible. The provisions are probably more acceptable in consent divorces (since the defendant's consent to a judgment with an acceleration provision could be interpreted as a waiver of the 21-day appeal period), than in true default divorces where the defendant never approves the judgment.

Until this issue is decided, just wait until the 21-day period is over before you seek enforcement or modification of the judgment.

After the 21-day appeal period expires, a divorce judgment can be enforced or modified, with the proper enforcement or modification grounds. It's the existence of grounds, not the passage of time, which is important. Thus, a very recent divorce judgment may be enforceable or modifiable with the necessary grounds, while a 10-year-old judgment cannot if the correct grounds don't exist.

How Much Time Do I Have to Enforce or Modify My Divorce Judgment?

You can enforce or modify the custody, parenting time or residence-of-children orders of your divorce judgment until each child attains the age of 18.* After that age, the children are adults and no longer subject to these orders.

Child support and alimony orders are basically orders to pay money, which become separate money judgments when support is due (weekly, monthly, etc.). In Michigan, money judgments are governed by a 10-year statute of limitations. This means you must sue to collect the support within a 10-year period, or you lose the right to sue (the support claim becomes "time-barred" in legal parlance).

There are two rules about when the 10-year clock begins ticking. For divorce judgments expiring before 1997 (judgments expire when the youngest child attains the age of 18), separate 10-year periods begin as each support payment becomes due and run out 10 years later. So, for example, an unpaid child support payment due in 1995 must be sued for by 2005 or it's time-barred.

Another rule applies for divorce judgments expiring in 1997 and afterward. For support payments from these judgments, the 10-year-clock starts when the final support payment is due under the judgment (regardless of actual payment) and runs out 10 years later. Take a divorce judgment with three minor children in which the last child support payment is due in 2000, when youngest child turns 18 and graduates from high school. Any and all support due under this judgment, even past-due amounts lingering from the 1980s or 1990s, must be sought by 2010 or it's time-barred.

As you can see, the statute of limitations rule for 1997-and-after divorce judgments is more generous. This rule excludes the period when the judgment is in effect (when the children are minors), which may be a long time, and starts the 10-year clock when the judgment expires.

There are several other limitation rules that can extend the 10-year period even further. Anytime a child support or alimony payer pays something—even a dollar—a new 10-year limitation period begins. This, incidentally, is one reason why the friend of the court is always anxious to have delinquent support payers pay something "on account."

---

* These orders can expire earlier if the children are emancipated by:
1) marriage 2) enlistment in the military 3) court order.

You can also refile a judgment ordering support, renewing the judgment, and receive another 10 years to sue. You can do this over and over, gaining new 10-year periods indefinitely.

As for modification of child support or alimony, the support can be modified anytime until expiration of the support order. Child support orders normally expire when children attain the age of 18.* Alimony orders expire according to their own terms, usually after a specified period of time or when the alimony recipient remarries or dies.

In either case, the court can normally modify future child support or alimony only, not past-due amounts, thanks to a ban on retroactive modification of support. See "Full Payment of Child Support" on page 116 for more about this full-payment rule and several exceptions to the rule.

Sometimes, divorce judgments place liens on real property to secure the payment of support or other obligations. These judgment-imposed liens are governed by a 15-year limitation period.

Can I Enforce or Modify My Divorce Judgment If I Didn't Contest It at Divorce?

Around 96% of Michigan divorces are uncontested. In these cases, one of the parties appears briefly to contest the case, but ultimately withdraws after a settlement, or else never appears at all. Whichever party you were, the active or passive one, you can enforce or modify your judgment after divorce without restriction or limitation.

Can I Enforce or Modify My Divorce Judgment across State Lines?

Interstate enforcement or modification of divorce judgments is a complex subject involving a number of hard-to-understand state and federal laws. Moreover, interstate proceedings are shaped by a variety of factual circumstances, such as which state granted the divorce, state where post-judgment relief is sought, residence of the parties, residence of the children, etc.

All these variables make generalizing about interstate proceedings difficult. Nevertheless, a few general rules are true:

- you can usually enforce a divorce judgment anywhere in the country, not just in the state that granted the divorce
- modification of out-of-state divorce judgment orders normally goes back to the state granting the divorce, with a few important exceptions

Each issue chapter in this book has a fuller explanation of interstate proceedings. These chapters also describe any special steps for enforcing or modifying out-of-state orders in Michigan.

---

*   Sometimes, child support can terminate before age 18 or last longer. See "Modification" on page 122 for more about these exceptions.

Thankfully, in most cases you won't have to worry much about interstate enforcement or modification because the friend of the court will do the paperwork for you. But even when the friend of the court takes the case, you still benefit by knowing a little about how interstate proceedings work. And sometimes, the friend of the court may decline to get involved and you must handle the interstate proceeding yourself.

Can I Enforce or Modify My Divorce Judgment during an Appeal?

If you or your ex was dissatisfied with your divorce judgment, one (or both) of you may have appealed the judgment. Ordinarily, an appeal must be filed within 21 days after entry (filing) of the judgment. But in exceptional cases late appeals are permissible.

While an appeal is pending, the divorce judgment is often frozen until the appeal is decided by the court of appeals, which can take months or even years. During an appeal, the judgment is enforceable, unless proceedings in the case are "stayed" by the divorce court or the court of appeals. In appeals, stays are often issued by courts or agreed to by the parties, effectively freezing the case until completion of the appeal.

With or without a stay, an appealed divorce judgment cannot normally be modified. Under some circumstances, the judgment can be modified by the court of appeals or by the agreement of the parties.

What If My Ex or I Am in the Military?

There are state and federal laws protecting *active-duty* military servicemembers from lawsuits and judgments (including divorce and post-judgment cases), which they cannot deal with because of their military service.

These military relief laws usually won't prevent enforcement or modification of a divorce judgment against a servicemember, although extra steps may have to be taken during the case to protect the servicemember. Appendix C on page 207 has more about post-judgment relief when you or your ex is in the military.

What If My Ex or I Am Imprisoned?

If your ex is an inmate at a Michigan prison, several special steps must be taken during a custody case. These guarantee the inmate due process when his/her parental custody rights are at stake. See "Special Motion Preparation When Your Ex Is Imprisoned" on page 67 for more about these special procedures.

You must follow these special procedures if you are filing a motion to enforce or modify custody against an incarcerated ex-spouse. If you are the prisoner, make sure you receive these due process protections during a custody case.

What If My Ex or I Am Native American?

If you or your ex are Native American, you may have been divorced in a regular state court. Or you might have received the divorce from a tribal court, which can also issue divorces.

When you got a tribal divorce, there are some special issues about enforcement or modification of the divorce judgment in Michigan courts.

The state has reciprocity agreements with most of the 16 legally-recognized Indian tribes in Michigan, allowing mutual enforcement of judgments in both court systems. If your tribal divorce judgment was issued by a participating tribe, it's enforceable in state court.

For custody modification, Indian tribes are treated like states, so the interstate custody modification rules described in "Interstate Enforcement and Modification" on page 62 apply to the motion. There is a federal law, the Indian Child Welfare Act, protecting the custody of Native American children. However, this law doesn't normally apply to divorce or post-judgment custody cases between parents. It does apply when nonparent third parties seek custody of Native American children.

> ### More Information
>
> About whether a Michigan Indian tribe has a reciprocity agreement with the state, contact the State Court Administrative Office at (517) 373-0130.

Can Special Arrangements Be Made for My Courthouse Appearance?

If you have a handicap (mobility, vision, speech or hearing impairment), court personnel can make special accommodations when you must appear at the courthouse for a hearing or other reason. For non-English-speakers, the court can appoint an interpreter to translate the court proceedings into your language.

Handicapper Accommodations

Tell court personnel about the handicap by preparing a Request for Accommodations (MC 70) (see the sample MC 70 at the end of this section). File or send the form to the clerk well ahead of your scheduled appearance. Court personnel will contact you before the appearance and discuss the accommodations you need.

Foreign Language Interpreters

The court can appoint a foreign language interpreter if you can't speak English well enough to understand the court proceedings. Use the Motion and Order for Appointment of Foreign Language Interpreter (MC 81) (a sample MC 81 appears at the end of this section). The judge may skip a hearing on this motion and simply sign the appointment order.

Must I Use My Divorce Lawyer When I File a Post-Judgment Case?

When a lawyer represents a client in a lawsuit, the lawyer's representation officially ends 21 days after entry (filing) of the judgment in the case. This 21-day rule applies to divorce. So three weeks after the divorce judgment is entered, your divorce lawyer, if you had one, leaves the case. Afterward, you are under no obligation to go back to that lawyer, or another one, for enforcement or modification of your divorce judgment.

Why Can't My Ex and I Modify Our Divorce Judgment Informally?

Suppose you and your ex agree amicably to modify your divorce judgment. You may wonder why you have to take the trouble of going back to court for approval of your informal modification. After all, why can't you modify between yourselves and leave the court out?

The main problem with an informal out-of-court modification is that it isn't legally binding. If something goes wrong, and you or your ex wants to enforce your informal modification, you can't get court enforcement.

There are other problems with informal modifications. For example, informally modified alimony might not qualify as alimony for tax purposes, and therefore cannot be claimed as an income tax deduction by the payer.

When Is My Divorce Judgment Defective?

As mentioned in "Modification" on page 5, several divorce issues—custody, parenting time, residence of children, child support and alimony—stay open after divorce and may be enforced or modified then.

But the end-of-marriage and property division issues are typically closed by a legally valid divorce judgment and cannot be touched afterward. There is an exception to this rule when the divorce judgment is legally defective. Then and only then may the end-of-marriage and property division issues be reviewed and possibly modified.

A divorce judgment can be defective for several reasons. The divorce case that produced the judgment may have been marred by legal irregularities, such as a lack of jurisdiction, improper service of divorce papers or other procedural problems. If these irregularities were serious, the entire divorce, including the judgment of divorce, is defective.

Or just the divorce judgment itself may be defective. A judgment can be tainted by fraud, misrepresentation, mistake, inequity or unfairness, existence of new evidence challenging the judgment, excusable neglect of the divorce by one party or misconduct by a party. For example, a party may have filed false divorce papers concealing property or debts. This kind of fraud or misrepresentation could have made the judgment defective, allowing reopening of the judgment's property division order.

In special situations, military servicemembers can reopen divorce judgments and possibly modify closed issues like end-of-marriage and property division. The federal Servicemembers Civil Relief Act (SCRA), which is explained in Appendix C on page 207, sometimes allows *nonresponding* defendant-servicemembers in default divorces to reopen divorce judgments issued during service (or within 60 days afterward), if the reopening request is made within 90 days of separation from service. This is a complicated issue. For more advice, contact a military legal assistance ("JAG") lawyer or civilian lawyer knowledgeable in military law.

How Much Does Post-Judgment Relief Cost?

More Information

About finding Michigan divorce judgments, contact Michigan's vital records office:

Department of Community Health
Vital Records & Health Statistics
P.O. Box 30195
Lansing, MI 48909
(517) 335-8496

Or order Michigan vital records online at www.michigan.gov/mdch

To find vital records offices in other states, order the booklet "Where to Write for Vital Records" (#107L), by sending a $4.25 check (payable to "Superintendent of Documents"), to:

R. Woods
CIC - 01A
P.O. Box 100
Pueblo, CO 81002

You can also order this booklet with a credit card by calling (888) 878-3256. Or you can read or print the booklet at this Web site: www.pueblo.gsa.gov.

If you and your ex do an agreed-to modification, by "stipulation," the modification costs nothing, except your time in preparing and submitting the modification papers to the court.

Contested enforcement or modification requires a motion and payment of a $20 motion filing fee. For modification of child support, an extra $40 fee must also be paid.

If a full-blown evidentiary hearing is necessary to decide the motion, there may be miscellaneous fees and costs, such as court attendance fees for subpoenaed witnesses ($12-15 per witness per day and travel mileage to and from the courthouse) and the cost of serving subpoenas on the witnesses ($0-40 according to the method used for service of the subpoena)

In a name change case for you and/or your children, there is a $10 filing fee and the variable cost of publishing a legal notice in the newspaper.

You can get an exemption from payment of many of these fees and costs if you are receiving public assistance or qualify as a low-income person. Appendix A on page 195 has instructions and the form to apply for a fee exemption.

Where Can I Get a Copy of My Divorce Judgment If I Lost the Document?

To enforce or modify your divorce judgment, you need a copy of the judgment for reference. If you lost the document, you can get another copy by contacting the clerk of the court that granted your divorce. In Michigan, that clerk is the clerk of the family court. See "Court System" on page 21 for more about locating the family court clerk in your county. For an out-of-state divorce, contact the clerk of the court that granted your divorce in that state.

Lawyers normally keep files from closed cases for many years. If you had a lawyer during your divorce, contact the lawyer and request a copy of your divorce judgment. The lawyer should provide the document to you as a courtesy.

Yet another way to trace divorce documents is through a state vital records office. Every state has a vital records office compiling records of births, deaths, marriages and divorces. By calling or writing that office in the state where your divorce was granted, you can find your divorce judgment. The vital records office will either have the judgment itself or can tell you which court clerk has the document on file and you can get it there.

How Do I Withdraw a Request for Post-Judgment Relief?

If you file an enforcement or modification motion and then want to withdraw it, dismissal of the motion is easy. You simply call or write the clerk and ask for withdrawal of your motion and cancellation of any scheduled motion hearing. Do this as soon as possible, so the clerk can reassign your motion hearing slot to another case.

Must I Have the Friend of the Court in My Case?

Ordinarily, the friend of the court, who is a family court official, must participate in all post-judgment divorce cases with minor children and/or alimony. The friend of the court performs a number of functions in these cases, including investigation and recommendation to the judge on post-judgment issues, refereeing, mediation, review of orders and modification and enforcement of the divorce judgment (see "Friend of the Court" on page 38 for more about the friend of the court and its duties).

In most cases, the friend of the court's participation is beneficial. The friend of the court is a neutral third party who can help settle any disputes that erupt. Its support bookkeeping is particularly useful. Nevertheless, some post-judgment cases are completely amicable and the parties don't need or want friend of the court services.

Under a 2002 law, it's now possible to "opt out" of the friend of the court system—totally, partially or in a limited way—and manage the post-judgment case yourself. This isn't always wise and many cases are ineligible for opt-out. Appendix D on page 215 has more about the pluses and minuses of opting out, the three types of opt-outs, opt-out restrictions and the instructions and forms for opting out.

Opting Back into the Friend of the Court System

Or you may want to go in the reverse direction: You've previously opted out of the friend of the court system and now you want to get back in. Appendix D on page 215 also has the form and information to do this.

What If the Friend of the Court Won't Help Me?

As explained above, the friend of the court does many things during post-judgment divorce (investigation and recommendation, refereeing, mediation, etc.).

Some of this activity is discretionary; the friend of the court can decide whether it should act. Other interventions are required by law. For example, the friend of the court must enforce custody, parenting time, residence-of-children and support orders. There are other times when the friend of the court must do something in post-judgment cases and these are described in the issue chapters.

When the friend of the court intervenes, it must treat the parties with politeness and courtesy. The friend of the court must also be impartial, avoiding bias or discrimination (because of race, color, disability, age, sex, marital status, religion, national origin or political belief) against the parties.

What can you do if the friend of the court refuses to act when it should or acts unprofessionally after intervention in your case? One solution is filing a grievance against the friend of the court. Use the Friend of the Court Grievance (FOC 1a) for your complaint. The reverse side of the form has complete filing instructions, and information about pursuing the grievance if the chief judge of the circuit court rejects it. A sample grievance form also appears at the end of this section.

As the FOC 1a instructions emphasize, you cannot grieve a legal decision by a friend of the court referee or the judge. If you're unhappy with a legal decision, you can object to a referee's recommendation or appeal the judge's decision on your motion to the court of appeals.

What If a Third Party Is Involved or Intervenes in My Case?

Post-judgment cases are usually between parent-parties only. But sometimes, so-called third parties, who may be grandparents, siblings, foster-parents or others, may already be present or appear in the case. These nonparent third parties may have or seek custody, parenting time, control of the children's residence and even child support in several situations:*

Involvement. When a post-judgment case is filed, a third party may already have court-ordered custody or parenting time from a pre-divorce case, the divorce case itself or a prior post-judgment case. Sometimes, parents voluntarily turn over custody to third parties informally, without court orders.

Intervention. A third party may not have custody or parenting time, but wants it. Ordinarily, Michigan law makes it very difficult for a third party to seek custody or parenting time of children from an intact family. But a divorce opens the door to some third-party claims for custody and/or parenting time. Except for "grandparenting time," a third party cannot normally file/bring the claim directly, but may intervene in a post-judgment case filed by a parent and seek custody or parenting time. Once in the case,

---

*   Third parties cannot seek child support without custody, but may ask for it after becoming a custodian of the children. See "Redirection and Termination of Child Support" on page 113 for more about directing child support to new custodians.

the third party faces more difficulty, because Michigan law strongly favors parents over third-party claimants.

Whichever way third parties appear—by prior involvement in your case or current intervention—they make a post-judgment case more complicated. In general, you have to treat a third party as an extra party to the case. You should add the third party to your post-judgment papers (some papers have a special caption box for them; for papers that don't, try to squeeze the third party's name and address into the defendant's caption box).

For a modification by stipulation, the third party must sign the modification order (again, some forms have a separate place for this; in others you will have to improvise). You must also serve a copy of the modification order on the third party after the judge signs it. In a contested case, the third party must receive all the modification papers filed in the case (motion, response to motion, order, etc.), and be allowed to participate in any motion hearings.

Can I Appeal the Decision on My Post-Judgment Motion?

When you want to appeal a final divorce judgment, you have the right to file an appeal with the court of appeals within 21 days after entry (filing) of the judgment, or seek a late appeal later. By contrast, most post-judgment motions to enforce or modify that same divorce judgment result in court orders that are not fully appealable.

Post-judgment decisions are considered nonfinal orders, which are appealable only by leave (special permission) of the court of appeals. There is an exception for post-judgment orders concerning custody; these are directly appealable to the court of appeals without prior leave of the court.

Whether your appeal is by leave or by right, the appeal is bound to be complicated and far beyond the scope of this book. Contact a lawyer who does appellate work if you're serious about filing an appeal of a post-judgment decision.

Original - Friend of the court/Chief judge/
Citizen Advisory Committee
1st copy - Grieving party (with response)
2nd copy - SCAO (with response)
3rd copy - Grieving party (on filing)

Approved, SCAO

| STATE OF MICHIGAN
JUDICIAL CIRCUIT
COUNTY | FRIEND OF THE COURT GRIEVANCE
☒ Friend of the Court   ☐ Chief Judge
☐ Citizen Advisory Committee | THIS SPACE FOR COURT USE ONLY
CASE NO.:
GRIEVANCE NO.:
DATE RECEIVED |

Friend of the Court address

Plaintiff's name and address

v

Defendant's name and address

> FILL OUT
> CAPTION ON THIS
> AND ALL OTHER
> PAPERS AS SHOWN
> IN "PAPERS" IN
> CHAPTER 1C.

County: OJIBWAY   This grievance is about   ☒ employee(s).
                                                          ☐ office operations.
                                                          ☐ a decision based on gender
                                                             rather than the best interests of
                                                             the child.

STATEMENT OF GRIEVANCE:

THE DEFENDANT HAS VIOLATED THE PARENTING TIME ORDER MANY TIMES, BY REFUSING TO RETURN THE CHILDREN ON TIME.

I COMPLAINED TO THE FRIEND OF THE COURT ABOUT THESE VIOLATIONS ON AUG. 2, 1998, SEPT. 30, 1998, OCT. 20, 1998 AND DEC. 10, 1998, BUT THE FRIEND OF THE COURT HAS REFUSED TO ENFORCE THE PARENTING TIME ORDER.

AFTER MY LAST COMPLAINT IN DECEMBER, MR. MILLER, MY FRIEND OF THE COURT CASEWORKER, WAS RUDE TO ME ON THE TELEPHONE.

1-1-99   772-0000   Darlene Lovelace
Date   Your telephone no.   Signature

SEE INSTRUCTONS ON BACK OF FORM

MCL 552.526; MSA 25.176(26)

FOC 1a (4/01) FRIEND OF THE COURT GRIEVANCE

Approved, SCAO

REQUEST FOR ACCOMMODATIONS	Court name and location OJIBWAY COUNTY CIRCUIT COURT– FAMILY DIVISION 200 N. MAIN LAKE CITY, MI 48800

Today's date 1-7-99	Instructions for completing form: Provide your name, address, and telephone number. Check the boxes which apply to you and provide any necessary details. When you have completed this request, please return it to the court at the above address.

1. **Name**
DARLENE A. LOVELACE

Address
121 S. MAIN

City LAKE CITY	State MI	Zip 48800	Telephone no. 772-0000

2. Court activity you need accommodations for:

☒ Hearing 2-15-99
Date

☐ Mediation meeting _____
Date

☐ Jury duty _____
Date(s)

☐ Other (specify): _____
Include dates if relevant

3. What is the nature of your disability? _____

☒ Physical mobility impairment (wheelchair, walker, crutches, etc.)

☐ Speech impairment (specify): _____

☐ Visual impairment _____

☐ Hearing impairment (specify)   ☐ deaf   ☐ hard of hearing

☐ Other (specify): _____

4. What type of accommodation are you requesting? _____

☐ Interpreter for deaf (specify whether ASL, tactile, oral, etc.) _____

☐ Assistive listening device (specify type of device) _____

☒ Physical location accessible for persons with a physical mobility concern.

☐ Other (specify) _____

For court use only

MC 70 (10/97) **REQUEST FOR ACCOMMODATIONS**

Original - Court file 1st copy - Assignment Clerk/Extra 2nd copy - Friend of the Court/Extra	3rd copy - Opposing party 4th copy - Moving party

Approved, SCAO

STATE OF MICHIGAN JUDICIAL DISTRICT JUDICIAL CIRCUIT COUNTY	MOTION AND ORDER FOR APPOINTMENT OF FOREIGN LANGUAGE INTERPRETER	CASE NO.
		Court telephone no.

Court address

Plaintiff name(s) ☐ moving party	v	Defendant name(s) ☐ moving party
Plaintiff's attorney, bar no., address, and telephone no.		Defendant's attorney, bar no., address, and telephone no.

MOTION

1. I state that I am unable to speak English sufficiently to understand and participate in the proceedings in this case.

2. ☐ I am represented by an attorney.   ☒ I am not represented by an attorney.

3. I request the court to appoint a foreign language interpreter to interpret for me.

4. I request an interpreter who speaks the _KOREAN_ language.

5. If required, place my request on the motion calendar.

Darlene Lovelace
Signature

_1-1-99_
Date

NOTICE OF HEARING

To be completed only if the court
requires a hearing on the motion

You are notified that a hearing has been scheduled on this matter for:

	Bar no.	Date	Time
Judge			
Hearing location			
☐ Court address above ☐			

If you require special accommodations to use the court because of disabilities, please contact the court immediately to make arrangements.

_____
Date

_____
Signature

CERTIFICATE OF MAILING

I certify that on this date I mailed a copy of this motion and notice of hearing (if applicable) to the other party at the last known address.

Darlene Lovelace
Signature

_1-2-99_
Date

ORDER

IT IS ORDERED the above motion is   ☒ granted.   ☐ denied.

Lester Tubbs
Judge

_1-2-99_
Date

MC 81 (10/01) **MOTION AND ORDER FOR APPOINTMENT OF FOREIGN LANGUAGE INTERPRETER**

> THE CLERK WILL SCHEDULE A HEARING ON THE MOTION IF NECESSARY.

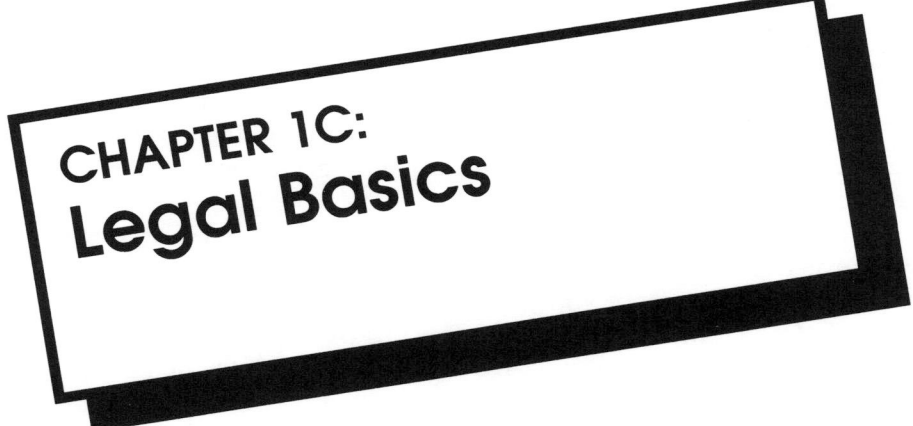

CHAPTER 1C:
Legal Basics

Ordinarily, it's difficult to represent yourself in court. You can never seem to find the right legal forms. And court personnel are often unable or unwilling to answer your questions.

Post-judgment divorce is different. You are actually encouraged to handle post-judgment matters yourself, without a lawyer. The state has issued do-it-yourself legal forms (many of these are included in this book), which county friends of the court must provide to divorced parents. The friend of the court is also required, by law, to assist in many kinds of post-judgment cases.

Despite all this help, nonlawyers filing post-judgment motions are often stumped by basic questions: Where do I go to file motion papers? How many copies of the papers do I need? On whom do I serve the papers? This section deals with all these problems and more, so you will be well-prepared and confident when you seek post-judgment relief.

Court System

Before 1998, divorce cases were handled by the general circuit courts of Michigan. On Jan. 1, 1998, Michigan's court system was reorganized and new family courts (which are actually divisions of the circuit courts) went into operation. Michigan family courts deal with all kinds of family-related cases: divorce (including post-judgment matters), annulment, separate maintenance, family support, custody, parenting time, paternity, domestic violence, child abuse and neglect, juvenile delinquency, guardianship/conservatorship, adoption, emancipation of minors and name change cases.

Family courts are designed to specialize in family law matters, unlike the general circuit courts which deal with all kinds of civil and criminal cases. Family courts also have a "one-family, one-judge" policy, which brings all of a family's cases before the same judge, who is familiar with the family and its problems.

The court reorganization may have an impact on where you go for post-judgment relief. If you got a divorce after Jan. 1, 1998, from one of the family courts, that's where you get post-judgment relief. But if you were divorced before Jan. 1, 1998, your case must be reassigned to a family court judge, unless it's already been reassigned. The clerk can tell you how to have a pre-1998 case reassigned to a family court judge.

Once you find the correct court, you will encounter the following court personnel with responsibility for your case:

Judge. Your post-judgment case is handled by a family court judge, who is either a circuit court or probate court judge on assignment to family court. There's a good chance the judge is the same one who handled your divorce, if you were divorced after Jan. 1, 1998, when Michigan's family court system began. But it could be a different judge if you were divorced before Jan. 1, 1998, and your case was reassigned to a family court judge. You will also get a new judge if your former judge has left the court because of death, disability, retirement, electoral defeat, reassignment to another court or some other reason.

Clerk. The family court clerk receives all your post-judgment papers and maintains a case file for them. Throughout this book, the family court clerk is simply called the clerk. In most counties, the county clerk is the clerk of the family court. But some counties have a special family court clerk, separate from the county clerk.

To find out who does the family court clerking in your county, call the county clerk and ask for information. Or simply look up the county government listing in the telephone book and see if there is a separate listing for a clerk of the family division of the circuit court.

Friend of the court. The friend of the court, as an agent of the family court, plays a number of roles in post-judgment divorce cases. The friend of the court enforces custody, parenting time, residence-of-children, child support and alimony orders. It may help in the modification of these orders. The friend of the court also investigates, referees and mediates contested post-judgment motions, in an effort to settle these motions before they go to the judge. The friend of the court was traditionally the collector and distributor of child support and alimony. But many of these duties have now been transferred to the state disbursement unit.

State disbursement unit. The SDU is a new state agency, in Lansing, which has taken over collection and distribution of child support and alimony from the local county friends of the court. See "Centralization of Child Support

Services" on page 116 for more about the SDU and the transfer of support-related duties from the friend of the court to the state unit.

Family Independence Agency. The FIA is a branch of state government (formerly the Department of Social Services (DSS)), in charge of public assistance like Family Independence Program (FIP) payments, Medicaid and other benefits. The FIA also helps in establishing and enforcing child support orders, particularly when a family is receiving public assistance.

Office of Child Support. The OCS is the division of the FIA which has taken over some of the support enforcement duties of the friend of the court.

Prosecuting attorney. In post-judgment cases, county prosecuting attorneys help friends of the court enforce divorce judgments. They also assist in interstate enforcement of child support.

Courtroom clerk. The courtroom clerk sits in the courtroom next to the judge while the court is in session. During a post-judgment motion hearing, the courtroom clerk marks and receives exhibits offered into evidence.

Assignment clerk. Several of the larger counties use special assignment clerks to schedule court hearings. In these counties, motion hearings may be scheduled by the assignment clerk.

Court reporter. The court reporter sits below the judge and records the court proceedings. During a motion hearing, the court reporter makes a record of the hearing, for reference or in case of an appeal.

Judge's secretary. Working in the judge's office, the judge's secretary may help submit papers to the judge for review.

Law clerk. Most judges have law clerks, who are often law students or new lawyers. Law clerks help judges with a number of tasks, including review of papers.

You will probably be familiar with these court personnel from your previous contact with them during your divorce. But the offices of some court personnel may have moved since then. Make sure you know where to find them now.

Papers

In most counties, it's your responsibility to prepare the papers (motions, responses to motions, orders, etc.) for post-judgment modifications. Sometimes, the friend of the court will help with the order deciding a motion. But even here, you must prepare the modification motion to get the order.

Preparing Papers

Whenever possible, type all post-judgment papers. But if you can't, it's permissible to print by hand in ink. Either way, make sure the papers are neat and legible.

The papers you file must also be accurate and honest. Judges can penalize those who intentionally or even carelessly file false legal papers. Ordinarily, these penalties are payments of money to opponents hurt by the false papers.

But for some papers, the penalties are severe. When you sign an affidavit, you swear to the notary public that the contents are true. You do much the same when you sign papers with a verification declaration ("I declare that the above statements are true to the best of my information, knowledge, and belief"). According to Michigan law, it's a crime to knowingly file a false affidavit; the intentional falsification of a verified document is a contempt of court. Don't be alarmed by these penalties; just make sure that your papers are accurate and honest.

The bulk of the papers have been issued by the State Court Administrative Office (SCAO). In fact, the basic motion, response to motion, and order forms are special do-it-yourself forms the SCAO released in early 1997. By law, the SCAO was required to design these forms, with instructions, and distribute them at county friend of the court offices. You can obtain copies of the SCAO post-judgment forms at your local friend of the court office if you need extras.

Comparison of the state-issued SCAO forms with the versions reprinted in this book reveals some differences. The SCAO forms include multi-page sets of instructions. To avoid repetition and save space, this book's SCAO forms' instructions have been edited. In particular, the sets of instructions each form comes with have been reorganized, expanded, summarized and appear just once, in this chapter. Similarly, the line-by-line instructions, which on the SCAO forms are keyed by letters of the alphabet to an instruction sheet, have also been summarized just once in this chapter and the letter keys on the forms have been removed.

The SCAO forms include Michigan court, probate court and friend of the court forms. These forms are coded in the lower left corner by type (MC, PC or FOC), number and date of release. A few counties, notably Wayne (number-coded), have local forms. To fill a few gaps in the SCAO forms, there are also several Grand River Press forms (code: GRP/number/date).

You may notice a difference in the type-size of the papers. On Jan. 1, 2004, a new court rule went into effect requiring that all court papers, except the state-issued SCAO forms, must be in 12-point type. Thus, the printing on all the GRP forms was increased to 12-point size. Also, when you fill in the papers, try to type or print in a larger size (no fine print) matching the printing on these forms.

The new court rule also specifies that all court papers must be 8½ x 11." Previously, this was the maximum size, but papers could be a little smaller. A prior edition of this book was 8½ x 11," making the perforated forms .25" smaller after detachment from the book (perforation of the forms causes a

.25" loss in the binding margin). Now, the book has been increased in overall width by .25" to make up this difference.

Captions of Papers

Every form has a special purpose and each is prepared differently. Yet all the forms share similar captions which are filled in as follows:

Approved, SCAO	Original - Court 1st copy - Other Party 2nd copy - Moving Party	3rd copy - Friend of the Court 4th copy - Proof of Service 5th copy - Proof of Service
STATE OF MICHIGAN JUDICIAL CIRCUIT OJIBWAY COUNTY	NOTICE OF HEARING TO ENTER ORDER	CASE NO. 89-00501- DM JUDGE TUBBS

Court address
200 N. MAIN, LAKE CITY, MI 48800

Court telephone no.
773-0000

Plaintiff's name, address, and telephone no. ☐ moving party DARLENE A. LOVELACE 121 S. MAIN LAKE CITY, MI 48800 772-0000	v	Defendant's name, address, and telephone no. ☒ moving party DUDLEY E. LOVELACE 900 S. MAPLE LAKE CITY, MI 48800 773-0004

Third party's name, address, and telephone no. ☐ moving party

A post-judgment motion is regarded as a continuation of the divorce case, not a new case. Thus, information from the divorce is carried over to the post-judgment case. For this, you must often refer to your divorce judgment. If you lost the judgment, see "Where Can I Get a Copy of My Divorce Judgment If I Lost the Document?" on page 14 for information about obtaining a copy of a lost judgment.

In the caption of the papers, the court/friend of the court address and telephone number (some forms ask for court information; some friend of the court information; others neither) will probably be the same as in your divorce case. But if your case has been reassigned to a new judge, in a different court, insert the new information. The case number is the same as your divorce case number.

The parties (plaintiff and defendant) also stay the same. So if you were the defendant in the divorce, you remain as defendant even when you are the moving party filing the post-judgment motion, which is normally an active plaintiff-type role.

Likewise, your names remain the same as in the divorce, although the ex-wife may have a new name from remarriage or a name change. You may, however, sign any papers using your new name. Your addresses and telephone numbers may have changed since the divorce and the new ones should be used in the captions.

Glossary

Moving party–the party filing a post-judgment motion.

Nonmoving party–the party against whom a post-judgment motion is filed and who may respond to it.

To Obtain

Extra copies of Wayne County forms, call the Wayne County Friend of the Court's form fax line at (313) 967-3662. The line has a menu where you can select the form you want, which is then faxed to a fax number you specify.

The Wayne County circuit court system also has a Web site, www.3rdcc.org, from which you can view and/or download forms.

You should have enough caption labels for all your papers. But if you run out, you can get more in the clerk's office in room 201 of the Coleman A. Young Municipal Center (CAYMC) (formerly the City-County Bldg.) at 2 Woodward Ave. in Detroit.

Keeping the parties and their names the same in the divorce and a post-judgment case helps the judge sort out the parties in the case. It also assists the clerk in keeping the case files straight.

Wayne County, which has the state's largest court system, has a special caption-labeling system to prevent mishandling of court papers. When you file a post-judgment motion in Wayne County, the clerk prints strips of caption labels for both parties. Notice how the clerk takes several of the labels and affixes them to the captions of your motion papers. As you file other papers, use labels from your strip to label them in the same way. Save the other strip of caption labels because you must give it to your ex when you serve the motion.

Copying Papers

As you prepare your papers, make three photocopies of each paper. After copying, put "FOC" (an abbreviation for friend of the court) in the upper left corner of one photocopy of each paper. The friend of the court gets copies of all your papers through the clerk. By earmarking your papers with "FOC," you ensure that these copies are directed to the friend of the court. In all, you should have enough papers and copies to distribute as follows:

- original - court (clerk)
- 1st copy - friend of the court
- 2nd copy - moving party
- 3rd copy - nonmoving party

When you photocopy papers, copy both sides of any two-sided forms because some papers have important information on the reverse. Most two-sided forms are tumble-printed with their reverse sides upside down. This makes it possible to read the reverse sides while the papers are fastened to a file folder by simply lifting them up. When you photocopy these two-sided forms, you might not be able to run your copies through the photocopier again to get a tumble-printed form. If so, just make the paper into a two-page form and staple the pages together.

With all these papers and copies, it's easy to get disorganized. To keep track of everything, make a file for all your papers. Not only will this file keep you organized during the post-judgment case, it will give you a complete record of the case afterward.

Filing Papers

When you file a post-judgment motion, the clerk will make a file for your case. As you file papers, the clerk will ordinarily use the following procedure:

- keep the original for the case file
- take the copy marked "FOC" and forward it to the friend of the court
- return a true copy* for the moving party
- return a true copy for the nonmoving party

You may file your post-judgment papers with the clerk personally, by mail or sometimes even by facsimile (fax). Despite these options, it's usually best to file in person whenever you can. By filing personally, you can pay any fees that are due and immediately get back copies of your papers for service on the other party.

For filing by mail, send your papers and any fees to the clerk along with a cover letter asking for filing and return of the copies you have enclosed. To get the copies back quickly, include a self-addressed envelope with postage.

Filing by fax isn't allowed when filing fees are due (unless you have paid in advance by depositing money with the clerk), because the clerk won't accept a filing without payment of the filing fee. Moreover, the clerk won't send or fax back copies of the papers you file, so there's no way to get copies. Thus, fax-filing should only be used in an emergency, when you have to file in a hurry to meet a filing deadline.

Serving Papers

When one party seeks post-judgment relief, the nonmoving party must receive notice of the request for relief. Notice is provided by serving the post-judgment papers on the nonmoving party.

Forms of Service

There are two basic ways for serving post-judgment papers: delivery and mail. The state-issued forms included in this book are designed for service by mail only, not delivery. Thus, service by mail, which is the easiest form of service anyway, will have to be used.

Service by Mail: Manner of Service and Time of Effectiveness

For service by mail, you simply send the post-judgment papers by ordinary first-class mail; certified or registered mailing isn't necessary.

Service by mail takes place when you *send* the papers, not when they're received. To allow for transit in the mail, the notice periods for papers served by mail are extended by a few days beyond the notice periods for service by delivery.

---

* When a clerk returns a copy of a paper to you, it may have a stamp or notation indicating that it's a true copy. This says that the copy is real. Try to get true copies of all papers you file, especially court orders.

Whom to Serve

Your post-judgment papers will probably be served on your ex-spouse. As explained in "Must I Use My Divorce Lawyer When I File a Post-Judgment Case?" on page 13, divorce lawyers officially stop representing clients 21 days after entry (filing) of a divorce judgment. After that 21-day period, the ex-spouses themselves become the parties of record in the case and must receive service of the post-judgment papers filed in the case.

The ex-spouses continue as the parties of record unless and until they retain lawyers to represent them. You will know when this happens because the lawyer normally will file a document called an appearance,* which is an official notice that the lawyer is representing a party in the case. After an appearance, the lawyer receives service of papers on behalf of his/her client.

In summary, if you are filing for post-judgment relief more than 21 days after entry of your divorce judgment, serve all the papers directly on your ex. If your ex gets a lawyer during the post-judgment case, serve all subsequent papers on the lawyer instead of your ex.

Where to Serve

For service by mail, serve the post-judgment papers on your ex at his/her last known mailing address. This could be your ex's residence or a different mailing address, such as a post office box.

You may know your ex's mailing address. But if you're in doubt, contact the friend of the court. Divorce judgments require both parties to keep current address information on file with the friend of the court, and you can usually get access to this information. The friend of the court also has special ways, such as the state and federal parent locator services, to find people on its own.

Sometimes, after an episode of domestic violence, a party may be allowed to keep his/her residence address confidential. Typically, the victim must maintain another mailing address, such as a post office box. If this has happened in your case, contact the friend of the court to find out the victim's mailing address.

The friend of the court can also assist when your ex is transient, without a current mailing address. There is a special court rule allowing the friend of the court to establish the mailing address of a transient party, including cases where the individual has disappeared and mail has been returned as undeliverable.

If your ex retains a lawyer who files an appearance in the case, serve the papers on the lawyer at the office address indicated in the appearance.

---

*   Some lawyers prefer to make their appearance by adding an appearance statement to the first motion papers they file, rather than by filing a separate appearance document.

You must also make a proof of service to show the court that your ex received the post-judgment papers. You prove service in the proof of service section (designated as the Certificate of Mailing in the motion and response-to-motion forms and as the Proof of Service in the order forms) at the bottom or on the reverse of each form.

After service, you should have remaining one copy of the paper you served. Fill out the proof of service section of this form. Make two photocopies of the form and earmark one with "FOC" in the upper left corner.

You must file the original (filled-in) proof of service copy of your form and the friend of the court's copy with the clerk, so a proof of service is on file for the judge to see. Keep a copy for yourself. Whenever possible, file the proof of service forms prior to the day of the court hearing since a proof of service should be filed before the hearing begins. In an emergency, you can file the proof forms on the day of the hearing, but absolutely no later than this time.

Fees

As described in "How Much Does Post-Judgment Relief Cost?" on page 14, there is a $20 fee for filing a post-judgment motion. If you file several post-judgment motions at the same time, a single $20 fee usually covers all filings. It costs $10 to file a name change case.

Besides filing fees, there may miscellaneous fees and costs, such as court attendance fees for subpoenaed witnesses and fees for serving subpoenas (seldom necessary), and the cost of publishing a legal notice in the newspaper during a name change case. For modification of child support, an extra $40 fee is due.

You pay the filing fees to the clerk when you file. Clerks usually accept cash, money orders and personal checks as payment (some clerks won't take checks from nonlawyers). After you pay, the clerk may give you a receipt, which you should keep as proof of payment.

Court attendance fees are payable to the subpoenaed witnesses personally. For service of subpoenas by delivery, the sheriff or process server serving the subpoenas receives the service fees. You pay the newspaper for publication of the legal notice in a name change case.

The law seems to require payment of the $40 child support modification fee when a modification order is filed. But some clerks may charge this fee up front, when a modification motion is filed.

If you qualify, you can get an exemption from payment of many of these fees and costs. You are exempt from payment if you are receiving public assistance or have a low income. Appendix A on page 195 has more about qualifying for a fee exemption, and instructions and the form to apply for the exemption.

Time

During a post-judgment case, there are several important time periods and deadlines, especially: 1) seven- or nine-day notice period for hearings on written motions 2) three- or five-day deadline for responding to a written motion 3) seven-day deadline for submitting a proposed order after a motion hearing 4) seven-day deadline for objecting to such a proposed order.

The court rules have detailed provisions to figure periods of time. For a time period of days, the period begins on the day after the day of an act (filing, service, motion hearing, etc.); the day of the act itself isn't counted. The last day of the period is counted, unless it falls on a Saturday, Sunday or legal holiday. In that case, the period extends to the next day that isn't a Saturday, Sunday or legal holiday.

Example: You serve your ex with a modification motion by mail on May 1. The nine-day notice period (for written motions served by mail) begins on May 2 (the day after the day of service). The first permissible date for the motion hearing is May 11, assuming May 11 isn't a Saturday, Sunday or legal holiday.

To avoid time problems, you can simply estimate the time period and then add a little more time for safety. For example, if you figure that a time period ends sometime during the first week of a month, you could wait until the middle of the month to take action, avoiding any danger of acting too quickly.

Stipulated Orders

If you and your ex agree on modification of your divorce judgment, you can stipulate (agree) to the change, go directly to the judge and get a modification order. With a stipulation, you don't need to file a modification motion, don't have to pay a motion filing fee (or the extra fee charged for child support modification) and can usually avoid court hearings. There are five steps to get an agreed-to stipulated order which are explained below.

1. Fill out the order form

Select the order form that matches the modification you want. There are several types of order forms:

- Order Regarding Custody and Parenting Time (FOC 89) for modification of custody alone or custody and parenting time together; add the Uniform Child Support Order (FOC 10/52) for modification of child support also
- Order Regarding Parenting Time (FOC 67) for modification of parenting time

- Order Regarding Residence of Children (GRP 22) for change of residence of children
- Uniform Child Support Order (FOC 10/52) for modification of child support
- Order Regarding Spousal Support (GRP 23) for modification of alimony (spousal support)
- Order Regarding Assignment of Dependency Exemptions (GRP 24) for reassignment of tax exemptions for dependent children

Some stipulations require multiple forms: a separate motion/stipulation form and the order form itself. If several forms are necessary for stipulation, keep the motion/stipulation together with the order as you prepare, submit (to the friend of the court and judge), file and serve the order as described below. Only a few post-judgment issues require a set of stipulation forms:

- Motion/Stipulation for Transferring Case (FOC 24) and Order Changing Venue and Transferring Case (FOC 25) to transfer a post-judgment case to another county in Michigan
- Motion/Stipulation to Opt Out of the Friend of the Court System (GRP 26) and Order Exempting Case from Friend of the Court Services (FOC 102) for total or partial opt-outs from the friend of the court system
- Agreement Suspending Immediate Income Withholding (FOC 63) and Order Suspending Immediate Income Withholding (FOC 64) for an agreed-to limited opt-out from the friend of the court system

Fill out the order as you and your ex have agreed, using the sample orders at the end of each issue chapter for guidance. Both of you must sign the order, to show that you are stipulating to it. At the beginning of the order, check the box indicating that the order is being entered "on stipulation" or "on stipulation of the parties." Then, at the end of the order, both parties must sign their names in the spaces provided.

If a stipulation requires a set of forms, you and your ex must sign the motion/stipulation form (such as the FOC 24, GRP 26 or FOC 63), while the judge alone signs the order form.

2. Obtain friend of the court approval of the order [if necessary]

In some counties, the friend of the court must review and approve all stipulated orders before a judge will sign them. Contact the friend of the court to find out the policy in your county.

If approval is necessary, drop off the order and all copies at the friend of the court's office. Ask when you can pick up the order, and then return and get the order when ready. On some forms, the friend of the court approves the order by signing at the bottom indicating that it is "Approved as to form." If something is wrong, find out the problem, correct it and resubmit the order to the friend of the court.

In Wayne County only, you must prepare a special form, the Certificate of Conformity for Domestic Relations Order or Judgment (#1225), with extra copies for the friend of the court and your ex, and file the certificate with the clerk when you file the stipulated order. The certificate tells the court that you prepared the order correctly.

3. Get the order signed by the judge

Your stipulated order must be signed by the judge before it can go into effect. Typically, you drop off the order and all copies at the judge's office, leaving it with the judge's secretary or law clerk. Ask when the judge will review the order and then return to pick up the order and copies. If the judge objects to something in the order, find out the problem, correct it and submit an amended order to the judge.

Sometimes, the judge's office will send the signed order and friend of the court copy to the clerk for you. If so, you can omit the next step.

4. File the order

After the judge signs the order, go to the clerk's office with the order and copies. The clerk will file the original order and keep a copy for the friend of the court, leaving you with two copies.

5. Serve the order

You must serve the order on your ex by sending a copy to him/her. See "Serving Papers" on page 27 for complete instructions for service by mail, including making and filing a proof of service.

Motions

When you and your ex can't agree on enforcement or modification of the divorce judgment, you must file a motion asking for what you want. A motion is a request to a court for some type of relief (enforcement, modification, etc.). The nonmoving party can respond to the motion by asking for denial of the requested relief or for different relief.

Meanwhile, the friend of the court may try to settle a contested motion by mediation, investigation into the dispute followed by a recommended decision or by refereeing the dispute during a simulated motion hearing known as a referee hearing.

If the friend of the court's settlement efforts fail, the motion is decided by the judge, in court, during a court session called a motion hearing. After the hearing, the judge grants or denies the motion.

Filing Motions

1. Fill out the motion form

To file a motion, select the motion form that matches the modification you want. There are several types of motion forms:

- Motion Regarding Custody (FOC 87) for modification of custody alone, or modification of custody, parenting time and child support together
- Motion Regarding Parenting Time (FOC 65) for enforcement and/or modification of parenting time
- Motion Regarding Residence of Children (GRP 20) for change of children's residence
- Motion Regarding Support (FOC 50) for modification of child support or alimony (spousal support), or reassignment of tax exemptions for dependent children
- Motion/Stipulation for Transferring Case (FOC 24) to transfer a case to another county in Michigan
- Motion/Stipulation to Opt Out of the Friend of the Court System (GRP 26) for total, partial or for-cause limited opt-outs from the friend of the court system

Fill out the motion forms as shown in the sample motions at the end of each issue chapter or appendix. Before you can complete the motion, you may have to make a settlement effort (required in a few counties) and will need to schedule a motion hearing (in all counties). These topics are covered in 1a. and b. below.

1a. Contact the nonmoving party and make a settlement effort [if required]

Genesee, Macomb, Oakland and Wayne Counties, large counties with busy courts, have local court rules requiring early efforts to settle all motions. In these counties, you must contact your ex and attempt to settle the dispute *before you file a motion*. To go forward with the motion, you must state on the motion (or other motion documents) that you tried to settle, but failed.

There's always a chance that you and your ex will settle your dispute after contact (that's the aim of these local rules). If you do, you can skip the motion and get relief by stipulation (see "Stipulated Orders" on page 30 for a full explanation of stipulated-to relief).

But more often, your ex won't consent to the post-judgment relief you want in your motion. Your ex may reject your request for relief outright. Or you may not be able to find and/or talk with your ex, after reasonable attempts to make contact. Either way, the failure to obtain consent allows the motion to go forward.

In the counties requiring prefiling settlement efforts, you must add a settlement effort statement, like the paragraph below, to the motion documents. The statement must describe your ex's direct denial of your request for relief (first clause) or your failure to contact him/her (second clause):

I hereby certify that I have made contact with [your ex] on [date of contact], requesting concurrence in the motion and that concurrence has been denied; or that I have made the following reasonable and diligent attempts to contact [your ex] requesting concurrence in the relief sought with this motion: [describe attempts]

In counties like Oakland and Wayne, this statement may already appear on the praecipes used to schedule motion hearings (see below). In other counties, you might have to add the statement to the praecipe or the motion itself. In Wayne County, you must also add another statement to the motion or praecipe (it's included on some forms):

I hereby certify that I have complied with all provisions of LCR 2.119(B) on motion practice. [your signature]

In Genesee County only, you must also attach a proposed motion-deciding order to your motion. See "Court Orders" on page 44 for more about orders. Prepare an order as explained there and write "Proposed" on the top of all the copies (but not the original order). Attach the original order to the original motion and copies of the proposed order to copies of the motion.

1b. Schedule a motion hearing

Before you complete your motion, you must schedule a hearing for the motion. Contact the clerk or the friend of the court to find out who schedules motion hearings in your county. Typically, motion hearings are arranged by the clerk or a special assignment clerk, with a simple request. But in some counties, you must file a written request for a motion hearing in a special request form known as a praecipe.

For example, Oakland County requires a praecipe to request a motion hearing. Oakland's Praecipe for Motion and Miscellaneous Docket (C-10) is a half-sheet form that you can get from the county clerk. In Oakland County, motions are typically heard on Wednesday mornings. You must file your motion praecipe with the assignment clerk at least nine days before the hearing (for service of the motion by mail). The clerk assigns the motion hearing by the next day for the next Wednesday.

Wayne County also uses praecipes for scheduling hearings. It has several kinds including: 1) Praecipe for Motion in Domestic Relations Action (#1016) for referee hearings (see "Friend of the Court" on page 38 for more about these) that must precede judge hearings for most post-judgment motions 2) Request for Hearing on a Motion (Praecipe), Order/Judgment (FD/FOC 4121) for direct-to-judge motion hearings.

All this is sorted out in an "Attorney Guide - Motion Practice in Wayne County Family Court." The guide also explains how, when and where to file the praecipes for hearings. You can get the guide and any praecipe forms from the Wayne County Clerk directly or through its fax or online services described on page 26.

As you schedule the motion hearing, estimate how much time the court will need to hear the motion. The type of motion hearing—whether it's nonevidentiary or evidentiary—dictates the amount of time necessary for the hearing (see "Motion Hearings" on page 41 for the difference between the two types of hearings).

A nonevidentiary hearing normally takes 15-30 minutes. Short hearings like this are often scheduled on the motion days that judges hold each week. An evidentiary hearing requires a bigger chunk of time, since it takes more time to receive evidence. You should be able to obtain bigger blocks of time during the judge's motion day or on a nonmotion day.

Make sure you schedule the motion hearing far enough in advance to give the nonmoving party proper notice, so s/he can respond to the motion. For motions served by mail, nine days' prior notice is necessary. Thus, as you schedule the motion hearing, allow for at least a nine-day interval between service of the motion by mail and the motion hearing. See "Time" on page 30 for information about figuring time periods of days.

After you get the information about the date, time and place of the motion hearing, insert this information in the Notice of Hearing section of your motion. Make three copies of the form.

2. File the motion

Take the motion and any other motion materials (such as praecipes) and all copies to the clerk. The clerk will charge you $20 to file the motion (see "Fees" on page 29 for more about payment of fees). The clerk will file the original motion and keep a copy for the friend of the court. The remaining two copies will be returned to you.

3. Serve the motion

You must serve the motion on your ex by sending a copy to him/her. See "Serving Papers" on page 27 for complete instructions for service by mail, including making and filing a proof of service.

In Wayne County only, when you send a motion to your ex, include in the mailing the extra strip of caption labels you received from the clerk when you filed the motion. See "Captions of Papers" on page 25 for more about caption-labeling in Wayne County.

Responding to a Motion

If you are served with a post-judgment motion, you can respond in several ways, either orally or in writing. Sometimes, you can even respond with your own "counter-motion" and become a moving party yourself.

When you agree with the motion completely, contact your ex as soon as possible and arrange to stipulate to a modification order. Any scheduled referee or motion hearings in the case should be canceled. See "Stipulated Orders" on page 30 for instructions about stipulating to orders.

Several paragraphs of the motion response forms also allow you to agree with modification motions. But why bother completing, filing and serving a response form when it's simpler and easier to stipulate to an order? It's also permissible to agree to modification orally at the motion hearing. But this also is a waste of scarce court time when agreement by stipulation is available.

Sometimes, you might agree with part of the modification motion while opposing the rest. For example, your ex may have moved for modification of custody, parenting time and child support. You may oppose modification of custody and parenting time, while agreeing with the proposed modification of child support.

All the response forms have check-boxes and spaces for partial agreement with motions. You or your ex should also point out the partial agreement to the friend of the court referee or judge at the hearing. The agreed-upon issues can then be eliminated from the hearing, so everyone can concentrate on the remaining contested ones.

If you oppose the motion, you can voice your opposition in two ways. You can file a written response to the motion or wait until the motion hearing and respond orally. A written response is better, because it's a clearer and more forceful way to state your view.

1. Fill out the response-to-motion form

Each motion in this book has a matching response form:

- Response to Motion Regarding Custody (FOC 88) for a response to a motion for modification of custody alone, or a response to a motion for modification of custody, parenting time and child support together
- Response to Motion Regarding Parenting Time (FOC 66) for responses to parenting time motions
- Response to Motion Regarding Residence of Children (GRP 21) for a response to a motion for change of residence of children
- Response to Motion Regarding Support (FOC 51) for responses to modification of child support or alimony (spousal support), a response to a motion for reassignment of tax exemptions for dependent children or to a for-cause limited opt out from the friend of the court system
- Response to Motion for Transferring Case (GRP 25) for a response to a motion to transfer the case to another Michigan county

Fill out the response form as shown in the sample responses at the end of each issue chapter or appendix. Make three copies of the form.

2. File the response

Take the response and copies to the clerk of the court where the motion was filed. The clerk will file your original response and keep a copy for the friend of the court. The remaining two copies will be returned to you.

3. Serve the response

When you respond to a motion, you must serve your response on the moving party, so s/he can take it into account during the motion hearing. See "Serving Papers" on page 27 for complete instructions for service by mail, including making and filing a proof of service.

A response to a motion must be served at least five days before the motion hearing, if served by mail. See "Time" on page 30 for information about figuring time periods of days.

Making a Counter-Motion

As you respond to a post-judgment motion, you can also make your own motion, in a kind of "counter-motion." You then become the moving party for your motion, while remaining the responding party with regard to the main motion.

To cite a common example, your ex may have moved for a decrease in child support. In your response, you not only deny his grounds for the decrease, but also move for an increase in child support.

All the response forms allow you to make those kinds of simple counter-motions. Typically, the last paragraph of a response lets you propose a different kind of modification for the issue(s) raised in the main motion. This, in essence, is a counter-motion. It's also possible to make a counter-motion orally, at the motion hearing. But putting it in writing is better, because it gives everyone prior notice of what you want.

A counter-motion piggybacks on the main motion. It uses the same hearing time allotted for the main motion (unless more time is necessary), and the same notice of hearing. You may have to pay another $20 fee to file a counter-motion.

Normally, a counter-motion deals with the same kind of issues raised in the main motion. But it's possible to seek completely new relief in a counter-motion and sometimes it makes sense to do this. For example, if your ex moves for modification of child support and you want adjustment of a specific parenting time schedule, why shouldn't you counter-move for modification of parenting time and have both issues decided in one hearing?

On the other hand, avoid bringing counter-motions for new relief when your counter-motion is incompatible with the main motion. For example, let's say your ex has moved for modification of child support and scheduled a 15-minute nonevidentiary motion hearing. You want to make a counter-motion for change of custody. Plainly, these motions are incompatible. A motion for modification of custody is a serious matter, typically requiring an evidentiary hearing of several hours, not minutes. The court could never consider both motions during the 15 minutes allotted for the main motion.

If you want to seek new relief in a counter-motion, you should: 1) file a response to the main motion 2) file a separate motion for your counter-motion, since the response forms really don't have enough space to bring a completely new motion. You can use the same hearing information from the main motion in the Notice of Hearing section of your counter-motion.

Friend of the Court

As explained before, the friend of the court plays several important roles in post-judgment divorce cases. Whenever a post-judgment motion is filed, the friend of the court can assume the role of mediator, investigator or referee—or even all three—to help the court settle or decide the motion.

Mediation and Other Settlement Services

There are several kinds of mediation and related settlement services available in post-judgment cases, one of which the friend of the court offers:

Informal mediation. The friend of the court provides informal mediation by a neutral mediator who tries to settle the contested issues. Participation in informal mediation is voluntary; you don't have to take part and aren't penalized if you refuse to participate.

The mediator is assigned from the friend of the court's own staff or is an outsider trained in mediation. Informal mediation is flexible, so the mediator can meet with the parties and the children in a comfortable setting.

If settlement of the dispute is reached, the friend of the court will help prepare and file a stipulated order. If mediation fails, the process ends and the case moves onto the next step.

Formal mediation. Courts also offer formal mediation by a domestic relations mediator, who must have training in family counseling, outside the friend of the court system. Formal mediation is really designed for settlement of divorce cases, but it can be used to mediate post-judgment motions.

The parties can agree to formal mediation, one party can ask for it or the judge can order it (the judge can also cancel the order for several reasons). After formal mediation is started, participation is mandatory; if you don't take part you lose by default.

In formal mediation, the parties usually submit factual and legal summaries to the mediator before the mediation session. They must attend the session and present their arguments.

During the session, the mediator tries to *facilitate* settlement of the dispute. If settlement is achieved, the agreement is put into a stipulated order. No settlement? The parties can ask the mediator to *evaluate* the case and recommend a settlement, which they can accept or reject. If the parties skip evaluation, the mediator simply reports to the court that mediation has failed.

Private mediation. The parties can agree, by contract, to submit their dispute to nonbinding private mediation, outside the court system.

Arbitration. In 2001, Michigan adopted a new law authorizing domestic relations arbitration. Like private mediation, arbitration happens outside the court system, after the parties agree to arbitrate. However, arbitration is usually binding, but subject to final court review.

Much as it does in a divorce, the friend of the court can investigate post-judgment motions and make a report and recommendation to the judge about the motion. During an investigation, the friend of the court investigator may contact the parties, the children and others to gather facts about the dispute. Or if you want input, you can request an interview during the investigation.

The investigator summarizes the facts in a report, which also contains a recommendation to the judge about deciding the motion. The investigator's report is sent to the parties and put in the case file for the benefit of the judge. The judge may consider the report and recommendation, but isn't bound by them.

Like mediation, refereeing is another way to settle post-judgment motions before a motion hearing. As referee, the friend of the court assumes a semi-judicial role, hears the motion in a simulated motion hearing and then issues a recommended decision. Either party can object to the recommendation, sending the case onto the judge.

Almost any post-judgment motion can be refereed. The parties can agree to refereeing, one party can ask for it or the judge can order it. But typically, family court judges in a county decide which kinds of post-judgment motions are suitable for refereeing and all these motions are routinely refereed. Some counties use refereeing selectively, while other counties, such as Wayne, require refereeing for every contested post-judgment motion.

In some ways, a referee hearing resembles a court hearing. Each side can have a lawyer, testimony may be taken, the rules of evidence apply and the proceedings are recorded. The difference is informality. A referee hearing is typically held in a conference room at the friend of the court's office or a similar casual setting, instead of a courtroom.

During a referee hearing, the moving party filing the post-judgment motion presents his/her case first, then the nonmoving party may oppose it. Both sides may offer limited evidence, usually their own testimony (seldom from other witnesses), or documents like paycheck stubs or W-2 forms.

Afterward, the friend of the court referee must make findings in the case and insert these in the record of the hearing or put them in a written report. The referee must also issue a recommended order deciding the motion. The parties may be satisfied with the recommendation, and then the recommended order will be signed by the judge as the final order.

Either party can object to the friend of the court's recommended order because of a perceived factual or legal error in the recommendation. An objector who objects merely to harass or delay can be assessed costs by the court.

Objecting to the Friend of the Court's Recommendation

You have 21 days to object to a referee's recommended order. This objection period begins when you receive the recommended order and the deadline is satisfied by filing an objection with the clerk (see "Time" on page 30 for more about figuring time periods of days).

1. Fill out the objection form

Use the Objection to Referee's Recommended Order (FOC 68) for an objection. Fill out the objection as shown in the sample form at the end of this section. Incidentally, the objector becomes the moving party for the purposes of the objection only.

1a. Schedule a motion hearing

If you object to a referee's recommended order, the dispute moves onto a motion hearing before a judge. As the objector, it's up to you to schedule this hearing.

Contact the friend of the court to find out who schedules motion hearings in your county. Typically, motion hearings are arranged by the clerk or a special assignment clerk, with a simple request. But some counties require written requests using forms known as praecipes (see "1b. Schedule a motion hearing" on page 34 about scheduling motion hearings with praecipes).

As you schedule the motion hearing, estimate how much time the court will need to hear the motion. The type of motion hearing—whether it's nonevidentiary or evidentiary—dictates the amount of time necessary for the hearing (see "Motion Hearings" below for the difference between the two types of hearings).

A nonevidentiary hearing normally takes 15-30 minutes. Short hearings like this are often scheduled on the motion days that judges hold each week. An evidentiary hearing requires a bigger chunk of time, since it takes more time to receive evidence. You should be able to obtain a bigger block of time on the judge's motion day or on a nonmotion day.

Make sure you schedule the motion hearing far enough in advance to give the nonobjector proper notice, so s/he can respond. For a motion or objection served by mail, nine days' notice is necessary. Thus, as you schedule the motion hearing, allow for at least a nine-day interval between service of the objection by mail and the motion hearing. See "Time" on page 30 for information about figuring time periods of days.

After you get the information about the date, time and place of the hearing, insert this information in the Notice of Hearing section of your Objection to Referee's Recommended Order (FOC 68). Make three copies of the form.

2. File the objection

Take the Objection to Referee's Recommended Order (FOC 68) and copies to the clerk. The clerk will file the original objection and keep a copy for the friend of the court. The remaining two copies will be returned to you.

3. Serve the objection

You must serve the objection on your ex by sending a copy to him/her. See "Serving Papers" on page 27 for complete instructions for service by mail, including making and filing a proof of service.

4. Prepare for and attend the motion hearing

After an objection is filed and served, the motion goes before the judge at the motion hearing the objector has scheduled. The judge considers the motion anew or "de novo" as the objection says. Previously, courts would start from scratch at de novo hearings, as if the refereeing had never happened. Today, courts can use material from the referee hearing, but the parties can supplement this with new or additional evidence. See "Motion Hearings" below for tips on how to prepare for and attend a motion hearing.

Motion Hearings

If mediation, investigation and refereeing don't work, the motion must be decided by the judge, in open court, during a motion hearing. There are two kinds of motion hearings: 1) nonevidentiary hearing where little or no evidence is introduced and the parties merely make legal arguments to the judge 2) evidentiary hearing where evidence, such as testimony, is presented.

Which type of motion hearing do you need? The test is whether you and your ex agree on the facts surrounding the motion. If these facts aren't in dispute, a nonevidentiary hearing will do; disputed facts signal the need for a full evidentiary hearing.

Preparing for a Motion Hearing

You must plan all parts of your case carefully. Your legal arguments must be well-organized, with convincing evidence to support them.

Securing evidence is by far the most important part of prehearing preparation. If you want testimony from witnesses, you must have them attend the hearing. Any documents or other things you want to introduce at the hearing must also be obtained beforehand.

Frequently, witnesses volunteer to testify and important documents are readily available. But sometimes, you must obtain this evidence by subpoena.

Subpoenas

A subpoena is a court order directing a witness to appear in court and testify. A subpoena can also order the witness to bring anything portable to court, such as documents, records or photographs. A subpoenaed witness must obey these orders or risk contempt of court.

Which people and things should you subpoena? It's always a good idea to subpoena witnesses who are unreliable or reluctant to testify for you. The subpoena should convince them to appear and give their testimony. If subpoenaed witnesses don't attend as ordered, you have the right to get a delay of the hearing until the witness appears.

For cooperative witnesses, like relatives or friends, you have a choice. You can just ask them to appear as witnesses, without a subpoena. Or you can both ask and subpoena them, as a precaution. The danger with a simple request is that the witness will renege on their promise to appear, leaving you without the testimony and no grounds for a delay. On the other hand, subpoenaing witnesses takes both time and money. You may decide this isn't worth the effort when you can really count on your witnesses.

If you need a subpoena, see Appendix E on page 229, which has complete instructions and forms for getting and serving subpoenas.

Motion Hearing Itself

Before a motion hearing, make sure you know the location of the hearing. Motion hearings take place in the courtroom of the judge assigned to your case, which is usually in the county courthouse or similar county office building.

Go to the place of the hearing on the scheduled day and time. Try to arrive around 30 minutes before the hearing, to take care of any last-minute details. By arriving early, you can also observe other hearings. Be prepared to spend most of the morning or afternoon at the hearing.

When your case is called by the courtroom clerk, step forward and identify yourself. Mention that you are representing yourself. Take a seat at one of the tables inside the bar (the gate) of the courtroom.

The format of the hearing hinges on whether your ex shows up for the hearing. If your ex is absent, the hearing should be brief, with you winning by default. A full hearing with arguments from both sides is necessary when your ex appears at the hearing.

Your Ex Doesn't Attend the Hearing

If your ex doesn't appear at the motion hearing, the judge may be curious about the absence. The judge will probably check the proof of service to make sure your ex was served with the motion. The judge may also question you about the service. If there were flaws in the service, the judge could delay the hearing until these are corrected.

Without opposition, you should get the relief you seek in your motion. But keep in mind that the judge always has the final say on issues like custody, parenting time, residence of children and child support. The judge can deny your motion whenever it's not in the best interests of the children or if it's unreasonable.

If the judge is satisfied with your motion, s/he should grant it without much ado. The judge will probably ask you some questions about the nature of your motion. S/he may ask to see documentary evidence you have brought. At an evidentiary hearing, the judge may even ask you to take the witness stand and, under oath, establish a factual foundation for your motion.

Whatever happens, the judge will likely grant your motion immediately, ruling "from the bench." Jot down notes on the judge's decision as s/he announces it, since it's your job to prepare the court order deciding the motion for the judge. See "Court Orders" below for information about preparing and filing the order.

Your Ex Attends the Hearing

Things won't be so easy when your ex is present at the hearing. Facing opposition, you will have to present your case forcefully to prevail on your motion. Or if you're opposing the motion, you will have to argue effectively for denial of the motion.

The judge will probably start the hearing with some informal questioning of both parties. For a nonevidentiary hearing, the judge will go right to the legal arguments, since evidence isn't necessary. Each side gets to present their legal arguments for or against the motion. After the first round of arguments, the judge may ask each side for rebuttal arguments, responding to what has already been said. After arguments, the judge decides the motion.

At an evidentiary hearing, evidence precedes legal argument. The judge will ask the moving party to go first. If that's you, you must take the witness stand, be sworn and give your testimony. You may also want to introduce documents during your testimony or call other witnesses, who may also have documents. Your ex and the judge may ask questions during your testimony or that given by your witnesses.

Then the reverse happens; your ex gives testimony and you and the judge can question him/her. Other witnesses or documentary evidence your ex presents is also subject to questioning and examination.

> ## Courtroom Etiquette
>
> During a court hearing, you should follow these rules of courtroom behavior:
>
> - Dress neatly and be well-groomed.
>
> - Be on time.
>
> - Be courteous to the judge and your ex.
>
> - Wait until called on to speak.
>
> - Don't interrupt while the judge or your ex is talking; you will get your chance to speak.
>
> - After the judge makes a decision, don't persist in arguing your view.

After all the evidence is received, the judge gives both parties the opportunity to present their legal arguments. The judge may then ask for another round of arguments, in rebuttal, allowing each party one last word.

When the arguments are finished, the judge decides the motion. The judge may rule immediately "from the bench," or take the case "under submission" and rule later. The judge's decision must then be put into a court order.

Court Orders

Win or lose, the moving party is responsible for preparing the order granting or denying the post-judgment motion. During the motion hearing, if the judge rules from the bench, the moving party should take notes on the judge's decision. S/he can prepare the order from these notes. If the judge issues a written opinion, the order must follow the opinion.

The nonmoving party has the right to review the order prepared by the moving party, to make sure it reflects the judge's oral or written decision. The nonmoving party has this right of review even if s/he was a no-show at the motion hearing. Usually, the nonmoving party agrees with the form of the order, and either consents to entry of the order or allows entry by doing nothing to oppose the order.

But sometimes the nonmoving party objects to the order, if s/he believes that the order is inaccurate or incomplete. In that case, an extra court hearing on the wording of the order is necessary. This is a very narrow issue, requiring a brief hearing.

The moving party must follow steps 1-5 below to get a court order granting or denying a post-judgment motion. These sections also explain how a nonmoving party may object to or oppose the order.

1. Fill out the order form

Select the order form that matches the modification the judge has ordered. There are several types of order forms:

- Order Regarding Custody and Parenting Time (FOC 89) for modification of custody alone or custody and parenting time together; add the Uniform Child Support Order (FOC 10/52) for modification of child support also
- Order Regarding Parenting Time (FOC 67) for modification of parenting time
- Order Regarding Residence of Children (GRP 22) for change of residence of children
- Uniform Child Support Order (FOC 10/52) for modification of child support
- Order Regarding Spousal Support (GRP 23) for modification of alimony (spousal support)
- Order Regarding Assignment of Dependency Exemptions (GRP 24) for reassignment of tax exemptions for dependent children
- Order Changing Venue and Transferring Case (FOC 25) to transfer a case to another county in Michigan
- Order Exempting Case from Friend of the Court Services (FOC 102) for a total or partial opt-out from the friend of the court system or Order Suspending Immediate Income Withholding (FOC 64) for a limited opt-out from that system

Fill out the order form as shown in the sample orders after each issue chapter or appendix.

2. Obtain friend of the court approval of the order [if necessary]

In some counties, the friend of the court must review and approve all orders before the judge will sign them. Contact the friend of the court to find out the policy in your county.

If approval is necessary, drop off the order and all copies at the friend of the court's office. Ask when you can pick up the order, and then return and get the order when ready. On some forms, the friend of the court approves the order by signing at the bottom indicating that it is "Approved as to form." If something is wrong, find out the problem, correct it and resubmit the order to the friend of the court.

In Wayne County only, you must prepare a special form, the Certificate of Conformity for Domestic Relations Order or Judgment (#1225), with extra copies for the friend of the court and your ex, and file the certificate with the clerk when you file the order. The certificate tells the court that you prepared the order correctly.

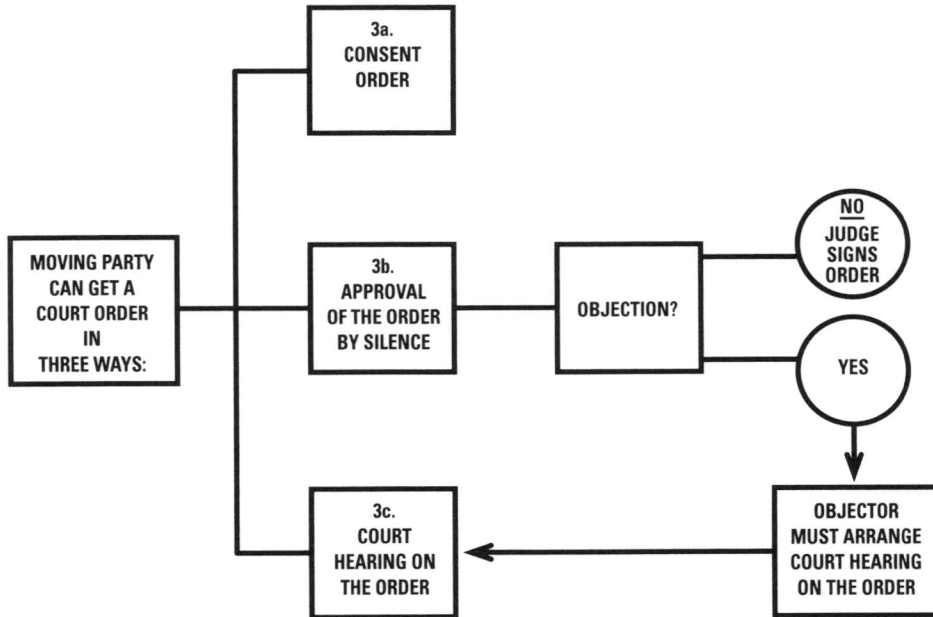

3. Get the order signed by the judge

There are three basic ways for getting an order signed by the judge after a motion hearing. These are listed below in increasing order of difficulty. A good plan is to start with the first method and then go to the others as necessary.

- the moving and nonmoving parties can consent to the order before submitting it to the judge for signing
- the moving party can send the order to the nonmoving party seeking "approval-by-silence" (where the order is considered approved if the nonmoving party doesn't object to it within seven days of mailing), and then submit the order to the judge for signing
- schedule a court hearing on the order, followed by the judge's signing the order

3a. Consent order [or 3b. or 3c.] (and steps 2-5 in "Stipulated Orders")

If you and your ex approve the order, you both must sign it. When you consent to an order, you're approving only the form of the order, not the legal decision contained in the order. Thus, you may lose at the motion hearing and still consent to the form of the order. Your consent won't affect your right to appeal the order.

For a consent order, check the box below the caption indicating that the order is being entered "on consent" or on the "consent of the parties." At the end of the order, both parties must sign their names in the spaces provided.

One efficient way to get a consent order is to obtain consent at the motion hearing. You can prepare the bulk of the order before the hearing (caption, factual section, etc.) and then complete the decisional part, which is often composed of check-boxes or fill-in-the-blanks, at the end of the hearing. If your ex consents to this order, s/he, you and the judge can sign it there.

Or you can prepare the order after the hearing, and obtain your ex's consent personally or through the mail a little later.

Either way, see steps 2-5 in "Stipulated Orders" on page 30 about submitting the order to the judge for signing, filing it with clerk and serving it on your ex. Use these steps as needed.

3b. Approval of the order by silence [or 3a. or 3c.] (and 3b.(1)-(5))

If your ex won't consent to the order, try the approval-by-silence method instead. You must do this within seven days of the hearing.

3b.(1) Propose the order

Take the order you prepared, make three copies and write "Proposed" on the top of all the copies (but not on the original order).

3b.(2) Fill out the notice to enter order form

Fill out the Notice to Enter Order without Hearing (FOC 54), as shown in the sample notice at the end of this section, and make three copies. Attach the original order to the original FOC 54 and three copies of the proposed order to three copies of the FOC 54.

3b.(3) File the notice papers with the clerk

Take all your papers to the clerk. The clerk will file the original FOC 54 (with attached original order) and keep a copy of this paper for the friend of the court. The remaining two copies will be returned to you.

3b.(4) Serve the notice papers

You must serve the notice on your ex by sending him/her a copy of the FOC 54 (with attached proposed order). The notice must be sent within seven days after the motion hearing. See "Serving Papers" on page 27 for complete instructions for service by mail, including making and filing a proof of service.

3b.(5) Get the order signed by the judge

3b.(5)(a) No objection to the order [or 3b.(5)(b)]

If the nonmoving party doesn't file an objection to the proposed order with the clerk within seven days after mailing (see "Time" on page 30 about how to compute time periods of days), the silence is regarded as approval of the order. The clerk will then submit the original order to the judge for signing. If the judge approves the order, s/he will sign it. The clerk will send a notice that the order is signed and ready to be picked up.

The moving party should return to the clerk and get the original order which has been signed by the judge. The moving party must make three copies of the signed original order. All should be filed with the clerk, who will keep the original order and a copy for the friend of the court and return the other two copies to you.

The moving party must serve one copy on the nonmoving party within seven days after the judge signs the order. See "Serving Papers" on page 27 for complete instructions for service by mail, including making and filing a proof of service.

If the judge objects to the proposed order, s/he won't sign it. The court will then set up a hearing on the order and notify the parties of the hearing. See "3c. Court hearing on the order" on page 49 about how to appear at this kind of hearing.

3b.(5)(b) Objection to the order [or 3b.(5)(a)] (and 3b.(5)(b)(1)-(6))

If the nonmoving party believes the proposed order is inaccurate and/or incomplete, s/he may object to the order. The objection must be filed with the clerk within seven days after the Notice to Enter Order without Hearing (FOC 54) with attached proposed order is sent. The nonmoving party, or objector, can use the Objection to Proposed Order (FOC 78) for the objection.

After an objector files an objection, much of the responsibility for obtaining an order shifts to the objector, as explained below.

3b.(5)(b)(1) Propose an alternate order

The objector must make a new order according to what s/he believes the judge really said in the oral decision or written opinion. See steps 1-2 in "Court Orders" on page 44 about how to prepare an order. Afterward, make three copies of the order and write "Alternate Proposed" on the top of all the copies (but not on the original order).

3b.(5)(b)(2) Fill out the objection form

Fill out the Objection to Proposed Order (FOC 78) like the sample objection at the end of this section and make three copies. There are two basic grounds for objection: accuracy and completeness. In the FOC 78, you must describe in detail why you believe the moving party's proposed order was inaccurate and/or incomplete. Incidentally, the objector becomes the moving party in the FOC 78 only.

3b.(5)(b)(3) Schedule a hearing on the orders

The moving party has proposed an order, and the objector has objected to it and proposed an alternate one. The court must decide which order to adopt during a hearing.

The objector must schedule the hearing on the orders and notify the moving party of the hearing. See 3c.(1)-(4) "Fill out the notice of hearing form" through "Serve the notice papers" below about how to do both things using the Notice of Hearing to Enter Order (FOC 53).

3b.(5)(b)(4) File the objection papers with the clerk

Take all these papers to the clerk. The clerk will file: 1) the original FOC 78 and keep a copy for the friend of the court 2) the original FOC 53 (with attached alternate proposed order) and keep a copy of this paper for the friend of the court. The remaining copies of these papers will be returned to you.

Remember, to object you must act quickly because the FOC 78 must be on file with the clerk within seven days after the FOC 54 with attached proposed order was *sent* to (not received by) you.

3b.(5)(b)(5) Serve the objection papers

You must serve the objection papers on the moving party. Send him/her copies of the FOC 78 and FOC 53 (with attached alternate proposed order). See "Serving Papers" on page 27 for complete instructions for service by mail, including making and filing a proof of service.

3b.(5)(b)(6) Prepare for and attend the hearing on the orders

During the hearing, the judge will have two orders to choose from: 1) the moving party's proposed order for which approval-by-silence was sought 2) the nonmoving party-objector's alternate order proposed after objection.

The issue is which of these orders most *accurately* and *completely* states the judge's decision on the motion. This is a very narrow issue; it isn't a chance to reargue the motion itself.

By filing an objection, the nonmoving party-objector has become the active party. The primary burden is therefore on the objector to show that his/her alternate order conforms to the judge's decision.

If the judge made an oral decision at the motion hearing, the transcript of the hearing is the best evidence of what the judge said. Before the hearing on the orders, the objector should contact the court reporter from the motion hearing and order a transcript of the hearing. Do this quickly after objection, because the court reporter needs time to transcribe his/her notes from the hearing.

Judges sometimes take their own notes during hearings and these can be extra proof of the judge's oral decision. The judge's notes should be in your case file at the clerk's office, which is a public record open for inspection.

Naturally, the judge's opinion is the best evidence of a written decision on a motion. When an opinion was issued, you can normally skip getting a transcript, unless the opinion is ambiguous and the transcript clears up the ambiguity. The opinion will be in the case file and should have also been sent to both parties after the motion hearing.

The moving party must attend the court hearing to support his/her proposed order. Once again, the moving party must refer to the transcript or opinion for support. Often, these documents will reveal the judge's decision, but it's a matter of interpretation about what the judge really meant.

After the issue is decided, the judge will probably sign one of the proposed orders, but could ask for a new corrected one. If correction is necessary, you might be able to do that right after the hearing and have the judge sign it in the courtroom. Or you can correct the order later and submit it to the judge at his/her office soon after the hearing. Make three copies of the signed order.

For information about filing the signed order with the clerk and serving it on your ex, follow steps 4-5 in "Stipulated Orders" on page 30.

3c. Court hearing on the order [or 3a. or 3b.] (and 3c.(1)-(5))

A court hearing on the order is necessary in two situations: 1) the moving party has sought the order by the approval-by-silence method and the nonmoving party has filed an objection to the proposed order 2) the moving party has skipped the consent and approval-by-silence methods for getting the order and gone directly to the court hearing method instead.

In a court hearing on an order, the issue is whether the proposed order *accurately* and *completely* states the judge's decision on the motion. This is a very narrow issue; it isn't a chance to reargue the motion itself.

During the hearing, the judge will decide whether the proposed order is acceptable and either adopt this order or ask for a corrected one. The steps for scheduling, preparing for and attending the hearing on the order are described below.

3c.(1) Fill out the notice of hearing form

Fill out the Notice of Hearing to Enter Order (FOC 53) as shown in the sample notice at the end of this section.

3c.(1)(a.) Schedule a hearing

Before you complete the notice, you must schedule a hearing on the order. Contact the clerk or friend of the court to find who schedules court hearings in your county. Typically, hearings are arranged by the clerk or a special assignment clerk, with a simple request. But some counties require written requests using forms known as praecipes (see "1b. Schedule a motion hearing" on page 34 about scheduling hearings with praecipes).

As you schedule the hearing on the order, estimate how much time the court will need for the matter. A hearing on an order should be nonevidentiary or with very limited evidence (such as the motion hearing transcript), requiring perhaps 15-30 mintues of court time. Short hearings like this are often scheduled on the motion days that judges hold each week.

Make sure you schedule the court hearing far enough in advance to give your opponent proper notice, so s/he can prepare a response at the hearing. For this type of hearing, nine days' notice is necessary. Thus, as you schedule the court hearing on the order, allow for at least a nine-day interval between service of the Notice of Hearing to Enter Order (FOC 53) and the court hearing on the order. See "Time" on page 30 for information about figuring time periods of days.

After you get the information about the date, time and place of the hearing, insert this information in paragraph #3 of the FOC 53. Make three copies of the form.

3c.(2) Propose the order

You must make the order you have prepared into a proposed order. Simply take this order, make three copies and write "Proposed" on the top of all the copies (but not on the original order). Attach the original order to the original Notice of Hearing to Enter Order (FOC 53) and three copies of the proposed order to three copies of the FOC 53.

3c.(3) File the notice papers with the clerk

Take all these papers to the clerk. The clerk will file the original FOC 53 (with attached original order) and keep a copy of this paper for the friend of the court. The remaining two copies will be returned to you.

3c.(4) Serve the notice papers

You must serve the notice on your ex by sending to him/her a copy of the FOC 53 (with attached proposed order). The notice should be sent promptly so the nine-day notice period is satisfied, giving your ex time to respond. See "Serving Papers" on page 27 for complete instructions for service by mail, including making and filing a proof of service.

3c.(5) Prepare for and attend the hearing on the order and have it signed by the judge

At the hearing, the moving party proposing the order has the burden of showing that the order *accurately* and *completely* follows the judge's decision. This is a very narrow issue; it isn't a chance to reargue the motion itself.

The moving party can prove conformity in several ways. If the judge made an oral decision at the motion hearing, the transcript of the hearing is the best evidence of what the judge said. Before the hearing on the order, the moving party should contact the court reporter from the motion hearing and order a transcript of the hearing. Do this quickly, because the court reporter needs time to transcribe his/her notes from the hearing.

Some judges take their own notes during hearings and these can be extra proof of the judge's oral decision. The judge's notes should be in your case file at the clerk's office, which is a public record open for inspection.

Needless to say, the judge's opinion is the best evidence of a written decision on a motion. When an opinion was issued, you can normally skip getting a transcript, unless the opinion is ambiguous and the transcript clears up the ambiguity. The opinion will be in the case file and should have also been sent to both parties after the motion hearing.

To challenge a proposed order, the nonmoving party must appear at the hearing on the order. S/he will argue that the order doesn't follow the judge's oral or written decision. In making this claim, the nonmoving party can cite from the motion hearing transcript, the judge's notes or a written opinion.

After the issue is decided, the judge will sign the proposed order or ask for a new corrected one. If correction is necessary, you might be able to do that right after the hearing and have the judge sign it in the courtroom. Or you can correct the order later and submit it to the judge at his/her office soon after the hearing. Make three copies of the signed order.

4. File the order

Take the original order and copies to the clerk. The clerk will file the original order and keep a copy for the friend of the court. The remaining two copies will be returned to you.

5. Serve the order

You must serve the order on your ex by sending a copy to him/her. See "Serving Papers" on page 27 for complete instructions for service by mail, including making and filing a proof of service.

Local Rules and Forms

The procedures for enforcing and modifying divorce judgments described in this book are supposed to be uniform, applying to every county in the state. Likewise, the modification forms issued by the state are designed for use statewide.

Nevertheless, you may encounter some local procedures and forms that aren't covered in this book. A few counties, Wayne in particular, have special rules and forms for filing motions. Don't be alarmed by these; ask the local authorities what the local practice is and adapt to it.

Sometimes, local practices can be beneficial. In some counties, the friend of the court will take charge when you want to modify your divorce judgment. In these counties, the friend of the court will file the necessary papers (which you still must prepare), serve them on the other party and schedule the motion hearing. You take over then and present the motion to the court.

New Laws, Rules, Forms and Fees

These days, family law is a very active area of the law. Congress and the Michigan Legislature are constantly passing new family laws. Added to this are hundreds of family law decisions issued by courts. Some of these new family laws affect post-judgment divorce.

As a result of this activity, parts of this book may become outdated. To keep the book current, Grand River Press offers an update about recent legal changes. See the order form in the front of this book for ordering information.

To Obtain

Laws, court rules and other legal information, visit a law library. Most county courthouses have law libraries which are open to the public. The divorce laws are in the MCLAs (Michigan Compiled Laws Annotated) and MSAs (Michigan Statutes Annotated); the court rules are published in *Michigan Rules of Court - State* by the West Group (this volume also includes all the local court rules).

Online, you can access Michigan law via www.michiganlegislature.org, using the search engine to search by section or subject. The basic divorce laws are MCL 552.1-552.1803 and 722.21-722.31 (Child Custody Act of 1970).

For court rules, go to www.courts.michigan.gov/supremecourt, scroll down and click on the "Court Rules Online" icon, and a table of contents will pop up with several choices: 1) under "Michigan Court Rules," select "Chapter 3 Special Proceedings and Actions" for the divorce court rules of MCR 3.201-3.219. 2) under "Local Court Rules," select "Circuit Courts" for local court rules arranged by county.

Approved, SCAO

CASE NO.

| STATE OF MICHIGAN
JUDICIAL CIRCUIT
COUNTY | OBJECTION TO
REFEREE'S RECOMMENDED ORDER | |
Court telephone no.

Court address

Plaintiff's name, address, and telephone no.   ☐ Moving party

v

Defendant's name, address, and telephone no.   ☒ Moving party

Third party's name, address, and telephone no.   ☐ Moving party

PARTY WHO OBJECTS TO ORDER IS MOVING PARTY HERE

I object to the entry of the referee's recommended order dated ___1-22-99___ and request a de novo hearing by the court. My objection is based on the following reason(s):

IN DECIDING CUSTODY, REFEREE DIDN'T CONSIDER ALL THE BEST INTEREST FACTORS. THE REFEREE OMITTED THE DOMESTIC VIOLENCE FACTOR, ALTHOUGH THERE WAS EVIDENCE OF SUCH ABUSE BY PLAINTIFF.

SAY WHY YOU BELIEVE REFEREE ERRED IN ITS DECISION

I declare that the statements above are true to the best of my information, knowledge, and belief.

___1-31-99___
Date

Dudley Lovelace
Signature of objecting party

DUDLEY LOVELACE
Name (type or print)

NOTICE OF HEARING

A hearing will be held on this objection before Hon. ___LESTER TUBBS___
Name of judge

on ___2-15-99___ at ___9:00 AM___ at ___OJIBWAY COUNTY COURTHOUSE___.
Date   Time   Place

If you require special accommodations to use the court because of a disability, please contact the court immediately to make arrangements.

CERTIFICATE OF MAILING

I certify that on this date I mailed a copy of this objection and notice of hearing on the other party(ies) by ordinary mail at the above address(es).

___1-31-99___
Date

Dudley Lovelace
Signature of objecting party

MCR 3.215(E)

FOC 68 (6/98) **OBJECTION TO REFEREE'S RECOMMENDED ORDER**

Approved, SCAO

Original - Court
1st copy - Other Party
2nd copy - Moving Party

3rd copy - Friend of the Court
4th copy - Proof of Service
5th copy - Proof of Service

STATE OF MICHIGAN JUDICIAL CIRCUIT COUNTY	NOTICE TO ENTER ORDER WITHOUT HEARING	CASE NO.

Court address

Court telephone no.

Plaintiff's name

☐ moving party

v

Defendant's name

☐ moving party

Third party's name

☐ moving party

1. On **2-15-99** a hearing was held on a motion regarding **CUSTODY**
   Date   Type of order
   and a decision was made.

2. The attached proposed order states what the judge or referee said at the hearing.

3. This is your notice that the proposed order will be given to the judge to sign. If you don't think that the order accurately states what was ordered in court, you must file your written objections with the court within 7 days of the date this notice was mailed. A form to use for filing objections is available at the friend of the court office. Contact the friend of the court and ask for form FOC 78.

4. If you do not file written objections to the proposed order within 7 days of the date of this notice, the judge may sign the proposed order without a hearing. If the judge decides that a hearing is needed, you will be notified of the hearing date.

5. If you file written objections to the proposed order, a hearing will be scheduled. You will be notified of the hearing date.

6. Parties may be represented by their attorneys in this matter.

2-16-99
Date

Dudley Lovelace
Signature of moving party

CERTIFICATE OF MAILING

I certify that on this date I mailed a copy of this notice proposed order on the other party(ies) by ordinary mail at the above address(es).

2-16-99
Date

Dudley Lovelace
Signature of moving party

FOC 54 (12/96) **NOTICE TO ENTER ORDER WITHOUT HEARING**

MCR 2.602(B)

Original - Court
1st copy - Moving Party
2nd copy - Objecting Party

3rd copy - Friend of the Court
4th copy - Proof of Service
5th copy - Proof of Service

CASE NO.

Approved, SCAO

STATE OF MICHIGAN
JUDICIAL CIRCUIT
COUNTY

OBJECTION TO PROPOSED ORDER

Court telephone no.

Court address

☒ Moving party

Plaintiff's name, address, and telephone no.

Defendant's name, address, and telephone no.

☐ Moving party

PARTY WHO OBJECTS TO PROPOSED ORDER IS MOVING PARTY HERE

Third party's name, address, and telephone no.   ☐ Moving part

I received a notice to enter a proposed order without a hearing dated _2-16-99_   My objection is based on the following reason(s):
I object to the entry of the proposed order and request a hearing by the court.

THE PROPOSED ORDER DOESN'T FOLLOW THE JUDGE'S DECISION ANNOUNCED IN COURT. SPECIFICALLY, THE JUDGE CHANGED SOLE CUSTODY FOR PLAINTIFF TO JOINT LEGAL CUSTODY FOR THE PARTIES WITH PHYSICAL CUSTODY TO PLAINTIFF. YET, THE PROPOSED ORDER GIVES BOTH PHYSICAL AND LEGAL CUSTODY TO THE PARTIES JOINTLY, CONTRARY TO JUDGE'S DECISION.

EXPLAIN WHY PROPOSED ORDER DOESN'T FOLLOW JUDGE'S ORAL OR WRITTEN DECISION

I declare that the statements above are true to the best of my information, knowledge, and belief.

_2-20-99_
Date

Darlene Lovelace
Signature of objecting party

DARLENE LOVELACE
Name (type or print)

CERTIFICATE OF MAILING

I certify that on this date I mailed a copy of this objection on the other party(ies) by ordinary mail at the above address(es).

_2-20-99_
Date

Darlene Lovelace
Signature of objecting party

MCR 2.602(B)

FOC 78 (12/96) **OBJECTION TO PROPOSED ORDER**

Approved, SCAO

Original - Court
1st copy - Other Party
2nd copy - Moving Party

3rd copy - Friend of the Court
4th copy - Proof of Service
5th copy - Proof of Service

STATE OF MICHIGAN
JUDICIAL CIRCUIT
COUNTY

NOTICE OF HEARING TO ENTER ORDER

CASE NO.

Court address

Court telephone no.

Plaintiff's name, address, and telephone no. ☐ moving party	Defendant's name, address, and telephone no. ☐ moving party

v

Third party's name, address, and telephone no. ☐ moving party

1. On _**2-15-99**_ _____ a hearing was held on a motion regarding _**CUSTODY**_
   Date   Type of order
   and a decision was made.

2. The attached proposed order states what the judge or referee said at the hearing.

3. This is your notice that a hearing will be held before _**LESTER TUBBS**_
                                                              Name of judge or referee
   _**3-15-99**_ _____ at _**9:00 AM**_ at _**OJIBWAY COUNTY COURTHOUSE**_ _____ on
   Date   Time   Place
   to have the proposed order signed. If you don't think that the order accurately states what was ordered in court, attend
   the scheduled hearing.

4. Parties may be represented by their attorneys in this matter.

_**2-25-99**_
Date

Dudley Lovelace
Signature of moving party

If you require special accommodations to use the court because of a disability, or if you require a foreign language interpreter
to help you fully participate in court proceedings, please contact the court immediately to make arrangements. When contacting
the court, provide your case number(s).

CERTIFICATE OF MAILING

I certify that on this date I mailed a copy of this notice of hearing and proposed order on the other party(ies) by ordinary mail
at the above address(es).

_**2-25-99**_
Date

Dudley Lovelace
Signature of moving party

FOC 53   (4/01) **NOTICE OF HEARING TO ENTER ORDER**

MCR 2.602(B)

STATE OF MICHIGAN
THIRD JUDICIAL CIRCUIT
WAYNE COUNTY

Penobscot Bldg. 645 Griswold Ave. Detroit, MI 48226

CERTIFICATE OF CONFORMITY FOR DOMESTIC RELATIONS ORDER OR JUDGMENT	CASE NO.
	313-224-5372

PLAINTIFF'S NAME

V.

DEFENDANT'S NAME

USE THIS FORM WHEN YOU SUBMIT A STIPULATED OR CONTESTED ORDER TO THE JUDGE FOR SIGNING IN WAYNE COUNTY ONLY.

I certify the attached Order or Judgment as presented for entry to be in full conformity with th[e] set forth by statute, INCLUDING A PROVISION FOR IMMEDIATE INCOME WITHHOLDING (WHICH SHALL BE IMPLEMENTED BY THE FRIEND OF THE COURT), THE PAYER'S SOCIAL SECURITY NUMBER AND THE NAME AND ADDRESS OF HIS/HER SOURCE OF INCOME IF KNOWN , UNLESS OTHERWISE ORDERED BY THE COURT, and with Michigan Court Rules 3.201 and following, and if applicable, includes all provisions of the Friend of the Court recommendation or is in conformity with the decision of

JUDGE LESTER TUBBS _____ rendered on the ___15TH___ day of

___FEB.___ , 19 _99_ .

_2-15-99_
Date

Dudley Lovelace
Attorney / Bar No.
DEFENDANT

Instructions :   Please sign and present this Certificate to the Court Clerk when the Order or Judgment is presented for entry. If an ex parte interim order is being presented to the Judge, please complete the "Certificate on Behalf of Plaintiff regarding Ex Parte Interim Support Order" and follow Local Court Rule 3.206.

#1225 (7/95) CERTIFICATE OF CONFORMITY FOR DOMESTIC RELATIONS ORDER OR JUDGMENT

CHAPTER 2:
Custody

Once established by a divorce judgment, custody of minor children cannot be changed casually. On the contrary, Michigan custody law aims for stability in the lives of children, and discourages custody modification in all but the most convincing cases. With a bias against change embedded in the custody law, most modification motions are bound to fail. Nevertheless, under the right circumstances it's possible to modify custody after your divorce.

Types of Custody

Since the debut of joint custody in 1980, Michigan custody comes in two parts: legal custody and physical custody. These two custody elements can be combined in various ways to provide for several types of custody:

Sole custody. Sole custody assigns both legal and physical custody of the children to the custodial parent. Since the custodial parent has physical custody, the children live with him/her. The noncustodial parent ordinarily has periodic parenting time.

As the children's legal custodian, the custodial parent makes all important child-rearing decisions. Routine decisions about the children are made by the parent in whose care the children are when the routine decision has to be made (usually this is the custodial parent, but it could be the noncustodial parent during parenting time).

Joint legal custody. With this arrangement, one parent has physical custody of the children, but both parents share legal custody. Like sole custody, the children live with the custodial parent (parent with physical custody); the noncustodial parent ordinarily has parenting time.

But because legal custody is joint, both parents must agree about important aspects of the children's medical care, education, religious instruction, etc. For example, if a child wanted to transfer from a public to a private school, both parents must consent to the transfer. But if the child needed a routine school permission form signed, the parent taking care of the child at the time could sign the form.

Joint physical custody. When parents have joint physical custody, they share physical and usually legal custody of the children. As joint legal custodians, the parents share decision-making for the children, as described above. And as joint physical custodians, both parents also share physical control of the children. But how can that be accomplished? After all, you can't physically divide the children in two, as King Solomon proposed in the Bible story. As it happens, there are several ways for parents to share physical custody of children:

¶ *Split-time custody.* With split-time custody, the children live with each parent for fairly short periods of time. For example, the children might reside with one parent for a week, then move to the other for the next week, and so on. Parents of young children have been known to exchange custody every few days or even every other day.

¶ *Block-time custody.* Block-time custody allows the children to spend large amounts of time with the parents. Typically, block-time custody is scheduled around the children's school year. In this arrangement, the children might reside with one parent for the nine-month school year and with the other parent during the three-month summer vacation.

¶ *"Bird's nest" custody.* Just as birds tend to their young in the nest, the children can stay in the home and the parents take turns moving in and out. Each parent exercises physical custody while living in the home with the children.

Split custody. Split custody divides the children between the parents so each parent has custody of one or more. You can split sole custody or joint legal custody by assigning physical custody of the children to different parents. In a way, joint physical custody is already split because the parents share custody of the children. But you can split joint physical custody even more by putting the children on different custody schedules, so they don't move together as their physical custody rotates.

Mixed custody. Ordinarily, parents get one type of custody for all their children. But it's possible to mix custody so there are different types of custody for the children of a family. For example, one parent might have sole custody of two children and joint physical custody of a third child with the other parent.

Third-party custody. When you divorce, you lose natural custody of your children to the court, which becomes their guardian. Normally, the court gives custody back to the parents. As a matter of fact, Michigan custody law favors parental custody (see "Modification and Third Parties" on page 65 for more about this tilt toward parents in the custody law). Nevertheless, in exceptional cases a court can award custody to a third party, instead of parents. The third party receiving custody might be a relative, such as a grandparent, or even a nonrelative like a foster parent or child welfare agency.

Given all these custody choices, how do courts decide custody? According to Michigan's child custody act of 1970, courts must determine custody according to the best interests of the children. The act defines children's best interests as the sum of the following factors:

- love, affection, and other emotional ties existing between the parties involved and the child
- capacity and disposition of the parties involved to give the child love, affection, and guidance and to continue the education and raising of the child in his or her religion or creed, if any
- capacity and disposition of the parties involved to provide the child with food, clothing, medical care or other remedial care recognized and permitted under the laws of this state in place of medical care, and other material needs
- length of time the child has lived in a stable, satisfactory environment, and the desirability of maintaining continuity
- permanence, as a family unit, of the existing or proposed custodial home or homes
- moral fitness of the parties involved
- mental and physical health of the parties involved
- home, school, and community record of the child
- reasonable preference of the child, if the court considers the child to be of sufficient age to express preference
- willingness and ability of each of the parties to facilitate and encourage a close and continuing parent-child relationship between the child and the other parent or the child and the parents
- domestic violence, regardless of whether the violence was directed against or witnessed by the child

- when joint custody is also at stake, the judge must also consider an extra factor: whether the parents will be able to cooperate and generally agree concerning important decisions affecting the welfare of the child
- any other factor considered by the court to be relevant to a particular child custody dispute

Note: In most cases, custody must be withheld from a parent who has committed criminal sexual conduct against any children in the family.

During a custody trial or hearing, the judge must address *all* of these best interest factors. The judge must make special factual findings and reach legal conclusions about each factor, even when it doesn't seem to apply.

Besides the best-interest factors, courts deciding custody are guided by two legal presumptions: custodial presumption and parental presumption.

To provide stability for children, the custodial presumption gives current custodians of children preference over noncustodians seeking custody. The presumption applies when children are living in an "established custodial environment." According to the custody law, a custodial environment exists when "over an appreciable time the child naturally looks to the custodian in that environment for guidance, discipline, the necessities of life and parental comfort."

In most post-judgment cases, enough time has passed since the divorce to establish a custodial environment with one parent. On the other hand, if physical custody has been exchanged frequently, either during the exercise of joint physical custody or after multiple custody modifications, no custodial environment may exist.

Sometimes, two custodial environments coexist. Michigan courts have ruled that joint physical custody can establish custodial environments with both parents, and each may invoke the custodial presumption. This creates a kind of custody stalemate that is difficult to change.

The parental presumption gives parents a custody edge over nonparents. The parental presumption is seldom an issue in post-judgment custody cases because it's usually the parents who are vying for custody. But sometimes, third parties may have previously received custody of the children or third-party noncustodians are able to intervene in a post-judgment case and ask for custody. In these situations, parents can invoke the parental presumption to get custody away from third-party custodians or ward off custody claims of intervening third parties.

Glossary

Legal presumption–a rule of evidence helping a party to prove something, or which makes it more difficult for another party to prove something.

Interstate Enforcement and Modification

Years ago, divorced parents routinely flouted custody orders by snatching their children and moving out of state. Once away, they could often avoid enforcement of the custody order. Making matters worse, fugitive parents could file a custody modification case in their new state and obtain custody legally, leaving the former custodial parent in the home state helpless.

Today, there are several state and federal laws, notably the Uniform Child Custody Jurisdiction and Enforcement Act (UCCJEA) and the Parental Kidnapping Prevention Act (PKPA), preventing state-hopping in custody cases. These laws encourage enforcement of the original custody order and limit modification of custody orders out of state. Nevertheless, modification of out-of-state custody orders is still permissible under the right circumstances. All this is summarized by the table below, which looks at interstate custody enforcement and modification from a Michigan point of view, as if a party were about to file a post-judgment motion in Michigan:

Interstate Custody Proceedings

	Michigan order	Out-of-state order
Both parents residing in Michigan when post-judgment relief is sought.	Enforcement in Michigan; modification in Michigan only.	Enforcement in Michigan; no modification in Michigan unless and until Michigan becomes children's home state or home-state substitute.
The children and one parent residing outside of Michigan when post-judgment relief is sought.	Enforcement in Michigan; no modification in Michigan.	Enforcement in Michigan; no modification in Michigan.
Children and both parents rsiding outside of Michigan when post-judgment relief is sought.	Enforcement in Michigan; no modification in Michigan.	Enforcement in Michigan; no modification in Michigan.

Assumptions	*Exceptions*	*Definitions*
Assumes that children live with the parties (not with third parties), and move with them.	Courts can decline jurisdiction they have because: 1) another state is more convenient/appropriate place 2) jurisdiction is based on misconduct.	The children's home state is where they are, or were recently, living during past 6 months. Home-state substitute exists when children are transient and other factors must be used to determine jurisdiction.

Dealing with an Out-of-State Order in Michigan

If your out-of-state custody order is enforceable and/or modifiable in Michigan, you must register the order before enforcement or modification can begin. Registration can be complicated, since it must consider custody jurisdiction and other technical issues. For help with registration, contact the friend of the court. The friend of the court, if it's able to help, can also combine registration and actual enforcement into one step.

After registration, your custody enforcement or modification motion is handled normally, almost as if you'd been divorced in Michigan and lived here ever since. The law of the divorce-granting state generally applies, but all the enforcement and modification procedures and remedies described below are available.

Modification out of State

When another state has control of your case, you must go there for modification of custody. Typically, this state is the divorce-granting state, although it could be the state where the children are now living now if everyone has moved out of the divorce-granting state.

Enforcement

For enforcement of a custody order, the first stop is always the friend of the court. By law, the friend of the court is responsible for enforcing custody orders. You should prepare a written complaint describing the custody violation and submit this to the friend of the court.

One enforcement remedy is informal mediation. The friend of the court will contact the parties and offer to settle/mediate their custody dispute before one of its mediators.

If a custody dispute cannot be mediated, the friend of the court may file a motion asking for a contempt citation against the custody violator. The penalties for contempt of court are stiff, and include a monetary fine, jail or both. The friend of the court can also ask the court to suspend the violator's driver's, occupational or sporting/recreational licenses.

If the friend of the court refuses to enforce a custody order, you can seek enforcement yourself. Contempt is the primary method of enforcement. Regrettably, you will probably need a lawyer to represent you in a contempt proceeding to enforce custody.

State and federal kidnapping laws are another effective way of enforcing custody orders. Among other things, these laws prohibit parents from holding children to frustrate the custody or parenting time rights of the other parent. There is also an international treaty, known as The Hague Convention, which the United States and many other countries have signed, prohibiting wrongful removal of children to foreign countries and providing for return of the children. If you want to obtain the protection of these criminal laws, call your local, state or federal law enforcement agencies.

State and federal authorities have special parent locator services available for finding missing children. These services are designed for child support collection, but they can be used to locate parents harboring abducted children. There are also state and national contact lines for locating missing children.

More Information

About finding missing children, use a state or federal parent locator service. Contact the friend of the court for access to these services, or call the federal parent locator service directly at (202) 401-9267.

Call state and national missing children contact lines:

Michigan State Police at (517) 333-4006

National Center for Missing and Exploited Children (NCMEC) at its 24-hour hotline: (800) 843-5678

Modification

A custody order can be modified with regard to a child while the order is in effect against the child. But after a child reaches the age of 18, the custody order expires as to the child and cannot be modified regarding the child (the order may still be operative and modifiable against younger siblings).

In modifying custody, the court can make minor custody changes, such as adjusting a block-time joint physical custody schedule from a 3½ days/3½ days split to a weekends/weekdays division. Or the court could make a fundamental change, modifying the type of custody or the custodian.

What's more, modifying custody often triggers changes in parenting time and child support. For example, changing from sole custody to joint physical custody might require less parenting time. As a result, custody modification is frequently combined with modification of parenting time or child support. See Chapters 3 and 5 for information about modifying parenting time and child support.

Modification and Third Parties

Sometimes, the parents have already lost custody to a third party before, during or after their divorce (so the third party is already "involved" in your post-judgment case). Or the parents may face a third-party custody claim now, post-judgment (the third party wants to "intervene" in your case).

These third-party scenarios are explained in "What If a Third Party Is Involved or Intervenes in My Case?" on page 16. That section also describes the special steps you must take to deal with a third party appearing in your case.

As a practical matter, third parties face enormous difficulty in obtaining custody. The parental presumption favors parents over nonparents. And recently, the Michigan Supreme Court raised the bar even further, ruling (in a parenting time case) that courts shouldn't give third parties extra rights according to the best interest test unless the parents are unfit. What the new legal standard for third-party rights will ultimately be is unclear right now, but it's bound to be tougher than before.

Guardian ad Litem

Another kind of third party could appear in your custody case: a guardian ad litem (GAL), representing the interests of the children. Courts now have the authority to appoint GALs to protect children in custody cases, although the y seldom do.

Stipulated Modification

You and your ex may agree on modifying custody. For example, a parent with sole custody may be overwhelmed with child-rearing and may now want to share custody with the other parent in a joint physical custody arrangement.

Regardless of what you and your ex stipulate to, the court has the final say on any modification of custody. It can reject your proposed modification if it believes the change isn't in the best interests of the children. Nevertheless, chances are good that the court will approve your proposed modification. This is especially true if you've stipulated to some type of joint custody, because Michigan custody law has a presumption in favor of joint custody when both parents want it.

You don't always need to file a motion or have a court hearing to modify custody by stipulation. You must prepare the Order Regarding Custody and Parenting Time (FOC 89) and have it approved by the court. See "Stipulated Orders" on page 30 for complete instructions about preparing a stipulated order, getting court approval of the order, filing it with the clerk and serving it on your ex.

As for the new custody provision, see "Types of Custody" on page 59 for the various custody options and "Custody Provisions for the Court Order" on page 70 about providing for all kinds of custody in the FOC 89. You can also adjust parenting time in the FOC 89. But if you also want to modify child support, you must add the Uniform Child Support Order (FOC 10/52) to the FOC 89.

Contested Modification

When your ex won't stipulate to modification of custody, you must file a motion asking for the change. Minor adjustments of a custody schedule, in which custody doesn't change hands, might not be very controversial. But when you want to change the type of custody or the custodian, you must have a very strong case to prevail. As explained before, the custodial presumption creates a bias toward the custody status quo. Only when you have powerful evidence for modification of custody does your motion have a chance for succeeding.

Motion

You can ask for custody modification in the Motion Regarding Custody (FOC 87). There is a sample FOC 87 at the end of this chapter, showing you how to complete the various parts of the motion. The core of the motion are paragraphs #4 and #5, which state the grounds for the motion, and paragraph #7 with your proposed custody modification.

In paragraph #4, cite which circumstances have changed in the lives of you, your ex and/or your children since your custody order was issued. As explained "Grounds for Modification" on page 5, change of circumstances is the customary grounds for modifying custody.

Paragraph #5 has the other grounds for modification: proper cause (see "Grounds for Modification" on page 5 for more about the double grounds for modification). Proper cause is often the factual change of circumstances plus application of a legal rule supporting modification. In this case, the legal rule is the best interest factors from the custody law that must be related to the facts making up the change of circumstances.

In paragraph #7, describe the new custody arrangement you are proposing. If the modification is small, you can describe it in the space provided; for a bigger change, particularly one with extra issues like parenting time or child support, attach an extra sheet to the motion and describe the modification there.

For complete information and instructions about preparing, filing and serving a motion like this, see "Papers" on page 23 and "Motions" on page 32.

Special Motion Preparation When Your Ex Is Imprisoned

When your ex is incarcerated in a Michigan prison, you must take several special steps during your custody case. The purpose of these rules is to make sure the inmate gets full due process (notice and opportunity to respond) in family cases when parental custody rights are at stake.

Before you do anything, you must know where your ex is imprisoned and have his/her prisoner identification number. You may already know these things; if not, use the state prison locator service to find out. After you have this information, you must follow these procedures:

> **More Information**
>
> To locate a Michigan prison inmate and/or obtain the inmate's prisoner identification number, call the state's prison locator service at (517) 335-7570.

¶ In the caption of your motion, add the following two items in or near your ex's caption box:

"[Plaintiff/defendant] is an inmate at [name of Michigan correctional facility] with prisoner identification number [prisoner identification number]."

"A telephone hearing with the inmate must be held as provided by MCR 2.004."

¶ Later, after you file and serve the motion, the court will issue an order scheduling a hearing or conference with your ex, by telephone, at his/her correctional facility.

During the telephone hearing, court officials must confirm that your ex was served with the motion papers, has access to a lawyer, if one is wanted, how s/he can communicate with the court and set future hearings in the case.

¶ After the telephone hearing, the case should continue normally and your ex may or may not appear at the motion hearing.

Responding to a Motion

If you receive a motion for modification of custody from your ex, you can respond orally or in writing, in several ways.

If you agree with the motion completely, contact your ex immediately and arrange to stipulate to a modification order. In paragraphs #4, #5, #6 and

#7 of the Response to Motion Regarding Custody (FOC 88), you can also indicate your agreement with the motion. But why do extra paperwork when it's easier to stipulate to a modification order? You could also appear at the hearing and agree to the motion, but this too wastes time when stipulation is available. See "Stipulated Modification" on page 65 for more about stipulations.

Sometimes, you may agree with part of the motion and disagree with the rest. It's important to signal your partial agreement as soon as possible because this narrows the issues in the case. If you file a Response to Motion Regarding Custody (FOC 88), check box #6b and describe the extent of your agreement with the motion in the space below. If you choose to respond orally, mention your partial agreement to the mediator, referee or judge, so the agreed-upon issues can be eliminated from the hearing.

When you oppose the motion, you can voice your disagreement in two ways. You can file a written response to the motion or wait until the motion hearing and respond orally. A written response is usually better, because it gets your views across more effectively.

Use the Response to Motion Regarding Custody (FOC 88) for a written response. In paragraphs #4 and #5, say why you oppose the motion. You may disagree that circumstances have changed and/or that it would be in the best interests of the children to modify custody.

If you've been the custodial parent for a while, don't forget the custodial presumption. As explained before, this presumption favors leaving current custody intact, forcing a noncustodian to come forward with extra evidence for modification of custody. This is a very difficult burden to satisfy, and gives the custodial parent an enormous advantage during the motion hearing.

For complete information and instructions about preparing, filing and serving a response, see "Responding to a Motion" on page 35.

You can also respond to a motion by making a counter-motion. Normally, if you oppose the motion with the Response to Motion Regarding Custody (FOC 88), you disagree with the grounds for the motion in paragraphs #4 and #5. Then, in paragraph #7 you oppose the proposed modification, as in the sample response at the end of this chapter.

But if you want a different kind of modification of custody (or different parenting time or child support from the kind proposed in the main motion), check box #7b and explain in the space below what you want. Whether you realize it or not, this request is a counter-motion.

In some cases, it's even possible to ask for completely new relief in a counter-motion. Add new issues carefully, because these can easily sidetrack the case. Nevertheless, it may make sense to seek new relief in a counter-motion when the new issues are compatible with the main motion.

For more about counter-motion tactics and how to counter-move for new relief, see "Making a Counter-Motion" on page 37.

Friend of the Court

Before a post-judgment motion is heard by the judge, the friend of the court may intervene to mediate, investigate or referee, in an attempt to settle the dispute. Modification of custody is usually a serious issue, so it's likely that several things will be used to settle the dispute.

There will almost certainly be an effort to mediate, either informally by the friend of the court or formally by a court-appointed mediator. Out-of-court private mediation or arbitration is also possible.

During a custody dispute, the friend of the court is usually required to investigate the issue, and make a report and recommendation about custody. It's also a good bet that the motion will be refereed by the friend of the court before the motion hearing.

See "Friend of the Court" on page 38 for more about the friend of the court's roles in post-judgment cases, and how to deal with mediation, investigation or refereeing by the friend of the court. This section also has information about formal mediation, private mediation and arbitration, which all take place outside the friend of the court system.

Motion Hearing

As explained in "Motion Hearings" on page 41, there are two kinds of motion hearings: 1) nonevidentiary hearing where facts aren't in dispute, evidence is seldom introduced and the parties merely make legal arguments to the judge 2) evidentiary hearing where facts are disputed and evidence, such as testimony from witnesses, must be introduced to establish the true facts.

Simple custody modifications like minor adjustments of a custody schedule can maybe get by with a nonevidentiary hearing. But most modifications will require full evidentiary hearings, because the parties seldom agree on the facts in these cases.

The moving party's task during a motion hearing is two-fold: 1) establish a change of circumstances justifying modification of custody 2) show that the modification is in the best interests of the children.

To prove the first issue, the moving party must show that the current custody arrangement isn't working out as planned. The reasons for this are limitless: the children are having academic problems at school, have high absenteeism, show poor discipline at school, in the home or in the community, are breaking the law and have police records, have health problems, are living in a bad environment, etc. Whatever the reasons, the moving party must present a convincing case that the custody status quo isn't working.

As explained before, the best interests of the children are determined by the 12 or 13 factors in the child custody act of 1970 (see "Types of Custody" on page 59 for a complete list). During the custody hearing, the judge must make factual findings about *all* of these best -interest factors. Consequently, you must address each factor whether you are the moving party or the opponent.

The two custody presumptions may also be important. The custodial presumption is often at issue because an established custodial environment may have developed since divorce. And the parental presumption can help parents regain custody from a third party or defend against third-party custody claims.

Glossary

Clear and convincing evidence–is strong evidence that makes something highly probable.

Or you could look at it this way: On an imaginary evidence scale, clear and convincing evidence falls somewhere between a preponderance of evidence (factual assertions are "more likely than not") standard used in ordinary civil cases, but less than the beyond-a-reasonable-doubt test in criminal cases.

Sometimes, both of these presumptions apply, as when a parent is trying to get custody back from a third party with an established custodial environment. In that case, courts have decided that the two presumptions cancel each other, but that the burden falls on the parent to show, by a mere preponderance of evidence, that the best interests of the children are for transferring custody to the parent.

When a presumption applies, "clear and convincing" evidence must be introduced to overcome the presumption. For example, in a custody dispute between a third party and a custodial parent invoking the parental presumption, the third party might show physical abuse of the children by the parent. This kind of evidence would probably qualify as clear and convincing evidence that the best interests of the children are for transferring custody from the parent to the third party.

Since a custody hearing is likely to be evidentiary, with important issues at stake, you must make careful preparations for the hearing. Preparation for the hearing should be extensive. You may even need to subpoena witnesses, such as teachers, counselors, social workers or neighbors. See "Preparing for a Motion Hearing" on page 41 for complete information about prehearing preparations.

The format of the hearing will be determined by whether your ex attends the hearing. If your ex is present, the hearing will be held as planned, with both sides presenting their evidence and arguments. In your ex's absence, you will probably win by default after an abbreviated hearing. "Motion Hearing Itself" on page 42 explains all this in detail.

Court Order

After the court hearing, the judge will decide the motion. The judge will either decide immediately and give an oral decision "from the bench," or take the case "under submission" and rule later by issuing a written decision.

Either way, the moving party must prepare the order granting or denying the motion. Use the Order Regarding Custody and Parenting Time (FOC 89) as the order for custody and parenting time modifications (see "Parenting Time Provisions for the Court Order" on page 88 about providing for parenting time and "Child Support Provisions for the Court Order" on page 129 for child support modifications, which must be added in the Uniform Child Support Order (FOC 10/52)).

The moving party must also get the order signed by the judge and filed with the clerk. There are several ways to do this. See "Court Orders" on page 44 for complete forms and instructions.

Custody Provisions for the Court Order

Inside the custody order, you must provide for the custody the judge has ordered, whether this was the custody you proposed in the motion or something else. You can provide for several types of custody in paragraph

#10 of the Order Regarding Custody and Parenting Time (FOC 89); but some types require extra provisions in an attachment to the order.

Sole, Joint Legal or Third-Party Custody

To select sole or joint legal custody, check the correct boxes in paragraph #10 of the FOC 89. The sample paragraph #10 below is an example of sole custody for the plaintiff. The full sample FOC 89 on page 77 shows joint legal custody (with sole physical custody to the plaintiff. For third-party custody, check the correct custody boxes, the third-party box and insert the third party's name in the space to the right.

☒ 10. Custody is granted as follows:
Name(s) of child(ren): DUANE W. LOVELACE AND DARRYL W. LOVELACE

☐ Joint legal to ☐ plaintiff ☐ defendant ☐ third party
Unless otherwise agreed, a parent whose custody or parenting time of a child is governed by this order shall not change the legal residence of the child except in compliance with section 11 of the Child Custody Act of 1970, 1970 PA 91, MCL 722.31.
☐ Joint physical to ☐ plaintiff ☐ defendant ☐ third party
☒ Sole legal to ☒ plaintiff ☐ defendant ☐ third party
☒ Sole physical to ☒ plaintiff ☐ defendant ☐ third party

Joint Physical Custody

Whenever you choose joint physical custody, you must decide whether to provide for a specific physical custody schedule or leave custody open and flexible. It's permissible to have open joint physical custody, allowing you and your ex to exchange custody as you go and at your convenience. If you want this arrangement, you needn't do any more than choose the joint physical custody option by checking the correct boxes in paragraph #10 of the Order Regarding Custody and Parenting Time (FOC 89). The sample paragraph #10 on the next page depicts joint physical custody for the parties (for an open order, delete the parenthesized statement in the lower right corner).

Joint physical custody is difficult to manage. If you anticipate problems, you should specify in advance how you and your ex will share physical custody. To provide for joint physical custody with a specific custody schedule, choose joint physical custody in paragraph #10 of the Order Regarding Custody and Parenting Time (FOC 89). Add a statement that the remainder of the joint physical custody is attached, as in the sample paragraph #10 below.

☒ 10. Custody is granted as follows:
Name(s) of child(ren): DUANE W. LOVELACE AND DARRYL W. LOVELACE

☒ Joint legal to ☒ plaintiff ☒ defendant ☐ third party
Unless otherwise agreed, a parent whose custody or parenting time of the child is governed by this order shall not change the legal residence of the child except in compliance with section 11 of the Child Custody Act of 1970, 1970 PA 91, MCL 722.31.
☒ Joint physical to ☒ plaintiff ☒ defendant ☐ third party   (SEE PARAGRAPH #10A ON
☐ Sole legal to ☐ plaintiff ☐ defendant ☐ third party   THE ATTACHED SHEET FOR
☐ Sole physical to ☐ plaintiff ☐ defendant ☐ third party   THE REMAINDER OF THE
                                                             JOINT PHYSICAL CUSTODY
                                                             ORDER.)

Then, in an attachment to the FOC 89, provide for specific joint physical custody. The provisions below are split-time, block-time and bird's nest joint physical custody provisions which you can adapt to your situation.

Split-Time Custody

You can arrange for split-time custody in many ways. The sample provision provides for weekday/weekend split-time custody, but you could substitute another schedule listed below, or any other schedule:

- day/day
- 3½ days/3½ days
- 3 days/4 days
- weekdays/weekend
- one week/one week
- two weeks/two weeks
- one week/three weeks
- month/month
- two months/two months
- etc.

10a. <u>Joint Physical Custody</u>. The parties shall have joint physical custody of their minor children as follows: Plaintiff shall have physical custody during weekdays from 8:30 a.m. Monday until 6:00 p.m. Friday. Defendant shall have physical custody during weekends from 6:00 p.m. Friday until 8:30 a.m. Monday.

Block-Time Custody: school year/summer vacation

10a. <u>Joint Physical Custody</u>. The parties shall have joint physical custody of their minor children as follows: Plaintiff shall have physical custody from [seven] days before the first day of school in the fall until [seven] days after the last day of school in the spring. Defendant shall have physical custody of the children during the remaining summer school vacation period.

"Bird's Nest" Custody

10a. <u>Joint Physical Custody</u>. The parties shall have joint physical custody of their minor children as follows: The parties will alternate residence in the family home [monthly]. Each party shall exercise physical custody while residing with the children at the family home.

When you choose joint physical custody, don't forget about parenting time. Some types of joint physical custody, such as frequent split-time or bird's nest custody, might not require any or much parenting time (except perhaps during holidays). But parenting time may be necessary for infrequent split-time or block-time custody. In that case, you should include a parenting time provision in paragraph #11 of the Order Regarding Custody and Parenting Time (FOC 89), unless your divorce judgment already has an adequate provision.

Paragraph #10 of the FOC 89 can't deal with split or mixed custody. As a result, insert a statement in the paragraph that the custody order is attached, as in the sample paragraph below. Then provide for split or mixed custody separately, in an attached provision.

☒ 10. Custody is granted as follows: *(SEE PARAGRAPH #10a ON THE ATTACHED SHEET*
Name(s) of child(ren): _____ *FOR THE CUSTODY ORDER)* _____
☐ Joint legal to   ☐ plaintiff   ☐ defendant   ☐ third party
    Unless otherwise agreed, a parent whose custody or parenting time of a child is governed by this order shall not change the legal residence of the child except in compliance with section 11 of the Child Custody Act of 1970, 1970 PA 91, MCL 722.31.
☐ Joint physical to   ☐ plaintiff   ☐ defendant   ☐ third party
☐ Sole legal to   ☐ plaintiff   ☐ defendant   ☐ third party
☐ Sole physical to   ☐ plaintiff   ☐ defendant   ☐ third party

You can split sole, joint legal or even joint physical custody of children. Split sole or joint legal custody by assigning physical custody to different parents (legal custody stays with each custodial parent in split sole custody; it's shared with split joint legal custody). The custody provision below depicts split sole custody:

10a. <u>Split Sole Custody</u>.   The parties shall have custody of their minor children as follows: Plaintiff shall have legal and physical custody of Duane Wesley Lovelace; defendant shall have legal and physical custody of Darryl Wendell Lovelace.

It's possible to split joint physical custody by putting the children on different custody schedules, so they don't move in sync between the parents. The custody provision below sets up split block-time joint physical custody:

10a. <u>Split Joint Physical Custody</u>.   The parties shall have custody of their minor children as follows:

(a) Plaintiff shall have physical custody of Duane Wesley Lovelace from [seven] days before the first day of school in the fall until [seven] days after the last day of school in the spring. Defendant shall have physical custody of Duane Wesley Lovelace during the remaining summer school vacation period.

(b) Defendant shall have physical custody of Darryl Wendell Lovelace from [seven] days before the first day of school in the fall until [seven] days after the last day of school in the spring. Plaintiff shall have physical custody of Darryl Wendell Lovelace during the remaining summer school vacation period.

(c) The parties shall have joint legal custody of these children.

You can mix custody by choosing different types of custody for the children within a family. The custody provision below mixes sole custody and joint physical custody:

10a. <u>Mixed Custody</u>. The parties shall have custody of their minor children as follows:

(a) Plaintiff shall have legal and physical custody of Duane Wesley Lovelace.

(b) The parties shall have joint legal and physical custody of Darryl Wendell Lovelace.

[A specific joint physical custody provision for Darryl is optional here, or his joint physical custody can be left open.]

THIS PARAGRAPH SEES WHETHER PARTIES AGREE ON THE MODIFICATION. IF YOU BOTH AGREE, SKIP FILING A MOTION AND JUST STIPULATE TO A MODIFICATION ORDER, AS EXPLAINED IN "STIPULATED ORDERS" IN CHAPTER 1C.

INCLUDE BOTH GROUNDS FOR MODIFICATION IN PARAGRAPHS #4 AND #5. SEE "MOTION" IN THIS CHAPTER FOR MORE ABOUT MODIFICATION GROUNDS.

Approved, SCAO

Original - Court
1st copy - Other Party
2nd copy - Moving Party

3rd copy - Friend of the Court
4th copy - Proof of Service
5th copy - Proof of Service

STATE OF MICHIGAN
JUDICIAL CIRCUIT
COUNTY

MOTION REGARDING CUSTODY

CASE NO.

Telephone no.

Friend of the Court address

Plaintiff's name, address, and telephone no.   ☐ moving party

Defendant's name, address, and telephone no.   ☐ moving party

v

Third party name, address, and telephone no.   ☐ moving party

1. ☒ a. On __7-1-90__ a judgment
   Date
   or order was entered regarding custody
   ☐ b. There is currently no order regarding

was ordered to have custody of the following child

☒ 2. The ☒ plaintiff ☐ defendant ☐ third party
   DUANE W. LOVELACE AND DARRYL W. LOVELACE

3. The child(ren) have been living with __DARLENE LOVELACE__
   Name(s)
   __121 S. MAIN, LAKE CITY, MI 48800__ since __6-1-95__
   Complete address   Date

4. Circumstances have changed as follows that require custody or a change in custody:
   Use a separate sheet to explain in detail what has happened and attach. Include all necessary facts.
   WITHOUT LEGAL CUSTODY, MY PARENTAL AUTHORITY IS DIMINISHED AND IT'S MORE DIFFICULT TO DISCIPLINE THE BOYS AS THEY GET OLDER.

5. Proper cause exists as follows that require custody or a change in custody: Use a separate sheet to explain in detail which
   factors of the Child Custody Act for determining best interests of the child(ren) are affected by the circumstances in 4. above. Include all necessary
   facts. MY DIMINISHED PARENTAL AUTHORITY IMPAIRS: 1) MY ABILITY TO PROVIDE
   GUIDANCE TO THE CHILDREN (FACTOR #2) 2) OVERALL PARENT-CHILD RELATIONSHIP (FACTOR #10)
   _____ and I agree to custody, support, and parenting time as follows:

☐ 6. _____
      Name
      Use a separate sheet to explain in detail what you have agreed on and attach. Include all necessary facts.

7. I ask the court to order that custody, parenting time, and support be as follows:
   Use a separate sheet to explain in detail what you want the court to order and attach.
   MODIFY PRESENT SOLE CUSTODY ORDER TO PROVIDE
   JOINT LEGAL CUSTODY FOR PLAINTIFF AND ME.

I declare that the above statements are true to the best of my information, knowledge, and belief.

__1-1-99__   _Dudley Lovelace_
Date   Moving party's signature

NOTICE OF HEARING

A hearing will be held on this motion before __LESTER TUBBS__
                                              Name of judge or referee
on __2-15-99__ at __9:00 AM__ at __OJIBWAY COUNTY COURTHOUSE__
   Date   Time   Place

NOTE: If you are the person receiving this motion, you may file a response. Contact the friend of the court office and request form FOC 88.

CERTIFICATE OF MAILING

I certify that on this date I mailed a copy of this motion and notice of hearing on the other party(ies) by ordinary mail at the above address(es).

__1-2-99__   _Dudley Lovelace_
Date   Moving party's signature

                                              MCL 722.21 et seq., MCR 2.119, MCR 3.213

FOC 87 (6/03) MOTION REGARDING CUSTODY

SEVERAL PARAGRAPHS TEST WHETHER YOU AGREE WITH MODIFICATION. IF YOU AGREE, COMPLETELY OR IN PART, SEE "RESPONDING TO A MOTION" IN THIS CHAPTER ABOUT YOUR RESPONSE OPTIONS.

YOU CAN MAKE A COUNTER-MOTION IN THIS PARAGRAPH. SEE "RESPONDING TO A MOTION" IN THIS CHAPTER FOR MORE ABOUT COUNTER-MOTIONS.

Approved, SCAO

Original - Court
1st copy - Moving Party
2nd copy - Responding Party

3rd copy - Friend of the Court
4th copy - Proof of Service
5th copy - Proof of Service

STATE OF MICHIGAN
JUDICIAL CIRCUIT
COUNTY

RESPONSE TO
MOTION REGARDING CUSTODY

CASE NO.

Friend of the Court address

Plaintiff's name, address, and telephone no.

☐ moving party

Telephone no.

Defendant's name, address, and telephone no.

☐ moving party

v

Third party name, address, and telephone no.

☐ moving party

1. ☒ a. On __7-1-90__
   Date

   or order was entered regarding custody.

   a judgment

   ☐ b. There is currently no order regarding custody.

☒ 2. The   ☒ plaintiff   ☐ defendant   ☐ third party
DUANE W. LOVELACE AND DARRYL W. LOVELACE
                                              was ordered to have custody of the following child(ren):

3. The child(ren) have been living with __DARLENE LOVELACE__
                                          Name(s)

__121 S. MAIN, LAKE CITY, MI 48800__   at
Complete address

4. I ☐ agree ☒ do not agree   that circumstances have changed as stated in the motion.   since __6-1-95__
                                                                                                   Date
Explain in detail what you do not agree with and why. Include all necessary facts. Use a separate sheet of paper if needed.
DEFENDANT WAS ALWAYS A POOR DISCIPLINARIAN OF THE BOYS. THIS WAS TRUE
DURING OUR MARRIAGE AND HASN'T CHANGED SINCE.

5. I ☐ agree ☒ do not agree   that proper cause exists as stated in the motion.
Explain in detail what you do not agree with and why. Include all necessary facts. Use a separate sheet of paper if needed.
DEFENDANT'S REASONS FOR MODIFICATION AREN'T ENOUGH TO OVERCOME THE
ESTABLISHED CUSTODIAL ENVIRONMENT PRESUMPTION. ANYWAY, GIVING LEGAL CUSTODY TO
DEFENDANT WON'T IMPROVE HIS GUIDANCE OF THE CHILDREN OR THE OVERALL PARENT-CHILD
RELATIONSHIP.

☐ 6. I agreed with the other party to custody, parenting time, and support:
   ☐ a. exactly as stated in the motion.
   ☐ b. but not as stated in the motion.
   If b. is checked, explain in detail what you did agree on. Include all necessary facts. Use a separate sheet of paper if needed.

7. ☐ a. I agree with what is being asked for in the motion.
   ☒ b. I do not agree with what is being asked for in the motion and ask the court to order custody, parenting time, and
       support as follows: If b. is checked, explain in detail why and what you want the court to order. Use a separate sheet of paper if needed.
DENY DEFENDANT'S MODIFICATION MOTION, AFFIRMING
CURRENT SOLE CUSTODY ARRANGEMENT.

I declare that the above statements are true to the best of my information, knowledge, and belief.
__2-1-99__
Date

Darlene Lovelace
Responding party's signature

CERTIFICATE OF MAILING

I certify that on this date I mailed a copy of this response on the other party by ordinary mail at the above address.
__2-1-99__
Date

Darlene Lovelace
Responding party's signature

FOC 88 (6/03) RESPONSE TO MOTION REGARDING CUSTODY

MCL 722.21 et seq., MCR 2.119

CHECK:
- 1ST BOX IF ORDER WAS CONTESTED AND GOTTEN AFTER COURT HEARING ON THE ORDER
- 2ND BOX IF NONMOVING PARTY CONSENTED TO ORDER
- 3RD BOX FOR STIPULATED ORDERS
- NO BOXES FOR APPROVAL OF THE ORDER BY SILENCE

Original - Court
1st copy - Other Party
2nd copy - Moving Party

3rd copy - Friend of the Court
4th copy - Proof of Service
5th copy - Proof of Service

ORDER REGARDING CUSTODY AND PARENTING TIME

CASE NO.

Telephone no.

Defendant's name, address, and telephone no.

v

Date: 2-15-99

Judge: LESTER TUBBS

Bar no.

1. This order is entered ☐ after hearing. ☒ on consent of the parties. ☐ on stipulation of the parties.

THE COURT FINDS:

☒ 2. A motion requesting custody, parenting time, and support or a change to custody, parenting time, and support was filed.

☒ 3. A response to the motion was filed.

☒ 4. A change of circumstances ☒ does ☐ does not exist which warrants a custody order or a change in custody.
☐ does not exist which warrants a custody order or a change in custody.

☒ 5. Proper cause ☒ does ☐ does not in the best interests of the child(ren) to ☐ establish ☐ change parenting time.

☐ 6. It ☐ is ☐ is not in the best interests of the child(ren) to ☐ establish ☐ change the support order.

☐ 7. A material change of circumstances exists which warrants a change in the support order.

☐ 8. It is in the best interests of the child(ren) to dismiss the motion.

IT IS ORDERED:

☐ 9. The motion regarding custody, parenting time, and support is dismissed. The prior order remains in effect.

☒ 10. Custody is granted as follows:
Name(s) of child(ren): DUANE W. LOVELACE AND DARRYL W. LOVELACE
☒ Joint legal to ☐ plaintiff ☒ defendant ☐ third party
Unless otherwise agreed, a parent whose custody or parenting time of a child is governed by this order shall not change the legal residence of the child except in compliance with section 11 of the Child Custody Act of 1970, 1970 PA 91, MCL 722.31.

☐ Joint physical to ☐ plaintiff ☐ defendant ☐ third party
☐ Sole legal to ☐ plaintiff ☐ defendant ☐ third party
☒ Sole physical to ☒ plaintiff ☐ defendant ☐ third party
☐ established ☐ changed as follows:

USE PARAGRAPH #11 AND/OR FOC 10/52 IF YOU'RE MODIFYING PARENTING TIME OR CHILD SUPPORT ALONG WITH CUSTODY.

11. Parenting time is
Explain in detail what the court has ordered.

12. The parents shall cooperate with respect to a child so as, in a maximum degree, to advance a child's health, emotional, and physical well-being and to give and afford a child the affection of both parents and a sense of security. Neither parent will, directly or indirectly, influence a child so as to prejudice a child against the other parent. The parents will endeavor to guide a child so as to promote the affectionate relationship between a child and the mother and a child and the father. The parties will cooperate with each other in carrying out the provisions of this order, or otherwise take action regarding a child, it seems necessary to adjust, vary or increase the time allotted to either party, or otherwise take action regarding a child, each of the parties shall act in the best interests of the child. Neither party shall do anything which may estrange the other from the child, injure the child's opinion of the other party, or which will hamper the free and natural development of the child for the other party.

13. The parent with primary physical custody shall notify the friend of the court in writing whenever the address of a minor child changes.

Lester Tubbs
Judge

2-15-99
Date

Support provisions ordered on form FOC 10 / 52.

MCL 552.14, MCL 552.517b(3), MCL 722.21 et seq., MCR 2.119

FOC 89 (6/03) **ORDER REGARDING CUSTODY AND PARENTING TIME**

CHAPTER 3:
Parenting Time

If you have parenting time problems after divorce, you're not alone. Parenting time, along with child support, accounts for most post-judgment cases, as parents frequently cannot adjust to the parenting time set by the divorce judgment.

Until 1996, when the terminology changed, parenting time was known as visitation (some older divorce judgments may still use this name). Whichever name it goes by, parenting time gives the children access to the noncustodial parent so the parent-child relationship can continue after divorce. Parenting time is actually a right possessed by children. This fact often gets lost when parents fight over it, trying to assert their parenting time "rights."

Ordinarily, parenting time is given to noncustodial parents whenever sole custody or joint legal custody is ordered. But parenting time might be necessary for custodial parents in some joint physical custody arrangements. For example, parents with split-time or block-time custody where custody is exchanged infrequently might need parenting time. On the other hand, frequent split-time or bird's nest custody probably doesn't require any parenting time.

Types of Parenting Time

Many states have just one kind of parenting time: specific parenting time. In Michigan, there are several parenting time options:

Reasonable parenting time. Reasonable parenting time is a flexible arrangement allowing parents to schedule parenting time as they please, at times and on terms that are convenient for them.

Specific parenting time. Specific parenting time fixes parenting time according to specific times, terms and conditions.

Supervised parenting time. If a parent is irresponsible, parenting time can be supervised by a trustworthy third party, such as a grandparent.

Long-distance parenting time. Courts are experimenting with forms of long-distance parenting time by telephone, video-conferencing and the Internet.

When a custodial parent wants to deny the noncustodial parent parenting time, the court must decide whether parenting time is in the best interests of the children. That's determined by the same multi-factor best interest test used in custody cases (minus the special joint custody factor):

- love, affection, and other emotional ties existing between the parties involved and the child
- capacity and disposition of the parties involved to give the child love, affection, and guidance and to continue the education and raising of the child in his or her religion or creed, if any
- capacity and disposition of the parties involved to provide the child with food, clothing, medical care or other remedial care recognized and permitted under the laws of this state in place of medical care, and other material needs
- length of time the child has lived in a stable, satisfactory environment, and the desirability of maintaining continuity
- permanence, as a family unit, of the existing or proposed custodial home or homes
- moral fitness of the parties involved
- mental and physical health of the parties involved
- home, school, and community record of the child
- reasonable preference of the child, if the court considers the child to be of sufficient age to express preference
- willingness and ability of each of the parties to facilitate and encourage a close and continuing parent-child relationship between the child and the other parent or the child and the parents
- domestic violence, regardless of whether the violence was directed against or witnessed by the child
- any other factor considered by the court to be relevant to a particular child custody dispute

Note: In most cases, parenting time must be withheld from a parent who has committed criminal sexual conduct against any children in the family.

Michigan law presumes that parenting time is in the best interests of children and can only be taken away from them when parenting time endangers their psychological or physical health. Judges also favor parenting time and are reluctant to withhold it. Even when a noncustodial parent is irresponsible, a court will often order supervised parenting time rather than deny it completely.

Thanks to this preference for parenting time, contesting *whether* parenting time should be ordered is unusual. Instead, most parenting time battles are fought over the type, frequency or duration of parenting time. In these disputes, the parenting time law says that the court may consider the following factors in making a parenting time order:

- existence of any special circumstances or needs of the child
- whether the child is a nursing child less than six months of age, or less than one year of age if the child receives substantial nutrition through nursing
- reasonable likelihood of abuse or neglect of the child during parenting time
- reasonable likelihood of abuse of a parent resulting from the exercise of parenting time
- inconvenience to, and burdensome impact or effect on, the child traveling to and from the parenting time
- whether the noncustodial parent can reasonably be expected to exercise parenting time in accordance with the court order
- threatened or actual detention of the child with the intent to retain or conceal the child from the other parent or from a third person who has legal custody. A custodial parent's temporary residence with the child in a domestic violence shelter may not be construed as evidence of the custodial parent's intent to retain or conceal the child from the other parent
- any other relevant factors

If you and your ex agree on parenting time, the court will almost always approve your arrangement. In fact, the parenting time law says that agreements about parenting time carry great weight. But like other divorce issues affecting child welfare, courts have the final word on parenting time and can reject your parenting time agreement if it isn't in the children's best interests.

In contested cases, the law says that a court must order specific parenting time whenever a parent asks for it. Even without such a request, courts in contested parenting time cases often order specific parenting time anyway, because they figure that reasonable parenting time is unsuitable for feuding parents.

Interstate Enforcement and Modification

Interstate enforcement or modification of parenting time is governed by the same laws that apply to custody, primarily the Uniform Child Custody Jurisdiction and Enforcement Act (UCCJEA) and the Parental Kidnapping Prevention Act (PKPA). See "Interstate Enforcement and Modification" on page 62 for a full explanation of interstate custody proceedings. Just substitute parenting time for custody in that section, to see how parenting time enforcement and modification are handled across state lines.

Dealing with an Out-of-State Order in Michigan

If your out-of-state parenting time order is enforceable and/or modifiable in Michigan, you must first register the order in Michigan before enforcement or modification can begin. See "Interstate Enforcement and Modification" on page 62 for more about registration difficulties and obtaining registration through the friend of the court.

Afterward, your motion is handled normally, almost as if you'd been divorced in Michigan and lived here ever since. The law of the divorce-granting state generally applies, but all the enforcement and modification procedures and remedies described below are available.

Modification out of State

When another state has control of your case, you must go there for modification of parenting time. Typically, this state is the divorce-granting state, although it could be the state where the children are living now if everyone has moved out of the divorce-granting state.

Enforcement

Before you can enforce a parenting time order, you must make sure the order is enforceable. Orders for reasonable parenting time are notoriously difficult to enforce because they are, by nature, vague. A poorly-worded order may also need clarification before enforcement.

You may be able to enforce the parenting time order in your divorce judgment with a simple complaint to the friend of the court. By law, the friend of the court is supposed to enforce all parenting time orders. If you believe your parenting time order is being violated, submit a written complaint to the friend of the court and it should respond. When it does, the friend of the court has several methods for enforcing parenting time orders:

Informal mediation. After receiving a parenting time complaint, the friend of the court will send the alleged violator a notice of the alleged violation and offer to settle/mediate the dispute informally, which may solve the problem.

Make-up parenting time. Give the noncustodial parent extra parenting time to make up for the lost time. Each family court must have a make-up parenting time policy allowing the noncustodial parent to choose substitute parenting time, of the same kind and duration as the lost time, within one year of the loss.

Modification of parenting time. The friend of the court can seek modification of parenting time, to avoid future violations. In a way, the friend of the court enforces parenting time by modifying it.

Contempt. After other enforcement remedies have failed, bring contempt proceedings against the violator. This can result in a fine of $100 or more, jail (with or without work release), suspension of a violator's driver's, occupational or sporting/recreational licenses or other penalties for the violator.

If the friend of the court won't enforce the parenting time order, you can try enforcement yourself. Enforcement by contempt is difficult because you may need a lawyer to file a contempt case. But you can enforce by seeking make-up parenting time or modification of the parenting time schedule.

State, federal and international kidnapping laws offer another means of enforcement. These laws have criminal penalties for serious and wilful violations of enforceable parenting time orders (vague orders may not qualify for criminal enforcement). State and federal authorities also have locator services for finding missing children. "Enforcement" on page 64 has more information about parental kidnapping laws and locator services. To use them, call your local, state or federal law enforcement agencies.

At one time, Michigan gave child support payers another powerful self-help remedy for enforcing parenting time: withholding child support. Today, Michigan law regards parenting time and child support as separate issues, with their own set of enforcement remedies. So even if the custodial parent is violating parenting time, the violation never excuses nonpayment of child support.

The Motion Regarding Parenting Time (FOC 65) is a dual-purpose form designed for either enforcement or modification. For enforcement alone, check as many boxes in paragraph #2 as apply, describing the parenting time violations. In paragraph #5, choose the enforcement remedy you want: check "changed" for modification or "made up" for make-up of parenting time. See "Contested Modification" on page 85 about how to file the motion and bring it before the court.

Modification

A parenting time order can be modified with regard to a child while the order is in effect against the child. But after a child reaches adulthood at age 18, the parenting time order expires as to the child and cannot be modified (the order may still be operative and modifiable against younger siblings).

In modifying parenting time, the court could simply clarify an unclear specific parenting time order. Or it can alter part of a specific parenting time order, leaving the rest of the order intact. Or the court can change the type of parenting time, going from specific parenting time to reasonable parenting time, or the reverse.

Modification and Third Parties

Sometimes, nonparent third parties have received parenting time before, during or after a divorce (so the third party is already "involved" in your post-judgment case). Or the parents may face a third-party parenting time claimnow, post-judgment (the third party wants to "intervene" in your case).

These third-party scenarios are explained in "What If a Third Party Is Involved or Intervenes in My Case?" on page 16. That section also describes the special steps you must take to deal with a third party in your case. See also "Modification and Third Parties" on page 65 about the trend away from the best interest test for third-party custody and parenting time claims toward a new yet-to-be-defined legal standard.

Recently, the parenting time rights of one category of third party have been clarified. In early 2005, a new "grandparenting time" law was passed allowing grandparents to file post-judgment motions for grandparenting time directly. The parents, assuming they are fit parents, can contest the grandparents' claim (if *both* parents object, the claim is dismissed). During a motion hearing, the judge can order grandparenting time if the grandparents can show that denial of the time would create a "substantial risk of harm to the child's mental, physical or emotional health."

Stipulated Modification

You and your ex may agree on modifying parenting time. For example, you may both realize that flexible reasonable parenting time isn't working and that a specific parenting time schedule would be better. Or you may decide that your specific parenting time schedule needs fine-tuning.

Regardless of what you and your ex stipulate to, the court has the final say about any modification of parenting time. It can reject your proposed modification if it believes the change isn't in the best interests of the children. Nevertheless, odds are good that the court will approve your proposal.

You don't need to file a motion or have a court hearing to modify parenting time by stipulation. All you have to do is prepare the Order Regarding Parenting Time (FOC 67) and have it approved by the court. See "Stipulated Orders" on page 30 for complete instructions about preparing a stipulated order, getting court approval of the order, filing it with the clerk and serving it on your ex.

As for the new parenting time provision, see "Types of Parenting Time" on page 79 for the basic parenting time options. "Parenting Time Provisions for the Court Order" on page 88 has suggested language for reasonable parenting time and two kinds of specific parenting time. Insert the provision in paragraph #7 of the Order Regarding Parenting Time (FOC 67). If there isn't enough space there, attach a blank sheet with the full provision.

Contested Modification

When you ex won't stipulate to modification of parenting time, you must file a motion for modification. Modification isn't guaranteed; the court will consider your motion during a hearing and either grant or deny it.

Motion

You can ask for parenting time modification in the Motion Regarding Parenting Time (FOC 65). There is a sample FOC 65 at the end of this chapter showing you how to complete the various parts of the motion. The core of the motion are paragraphs #2 and #4, which state the grounds for the motion, and paragraph #5 describing your proposed parenting time modification.

Has your ex violated the parenting time order? If there have been serious violations, describe these in paragraph #2 by checking as many boxes as apply and attaching a full explanation. These violations show that the order isn't working as planned, providing grounds for modification (or enforcement) of parenting time.

On the other hand, you and your ex may have obeyed the parenting time order, but you now believe it needs to be modified. In paragraph #4, you must show why changing parenting time is in the best interests of your children. This information establishes grounds for modification.

In paragraph #5, describe the new parenting time arrangement you want. If the modification is brief, you can describe it in the small space provided; for a bigger change, describe this fully in an attachment to the FOC 65.

For complete information and instructions about preparing, filing and serving a motion like this, see "Papers" on page 23 and "Motions" on page 32.

Responding to a Motion

If you receive a motion for modification of parenting time from your ex, you can respond orally or in writing, in several ways.

If you agree with the motion completely, contact your ex immediately and arrange to stipulate to a modification order. In paragraphs #2, #3, #4 and #5 of the Response to Motion Regarding Parenting Time (FOC 66), you can also indicate your agreement with the motion. But why do extra paperwork when it's easier to stipulate to a modification order? You could also appear at the hearing and agree to the motion, but this too wastes time when stipulation is available. See "Stipulated Modification" on page 84 for more about stipulations.

Sometimes, you may agree with part of the motion and disagree with the rest. It's important to signal your partial agreement as soon as possible because this narrows the issues in the case. If you file a Response to Motion Regarding Parenting Time (FOC 66), check box #3b and describe the extent of your agreement with the motion in the space below. If you choose to respond orally, mention your partial agreement to the mediator, referee or judge, so the agreed-upon issues can be eliminated from the hearing.

When you oppose the motion, you can voice your disagreement in two ways. You can file a written response to the motion or wait until the motion hearing and respond orally. A written response is usually better, because it gets your views across more effectively.

Use the Response to Motion Regarding Parenting Time (FOC 66) for a written response. In paragraphs #2, #4 or both, say why you oppose the motion. You may dispute that you have violated the parenting time order and/or disagree that it is in the best interests of the children to modify parenting time.

For complete information and instructions about preparing, filing and serving a response, see "Responding to a Motion" on page 35.

You can also respond to a motion by making a counter-motion. Normally, if you oppose the motion with the Response to Motion Regarding Parenting Time (FOC 66), you disagree with the grounds for the motion in paragraphs #2 and #4. Then, in paragraph #5 you oppose the proposed modification, as in the sample response at the end of this chapter.

But if you want a different kind of change of parenting time, check the second and fourth boxes in paragraph #5, and then explain in the space below what you want. Whether you realize it or not, this request is a counter-motion.

In some cases, it's even possible to ask for completely new relief in a counter-motion. Add new issues carefully, because these can easily sidetrack the case. Nevertheless, it may make sense to seek new relief in a counter-motion when the new issues are compatible with the main motion.

For more about counter-motion tactics and how to counter-move for new relief, see "Making a Counter-Motion" on page 37.

Friend of the Court

Before a post-judgment motion is heard by the judge, the friend of the court may intervene to mediate, investigate or referee, in an attempt to settle the dispute.

A parenting time dispute will almost certainly be sent to mediation, because courts figure that parenting time is well-suited for mediation. Even in the bitterest disputes over parenting time, the parents must ultimately cooperate to exercise parenting time. Courts try to encourage this kind of cooperation by mediation of disputes.

The mediation will probably be informal mediation by the friend of the court. But formal mediation outside the friend of the court system is also possible; outside private mediation or arbitration is unlikely. During a parenting time dispute, the friend of the court is usually required to investigate the issue, and make a report and recommendation about parenting time. It's also possible that the motion will be refereed by the friend of the court prior to the motion hearing.

See "Friend of the Court" on page 38 for more about the friend of the court's roles in post-judgment cases, and how to deal with mediation, investigation or refereeing by the friend of the court. This section also has information about formal mediation, private mediation and arbitration, which all take place outside the friend of the court system.

As explained in "Motion Hearings" on page 41, there are two kinds of motion hearings: 1) nonevidentiary hearing where facts aren't in dispute, evidence is seldom introduced and the parties merely make legal arguments to the judge 2) evidentiary hearing where facts are disputed and evidence, such as testimony from witnesses, must be introduced to establish the true facts.

Some parenting time modifications require full evidentiary hearings, such as when a parent faces a complete loss of parenting time or a change to supervised parenting time. But with most modifications, when simple adjustment of parenting time is sought, a nonevidentiary hearing should be enough.

During the motion hearing, the moving party must establish the grounds for modification by showing either: 1) violation of the parenting time order, or 2) it's in the best interests of the children to modify parenting time.

To prove the first grounds, the moving party must show that the current parenting time order has been violated seriously (more than minor infractions). The other grounds for modification are established by evidence that the parenting time arrangement isn't working and that it's in the best interests of the children to change it.

As explained before, the best interests of the children are determined by the 12 factors (minus the special joint custody factor) from the child custody act of 1970 (see "Types of Parenting Time" on page 79 for a complete list). During a hearing on parenting time, courts have customarily been required to make factual findings on *all* the best- interest factors. Consequently, you must address each factor whether you are the moving party or the opponent.

If the parenting time hearing is evidentiary, you must make careful preparations for the hearing. You may even need to subpoena witnesses, such as teachers, counselors, social workers or neighbors. See "Preparing for a Motion Hearing" on page 41 for complete information about prehearing preparations. A nonevidentiary hearing, by contrast, won't require such extensive preparation. For example, you probably won't have to subpoena or bring witnesses to the hearing.

The format of the hearing will be determined by whether your ex attends the hearing. If your ex is present, the hearing will be held as planned, with both sides presenting their cases. In your ex's absence, you will probably win by default after an abbreviated hearing. "Motion Hearing Itself" on page 42 explains all this in detail.

After the motion hearing, the judge will decide the motion. The judge will either decide immediately and give an oral decision "from the bench," or take the case "under submission" and rule later by issuing a written decision.

Either way, the moving party must prepare the order granting or denying the motion. Use the Order Regarding Parenting Time (FOC 67) for the modification. "Parenting Time Provisions for the Court Order" below has suggested language for reasonable parenting time and two kinds of specific parenting time.

The moving party must also get the order signed by the judge and filed with the clerk. There are several ways to do this. See "Court Orders" on page 44 for complete instructions and forms.

Parenting Time Provisions for the Court Order

Reasonable Parenting Time

If you want the flexible type of parenting time known as reasonable parenting time, insert "The parties shall have reasonable parenting time" in paragraph #7 of the Order Regarding Parenting Time (FOC 67). By selecting this option, you and your ex can schedule parenting time as you wish.

Specific Parenting Time

To fix parenting time according to a specific schedule, insert "The parties shall have specific parenting time according to the attached schedule" in paragraph #7 of the FOC 67. Then attach a specific parenting time provision to the order on a separate sheet. In this provision, you can specify the times, terms and conditions of the parenting time. Naturally, the provision must suit you and your children, but you should be able to adapt one of the following examples to your situation.

7a. <u>Specific Parenting Time Schedule.</u>   Defendant shall have parenting time during:

(a) alternate weekends from 6:00 p.m. Friday until 6:00 p.m. Sunday. If a state holiday falls on a Monday following a weekend visitation, the visitation shall extend to 6:00 p.m. on that Monday holiday

(b) in even-numbered years, from 6:00 p.m. on the last day before Christmas school vacation until noon on Christmas Day

(c) in odd-numbered years, from noon on Christmas Day until 6:00 p.m. on the day before school resumes

(d) in odd-numbered years, from 6:00 p.m. on the Wednesday before Thanksgiving Day until 6:00 p.m. on the following Sunday

(e) Easter Sunday in even-numbered years

(f) in even-numbered years, from 6:00 p.m. on the last day before spring school vacation until 6:00 p.m. on the day before school resumes

(g) in even-numbered years, the children's birthdays

(h) [Two] weeks during the children's summer school vacation, beginning not less than 30 days after written notice to plaintiff and ending at least seven days before school resumes.

(i) other times as the parties may agree upon

At the beginning of any period of parenting time, plaintiff shall have the children ready at the time specified and defendant shall return them promptly at the end of the parenting time. Plaintiff shall be responsible for transporting the children to begin parenting time and defendant shall be responsible for returning them from parenting time.

The parenting time provision above is designed for parents who live close to each other after their divorce. For parents living far apart, parenting time on alternating weekends and split holidays is impractical. In these cases, parents should choose infrequent parenting time, where the noncustodial parent has extended periods of parenting time instead of more frequent access. The provision below is designed for parents who live a considerable distance from each other, requiring airplane travel for the parenting time:

7a. <u>Specific Parenting Time Schedule</u>.   Defendant shall have parenting time during:

(a) in even-numbered years, Christmas school vacation

(b) in odd-numbered years, Thanksgiving school vacation

(c) in odd-numbered years, spring school vacation

(d) [Four] weeks during the children's summer school vacation, beginning not less than 30 days after written notice to plaintiff and ending at least seven days before school resumes.

(e) other times as the parties may agree upon

At the beginning of any period of parenting time, plaintiff shall have the children ready at the time specified and defendant shall return them promptly at the end of the parenting time. [Plaintiff/defendant] shall be responsible for [or share equally] the cost of transporting the children to and from the parenting time.

PARAGRAPH #2 IS PRIMARILY AN ENFORCEMENT SECTION, AFTER PARENTING TIME VIOLATIONS. CHECK CORRECT BOXES AND DESCRIBE VIOLATIONS IN SPACE BELOW BOXES. REMEDIES FOR PARENTING TIME VIOLATIONS INCLUDE MODIFYING PARENTING TIME OR MAKING UP LOST TIME, BOTH OF WHICH YOU ASK FOR IN PARAGRAPH #5.

THIS PARAGRAPH SEES WHETHER PARTIES AGREE ON THE MODIFICATION. IF YOU BOTH AGREE, SKIP FILING A MOTION AND JUST STIPULATE TO A MODIFICATION ORDER, AS EXPLAINED IN "STIPULATED ORDERS" IN CHAPTER 1C.

PARAGRAPH #4 IS A MODIFICATION SECTION WHERE YOU DESCRIBE GROUNDS FOR MODIFICATION. SEE "MOTION" IN THIS CHAPTER FOR MORE ABOUT MODIFICATION GROUNDS.

Original - Court
1st copy - Other Party
2nd copy - Moving Party

4th copy - Proof of Service
5th copy - Proof of Service

MOTION REGARDING PARENTING TIME

CASE NO.

Court telephone no.

☐ moving party

v

☐ moving party

Defendant's name, address, and telephone no.   ☐ moving party

☐ moving party

1. ☒ a. On ___7-1-90___ a judgment
   Date
   or order was entered regarding parenting time.
   ☐ b. There is currently no order regarding parenting time.

___ has disobeyed the parenting time order.

2. ☐ _____
   Name
   ☐ a. he/she has denied me parenting time with the child(ren) as follows:
   ☐ b. he/she has not had parenting time with the child(ren) as follows:
   ☐ c. he/she has made changes in parenting time without court order as follows:
   ☐ d. he/she has not followed the specific conditions of parenting time as follows:
   Use a separate sheet to explain in detail what has happened and attach. Include all necessary fact

   ___ and I have agreed

3. ☐ _____
   Name
   Use a separate sheet to explain in detail what you have agreed on and attach. Include all necessary

4. It is in the best interests of the child(ren) to ☐ establish parenting time ☒ change parenting time because: I'M NOW WORKING ON SAT. AND SUN.,
   Use a separate sheet to explain why it is in the best interests of the child(ren) and attach. MAKING THE CURRENT WEEKEND PARENTING TIME IMPOSSIBLE. IN ORDER TO GIVE THE CHILDREN GUIDANCE (FACTOR #2) AND MAINTAIN A PARENT-CHILD RELATIONSHIP (FACTOR #10), I NEED PARENTING TIME ON WEEKDAYS.

5. **I ask the court to order that parenting time be** ☐ established ☒ changed ☐ made up as follows:
   Use a separate sheet to explain in detail what you want the court to order and attach. CURRENT SEMI-MONTHLY WEEKEND PARENTING TIME BE CHANGED TO SEMI-MONTHLY TWO-DAY BLOCKS OF PARENTING TIME ON MONDAYS AND TUESDAYS WHEN I'M NOT WORKING. REST OF PARENTING TIME SCHEDULE STAYS THE SAME.

I declare that the above statements are true to the best of my information, knowledge, and belief.

___1-1-99___   _Dudley Lovelace_
Date   Moving party's signature

NOTICE OF HEARING

A hearing will be held on this motion before FRED PINCH, ASST. FOC
                                              Name of judge or referee

on ___1-15-99___ at ___9:00 AM___ at FOC OFFICE, OJIBWAY COUNTY COURTHOUSE
   Date   Time   Place

NOTE: If you are the person receiving this motion, you may file a response. Contact the friend of the court office and request form FOC 66.

CERTIFICATE OF MAILING

I certify that on this date I mailed a copy of this motion and notice of hearing on the other party(ies) by ordinary mail at the above address(es)

___1-2-99___   _Dudley Lovelace_
Date   Moving party's signature

                                              MCL 552.14, MCR 2.119

FOC 65 (11/02) **MOTION REGARDING PARENTING TIME**

USE PARAGRAPH #2 TO RESPOND TO ACCUSATION OF VIOLATION OF PARENTING TIME ORDER.

SEVERAL PARAGRAPHS TEST WHETHER YOU AGREE WITH MODIFICATION. IF YOU AGREE, COMPLETELY OR IN PART, SEE "RESPONDING TO A MOTION" IN THIS CHAPTER ABOUT YOUR RESPONSE OPTIONS.

YOU CAN MAKE A COUNTER-MOTION IN THIS PARAGRAPH. SEE "RESPONDING TO A MOTION" IN THIS CHAPTER FOR MORE ABOUT COUNTER-MOTIONS.

Approved, SCAO

Original - Court
1st copy - Moving Party
2nd copy - Responding Party

3rd copy - Friend of the Court
4th copy - Proof of Service
5th copy - Proof of Service

STATE OF MICHIGAN
JUDICIAL CIRCUIT
COUNTY

RESPONSE TO
MOTION REGARDING PARENTING TIME

CASE NO.

Court address

Court telephone no.

Plaintiff's name, address, and telephone no. ☐ moving party

Defendant's name, address, and telephone no. ☐ moving party

v

address, and telephone no. ☐ moving party

1. ☒ a. On __7-1-90__ — a judgment
   Date
   or order was entered regarding parenting time.
   ☐ b. There is currently no order regarding parenting time.

☐ 2. I ☐ have ☐ have not disobeyed the parenting time order as stated in the motion.
Explain in detail what you do not agree with in item 2. of the motion and why. Include all necessary facts. Use a separate sheet of paper if needed.

☐ 3. ☐ a. I agreed with the other party to start or make changes in parenting time as stated in the motion.
   ☐ b. I agreed with the other party to start or make changes in parenting time as stated in the motion.
   ☒ c. I did not agree with the other party to start or make changes in parenting time. They were not what was stated in the motion.
   If b. is checked, explain in detail what you did agree on. Include all necessary facts. Use a separate sheet of paper if needed.

4. I ☐ agree ☒ do not agree that it is in the best interests of the child(ren) to ☐ establish ☒ change parenting time as stated in the motion.
If you do not agree with the motion, explain why it is in the best interests of the child(ren). Use a separate sheet of paper if needed.
GIVING DEFENDANT PARENTING TIME ON WEEKDAYS WILL DISRUPT THEIR SCHOOL ROUTINE, HARMING THEIR EDUCATION (CONTRARY TO FACTOR #8)

5. I ask the court to order that parenting time ☐ be ☒ not be ☐ established ☒ changed ☐ m as stated in the motion.
If you do not agree with the request in the motion, explain in detail what you want the court to order. Use a separate sheet of paper if needed.
DENY DEFENDANT'S MODIFICATION MOTION AND LET HIM AND HIS EMPLOYER ADJUST HIS WORK SCHEDULE TO CURRENT PARENTING TIME SCHEDULE

I declare that the above statements are true to the best of my information, knowledge, and belief.

__1-12-99__
Date

Darlene Lovelace
Responding party's signature

CERTIFICATE OF MAILING

I certify that on this date I mailed a copy of this response on the other party(ies) by ordinary mail at the above address(es).

__1-12-99__
Date

Darlene Lovelace
Responding party's signature

FOC 66 (12/96) **RESPONSE TO MOTION REGARDING PARENTING TIME**

MCL 552.14; MSA 25.94, MCR 2.119

CHECK:
- 1ST BOX IF ORDER WAS CONTESTED AND GOTTEN AFTER COURT HEARING ON THE ORDER
- 2ND BOX IF NONMOVING PARTY CONSENTED TO ORDER
- 3RD BOX FOR STIPULATED ORDERS
- NO BOXES FOR APPROVAL OF THE ORDER BY SILENCE

Original - Court
1st copy - Other Party
2nd copy - Moving Party

3rd copy - Friend of the Court
4th copy - Proof of Service
5th copy - Proof of Service

Approved, SCAO

ORDER REGARDING PARENTING TIME

CASE NO.

Court telephone no.

Defendant's name, address, and telephone no.

v

Date: 1-28-99

Judge: LESTER TUBBS

1. This order is entered ☐ after hearing.   ☒ on consent of the parties.   ☐ on stipulation of the parties.

THE COURT FINDS:

☒ 2. A motion requesting parenting time/change to parenting time was filed.

☒ 3. A response to the motion was filed.

☒ 4. It ☒ is ☐ is not   in the best interests of the child(ren) to ☐ establish ☒ change   parenting time.

☐ 5. It is in the best interests of the child(ren) to dismiss the motion.

IT IS ORDERED:

☐ 6. The motion is dismissed. Parenting time is unchanged and the existing order remains in effect.

☒ 7. Parenting time is ☐ established ☒ changed ☐ to be made up   as follows:
Explain in detail what the court has ordered.
INSTEAD OF WEEKEND PARENTING TIME, DEFENDANT SHALL HAVE PARENTING TIME DURING ALTERNATE MONDAY-TUESDAY COMBINATIONS, BEGINNING AT 6:00 PM ON SUNDAYS BEFORE THIS PERIOD AND CONTINUING UNTIL 6:00 PM ON TUESDAY AT THE END OF THE PERIOD.

8. Except as changed in this order, the prior order (if one) remains in effect.

THE PARTIES MUST SIGN A STIPULATED ORDER OR ONE OBTAINED BY CONSENT. PARTIES DON'T SIGN AN ORDER OBTAINED THROUGH "APPROVAL-BY-SILENCE" OR AFTER A COURT HEARING ON THE ORDER.

Darlene Lovelace
Plaintiff's signature (consent/stipulation)

Dudley Lovelace
Defendant's signature (consent/stipulation)

Third party's signature (consent/stipulation)

Approved as to form: _Fred Pinch_
Friend of the court signature (only if required)

Lester Tubbs
Circuit court judge

1-28-99
Date

PROOF OF SERVICE

I certify that on this date I mailed a copy of this order on the other party(ies) by ordinary mail at the above address(es).

Dudley Lovelace
Signature

1-28-99
Date

MCL 552.14; MSA 25.94; MCR 2.119

FOC 67 (12/96)   **ORDER REGARDING PARENTING TIME**

CHAPTER 4:
Residence of Children

The residence (also known as domicile) of minor children used to be a minor issue during and after divorce. Divorce judgments did bar custodial parents from taking children out of state. But otherwise, divorced parents were free to move around the state with their children as they pleased.

This freedom of movement worked all right in an era when sole custody was the norm. But as joint custody became more common, it was difficult to reconcile freedom of movement with joint custody rights. Imagine a parent moving with children from Detroit to Copper Harbor in the Upper Peninsula (a distance of over 600 miles), and the effect this move would have on the other parent's joint custody or parenting time back in Detroit.

As a result, in 2001 Michigan adopted a new law governing children's residence. The law tries to harmonize—not always successfully—parents' rights of movement and custody and parenting time arrangements for children.

Establishing Residences of Children

The 2001 law establishes local residences of minor children during divorce. These residences are created when a case is filed. A divorce-filing actually establishes two local residences of the children: one with each parent, at the parental homes (the initial divorce papers will cite these addresses). Dual residences exist even if one parent ends up with most, or all, custody later. At that point, residence is a totally separate issue from custody and is fixed without regard to custody.

Since divorce, the children's actual residences may have changed under one of the exclusions or exceptions described below or through a change-of-residence motion. But the local residences of children established at the beginning of the divorce remain important because they serve as a permanent reference point for the exceptions under the 2001 law (see below).

Like a custody or parenting time order, a divorce judgment's residence provisions cover the minor children until they reach the age of 18, and then expires for each of them. On its face, this residence order applies to the children only. But it also applies indirectly to the parents, since the parents mustn't move the children's residences which are also their own.

All this may sound rather restrictive and confining. But in fact, parents have quite a lot of freedom to move, thanks to an elaborate system of exclusions and exceptions under the 2001 law.

Exclusions

Some kinds of intrastate moves are excluded outright from the 2001 law. Parents covered by these exclusions are free to move around the state without prior court approval. These moveaways are excluded from the residence law:

- move in Michigan when a parent has received sole custody (sole legal and sole physical custody)*
- move by a parent in Michigan when the other parent consents to the move
- move in Michigan caused by a flight from domestic violence

Exceptions

Besides excluded moves, other moves are excepted from the residence law. Moveaways covered by these exceptions are based on distance, so you must know the children's two local residences established at divorce-filing (see above for more about these). It's also helpful to have a good map of Michigan (such as a road map or atlas) and an inexpensive compass, like the ones geometry students use. Like excluded moves, these moves are exempted from the 2001 residence law and may take place without court review:

- move in Michigan if the children's local residences are more than 100 miles apart

On your map, you can use the scale to measure the distance in miles from the children's two residences. If these residences are more than 100 miles apart, you can move anywhere in Michigan.

---

*   Curiously, the 2001 law only mentions sole legal custody. But since sole legal custody is incompatible with any kind of joint custody, this ties the exclusion to sole custody cases; and by implication, this exclusion also makes the 2001 law apply to joint custody cases only.

- move by a parent inside his/her own 100-mile local residence zone in Michigan

The exception above can be a little difficult to judge. On your map, find the local residence of the relocating parent. Using the map scale, measure a 100 miles on the compass and lock it. Put the pointed end on the residence and draw a 100-mile circle around this point. A move within this circle or zone is permissible under this exception.

> *Example*: A wife gets a divorce in Lansing against her husband living in Mt. Pleasant. Dual residences for the children exist in both cities. According to this exception, the wife could move inside a zone of 100 miles radius around Lansing (or the husband, if he wished to move, could move within a 100-mile zone around Mt. Pleasant).

- move in Michigan if the move actually brings the local residences closer together; a move creating more distance is barred

This final exception is even harder to visualize. Using a map and compass, place the two ends (pointed and pencil) of the compass on each parent's residence and lock the compass. Then, put the pointed end on the stay-behind parent's residence and draw a circle around this residence. This is the area into which the relocating parent can move under this exception.

> *Example*: A wife gets a divorce in Lansing against her husband in Clare. The distance between these local residences is 80 miles. The wife could move into a zone 80 miles around Clare, because this move wouldn't create more distance than existed before during the divorce. Similarly, the husband could move into an 80-mile zone around Lansing.

Limits on Exclusions and Exceptions

Before the 2001 residence law was adopted, Michigan had a court rule preventing a custodial parent from moving out of state with the children, except with court approval. This approval was required so courts wouldn't lose control of the children, making it more difficult to enforce the custody-related provisions of divorce judgments.

It's not entirely clear how the 2001 residence law and the old court rule mesh. But it seems that they fit together in such a way that custodial parents who wish to move with children out of state must *always* obtain court permission, even when the move would normally be excluded or excepted under the 2001 law.

> *Example*: A couple divorces in Menominee, Michigan, and the mother gets sole custody of the children. She wants to move a few miles across the river to adjacent Marinette, Wisconsin.

Ordinarily, an exclusion (sole custody exclusion) and an exception (moving within one's 100-mile local residence zone) would plainly exempt this move from court review. But because it's across state lines, prior court permission is necessary for the move.

When a parent wants to change the children's residence and none of the exclusions or exceptions applies, s/he must file a change-of-residence motion. The motion must be granted before the move takes place; you can't move first and seek approval later.* At the hearing on the motion, the court must consider the following factors:

- whether the legal residence change has the capacity to improve the quality of life for both the child and the relocating parent
- the degree to which each parent has complied with, and utilized his or her time under, a court order governing parenting time with the child, and whether the parent's plan to change the child's legal residence is inspired by that parent's desire to defeat or frustrate the parenting time schedule
- the degree to which the court is satisfied that, if the court permits the legal residence change, it is possible to order a modification of the parenting time schedule and other arrangements governing the child's schedule in a manner that can provide an adequate basis for preserving and fostering the parental relationship between the child and each parent; and whether each parent is likely to comply with the modification
- the extent to which the parent opposing the legal residence change is motivated by a desire to secure a financial advantage with respect to a support obligation
- domestic violence, regardless of whether the violence was directed against or witnessed by the child

When parents want to take children not just out of state but outside the country, extra factors may be considered. For international moves, courts look at international relations between the U.S and the destination foreign country, cultural factors, the severe impact the move will likely have on joint custody and parenting time and the enforceability of custody orders in the foreign country.

Whether the move is intrastate, interstate or even overseas, courts frequently allow changes of residence for children. After all, parents often have good reasons for moving—to remarry, take a new job, return to school to acquire new job skills—and courts don't want to stand in the way of these opportunities.

---

*   There is an exception to this rule when the relocating spouse is fleeing the threat of domestic violence. In that case, the spouse can move before the motion is decided.

Enforcement

If a parent wrongfully moves around inside Michigan, the divorce judgment may have been violated. The same goes for a move with minor children out of state without prior court permission.

The customary remedy for a violation is a contempt citation against the moving parent. Contact the friend of the court if your ex makes an unauthorized moveaway. It's also possible that a wrongful move with children is a violation of the state, federal or international kidnapping laws described in "Enforcement" on page 64. To receive the protection of these laws, contact local, state or federal law enforcement agencies.

Modification

You don't need anyone's permission to move down the block or even across town. But you may need court approval for longer moves inside Michigan (see "Establishing Residences of Children" on page 93 for the change-of-residence rules, with important exclusions and exceptions). And you always need court say-so to move with the children outside Michigan or internationally.

The court's approval of your proposed move is, in essence, a modification of the residence (also known as domicile) order in the divorce judgment. A change of residence can also trigger modification of other parts of the judgment, since custody and/or parenting time may have to be modified to accommodate the move.

Stipulated Modification

Like other post-judgment issues, the parties can stipulate (consent) to a change of children's residence (the 2001 residence law also permits this). Despite the agreement, the court has the final say on all moves subject to review and can prevent the move. Nevertheless, courts typically approve most change-of-residence stipulations.

It isn't necessary to file a motion or have a court hearing to change children's residence by stipulation. All you have to do is prepare the Order Regarding Residence of Children (GRP 22) and have it approved by the court. The change-of-residence provisions in the GRP 22 are covered in "Court Order" on page 101. See "Stipulated Orders" on page 30 for complete instructions about preparing a stipulated order, getting court approval of the order, filing it with the clerk and serving it on your ex.

Sometimes, changing the children's residence requires modification of their joint physical custody and/or parenting time. In particular, a move may rule out arrangements where the children are exchanged frequently, and spell the need instead for infrequent, but longer, exchanges. See "Custody Provisions for the Court Order" on page 70 and "Parenting Time Provisions for the Court Order" on page 88 for other options.

For any modification of joint physical custody, you must use the Order Regarding Custody and Parenting Time (FOC 89) with the Order Regarding

Residence of Children (GRP 22). You can also modify parenting time along with custody in the FOC 89. But if you want to modify parenting time without touching custody, you may do that in paragraph #9 (or an attachment) of the GRP 22 when you change the children's residence.

Contested Modification

If you and your ex can't agree about your proposed move, you must file a motion for modification of the children's residence. Approval isn't guaranteed; the court will consider the motion during a hearing and either grant or deny it.

Don't wait until the last minute to file your modification motion. A contested change of residence motion can take several months, particularly if the friend of the court investigates or referees the matter. As a result, file the motion months far ahead of your planned date of departure, or you may not get a final decision by that time.

Motion

You can ask for change of residence in the Motion Regarding Residence of Children (GRP 20). There is a sample GRP 20 at the end of this section, showing you how to complete the various parts of the motion. The core of the motion are paragraphs #3 and #4, which state the grounds for the motion, and paragraph #6 describing your proposed move.

In paragraph #3, cite which circumstances have changed in the lives of you, your ex and/or your children since the children's residences were established during the divorce. As explained in "Grounds for Modification" on page 5, change of circumstances is the customary grounds for modifying a divorce judgment, including residence-of-children provisions.

Paragraph #4 has the other grounds for modification: proper cause (see "Grounds for Modification" on page 5 for more about the double grounds for modification). Proper cause is often the factual change of circumstances plus application of the legal rule supporting modification. In this case, the legal rule is the five-factor test described on page 96, which must be related to the facts making up the change of circumstances.

Typically, the moving party's best strategy is to emphasize the first factor in the test for intrastate and interstate moves. Be specific and cite quality-of-life improvements from the proposed move: better pay and benefits at work, superior schools, safer environment, etc. By contrast, vague reasons like wanting a new life or fresh start somewhere else won't convince the court the move is justifiable.

In paragraph #6, describe where you want to move (citing the street address, if known) and how parenting time can be modified to maintain contact between the children and the other parent.

For complete information and instructions about preparing, filing and serving a motion like this, see "Papers" on page 23 and "Motions" on page 32.

If you receive a motion for change of residence from your ex, you can respond orally or in writing, in several ways.

If you agree with the motion completely, contact your ex immediately and arrange to stipulate to a modification order. In paragraphs #2, #3, #4 and #5 of the Response to Motion Regarding Residence of Children (GRP 21), you can also indicate your agreement with the motion. But why do extra paperwork when it's easier to stipulate to a modification order? You could also appear at the hearing and agree to the motion, but this too wastes time when stipulation is available. See "Stipulated Modification" on page 97 for more about stipulations.

Sometimes, you may agree with part of the motion and disagree with the rest. It's important to signal your partial agreement as soon as possible because this narrows the issues in the case. If you file a Response to Motion Regarding Residence of Children (GRP 21), check box #4b and describe the extent of your agreement with the motion in the space below. If you choose to respond orally, mention your partial agreement to the mediator, referee or judge, so the agreed-upon issues can be eliminated from the hearing.

When you oppose the motion, you can voice your disagreement in two ways. You can file a written response to the motion or wait until the motion hearing and respond orally. A written response is usually better, because it gets your views across more effectively.

Use the Response to Motion Regarding Residence of Children (GRP 21) for a written response. In paragraphs #2 and #3, say why you oppose the motion. You may dispute that circumstances have changed, disagree that your ex's and children's lives would improve with the move or cite other factors in your favor.

Opposing a change of residence motion is often difficult because you might not know enough about the proposed new residence to make a comparison with the current one. In that case, the best line of defense may be to focus on any loss of joint custody or parenting time the move would cause. In fact, you may want to emphasize this issue by making a counter-motion for modification of custody and/or parenting time (see below for more about this tactic).

For complete information and instructions about preparing, filing and serving a response, see "Responding to a Motion" on page 35.

You can also respond to a motion by making a counter-motion. Normally, if you oppose the motion with the Response to Motion Regarding Residence of Children (GRP 21), you disagree with the grounds for the motion in paragraphs #2 and #3. Then, in paragraph #5 you oppose the proposed modification, as in the sample response at the end of this chapter.

But if you want a different kind of change of residence, check box #5b and explain in the space below what you want. Whether you realize it or not, this request is a counter-motion.

In some cases, it's even possible to ask for completely new relief in a counter-motion. Add new issues carefully, because these can easily sidetrack the case. Nevertheless, it may make sense to seek new relief in a counter-motion when the new issues are compatible with the main motion.

For more about counter-motion tactics and how to counter-move for new relief, see "Making a Counter-Motion" on page 37.

Counter-Motion: Modifying Custody and/or Parenting Time

One effective strategy is to counter-move for modification of custody and/or parenting time when faced with a residence modification motion. In many cases, when a joint custodial parent moves for a change of residence, the effect of the motion—whether intentional or not—is to modify custody and/or parenting time. That's because the change of residence will upset the current joint custody or parenting time. And if that's true, different standards of proof (the full best interest test, custodial presumptions, etc.) and procedures (automatic accelerated appeal) should be applied.

Michigan law has difficulty dealing with this problem. In some states, when a change-of-residence motion affects custody and/or parenting time, it's converted into a custody modification motion. Michigan doesn't have a similar provision in its law.

Naturally, the moving party will usually try to keep the motion as a residence modification and minimize the effects of the motion on the other party's custody and/or parenting time. But you can force the issue out in the open by counter-moving for custody and/or parenting time modification. This can be especially helpful if you have an established custodial environment or other custody factors in your favor.

Friend of the Court

Before a post-judgment motion is heard by the judge, the friend of the court may intervene to mediate, investigate or referee, in an attempt to settle the dispute.

Because a change of residence is linked to custody and parenting time, there will probably be mediation of the dispute. This is most likely to be informal mediation, but it could be formal mediation; out-of-court private mediation or arbitration, which is expensive, is unlikely.

During a dispute over the children's residence, you can usually expect an investigation, report and recommendation about the issue by a friend of the court investigator. It's also likely that the motion will be refereed by the friend of the court prior to the motion hearing.

See "Friend of the Court" on page 38 for more about the friend of the court's roles in post-judgment cases, and how to deal with mediation, investigation or refereeing by the friend of the court. This section also has information about formal mediation, private mediation and arbitration, which all take place outside the friend of the court system.

Motion Hearing

As explained in "Motion Hearings" on page 41, there are two kinds of motion hearings: 1) nonevidentiary hearing where facts aren't in dispute, evidence is seldom introduced and the parties merely make legal arguments to the judge 2) evidentiary hearing where facts are disputed and evidence, such as testimony from witnesses, must be introduced to establish the true facts.

Changing the residence of children normally requires a nonevidentiary hearing, or if the issues are complicated, a limited evidentiary hearing. Typically, the basic facts of residence are fixed and known, so evidence isn't always necessary.

You will notice that several change-of-residence factors concern reasons or motives for seeking or opposing the move. It's possible to get this state-of-mind evidence by asking the other party about his/her motives. But few people are candid enough to confess their motives, and even if they were, you have to be a skillful questioner to draw out this information.

Instead, you normally prove motives by inferences from known facts. For example, let's say your ex claims that s/he opposes your move because of a fear of losing parenting time. You could refute this claim by showing that s/he has had a spotty record of using parenting time (your case file will show this). This creates a reasonable inference that your ex really doesn't care about parenting time and that the real reason for opposing the moveaway is simply to stop it.

The moving party's task during the motion hearing is to establish grounds for the motion by showing that: 1) there has been a change of circumstances regarding residence since the divorce 2) proper cause exists for the change of residence.

To prove the first grounds, the moving party must offer a good reason for a change of residence. Typically, the moving party wants to move to remarry, for a new job or opportunity for education, and this satisfies the changed circumstances requirement. Proper cause for change of residence is established by showing that the move is justified by the five-factor test from the 2001 residence law (see "Establishing Residences of Children" on page 93 for a list of these factors). These factors are fairly self-explanatory and should be easy to apply to your case during the motion hearing.

Since the hearing is likely to be nonevidentiary, you won't have to prepare for the hearing as much as you would for a full evidentiary hearing. For example, you probably won't have to subpoena or bring witnesses to the hearing.

The format of the hearing will be determined by whether your ex attends the hearing. If your ex is present, the hearing will be held as planned, with both sides presenting their arguments. In your ex's absence, you should win by default after an abbreviated hearing. "Motion Hearing Itself" on page 42 explains all this in detail.

Court Order

After the motion hearing, the judge will decide the motion. The judge will either decide immediately and give an oral decision "from the bench," or take the case "under submission" and rule later by issuing a written decision.

Either way, the moving party must prepare the order granting or denying the motion. Use the Order Regarding Residence of Children (GRP 22) as the order. See "Court Orders" on page 44 for complete information about preparing, filing and serving an order like this.

As for the change-of-residence provision inside the GRP 22, state the effective date of the move, the names of the children moving, which parent is relocating and their old and new addresses (citing the new street address, if known).

Sometimes, changing the children's residence requires modification of their joint physical custody and/or parenting time. In particular, the move may rule out arrangements where the children are exchanged frequently, and spell the need instead for infrequent, but longer, exchanges. See "Custody Provisions for the Court Order" on page 70 and "Parenting Time Provisions for the Court Order" on page 88 for other options.

For any modification of joint physical custody, you must use the Order Regarding Custody and Parenting Time (FOC 89) with the Order Regarding Residence of Children (GRP 22). You can also modify parenting time along with custody in the FOC 89. But if you want to modify parenting time without touching custody, you may do that in paragraph #9 (or an attachment) of the GRP 22 when you change the children's residence.

After a Change of Residence

After a stipulation or successful motion for modification of children's residence, the relocating parent may move to another part of Michigan or out of state. The parent must promptly notify the friend of the court, in writing, of his/her new address and that of the children (if they are moving with the relocating parent) after the move, as required by the judgment of divorce.

For your convenience, there is a form, Change in Personal Information (FOC 108), which you can use for change of address. In paragraph #1, you can file an address change for you and your children. You can also use the FOC 108 to change other personal information on file with the friend of the court (employment, social security number, licenses, etc.). You file the FOC 108 with the friend of the court only, not the court.

After an intrastate move, the court that granted the divorce will continue to handle the case. This may now be inconvenient if the relocating parent has moved a great distance. For convenience, you can sometimes transfer your divorce case to the Michigan county where you and your children now live. Appendix B on page 199 has the details and forms for case transfer.

For a move with the children out of state, the friend of the court will often contact a sister agency in the state (most states have friend of the court-type agencies). The out-of-state agency will provide similar supervision in the case.

The divorce case itself will remain in Michigan. But after the children have resided in the new state for a while, Michigan could lose control of the case. This might allow modification of custody and parenting time in the new state. See "Interstate Enforcement and Modification" on page 62 for more about this issue.

STATE OF MICHIGAN
Circuit Court - Family Division
_____ COUNTY

MOTION REGARDING
RESIDENCE OF CHILDREN

CASE NO.

Plaintiff: ☐ moving party

v

Defendant: ☐ moving party

1. (Names) DUANE W. LOVELACE AND DARRYL W. LOVELACE
after the parties' divorce on 7-1-90 , currently have legal residences with:
plaintiff at 121 S. MAIN, LAKE CITY, MI, 48800
defendant at 900 S. MAPLE, LAKE CITY, MI 48800
third party (named) at _____

2. I want to change these minor children's legal residence with me:

   ☐ inside the state of Michigan but the move isn't permitted by MCL 722.31 without a court o___

   ☒ outside the state of Michigan;

   to CHICAGO, IL

   on 4-1-99

3. Circumstances have changed as follows that require a change of residence as proposed above:
I HAVE BEEN OFFERED A JOB IN CHICAGO, IL BY THE ABC CORP., AND
I WANT TO MOVE THERE WITH THE CHILDREN AND TAKE THIS JOB.

4. Proper cause exists as follows that requires a change of residence:
   SEE ATTACHMENT

   ☐ 5. _____ and I agree to a change of residence and parenting time as follows:

6. **I ask the court to order a change of residence and parenting time** as follows:
CHANGE THE RESIDENCE OF THE CHILDREN WITH ME FROM LAKE CITY, MI,
TO CHICAGO, IL, AND MODIFY PARENTING TIME TO: 1) ONE WEEKEND
PER MONTH, 2) SIX WEEKS IN SUMMER.

I declare that the above statements are true to the best of my information, knowledge and belief.

Moving party _Darlene Lovelace_

Date 1-1-99

NOTICE OF HEARING

A hearing will be held on this motion before (judge ~~or referee~~) LESTER TUBBS
on 2-15-99 at (time) 9:00 AM at (place) OJIBWAY COUNTY COURTHOUSE

Note: If you are the person receiving this motion, you may file a response.

CERTIFICATE OF MAILING

I certify that on this date I mailed a copy of this motion and notice of hearing to the other party(ies) by
ordinary mail at the above address(es).

Moving party _Darlene Lovelace_

Date 1-2-99

GRP 20 (9/04) **MOTION REGARDING RESIDENCE OF CHILDREN**

THIS PARAGRAPH SEES WHETHER PARTIES AGREE ON THE MODIFICATION. IF YOU BOTH AGREE, SKIP FILING A MOTION AND JUST STIPULATE TO A MODIFICATION ORDER, AS EXPLAINED IN "STIPULATED ORDERS" IN CHAPTER 1C.

INCLUDE BOTH GROUNDS FOR CHANGE OF RESIDENCE IN PARAGRAPHS #3 AND #4. SEE "MOTION" IN THIS CHAPTER FOR MORE ABOUT GROUNDS.

4a. MY REASON FOR THE PROPOSED MOVE IS TO ACCEPT A JOB OFFERED BY THE ABC CORP., CHICAGO, IL. BY TAKING THE JOB, MY ANNUAL INCOME WILL INCREASE BY OVER 30% AND I WILL BE ELIGIBLE FOR BETTER HEALTH CARE COVERAGE. BOTH THINGS WILL BENEFIT ME AND THE CHILDREN.

AFTER THE MOVE THE SEMI-MONTHLY WEEKEND PARENTING TIME DEFENDANT NOW HAS WOULD NOT BE PRACTICAL. HOWEVER, I SUGGEST THAT HE RECEIVE PARENTING TIME ON ONE WEEKEND A MONTH, AND EXTRA PARENTING TIME IN THE SUMMER TO MAKE UP FOR THE TIME LOST DURING THE REST OF THE YEAR.

STATE OF MICHIGAN Circuit Court - Family Division COUNTY	RESPONSE TO MOTION REGARDING RESIDENCE OF CHILDREN	CASE NO.

Plaintiff: ☐ moving party

Defendant: ☐ moving party

v

1. A motion has been filed to change the legal residence of these minor children:
(names) *DUANE W. LOVELACE AND DARRYL W. LOVELACE*

    ☐ inside the state of Michigan.

    ☒ outside the state of Michigan.

SEVERAL PARAGRAPHS TEST WHETHER YOU AGREE WITH MODIFICATION. IF YOU AGREE, COMPLETELY OR IN PART, SEE "RESPONDING TO A MOTION" IN THIS CHAPTER ABOUT YOUR RESPONSE OPTIONS.

2. I ☐ agree ☒ do not agree that circumstances have changed as stated in the motion. *I DON'T HAVE ANY KNOWLEDGE ABOUT JOB OFFERS PLAINTIFF MAY HAVE RECEIVED LATELY.*

3. I ☐ agree ☒ do not agree that proper cause exists as stated in the motion. *MOVING THE CHILDREN TO CHICAGO WILL UPROOT THEM FROM THEIR SCHOOL AND COMMUNITY WHERE THEY HAVE LIVED SINCE BIRTH. THE MOVE WOULD ALSO SEPARATE THEM FROM ME AND OTHER RELATIVES IN THE AREA.*

4. ☐ I agreed with the other party to a change of residence and parenting time:

    ☐ a. exactly as stated in the motion.

    ☐ b. but not as stated in the motion. (Describe agreement)

YOU CAN MAKE A COUNTER-MOTION IN THIS PARAGRAPH. SEE "RESPONDING TO A MOTION" IN THIS CHAPTER FOR MORE ABOUT COUNTER-MOTIONS.

5. ☐ a. I agree with what is being asked for in the motion.

    ☒ b. I do not agree with what is being asked for in the motion and ask the court to m[...]
regarding residence of children and parenting time as follows: *DENY PLAINTIFF'S MOTION KEEPING THE CHILDREN'S RESIDENCE WITH HER IN LAKE CITY, MI, WITH CURRENT PARENTING TIME SCHEDULE INTACT.*

I declare that the above statements are true to the best of my information, knowledge and belief.

Date *2-1-99*   Responding party *Dudley Lovelace*

CERTIFICATE OF MAILING

I certify that on this date I mailed a copy of this response to the other party(ies) by ordinary mail at the above address(es).

Responding party *Dudley Lovelace*

Date *2-1-99*

GRP 21 (9/04) RESPONSE TO MOTION REGARDING RESIDENCE OF CHILDREN

> CHECK:
> • 1ST BOX IF ORDER WAS CONTESTED AND GOTTEN AFTER COURT HEARING ON THE ORDER
> • 2ND BOX IF NONMOVING PARTY CONSENTED TO ORDER
> • 3RD BOX FOR STIPULATED ORDERS
> • NO BOXES FOR APPROVAL OF THE ORDER BY SILENCE

STATE OF MICHIGAN uit Court - Family Division COUNTY	ORDER REGARDING RESIDENCE OF CHILDREN	CASE NO.
f:		
	Defendant:	
	v	

Date of hearing __2-15-99__

1. This order is entered ☐ after hearing. ☒ on consent. ☐ on stipulation.   Judge __LESTER TUBBS__

THE COURT FINDS:

☒ 2. A motion to change the legal residence of the parties' minor children was filed.

☒ 3. A response to the motion was filed.

☒ 4. A change of circumstances ☒ does ☐ does not exist warranting a change of residence.

☒ 5. Proper cause ☒ does ☐ does not exist which warrants a change of residence.

☐ 6. The parties have agreed to the change of the children's residence.

IT IS ORDERED:

☐ 7. The motion to change the legal residence of the minor children is dismissed, leaving the current residences intact.

☒ 8. a. Starting __4-1-99__, the legal residence of the following minor children:
(names) __DUANE W. LOVELACE AND DARRYL W. LOVELACE__
shall be changed from their current residence with:
☒ plaintiff ☐ defendant ☐ third party (named): _____
at __121 S. MAIN, LAKE CITY, MI 48800__
to __CHICAGO, IL__

b. Except as permitted above, the minor children's residence (domicile) shall not be moved from the state of Michigan without the prior approval of the court.

c. The person awarded custody shall promptly notify the friend of the court in writing when the minor is moved to another address.

9. The parenting time order dated __7-1-90__ is modified to provide that ☐ plaintiff ☒ defendant ☐ third party shall have parenting time with the minor children as follows:
ONE WEEKEND PER MONTH AND SIX WEEKS DURING THE CHILDREN'S SUMMER SCHOOL VACATIONS, ACCORDING TO TERMS SET BY THE PARTIES' DIVORCE JUDGMENT. THE HOLIDAY PARENTING-TIME SCHEDULE REMAINS UNCHANGED. PLAINTIFF SHALL ALSO PAY ALL COSTS OF TRANSPORTATION FOR PARENTING TIME.

Date/plaintiff __2-15-99__ _Darlene Lovelace_

Date __2-15-99__

Date/defendant __2-15-99__ _Dudley Lovelace_

Judge _Lester Tubbs_

PROOF OF SERVICE

I certify that on this date I mailed a copy of this order to the other party(ies) by ordinary mail at the above address(es).

Date __2-15-99__

Signature _Darlene Lovelace_

GRP 22 (9/04)   **ORDER REGARDING RESIDENCE OF CHILDREN**

> THE PARTIES MUST SIGN A STIPULATED ORDER OR ONE OBTAINED BY CONSENT. PARTIES DON'T SIGN AN ORDER OBTAINED THROUGH "APPROVAL-BY-SILENCE" OR AFTER A COURT HEARING ON THE ORDER.

Original - Friend of the court
Copy - Filing party

CASE NO.

Approved, SCAO

**STATE OF MICHIGAN
JUDICIAL CIRCUIT
COUNTY**

CHANGE IN PERSONAL INFORMATION

Friend of the Court address

Please type or print information. Complete only those sections that apply. You can only file changes for yourself or those minor children of whom you have physical custody. Use another form when making changes for more than one person. **YOU MUST SIGN THIS FORM.**

☒ for party and minor child(ren)   ☐ for party only
☐ for minor child _____   no longer living with custodial parent

Name

1. New Address and/or Telephone Number

Street address			
6701 S. PULASKI	State	Zip	Area code and telephone number
City	IL	60621	(312)336-9007
CHICAGO			

I understand that by filing this change of address, it will be used to automatically update address information on any other child support cases I have in Michigan. This change is effective for (check all that apply)
☐ mailing address only (where I receive mail)
☐ legal address only (where I want legal notices to be sent)
☒ all addresses you have listed for me
☐ residence address only (where I live)
☐ an address that is confidential by court order and which remains confidential with this change

2. Alternate Address
The court has entered an order making my address confidential under Michigan Court Rule 3.203(F). The following is an alternate address for the court, the friend of the court office, and the other party to use in serving me with notice and other court papers.
I will retrieve all my mail regarding this case from this alternate address.

Street address	City	State	Zip

3. Name Change (attach order changing name or certificate of marriage)

New name

4. New Employer   ☐ employer information is confidential by court order

Employer name	Street address		Area code and telephone number
City	State	Zip	

5. New Driver License

Issuing state	License number	Expiration date

6. New Occupational License

Issuing state	Type of occupation	License number	Expiration date

7. New Social Security Number   ☐ for you   ☐ for minor child _____ Name

Social security number

8. Health Care Insurance Provider

Name	Type	Contract number

9. Other Information: (to be provided as ordered by the court) (attach separate sheet)

	Social security number	Date of filing
	380-16-1010	4-10-99

Name of party filing the change (type or print)	Name of other party (type or print)
DARLENE LOVELACE	DUDLEY LOVELACE

Signature of party filing the change

Darlene Lovelace

FOC 108 (10/04) **CHANGE IN PERSONAL INFORMATION**

CHAPTER 5:
Child Support

For years, child support collection was neglected by the legal system. To be sure, courts ordered child support during divorces, but they were often guilty of lax enforcement afterward.

At that time, courts had few effective ways of collecting child support, and even these weren't used as forcefully as they should have been. And when delinquent child support payers were haled into court, judges often regarded child support as negotiable, settling for partial payment and cancellation of the rest.

As a result of this neglect, child support recipients often didn't get full payment, driving them onto welfare. Alarmed by rising welfare costs, state and federal lawmakers began paying more attention to child support during the 1980s. What followed were a number of important laws and reforms revolutionizing the way child support is figured and paid.

Child Support Obligations

Among these new support laws was a 1985 federal law requiring all states to adopt uniform child support guidelines and formulas. Hitherto, judges could set child support themselves on a case-by-case basis. In Michigan, judges typically used a rough method of allotting 20% of the payer's income for one child, 30% for two children and 40% for three or more.

Michigan Child Support Formula

More Information
The *Michigan Child Support Formula Manual* is reproduced in Appendix F on page 237. The manual is divided into a text portion explaining basic concepts like income, deductions from income, etc., and a schedules supplement. The schedules supplement has two sets of schedules: 1) percentage-of-incomes schedules showing noncustodial parents' percentage share of total family income (you subtract this percentage from a 100% to find the custodial parent's share) 2) child support schedules. You use the percentage-of-incomes schedules to determine parental sharing of things like health care coverage premiums, ordinary and extraordinary uninsured health care expenses, according to their incomes. The child support schedules are used to figure base child support. The manual reproduced in this book is the 2004 edition, which went into effect on Oct. 1, 2004. Recently, publication of the manual has become irregular, so it's difficult to say when a new one will be issued. But expect a revised edition in late 2005 or early 2006. The state used to print and sell the manual. In 2002, it discontinued sales of the manual. The state provides a limited number of printed copies to friends of the court and libraries, including most law libraries. You may be able to examine a copy of the manual there. The state's Friend of the Court Bureau also provides the manual online for free. It's available there to view or you can download a file and print your own copy. The bureau's Web site is: www.courts.michigan.gov/scao/services/focb/focb.htm The bureau's Web site also has a handy child support calculator program, called MarginSoft Child Support 2004, which you can download from the site.

Bowing to the federal law, Michigan devised its child support formula in 1987. Michigan's formula assumes that the needs of children can be fixed as a percentage of a family's total income, which varies with the amount of family income and the number and ages of the children,. According to the formula, these needs must be shared by the parents according to their incomes. The child support recipient pays his/her share by direct spending on the children, while the payer-parent contributes in the form of child support payments.

The Michigan child support formula has also been converted into easy-to-use child support schedules. These schedules match up the incomes of the recipient and payer, yielding a base amount of child support that provides for the needs of the children.

At first, the Michigan child support formula was merely an optional guideline which judges could follow as they wished. But in 1991, the formula became mandatory so all Michigan child support is supposed to be set by the formula, with a few exceptions described below.

Figuring Base Child Support

Before you can figure base child support, you must determine the monthly gross and net incomes of both parents. Simply put, gross income includes wages, salary, commissions and most other types of gain. However, the following items are not regarded as income: 1) gifts 2) inheritances 3) many public benefits, such as FIP payments, TANF, SSI and food stamps. Pages 7-8 of the manual explain the concept of income (including a list of 33 kinds of income) and pages 10-13 describe items excluded from income.

After establishing your gross income, you must deduct allowable deductions from monthly gross incomes to find your monthly net incomes. As explained on pages 17-19, the formula permits the following deductions from gross income:

- FICA
- federal, state and local taxes
- mandatory deductions from income (most union dues and some retirement plan contributions)
- pre-existing support obligations (such as child support) from a previous marriage or relationship (but not payments on child support arrearages)

The formula manual recommends that income be determined from actual tax returns whenever possible. This shouldn't be very difficult for wage- and salary-earners. They can take annual gross wages/salary from their W-2 forms, subtract the annual amount of deductions from income listed above and derive annual net income. Divide this figure by 12 to get monthly net income.

When people receive income from other sources (such as self-employment, commissions, interest and dividends), determining net income is much harder. Nevertheless, you can use that person's most recent federal income tax return to estimate his/her net income. Take the adjusted gross income from the return and subtract the total annual amount of deductions listed above. Divide the remainder by 12 to find monthly net income.

After you establish the monthly net incomes of both you and your ex, use the formula manual's child support schedules to figure base child support in a three-step procedure:

1) Take the monthly net incomes of you and your ex and round the amounts off to the nearest increment of $50 (so, for example, 265 becomes 250 and 285 becomes 300).

2) Locate the correct schedule according to the number of minor children you have. Using that schedule, find the custodial parent's income along the top row and the noncustodial parent's income in the left column. The number where the row and column intersect is the current base child support amount.

3) Besides current child support, you must also show how the base child support will decrease in the future as each child becomes independent. Go back to the child support schedules and figure the base child support with one less child, two less children, etc., down to one child. These amounts can be plugged into the child support order.

Adjusting the Formula

Not every divorce case fits neatly within the Michigan child support formula. The designers of the formula anticipated many of these exceptional cases, such as parents with low or high incomes, shared caretaking and special types of custody, and provided adjustments to the formula.

Parents with Low or High Incomes

The Michigan child support formula believes that low-income parents shouldn't be discouraged from continuing or seeking work by imposing burdensome child support obligations upon them. The formula considers a parent with a monthly net income of $776 or less as a low-income parent. For low-income noncustodial parents, the formula generally recommends that they pay around 10% of their monthly net incomes as child support, regardless of the number of children. Low-income custodial parents get a break by having the bulk of their income disregarded when child support is figured. Pages 26-28 of the formula manual explain in detail these low-income adjustments.

Needless to say, low-income adjustments could be abused by parents. Noncustodial parents might quit working or reduce their income to avoid paying child support. Custodial parents might also pass up income to get more child support.

The formula recognizes this problem and provides that income can be imputed (assigned) to parents who have voluntarily and unjustifiably reduced their income. A judge decides whether income must be imputed to a parent. If so, parents can have income imputed to them according to what they could earn, rather than what they do earn. To determine parents' unused earning ability, judges must consider their prior employment experience, educational level, special skills and training, the employment market in the area and several other factors.

Another type of adjustment must be made when a parent's monthly net income is "off the charts," exceeding the amounts in the applicable child support schedule. The formula believes that children shouldn't share fully in parents' great wealth, so it attempts to cap support for children of affluent parents to a reasonable amount. Pages 29-30 of the formula manual explains the adjustment for high earners.

Shared Caretaking: Abatement of Child Support and the SERF

The Michigan child support formula is based on the idea that custodial parents support their children with direct spending on food, clothing, shelter, etc., while noncustodial parents provide support indirectly by paying child support. This arrangement breaks down when noncustodial parents have extended periods of parenting time or share physical custody of the children. When noncustodial parents are also taking care of the children, it's unfair to make them provide support by both direct spending and paying child support. With this in mind, the formula has adjustments to child support for parents with extended parenting time or joint physical custody.

On pages 31-32, the formula manual recommends a 50% abatement (decrease) of child support whenever the children spend six or more consecutive overnights with the noncustodial payer-parent. Other percentages are permissible.

The formula manual also has a special "shared economic responsibility formula" (SERF) to figure base child support in some joint physical custody cases. The SERF applies when the divorce judgment (as originally issued or as modified) provides the noncustodial payer 128 overnights with the children (from joint physical custody, parenting time or a combination of the two*) annually. Pages 30-31 of the manual explain this concept and the special calculation of base child under the SERF.

---

* If you use the SERF, don't abate child support because the SERF already takes abatement into account.

Special Types of Custody: Split, Mixed or Third-Party Custody

Split, mixed and third-party custody pose similar problems. With split or mixed custody, both parents have custody of one or more children. Since the parents are simultaneously custodial and noncustodial parents, each might owe and be owed child support. In that case, the formula provides a way to set off the parents' child support obligations and arrive at a net amount due one parent. This set-off is explained on pages 41-43 of the formula manual.

For third-party custody, both parents may become support payers to the third-party custodian. Page 41 of the manual explains the calculation both when the children are living with one third party or when they are assigned to multiple third-party custodians.

Redirection and Termination of Child Support

If the children's custodian has changed, child support must be redirected to the new custodian. Sometimes, child support must be cut off for children at adulthood if they drop out of high school or for other reasons. Divorce judgments usually have provisions dealing with both redirection and termination of child support.

Departing from the Formula

The Michigan child support formula was designed to fit most cases. Nevertheless, the formula can't cover everything, even with the adjustments described above. In exceptional cases, when application of the formula is "unjust or inappropriate," the court can allow you (with or without the agreement of your ex) to depart from the formula and set child support at a nonformula amount. Pages 3-4 of the manual list some of the situations (children have special needs, parents are imprisoned, etc.) in which departure may be justified.

Other Kinds of Child Support: Health Care, Child Care and Educational Expenses

Base child support covers the basic needs of children (food, clothing and shelter). But this leaves things like health care, child care and educational expenses, which are also vital to children's well-being. In 1985, Congress passed a law expanding the concept of child support to include these extra expenses.

Health Care

Years ago, when medical costs were less, divorce judgments paid little attention to health care coverage for children. But these days, this coverage is vital and there are several ways judgments provide it.

Health Care Coverage

According to most divorce judgments, one or both parents are required to continue, or obtain, health care coverage (health insurance, HMO, PPO, etc.)

More Information

As explained here, the Michigan child support formula has ways to cover small (ordinary) and large (extraordinary) uninsured health care expenses. But you want to obtain health care coverage and avoid uninsured expenses whenever possible. Look into some of these coverage options:

Medicaid (Healthy Kids). Children in low-income families should qualify for Medicaid (called the Healthy Kids program in Michigan), which provides full health care coverage. Children receiving Family Independence Program (FIP) payments automatically qualify for Medicaid. In Michigan, the family income ceilings for Medicaid are higher than those for the FIP, allowing children to get Medicaid even if they don't qualify for the FIP.

Children's Health Insurance Program (MIChild). All states now have special health care coverage for children from families without employer-provided coverage but who make too much to qualify for Medicaid. Michigan's program is called MIChild (pronounced "my child").

COBRA-coverage. A 1985 law, the Consolidated Omnibus Budget Reconciliation Act, or COBRA for short, can provide health care coverage. Immediately after divorce, COBRA allows you to obtain health care coverage for you and/or dependent children from your ex's employer-provided group plan (if the employer has 20 or more employees), which can last for a maximum of three years. What's more, you don't have to show medical insurability to get COBRA-coverage, so for example, you can get coverage immediately when you have high medical risks or pre-existing conditions.

One drawback to COBRA: You may have to pay the plan premiums (both the employer and employee shares) yourself. But fortunately, the premiums must be charged at group rates, which are usually lower than individual rates.

County health plans. Ingham County has devised a health plan for those without health care coverage. It provides coverage for doctor visits and prescription drugs, but not hospitalization. Other counties have signed on to Ingham's plan extending it all over the state.

Michigan Prescription Discount Plan (MIRx). Michigan recently created this prescription drug discount plan for the same group as MIChild: low-income people without health care coverage but who don't qualify for Medicaid. The plan offers discounts averaging 20%.

Hill-Burton program. Years ago, the federal government provided loans and grants to many hospitals for construction and modernization under the Hill-Burton Act. In return, these Hill-Burton hospitals promised to provide a certain amount of reduced-cost or free care to low-income patients. Many hospitals have fulfilled their Hill-Burton obligations and don't have to provide this care any more; others still must (as of 2001, there were still around 50 Hill-Burton health care facilities in Michigan). If you are hospitalized at a Hill-Burton hospital, you may qualify for uncompensated care.

Individual policy. You can go into the open market and obtain an individual health plan. This type of care can be expensive, but you can limit the cost by choosing higher deductibles and co-payments.

Health Savings Plans. These savings plans, similar to 401(k)s, include: 1) Health Savings Account (HSA) into which you (and your employer) can put pretax money and withdraw it later tax-free to pay for uninsured health care expenses left by a high-deductible health care plan 2) Health Reimbursement Account (HRA) funded by employers only, which can also pay for uninsured health care expenses 3) Flexible Spending Account (FSA) resembling HRAs, but whose unused balances revert to the employer at the end of the year.

when available at a reasonable cost. Employees can often get coverage for their children as a benefit of employment. Self-employed parents must provide coverage if the insurance is affordable; self-employeds don't have to provide coverage they can't afford. Page 34 of the manual has guidelines for determining whether the cost of individual health care coverage is reasonable.

If the parties have to pay for health care coverage out of pocket, this cost can be shared by the parties according to their incomes, and added to or subtracted from the base amount of child support. The percentage-of-incomes schedules in the formula manual provides the percentages, and these can be used to allocate the net health care premium for the children to the parties. Page 34-35 of the manual explains this rather complicated calculation (if you need help, contact the friend of the court).

Health Care Expenses

Besides the cost of health care coverage, the formula manual attempts to deal with the three remaining categories of health care expenses:

Routine expenses. These expenses include everyday items like vitamins, first-aid supplies, cough syrup, etc. They are included in base child support and aren't separately reimbursable.

Ordinary expenses. Ordinary expenses include known or predictable expenses not paid for by primary health care coverage, such as deductibles, co-payments, orthodontics, etc. Page 36 of the manual has a chart estimating the annual and monthly amounts of ordinary expenses per child. You can take this amount and divide it between the parents according to their incomes (using the percentage-of-incomes schedules). The support payer's percentage share is added as a separate line item to base child support; the recipient pays his/her share directly to health care providers.

Extraordinary expenses. These are uninsured health care expenses over and above the annual amount of the ordinary expenses. The manual, on page 37, recommends that parents share these extraordinary expenses according to their incomes. Typically, this percentage sharing formula is inserted in the child support order.

Child Care

The Michigan child support formula offers extra support for child care, which is added to the base amount of child support. To qualify for the add-on, a parent must obtain child care services from a babysitter or day care center because of: 1) work 2) an opportunity to look for work 3) education to prepare for work. Ordinarily, custodial parents use child care the most. But noncustodial parents may also need it during parenting time. Both can qualify for child care add-ons.

The child care addition is available to take care of children up to the start of the school year following their 12th birthdays. The add-on can sometimes be obtained for older children when they need supervision for health or safety reasons.

Pages 37-39 of the formula manual explain the child care addition and how to figure it. Generally, you take the actual child care expenses, deduct any tax credits, subsidies or reimbursement available for them and divide the remaining net cost between the parents according to their incomes. The noncustodial payer-parent pays his/her share as an addition to base child support.

Educational Expenses

Educational expenses of the children, such as private school tuition, tutoring, music lessons, summer camps, athletics, scouting, etc., can be assigned to the parties according to their incomes or in other percentages they choose.

Payment of Child Support

Immediate Income Withholding

Around the time Michigan developed its child support formula, the state adopted a new method of collecting child support. Previously, child support

---

More Information

About the Healthy Kids, MIChild or MIRx programs, contact your local county health department, the FIA or the Michigan **Department of Community Health** at (888) 988-6300.

About COBRA, send a self-addressed stamped envelope to:

Insurance Continuation
Older Women's League (OWL)
666 11th St. NW
Washington, DC 20001

For information about local county health programs like Ingham's, call your local county health department.

About the Hill-Burton program, ask the hospital administration if the hospital is a Hill-Burton facility.

To look into individual coverage, go to Quotesmith.com for lists of health plan providers with premium estimates, without having to submit personal data.

After you find a possible provider, make sure the company is licensed and reliable by checking with Michigan's **Office of Financial and Insurance Services** at:
P.O. Box 30004
Lansing, MI 48909
(517) 373-0220

was typically paid under the honor system, with payers voluntarily making support payments to the friend of the court. Only when payers got behind was an income withholding order issued directing their source of income (usually employers) to withhold money and pay it to the friend of the court.

As child support debts began piling up, it became apparent that the honor system of payment wasn't working. In 1991, this system was replaced by immediate income withholding. Under the new method, income withholding normally starts soon after a child support order goes into effect. At that time, court officials contact the payer's employer or other source of income and sets up withholding.

Immediate income withholding is designed for the bulk of cases. Courts and child support recipients prefer this method of payment because it's reliable. On the other hand, some child support payers dislike the payment method since it means extra paperwork for their employers.

In some cases, you can drop immediate income withholding and choose another method of payment. You can do this by opting out of the friend of the court system, either totally, partially or in a limited way. See Appendix D on page 215 for more about the types of opt-outs and whether you qualify.

After opting out of immediate income withholding, the new method of payment continues as long as the payer makes regular payments. But if the payer falls behind by a month's worth of payments, the friend of the court must act to put immediate income withholding back in effect. The friend of the court will schedule a hearing on the payment issue and the court will decide which method of payment should be used.

Full Payment of Child Support

One of the worst things about the old child support collection system was cancellation of unpaid child support. When delinquent payers were brought into court, judges often allowed them to pay just a fraction of the debt, canceling the rest.

This kind of cancellation, or retroactive modification, of child support is now generally forbidden by law. These days, each child support payment becomes a separate judgment when due and full payment is expected.

There are a few exceptions to the full-payment rule. Past-due child support can be modified or even canceled when: 1) there is a court-approved retroactive modification agreement between the parties 2) one party has hidden income, then the debt can be modified to compensate for the fraud.

And just recently, a child support debt relief law went into effect allowing a payer to seek court approval for a debt payment plan which can modify or cancel child support arrearages. The provisions of this law are complicated with all sorts of restrictions and consents (from the child support recipient and/or state) necessary before a plan may be approved. Contact the friend of the court for more information about this relief.

Centralization of Child Support Services

For years, county friends of the court were the primary collectors and distributors of support (both child support and alimony). Today, a new state agency in Lansing, the state disbursement unit (SDU), has taken over these duties.

Under the new centralized system, support payers (employers deducting support under immediate income withholding or payers paying support themselves) will send all payments to the SDU. The SDU is supposed to distribute this money to support recipients across the state within two days after arrival in Lansing.

The aim of the SDU is quicker payment, more accurate record-keeping and ultimately better enforcement. Right now, most enforcement stays with local friends of the court, but more and more enforcement responsibility is being shifted to the state.

Interstate Enforcement and Modification

Years ago, one sure way to avoid paying child support was to move out of state. Interstate enforcement of support was notoriously lax, allowing many payers to escape payment. What's more, a fugitive payer could often modify the child support in the new state, leaving the child support recipient back home with a worthless child support order.

Beginning in the 1950s, states enacted interstate support enforcement laws providing for enforcement of support orders across state lines. Recently, a new generation of these laws, such as the Uniform Interstate Family Support Act (UIFSA) and the Interstate Income Withholding Act (IIWA), has gone into effect with expanded enforcement powers. In addition, the new

Interstate Child Support Proceedings

	Michigan order	Out-of-state order
Both parties residing in Michigan when post-judgment relief is sought.	Enforcement and modification in Michigan.	Enforcement and modification in Michigan.
Moving party residing in Michigan when post-judgment relief is sought; non-moving party residing outside of Michigan then.	Enforcement and modification in Michigan.	Limited enforcement in Michigan; no modification in Michigan.*
Moving party residing outside of Michigan when post-judgment relief is sought; moving party residing in Michigan then.	Enforcement and modification in Michigan.	Enforcement in Michigan; no modification in Michigan unless and until moving party moves out of divorce-granting state,* then modification here.
Both parties residing outside of Michigan when post-judgment relief is sought.	Limited or residual enforcement in Michigan; no modification in Michigan.	Limited enforcement in Michigan; no modification in Michigan.

Assumptions	*Exceptions*	*Definitions*
Assumes that children live with the parties (not with third parties), and move with them.	*Modification permissible if the parties consent to modification in Michigan and file the consent with the divorce-granting court.	Limited enforcement is over any property nonresident owns in Michigan. Residual enforcement is only for collection of child support due before parties moved out of Michigan.

laws place strict limits on interstate modification of support, although this is still permissible under some circumstances.

This new interstate enforcement and modification scheme is summarized by the table on the previous page, which looks at interstate proceedings for child support from a Michigan point of view, as if a party were about to file a post-judgment motion in Michigan.

Dealing with an Out-of-State Order in Michigan

If your out-of-state child support order is enforceable or modifiable in Michigan, the UIFSA and IIWA provide several options. Before you choose one, contact the friend of the court because it will often handle enforcement and maybe even modification for you. But if the friend of the court declines to act, you have the right to file under either act.

The first step toward full enforcement and/or modification is registration of the support order here in Michigan. Registration is complicated because it must deal with technical legal issues and allow your ex to respond to your registration request. Here again, the friend of the court can help. It can assist with registration or even combine registration and enforcement or modification into one step.

Enforcement

After registration, an out-of-state child support order is ready for enforcement. Many of the enforcement remedies listed below are available to enforce the order, just like a Michigan order.

Rapid Enforcement of an Income Withholding Order

The UIFSA also permits enforcement of income withholding within an out-of-state support order (all states now use income withholding to collect support) quickly without going to court. All you have to do is send the income withholding order to the child support payer's Michigan employer. The employer must comply with the order and begin deducting support payments from the payer's paycheck. The payer can contest the withholding by notifying the out-of-state support agency handling the order, the employer and the child support recipient.

Another law, the Interstate Income Withholding Act (IIWA), also provides for interstate enforcement of income withholding orders. But the IIWA's procedures are complicated and time-consuming compared to the UIFSA's quick and efficient enforcement method.

Modification

Following registration, you can seek modification of an out-of-state order in Michigan. The motion would be handled normally, as described in the modification section on page 122, except modification must be compatible with the divorce-granting state's law.

Enforcement and Modification out of State

As depicted by the table above, there are situations in which you cannot fully enforce or modify an out-of-state child support order in Michigan. If so, you may be able to file where your ex is living, whether this is the divorce-granting state or some other state s/he has moved to since the divorce. The problem is, it's often inconvenient to file out of state when you live in Michigan.

One option is to enforce or modify out of state from Michigan. The UIFSA allows you to initiate an enforcement and/or modification case here which is then forwarded to a the state where your ex is living. The friend of the court can explain and help in this kind of two-state case.

Enforcement

Enforcing Payment of Child Support

The friend of the court is responsible for enforcement of your child support. According to Michigan law, the friend of the court must begin enforcement when past-due support reaches a month or more of payments. This responsibility extends to health care, child care and educational expense provisions in divorce judgments, which are now regarded as forms of child support.

Friends of the court, and now increasingly state agences tasked with enforcement, tend to be aggressive in enforcing child support because tough enforcement means lower welfare costs. During enforcement, these agencies have some powerful enforcement remedies, including:

Immediate income withholding. An order requiring the child support payer's source of income (usually an employer) to withhold money (such as wages or salary) owed to the payer, and to send it onto the SDU for payment to the child support recipient. Since 1991, all child support must be paid by immediate income withholding, unless the court approves another method of payment.

Contempt. The friend of the court may ask the court to hold the child support payer in contempt of court for nonpayment of support. The payer can defend by citing various excuses (unemployment, illness, etc.) for nonpayment. If contempt is established, the payer can be incarcerated in a county jail (with or without work release) or a nonprison state correctional facility, ordered to participate in work activity or face loss of a driver's, occupational or sporting/recreational license. Any penalties may continue until the support is paid.

More Information

About Michigan child support, ask for the booklet "Michigan Child Support Services and You" from:

State Court Administrative Office
P.O. Box 30048
Lansing, MI 48909

For general information about child support enforcement and the Michigan Attorney General's new role in enforcing high-debt cases, call the AG's child support unit at (866) 729-5437 or visit its Web site: www.paykids.com.

Regarding child support enforcement froma support recipient's point of view, contact:

Association for Children for Enforcement of Support (ACES)
2260 Upton Ave.
Toledo, OH 43606
(800) 738-2237
www.childsupport-aces.org

Contact the fathers' rights groups cited on page 60 for information about fathers and child support.

Criminal nonsupport. In Michigan, failure to pay child support in the amount due or on time is a felony. A federal law also makes it a crime for child support payers owing large arrearages to: 1) avoid out-of-state child support obligations 2) cross state lines or national boundaries with an intent to avoid their child support obligations. These offenses are seldom prosecuted, but they're sometimes invoked if nonpayment of support is massive and wilful or as leverage to get payment

License revocation. License suspension (of a driver's, occupational or sporting/recreational license) is a penalty for contempt. But it's also a separate enforcement remedy when nonpayment of support exceeds two months.

Consumer reporting. The friend of the court can report nonpayment of child support to consumer reporting agencies, such as credit agencies. The payer has various rights to prevent the reporting of false information which might unfairly damage his/her credit. Or the payer can avoid consuer reporting by paying the arrearage in full.

Loss of passport. When unpaid child support exceeds $5,000, the state can notify the U.S. State Department and it can deny or revoke the payer's passport, preventing international travel. Passport suspension happens automatically, after state certification of the large arrearage.

Tax refund interception. Using information from the SDU, the state Office of Child Support may seize a child support payer's state and/or federal income tax refunds.

Surcharge. When child support is in arrears, a surcharge is tacked onto the debt at a floating interest rate tied to U.S. treasury notes. These surcharges are added automatically by the friend of the court every Jan. 1 and July 1.

In 2005, a new surcharge relief law goes into effect allowing: 1) waiver of current surcharges when the payer has paid at least 90% of recent support and any arrearage isn't growing 2) waiver of current and past surcharges (but no relief is allowed for surcharges accumulating before July 1, 2005) under an arrearage payment plan filed by the payer or friend of the court and approved by the court.

Fraudulent transfer. Like other debtors, child support payers sometimes transfer property to others at less than fair value, to prevent seizure of the property. The state FIA can have this kind of transfer set aside under Michigan's fraudulent transfer law.

Liens and other security. Automatically, by law, a lien for unpaid child support attaches to the payer's real and personal property. This lien can be foreclosed by having the property seized and sold to satisfy the support arrearage. In a common technique, liens are placed on checking or savings accounts at financial institutions (banks, savings and loans, credit unions, etc.) by a computer program matching delinquent payers to account-holders.

Courts can also require child support payers to post cash bonds or other security to guarantee payment. These bonds are sometimes required when child support is in arrears and the payer has suddenly received a large sum of money, such as an inheritance, legal settlement or lottery prize, from which the cash bond can be taken. A court can also appoint a receiver to take control of the payer's property and use the assets to pay off the child support debt.

Debt collection. These days, unpaid child support is just like any other debt and all the normal debt collection remedies available to creditors may be used to collect the child support. For example, garnishment may be used against a delinquent payer's wages or bank account, or the payer's personal property may be executed against (seized) and sold.

> ## More Information
>
> About private collection of child support, contact local debt collection firms listed under "Collection Agencies" in the yellow pages.
>
> Or call a national company, with local collection lawyers, specializing in collection of support orders:
>
> **The Accounts Retrievable System**
> 2050 Bellmore Ave.
> Bellmore, NY 11710
> (516) 783-6566

Most of these enforcement remedies are reserved for the friend of the court or other state enforcement agencies. But after nonpayment of support, you may seek enforcement by contempt or debt collection remedies.

Some of these enforcement remedies are complicated, and you may have difficulty asking for a contempt of court, garnishment or execution without a lawyer. One solution is to turn the child support debt over to a private debt collection agency. These firms usually charge contingency fees against the amount collected: Nothing if nothing is recovered, or 20-30% of any child support collected. The contingency fees give collection agencies an incentive to pursue the child support payer aggressively.

At one time, Michigan gave custodial parents another powerful self-help remedy for enforcing child support: withholding parenting time. Michigan was one of a handful of states allowing this. Most states treat child support and parenting time as separate issues, and don't permit denial of parenting time as a means of enforcing child support. Several years ago, Michigan joined the majority and now forbids linking child support to parenting time. Even if child support is seriously behind, the nonpayment never excuses withholding of parenting time.

Enforcing Health Care Obligations

With the high cost of health care these days, courts cannot allow parents to renege on health care obligations to their children. Courts have several ways to enforce these duties.

Typically, divorce judgments require parents to continue or obtain health care coverage when available at a reasonable cost. This obligation can be backed up by the judgment-enforcement powers of the court. Laws can force balky parent-employees (and their employers) to enroll/maintain children in available employer-provided plans. These laws can also order payment of any employee-paid plan premium payments from the employee's wages or salary by immediate income withholding. To take advantage of these enforcement remedies, contact the friend of the court.

This leaves the knotty problem of uninsured health care expenses. As explained in "Health Care Expenses" on page 114, the Michigan child support formula classifies these as either ordinary expenses (left by deductibles, co-payments or other gaps in coverage) or extraordinary expenses (similar expenses exceeding the annual amount of ordinary expenses).

Ordinary health expenses are normally covered by an addition to the base amount of child support. Divorce judgments usually assign extraordinary health care expenses to parents in specified percentages (typically, in a ratio according to their incomes).

Ordinary health care expenses can be collected like the base amount of child support. Collection of extraordinary health care expenses is more complicated. You must first make sure the annual amount fixed for ordinary health care expenses has been exceeded for the year. The excess must be allocated between the parents according to the percentages specified by the divorce judgment. Your ex is responsible for his/her share.

When your ex fails to pay his/her share, you must make a demand for payment. You can use the Request for Health Care Expense Payment (FOC 13). Complete the form like the sample and send it to your ex within 28 days after the health care plan either made partial payment or denied coverage (leaving extraordinary uninsured expenses). Make several copies of the form. Your ex has 28 days after demand for payment.

If your ex doesn't pay, contact the friend of the court. It will confirm your claim and seek payment from your ex. Act quickly because there are several deadlines specified in months.

Modification

A court can modify the child support order of a divorce judgment while the order is in effect. Ordinarily, a child support order lasts until each child reaches adulthood, around the age of 18.

By law, child support lasts beyond age 18, to a maximum of 19½ years of age, when a child is: 1) regularly attending high school on a full-time basis with a reasonable expectation of completing sufficient credits to graduate from high school 2) residing on a full-time basis with the support recipient or at an institution. What's more, a child support payer can *voluntarily* agree in the divorce judgment to pay support for even longer periods, such as while a child attends college. If child support continues beyond age 18, it's modifiable during this period.

On the other hand, child support stops before age 18 for emancipated children. A minor child can be emancipated by: 1) marriage 2) enlistment in the military 3) court order. After emancipation, the child's support terminates and cannot be modified.

Modifying Amount of Child Support

A court can modify a child support order by raising or lowering the base amount of child support. The modified child support may be a formula amount, with or without adjustment for factors like low or high income, shared caretaking or special types of custody. Or departure from the formula may be permitted in special cases.

The court could also modify the add-on for ordinary health care expenses, the percentages for sharing extraordinary health care expenses or child care or educational expenses. All these things are now considered forms of child support and can be part of child support modification.

Keep in mind that child support can only be modified for the future, not the past, thanks to Michigan's ban on retroactive modification of support (see "Full Payment of Child Support" on page 116 for more about this). Thus, a child support recipient cannot seek more child support for the past. But by acting quickly, the recipient may be able to get more child support for the future.

Modification is doubly important for child support payers seeking to pay less. With the ban on retroactive modification of support, a payer can't normally ask for cancellation of unpaid child support. All the law allows is modification for the future, beginning the date the modification motion is served. This emphasizes the need for quick action when you feel modification of your child support order is justified.

Modifying Child Support Payment Method

As explained before, these days most child support is paid by immediate income withholding, usually from the payer's employer. Child support is generally paid monthly, in advance, on the first day of the month.

Sometimes, you can avoid immediate income withholding and set up another method of child support payment. The easiest way to do this is by opting out of the friend of the court system, either totally, partially or in a limited way (see Appendix D on page 215 for more about opt-outs). If you avoid immediate income withholding, you might also be able to have child support paid at different intervals than monthly.

Modification of Child Support Amount through the Friend of the Court

By law, the friend of the court is responsible for reviewing child support periodically. During a review, the friend of the court must decide whether an increase or decrease of base child support is justified. The friend of the court can also look at child support extras (for health care, child care and educational expenses), and see if they need to be modified.

If a modification is necessary,* the friend of the court must bring a motion for the modification. In this way, child support recipients can get an increase, or payers a decrease, by letting the friend of the court do most of the work.

---

* If the modification is small, the friend of the court doesn't have to act. It must move for modification only when the amount of child support would change by the *lesser* of: 1) 10% or more of the current order 2) $25 per month (or equivalent for nonmonthly payments).

The friend of the court is supposed to review child support orders at least once every two years (this period increases to three years after June 30, 2005) when children are receiving public assistance. Or the friend of the court may do such a "periodic review" whenever it believes there are grounds for modification.

The modification grounds for period reviews by the friend of the court have previously been a change of circumstances since the judgment of divorce. These change of circumstances grounds will continue to apply to periodic reviews of divorces completed before July 1, 2005. For divorces completed on or after that date, new modification grounds apply: "reasonable grounds" for modification of child support. The law defines reasonable grounds to include:

- informal changes of the custody of children, not ordered by the court, indicating that child support should be redirected to the new custodian
- changes in the needs of children
- changes in the incomes of parents (including application for or receipt of public assistance, unemployment or workers' compensation)
- probable access of parents to employer-provided health care coverage
- imprisonment or a parent or release of a parent from prison

The child support recipient or payer can also request a periodic review. The request must be in writing. The friend of the court must respond to one review request from each party once every two years (three years after June 30, 2005). The friend of the court may disregard extra requests during that period. The court can also order a periodic review anytime.

The friend of the court must notify the parties that a review is going on, and allow the parties to comment or provide information about a possible modification. Typically, the parties will receive a Notice of Child Support Review (FOC 71) at the beginning of the review.

If the friend of the court decides to move for modification of child support after a periodic review, it will prepare the modification motion and schedule the motion hearing. At the hearing, the friend of the court will present evidence and argue for an increase or decrease in child support. During the modification case, the friend of the court cannot side with either party and advocate for them, as a lawyer would, but must merely defend its position on the proposed modification.

On the other hand, after reviewing child support the friend of the court may decide that no modification is necessary. You can object to this decision by filing the Objection to Child Support Review (FOC 79). The objection must be filed with the clerk within 30 days (this period is shortened to 21 days after June 30, 2005) after receiving the friend of the court's no-modification recommendation. There is a sample FOC 79 at the end of this chapter.

After you object, the court will schedule a motion hearing on your request for an increase or decrease. See "Contested Modification" below for information about appearing at the hearing and arguing your position.

Stipulated Modification

You and your ex can agree, or stipulate, to modification of the amount of child support or the method for paying it. Since the issue impacts the children, the court must review your proposed modification.

You don't need to file a motion or have a court hearing to modify child support by stipulation. All you have to do is prepare the correct modification order (explained below) and have it approved by the court. See "Stipulated Orders" on page 30 for complete instructions about preparing a stipulated order, getting court approval of the order, filing it with the clerk and serving it on your ex.

Amount of Child Support

You and your ex can agree to modify base child support according to the formula, with or without adjustment for special factors like low or high incomes, shared caretaking or special types of custody. Or you could, with court permission, depart from the formula and agree to a nonformula amount.

You can also deal with other forms of child support by stipulation. You can modify health care, child care and educational expense payments or sharing arrangements.

All these topics are covered in "Child Support Obligations" on page 109. "Child Support Provisions for the Court Order" on page 129 explains how to modify base child support in the Uniform Child Support Order (FOC 10/52), or deal with the other kinds of support in this order.

Method of Payment

If you don't have immediate income withholding and you and your ex want it, contact the friend of the court. The friend of the court, which has exclusive authority to start immediate income withholding, will be happy to set up this method of payment for you.

More is necessary when you want to avoid immediate income withholding now in effect and adopt another payment method. Other payment options include payment monthly or at some other interval directly to the SDU or support recipient.

The best way to avoid immediate income withholding is by stipulating to an opt-out from the friend of the court system, either totally, partially or in a limited way (for support payments only). Appendix D on page 215 explains how to do this and which forms to use.

Contested Modification

When your ex won't stipulate to modification of child support, you must file a motion asking for the change. Modification isn't guaranteed; the court will consider your motion during a hearing and either grant or deny it.

For a modification, you must pay an extra $40 fee. The laws seems to require payment of the child support modification fee when the modification order is filed. But some clerks may charge the fee up front, when a modification motion is filed.

Motion

Amount of Child Support

You can ask for modification of the amount of child support in the Motion Regarding Support (FOC 50). There is a sample FOC 50 at the end of this chapter, showing you how to complete the various parts of the motion. The core of the motion is paragraph #5, which explains the grounds for modification, and paragraph #7 describing your proposed modification.

The customary grounds for modifying child support are change of conditions or circumstances in the lives of you, your ex and/or children. Your income may have risen or fallen, affecting your ability to pay child support (as payer) or impacting your need for it (as recipient) on behalf of the children.

These simple change-of-circumstances grounds will continue to apply to party-filed modification motions for divorce cases completed before July 1, 2005. For divorces completed on or after that date, a new law requires a *substantial* change of circumstances for modification.* The new law appears to toughen the standard for party-filed modifications a bit. In reality, the reasons will continue to be much the same (change in parties' incomes, different needs of children, etc.), with maybe a slightly more convincing case necessary for modification now.

In some cases, revision of the Michigan child support formula qualifies as a change of conditions (the formula's schedules are revised every year or so; the formula itself is revised less frequently). If your child support has gotten seriously out of step with the formula, you can cite this as the grounds for modification. See "Michigan Child Support Formula" on page 110 for more about the formula and child support schedules.

You may need now to adjust your base child support under the formula. Adjustments are allowed when the parties have low or high incomes, shared caretaking of children (resulting in abatement of support or use of the SERF) or special types of custody, such as split, mixed or third-party custody. See "Adjusting the Formula" on page 111 for more about these issues.

In extraordinary situations, you may ask for permission to depart from the formula and set base child support at a nonformula amount (see "Departing from the Formula" on page 113 for more about departure reasons). If you believe departure is justified in your case, you must show that the formula amount is "unjust or inappropriate" in your case. You must add the departure reason to the modification grounds in paragraph #5 of the Motion Regarding Support (FOC 50).

---

*   As described in "Modification of Child Support Amount through the Friend of the Court" on page 123, new grounds also apply to modification motions filed by the friend of the court after a periodic review.

Finally, you could deal with other kinds of child support in your modification motion. You might ask for modification of health care, child care or educational expense payments or sharing arrangements. These topics are covered in "Other Kinds of Child Support: Health Care, Child Care and Educational Expenses" on page 113.

For complete information and instructions about preparing, filing and serving post-judgment motions such as a Motion Regarding Support (FOC 50), see "Papers" on page 23 and "Motions" on page 32.

Method of Payment

If you want to ask for another method of paying child support, it's best to do this by an opt-out from the friend of the court system, either totally, partially or in a limited way (for support payments only). Appendix D on page 215 explains how to do this and which forms to use.

Responding to a Motion

If you receive a motion for modification of child support from your ex, you can respond orally or in writing, in several ways.

If you agree with the motion completely, contact your ex immediately and arrange to stipulate to a modification order. In paragraphs #5, #6 and #7 of the Response to Motion Regarding Support (FOC 51), you can also indicate your agreement with the motion. But why do extra paperwork when it's easier to stipulate to a modification order? You could also appear at the hearing and agree to the motion, but this too wastes time when stipulation is available. See "Stipulated Modification" on page 125 for more about stipulations.

Sometimes, you may agree with part of the motion and disagree with the rest. It's important to signal your partial agreement as soon as possible because this narrows the issues in the case. If you file a Response to Motion Regarding Support (FOC 51), check box #6b and describe the extent of your agreement with the motion in the space below. If you choose to respond orally, mention your partial agreement to the mediator, referee or judge, so the agreed-upon issues can be eliminated from the hearing.

When you oppose the motion, you can voice your disagreement in two ways. You can file a written response to the motion or wait until the motion hearing and respond orally. A written response is usually better, because it gets your views across more effectively.

Use the Response to Motion Regarding Support (FOC 51) for a written response. In paragraph #5, say why you oppose the motion. You may challenge the moving party's factual claims about loss or gain of income, or how this impacts the party's ability to pay support or the children's need for it. Or you might dispute that the formula needs adjustment. If departure from the formula has been sought, you could question whether the case is exceptional enough to permit departure. When other kinds of child support (health care, child care and educational expenses) are at issue, you might oppose the claims for these as well.

Is your ex is seeking a change in the method of paying child support? If your ex is seeking this relief in a support modification motion, you can cite reasons (history of late payments, etc.) against this in paragraph #5 of the FOC 51. If the request is for a limited opt-out, see "Responding to a Motion" on page 220 in Appendix D about how to respond.

For general information and instructions about preparing, filing and serving a response, see "Responding to a Motion" on page 35.

You can also respond to a motion by making a counter-motion. Normally, if you oppose the motion with the Response to Motion Regarding Support (FOC 51), you disagree with the grounds for the motion in paragraph #5. Then, in paragraph #7 you oppose the proposed modification, as in the sample response at the end of this chapter.

But if you want a different kind of child support modification, check box #7b and explain in the space below what you want. For example, it's not uncommon for a child support recipient to move for an increase of child support and for the child support payer to respond by asking for a decrease. The payer's request for a decrease is, in essence, a counter-motion.

In some cases, it's even possible to ask for completely new relief in a counter-motion. Add new issues carefully, because these can easily sidetrack the case. Nevertheless, it may make sense to seek new relief in a counter-motion when the new issues are compatible with the main motion.

For more about counter-motion tactics and how to counter-move for new relief, see "Making a Counter-Motion" on page 37.

Friend of the Court

Before a post-judgment motion is heard by the judge, the friend of the court may intervene to mediate, investigate or referee, in an attempt to settle the dispute.

Previously, child support disputes weren't eligible for informal mediation or settlement. But after June 30, 2005, these disputes may be submitted to informal settlement by the friend of the court. Referral of the dispute to formal mediation is also possible. Private mediation or arbitration, which is expensive, is unlikely.

During a child support dispute, the friend of the court is usually required to investigate the issue, and make a report and recommendation about child support. The friend of the court's child support recommendation must follow the Michigan child support formula. It's also possible that the motion will be refereed by the friend of the court prior to the motion hearing.

See "Friend of the Court" on page 38 for more about the friend of the court's roles in post-judgment cases, and how to deal with mediation, investigation or refereeing by the friend of the court. This section also has information about formal mediation, private mediation and arbitration, all of which take place outside the friend of the court system.

Motion Hearing

As explained in "Motion Hearings" on page 41, there are two kinds of motion hearings: 1) nonevidentiary hearing where facts aren't disputed, evidence is seldom introduced, and the parties merely make legal arguments to the judge 2) evidentiary hearing where facts are disputed and evidence, such as testimony from witnesses, must be introduced to establish the true facts.

Most child support modifications require nonevidentiary hearings or, at most, limited evidentiary hearings. Many times, the parties agree on their incomes, so evidence about earnings isn't necessary. If there's disagreement, some evidence, such as paycheck stubs, W-2 forms or income tax returns, may be required to establish income. Witness testimony is seldom necessary. See "Motion Hearings" on page 41 for information about preparing for and appearing at a nonevidentiary hearing.

Court Order

After the motion hearing, the judge will decide the motion. The judge will either decide immediately and give an oral decision "from the bench," or take the case "under submission" and rule later by issuing a written decision.

Either way, the moving party must prepare the order granting or denying the motion. Use the Uniform Child Support Order (FOC 10/52) for the modification. You may have gotten, or are getting, a total or partial opt-out from the friend of the court system. If you are opting out, you should use a special version of the child support order, the Uniform Child Support Order, No Friend of Court Services (FOC 10a/52a), which is identical to the FOC 10/52 but deletes all references to the friend of the court. There is a blank FOC 10a/52a among the opt-out forms in the forms section.

The moving party must get the order signed by the judge and filed with the clerk. There are several ways to do this. See "Court Orders" on page 44 for complete instructions and forms.

In Wayne County only, you must also prepare an Order Data Form-Support (FD/FOC 4002). The data form asks for basic information about the parties, their children and the child support. This data is entered by the Wayne County Friend of the Court into its computer system for enforcement of support later. You must give the FD/FOC 4002 to the clerk when you file the child support order and it will forward the form to the Wayne County Friend of the Court.

Child Support Provisions for the Court Order

You insert the base child support amount in the big box in paragraph #3 of the Uniform Child Support Order (FOC 10/52). Typically, the judge will order different amounts for as many minor children as there are in the family (so child support declines as children become independent), and you can insert these amounts in the box. The base child support amount ordered in the judge's decision may be taken directly from the formula or it may have been adjusted for special factors(low or high incomes, abatement/SERF, etc.).

If the SERF was used, you must mention this in the order. In the big box in paragraph #3 of the Uniform Child Support Order (FOC 10/52), check the box indicating that support was set according to the shared economic responsibility formula and insert the number of overnights (128-night minimum) of physical custody and/or parenting time causing application of the SERF. Just above this, you can also provide for abatement (at a rate of 50% after six consecutive overnights with the payer) if your divorce judgment has omitted this (most recent judgments provide for abatement).

At the bottom of the box, indicate whether the child support amounts follow or do not follow the child support formula. If they do not, you must cite several factors justifying departure, which are listed below:

- the child support specified by the formula for your case
- how your child support departs from the formula
- the reason for the departure
- the value of any property or other concessions made in lieu of support

These departure factors must be included in your child support order. You can add these in paragraph #12 or an attachment to the FOC 10/52, as in the following example:

12. <u>Departure from Child Support Formula</u>.   The child support in paragraph #3 departs from the amount specified in the child support formula. Nevertheless, the court approves the departure because it is unjust or inappropriate to order child support according to the formula. The court also finds that:

(a) the monthly child support specified in the formula is [$400]

(b) the amount ordered is [$500] per month, which is [$100 more] than the formula amount

(c) the reason for the departure is [the parties' daughter Deborah is visually impaired and needs extra support]

(d) the child support recipient received [no property or alimony] in lieu of child support

Other forms of child support may have been decided by the judge. As explained in "Health Care" on page 113, one or both parents can be ordered to provide primary health care coverage for the children if available at a reasonable cost. In paragraph #4 of the Uniform Child Support Order (FOC 10/52), you can reassign this responsibility to cover. And you can impose reasonable dollar-caps on shouldering the cost of individual (nonemployer-provided) coverage.

If the parents do have to pay some or all of the health care coverage premiums, this cost can be allocated between them and the child support payer's share can be added (or subtracted) from base child support. If this has happened, describe the premium-sharing in the third check-box inside the big box in paragraph #3 of the FOC 10/52.

You can also provide for uninsured health care expenses in the FOC 10/52. There may already be an addition to base child support for ordinary health care expenses. Or the judge may have ordered this to start. Either way, you can adjust or add this extra amount in the big box in paragraph #3. To the right of the "Ordinary medical" line, insert amounts for each child. Take the total amount set annually for these ordinary health care expenses (for all the children) and insert this figure in the space in paragraph #5 of the FOC 10/52. This figure creates a floor for calculation of extraordinary health care expenses.

You can deal with extraordinary health care expenses in paragraph #5 of the Uniform Child Support Order (FOC 10/52). The judge may have ordered an adjustment to the sharing percentages for extraordinary health care expenses, and you can adjust this in paragraph #5.

Child care expenses can be adjusted or added in the big box in paragraph #3 of the FOC 10/52. See "Child Care" on page 115 about figuring a child care add-on. This amount can be added to the "Child care" line in the box.

The Uniform Child Support Order (FOC 10/52) doesn't have a paragraph for children's educational expenses. But you can add a sharing provision in paragraph #12 or an attachment to the order, like this:

12. <u>Educational Expenses</u>. In addition to base child support, plaintiff shall pay [20%] and defendant shall pay [80%] of the [annual tuition at St. Francis Elementary School, Lake City, Michigan,] for the parties' children.

Method of Payment

Normally, you can ask for another method of payment as part of an opt-out from the friend of the court system. And if you are allowed to opt out, you use an opt-out order to set up the new method of payment. See Appendix D on page 215 about opt-outs.

Original - Court
1st copy - Other Party
2nd copy - Moving Party

3rd copy - Friend of the Court
4th copy - Proof of Service
5th copy - Proof of Service

Approved, SCAO

STATE OF MICHIGAN
    JUDICIAL CIRCUIT
        COUNTY

MOTION REGARDING SUPPORT

CASE NO.

Court telephone no.

Court address

Plaintiff's name, address, and telephone no.   ☐ moving party

v

Defendant's name, address, and telephone no.   ☐ moving party

Third party name, address, and telephone no.   ☐ moving party

1. ☒ a. On ___7-1-90___ a judgment
           Date
    or order was entered regarding support.
  ☐ b. There is currently no order regarding support.

> THIS PARAGRAPH SEES WHETHER PARTIES AGREE ON THE MODIFICATION. IF YOU BOTH AGREE, SKIP FILING A MOTION AND JUST STIPULATE TO A MODIFICATION ORDER, AS EXPLAINED IN "STIPULATED ORDERS" IN CHAPTER 1C.

☒ 2. The ☐ plaintiff ☒ defendant is ordered to pay support of $ ___480___ each ___MONTH___
                                                  week, month, etc.

☐ 3. The ☐ plaintiff ☐ defendant is ordered to pay child care of $ _____ each _____
                                                 week, month, etc.

☐ 4. The ☐ plaintiff ☐ defendant is ordered to pay health care of $ _____ each _____
                                                 week, month, etc.

> DESCRIBE GROUNDS FOR MODIFICATION.

☒ 5. Conditions regarding support have changed as follows: Include all necessary facts. AT WORK, MY SALES COMMISSION
Use a separate sheet to explain in detail what has happened and attach. HAS BEEN CUT FROM 10% TO 5% CAUSING LOSS OF NET INCOME AVERAGING $200
PER MONTH. THIS LOSS OF INCOME JUSTIFIES A REDUCTION OF CHILD SUPPORT.
    and I have agreed to support as follows:

☐ 6. _____
    Name
    Use a separate sheet to explain in detail what you have agreed on and attach. Include all necessary facts.

7. **I ask the court to order that support be** paid as follows: ☐ See 6. above for details.
    Use a separate sheet to explain in detail what you want the court to order and attach.
REDUCE MONTHLY CHILD SUPPORT FROM $480 TO $420 FOR
SUPPORT OF TWO CHILDREN, AND $312 TO $272 FOR SUPPORT
OF ONE CHILD.

I declare that the above statements are true to the best of my information, knowledge, and belief.

___1-1-99___   _Dudley Lovelace_
Date   Moving party's signature

NOTICE OF HEARING

LESTER TUBBS
A hearing will be held on this motion before _____
                                   Name of judge or referee

on ___2-15-99___ at ___9:00 AM___ at ___OJIBWAY COUNTY COURTHOUSE___.
    Date   Time   Place

NOTE: If you are the person receiving this motion, you may file a response. Contact the friend of the court office and request form FOC 51.

CERTIFICATE OF MAILING

I certify that on this date I mailed a copy of this motion and notice of hearing on the other party(ies) by ordinary mail at the above address(es).

___1-2-99___   _Dudley Lovelace_
Date   Moving party's signature

MCL 552.14; MSA 25.94; MCR 2.119; MCR 3.213

FOC 50 (12/96) **MOTION REGARDING SUPPORT**

Approved, SCAO

Original - Court
1st copy - Moving Party
2nd copy - Responding Party

3rd copy - Friend of the Court
4th copy - Proof of Service
5th copy - Proof of Service

STATE OF MICHIGAN
JUDICIAL CIRCUIT
COUNTY

Court address

RESPONSE TO
MOTION REGARDING SUPPORT

CASE NO.

Plaintiff's name, address, and telephone no.   ☐ moving party

v

Court telephone no.

Defendant's name, address, and telephone no.   ☐ moving party

Third party name, address, and telephone no.   ☐ moving party

1. ☒ a. On _____7-1-90_____ a judgment
   Date
   or order was entered regarding support.
   ☐ b. There is currently no order regarding support.

☒ 2. The ☐ plaintiff ☒ defendant   is ordered to pay support of $ ____480____ each __MONTH__
                                                                                        week, month, etc.

☐ 3. The ☐ plaintiff ☐ defendant   is ordered to pay child care of $ _____ each _____
                                                                                        week, month, etc.

☐ 4. The ☐ plaintiff ☐ defendant   is ordered to pay health care of $ _____ each _____
                                                                                        week, month, etc.

☒ 5. I ☐ agree ☒ do not agree   that conditions regarding support have changed as stated in the motion.
Explain in detail what you do not agree with and why. Include all necessary facts. Use a separate sheet of paper if needed.
I DON'T HAVE ANY KNOWLEDGE ABOUT DEFENDANT'S SALES COMMISSIONS.
BUT I HAVE OBSERVED THAT DEFENDANT IS WORKING MORE HOURS
THAN BEFORE, WHICH COULD OFFSET ANY LOSS OF SALES COMMISSIONS.

SEVERAL PARAGRAPHS TEST WHETHER YOU AGREE WITH MODIFICATION. IF YOU AGREE, COMPLETELY OR IN PART, SEE "RESPONDING TO A MOTION" IN THIS CHAPTER ABOUT YOUR RESPONSE OPTIONS.

☐ 6. I agreed with the other party to start/change support:
   ☐ a. exactly as stated in the motion.
   ☐ b. but not as stated in the motion.
   If b. is checked, explain in detail what you did agree on. Include all necessary facts. Use a separate sheet of paper if needed.

7. ☐ a. I agree with what is being asked for in the motion.
   ☒ b. I do not agree with what is being asked for in the motion and ask the court to order that support be pa
   If you do not agree with the request in the motion, explain in detail why and what you want the court to order. Use a separate sheet of pa
   DENY DEFENDANT'S MOTION FOR A REDUCTION OF CHILD SUPPORT
   KEEPING CHILD SUPPORT AT ITS CURRENT LEVEL.

YOU CAN MAKE A COUNTER-MOTION IN THIS PARAGRAPH. SEE "RESPONDING TO A MOTION" IN THIS CHAPTER FOR MORE ABOUT COUNTER-MOTIONS.

I declare that the above statements are true to the best of my information, knowledge, and belief.

____2-1-99____
Date

Darlene Lovelace
Responding party's signature

CERTIFICATE OF MAILING

I certify that on this date I mailed a copy of this response on the other party(ies) by ordinary mail at the above address(es).

____2-1-99____
Date

Darlene Lovelace
Responding party's signature

FOC 51 (12/96) **RESPONSE TO MOTION REGARDING SUPPORT**

MCL 552.14; MSA 25.94, MCR 2.119

		2nd copy - Defendant
	Original - Court	3rd copy - Friend of the Court
	1st copy - Plaintiff	

Approved, SCAO

STATE OF MICHIGAN	**UNIFORM CHILD SUPPORT ORDER**	**CASE NO.**
JUDICIAL CIRCUIT	(PAGE 1)	
COUNTY	☒ MODIFICATION	

FAX no.   Court telephone no.

Court address

Plaintiff's name, address, and telephone no.		Defendant's name, address, and telephone no.
	v	
Plaintiff's attorney name, address, telephone no., and bar no.		Defendant's atttorney name, address, telephone no., and bar no.
Plaintiff's source of income name, address, and telephone no.		Defendant's source of income name, address, and telephone no.

Unless otherwise ordered:

1. This order continues until each child is age 18 or graduates from high school, as provided by MCL 552.605b, whi[ch] but no longer than age 19 1/2. Child care for each child terminates effective September 1 following each child's [...] [text cut off]

2. Income withholding shall take immediate effect. All payments shall be made through the friend of the court or State [...] Unit.

3. **Support.**   The payer has a monthly support obligation as follows:

Payer: DUDLEY LOVELACE   Payee: DARLENE LOVELACE   Effective date: 1-2-99

Children's names and birth dates: DUANE W. LOVELACE 6-1-86
DARRYL W. LOVELACE 7-1-87

	1 child	2 children	3 children	4 children	5 or more children
Children supported:					
Base support:	$ 272	$ 420	$	$	$
Ordinary medical:	$	$	$	$	$
Child care:	$	$	$	$	$
Other:	$	$	$	$	$
Total:	$ 272	$ 420	$	$	$

☐ Base support shall abate 50% after 6 consecutive overnights with the payer _____ overnights of parenting time.
☐ Support was set based on the shared economic responsibility formula using _____ paid by plaintiff and $_____ paid by defendant.
☐ Base support considers health care premiums of $_____ ☒ do   ☐ do not   follow the child support formula.
The above ordered support provisions

4. **Insurance.** For the benefit of the children, ☐ plaintiff ☐ defendant   shall maintain health care coverage through an insurer [as defined in MCL 552.602(o)] that includes payment for hospital, dental, optical, and other medical expenses when that coverage is available through an employer or under an existing individual policy at the following reasonable cost:
☐ up to a maximum of $_____ for plaintiff.   ☐ up to a maximum of $_____ for defendant.
☐ not to exceed 5% of the plaintiff's/defendant's gross income.

(see Page 2 for remainder of order)

FOC 10 / 52 (9/04) **UNIFORM CHILD SUPPORT ORDER, PAGE 1**   MCL 552.14, MCL 552.517, MCL 552.517b(3), MCR 3.211

[Speech bubble:] IN THIS SECTION, YOU CAN PROVIDE FOR ABATEMENT OF CHILD SUPPORT OR APPLY THE SHARED ECONOMIC RESPONSIBILITY FORMULA (SERF), WHEN NECESSARY.

[Speech bubble:] SUPPORT MODIFICATION CAN DATE BACK TO WHEN MODIFICATION MOTION WAS SERVED

[Speech bubble:] IN PARAGRAPHS #4 AND #5, YOU CAN ADJUST HEALTH CARE OBLIGATIONS. IF NOT, SKIP THESE PARAGRAPHS

Approved, SCAO

	Original - Court 1st copy - Plaintiff	

STATE OF MICHIGAN
JUDICIAL CIRCUIT
COUNTY

Court address

UNIFORM CHILD SUPPORT ORDER
(PAGE 2)
☒ **MODIFICATION**

2nd copy - Defendant
3rd copy - Friend of the Court

CASE NO.

Plaintiff's name

FAX no.   Court telephone no.

v

Defendant's name

5. **Uninsured Medical Expenses.** All uninsured health care expenses exceeding the ordinary medical amount will be paid _____% by the plaintiff and _____% by the defendant. Uninsured expenses exceeding the ordinary medical amount for the year they are incurred that are not paid within 28 days of a written payment request may be enforced by the friend of the court. The ordinary medical amount is $ _____ year.

6. **Qualified Medical Support Order.** This order is a qualified medical support order under 29 USC 1169. To qualify this order, the friend of the court shall issue a notice to enroll under MCL 552.626b. A parent may contest the notice by requesting a review or hearing concerning availability of health care at a reasonable cost.

7. **Retroactive Modification, Surcharge for Past Due Support, and Liens for Unpaid Support.** Support is a judgment the date it is due and is not modifiable retroactively. A surcharge will be added to past due support. Unpaid support is a lien by operation of law and the payer's property can be encumbered or seized if an arrearage accrues for more than the periodic support payments payable for two months under the payer's support order.

8. **Change of Address, Employment Status, Health Insurance.** Both parties shall notify the friend of the court in writing, within 21 days of any change in: a) their mailing or residence address and telephone number; b) the name, address, and telephone number of their sources of income; c) their health maintenance or insurance company, insurance coverage, persons insured, or contract number; d) their occupational or driver licenses; and e) their social security number unless exempt by law under MCL 552.603.

9. **Redirection and Abatement:** Subject to statutory procedures, the friend of the court : 1) may redirect support paid for a child to the person who is legally responsible for that child; 2) shall abate support charges for a child who resides on a full-time basis with the payer of support; or 3) shall redirect support to the Family Independence Agency for a child placed in foster care.

10. **Fees.** The payer of support shall pay statutory and service fees as required by law.

11. **Prior Orders.** Except as changed in this order, prior provisions remain in effect. Support payable under any prior order is preserved.

12. **Other:** (attach separate sheets as needed)

> THE PARTIES MUST SIGN A STIPULATED ORDER OR ONE OBTAINED BY CONSENT. PARTIES DON'T SIGN AN ORDER OBTAINED THROUGH "APPROVAL-BY-SILENCE" OR AFTER A COURT HEARING ON THE ORDER.

IT IS SO ORDERED:

Darlene Lovelace 2-15-99
Plaintiff (if consent/stipulation)   Date

2-15-99
Date

Dudley Lovelace 2-15-99
Defendant (if consent/stipulation)   Date

Lester Jubbs
Judge   Bar no.

CERTIFICATE OF MAILING

I certify that on this date I served a copy of this order on the parties by first class mail addressed to their last known addresses as defined in MCR 3.203.

2-15-99
Date

Dudley Lovelace
Signature

FOC 10 / 52 (9/04) **UNIFORM CHILD SUPPORT ORDER, PAGE 2**

MCL 552.14, MCL 552.517, MCL 552.517b(3), MCR 3.211

Original - Obligor

The following expenses have been incurred for the health care of a minor child for whom you are obligated to provide health care support.

Name of Child Receiving Service	Name of Medical Provider	Date of Service	Type of Service	Total Medical Cost	Amt. Paid by Insurance	Balance Due*	Obligor's %	Amt. Owed by Obligor
DUANE LOVELACE	LAKE CITY COMM. HOSPITAL	1-10-99	(SEE ATTACHED)	$1,100	$800	$300	66%	$198

I declare that the above statements are true to the best of my information, knowledge, and belief and that on this date I mailed a copy
Payment to the obligor at his or her last known address.

Date 1-30-99

Signature _Darlene Lovelace_

*Balance due means balance owed after payment by insurance and any adjustments to the total medical cost.

> THE AMOUNT YOU REQUEST HERE IS THE OBLIGOR'S PERCENTAGE SHARE OF THE UNINSURED REMAINDER OF THE TOTAL COST OF THE HEALTH CARE SERVICE.

Approved, SCAO

STATE OF MICHIGAN
JUDICIAL CIRCUIT
COUNTY

REQUEST FOR
EXPENSE

Friend of the Court address

Plaintiff

INSTRUCTIONS FOR REQUESTING PARTY:
The following is important information should you later seek t
expenses (medical, dental, and other health care expenses

1. Your court order must require the other party to pay a po
2. The expense must exceed any amounts your child supp
3. You must submit your request for payment to the other pa
   or the date insurance denies payment.
4. If you and the other party reach an agreement concernin
   be paid, state the total amount to be paid, and provide
5. The bills must be presented to the friend of the court on o
   after the insurer's final denial of coverage for the expen
   were completed within 2 months after the expense was
   forth above. You will need to fill out a second form to re
6. In the event it is necessary for the friend of the court to
   receipts for the expenses you list. You will be responsi
   documentation to all court hearings where medical ex
7. Attach a copy of all bills and insurance notifications to
8. **You must keep a copy of this form and all attachme
   is necessary.**

TO: Obligor's name and address
DUDLEY LOVELACE
900 S. MAPLE
LAKE CITY, MI 48800

Complete expenses incurred on the other side of this f

FOC 13 (6/03) REQUEST FOR HEALTH CARE EXP

Original - Court (A)
1st copy - Other Party (B)
2nd copy - Moving Party (C)

3rd copy - Friend of the Court (D)
4th copy - Proof of Service (E)

Approved, SCAO

STATE OF MICHIGAN
JUDICIAL CIRCUIT
COUNTY

OBJECTION TO CHILD SUPPORT REVIEW

CASE NO.

FAX no.   Court telephone no.

PARTY WHO OBJECTS TO FRIEND OF THE COURT'S REVIEW IS THE MOVING PARTY HERE.

Court address

Plaintiff's name, address, and telephone no.   ☐ Moving party

v

Defendant's name, address, and telephone no.   ☒ Moving party

I received a notice of child support review from the friend of the court dated ___1-1-99___
I object to the to the determination that no change in the child support/health care order should occur and request a hearing by the court. My objection is based on the following reason(s):

MY NET INCOME HAS DECLINED BY AN AVERAGE OF $200 MONTHLY BECAUSE MY SALES COMMISSION PERCENTAGE WAS REDUCED FROM 10% TO 5%. THIS LOSS OF INCOME JUSTIFIES REDUCTION OF MONTHLY CHILD SUPPORT FROM $480 TO $420 FOR SUPPORT OF TWO CHILDREN AND $312 TO $272 FOR ONE CHILD.

I declare that the statements above are true to the best of my information, knowledge, and belief.

___1-20-99___
Date

Dudley Lovelace
Signature of objecting party

DUDLEY LOVELACE
Name (type or print)

CERTIFICATE OF MAILING

I certify that on this date I mailed a copy of this objection on the other party by ordinary mail at the above address.

___1-20-99___
Date

Dudley Lovelace
Signature of objecting party

FOC 79 (6/96) **OBJECTION TO CHILD SUPPORT REVIEW**

MCL 552.517; MSA 25.176(17), MCL 552.517b; MSA 25.176(17b)

PAGE 1 OF 2

> USE THIS FORM IN A CHILD SUPPORT MODIFICATION IN WAYNE COUNTY ONLY. SEE THE BLANK FORM WHICH HAS A TWO-PAGE PREFACE WITH MORE INSTRUCTIONS.

STATE OF MICHIGAN
COUNTY OF WAYNE
THIRD JUDICIAL CIRCUIT COURT
FAMILY DIVISION

ORDER DETAILS

ORDER DATA FORM-SUPPORT
Re: SUBMISSION FOR LOADING ATTACHED SUPPORT ORDER INTO MiCSES ON FOC COMPUTER SYSTEM

THE ORDER WAS ENTERED ON:
2-15-99
(DATE ON ORDER STAMPED BY JUDGE'S CLERK)

_____
JUDGE

*INDICATES REQUIRED INFORMATION

CHECK ONLY THE BOXES WHICH APPLY TO PROVISIONS IN THE SUBMITTED ORDER

* PLAINTIFF NAME:
DARLENE A. LOVELACE

*THIS ORDER IS:
☐ EX PARTE (PROOF OF SERVICE REQUIRED)

* DEFENDANT NAME:
DUDLEY E. LOVELACE

*WERE CHILD SUPPORT GUIDELINES FOLLOWED? ☒ YES ☐ NO

☐ TEMPORARY ☐ JUDGMENT ☒ MODIFICATION

*THE CHILD SUPPORT PAYER IS ☐ PLAINTIFF ☒ DEFENDANT ☐ NOT APPLICABLE.

☒ CHILD SUPPORT. COMMENCEMENT DATE IS **1-2-99**
☐ PAY DIRECT, NOT THROUGH FOC.

* 5 CHILDREN PER WEEK CHILD SUPPORT AMOUNT	* 4 CHILDREN PER WEEK CHILD SUPPORT AMOUNT	* 3 CHILDREN PER WEEK CHILD SUPPORT AMOUNT	* 2 CHILDREN PER WEEK CHILD SUPPORT AMOUNT	* 1 CHILD PER WEEK CHILD SUPPORT AMOUNT
$	$	$	$ **420**	$ **272**

☒ INCOME WITHHOLDING: ☒ PROCESS AT GUIDELINE AMOUNT ☐ PROCESS AT $ _____ PER WEEK

☒ CHILD SUPPORT ARREARAGE:
☒ PRESERVED ☐ CANCELED AS OF DATE: _____

☐ CHILD CARE EXPENSES: $ _____
END DATE IS ☐ GUIDELINE DATE **OR** ☐ DATE: _____ PER WEEK, COMMENCEMENT DATE IS _____ ☐ SET AT $ _____ AS OF DATE:

☐ CHILD CARE ARREARAGE:
☐ PRESERVED ☐ CANCELED AS OF DATE: _____

☐ ARREARAGE ADJUSTMENT:
☐ DIRECT CREDIT IN AMOUNT OF $ _____ ☐ SET AT $ _____ AS OF DATE:

☒ MEDICAL INSURANCE IN ORDER. ☐ ADD ADDITIONAL OBLIGATION IN AMOUNT OF $ _____
☐ CHILD SUPPORT PAYER RESPONSIBLE FOR _____ % OF UNINSURED MEDICAL EXPENSES.

☐ PARENTING TIME ABATEMENT:
☐ PARENTING TIME ORDERED: (CHECK ONE): _____ % PARENTING TIME CREDIT AFTER ___ CONSECUTIVE OVERNIGHTS.
☐ REASONABLE ☐ SPECIFIC ☐ SUPERVISED ☐ RESERVED ☐ REFER TO FAMILY COUNSELING/OTHER

*THE SPOUSAL SUPPORT PAYER IS ☐ PLAINTIFF ☐ DEFENDANT ☐ NOT APPLICABLE.

☐ SPOUSAL SUPPORT: ☐ $ _____ PER WEEK, COMMENCEMENT DATE: _____
☐ PERMANENT ☐ END DATE _____ ☐ PAY DIRECT, NOT THROUGH FOC

☐ SPOUSAL SUPPORT ARREARAGE:
☐ PRESERVED ☐ CANCELED AS OF DATE: _____ ☐ SET AT $ _____ AS OF DATE:

☐ ORDER REFERS MATTERS TO DIVORCE INVESTIGATION/MODIFICATION FOR FURTHER INVESTIGATION.

I CERTIFY THAT THE ABOVE INFORMATION IS TRUE TO THE BEST OF MY KNOWLEDGE, INFORMATION AND BELIEF, AND IS IN FULL CONFORMITY WITH THE REQUIREMENTS SET FORTH BY STATUTE AND COURT RULE AND THE DECISION OF THE COURT. (NOTE: FOC WILL NOT READ THE ORDER WHEN ENTERING IT ON MiCSES.)

DATE: **2-15-99**

PLEASE PRINT:

SIGNATURE OF ATTORNEY *Dudley Lovelace*

ATTORNEY NAME
DUDLEY LOVELACE

BAR NO.

ADDRESS
900 S. MAPLE

CITY/STATE/ZIP
LAKE CITY, MI 48800

FD/FOC 4002 (11/06/02) ORDER DATA FORM-SUPPORT

773-0011
TELEPHONE NO.

PAGE 2 OF 2

DEMOGRAPHICS

STATE OF MICHIGAN
COUNTY OF WAYNE
THIRD JUDICIAL CIRCUIT
COURT
FAMILY DIVISION

ORDER DATA FORM-SUPPORT
Re: SUBMISSION FOR LOADING
ATTACHED SUPPORT ORDER INTO
MiCSES ON FOC COMPUTER SYSTEM

THE ORDER WAS ENTERED ON:
2-15-99
(DATE ON ORDER STAMPED BY JUDGE'S CLERK)

(PLACE LABEL HERE)

CASE #:
_____

JUDGE

*INDICATES REQUIRED INFORMATION
CHECK ONLY THE BOXES WHICH APPLY TO PROVISIONS IN THE SUBMITTED ORDER

* PLAINTIFF NAME:	* DEFENDANT NAME:
DARLENE A. LOVELACE	DUDLEY E. LOVELACE

* NAME(S) OF CHILDREN (OLDEST TO YOUNGEST)	* DATE(S) OF BIRTH	* SOCIAL SECURITY NUMBER(S)
DUANE W. LOVELACE	6-1-86	466-10-1001
DARRYL W. LOVELACE	7-1-87	469-00-4411

(ADD ADDITIONAL CHILDREN ON SEPARATE SHEET)

NON-CUSTODIAL PARENT (OR FATHER IF JOINT CUSTODY) ☐ PLAINTIFF ☒ DEFENDANT

* NAME: DUDLEY E. LOVELACE	* DATE OF BIRTH: 6-15-64	* SOC. SEC. NO. 379-10-5567	HOME TELEPHONE NO: 773-0011
* RESIDENTIAL ADDRESS: 900 S. MAPLE	* CITY, STATE, ZIP LAKE CITY, MI 48800	OTHER TELEPHONE NUMBERS: ☒ WORK ☐ MOBILE 773-3004	FIA/TANF NO.: NOW ACTIVE: ☐ YES ☐ NO
* EMPLOYER: WATERBED WORLD	* EMPLOYER ADDRESS: 1000 SERVICE RD. LAKE CITY, MI 48800	EMPLOYER TELEPHONE NO.: 773-3004	EMPLOYER FED I.D. NO.: 06-1192796

CUSTODIAL PERSON (OR MOTHER IF JOINT CUSTODY) ☒ PLAINTIFF ☐ DEFENDANT

* NAME: DARLENE A. LOVELACE	* DATE OF BIRTH: 5-1-65	* SOC. SEC. NO. 380-16-1010	HOME TELEPHONE NO: 772-0011
* RESIDENTIAL ADDRESS: 121 S. MAIN	* CITY, STATE, ZIP LAKE CITY, MI 48800	OTHER TELEPHONE NUMBERS: ☒ WORK ☐ MOBILE 772-0000	FIA/TANF NO.: NOW ACTIVE: ☐ YES ☐ NO
* EMPLOYER: 10,000 PANCAKES	* EMPLOYER ADDRESS: 111 M-78 LAKE CITY, MI 48800	EMPLOYER TELEPHONE NO.: 772-0000	EMPLOYER FED I.D. NO.: 04-1510060

I CERTIFY THAT THE ABOVE INFORMATION IS TRUE TO THE BEST OF MY KNOWLEDGE, INFORMATION AND BELIEF, AND IS IN FULL CONFORMITY WITH THE REQUIREMENTS SET FORTH BY STATUTE AND COURT RULE AND THE DECISION OF THE COURT. (NOTE: FOC WILL NOT READ THE ORDER WHEN ENTERING IT ON MiCSES.)

2-15-99
DATE:

Dudley Lovelace
SIGNATURE OF ATTORNEY

BAR NO.

PLEASE PRINT: DUDLEY LOVELACE
ATTORNEY NAME

FD/FOC 4002 (11/06/02) ORDER DATA FORM-SUPPORT

CHAPTER 6:
Alimony

Child support and alimony are two different kinds of support: Child support pays for the support of children; alimony is spouse-support. As a matter of fact, "spousal support" is the correct name for alimony in Michigan. State support laws use this name, as do the support forms in this book. However, most people still refer to spousal support as alimony, so this word will be used in the text of this book.

Originally, alimony was payable to wives or ex-wives only. In 1970, Michigan revised the support law and made alimony available to men and women alike. Even so, women are typically the alimony recipients and men the alimony payers.

As a form of support, alimony can be enforced after divorce much like child support. But while child support is always open to future modification, not every alimony order is modifiable. To know which is modifiable and which isn't, you must examine the alimony order in your divorce judgment and determine the type of alimony you have.

Types of Alimony

Alimony is a slippery word because Michigan divorce law, federal tax law and federal bankruptcy law all define the concept differently.

Michigan divorce law regards as alimony any divorce-related payments of money or other property from one (ex) spouse to the other for purposes of support. Alimony usually takes the form of cash payments paid periodically (weekly, monthly, etc.). There is another kind of so-called alimony, alimony-in-gross, which is often paid in several lump-sum payments.

Despite its name, alimony-in-gross is a division of a liquid asset: money. Thus, alimony-in-gross is really property division and not true alimony.

Federal law has its own rules for defining alimony. The federal tax law generally disregards what parties call their payments. Instead, it considers support payments as alimony if they:

- are paid in cash (including checks or money orders)
- made to a spouse or to someone on his/her behalf
- made in a divorce document (such as a divorce judgment)
- made when the spouses are living apart (subject to several exceptions, including payment of temporary alimony)
- end on the death of the recipient-spouse
- are not provided as child support
- are not designated as something other than alimony

These tax rules are important because payments qualifying as alimony get special tax treatment. The payments are deductible by the payer and counted as income for the recipient.

Federal bankruptcy law has yet another definition of alimony. According to bankruptcy law, support payments are alimony if they are: 1) intended by the parties as alimony 2) actually used for support 3) a reasonable amount of support. When payments are treated as alimony under bankruptcy law, they're protected from elimination or "discharge" during bankruptcy of the payer. If the payments don't qualify as alimony, the payer can sometimes discharge them in bankruptcy.

When someone claims alimony during a divorce or afterward, the court must consider the following factors in deciding whether alimony should be paid:

- length of the marriage
- ability of the parties to work
- source of and amount of property awarded to the parties
- age of the parties
- ability of the parties to pay alimony
- present situation of the parties
- needs of the parties
- health of the parties
- prior standard of living of the parties and whether either is responsible for the support of others
- past relations and conduct of the parties
- general principles of equity

The procedure for deciding alimony is flexible, so a court may apply these factors as it chooses. It can weigh the factors unequally, disregard ones that don't apply or add others that seem important through the catch-all "general principles of equity" factor.

After a court decides that alimony is due, it must then determine the amount. In Michigan, there are no uniform alimony guidelines as there are for child support. So most judges set alimony on a case-by-case basis using the following factors:

- length of the marriage
- contributions of the parties to the joint estate
- age and health of the parties
- parties' stations in life
- necessities of the parties
- earning ability of the parties

Several years ago, Washtenaw County rejected the case-by-case approach and adopted an alimony formula. It judges the strength of an alimony claim (length of the marriage, age, income and job skills are the most important factors), adjusts the claim for other factors and then provides for a mathematical computation of alimony. Recently, other counties have begun using Washtenaw's alimony formula or adaptations of it. This suggests a need for a uniform statewide alimony formula, which may be developed in the future.

For all the fuss over alimony, few divorce judgments actually order alimony. Historically, alimony was awarded only in a small fraction of divorces. This is also true today. What's more, modern alimony tends to be shorter-term, instead of the open-ended awards that once were common. Nowadays, alimony is likely to be for a limited time—maybe a year or two—to help the recipient get back on his/her feet after divorce. This kind of short-term alimony is sometimes referred to as rehabilitative or transitional alimony.

The means for ending short-term alimony are conditions attached to the alimony order in the judgment of divorce. These conditions are negotiable during the divorce. But most divorce judgments contain several of the following conditions:

Death. Alimony is almost always made to end when the recipient dies (as explained above, there are also sound tax reasons for imposing this condition). Alimony doesn't automatically end when the payer dies, and it can survive and become a debt of his/her estate. Nevertheless, judgments often terminate alimony when payers die.

Remarriage. Alimony often ends when the recipient remarries, but seldom ends if the payer remarries.

Cohabitation. To prevent recipients from choosing cohabitation over remarriage as a way to keep alimony, the alimony may end if the recipient cohabitates with a member of the opposite sex.

Date. Alimony may end on a specific date.

Modification. In Michigan, true alimony has customarily been open to future modification when there has been a change in the parties' circumstances. A modification could result in an increase, decrease or even termination of the alimony.

A few years ago, Michigan law was changed to allow nonmodifiable alimony. To get nonmodifiability, the parties must carefully negotiate and reach a settlement on the issue. The divorce judgment's alimony order must cite this agreement and say that the alimony is nonmodifiable.

Although few divorce judgments contain alimony, all must address the issue. Michigan court rules state that every divorce judgment must either grant, deny or reserve (leave open) alimony *for both spouses.* If a judgment neglects this rule, and says nothing about alimony for one or both spouses, alimony is automatically reserved for the party or parties omitted from the alimony provision of the judgment.

Payment of Alimony

Like child support, alimony is normally paid by immediate income withholding from the payer's source of income to a central collection and distribution agency in Lansing, the state disbursement unit (SDU). But it's possible to set up other payment methods and have alimony paid to the SDU without immediate income withholding or directly to the alimony recipient.

Interstate Enforcement and Modification

Interstate enforcement and modification of alimony are governed by the same laws that apply to child support, primarily the Uniform Interstate Family Support Act (UIFSA) and the Interstate Income Withholding Act (IIWA). See "Interstate Enforcement and Modification" on page 117 for an explanation of interstate support proceedings. Just substitute alimony for child support in that section to see how alimony is handled across state lines.

There is one major difference between the interstate treatment of child support and alimony: You cannot modify an alimony order outside of the state where it was issued. As a result, you must go back to the divorce-granting state for any modification of the order.

If your out-of-state alimony order is enforceable in Michigan, the UIFSA provides two enforcement options: 1) enforcement after registration of the out-of-state order in Michigan 2) rapid enforcement of the out-of-state order's income withholding order, if one was issued. "Interstate Enforcement and Modification" on page 117 explains these options in detail.

Before you choose, contact the friend of the court because it will often handle enforcement for you. But if the friend of the court declines to act, you have the right to seek enforcement under the UIFSA yourself.

Enforcement

Enforcing Payment of Alimony

Enforcement of alimony begins and often ends with the friend of the court. The friend of the court is responsible for enforcing all kinds of support orders, including alimony. Actual enforcement should begin when past-due alimony equals one month or more of payments.

Regrettably, some friends of the court pay more attention to enforcement of child support than alimony. Thus, you may have to prod the friend of the court for enforcement. If the friend of the court won't help at all, see "What If the Friend of the Court Won't Help Me?" on page 15 for advice about filing a grievance against the friend of the court.

Once enforcement begins, the friend of the court and other state agencies responsible for enforcement have several powerful enforcement remedies:

Immediate income withholding. An order requiring the alimony payer's source of income (usually an employer) to withhold money (such as wages or salary) owed to the payer, and to send it onto the SDU for payment to the alimony recipient. Since 1991, all alimony must be paid by immediate income withholding, unless the court permits another method of payment.

Contempt. The friend of the court may ask the court to hold the alimony payer in contempt of court for nonpayment of alimony. The payer can defend by citing various excuses (unemployment, illness, etc.) for nonpayment. If contempt is established, the payer can be incarcerated in a county jail (with or without work release) or a nonprison state correctional facility, ordered to participate in work activity or face loss of driver's, occupational or sporting/recreational licenses. Any penalties can continue until the alimony is paid.

Criminal nonsupport. In Michigan, failure to pay alimony in the amount due or on time is a felony. A federal law also makes it a crime for alimony payers owing large arrearages to: 1) avoid out-of-state alimony obligations 2) cross state lines or national boundaries with an intent to avoid alimony. These offenses are seldom prosecuted, but they're sometimes invoked if nonpayment of alimony is massive and wilful.

License suspension. License suspension (of a driver's, occupational or sporting/recreational license) is a penalty for contempt. But it's also a separate enforcement remedy when nonpayment of alimony exceeds two months.

Consumer reporting. The friend of the court can report nonpayment of alimony to consumer reporting agencies, such as credit agencies. The payer has various rights to prevent the reporting of false information which might unfairly damage his/her credit. Or the payer can avoid consumer reporting by paying the arrearage in full.

Tax refund interception. Using information from the SDU, the state Office of Child Support may seize an alimony payer's state and/or federal income tax refund. The payer must be notified of an impending interception and has the right to contest it.

Surcharge. When alimony is in arrears, a surcharge is tacked onto the debt at a floating interest rate tied to U.S. treasury notes. These surcharges are added automatically by the friend of the court every Jan. 1 and July 1.

In 2005, a new surcharge relief law goes into effect allowing: 1) waiver of current surcharges when the payer has paid at least 90% of recent support and any arrearage isn't growing 2) waiver of current and past surcharges (but no relief is allowed for surcharges accumulating before July 1, 2005) under an arrearage payment plan filed by the payer or friend of the court and approved by the court.

Fraudulent transfer. Like other debtors, alimony payers sometimes transfer property to others at less than fair value, to prevent seizure of the property. The state FIA can have this kind of transfer set aside under Michigan's fraudulent transfer law.

Liens and other security. Automatically, by law, a lien for unpaid alimony attaches to the payer's real and personal property. This lien can be foreclosed by having the property seized and sold to satisfy the support arrearage. In a common technique, liens are placed on checking or savings accounts at financial institutions (banks, savings and loans, credit unions, etc.) by a computer program matching delinquent payers to account-holders.

Courts can also require alimony payers to post cash bonds or other security to secure payment. These bonds are sometimes required when alimony is in arrears and the payer has suddenly received a large sum of money, such as an inheritance, legal settlement or lottery prize, from which the cash bond can be taken. A court can also appoint a receiver to take control of the payer's property and use the assets to pay off the alimony debt.

Debt collection. These days, unpaid alimony is just like any other debt and all the normal debt collection remedies available to creditors may be used to collect the alimony. For example, garnishment may be used against a delinquent payer's wages or bank account, or the payer's personal property may be executed against (seized) and sold.

More Information

About private collection of alimony, contact local debt collection firms listed under "Collection Agencies" in the yellow pages.

Or call a national company, with local collection lawyers, specializing in collection of support orders:

The Accounts Retrievable System
2050 Bellmore Ave.
Bellmore, NY 11710
(516) 783-6566

Most of the enforcement remedies are reserved for the friend of the court or other state enforcement agencies. But after nonpayment of alimony, you may seek enforcement by contempt or debt collection remedies.

Some of the enforcement remedies are complicated and you may have difficulty asking a court for a contempt of court, garnishment or execution without a lawyer. One solution is to turn the alimony debt over to a private debt collection agency. These firms typically charge contingency fees against the amount collected: Nothing if nothing is recovered, or 20-30% of any support collected. The contingency fees give collection agencies an incentive to pursue the alimony payer aggressively.

Modification

Alimony isn't always open to modification. Alimony is only modifiable if the alimony order is "live" (still in effect) or can be revived. In addition, the alimony must be the kind that is modifiable, since these days some types are nonmodifiable.

Effectiveness of Alimony Order

In most cases, divorce judgments "bar" or deny alimony for one or both parties. If the judgment denied alimony for you, you cannot ask for it later, unless you can show that the judgment is defective (see "When Is My Divorce Judgment Defective?" on page 13 for more about this exception).

If the divorce judgment contained an alimony order, the alimony may be modified as long as the order is in effect. But the order may have expired by its own terms or because of the occurrence of conditions.

As explained before, alimony is often subject to conditions that can terminate it. These conditions can be imposed by law (for example, in Michigan alimony automatically ends when the alimony recipient dies). Or conditions can be attached by the divorce judgment (death of the alimony recipient or payer and remarriage of the recipient are popular ones). When these conditions are triggered, alimony terminates and cannot be modified.

There's a third possibility: reservation of alimony, intentionally or by omission. If the divorce judgment reserved alimony for you, you can ask for it after divorce. Reservation can also happen by accident. The court rules say that divorce judgments must grant, deny or reserve alimony for both parties; failure to do any of these results in reservation for the omitted party or parties.

Either way, when alimony is reserved for you, you may ask for an original alimony order after divorce. This doesn't guarantee that you will get alimony. But the court will look at the issue anew, as it would have during the divorce. Without reservation of alimony, you would have to show a change of conditions or circumstances for such a post-judgment modification.

Modifiability of Alimony Order

Keep in mind that not every type of alimony is modifiable. As explained before, alimony-in-gross is really part of property division and is therefore nonmodifiable, except when the judgment of divorce is defective.

For years in Michigan, true alimony was always modifiable. This is no longer so. Since Michigan law was changed in 2000, divorce parties can negotiate and agree to make alimony nonmodifiable. Few older divorce judgments do this. Newer ones (after-2000) may, but the alimony order must clearly say that the alimony is nonmodifiable. See "Types of Alimony" on page 141 for more about the different kinds of modifiable and nonmodifiable alimony.

Modifying Alimony

In a modification motion, you can ask the court to change the amount of the alimony. This could raise, lower or even terminate the alimony.

One thing you can't normally do is modify past alimony. Michigan law generally bans so-called retroactive modification of support, preventing an alimony recipient from asking for more past alimony or a payer's seeking reduction or cancellation of past-due amounts. All the law allows is modification of future alimony, effective the date the modification motion is served.

There are a few exceptions to the full-payment rule. Past-due alimony can be modified or even canceled when: 1) there is a court-approved retroactive modification agreement between the parties 2) one party has hidden income, then the debt can be modified to compensate for the fraud.

And just recently, a support debt relief law went into effect allowing a payer to seek court approval for a debt payment plan which can modify or cancel alimony arrearages. The provisions of this law are complicated with all sorts of restrictions and consents (from the alimony recipient and/or state) necessary before a plan may be approved. Contact the friend of the court for more information.

These days, most alimony is paid by immediate income withholding. According to this method, the alimony is deducted from the payer's source of income (usually an employer) and sent to the SDU, which forwards it to the alimony recipient.

Income withholding is popular with alimony recipients and courts because it's reliable. But some alimony payers may dislike this payment method since it means more paperwork for their employers. They may want to avoid immediate income withholding and set up a different method of payment.

Stipulated Modification

You and your ex can agree, or stipulate, to modification of the amount of alimony or the method for paying it.

You don't need to file a motion or have a court hearing to modify alimony by stipulation. All you have to do is prepare the correct modification order (explained below) and have it approved by the court. See "Stipulated Orders" on page 30 for complete instructions about preparing a stipulated order, getting court approval of the order, filing it with the clerk and serving it on your ex.

Amount of Alimony

You and your ex may stipulate to an increase, decrease or termination of the alimony. The court must review and approve the proposed modification.

But the court will likely approve your agreement because you have more control over alimony, since children's welfare isn't directly at stake.

Use the Order Regarding Spousal Support (GRP 23) for your alimony stipulation. For modification of an existing alimony order, check the "modified" box in paragraph #7 of the GRP 23 and describe the modification in the space below, as in the sample order at the end of this chapter. Use paragraph #7 also for entry of an original alimony order (check the box indicating that the order is "original"), after reservation of alimony in the divorce judgment. See "Alimony Provisions for the Court Order" on page 152 for sample short- and long-term alimony orders which you can adapt as your original alimony order.

If overdue support has accumulated into an arrearage, specify how this must be paid off in paragraph #9b of the Order Regarding Spousal Support (GRP 23). For example, the alimony payer could agree to pay a certain amount per week or month in addition to the base alimony. Keep in mind that normally you cannot reduce or cancel the arrearage, thanks to the ban on retroactive modification of support described earlier.

Method of Payment

If you don't have immediate income withholding and you and your ex want it, contact the friend of the court. The friend of the court, which has exclusive authority to start immediate income withholding, will be happy to set up this method of payment for you.

More is necessary when you want to avoid immediate income withholding now in effect and adopt another payment method. Other payment options include payment directly to the SDU or alimony recipient. You could also change the payment intervals (semi-monthly instead of monthly, etc.).

The best way to avoid immediate income withholding is by stipulating to an opt-out from the friend of the court system, either totally, partially or in a limited way (for alimony payment only). Appendix D on page 215 explains how to do this and which forms to use.

Contested Modification

When your ex won't stipulate to modification of alimony, you must file a motion asking for the change. Modification isn't guaranteed; the court will consider your motion during a hearing and either grant or deny it.

Motion

Amount of Alimony

You can ask for alimony modification in the Motion Regarding Support (FOC 50). There is a sample FOC 50 at the end of this chapter, showing you how to complete the various parts of the motion. The core of the motion is paragraph #5, which explains the grounds for modification, and paragraph #7 describing your proposed modification.

The customary grounds for modifying the amount of alimony are change of conditions or circumstances in the lives of you and your ex. For modification of an existing alimony order, the changed conditions or circumstances must concern the short-list of amount-of-alimony factors described on page 143. For example, an alimony recipient may ask for more alimony because her financial needs have increased or her earning ability has been diminished. An alimony payer could plead loss of income or financial hardship in seeking a decrease in alimony.

When the motion concerns an original alimony order, after reservation of the issue in the divorce judgment, both sets of alimony factors must be used (some of these factors overlap). The long-list of alimony factors cited on page 142 must be invoked to convince the court that alimony should be ordered. Then, the short-list of factors on page 143 is used to determine the amount of alimony. As a result, the grounds for entry of an original alimony order in paragraph #5 of the Motion Regarding Support (FOC 50) should refer to both sets of factors, citing the relevant factors.

Whichever kind of alimony order you want—modified or original—describe the new amount of alimony you are seeking in paragraph #7 of the Motion Regarding Support (FOC 50).

For complete information and instructions about preparing, filing and serving a motion like this, see "Papers" on page 23 and "Motions" on page 32.

Method of Payment

If you want to ask for another method of paying alimony, it's best to do this through a limited opt-out from the friend of the court system. See Appendix D on page 215 for instructions and forms.

Responding to a Motion

If you receive a motion for modification of alimony from your ex, you can respond orally or in writing, in several ways.

If you agree with the motion completely, contact your ex immediately and arrange to stipulate to a modification order. In paragraphs #5, #6 and #7 of the Response to Motion Regarding Support (FOC 51), you can also indicate your agreement with the motion. But why do extra paperwork when it's easier to stipulate to a modification order? You could also appear at the hearing and agree to the motion, but this too wastes time when stipulation is available. See "Stipulated Modification" on page 148 for more about stipulations.

Sometimes, you may agree with part of the motion and disagree with the rest. It's important to signal your partial agreement as soon as possible because this narrows the issues in the case. If you file a Response to Motion Regarding Support (FOC 51), check box #6b and describe the extent of your agreement with the motion in the space below. If you choose to respond orally, mention your partial agreement to the mediator, referee or judge, so the agreed-upon issues can be eliminated from the hearing.

When you oppose the motion, you can voice your disagreement in two ways. You can file a written response to the motion, or wait until the motion hearing and respond orally. A written response is usually better, because it gets your views across more effectively.

Use the Response to Motion Regarding Support (FOC 51) for a written response. In paragraph #5, say why you oppose the motion. You must challenge whichever alimony factors were cited in the motion as grounds for a modified or original alimony order. You could also dispute whether the proposed amount of alimony is reasonable, again with reference to the amount-of-alimony factors.

Is your ex seeking a change in the method of paying alimony? If your ex is asking for this in a support modification motion, you can cite reasons (history of late payments, etc.) against this in paragraph #5 of the FOC 51. If the request is for a limited opt-out, see "Responding to a Motion" on page 220 in Appendix D about how to respond.

For general information and instructions about preparing, filing and serving a response, see "Responding to a Motion" on page 35.

You can also respond to a motion by making a counter-motion. Normally, if you oppose the motion with the Response to Motion Regarding Support (FOC 51), you disagree with the grounds for the motion in paragraph #5. Then, in paragraph #7 you oppose the proposed modification, as in the sample response at the end of this chapter.

But if you want a different kind of change of alimony, check box #7b and explain in the space below what you want. For example, it's not uncommon for an alimony recipient to move for an increase of alimony and for the alimony payer to respond by asking for a decrease. The payer's request for a decrease is, in essence, a counter-motion.

In some cases, it's even possible to ask for completely new relief in a counter-motion. Add new issues carefully, because these can easily sidetrack the case. Nevertheless, it may make sense to seek new relief in a counter-motion when the new issues are compatible with the main motion.

For more about counter-motion tactics and how to counter-move for new relief, see "Making a Counter-Motion" on page 37.

Friend of the Court

Before a post-judgment motion is heard by the judge, the friend of the court may intervene to mediate, investigate or referee, in an attempt to settle the dispute.

Previously, alimony disputes weren't eligible for informal mediation or settlement. But after June 30, 2005, these disputes may be submitted to informal settlement by the friend of the court. Referral of the dispute to formal mediation is also possible. Private mediation or arbitration, which is expensive, is unlikely.

During a dispute over the amount of alimony, the friend of the court is often required to investigate the issue, and make a report and recommendation about the issue. Friend of the court referees aren't supposed to hear motions for modification of the amount of alimony. But as with informal mediation, courts often bend the rules a little and send alimony motions for refereeing anyway.

See "Friend of the Court" on page 38 for more about the friend of the court's roles in post-judgment cases, and how to deal with mediation, investigation or refereeing by the friend of the court. This section also has information about formal mediation, private mediation and arbitration, which all take place outside the friend of the court system.

Motion Hearing

As explained in "Motion Hearings" on page 41, there are two kinds of motion hearings: 1) nonevidentiary hearing where facts aren't in dispute, evidence is seldom introduced and the parties merely make legal arguments to the judge 2) evidentiary hearing where facts are disputed and evidence, such as testimony from witnesses, must be introduced to establish the true facts.

Most alimony modifications will require nonevidentiary hearings or, at most, limited evidentiary hearings. Many times, the parties agree on their incomes, so evidence about earnings isn't necessary. If there's disagreement, some evidence, such as paycheck stubs, W-2 forms or income tax returns, may be required to establish income. Witness testimony is seldom necessary. See "Motion Hearings" on page 41 for information about preparing for and appearing at a nonevidentiary hearing.

Court Order

After the motion hearing, the judge will decide the motion. The judge will either decide immediately and give an oral decision "from the bench," or take the case "under submission" and rule later by issuing a written decision. Either way, the moving party must prepare the order granting or denying the motion using the Order Regarding Spousal Support (GRP 23). See "Court Orders" on page 44 for complete information about preparing, filing and serving an order like this.

In Wayne County only, you must also prepare an Order Data Form-Support (FD/FOC 4002). The data form asks for basic information about the parties and the alimony. This data is entered by the Wayne County Friend of the Court into its computer system for enforcement of alimony later. You must give the FD/FOC 4002 to the clerk when you file the alimony order and it will forward the form to the Wayne County Friend of the Court. There is a sample FD/FOC 4002 at the end of Chapter 5 on page 138.

Alimony Provisions for the Court Order

For modification of the amount of alimony, use the Order Regarding Spousal Support (GRP 23). Check the first box in paragraph #2 to modify an existing alimony order; check the second box in that paragraph for entry of an original alimony order after reservation of alimony in the divorce judgment.

In paragraph #7, check the correct box to indicate whether the order is for modification or an original alimony order. Describe a modification in the blank space below paragraph #7, as in the sample order at the end of this chapter. An original alimony order goes in the same paragraph (or in an attachment to the GRP 23, if the order won't fit in the space). You can adapt one of the following provisions as your original alimony order.

Short-Term Alimony

7a. <u>Spousal Support</u>.   Defendant shall pay to plaintiff $200 monthly in advance on the first day of the month. This spousal support shall be modifiable. Payment of this support shall begin on Feb. 15, 1999 and end immediately on the happening of any of the following events:

(a) [July 1, 2001]

(b) death of plaintiff

(c) death of defendant

(d) remarriage of plaintiff

(e) cohabitation by plaintiff with a member of the opposite sex

After plaintiff's spousal support ends, it shall be forever barred to her.

Long-Term Alimony

7a. <u>Spousal Support</u>.   Defendant shall pay to plaintiff $200 monthly in advance on the first day of the month. This spousal support shall be modifiable. Payment of this support shall begin on Feb. 15, 1999 and end immediately on the happening of any of the following events:

(a) death of plaintiff

(b) death of defendant

(c) remarriage of plaintiff

(d) cohabitation by plaintiff with a member of the opposite sex

After plaintiff's spousal support ends, it shall be forever barred to her.

If overdue support has accumulated into an arrearage, specify how this must be paid off in paragraph #9b of the Order Regarding Spousal Support (GRP 23). For example, the alimony payer might be ordered to pay a certain amount per week or month in addition to the base alimony. Keep in mind that normally you cannot reduce or cancel the arrearage, thanks to the ban on retroactive modification of support described earlier.

Method of Payment

Normally, you can ask for another method of payment as part of an opt-out from the friend of the court system. And if you are allowed to opt out, you use an opt-out order to set up the new method of payment. See Appendix D on page 215 about opt-outs.

THIS PARAGRAPH SEES WHETHER PARTIES AGREE ON THE MODIFICATION. IF YOU BOTH AGREE, SKIP FILING A MOTION AND JUST STIPULATE TO A MODIFICATION ORDER, AS EXPLAINED IN "STIPULATED ORDERS" IN CHAPTER 1C.

DESCRIBE GROUNDS FOR MODIFICATION.

3rd copy - Friend of the Court
4th copy - Proof of Service
5th copy - Proof of Service

Original - Court
1st copy - Other Party
2nd copy - Moving Party

CASE NO.

Approved, SCAO

STATE OF MICHIGAN
JUDICIAL CIRCUIT
COUNTY

MOTION REGARDING SUPPORT

Court telephone no.

Court address

Plaintiff's name, address, and telephone no.   ☐ moving party

v

Defendant's name, address, and telephone no.   ☐ moving party

Third party name, address, and telephone no.   ☐ moving party

1. ☒ a. On ___7-1-90___ a judgment
Date
or order was entered regarding support.
☐ b. There is currently no order regarding support.

SPOUSAL   MONTH
is ordered to pay support of $ ___200___ each ___week, month, etc.___

☒ 2. The ☐ plaintiff ☒ defendant

☐ 3. The ☐ plaintiff ☐ defendant   is ordered to pay child care of $ _____ each ___week, month, etc.___

☐ 4. The ☐ plaintiff ☐ defendant   is ordered to pay health care of $ _____ each ___week, month, etc.___

☒ 5. Conditions regarding support have changed as follows: I WAS LAYED OFF RECENTLY
Use a separate sheet to explain in detail what has happened and attach. Include all necessary facts. FOR ONE YEAR TO OBTAIN/
AND NOW NEED TO RETURN TO COMMUNITY COLLEGE FOR ONE YEAR TO OBTAIN/
MY ASSOCIATES DEGREE, SO I CAN GET A NEW AND BETTER JOB. I NEED
_____ and I have agreed to support as follows: MORE
SPOUSAL SUPPORT
☐ 6. _____
Name   TO PAY MY LIVING
Use a separate sheet to explain in detail what you have agreed on and attach. Include all necessary facts. EXPENSES WHILE
I ATTEND COLLEGE
AND WORK PART-TIME.

7. **I ask the court to order that support** be paid as follows: ☐ See 6. above for details.
Use a separate sheet to explain in detail what you want the court to order and attach.
INCREASE SPOUSAL SUPPORT FROM $200 TO $300 PER MONTH
UNTIL SPOUSAL SUPPORT EXPIRES ON JULY 1, 2000.

I declare that the above statements are true to the best of my information, knowledge, and belief.

___1-1-99___   _Darlene Lovelace_
Date   Moving party's signature

NOTICE OF HEARING

LESTER TUBBS
A hearing will be held on this motion before ___Name of judge or referee___

on ___2-15-99___   at ___9:00 AM___ at ___OJIBWAY COUNTY COURTHOUSE___
Date   Time   Place

NOTE: If you are the person receiving this motion, you may file a response. Contact the friend of the court office and request form FOC 51.

CERTIFICATE OF MAILING

I certify that on this date I mailed a copy of this motion and notice of hearing on the other party(ies) by ordinary mail at the
above address(es).

___1-2-99___   _Darlene Lovelace_
Date   Moving party's signature

MCL 552.14; MSA 25.94, MCR 2.119, MCR 3.213

FOC 50 (12/96) **MOTION REGARDING SUPPORT**

Approved, SCAO

STATE OF MICHIGAN
JUDICIAL CIRCUIT
COUNTY

Original - Court
1st copy - Moving Party
2nd copy - Responding Party

3rd copy - Friend of the Court
4th copy - Proof of Service
5th copy - Proof of Service

RESPONSE TO MOTION REGARDING SUPPORT

CASE NO.

Court address

Plaintiff's name, address, and telephone no. ☐moving party

v

Defendant's name, address, and telephone no. ☐moving party

Court telephone no.

Third party name, address, and telephone no. ☐moving party

1.☒ a. On __7-1-90__ a judgment or order was entered regarding support.
☐ b. There is currently no order regarding support.

☒2. The ☐plaintiff ☒defendant is ordered to pay support of $ __200__ SPOUSAL each __MONTH__ week, month, etc.

☐3. The ☐plaintiff ☐defendant is ordered to pay child care of $ _____ each _____ week, month, etc.

☐4. The ☐plaintiff ☐defendant is ordered to pay health care of $ _____ each _____ week, month, etc.

☒5. I ☐agree ☒do not agree that conditions regarding support have changed as stated in the motion.
Explain in detail what you do not agree with and why. Include all necessary facts. Use a separate sheet of paper if needed.

IN HER PREVIOUS JOB, PLAINTIFF HAD A TUITION BENEFIT PROGRAM AVAILABLE TO HER BUT NEVER USED IT. DEFENDANT BELIEVES PLAINTIFF MAY BE ELIGIBLE FOR GRANTS AND LOANS TO PAY FOR HER EDUCATION. IN ADDITION, I DON'T HAVE FINANCIAL ABILITY TO PAY MORE SPOUSAL SUPPORT.

☐6. I agreed with the other party to start/change support:
☐ a. exactly as stated in the motion.
☐ b. but not as stated in the motion.
If b. is checked, explain in detail what you did agree on. Include all necessary facts. Use a separate sheet of paper if needed.

7. ☐ a. I agree with what is being asked for in the motion.
☒ b. I do not agree with what is being asked for in the motion and ask the court to order that support be paid
If you do not agree with the request in the motion, explain in detail why and what you want the court to order. Use a separate sheet of paper

DENY PLAINTIFF'S MOTION FOR MORE SPOUSAL SUPPORT, LEAVING SUPPORT AT CURRENT LEVEL UNTIL IT EXPIRES ON JULY 1, 2000.

I declare that the above statements are true to the best of my information, knowledge, and belief.
__2-1-99__ Date

Dudley Lovelace
Responding party's signature

CERTIFICATE OF MAILING

I certify that on this date I mailed a copy of this response on the other party(ies) by ordinary mail at the above address(es).
__2-1-99__ Date

Dudley Lovelace
Responding party's signature

FOC 51 (12/96) **RESPONSE TO MOTION REGARDING SUPPORT**

MCL 552.14; MSA 25.94; MCR 2.119

(Callout) SEVERAL PARAGRAPHS TEST WHETHER YOU AGREE WITH MODIFICATION. IF YOU AGREE, COMPLETELY OR IN PART, SEE "RESPONDING TO A MOTION" IN THIS CHAPTER ABOUT YOUR RESPONSE OPTIONS.

(Callout) YOU CAN MAKE A COUNTER-MOTION IN THIS PARAGRAPH. SEE "RESPONDING TO A MOTION" IN THIS CHAPTER FOR MORE ABOUT COUNTER-MOTIONS.

CHECK:
- 1ST BOX IF ORDER WAS CONTESTED AND GOTTEN AFTER COURT HEARING ON THE ORDER
- 2ND BOX IF NONMOVING PARTY CONSENTED TO ORDER
- 3RD BOX FOR STIPULATED ORDERS
- NO BOXES FOR APPROVAL OF THE ORDER BY SILENCE

MICHIGAN Family Division COUNTY	ORDER REGARDING SPOUSAL SUPPORT	CASE NO.

Defendant:

v

Judge LESTER TUBBS

Date of hearing __2-15-99__

1. This order is entered ☐ after hearing. ☒ on consent. ☐ on stipulation.

THE COURT FINDS:

☒ 2. A motion requesting ☒ change of spousal support ☐ entry of an original spousal support order was filed.

☒ 3. A response to the motion was filed.

☒ 4. A change of circumstances ☒ does ☐ does not exist which warrants a change in the spousal support order.

☐ 5. Spousal support, previously reserved, is now granted for ☐ plaintiff ☐ defendant below.

IT IS ORDERED:

☐ 6. The motion regarding spousal support is dismissed.

☒ 7. On __1-2-99__, this ☒ modified ☐ original spousal support order shall take effect: MONTHLY SPOUSAL SUPPORT SHALL INCREASE FROM $200 TO $300, STAYING AT THAT LEVEL UNTIL SPOUSAL SUPPORT EXPIRES ON JULY 1, 2000.

8. Income withholding shall continue or be implemented immediately upon entry of this order.

9. a. Spousal support is an order the date it is due and shall not be modified retroactively except as allowed by MCL 552.603 and 552.603b.

b. Unpaid spousal support is a lien on the payer's property by operation of law and the payer's property can be encumbered or seized if past-due support exceeds two times the monthly of periodic support payments. In a friend of the court case, a surcharge will be added to support as provided by MCL 552.603a. Currently past-due spousal support is preserve be paid as follows _____

10. While this case is a friend of the court case, the support payer shall pay friend of the c fees and other statutory fees.

11. The parties have previously provided information about their addresses, telephone and security nos., driver's and occupational licenses, sources of income and health care cov a friend of the court case, the parties must inform the friend of the court of any change formation, reporting changes in their residence information in writing within 21 days of a change.

Date/plaintiff 2-15-99 Darlene Loveface   Date/defendant 2-15-99 Dudley Loveface

Date __2-15-99__   Judge Lester Tubbs

PROOF OF SERVICE

I certify that on this date I mailed a copy of this order to the other party by ordinary mail at his/her address above.

Date __2-15-99__   Signature Darlene Loveface

GRP 23 (9/04)   ORDER REGARDING SPOUSAL SUPPORT

SUPPORT MODIFICATION CAN DATE BACK TO WHEN MODIFICATION MOTION WAS SERVED

THE PARTIES MUST SIGN A STIPULATED ORDER OR ONE OBTAINED BY CONSENT. PARTIES DON'T SIGN AN ORDER OBTAINED THROUGH "APPROVAL-BY-SILENCE" OR AFTER A COURT HEARING ON THE ORDER.

CHAPTER 7:
Name Change

When a family breaks up during divorce, spouses may want to change their names. Women do this most often, dropping their married names and resuming maiden or former married names. It's easy for a woman to get a name change during divorce. They can ask for a change of name (of surname or last name only) in the divorce papers, and the judgment of divorce can order the change at the end of the divorce.

But not all woman who ultimately want name changes gets these during divorce. Some simply neglect to do it during the divorce; later, it's too late. Women often want to keep their married names for a while so they match the names of their children. Then when the children are older, these women may be ready to change their names.

Name Change for Women

Women have several post-divorce name change options. These choices include informal out-of-court name change and two court procedures for changing names.

Common Law Name Change

You can change your name by simply adopting a new name and using it regularly; no court order is necessary for the change. This kind of common law name change by usage is legal as long as you're not adopting a new name for a fraudulent or improper purpose.

Few people know about the usage method of name change. But in fact, it happens every day. When women marry, they often assume their husbands' surnames, without a court order. This is an example of common law name change by usage, which everyone recognizes as legal.

For some reason, society is less willing to accept common law name change after divorce, so not everyone recognizes this kind of name change. This is especially true today with general anxiety about security and special concern about identity theft. Authorities want official proof of name changes and informal common law name changes aren't acceptable any more. As a result, most women choose formal court-ordered name changes.

Court-Ordered Name Change

There are two kinds of post-divorce name changes available from courts. In contrast to a common law name change, court-ordered name changes are recognized by everyone.

Name Change "Nunc Pro Tunc"

If a court believes that one of its judgments contains an error, the court can issue an order correcting the error. Typically, the corrective order is issued *nunc pro tunc* (a Latin phrase meaning "now for then"), so the correction is retroactive to the time the judgment was entered.

Some divorce courts have been willing to issue *nunc pro tunc* orders changing women's names post-divorce. These courts reason that omission of the name change from the divorce was an error, and that the *nunc pro tunc* order corrects the error. This is really a legal fiction and abuse of the power of courts to correct their judgments. Thus, courts have been discouraged from issuing name changes this way.

Name Change Case

A person can change his/her name by filing and completing a name change case in family court. This is the surest and best name change method, avoiding the lack of recognition given common law name change and the legal uncertainty of a *nunc pro tunc* name change.

To file a name change case, you must have lived in the county where you file for at least one year immediately before filing. You must also have a "sufficient reason" for the name change. For divorced filers, the wish to resume a maiden or former married name should satisfy this requirement.

You mustn't seek a name change with a "fraudulent intent." For example, you can't get a name change to avoid past debts or hide from law enforcement officials. Filers with criminal records are presumed to have fraudulent intentions, but this can be rebutted with evidence of good intentions.

Use the Petition to Change Name (PC 51), which comes with a helpful instruction sheet, to change your name. For an adult's name change, complete paragraphs #1-6 and #8, skipping paragraph #7 which applies to minors. Make three copies of the petition.

File the Petition to Change Name (PC 51) in the family court of your county. For reasons explained below, bring a self-addressed stamped envelope (SASE) when you file. There is a $10 filing fee. Poor people can get an exemption from payment of the filing fee and cost of publishing the notice of hearing (publication is also described below). See Appendix A on page 195 for more about fee exemptions.

Needless to say, criminals could seek name changes to avoid detection and prosecution. To make sure this doesn't happen, you must submit to a criminal background check when you file for a name change.

The instruction sheet for the Petition to Change Name (PC 51) explains the investigation procedure. You must go to your local police department with a copy of the PC 51. The police will take your fingerprints and charge you a small fee (around $5-10) for this service.

After fingerprinting, send a copy of your Petition to Change Name (PC 51), the fingerprint card and a fee cited by the police department (usually around $50-70) to the Michigan State Police in Lansing (the mailing address appears in the instruction sheet for the PC 51).

The state police will do a criminal background check and then electronically transmit your fingerprint card to the FBI. After the FBI check, the state police will mail a report about the investigation to the clerk of your family court.

All this can take several weeks, so don't expect to have the court hearing on your name change petition right away. Typically, the clerk will schedule the hearing when it receives the state police report. The clerk will send you a notice in the SASE you provided at filing, indicating that the report has been received and that a hearing time and date have been selected. Afterward, you can give the notice of the court hearing as described below.

In a name change of an adult, there isn't anyone with a direct interest in the name change who must be personally notified of the court hearing on your name change petition. As a result, you don't have to send a personal notice of the hearing to anyone and prove service of the notice, as you do when changing children's names.

In most cases, there must be a public notice of the court hearing on a proposed name change. The notice allows indirectly interested parties, such as other people with similar names or creditors of the petitioner, to oppose the name change or at least know about it.

Use the Publication of Notice of Hearing (PC 563) for the public notice. The PC 563 must be published once at least 14 days before the court hearing on the name change. The notice must appear in a newspaper qualified to publish legal advertisements in the county where you live. The clerk can tell you which newspapers are qualified in your area.

Take the Publication of Notice of Hearing (PC 563) to the newspaper. The newspaper will create a legal advertisement using the PC 563 and publish the ad once. After publication, the newspaper will bill you for the cost of publication, which will be a minimum of around $40 and possibly more. When you pay the bill, the newspaper will prepare an affidavit of publication and send it to the family court, as proof of publication.

Excusing Public Notice

There is a special rule excusing public notice for "good cause." Good cause includes evidence that public notice would put you or someone else (such as your children) in physical danger, based on victimization in the past. If you have a reasonable fear of such danger, or similar risks, ask the clerk for an affidavit to file with your PC 51 to excuse public notice. It's also possible to have the name change case file remain confidential.

Court Hearing

The court hearing will probably take place with just court personnel and you, because adult name changes are seldom contested. But it's possible that somebody, such as a creditor or a person whose name is similar to your proposed new name, could appear to contest your petition.

During the hearing, you must give the court a "sufficient reason" for your proposed name change. For a divorcee, the wish to shed her married name and adopt another name should provide the sufficient reason.

As for the new name, the petitioner can resume her maiden name, a former married name or even a completely new name. Typically, petitioners change their surnames only. But you could also change your first or middle names or any combination of names.

There are few restrictions on naming in the United States. Other countries control naming tightly and reject names that are exotic or strange. For example, in Germany names must be Germanic in origin and spelling, or the local registry won't register the name. In America you can adopt any name, no matter how unusual, unless the name is obscene or scandalous.

The court will reject your name change petition if it's sought with "fraudulent intent." If the police report reveals a criminal record, the court presumes the name change is fraudulent. You must rebut this presumption. For example, you could show that you want to resume a former name after divorce, and that the name change is not linked to your past criminal activity.

Win or lose, you must submit the Order Following Hearing on Petition to Change Name (PC 52) to the judge at the end of the hearing. After signing by the judge, file the order with the clerk. While you're at the clerk's office, it's convenient to get several post-name change documents as explained in "After a Name Change" on page 164.

Name Change for Children

Like adults, minor children have several name change options: 1) common law name change by usage 2) name change case 3) correction of birth certificate at the Michigan Department of Community Health.

The common law method has the same flaw as an adult name change by this method: lack of legal recognition. Birth certificate correction is normally used for adding omitted information (such as missing names) or correcting erroneous information (such as misspelled names) rather than changing complete or correct names of children. This leaves a name change case as the best way for changing children's names.

Name Change Case

A parent can seek a minor child's name change when she petitions for her own name change. Or a parent may ask for a minor child's name change separately, in a name change case for the children alone.

Ordinarily, both parents* must consent to their minor child's name change by co-signing the Petition to Change Name (PC 51). However, there are several exceptional situations when joint parental consent isn't necessary:

- if one parent is dead, the surviving parent alone may consent
- if both parents are dead, the guardian of the child may consent
- if one parent is unavailable, the available parent alone may consent
- a custodial parent alone may consent if:
  1) the noncustodial parent has a record of nonsupport and nonvisitation during the previous two years, or
  2) the noncustodial parent has been convicted of child abuse against any children in the family

Sometimes, the child must consent to or have a say in the name change proposed for him/her. According to Michigan law, a child over 14 has a veto against a name change his/her parents may seek. The child exercises this

---

* If a parent has been declared mentally incompetent, the parent's guardian may give consent.

veto by refusing to sign paragraph #11 of the Petition to Change Name (PC 51), which effectively blocks the name change.

Mature under-14 children (a child 7 or younger is presumed to be immature, but this presumption can be rebutted) may approve or disapprove the name change. After establishing the child's maturity, the judge must consider the child's wishes, but isn't bound by them.

Filing a Name Change Case

Use the Petition to Change Name (PC 51) for minor children's name changes. You may use the same form for changing the names of you and your minor children together, or for changing the names of the children only. The PC 51 comes with a helpful instruction sheet.

Complete those paragraphs #1-12 of the Petition to Change Name (PC 51) which apply to your case. If your ex consents to the name change for the children, s/he should co-sign the petition in paragraph #10.

Normally, both parents must consent to their children's name change. But see above for several exceptional situations (death of other parent, unavailability of other parent, etc.) in which one parent alone may petition for a name change. After divorce, the custodial parent may also seek a name change alone when there has been habitual nonsupport and nonvisitation or child abuse by the noncustodial parent against children in the family. You describe these exceptional situations in paragraph #7 of the PC 51.

An over-14 child must sign the petition, giving consent to the name change, in paragraph #11. The signature must take place in court, before court personnel. A mature under-14 child can sign the petition in paragraph #12 (the signature can be in or out of court), signaling the child's preference for (approval of) the proposed name change. If an under-14 child disapproves of the name change, s/he shouldn't sign the PC 51 and should let the judge know about this disapproval at the hearing.

You file the Petition to Change Name (PC 51) in the family court in the county where the children live. There is a $10 filing fee. Poor people can get an exemption from payment of the filing fee and cost of publishing the notice of hearing (described below). See Appendix A on page 195 for more about fee exemptions.

When you file, you may or may not schedule a hearing for the petition. Parents 22 years of age or older who are seeking a name change jointly with their children must also submit to a background investigation (see "Criminal Background Check" on page 159 for more about this investigation and how to request it). If a criminal background check is necessary, the case can't go forward until the clerk receives the results of the check in a state police report. At that time, the clerk will schedule the hearing and send you a notice.

Parent-petitioners under 22 and the minor children themselves don't face background investigations. In that case, you should be able to schedule the hearing when you file the petition. Make sure it's several weeks in the future, because you must give some notices and maybe serve some papers in the meantime.

Unlike an adult's name change, there's always someone with a direct interest in a name change for children: the other parent. In some cases, you must give the other parent a personal notice of the name change petition and the hearing for it. Whether or not a personal notice is necessary, you must always provide a public notice of the case.

Personal Notice

Naturally, no personal notice is necessary when the other parent is dead or unavailable. If the other parent is mentally incompetent, the notice must be given to this parent's guardian.

If your ex has consented to the children's name change by co-signing the Petition to Change Name (PC 51), s/he knows about the case. But s/he may not know about the court hearing on the petition. As a result, you should send, by ordinary first-class mail, both the PC 51 and Notice of Hearing (PC 562) to your ex. Prove this service by filling out and filing with the clerk a Proof of Service (PC 564).

If possible, personal notice must be given to unconsenting noncustodial parents in the exceptional cases (habitual nonsupport and nonvisitation or family child abuse) when consent isn't necessary. The notice informs the noncustodial parent of the proposed name change, allowing him/her to contest it.

If you know your ex's address or whereabouts, you must send the Petition to Change Name (PC 51) and Notice of Hearing (PC 562) to your noncustodial ex. This personal notice and proof of it are described above. But when you don't know your ex's current address or whereabouts, you can skip personal notice and give notice by publication, as described below.

Public Notice

Whether you give personal notice or not, you must usually publish a public notice about the name change you are seeking for your children (but see "Excusing Public Notice" on page 160 about excusing public notice when there is a danger of physical violence against you or others). This notice gives interested parties, such as a disappeared ex-spouse, other people with similar names or creditors, the opportunity to appear at the name change hearing and oppose your petition.

Use the Publication of Notice of Hearing (PC 563) for the public notice. If your ex has disappeared, make sure you insert his/her full name in the blank space at the top of the form, as shown in the sample PC 563.

The Publication of Notice of Hearing (PC 563) must be published once at least 14 days before the court hearing on the name change(s). The notice must appear in a newspaper qualified to publish legal advertisements in the county where you filed the petition. The clerk can tell you which newspapers are qualified in your area.

Take the Publication of Notice of Hearing (PC 563) to the newspaper. The newspaper will create a legal advertisement using the PC 563 and publish the ad once. After publication, the newspaper will bill you for the cost of publication, which will be a minimum of around $40 and possibly more. When you pay the bill, the newspaper will prepare an affidavit of publication and send it to the family court, as proof of publication.

Court Hearing

As the petitioner, you must attend the court hearing; your ex can choose whether to attend. You should bring the children whose names are to be changed. The children can sign the Petition to Change Name (PC 51), giving their consent to (for over-14 children) or stating their preference for (for mature under-14 children) the name change before court personnel, if they haven't already done this. Otherwise, the judge may question the children briefly about the name change at the hearing.

During the hearing, you must give a "sufficient reason" for changing your children's names. As an example, you may have resumed your maiden or former married name during or after a divorce, and now want your children's last names to match yours. You must also make it clear that you aren't seeking the name changes with any fraudulent intent.

To Obtain

A certified copy of a PC 52, you must pay a $10 fee to have the copy issued, plus $1 for each page of the document.

As for the children's new names, you will probably change their surnames only. But you could also change their first or middle names or any combination of names.

There are few restrictions on naming in the United States. Other countries control naming tightly and reject names that are exotic or strange. For example, in Germany names must be Germanic in origin and spelling, or the local registrar won't register the name. By contrast, in America you can adopt almost any name, no matter how unusual, unless the name is obscene or scandalous.

Court Order

Win or lose, you must submit the Order Following Hearing on Petition to Change Name (PC 52) to the judge at the end of the hearing. After signing by the judge, file the order with the clerk. While you're at the clerk's office, it's convenient to obtain several post-name change documents as explained below.

After a Name Change

Before you leave the clerk's office, it might be a good idea to get several certified copies of the Order Following Hearing on Petition to Change Name (PC 52). You can use these copies to prove your change of name at the following offices and agencies, so documents issued by them can be revised:

- friend of the court (personal information on file with the friend of the court) (you can attach the PC 52 to the Change in Personal Information (FOC 108) and complete paragraph #3 of this form; see sample FOC 108 on page 107)

- Michigan Secretary of State (driver's license and voter registration)
- Social Security Administration (social security card)
- passport acceptance agency (U.S. Post Office, county clerk, etc.) (passport)
- financial institutions (bank accounts, credit cards, etc.)
- insurance companies (life, disability and health insurance policies and documents)
- health care providers (health care files and documents at doctor, dentist, etc.)
- utilities (accounts with utilities, telephone companies, cable television, etc.)
- employer (employee benefits documents)
- schools and alumni associations (school records, alumni directories, etc.)
- airlines (frequent flier programs)

Typically, you must visit many of these offices and agencies in person to change your name; it's difficult or impossible to make the change over the telephone or Internet.

You must also give a special notice of name changes for you and/or your children to the Michigan Department of Community Health. This notice allows the department to add the PC 52 to your birth records. Ask the clerk for an Application to Record Court-Ordered Legal Name Change to a Michigan Birth Record (DCH-0850). File one form for each person according to the instructions in the form.

OSM CODE: NAM

Approved, SCAO

	FILE NO.
STATE OF MICHIGAN JUDICIAL CIRCUIT - FAMILY DIVISION COUNTY	**PETITION TO CHANGE NAME**

In the matter of the name change of _DARLENE A. LOVELACE, DUANE WESLEY LOVELACE AND DARRYL_
Present first name(s), middle name(s), and last name(s) (type or print)   _WENDELL LOVELACE_

to _DARLENE ANN ALBRIGHT, DUANE WESLEY ALBRIGHT AND DARRYL WENDELL ALBRIGHT_
Requested new first name(s), middle name(s), and last name(s) (type or print)

☒1. An action within the jurisdiction of the family division of circuit court involving the family or family members of the above named

person(s) has been previously filed in _OJIBWAY CO. CIRCUIT_ Court, Case Number _89-00501-DM_ , was

assigned to Judge _LESTER TUBBS_ , and   ☒remains ☐is no longer   pending.

2. The name change is for:
☐a. a married person who wishes to also include a name change for:
  ☐his/her spouse.   ☐his/her minor child(ren), of whom the petitioner has legal custody.
☒b. an adult.
☒c. a minor, whose natural or adopted parents are: _DARLENE ANN LOVELACE_ and
                                                    Mother

  DUDLEY E. LOVELACE
  Father

  Both parents are deceased. The guardian is _____ . (attach letters of guardianship)
                                              Name

3. The name change is for the following reason: _DIVORCED MOTHER WANTS TO RESUME MAIDEN NAME_
                                                 AND HAVE CHILDREN'S NAMES MATCH.
4. The name change is not sought for any fraudulent intent.

5. The following person(s) seeking a name change have a criminal record: _____

6. Each person for whom a name change is sought has been a resident of the county for at least one year.
[Complete item 7. only if the name change is for a minor. Please see other side for remainder of petition.]
☒7. I have legal custody of the minor.
  ☒a. The noncustodial parent has had the ability to visit, contact, or communicate with the child and has regularly and
  substantially failed or neglected to do so for a period of two years or more before the filing of this petition **and either:**
    ☒a support order has been entered, and the noncustodial parent has failed to substantially comply with the order for
    a period of two years or more before the filing of this petition; **or**
    ☐a support order has not been entered and the noncustodial parent, having the ability to support or assist in supporting
    the child, has failed or neglected to provide regular and substantial support for two years or more before the filing of
    this petition.
  ☐b. The noncustodial parent has been convicted of child abuse (MCL 750.136b), criminal sexual conduct (MCL 750.520b,
  MCL 750.520c, 750.520d, or 750.520e), or assault with intent to commit criminal sexual conduct (MCL 750.520g) and the child or
  a sibling of the child was the victim. (attach judgment of sentence)
  c. The last known address of the noncustodial parent is: _900 S. MAPLE, LAKE CITY, MI 48800_

  ☐ The noncustodial parent is not living at the above address, and I have taken the following steps to locate him/her:
  _____

(PLEASE SEE OTHER SIDE)

Do not write below this line - For court use only

MCL 333.2872, MCL 711.1, MCR 3.613

PC 51 (9/03) **PETITION TO CHANGE NAME**

CHECK #2B FOR A NAME CHANGE FOR YOU ALONE, #2C FOR YOUR CHILD(REN) ONLY, AND #2B AND #2C FOR YOU AND YOUR CHILD(REN) TOGETHER.

IF YOUR EX IS CONSENTING TO NAME CHANGE FOR CHILDREN, CHECK BOX LEFT OF #7, AND INSERT ADDRESS OF NONCUSTODIAL PARENT IN #7C. LEAVE REMAINING BOXES IN THIS PARAGRAPH UNCHECKED.

IF YOUR EX HAS DISAPPEARED, CHECK BOX HERE AND DESCRIBE YOUR EFFORTS TO FIND HIM/HER.

8. I request the following name change(s): (type or print first name, middle name, and last name)

Petitioner	FROM	TO	DATE OF BIRTH
Spouse	DARLENE ANN LOVELACE	DARLENE ANN ALBRIGHT	month, day, year 5-1-65
Minor child	DUANE WESLEY LOVELACE	DUANE WESLEY ALBRIGHT	month, day, year
Minor child	DARRYL WENDELL LOVELACE	DARRYL WENDELL ALBRIGHT	6-1-86
Minor child			7-1-87
Minor child			

If you want a new live birth certificate, check item 9. A special order is not needed if you only want to add the changed name(s) to the original certificate(s).

☐ 9. I request the court to order the State Registrar to create a new live birth certificate that does not disclose the name of

_____ at birth and to seal the original certificate.
Name

I declare that this petition has been examined by me and that its contents are true to the best of my information, knowledge, and belief.

1-1-99
Date

Darlene Lovelace
Petitioner signature

DARLENE LOVELACE
Name (type or print)

121 S. MAIN
Address

LAKE CITY, MI 48800   772-0000
City, state, zip   Telephone no.

_____
Date

_____
Petitioner signature

_____
Name (type or print)

_____
Address

_____
City, state, zip   Telephone no.

☐ 10. I am the spouse of the petitioner or the non-custodial parent of the minor and consent to the granting of this petition to change name.

Date

_____
Signature

☐ 11. I am _____ the granting of this petition to change my name.

Date

Date

☒ 12. I am a minor under 14 years of age, and I state my preference to the name change above.

1-1-99
Date

_____
Minor's signature

_____
Minor's signature

1-1-99
Date

Duane Lovelace
Minor's signature

Darryl Lovelace
Minor's signature

_____
Attorney signature

_____
Attorney name (type or print)   Bar no.

_____
Address

_____
City, state, zip   Telephone no.

> IF YOUR EX CONSENTS TO NAME CHANGE FOR CHILDREN, CHECK BOX AT #10 AND HAVE EX DATE AND SIGN THESE LINES.

OSM CODE: NOH

Approved, SCAO		FILE NO.
STATE OF MICHIGAN **PROBATE COURT** **COUNTY** CIRCUIT COURT - FAMILY DIVISION	**NOTICE OF HEARING**	

In the matter of THE NAME CHANGE OF DARLENE ANN LOVELACE, DUANE WESLEY LOVELACE AND DARRYL WENDELL LOVELACE

TAKE NOTICE: A hearing will be held on 3-15-99 _____ at 9:00 A m.,
                                              Date   Time

at OJIBWAY COUNTY COURTHOUSE _____ before Judge LESTER TUBBS _____ Bar no.
   Location

for the following purpose(s): state the nature of the hearing

PETITION OF DARLENE ANN LOVELACE TO CHANGE HER
NAME AND HER CHILDREN'S NAMES FROM DARLENE ANN
LOVELACE TO DARLENE ANN ALBRIGHT, DUANE WESLEY
LOVELACE TO DUANE WESLEY ALBRIGHT AND DARRYL
WENDELL LOVELACE TO DARRYL WENDELL ALBRIGHT.

If you require special accommodations to use the court because of a disability, or if you require a foreign language interpreter to help you fully participate in court proceedings, please contact the court immediately to make arrangements.

2-1-99
Date
DARLENE LOVELACE

Attorney name	Bar no.	Petitioner name
		121 S. MAIN
Address		Address
		LAKE CITY, MI 48800 772-0000
City, state, zip	Telephone no.	City, state, zip Telephone no.

The law provides that you should be notified of this hearing. Unless the check box below is marked, you are not required to attend the hearing, but it is your privilege to do so.

☐ You are required to attend this hearing.

Do not write below this line - For court use only

MCL 700.1401, MCL 710.20, et seq., MCR 5.102

PC 562 (9/03) **NOTICE OF HEARING**

Approved, SCAO

STATE OF MICHIGAN PROBATE COURT _____ COUNTY CIRCUIT COURT - FAMILY DIVISION	PROOF OF SERVICE	FILE NO.	OSM CODE: PSV

In the matter of THE NAME CHANGE OF DARLENE ANN LOVELACE, DUANE WESLEY

1. Titles of the papers served or mailed: LOVELACE AND DARRYL WENDELL LOVELACE
PETITION TO CHANGE NAME AND NOTICE
OF HEARING

☒ 2. I served by ☒ ordinary mail the papers described above on: ☐ registered mail (copy of return receipt attached) ☐ certified mail (copy of return receipt attached)

Name	Complete address of service	Date
DUDLEY LOVELACE	900 S. MAPLE, LAKE CITY, MI 48800	2-2-99

☐ 3. I served by **personal service** the papers described above on:

Name	Complete address of service	Date and Time

☐ 4. After diligent search and inquiry, I have been unable to find and serve the following interested persons:

_____

I have made the following efforts in attempting to serve process: _____

I declare under the penalties of perjury that this proof of service has been examined by me and that its contents are true to the best of my information, knowledge, and belief.

Service fee $	Miles traveled	Mileage fee $	Total fee $

Date 2-2-99

Signature *Darlene Lovelace*

Do not write below this line - For court use only

PC 564 (9/02) **PROOF OF SERVICE**

MCL 700.1306, MCL 700.1401, MCR 5.104(A), MCR 5.105, MCR 5.107

OSM CODE: PNH

Approved, SCAO

STATE OF MICHIGAN **PROBATE COURT** **COUNTY** CIRCUIT COURT - FAMILY DIVISION	**PUBLICATION OF NOTICE OF HEARING**	FILE NO.

In the matter of THE NAME CHANGE OF DARLENE ANN LOVELACE, DUANE WESLEY LOVELACE AND DARRYL WENDELL LOVELACE

TO ALL INTERESTED PERSONS including:*

IF YOUR EX HAS DISAPPEARED, INSERT HIS/HER NAME IN THIS SPACE.

whose address(es) are unknown and whose interest in the matter may be barred or affected by the following:

TAKE NOTICE: A hearing will be held on 3-15-99 at 9:00 A m.
                                          Date   Time

at OJIBWAY COUNTY COURTHOUSE before Judge LESTER TUBBS
   Location   Bar no.

for the following purpose:

ON THE PETITION OF DARLENE ANN LOVELACE TO CHANGE HER NAME AND HER CHILDREN'S NAMES FROM DARLENE ANN LOVELACE TO DARLENE ANN ALBRIGHT, DUANE WESLEY LOVELACE TO DUANE WESLEY ALBRIGHT AND DARRYL WENDELL LOVELACE TO DARRYL WENDELL ALBRIGHT.

2-1-99
Date
DARLENE LOVELACE
Petitioner name (type or print)

Attorney name (type or print)	Bar no.	121 S. MAIN
		Address
Address		LAKE CITY, MI 48800 772-0000
City, state, zip	Telephone no.	City, state, zip Telephone no.

PUBLISH ABOVE INFORMATION ONLY

Publish ONE time(s) in OJIBWAY TIMES in OJIBWAY County
                        Name of publication

Furnish ONE copies to PETITIONER

Furnish affidavit of publication to the court.

Forward statement for publication charges to PETITIONER

***NOTE TO PREPARER:** This notice may be combined with the Notice to Creditors (form PC 574) by adding the language from the Notice to Creditors.

Do not write below this line - For court use only

MCL 700.1401(1), MCL 700.3403, MCL 700.5405, MCR 5 105(A)(3), MCR 5.106, MCR 5.306, MCR 5.308(C), (D)

PC 563 (9/02) **PUBLICATION OF NOTICE OF HEARING**

Approved, SCAO

STATE OF MICHIGAN JUDICIAL CIRCUIT - FAMILY DIVISION COUNTY	ORDER FOLLOWING HEARING ON PETITION TO CHANGE NAME	FILE NO.

In the matter of the name change of **DARLENE ANN LOVELACE, DUANE WESLEY LOVELACE AND DARRYL**
WENDELL LOVELACE
Present first name(s), middle name(s), and last name(s) (type or print)
to **DARLENE ANN ALBRIGHT, DUANE WESLEY ALBRIGHT AND DARRYL WENDELL ALBRIGHT**
Requested new first name(s), middle name(s), and last name(s) (type or print)

1. Date of Hearing: **3-15-99**   Judge: **LESTER TUBBS**

Bar no

THE COURT FINDS:

2. A petition for name change has been filed.

3. Notice of hearing was given by publication.

4. Each person for whom a name change is sought has been a resident of the county for at least one year.

☒ 5. The court has received the required criminal record report(s) from the Michigan Department of State Police.

☐ 6. _____
Name(s) (type or print)

7. ☐ a. The request for name change of _____ has a criminal record.
made with fraudulent intent.   Name(s) (type or print)

   ☒ b. The request for name change of **DARLENE ANN LOVELACE, DUANE WESLEY LOVELACE** is not
made with fraudulent intent.   Name(s) (type or print)   **AND DARRYL WENDELL LOVELACE**

☐ 8. The petitioner, having legal custody, requests the name change of a minor. The noncustodial parent has consented to
the change.

☒ 9. The petitioner requests the name change of a minor. The custodial parent has consented to the name change. The
noncustodial parent was given notice of the hearing.

   ☒ a. The noncustodial parent has had the ability to visit, contact, or communicate with the minor but has regularly and
   substantially failed or neglected to do so for the past two years, **and**
      ☒ a support order has been entered, and the noncustodial parent has failed to substantially comply with the order
      for a period of two years or more before the filing of the petition for name change; **or**
      ☐ a support order has not been entered and the noncustodial parent, having the ability to support or assist in supporting
      the child, has failed or neglected to provide regular and substantial support for two years or more before the filing of
      the petition for name change.

   ☐ b. The noncustodial parent has been convicted of child abuse (MCL 750.136b), criminal sexual conduct (MCL 750.520b, 750.520c
   750.520d, or 750.520e), or assault with intent to commit criminal sexual conduct (MCL 750.520g) and the child or a sibling of the
   child was the victim.

☒ 10. The minor(s) under the age of 14 have stated their preference to a name change.

☐ 11. The minor(s) is/are not of sufficient age to express their preference to a name change.

(PLEASE SEE OTHER SIDE)

Do not write below this line - For court use only

PC 52 (9/97) ORDER FOLLOWING HEARING ON PETITION TO CHANGE NAME   MCL 333.2872; MSA 14.15(2872), MCL 711.1; MSA 27.3178(561), MCR 5.781

> IF YOUR EX HAS CONSENTED TO CHILD(REN)'S NAME CHANGE BY SIGNING THE PC 51, CHECK BOX IN #8.

IT IS ORDERED:

12. The name(s) of the following person(s) are changed:

From:

DARLENE ANN LOVELACE

DUANE WESLEY LOVELACE

DARRYL WENDELL LOVELACE

To:

DARLENE ANN ALBRIGHT

DUANE WESLEY ALBRIGHT

DARRYL WENDELL ALBRIGHT

☐ 13. The State Registrar shall create a new live birth certificate for _____

which does not disclose the name at birth and shall seal the original certificate.

☐ 14. The request to change the name of _____ is denied.

☐ 15. The request is denied and the petition is dismissed.

LESTER TUBBS
_____
Judge

3-15-99
_____
Date

_____   Bar no.
Attorney name (type or print)

_____
Address

_____   Telephone no.

City, state, zip

NOTE TO PETITIONER: You must provide this order to the State Registrar if you want to change your birth certificate.

Note to Clerk: Under MCL 711.1(3), if the court enters an order to change the name of a person who has a criminal record, the court shall forward the order to the central records division of the Michigan State Police and to 1 or more of the following:

- The Department of Corrections if the person named in the order is in prison or on parole or has been imprisoned or released from parole in the immediately preceding 2 years.

- The sheriff of the county in which the person named in the order was last convicted if the person was incarcerated in a county jail or released from a county jail within the immediately preceding 2 years.

- The court that has jurisdiction over the person named in the order if the person named in the order is under the jurisdiction of the family division of the circuit court, or until January 1, 1998, the probate court, or has been discharged from the jurisdiction of that court within the immediately preceding 2 years.

CHAPTER 8:
Tax Problems

As if going through a divorce weren't bad enough, divorce once had many unpleasant tax consequences. To cite just one example, the transfer of property during or soon after a divorce could create capital gains, resulting in a nasty post-divorce tax bill.

Many of these divorce tax traps were eliminated by the Tax Reform Act of 1984. The Taxpayer Relief Act of 1997 eased the tax burden even more. Today, divorce isn't the tax nightmare it once was. Nevertheless, there are still a few tax problems that can crop up after divorce.

Sale of Property

Ever since the Tax Reform Act of 1984, the transfer of property, such as a marital home, between spouses during or soon after a divorce isn't taxable. However, the transferee-spouse sometimes still got stuck with capital gains if s/he sold the home to a third party later.

This happens less often now after introduction of a homestead exclusion by the Taxpayer Relief Act of 1997. This exclusion, worth $250,000 for a single taxpayer and $500,000 for married taxpayers, covers capital gains from the sale of a "principal residence" (defined as a home owned and used by you as your principal residence for two of the five years before the sale).

The homestead exclusion can be used once every two years, or more frequently but at a reduced amount in hardship cases. Thanks to this generous exclusion, most capital gains from a post-divorce sale of a former marital home should now be exempt from taxation.

Filing Status

If your divorce is final by the end of a year, even as late as Dec. 31, the tax law considers you divorced for the *entire* year. As a result, you must file as a single person (either as a regular single person or with a special filing status of head of household) for that year (unless you remarry during the year).

A divorce case can straddle two tax years. You may file for divorce one year and finalize it during the next year. In this situation, the tax law regards you as married during the divorce-filing year, but divorced the next year. For the divorce-filing year, you have the option, as all married couples do, of filing a joint or separate income tax return.

Filing jointly usually results in a smaller net tax bill than with both spouses filing separately. But there are risks with joint returns, especially amid a divorce. Joint income tax returns mean joint liability for tax deficiencies, so each of you is 100% liable for any unpaid tax, interest and penalties. This is true even if the tax problems were caused by your spouse alone, without your knowledge, or concern his/her income and not yours.

Joint liability tax problems can happen anytime during marriage. But they are usually worse around divorce, when family financial discipline often breaks down. Making matters worse, the IRS seldom audits returns until several years after filing. Thus, the agency may audit a divorced couple's joint return well after divorce and find a tax deficiency, with accumulated interest and penalties.

Needless to say, all this can cause hardship for a spouse who signs a joint tax return unaware of the other spouse's tax cheating. Luckily, the tax law offers three remedies for relief:

Innocent spouse relief. The tax law provides relief from joint tax liability to so-called innocent spouses, who didn't know about the guilty spouse's understatement of tax. To qualify as an innocent spouse (or ex-spouse), you must satisfy the following requirements:

- you must have filed a joint return that understated tax because of either:
  1) omission of income, or
  2) claiming a tax deduction, credit or basis in property without factual or legal justification
- you did not know, and had no reason to know, of the tax understatement by the guilty spouse
- it would be "unfair" to hold you liable for the tax deficiency because:
  1) you didn't receive any significant benefit from the tax understatement, or
  2) the guilty spouse divorced or deserted you

In some cases, you can claim partial innocent spouse relief and avoid a portion of the joint tax liability. The innocent spouse rules now allow you to claim innocent spouse status for understatements of tax you didn't know about, while remaining jointly liable for tax deficiencies of which you were aware.

More Information

About divorce and taxes in general, obtain "Tax Information for Divorced or Separated Individuals" (Pub. 504).

About avoiding joint tax liability, get "Innocent Spouse Relief" (Pub. 971).

These booklets are available from any IRS office by calling the agency at (800) 829-3676, or you can view or download them at the IRS' Web site: www.irs.gov.

Separation of liability. Separation of liability is a new remedy, adopted in 1998, which attempts to match liability with responsibility for a tax understatement. To qualify for separate liability relief, you must:

- seek relief either:
  1) when divorced or legally separated from the spouse with whom you filed jointly, or
  2) you must not have been a member of the same household as the spouse with whom you filed jointly during the previous 12 months before filing for relief
- not have known about the incorrect item in the joint return and not have transferred property with your spouse or ex-spouse fraudulently or to avoid taxes

If separation is permitted, the qualifying spouse's liability is limited to taxes due on their own income, not for the full joint liability. To find the limit of liability, you look at what the taxes would have been had the qualifying spouse filed a separate tax return and this becomes the cap on liability in the joint return.

Equitable relief. Equitable relief is a fairness doctrine of last resort. It provides relief when, taking all the facts and circumstances into account, it's unfair to impose joint tax liability on you. Equitable relief is available only when you aren't eligible for relief under the innocent spouse or separation of liability rules described above.

On the other hand, equitable relief is broader in scope because it offers relief from both understatement of tax (false reporting of tax liabilities) and underpayment of tax (correct reporting of tax, but failure to pay the tax due). The innocent spouse and separate liability remedies apply to understatements only.

As you can see, the relief remedies from joint tax liability are complicated, with many qualifications and exceptions, making them difficult to invoke. Therefore, the best plan is to avoid filing joint tax returns when you suspect that your spouse has been cheating on taxes. File separately instead. And then later (within three years), if your ex was honest, you can always amend and file a joint return.

In the year of your divorce and later years, you must file a separate return as a single person, unless and until you remarry. You can file a regular single-person return. Or if you are a custodial parent, you may qualify for special head-of-household status. This filing status gives you a bigger standard deduction, lower tax rates and other tax advantages that ordinary single filers don't have.

To qualify as an unmarried head of household, you must pay more than half the cost of maintaining your home. This home must also be the principal residence of at least one child or other dependent for more than half the year.

Dependency Exemptions

When parents do their income taxes, they can claim extra exemptions for dependent children. In 2004, the federal and Michigan dependency exemptions are each worth $3,100 per child. These exemptions, which are increased periodically, are valuable because they act like deductions and reduce income tax.

Since the Taxpayer Relief Act of 1997, dependency exemptions are more valuable than ever because they are tied to a new child tax credit. Parents may take tax credits for children under the age of 17 for whom they can claim dependency exemptions. The child tax credit is now worth up to $1,000 per child.

Assignment of Dependency Exemptions

After divorce, the tax law says that the custodial parent is entitled to the dependency exemptions for the children. The custodial parent gets these exemptions even if the noncustodial parent pays more child support. When parents have joint custody, the custodial parent is the one who has physical custody for the most days during a year.

The tax law also allows a custodial parent to give the dependency exemptions to the noncustodial parent. In addition, Michigan law permits divorce courts to assign the exemptions when the issue is contested. Either way, the judgment of divorce should make the assignment.

Your divorce judgment may have assigned the dependency exemptions to the noncustodial parent those ways. If so, the custodial parent must complete the IRS assignment form, Release of Claim to Exemption for Child of Divorced or Separated Parents (Form 8332), as required by the judgment. After release, the noncustodial parent attaches this form to his/her income tax returns to claim the dependency exemptions.

Form 8332 permits assignment of dependency exemptions annually, for several years or permanently. From an assigning custodial parent's point of view, it's usually best to assign annually. That way, the assignment can be tied to payment of child support. And if the support isn't fully paid by the end of the year, the custodial parent can withhold the assignment. This serves as an informal mechanism for enforcing child support.

> ## Glossary
>
> *Dependency*–before either parent can claim dependency exemptions for their children, the dependency of the children on the parents must exist by:
>
> - the parents' together having custody of the children for more than half the year; and,
>
> - the parents' providing more than half the support for the children (money from a new spouse is ascribed to the remarried parent)

Enforcement of Assignment

The contempt power is probably the chief way to enforce an assignment of dependency exemptions. So if, for example, the custodial parent reneges on providing Form 8332, the noncustodial parent can ask the court to threaten the custodial parent with contempt of court until the form is provided.

Modifying Assignment of Dependency Exemptions

If your judgment of divorce assigns dependency exemptions, the assignment may or may not be modifiable. Modifiability hinges on whether the assignment provision is tied to the child support or property division provision of the divorce judgment.

As explained in "Modification" on page 5, child support is modifiable while it lasts. Property division, by contrast, is usually final at divorce and isn't open to modification unless the divorce judgment is defective.

A dependency exemption assignment can be part of child support or property division. You must examine and interpret your divorce judgment to see where it belongs. If the assignment provision is labeled as child support or property division, or falls under one of these headings, this designation usually controls whether it can be modified. If your dependency exemption assignment is tied to child support, it's modifiable on grounds of a change of conditions or circumstances.

As with other modifications, you and your ex can stipulate to modification of the dependency exemption assignment. Or you can seek modification by motion.

Stipulated Modification

You and your ex can agree, or sitpulate, to modification of the dependency exemption assignment in your judgment of divorce. The court must review and approve the change since it affects the welfare of children. The court could possibly reject your proposed modification, but will likely approve it.

You don't need to file a motion or have a court hearing to modify an assignment of dependency exemptions by stipulation. All you have to do is prepare the Order Regarding Assignment of Dependency Exemptions (GRP 24) and have it approved by the court. See "Stipulated Orders" on page 30 for complete instructions about preparing a stipulated order, getting approval of the order, filing it with the clerk and serving it on your ex.

As for the modification itself, simply reassign the dependency exemptions in paragraph #6 of the Order Regarding Assignment of Dependency Exemptions (GRP 24), as in the sample order at the end of this chapter.

Contested Modification

When your ex won't stipulate to modification of the assignment of dependency exemptions, you must file a motion asking for the change. Modification isn't guaranteed; the court will consider your motion during a hearing and either grant or deny it.

Motion

You can ask for dependency exemption modification in the Motion Regarding Support (FOC 50). There is a sample FOC 50 on page 132, showing you how to complete the various parts of the motion. The core of the motion is paragraph #5, which explains the grounds for modification, and paragraph #7 with the proposed reassignment.

The customary grounds for modifying child support-related issues are change of conditions or circumstances in the lives of you, your ex and/or children. For example, the custodial parent may have given up the dependency exemptions when she had no income and didn't need them. Now the custodial parent may have a job and needs the exemptions to offset income tax. See "Motion" on page 126 for more about the grounds for child support modifications and the shift to new grounds in 2005.

For complete information and instructions about preparing, filing and serving a motion like this, see "Papers" on page 23 and "Motions" on page 32.

Responding to a Motion

If you receive a motion for modification of assignment of dependency exemptions from your ex, you can respond orally or in writing, in several ways.

If you agree with the motion completely, contact your ex immediately and arrange to stipulate to a modification order. In paragraphs #5, #6 and #7 of the Response to Motion Regarding Support (FOC 51), you can also indicate your agreement with the motion. But why do extra paperwork when it's easier to stipulate to a modification order? You could also appear at the hearing and agree to the motion, but this too wastes time when stipulation is available. See "Stipulated Modification" above for more about stipulations.

Sometimes, you may agree with part of the motion and disagree with the rest. It's important to signal your partial agreement as soon as possible because this narrows the issues in the case. If you file a Response to Motion Regarding Support (FOC 51), check box #6b and describe the extent of your agreement with the motion in the space below. If you choose to respond orally, mention your partial agreement to the mediator, referee or judge, so the agreed-upon issues can be eliminated from the hearing.

When you oppose the motion, you can voice your disagreement in two ways. You can file a written response to the motion, or wait until the motion hearing and respond orally. A written response is usually better, because it gets your views across more effectively.

Use the Response to Motion Regarding Support (FOC 51) for a written response. In paragraph #5, say why you oppose the motion. You might disagree that conditions or circumstances have changed and/or that reassignment of the dependency exemptions is necessary.

For complete information and instructions about preparing, filing and serving a response, see "Responding to a Motion" on page 35.

You can also respond to a motion by making a counter-motion. You could bring a child support-related counter-motion by checking box #7b in the FOC 51, and then explain what you want in the space below. Or you could seek completely new relief by filing a separate motion form. For more about counter-motion tactics, and how to file a counter-motion, see "Making a Counter-Motion" on page 37.

Before a post-judgment motion is heard by the judge, the friend of the court may intervene to mediate, investigate or referee, in an attempt to settle the dispute.

Previously, child support-related disputes weren't eligible for informal mediation or settlement. But after June 30, 2005, these disputes may be submitted to informal settlement by the friend of the court. Referral of the dispute to formal mediation is also possible. Private mediation or arbitration, which is expensive, is unlikely.

While the modification motion is pending, the friend of the court is often asked to investigate the dispute, and make a report and recommendation about the issue. The motion may also be refereed by the friend of the court before the motion hearing.

See "Friend of the Court" on page 38 for more about the friend of the court's roles in post-judgment cases, and how to deal with mediation, investigation or refereeing by the friend of the court. This section also has information about formal mediation, private mediation and arbitration, all of which take place outside the friend of the court system.

As explained in "Motion Hearings" on page 41, there are two kinds of motion hearings: 1) nonevidentiary hearing where facts aren't in dispute, evidence is seldom introduced and the parties merely make legal arguments to the judge 2) evidentiary hearing where facts are disputed and evidence, such as testimony from witnesses, must be introduced to establish the true facts.

A motion to modify assignment of dependency exemptions will require a nonevidentiary hearing or, at most, a limited evidentiary hearing with a few documents like income tax returns. See "Motion Hearings" on page 41 for information about preparing for and appearing at nonevidentiary and evidentiary hearings.

After the motion hearing, the judge will decide the motion. The judge will either decide immediately and give an oral decision "from the bench," or take the case "under submission" and rule later by issuing a written decision.

Either way, the moving party must prepare the order granting or denying the motion. Use the Order Regarding Assignment of Dependency Exemptions (GRP 24) as the order. As for the modification itself, simply reassign the dependency exemptions in paragraph #6 of the GRP 24, as in the sample order at the end of this chapter.

The moving party must also get the order signed by the judge and filed with the clerk. There are several ways to do this. See "Court Orders" on page 44 for complete instructions and forms.

Earned Income Tax Credit

For lower-income parents, there is yet another tax credit that can be more valuable than dependency exemptions and child tax credits combined: the earned income tax credit (EITC). What makes the EITC so valuable is not only the amount of the credit, which can be sizable (a maximum of $4,300 in 2004), but that it can be converted into a cash payment to you even if you don't owe any income tax.

Most tax exemptions and credits merely reduce tax owed and are wasted if you don't owe any income tax. Many low-income people fall into this category; they're eligible for tax exemptions and credits they cannot use because their incomes are low enough to escape income taxation.

The EITC is different. If you qualify for the credit, but don't owe any income tax, the EITC can come back to you in the form a cash payment from the federal government. For low-income taxpayers owing some income tax, the EITC can offset the tax, with any remainder payable in cash. In some cases, you can even get an advance on next year's EITC, and have your employer add a portion of the credit to each paycheck you receive during the year.

The EITC was originally designed for custodial parents living with and taking care of children. Lower-income custodial parents may usually claim EITCs if the children (who are subject to several age limits, but are defined very liberally to include all kinds of dependents) live with them for more than half the year. Since 1994, noncustodians can also qualify for EITCs if they have a low income and satisfy several other requirements. The amount of an EITC is much less for these noncustodians.

Either way, there are complicated rules for qualifying for an EITC, which are explained in the IRS' EITC publication. If you need help claiming the credit, look for a local nonprofit tax clinic or program. Watch out for commercial tax preparation companies which charge a lot for tax return preparation and offer "advances" (loans really) against your EITC. These services can take a big bite (30% or more) out of your credit.

More Information

About the EITC, obtain "Earned Income Credit" (Pub. 596), from any IRS office or by calling the agency at (800) 829-3676. You can also view or download the publication at the IRS' Web site: www.irs.gov

The IRS has a Volunteer Income Tax Assistance (VITA) program of over 14,000 walk-in tax clinics which can help you claim an EITC. Call (800) 829-1040 for referral to a VITA participant near you.

CHECK:
- 1ST BOX IF ORDER WAS CONTESTED AND GOTTEN AFTER COURT HEARING ON THE ORDER
- 2ND BOX IF NONMOVING PARTY CONSENTED TO ORDER
- 3RD BOX FOR STIPULATED ORDERS
- NO BOXES FOR APPROVAL OF THE ORDER BY SILENCE

F MICHIGAN Family Division COUNTY	ORDER REGARDING ASSIGNMENT OF DEPENDENCY EXEMPTIONS	CASE NO.

Defendant:

v

Date of hearing ___2-15-99___   Judge ___LESTER TUBBS___

1. This order is entered ☐ after hearing. ☒ on consent. ☐ on stipulation.

THE COURT FINDS:

☒ 2. A motion for assignment of dependency exemptions for the parties' children was filed.

☒ 3. A response to the motion was filed.

☒ 4. A change of circumstances ☒ does ☐ does not exist which warrants assignme

dependency exemptions.

IT IS ORDERED:

☐ 5. The motion for assignment of dependency exemptions is dismissed.

☒ 6. Starting the tax year of ___2000___ , the dependency exemptions for the pa
shall be assigned to ☐ plaintiff ☒ defendant and the other party shall no longer cl
exemptions. The assigning party shall also sign and submit to the assignee-party IRS F
to carry out the assignment.

Date/plaintiff _2-15-99_ _Darlene Lovelace_   Date/defendant _2-15-99_ _Dudley Lovelace_

Date ___2-15-99___   Judge _Lester Tubbs_

THE PARTIES MUST SIGN A STIPULATED ORDER OR ONE OBTAINED BY CONSENT. PARTIES DON'T SIGN AN ORDER OBTAINED THROUGH "APPROVAL-BY-SILENCE" OR AFTER A COURT HEARING ON THE ORDER.

PROOF OF SERVICE

I certify that on this date I mailed a copy of this order to the other party by ordinary mail at his/her ad-dress above.

Date ___2-15-99___   Signature _Dudley Lovelace_

GRP 24 (9/04)   ORDER REGARDING ASSIGNMENT OF DEPENDENCY EXEMPTIONS

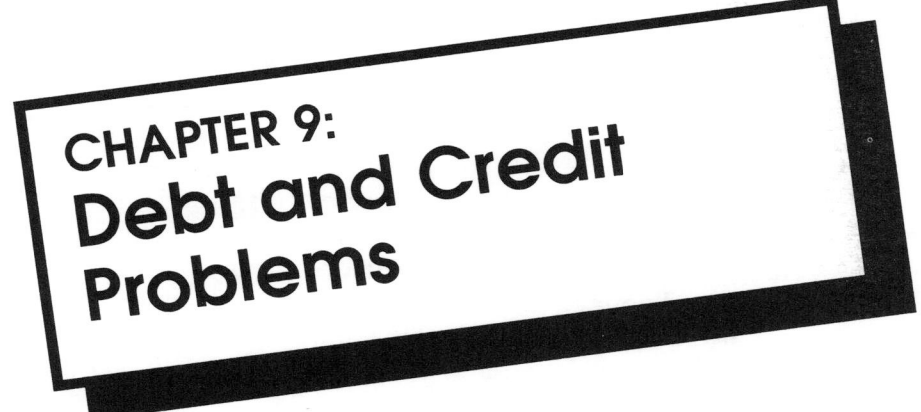

CHAPTER 9: Debt and Credit Problems

Debts and divorce seem to go together, because financial problems are one of the root causes of divorce. These financial problems can persist after divorce, leading to debt and credit problems—especially for women.

Debts

If your divorce papers don't say anything about debts, the following general rules govern liability for sole debts (debts incurred by a spouse alone) and joint debts (debts taken on by spouses together):

Sole debt. The spouse who incurred the debt (debtor-spouse) remains liable for it after the divorce. The nondebtor-spouse generally won't be liable for the debt unless s/he gave the debtor-spouse authority, as an agent, to incur debts of the nondebtor-spouse's behalf. The agent's authority can be express, implied or even given after the fact, by ratification of what the debtor-spouse did.

Joint debt. Because both spouses incurred joint debts, each remains liable for these after divorce.

A divorce judgment can modify this liability scheme to an extent. A debt provision in a judgment can shift the liability for a sole debt from the debtor-spouse to the other spouse. It could also have one spouse assume liability for a joint debt or a sole debt for which both spouses are liable under the agency exception described above.

Not all debts may be reassigned that way. Educational and personal loans are often left with those incurring them, since they have a greater incentive to pay them. Likewise, debts secured by property (mortgages, land contracts and other liens) are customarily transferred to the recipients of the secured property. On the other hand, general unsecured debts, such as credit card or charge account debts, are often divided during divorce.

Although you and your ex may have rearranged debts in your divorce judgment, your arrangements won't affect the rights of the creditors holding the debts. Your creditors will have the same rights after your divorce as they had before.*

> *Example:* A couple got a joint car loan from a bank (creditor). In their divorce, the wife received ownership of the car and the car loan was assigned to her by a debt provision in the divorce judgment. She falls behind on the car payments. The bank could sue the husband because the debt division didn't affect his liability to the bank.

If a debt division won't change creditors' rights, why do divorce parties go to the trouble of dividing debts in their divorce judgments? The advantage of debt division is that it provides a legal claim, known as indemnity, against the spouse assuming the debt. The indemnity can then be used as a defense or as direct claim.

> *Example:* A couple gets a joint car loan from a bank (creditor). In their divorce, the wife receives ownership of the car and agrees to pay the loan off in a debt division provision. After she falls behind in car payments, the bank sues both spouses. The husband could cite the indemnity from the debt division and shift liability to the wife. Had the bank sued the husband alone, he could add the wife to the case and raise the indemnity claim against her.

Debts after Divorce

Although it's difficult to think of debts as property, debt division is really part of the property division of a divorce. As such, it's a closed issue and cannot be reopened after the divorce, except when the divorce judgment is defective (see "When Is My Divorce Judgment Defective?" on page 13 for more about this exception). Thus, if you didn't divide debts during your divorce it's usually too late to do this afterward.

All you can do later is close or freeze joint accounts (credit cards, charge accounts, etc.). You can close a joint account if no debts remain in the account.

---

*   A creditor can agree to release a spouse from liability for a joint debt. In that case, the released spouse would no longer be liable to the creditor for the debt. Nevertheless, most creditors won't consent to such releases because they prefer to have two debtors rather than one.

If debts exist, you can pay these off or sometimes transfer these to individual accounts. Another option is to freeze the account, so no new debt can be added, and then pay off the account later.

Credit Problems

Today, in our consumer economy credit is more important than ever. As always, lenders look at credit reports (tracking a person's borrowing and payment habits) when making lending decisions. But more and more, automobile and homeowner insurance companies are using credit histories to determine insurability and premiums, and mortgage companies base interest rates on creditworthiness.

After divorce, many women discover that they can't get credit because they have no credit history. A woman may lose credit if her credit was reported in her previous married name. Even women who don't change their names may suffer a loss of credit if they got credit through their husbands' credit reports.

The solution to these credit woes is building a credit history in your own name. If you had credit under your former married name, you can add this information to your credit file. Joint accounts with your husband may have been reported in your husband's name only (all joint accounts opened after June 1, 1977, are supposed to reported in both spouses' names). If so, you can sometimes persuade credit reporting agencies to add these credit references to your file.

In addition, you can apply for new credit from banks, retailers and other creditors to build a credit history. A federal law, the Equal Credit Opportunity Act (ECOA), bars creditors from canceling old credit accounts you had during marriage if you still meet their lending standards (you may have to submit new information to prove your creditworthiness). The ECOA also guarantees creditworthy persons access to credit regardless of sex or marital status, and outlaws various discriminatory credit practices.

As you build a credit history, make sure you pay your bills on time, because this factor has the biggest impact on credit. It's also smart to have a good mix of credit, with both revolving (credit cards, charge accounts, etc.) and installment (mortgages, loans, etc.) debt.

One thing to avoid are credit repair services. These firms often charge a lot for meager results. Even worse, they can sometimes commit illegal practices for which you can be liable.

More Information

Credit agencies receive credit information from lenders and merchants, compile this information into credit reports and sell these to lenders and others. To check on your credit status, get copies of your credit reports from the three main credit reporting agencies:

Equifax: P.O. Box 105873, Atlanta, GA 30348, (800) 685-1111 or www.equifax.com

Experian: P.O. Box 2104, Allen, TX 75013, (888) 397-3742 or www.experian.com

TransUnion: TransUnion LLC, Consumer Disclosure Center, P.O. Box 1000, Chester, PA 19022, (800) 888-4213 or www.transunion.com

Each report is around $10, but consumers are entitled to one free report per year from each company under the new Fair and Accurate Credit Transactions Act. You can request the free reports from:

Annual Credit Report Request Service
P.O. Box 105281
Atlanta, GA 30348

Or call the service at (877) 322-8228 or go to www.annualcreditreport.com

For more information about credit and credit reporting, go to the **Federal Trade Commission's** Web site at www.ftc.gov and look for publications like "Building a Better Credit Report" and "Fair Credit Reporting" through the Credit/For Consumers/Credit Reports pathway.

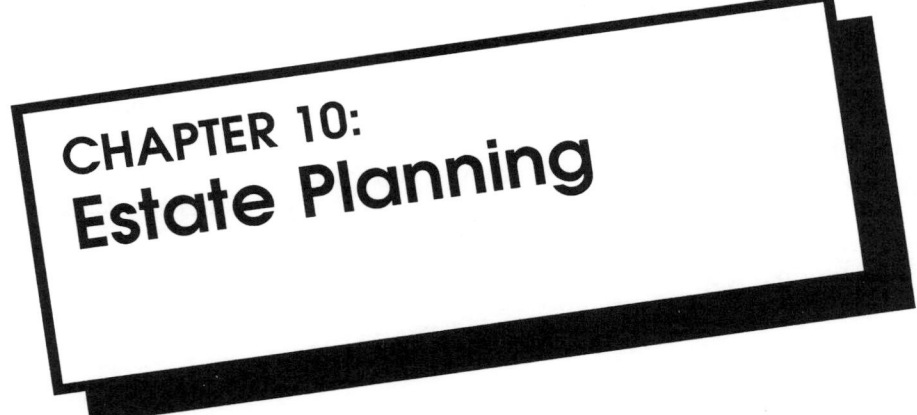

CHAPTER 10:
Estate Planning

The change in marital status caused by divorce has far-reaching effects on your estate plan. This may require reorganization of your life insurance and retirement benefits or revision of estate planning documents like powers of attorney, trusts and wills.

Your divorce judgment should cut off each spouse's interest in the life insurance, retirement benefits and estate of the other (unless the judgment says otherwise). These extinguishment provisions are required in all Michigan divorce judgments.

In 2000, Michigan adopted a new will, inheritance and probate law, called the Estates and Protected Individuals Code (EPIC). The EPIC says that divorce revokes all property transfers to and appointments of (as agent, beneficiary, trustee, personal representative, etc.) an ex-spouse and his/her relatives, such as your stepchildren, in all sorts of estate planning devices, including:

- life insurance
- all kinds of retirement plans
- power of attorney
- trust
- will
- miscellaneous (such as pay-on-death (POD) bank accounts)

Despite this helpful provision in the EPIC, it's still necessary to follow up after divorce and review or revise many estate planning documents.

Life Insurance and Retirement Benefits

Divorce judgments and the EPIC both revoke an ex-spouse's beneficiary rights in the other's life insurance and retirement benefits. But because of a peculiarity in the law, these revocations aren't always effective (especially for employer-provided life insurance and retirement benefits), making individual revocation necessary. Contact your insurance agent, retirement plan administrator or benefits office at work to make changes. As you make the revocations, it's convenient to name new beneficiaries, such as your children or others.

Power of Attorney

The EPIC revokes appointments of an ex-spouse (and relatives) as agent under two popular kinds of powers of attorney: 1) durable power of attorney (DPA) for financial affairs 2) patient advocate designation (PAD) for health care decision-making, often including the power to terminate life-sustaining treatment.

With both kinds of powers of attorney, revocation of your ex as agent often means promotion of successor agents to first-choice status (frequently, spouses designate each other as first-choice agents, with successors named as back-ups). Nevertheless, it's a good idea to make new powers of attorney with new sets of first-choice and successor agents after divorce.

Trust

Trusts are another popular estate planning devices which come in two varieties: 1) living, or *inter vivos*, trust 2) testamentary trust in a will. The EPIC says that divorce revokes an ex-spouse (and relatives) as beneficiary of a trust and as trustee. Even so, it's still smart to amend the trust and remove your ex from the trust.

Will

Both your divorce judgment and the EPIC revoke rights that your ex (and relatives) have in your will, including: 1) will gifts and other property transfers 2) appointments as personal representative, trustee (of a testamentary trust) or other roles.

But besides these selected will provisions, divorce doesn't touch other parts of a will. The will, minus the provisions benefiting an ex-spouse (and relatives), remains in force. Nevertheless, you should carefully review your will after divorce. The removal of your ex from the will may have upset your scheme of property distribution and appointments. After review, you may decide that your will needs revision or even replacement.

Guardian and Conservator Appointments

After a bitter divorce, divorced parents may want someone besides the other parent to serve as guardian of their minor children if they should die. With this in mind, the parent may hope to use a guardian appointment in a will as a means of taking custody of a child away from the other parent and giving custody to a nonparent third party, such as a new spouse, family member or friend.

What divorced parents often forget is that guardians are only necessary for orphaned children. If one parent survives, s/he automatically gets or keeps custody as the natural guardian of the children (unless the survivor is legally incapacitated). Moreover, the surviving parent can control the future custody of the children by making guardian appointments in a will (since the guardian appointments of the last parent to die prevail).

Divorced parents can still appoint the third parties they want as guardians. But they must realize that these appointments will take effect only if the other parent: 1) is legally incapacitated 2) dies first 3) dies last but didn't make guardian appointments in a will.

> *Example:* Darlene and Dudley went through a bitter divorce. Darlene got custody of their two sons. Darlene would like to deprive Dudley of custody of the boys after her death by naming her brothers as guardians in her will.

> Darlene discovers that Dudley, if he survives her, will get custody of the boys regardless of her will appointments. Thus, Darlene makes a will naming her brothers as the boys' guardians and conservators. She realizes that the guardian appointments will take effect only in the three exceptional situations described above.

Appointing a third party as conservator has a better chance of success. The surviving parent doesn't automatically become conservator, although parents have high priority for appointment. Thus, an appointed third party could possibly vie with the surviving parent for appointment as conservator and win.

More Information

About estate planning, including more information for single parents about naming guardians for minor children after divorce, order *The Michigan Estate Planning Book: A Complete Do-It-Yourself Guide to Planning an Estate in Michigan*, using the order form at the front of this book.

Miscellaneous

You should also remove your ex as beneficiary of pay-on-death (POD) bank accounts, brokerage accounts and bonds. If you hold a safe deposit box jointly with your ex, you should terminate this arrangement. As with other estate planning devices, the EPIC terminates spousal rights in these things, but it's still advisable to do this in fact.

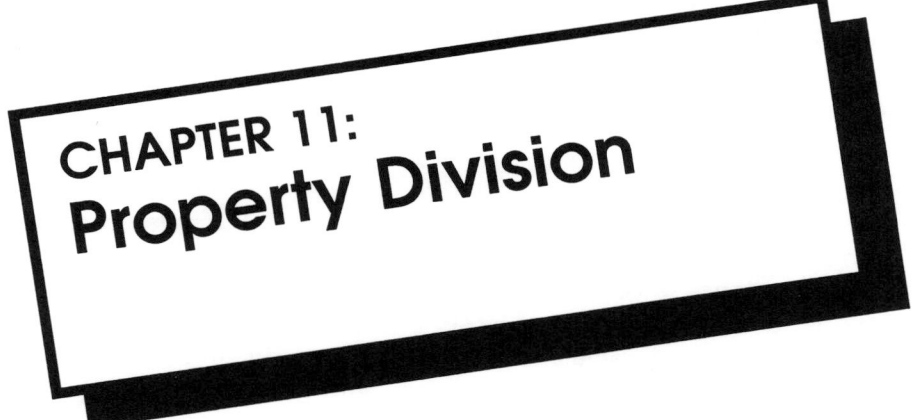

CHAPTER 11:
Property Division

As explained in "Modification" on page 5, the property division of a divorce is final and cannot be modified later, except when the judgment of divorce is defective. However, after divorce the judgment's property division must still be carried out and enforced.

The divorce judgment may have divided property on paper, but the property must actually be transferred between the spouses. For example, one spouse may have been awarded something in the other spouse's possession. This item must be transferred to the spouse designated in the judgment. If the item has a title, showing ownership, this document must also be changed.

Enforcement

Court Enforcement

Courts will always enforce the property divisions of their divorce judgments. Remedies like garnishment, execution (seizure of property) and receivership are available for enforcement. In extreme cases, such as when a party wilfully refuses to transfer property, the court's contempt power can be used for enforcement.

The trouble is, these court enforcement remedies are available only by filing a specialized enforcement motion with the divorce court. Unlike other divorce issues, the friend of the court has no authority to help with enforcement of property divisions. And filing an enforcement motion yourself, without legal guidance, is difficult. Luckily, there are several self-help enforcement remedies available without going to court.

Self-Help Enforcement

Personal property without titles (clothing, household goods, etc.) can be transferred by simply changing possession of the items. But both possession and title must be transferred for personal property with titles (bank accounts, stocks, bonds, motor vehicles, etc.).

You can transfer bank accounts by submitting to the financial institution a copy of the divorce judgment and a letter asking for division of the account. In the letter, you should specify how the account should be divided (by percentage, fractional or dollar shares), and whether the account should be closed/liquidated (and where this money goes) or kept open for one party. Both parties should sign this closing letter and sometimes these signatures must be guaranteed (reviewed by an officer at the financial institution).

You can transfer stocks and bonds by using the transfer procedure described on the back of the stock or bond certificates. Transfer agents, which are usually banks or special transfer companies, but sometimes the stock- or bond-issuing company itself, handle transfer. As with financial accounts, you may have to get signature guarantees when you sign the back of stock or bond certificates during transfer.

> ### To Obtain
>
> A certified copy of your divorce judgment, go to the clerk of the court that granted your divorce.
>
> There is a $10 fee for issuing a certified copy, plus $1 for each page of the document.

Transfer titles to motor vehicles through a secretary of state office by applying for a new title after the current owner has signed off on the back of the old certificate of title. If the owner refuses to cooperate, you can use a certified copy of the judgment of divorce for transfer of title. When you apply for a new title at the secretary of state, submit a certified copy of the judgment and you won't need your ex's signature on the old certificate of title.

Ownership of real property must be transferred by deed. For post-divorce transfers between ex-spouses, a simple form of deed called a quit claim deed is customarily used. Lawyers or real estate brokers can prepare these deeds for a small fee.

If your ex is uncooperative or unavailable for transfer, you can sometimes use the judgment of divorce to transfer ownership of real property yourself. To use the judgment this way, it must describe the property in detail, with a full legal description. You must also have a certified copy of the judgment of divorce for the transfer.

You can transfer Michigan real property by recording a certified copy of the divorce judgment with the register of deeds for the county where the property is located. This transfer method isn't available for out-of-state real property.

Appendix A: Fee Exemption

Appendix B: Case Transfer

Appendix C: Military Relief Laws

Appendix D: Opting Out of the Friend of the Court System

Appendix E: Subpoena

Appendix F: Michigan Child Support Formula Manual

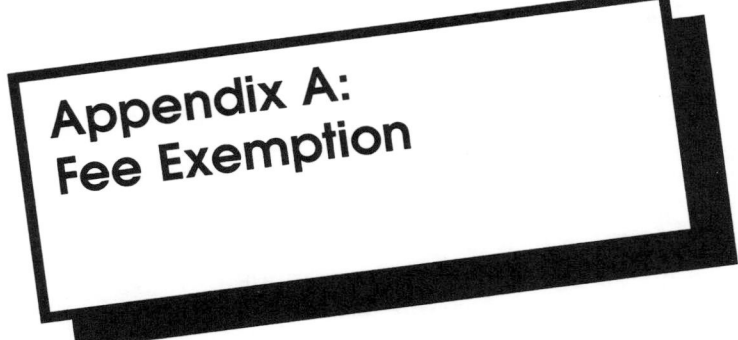

Appendix A: Fee Exemption

Michigan law exempts some poor people from payment of many of the fees and costs of using the legal system. In post-judgment cases, a fee exemption covers most of the fees and costs of the procedures (see "How Much Does Post-Judgment Relief Cost?" on page 14 for a summary of these expenses).

If you qualify for an exemption, you won't have to pay any motion filing fees or the extra fee charged for child support modification motions. If you subpoena witnesses for a motion hearing, and must use a sheriff for service of the subpoenas, the exemption covers the sheriff's service fees, but not the court attendance fees for witnesses. In a name change case, the exemption includes both the filing fee and the cost of publishing the notice of hearing in the newspaper.

Who can qualify for a fee exemption? The court rules say that persons receiving "any form of public assistance" are automatically entitled to a fee exemption. The rules don't define public assistance, but presumably it includes the main means-tested public welfare programs: 1) Family Independence Program (FIP) payments (formerly AFDC) 2) Temporary Assistance for Needy Families (TANF) 3) Supplemental Security Income (SSI) 4) food stamps 5) Medicaid.

In addition, the court rules say that indigent persons may qualify for fee exemptions. Indigent is just another word for poor. In Michigan, judges determine indigency on a case-by-case basis after they have reviewed applicants' financial information (income and assets versus obligations).

Obtaining a Fee Exemption

Fee exemption is normally a two-step procedure: 1) initial suspension of fees when a motion or case is filed 2) final exemption (or payment) of the suspended fees when the motion or case is finally decided by the judge.

To get fees suspended initially, prepare the Affidavit section of the Affidavit and Order, Suspension of Fees/Costs (MC 20), and submit it to the clerk when you file a motion or a name change case. The fee exemption request itself is a kind of motion, for which a motion filing fee would ordinarily be paid. However, the court rules say that no filing fee is due for these requests.

The clerk gives an automatic fee exemption to anyone receiving public assistance. If you claim indigency, the clerk will pass the Affidavit and Order, Suspension of Fees/Costs (MC 20) onto the judge for review. If the judge agrees that you're indigent, s/he will order a fee suspension on the reverse of the MC 20. A denial of your application will be indicated in the same place.

At the hearing on a motion or name change petition, the court will take another look at your financial condition and make a final decision about the fees and costs. The same standards apply then as before; those receiving public assistance get an automatic exemption, while those claiming indigency must cite facts to prove it.

If the judge finds that you cannot pay the suspended fees, s/he will order a final exemption. But if you can now pay, the judge will order payment. If that happens, you should add a fee payment provision to the final order (such as the Order Regarding Custody and Parenting Time (FOC 89), Order Regarding Parenting Time (FOC 67), etc.), like this:

14. <u>Court Fees</u>. Plaintiff shall immediately pay the suspended motion filing fee of [$20] to the court clerk.

Original - Court
1st copy - Applicant

2nd copy - Opposing party
PROBATE OSM CODE: OSF

CASE NO.

Approved, SCAO

STATE OF MICHIGAN
JUDICIAL DISTRICT
JUDICIAL CIRCUIT
COUNTY PROBATE

**AFFIDAVIT AND ORDER
SUSPENSION OF FEES/COSTS**

Court telephone no.

Court address

Plaintiff/Petitioner name, address, and telephone no.

Defendant/Respondent name, address, and telephone no.

v

Plaintiff's/Petitioner's attorney, bar no., address, and telephone no

Defendant's/Respondent's attorney, bar no., address, and telephone no.

☐ Probate   In the matter of _____

NOTE: Requests for waiver/suspension of transcript
costs must be made separately by motion.

[**AFFIDAVIT**]

1. The attached pleading is to be filed with the court by or on behalf of DARLENE LOVELACE
   Name

   applicant, who is   ☒ plaintiff/petitioner.   ☐ defendant/respondent.

2. The applicant is entitled to and asks the court for suspension of fees and costs in the action for the following reason:

   ☒ a. S/he is currently receiving public assistance: $ ____400____ per MONTH Case No. UI336092B

   ☒ b. S/he is unable to pay those fees and costs because of indigency, based on the following facts:

   INCOME: 10,000 PANCAKES, 111 M-78, LAKE CITY, MI 48800
           Employer name and address
   1 YR. $250 $225   per ☒ week. ☐ month. ☐ two weeks.
   Length of employment   Average gross pay   Average net pay

   ASSETS: State value of car, home, bank deposits, bonds, stocks, etc.
            HOUSEHOLD GOODS $1,000
                            CAR $1,000

   OBLIGATIONS: Itemize monthly rent, installment payments, mortgage payments, child support, etc.
                 CAR PAYMENT $75
                 RENT $250
                 FOOD $200

   ☐ 3. (in domestic relations cases only) The applicant is entitled to an order requiring his/her spouse to pay attorney fees.

   REIMBURSEMENT: It is understood that the court may order the applicant to pay the fees and costs when the reason for their
   waiver or suspension no longer exists.

   Darlene Lovelace
   Affiant signature

   Subscribed and sworn to before me on 1-1-99   OJIBWAY   County, Michigan.
                                          Date

   My commission expires: 12-30-99   Signature: Loretta Smiley
                          Date   Deputy clerk/Register/Notary public

   Notary public, State of Michigan, County of OJIBWAY

   (SEE REVERSE SIDE FOR ORDER)

   MCR 2.002

MC 20 (6/04) AFFIDAVIT AND ORDER, SUSPENSION OF FEES/COSTS

COMPLETE #2a IF YOU ARE RECEIVING PUBLIC ASSISTANCE.

COMPLETE #2b. INSTEAD IF YOU ARE CLAIMING INDIGENCY.

PRISONERS CLAIMING INDIGENCY SHOULD CHECK BOX #2b., SKIP REST OF THE SECTION, AND ATTACH CERTIFIED COPY OF THEIR INSTITUTIONAL ACCOUNT FOR PRIOR YEAR.

IF YOU MUST PUBLISH A NOTICE OF HEARING IN A NAME CHANGE CASE, OR USE A SHERIFF TO SERVE A SUBPOENA, EXPLAIN THAT ON A SHEET ATTACHED TO THIS FORM.

CERTIFICATION OF ATTORNEY

1. I have reviewed the affidavit of indigency, and I certify that its contents are true to the best of my information, knowledge, and belief.

2. I will bring to the court's attention the matter of suspended costs and fees and the availability of funds to pay them before any disposition is entered. I will report at that time any changes in the information contained in the affidavit of indigency or any other information regarding the affiant's financial status or alterations of the fee arrangement.

Date _____

Attorney signature _____

Attorney name (type or print) _____

Bar no. _____

CERTIFICATION BY PERSON OTHER THAN PARTY

1. I have personal knowledge of the facts appearing in the affidavit.

2. The person in whose behalf the petition is filed is unable to sign it because of

☐ minority: _____
Date of birth

Relationship: _____   ☐ other disability: _____
                                                                    Nature of disability

Date _____

Affiant signature _____

Affiant name (type or print) _____

Address _____

City, state, zip _____

Telephone no. _____

ORDER

IT IS ORDERED:

☒ 1. Fees and costs in this action required by law or court rule are waived/suspended until further order of the court. Before any final disposition or discontinuance is entered, the moving party shall bring the fee and costs suspension to the attention of the judge for final disposition.

☐ 2. The applicant's spouse shall pay the fees and costs required by law or court rule.

☐ 3. This application is denied.

Date 1-2-99

Judge _Lester Tubbs_   Bar no. _____

(Handwritten note: LEAVE CERTIFICATIONS BLANK.)

(Handwritten note: JUDGE WILL SUSPEND FEES OR DENY FEE SUSPENSION BELOW.)

(Handwritten note: JUDGE WILL DATE AND SIGN.)

Appendix B: Case Transfer

For post-judgment relief, you normally go back to the court granting your divorce (see "Where Do I Go to Enforce or Modify My Divorce Judgment?" on page 8 for more information). But sometimes, you can transfer your divorce case to the Michigan county where you live now and then seek post-judgment relief there. Transfer isn't automatic; you must satisfy several residence requirements and have the correct grounds for transfer:

Residence requirements for transfer. There are several residence requirements for transfer, *all* of which must be satisfied before a case is eligible for transfer:

- both you and your ex must have moved out of the county where the divorce case is now (called the county of current jurisdiction) and resided elsewhere for at least six months
- the Michigan county where you seek transfer (known as the transfer county) isn't directly adjacent to the county of current jurisdiction
- either you or your ex has lived in the transfer county for at least six months before the transfer motion is filed

Grounds for transfer. You can obtain a transfer because of a change of residence and for the convenience of you, your ex and/or your children. The transfer must also be in the best interests of the children.

Stipulated Transfer

You and your ex can stipulate to transfer of the divorce case to another Michigan county. The transfer county could be either where you live or your ex lives, as long as you satisfy the residence requirements described above. Despite your agreement, the court could reject the proposed transfer if it isn't in the best interests of your children.

You don't need to have a court hearing to transfer a case by stipulation. All you have to do is prepare the Motion/Stipulation for Transferring Case (FOC 24) and the Order Changing Venue and Transferring Case (FOC 25), and have the order approved by the court in the county of current jurisdiction. For guidance in preparing the FOC 24 and FOC 25, see the sample forms at the end of this appendix. See also "Stipulated Orders" on page 30 for complete instructions about preparing a stipulated order, getting court approval of the order, filing it with the clerk and serving it on your ex.

Before you submit the stipulated order to the judge, have the friend of the court review the FOC 24 and FOC 25. This review allows the friend of the court to determine whether any past-due child support is owed. If support is overdue, the court of current jurisdiction may make arrangements for payment before giving up control of the case.

After the Order Changing Venue and Transferring Case (FOC 25) has been filed, the clerk in the county of current jurisdiction will transfer the case file to the clerk in the transfer county. The case will be assigned to a family court judge in that county, and you can seek post-judgment relief before the new judge there.

Contested Transfer

When your ex won't stipulate to a case transfer, you must file a motion asking for transfer. Presumably, you will seek transfer to your county, where you must have lived at least six months before you file the transfer motion.

Motion

You can ask for a case transfer in the Motion/Stipulation for Transferring Case (FOC 24). The FOC 24 is a combined stipulation and motion, but in this instance you use it as a motion only. There is a sample FOC 24 at the end of this appendix showing you how to complete the motion. The core of the motion is paragraph #1 describing the eligibility of the case for transfer and the grounds for transfer. Both topics are covered at the beginning of this appendix.

For information and instructions about preparing, filing and serving a motion like this, see "Papers" on page 23 and "Motions" on page 32.

Responding to a Motion

If you receive a motion for transferring a case from your ex, you can respond orally or in writing, in several ways.

If you agree with the motion completely, contact your ex immediately and arrange to stipulate to a transfer. In paragraphs #2, #3, #4 and #5 of the Response to Motion for Transferring Case (GRP 25), you can also indicate your agreement with the motion. But why do extra paperwork when it's easier to stipulate to a modification order? You could also appear at the hearing and agree to the motion, but this too wastes time when stipulation is available. See "Stipulated Transfer" on page 199 for more about stipulations.

Sometimes, you may agree with part of the motion and disagree with the rest. It's important to signal your partial agreement as soon as possible because this narrows the issues in the case. If you file a Response to Motion for Transferring Case (GRP 25), check box #4b and describe the extent of your agreement with the motion in the space below. If you choose to respond orally, mention your partial agreement to the mediator, referee or judge, so the agreed-upon issues can be eliminated from the hearing.

When you oppose the motion, you can voice your disagreement in two ways. You can file a written response to the motion or wait until the hearing on the motion and respond orally. A written response is usually better, because it gets your views across more effectively.

Use the Response to Motion for Transferring Case (GRP 25) for a written response. In paragraphs #2 and #3, say why you oppose the motion. In paragraph #2, you can argue that the case is ineligible for transfer by showing that the residence requirements for transfer haven't been satisfied. Or you could dispute that the proposed transfer is more convenient for the parties or in the best interests of the children, in paragraph #3.

For complete information and instructions about preparing, filing and serving a response, see "Responding to a Motion" on page 35.

You can also respond to a motion by making a counter-motion. Normally, if you oppose the motion with the Response to Motion for Transferring Case (GRP 25), you disagree with the elibibility and/or grounds for the motion in paragraphs #2 and #3. Then, in paragraph #5 you oppose the proposed transfer, as in the sample response at the end of this chapter.

But if you want a different kind of case transfer, check box #5b and explain in the space below what you want. For example, you may want to transfer the case to the county where you live, instead of the county where the moving party seeks transfer. Whether you realize it or not, this request is a counter-motion.

In some cases, it's even possible to ask for completely new relief in a counter-motion. Add new issues carefully, because these can easily sidetrack the case. Nevertheless, it may make sense to seek new relief in a counter-motion when the new issues are compatible with the main motion.

For more about counter-motion tactics and how to counter-move for new relief, see "Making a Counter-Motion" on page 37.

Friend of the Court

Before a post-judgment motion goes to the judge, the friend of the court may intervene to mediate, investigate or referee, in an attempt to settle the dispute. See "Friend of the Court" on page 38 for more about the friend of the court's roles in post-judgment cases, and how to deal with mediation, investigation or refereeing by the friend of the court.

For a case transfer, which is a minor issue, it's doubtful that the motion would be sent to mediation or refereeing. But the friend of the court will probably do an investigation, to determine if child support is past due, and file a report. If support is overdue, the court of current jurisdiction may make arrangements for payment before giving up control of the case.

Motion Hearing

As explained in "Motion Hearings" on page 41, there are two kinds of motion hearings: 1) nonevidentiary hearing where facts aren't in dispute, evidence is seldom introduced and the parties merely make legal arguments to the judge 2) evidentiary hearing where facts are disputed and evidence, such as testimony from witnesses, must be introduced to establish the true facts.

A case transfer motion normally requires a nonevidentiary hearing, because the basic facts are fixed and the issues concern reasons for the proposed transfer.

During the motion hearing, the moving party must first establish the residence requirements for transfer, making the case eligible for transfer. Then, the moving party must show that: 1) transferring the case will be more convenient for the parties and children 2) transfer is in the best interests of the children (see page 61 for a list and explanation of the best-interest factors).

The other party can oppose the transfer by showing that the residence requirements for transfer haven't been satisfied. Or s/he can argue that keeping the case in the court of current jurisdiction is more convenient for everyone and in the best interests of the children. See "Motion Hearings" on page 41 for information about preparing for and appearing at a nonevidentiary hearing.

Court Order

After the court hearing, the judge will decide the motion. The judge will either decide immediately and give an oral decision "from the bench," or take the case "under submission" and rule later by issuing a written decision.

Either way, the moving party must prepare the order granting or denying the motion. Use the Order Changing Venue and Transferring Case (FOC 25) as the order. A sample FOC 25 appears at the end of this appendix. See also "Court Orders" on page 44 for complete information about preparing, filing and serving an order like this.

After the FOC 25 has been filed, the clerk in the county of current jurisdiction will transfer the case file to the clerk in the transfer county. The case will be assigned to a family court judge in that county, and you can seek post-judgment relief before the new judge there.

Original - Originating court
1st copy - Receiving court
2nd copy - Friend of the court

3rd copy - Plaintiff
4th copy - Defendant

Approved, SCAO

**STATE OF MICHIGAN
JUDICIAL CIRCUIT
COUNTY**

**MOTION/STIPULATION
FOR TRANSFERRING CASE
(Post Judgment)**

CASE NO.

Court telephone no.

Court address

Plaintiff's name, address, and telephone no.

v

Defendant's name, address, and telephone no.

☒ **MOTION** ☐ **STIPULATION**

☒ 1. I, ☒ the plaintiff, ☐ the defendant, ☐ the court-ordered custodian, request transfer of this case to

SUPERIOR _____ County.

a. This transfer is requested on the basis of residence and for the convenience of the parties and is in the best interests of the minor child(ren).
b. All parties have resided in counties other than the county of current jurisdiction for more than six months.

DARLENE LOVELACE _____ has resided in the county to which the transfer is
Name of plaintiff/~~defendant~~

requested for at least six months.
d. The county to which the transfer is requested is not adjacent to the county of current jurisdiction.

☐ We stipulate to the transfer of this case.
☐ 2. I, the friend of the court, request transfer of this case to _____ County for the following reasons:

> IF YOU AGREE ON CASE TRANSFER AND WANT TO STIPULATE TO IT, CHECK THIS BOX AND STIPULATION BOX JUST BELOW CAPTION. THEN, PREPARE FOC 25 AND PRESENT TO THE JUDGE AS EXPLAINED IN "STIPULATED ORDERS" IN CHAPTER 1C.

I declare that the statements above are true to the best of my information, knowledge, and belief.

1-1-99 _____
Date

Darlene Lovelace
Signature
DARLENE LOVELACE _____
Name and title (type or print)

_____
Signature

_____
Name and title (type or print)

_____
Name and title (type or print)

NOTICE OF HEARING

A hearing will be held on the above motion on 2-15-99 at 9:00 AM at the above court address.
Date   Time

If you require special accommodations to use the court because of a disability, please contact the court immediately to make arrangements.

CERTIFICATE OF MAILING

I certify that on this date I mailed a copy of this motion and notice of hearing on the other party by ordinary mail addressed to his/her last known address.

1-1-99 _____
Date

Darlene Lovelace
Signature

MCR 3.21

FOC 24 (6/98) **MOTION/STIPULATION FOR TRANSFERRING CASE (Post Judgment)**

STATE OF MICHIGAN
Circuit Court - Family Division
COUNTY

RESPONSE TO MOTION
FOR TRANSFERRING CASE

CASE NO.

Plaintiff: ☐ moving party

Defendant: ☐ moving party

v

1. A motion has been filed for transfer of this case to another county in Michigan.

2. I ☐ agree ☒ do not agree   that this case is eligible for transfer.
I LIVED IN THE COUNTY OF CURRENT JURISDICTION AS RECENTLY AS
THREE MONTHS AGO, SO BOTH PARENTS HAVE NOT BEEN ABSENT
FROM THAT COUNTY FOR AT LEAST SIX MONTHS AS REQUIRED BY
THE CASE TRANSFER RULES.

3. I ☐ agree ☒ do not agree   that proper cause exists for transfer.
TRANSFER OF THIS CASE TO SUPERIOR COUNTY, WHICH IS OVER 400
MILES FROM COUNTY OF CURRENT JURISDICTION, NEAR WHERE
I NOW LIVE, WILL MAKE IT DIFFICULT FOR ME TO FILE OR RESPOND
TO POST-JUDGMENT MOTIONS IN THIS CASE.

☐ 4. I agreed with the other party for transfer of this case to another county.
  ☐ a. exactly as stated in the motion.
  ☐ b. but not as stated in the motion. (Describe agreement)

SEVERAL
PARAGRAPHS TEST
WHETHER YOU AGREE
WITH MODIFICATION.
IF YOU AGREE,
COMPLETELY OR IN PART,
SEE "RESPONDING TO A
MOTION" IN THIS
CHAPTER ABOUT YOUR
RESPONSE OPTIONS.

YOU CAN MAKE A
COUNTER-MOTION IN THIS
PARAGRAPH. SEE "RESPONDING
TO A MOTION" IN THIS CHAPTER
FOR MORE ABOUT COUNTER-
MOTIONS.

5. ☐ a. I agree with what is being asked for in the motion.
  ☒ b. I do not agree with what is being asked for in the motion and ask the court t̶̶̶̶̶̶̶̶̶̶̶
  regarding case transfer as follows:
  DENY PLAINTIFF'S MOTION FOR CASE TRANSFER, LEAVING CASE
  WHERE IT IS NOW.

I declare that the above statements are true to the best of my information, knowledge and belief.

Date ___2-1-99___

Responding party _Dudley Lovelace_

CERTIFICATE OF MAILING

I certify that on this date I mailed a copy of this reponse to the other party(ies) by ordinary mail at the
above address(es).

Date ___2-1-99___

Responding party _Dudley Lovelace_

GRP 25 (9/04)   **RESPONSE TO MOTION FOR TRANSFERRING CASE**

Original - Originating court
1st copy - Receiving court
2nd copy - Friend of the court

3rd copy - Plaintiff
4th copy - Defendant

Approved, SCAO

CASE NO.

**STATE OF MICHIGAN
JUDICIAL CIRCUIT
COUNTY**

**ORDER CHANGING VENUE AND
TRANSFERRING CASE
(Post Judgment)**

Court telephone no.

Court address

Plaintiff's name and address

CERTIFICATE OF ARREARAGE

1. I certify that as of _____
   Date

the arrears on the records of the friend of the court

were $ _____ .

v

Defendant's name and address

Friend of the court

ORDER

2. Date of hearing: __2-15-99__ Judge: __LESTER TUBBS__ Bar no.

3. **THE COURT FINDS** that there are arrearages in the amount of $ _____ as certified above by the friend of the court.

IT IS ORDERED:

4. Venue is changed and this case shall be transferred to __SUPERIOR COUNTY__

   by __3-1-99__ .
   Date

☐ 5. Before the date of transfer _____ shall pay to the court of current
   Name

   jurisdiction all past due fees and costs in the amount of $ _____ .

6. ☐ a. ☐ Plaintiff ☐ Defendant ☐ Both parties equally _____ shall pay the statutory filing fee to the court of current
   jurisdiction before the date of transfer. The court of current jurisdiction shall submit the filing fee to the court to which
   the case is transferred. The case shall not be transferred until the fee is paid.

   ☐ b. The statutory filing fee is waived because ☐ the transfer was initiated by the court or friend of the court.
   ☐ the parties are indigent.

☐ 7. The transferring office of the friend of the court and/or the Michigan State Disbursement Unit shall continue to process support
   payments under the current support order until it receives notice that the case has been accepted for filing by the transferee
   office of the friend of the court. Any payments received during this interim period shall be credited to the payer's account.

__2-15-99__
Date

__Lester Tubbs__
Judge

MCR 3.212

FOC 25 (10/04) **ORDER CHANGING VENUE AND TRANSFERRING CASE (Post Judgment)**

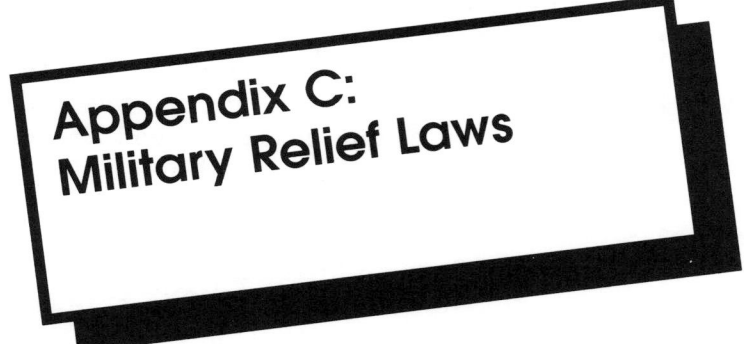

Appendix C: Military Relief Laws

You may have encountered the military relief laws protecting servicemembers from lawsuits during your divorce if a spouse was in active-duty military service then. Or the issue may be new and unfamiliar if you or your ex enlisted after the divorce.

Either way, you should know that there are actually two laws giving servicemembers relief from lawsuits: the federal Servicemembers Civil Relief Act (SCRA) and a similar Michigan relief law. These laws were really designed for ongoing lawsuits, such as pre-judgment divorce. But their protections have been extended to post-judgment divorce proceedings.

Federal Servicemembers Civil Relief Act (SCRA)

The SCRA, which has the widest scope, covers servicemembers in the active duty of the U.S. military (see the sidebox on the next page for which personnel are covered by the act). The SCRA offers several forms of relief to servicemembers protecting them from some kinds of debts, taxes, installment contracts, lawsuits, etc. The intent of the SCRA is to protect servicemembers from these obligations so they can focus on their military duties.

It's the lawsuit relief protections of the SCRA that have an impact on divorce. In essence, these protections shield servicemembers from hard-to-handle lawsuits, including divorces. The SCRA has a special section dealing with post-judgment cases, and provides a remedy, called a stay, against unfair enforcement or modification of judgments.

A stay is a freeze of a lawsuit, stopping the case until a later date. When the remedy is correctly invoked, a court must grant a stay if the

More Information

(1) The SCRA covers all five service branches of the U. S. military:

- **Army**
- **Navy**
- **Marine Corps**
- **Air Force**
- **Coast Guard**

The act also covers commissioned officers in the Public Health Service and the National Oceanic and Atmospheric Administration.

The SCRA protects servicemembers in the *active duty* of the U.S. military which are made up of two components:

Active component. Members of regular units (Regular Army, Regular Navy, etc.).

Reserve component. Servicemembers *activated* from the two segments of the military reserve:

- *Reserves*. Each service branch has its own reserve units (Army Reserve (Army), Naval Reserve (Navy), etc.), which are always under federal command.

- *National Guard*. State Army National Guard (attached to the Army) and Air National Guard (attached to the Air Force) units, including Michigan's army and air units.
  National Guard units fall under state control, unless they have been called to federal active duty by the president. After 30 consecutive days of federal service, guardmembers are protected by the SCRA.

The SCRA protects servicemembers lawfully away from active duty, such as during a period of leave or hospitalization. The act also covers military inductees (after receiving induction orders). The act doesn't apply to civilians working for the military.

(2) Michigan's military relief law covers members in Michigan's two National Guard units:

- **Army National Guard**
- **Air National Guard**

The law protects guardmembers in *active duty* for more than seven days after activation by the governor: 1) to support civilian authority (such as during a riot, flood, etc.) 2) for a war or emergency of the state or nation.

The protections of the law extend beyond the period of active duty for some things, but not for lawsuit relief which is the focus here.

Note: Other states have similar military relief laws protecting their National Guardmembers, which could be an issue if a party is in the active duty of an out-of-state unit.

servicemember's ability to comply with the judgment is "materially affected" by military service. The length of the stay is up to the court, but it can last no more than 90 days beyond the end of military service. Typically, a stay will last only until the servicemember can get leave so s/he can deal with the lawsuit.

During wartime, SCRA stays can be expanded by Congress to freeze *all* lawsuits against protected servicemembers. This happened during the 1990-91 Persian Gulf War, and could happen again in a future conflict.

Michigan's Military Relief Law

Many people don't know it, but Michigan has a military relief law similar to the federal SCRA. The state law covers Michigan National Guardmembers in active duty (see the sidebox for the scope of coverage). Like the federal law, Michigan's law offers protection from some debt collection, foreclosures, utility shutoffs and lawsuits.

Unlike the SCRA, Michigan's relief law offers absolute protection from lawsuits without regard to hardship for the servicemember. After a seven-day activation of guardmembers, Michigan's law effectively freezes lawsuits against them until termination of their active-duty service for the state.

Post-Judgment Motions and the Military Relief Laws

Soon after filing the moving party often faces a practical problem of serving the papers on the servicemember. The servicemember must decide whether to invoke the SCRA, and the moving party must respond to this decision.

Serving Papers on Servicemembers

When you seek post-judgment relief against a servicemember, you must know your ex's mailing address (APO (American post office) or FPO (foreign post office)), so the post-judgment papers can be served on him/her. This can be difficult if your ex has been transferred frequently or is stationed at a faraway military base.

Divorced parties are supposed to keep the friend of the court informed of all changes of address within 21 days of moving. Contact the friend of the court first and see if your ex has filed a change of address. Or the friend of the court may able to find the new address by using the parent locator services or other means. If not, the friend of the court has the authority to establish the address of a transient servicemember (see "Where to Serve" on page 28 for when and how the friend of the court does this).

After you find your ex's mailing address, you can serve the post-judgment papers by mail, because the U.S. Postal Service delivers to all military bases worldwide. Military mail can be slow with delivery taking several weeks instead of several days, so allow extra time for service when you schedule hearings. See "Serving Papers" on page 27 for more about service by mail, including making and filing a proof of service.

> ## More Information
>
> For advice about options under the military relief laws, servicemembers should consult a military legal assistance lawyer. Most large military bases have a judge advocate general's legal office staffed with these military legal assistance or so-called judge advocate general (JAG) lawyers.
>
> Typically, military legal assistance lawyers only advise; they don't provide direct in-court legal representation. For this, they may recommend a civilian lawyer.

Satisying the Military Relief Laws

After receiving a post-judgment motion, a servicemember has several options for responding: 1) waiver of military relief law protections 2) requesting a stay under the SCRA 3) no response. Once the servicemember chooses, the civilian moving party must bring the motion forward while complying with the military relief laws.

Waiver of Military Relief Law Rights

As with other legal rights, a servicemember can voluntarily waive (give up) his/her lawsuit relief rights provided by the military relief laws. The waiver cuts off these rights, allowing the motion to go ahead normally.

Waiver is the only way to satisfy Michigan's military relief law and the SCRA when it has imposed a temporary-but-total wartime freeze on lawsuits. But even if the SCRA applies in its flexible peacetime form, waiver always makes it easier for the motion to proceed.

If the servicemember is willing to waive, s/he should sign a waiver form. The Waiver of Military Relief Law Rights (GRP 27) is provided in this book for that purpose. After signing, the servicemember should return the waiver form to the moving party. The moving party should file the waiver form with the clerk and bring it to the attention of the referee or judge at the referee or motion hearing.

Servicemember Requests a SCRA Stay

After receiving a motion, the servicemember might contact the court and request a stay under the SCRA. The servicemember may ask for this personally, with the help of a military legal assistance lawyer or through a civilian lawyer.

A stay request may be informal, such as a letter from the servicemember to the court, or a formal request. The Request for Stay under the Servicemembers Civil Relief Act (GRP 28) in this book is available for a formal request.

In considering a request for a stay, the judge must determine if the servicemember's military service has a material effect on his/her ability to comply with the divorce judgment. Courts have defined material effect in terms of two main factors:

Geographical distance. This is probably the most important factor. If the servicemember is at sea or stationed overseas, a good argument can be made that military service is hindering the servicemember in the post-judgment case. On the other hand, leave can cancel distance, since the servicemember can often use the leave to return home and participate in the case. Thus, the availability of leave is often the deciding issue for a stay request. It's also important for determining the length of the stay, if one is issued.

Financial hardship. Courts want to know if military service has caused a financial hardship for the servicemember, which has impaired the ability to respond and comply. This typically isn't as much an issue for career servicemembers as it is for activated reservists or recent enlistees, since they may have suffered a loss of income after activation or enlistment.

Sometimes, the servicemember or his/her lawyer will include facts about distance (including availability of leave) and hardship in the stay request (the GRP 28 contains both items). Other times, the stay request may be brief, with few facts. If the facts are sketchy, the court may not have enough information to rule on the request. You can step in and ask the servicemember for the necessary information, including:

- When does your present enlistment expire?
- When do you expect to be released from active duty?
- When are you due to be transferred from you present duty station?
- Do you know where you will be assigned after you complete your current tour of duty?
- What ordinary or emergency leave do you have available?
- Describe any efforts you have made to obtain leave to participate in this case.
- If you joined active-duty service during the prior two years, what is the difference between your pre-service and in-service annual income?

You can ask for this information in an informal letter to the servicemember or his/her lawyer. If the member won't respond, you can ask for the information from the servicemember's commanding officer. It's customary to start with his/her immediate commander and then work up the chain of command until you get a response. Any response received should be filed with the clerk and brought to the attention of the judge if a stay becomes an issue.

Although courts are inclined toward granting SCRA stays, they have ruled that servicemembers cannot use the act as an excuse to avoid judgment obligations. The military is especially concerned about servicemembers' payment of child support and alimony. The military provides extra housing and living allowances to personnel for support of dependents, which servicemembers without dependents don't get. So when servicemembers renege on support, they are cheating both their dependents and the government paying the extra support allowances.

> ## More Information
>
> About an involuntary allotment, contact the Defense Finance and Accounting Service (DFAS):
>
> **DFAS-DE/FRB**
> 6760 E. Irvington Place
> Denver, CO 80279
> (800) 435-3396
> www.dfas.mil

After a record of nonsupport is established, the servicemember's commanding officer can ask or order the member to pay the support. Failure to obey can result in discipline, including even court martial or discharge. Or the military can make an involuntary allotment from the servicemember's pay. An allotment can be set up through the Department of Defense's financial center, DFAS.

If the court grants the servicemember's stay request, the stay will merely delay the motion, not end it. The court should grant the stay only until the servicemember has time to deal with the motion. This could be until the next period of leave or when the servicemember leaves the service, if separation is imminent. You can wait until the stay expires and then resume the motion where you left off. If the stay is long, you may want to withdraw the motion and refile it after the stay expires.

No Response

A servicemember might not respond to the motion. The servicemember may neglect or refuse to respond. Or s/he may have good reasons for not responding, such has absence aboard a ship or service in combat.

Either way, the court must decide how to protect the servicemember. The court could issue a stay on its own, which is something the SCRA allows, after deciding that the grounds for a stay (geographical distance and financial hardship) exist. Or the court could let the motion go forward, if it believes the servicemember can comply with the judgment.

STATE OF MICHIGAN Circuit Court - Family Division COUNTY	WAIVER OF MILITARY RELIEF LAW RIGHTS	CASE NO.

Plaintiff: ☐ moving party

v

Defendant: ☐ moving party

1. On __1-1-99__, the moving party filed a motion for __INCREASE OF CHILD SUPPORT__

2. I am in active-duty military service currently assigned to:
   THE 333RD MILITARY POLICE COMPANY, MICHIGAN ARMY NATIONAL GUARD

3. I waive the following military relief law rights and protections available to me during the motion cited above:

   ☒ a. judgment-stay protections provided by sec. 524 of the federal Servicemembers Civil Relief Act (50 USC App. 501 et seq.).

   ☒ b. general lawsuit relief provided by Michigan's military relief law (MCL 32.517) or a similar military relief law from another state.

Nonmoving party _Dudley Lovelace_

Date __1-15-99__

GRP 27 (9/04)   WAIVER OF MILITARY RELIEF LAW RIGHTS

STATE OF MICHIGAN Circuit Court - Family Division COUNTY	REQUEST FOR STAY UNDER THE SERVICEMEMBERS CIVIL RELIEF ACT	CASE NO.

Plaintiff: ☐ moving party

v

Defendant: ☐ moving party

1. Following the parties' divorce, the moving party has filed a motion for _INCREASE OF CHILD SUPPORT_ and a hearing before a judge/~~referee~~ has been scheduled for _2-15-99_

2. I am in active-duty military service and am currently assigned to _THE 333RD MILITARY POLICE_ at _FORT CARSON, COLORADO SPRINGS, CO_ _CO., MICHIGAN ARMY NATIONAL GUARD_ I expect to remain at that duty station until _7-1-99_ , followed by reassignment to this unit and unit location (if known) _UNKNOWN_

My current enlistment expires on _12-1-99_

3. My military service has materially affected my ability to comply with post-judgment motion requirements, particularly attendance at the motion hearing, for these reasons:

☒ A. Geographical distance:

1. My current duty station is distant from the court in this case preventing my attendance at the hearing without leave.

2. I have tried to obtain ordinary or emergency leave to attend the hearing but: _MY REQUESTS FOR LEAVE WERE DENIED BECAUSE. I'M SCHEDULED FOR SPECIAL TRAINING FOLLOWED BY COMPANY FIELD EXERCISES UNTIL JUNE 1999, WITH LEAVE POSSIBLE THEN._

DESCRIBE (UN)AVAILABILITY OF LEAVE.

☒ B. Financial hardship:

1. My pre-enlistment annual income was _$15,600_ and my in-service annual income is _$14,000_ and the loss of income makes it difficult to afford a local nonmilitary lawyer in Michigan to represent me in this matter.

4. **I request a stay of the motion** under sec. 524 of the Servicemembers Civil Relief Act until:
☒ date: _7-1-99_ ☐ duration of my military service ☐ duration of my military service plus 90 days.

I declare that the above statements are true to the best of my information, knowledge and belief.

Date _1-15-99_

Nonmoving party _Dudley Lovelace_

CERTIFICATE OF MAILING

I certify that on this date I mailed a copy of this request to the other party(ies) by ordinary mail at the above address(es).

Date _1-15-99_

Nonmoving party _Dudley Lovelace_

TO THE CLERK OF THE COURT:

Please notify me about whether this request is granted or denied.

GRP 28 (9/04) REQUEST FOR STAY UNDER THE SERVICEMEMBERS CIVIL RELIEF ACT

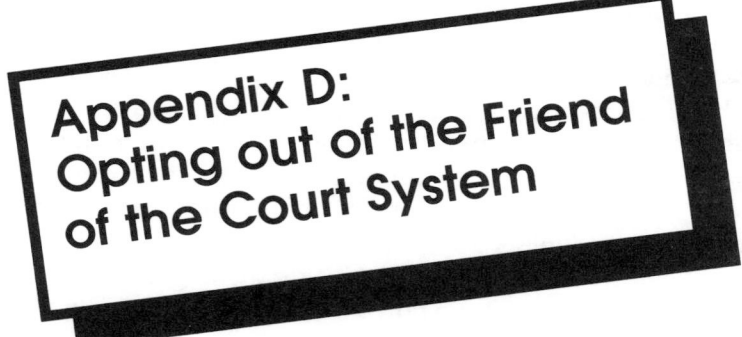

Appendix D:
Opting out of the Friend
of the Court System

The friend of the court has been a part of Michigan family law since 1919. The office provides a number of services in divorce cases, including investigation and recommendation to the judge on divorce issues, refereeing and mediation of disputes, and review, modification and enforcement of orders. All in all, the friend of the court has served the state and divorce families well over the years.

But recently, cracks in the friend of the court system have developed. In 2001, a major *Detroit News* investigation found that many county friends of the court were struggling with a backlog of cases and provided poor service. The next year, Michigan lawmakers tried to improve the system, passing a package of laws reforming friend of the court operations.

In the biggest break from the past, a new law allows divorce parties to "opt out" of the friend of the court system. Lawmakers had found that more than a half of divorce cases go smoothly, with parents meeting all obligations. They decided to remove some of these cases from the system, letting the friend of the court concentrate on problem cases.

In fact, the opt-out law, which is explained below, is a good deal more complicated than that. There are several types of opt-outs. And there are many restrictions on opting out and automatic triggers for bringing cases back under friend of the court control.

Is it worth considering an opt-out? Supporters of the opt-out law say that friend of the court intervention in a divorce isn't necessary if the spouses are cooperative. Opponents of the law argue that threat of friend of the court enforcement makes parents more agreeable, and without this leverage there will be more disputes during divorce and judgment violations afterward.

There is such a thing as an amicable divorce and parents often cooperate during and after divorce. However, the friend of the court performs several valuable functions, which shouldn't be underestimated. More than anything, the friend of the court is supposed to be an honest broker amid divorce. If there's a dispute over something, it has record of what went wrong; otherwise, it's one parent's word against the other. In particular, the friend of the court performs an important bookkeeping function, keeping track of support payments (support and parenting time are the source of most post-judgment violations).

Maybe the best approach is to stay inside the friend of the court system for a while after divorce and see how you like it. If you don't, you can then see about opting out. Or if you decide to opt out, consider either a partial or limited opt-out, instead of a total one.

Opting Back into the Friend of the Court System

It's also permissible to opt back into the friend of the court system. You may have opted out of the system at some point and now want back in. All you have to do is file the Request to Reopen Friend of the Court Case (FOC 104) (you must also attach a Verified Statement and Application for IV-D Services (FOC 23), which you can get from the friend of the court); no motion is necessary for this relief.

Types of Opt-Outs

The 2002 opt-out law allows several kinds of opt-outs from the friend of the court system:

- *total* opt-out from all friend of the court services
- *partial* opt-out from all friend of the court services except collection and distribution of support through the state disbursement unit (SDU) (with or without immediate income withholding as the method of payment)
- *limited* opt-out from immediate income withholding only, but receipt of all other friend of the court services

Total Opt-Out

In some cases, you can opt out of the friend of the court system completely, giving up all friend of the court services in your case. The friend of the court will then close its file for your case and withdraw from it. Afterward, you are responsible for all future management of your case, including payment of support (you lose SDU-payment of support with a total opt-out).

You must have the consent of your ex to get (and keep) a total opt-out. And the judge must review and approve your opt-out request. Even with this approval, not every case is eligible for total opt-out. The 2002 law puts several restrictions on opt-outs, barring total opt-out when:

- a party objects to opting out
- a party is eligible to receive FIA services (also known as title IV-D services) because the party receives public assistance
- a party is eligible to receive FIA services because the party received public assistance and an arrearage is owed to the state
- no support arrearage or custody or parenting time order violation has occurred during the last 12 months
- neither party has reopened a friend of the court case during the last 12 months
- there is evidence of: 1) domestic violence, or 2) uneven bargaining position between the parties; and evidence that a party is opting out against the best interests of that party or the children

A total opt-out must have the consent of your ex. As a result, you cannot obtain the opt-out by filing a contested motion; you must proceed by stipulation instead.

Ordinarily for a stipulation, you can simply consent (stipulate) to an order and no motion is necessary. A total or partial opt-out is different. The 2002 opt-out law requires an (uncontested) motion for these types of opt-outs. So a special combined motion/stipulation form is provided in this book to get the opt-out order. Opt-outs require several other forms. In all, you need the following forms and two copies of each form:

- Motion/Stipulation to Opt Out of the Friend of the Court System (GRP 26)
- Advice of Rights Regarding Use of Friend of the Court Services (FOC 101)
- Order Exempting Case from Friend of the Court Services (FOC 102)

The GRP 26 is the motion/stipulation to opt out. Just below the caption, check both boxes indicating that it's both a motion and stipulation. In paragraph #1, select the opt-out you want: #1a for a total opt-out, #1b for a partial opt-out and #1c for a limited opt-out. Both you and your ex must date and sign this form.

The FOC 101 warns you which services you lose by opting out. You and your ex must receive separate copies of the FOC 101, and both of you must date and sign the original form, which should be attached to the original GRP 26 and filed with the court.

The FOC 102 is the actual opt-out order. You select a total opt-out by leaving the boxes at paragraph #13a and b unchecked. The sample form shows you how to make this choice.

You may be stipulating to an opt-out only, or doing it while you are stipulating to another order (custody, parenting time, etc.). Either way, all you have to do is present the opt-out papers listed above to the judge, like other stipulations. See "Stipulated Orders" on page 30 for complete instructions about preparing a stipulated order, getting court approval of the order, filing it with the clerk and serving it on your ex.

After opting out, the friend of the court won't help with any post-judgment enforcement or modification. As a result, disregard all references in the other sections of this book to the friend of the court's receiving papers, investigating, recommending, refereeing, mediating or reviewing orders.

But later, if you want the friend of the court back in your case, just file the Request to Reopen Friend of the Court Case (FOC 104). The friend of the court will also re-enter the case automatically if: 1) either party requests friend of the court services 2) a party applies for public assistance.

Partial Opt-Out

Ordinarily, when you opt-out totally from the friend of the court system you give up all friend of the court services, including payment of support (child support and/or alimony) through the SDU. (See "Court System" on page 21 for more about SDU operations.) SDU-payment is an efficient means of collecting and distributing support, and not everyone opting out wants to lose this.

Luckily, the 2002 opt-out law allows partial opt-outs: You give up all friend of the court services except payment of support to the SDU. If you choose this option, you also have two subchoices: 1) SDU-payment by immediate income withholding 2) SDU-payment without immediate income withholding and payment from the payer directly to the SDU.

More Information
Ordinarily, the friend of the court helps set up payment of support to the SDU. If you opt out, the friend of the court won't do this and you have to contact the SDU yourself.
You can call the SDU at (866) 540-0008 or use its Web site: www.mi-sdu.com
The SDU will help you set up (or continue) immediate income withholding, if you chose that option, or issue a payment coupon book to the payer if you've selected direct payment to the SDU.

A partial opt-out is a lot like a total opt-out (they're really just different choices in the Order Exempting Case from Friend of the Court Services (FOC 102)), and they share similar procedures. And the same six restrictions (party's objection, eligibility for FIA services, etc.) apply. See "Total Opt-Out" on page 216 for more about these procedures and restrictions.

There is a difference in the paperwork. In the Motion/Stipulation to Opt Out of the Friend of the Court System (GRP 26), check paragraph #1b for a partial opt-out. Inside that paragraph, check the box describing the other method of payment (immediate income withholding or direct payment to the SDU) you want.

As you prepare the Order Exempting Case from Friend of the Court Services (FOC 102), pay close attention to paragraph #13 (unused in a total opt-out). This is where a partial opt-out occurs.

Having opted out of the friend of the court system, you, in essence, opt back in for SDU-payment. By checking the first box, #13a, you get SDU-payment by immediate income withholding. With choice #13b, you elect payment from the payer to the SDU, without immediate income withholding.

Limited Opt-Out

You may be happy with the friend of the court's services for custody, parenting time and support; all you want is a different method of support (child support and/or alimony) payment. The law allows you to opt out of immediate income withholding only, which is the normal means of paying support, and choose another payment method. Other payment options include: 1) payment to the SDU directly 2) direct payment to the support recipient.

After a limited opt-out, you will have access to the usual friend of the court services. You may or may not have SDU-collection and -distribution of support. But either way, the friend of the court will monitor payments and enforce support obligations, including health care coverage.

There are two ways to avoid immediate income withholding through a limited opt-out: 1) by agreement between you and your ex 2) for "good cause," without the consent of your ex. Either kind requires court approval.

As with total and partial opt-outs, there are some restrictions, although fewer ones, on limited opt-outs. You can't opt out for good cause if: 1) it's in the best interests of the children to have immediate income withholding 2) support is already past due.

An agreed-to limited opt-out is similar to a stipulation, while a for-cause limited opt-out resembles a contested motion. These procedures are described below.

Limited Opt-Out by Agreement

You don't need to file a motion or have a court hearing to get a limited opt-out by agreement. But you must prepare two opt-out papers and make three copes of each (the friend of the court, which remains in the case, gets one set of copies):

- Agreement Suspending Immediate Income Withholding (FOC 63)
- Order Suspending Immediate Income Withholding (FOC 64)

In an agreed-to opt-out, both you and your ex must sign the FOC 63. Indicate the alternate method of payment you want in paragraph #2 of that form. The FOC 64, which is the actual limited opt-out order, is used in both agreed-to and for-cause limited opt-outs. The sample FOC 64 shows you how to make the correct choice.

See "Stipulated Orders" on page 30 for complete information about preparing an order like the FOC 64, getting court approval of the order, filing it with the clerk and serving it on your ex.

Limited Opt-Out for Good Cause

If your ex won't agree to a limited opt-out, you must file a motion asking for the change. You could add this request to a motion for modification of the amount of child support. By combining both motions, you could use one motion hearing and pay one motion fee. Or you could seek the opt-out separately, without touching the amount of child support.

Motion

You can move for a limited opt-out in the Motion/Stipulation to Opt Out of the Friend of the Court System (GRP 26). Check paragraph #1c for a limited opt-out, and a box inside the paragraph describing the other method of payment you want (payment to the SDU or payment to the recipient).

Paragraph #3 describes the good cause for the opt out. Good cause is made up of two factors: 1) it's in the best interests of the children to avoid immediate income withholding 2) support has always been paid on time. Typically, the best interests of the children are served when something makes immediate income withholding difficult. For example, the payer may now have an irregular income, from self-employment or unemployment, making immediate income withholding impractical or impossible. Good cause also means that support has been paid when due.

For information and instructions about preparing, filing and serving a motion like this, see "Papers" on page 23 and "Motions" on page 32.

Responding to a Motion

If you receive a motion for a limited opt-out, you can respond orally or in writing, in several ways.

If you agree with the motion completely, contact your ex immediately and arrange to stipulate to the modification in the Agreement Suspending Immediate Income Withholding (FOC 63) and Order Suspending Immediate Income Withholding (FOC 64). Stipulation this way is more efficient than showing your agreement to the motion in the Response to Motion Regarding Support (FOC 51), or by waiting until the motion hearing and informing the court of your agreement. See "Limited Opt-Out by Agreement" above for more about stipulations.

Sometimes, you may agree with part of the motion and disagree with the rest. For example, you may agree with your ex's motion to opt out of immediate income withholding, but want payment through the SDU instead of payment to the recipient s/he proposed in the motion.

Whenever you agree in part, it's important to signal your partial agreement as soon as possible because this narrows the issues in the case. If you file a Response to Motion Regarding Support (FOC 51), check box #6b and describe the extent of your agreement with the motion in the space below. If you respond orally, mention your partial agreement to the mediator, referee or judge, so the agreed-upon issues can be eliminated from the hearing.

When you oppose the motion, you can voice your disagreement in two ways. You can file a written response to the motion or wait until the motion hearing and respond orally. A written response is usually better, because it gets your views across more effectively.

Use the Response to Motion Regarding Support (FOC 51) for a written response. In paragraph #5, say why you oppose the motion. You could argue that good cause for avoiding immediate income withholding doesn't exist because: 1) it's in the best interests of the children to continue immediate income withholding 2) support hasn't always been paid on time.

For complete information and instructions about preparing, filing and serving a response, see "Responding to a Motion" on page 35.

You can also respond to a motion by making a counter-motion. Normally, if you oppose the motion with the Response to Motion Regarding Support (FOC 51), you disagree with the grounds for the motion in paragraph #5. Then in paragraph #7, you oppose the proposed modification, as in the sample response on page 133.

But if you want a different kind of change in payment of child support, check box #7b and explain in the space below what you want. Whether you realize it or not, this request is a counter-motion.

In some cases, it's even possible to ask for completely new relief in a counter-motion. For example, if your ex moves for a limited opt-out, you could counter-move to increase or decrease the amount of child support or alimony. Add new issues carefully, because these can easily sidetrack the case. Nevertheless, it may make sense to seek new relief in a counter-motion when the new issues are compatible with the main motion.

For more about counter-motion tactics and how to counter-move for new relief, see "Making a Counter-Motion" on page 37.

Friend of the Court

Before a post-judgment motion goes to the judge, the friend of the court may intervene to mediate, investigate or referee, in an attempt to settle the dispute. See "Friend of the Court" on page 38 for more about the friend of the court's roles in post-judgment cases, and how to deal with mediation, investigation or refereeing by the friend of the court.

Any post-judgment motion can be referred to mediation, investigation or refereeing. For a contested limited opt-out motion, there could be an investigation into the payer's record of payment and other facts, followed by a recommendation from the friend of the court. But it's doubtful mediation or refereeing would be used to settle a minor issue like this.

Motion Hearing

As explained in "Motion Hearings" on page 41, there are two kinds of motion hearings: 1) nonevidentiary hearing where facts aren't in dispute, evidence is seldom introduced and the parties merely make legal arguments to the judge 2) evidentiary hearing where facts are disputed and evidence must be introduced to establish the true facts.

A motion for a limited opt-out from the friend of the court system will normally be decided during a nonevidentiary hearing. The issues are quite narrow: Is the current method of payment effective and has support been paid on time? These questions can usually be answered in a nonevidentiary hearing, with no or minimal evidence. See "Motion Hearings" on page 41 for information about preparing for and appearing at a nonevidentiary hearing.

Court Order

After the motion hearing, the judge will decide the motion. In this case, the judge will probably "rule from the bench" and give an oral decision immediately after the hearing.

The moving party must prepare the order granting or denying the motion. If the motion is granted, use the Order Suspending Immediate Income Withholding (FOC 64) (there is a sample FOC 64 at the end of this chapter). At the end of paragraph #3, add a short statement setting up the new method of payment, such as "Support shall be paid directly to the [SDU/recipient]." For a denial of your motion, the court should issue an general denial order.

The moving party must also get the order signed by the judge and filed with the clerk. There are several ways to do this. See "Court Orders" on page 44 for complete instructions and forms.

After a limited opt-out by agreement or for cause, the friend of the court will participate in your case, as in other post-judgment cases. The only difference is that child support and/or alimony won't by paid by immediate income withholding.

If payment to the SDU has been ordered, the friend of the court can help you set up this method of payment. Typically, the friend of the court will notify the SDU of the new payment method and the SDU will send the payer a payment coupon book. For payment from the payer directly to the recipient, the parties will have make their own payment arrangements.

Later, if the payer gets behind in payment by a month or more, you can ask for reinstatement of immediate income withholding. Contact the friend of the court and it should take the necessary steps for getting immediate income withholding back.

STATE OF MICHIGAN
Circuit Court - Family Division
COUNTY

MOTION/STIPULATION
TO OPT OUT OF THE
FRIEND OF THE COURT SYSTEM

CASE NO.

☐ moving party

Defendant: ☐ moving party

v

CHECK BOX AT:
- *1a. FOR TOTAL OPT-OUT*
- *1b. FOR PARTIAL OPT-OUT*
- *1c. FOR LIMITED OPT-OUT*

☒ **MOTION** ☒ **STIPULATION**

1. I request to opt this post-judgment divorce case out of these friend of the court services:
☒ a. all friend of the court services.
☐ b. all friend of the court services except payment of support through the state disbursement unit
(SDU) by: ☐ immediate income withholding. ☐ payment directly from payer.
☐ c. immediate income withholding only, with support payment directly to: ☐ SDU. ☐ recipient.

☒ 2. For an opt-out under 1a. or 1b., this case is eligible for opt-out because:
a. neither party receives public assistance for a child in this case;
b. no money is due the state because of past public assistance for a child in this case;
c. no child support arrearage or custody or parenting time violation has occurred during the previous 12 months in this case;
d. neither party has reopened a friend of the court case during the previous 12 months;
e. there is no evidence: (1) of domestic violence or unequal bargaining position between the parties, or (2) that a party has chosen to opt out against the best interests of the party or the party's child;
f. the parties are filing a form signed by them advising about the friend of the court services they will lose if this motion is granted. (FOC 101 is attached)
g. the parties stipulate to the opt-out selected in 1a. or 1b by co-signing below.

FOR A LIMITED OPT-OUT, YOU MUST EXPLAIN GOOD CAUSE FOR OPT-OUT IN PARAGRAPH #3.

☐ 3. For an opt-out under 1c., there is good cause for opt-out because:
a. it is in the best interests of the children for immediate income withholding to stop be[...]
b. the file in this case shows that previously ordered support has been paid on time;
c. in a friend of the court case, the payer of support agrees to keep the friend of the c[...]
of: 1) current sources of income 2) health care coverage.

BOTH PARTIES MUST SIGN FOR A TOTAL OR PARTIAL OPT-OUT.

I declare that the above statements are true to the best of my information, knowledge and belief.
Date/plaintiff 1-1-99 *Darlene Lovelace* Date/defendant 1-1-99 *Dudley Lovelace*

NOTICE OF HEARING

A hearing will be held on this motion before (judge or referee) _____
on _____ at (time) _____ at (place) _____
Note: If you are the person receiving this motion, you may file a response.

CERTIFICATE OF MAILING

I certify that on this date I mailed a copy of this motion and notice of hearing to the other party(ies) by ordinary mail at the above address(es).
Date 1-2-99 _____ Moving party *Darlene Lovelace*

GRP 26 (9/04) **MOTION/STIPULATION TO OPT OUT OF THE FRIEND OF THE COURT SYSTEM**

Advice of Rights Regarding Use of Friend of the Court Services, continued from page 1

e. Custody and Parenting Time Enforcement Services

For friend of the court cases, the friend of the court must enforce custody and parenting time when a party complains that it is violated. Child custody and parenting time enforcement services include:

- Asking the court to order the noncooperating party to come to the court to explain the failure to obey the parenting time order.
- Suspending the licenses of individuals who deny parenting time.
- Awarding makeup parenting time.
- Joint meetings to resolve complaints.

f. Custody and Parenting Time Investigation Services

For disputes about custody or parenting time in friend of the court cases, the friend of the court sometimes must investigate and provide reports to the parties and the court.

g. Mediation Services

Friend of the court offices must provide mediation services to help parties with friend of the court cases settle custody and parenting time disputes.

3. State Disbursement Unit and IV-D Services

a. State Disbursement Unit (SDU)

If you choose not to receive friend of the court services, you may continue to make payments to, and receive payments through, the state disbursement unit (SDU). The SDU will keep track of the amount paid and sent out. However, the SDU cannot provide you with all of the accounting functions the friend of the court provides.

All payments made through the SDU must be distributed to the amounts due as required by federal law. When a payer has more than one case, federal law determines how a payment is divided among the cases. **Even if you choose not to receive friend of the court services, payments through the SDU must be divided among all a payer's cases and distributed in the same manner as payments on FOC cases. You cannot discontinue friend of the court services if you want to use the SDU unless you first provide to the SDU all the information that the SDU needs to set up an account.**

b. Your Rights Under Title IV-D of the Social Security Act

Title IV-D of the Social Security Act provides federal government resources to collect child support and it allows certain funding to be used for parenting time and custody services. In Michigan, critical title IV-D services are delivered by the friend of the court. **If you choose not to receive friend of the court services, you cannot receive most IV-D services.**

ACKNOWLEDGMENT REGARDING SERVICES

Check below only if you do not want to receive friend of the court services. Then date, print name, and sign.

I have read this advice of rights and I understand the friend of the court services I am entitled to receive.

☒ I acknowledge that by signing below **I am choosing not to receive** any friend of the court services. I understand that before this choice can take effect, a motion requesting this choice and the other party's agreement must be filed with the court for approval. I also understand that the court may deny this choice if certain conditions are not met as stated in this advice of rights.

DARLENE LOVELACE   DUDLEY LOVELACE
_____   _____
Name (type or print)   Name (type or print)
Darlene Lovelace   1-1-99   _Dudley Lovelace_   1-1-99
Signature   Date   Signature   Date

If you did not check the above, you are choosing to receive friend of the court services. **For the most effective friend of the court services,** you can request IV-D services by dating and signing below.

I request IV-D services through the friend of the court office.

_____   _____
Date   Signature

See other side   MCL 552.505a

FOC 101 (10/04) **ADVICE OF RIGHTS REGARDING USE OF FRIEND OF THE COURT SERVICES**

Original - Court
1st copy - Plaintiff

2nd copy - Defendant
3rd copy - Friend of the Court

CASE NO.

Approved, SCAO

STATE OF MICHIGAN
JUDICIAL CIRCUIT
COUNTY

ORDER EXEMPTING CASE FROM
FRIEND OF THE COURT SERVICES

FAX no.   Telephone no.

Friend of the Court address

Plaintiff's name and address

v

Defendant's name and address

Attorney:

Attorney:

Attorney: LESTER TUBBS   Bar no.

Date of hearing: 1-2-99   Judge: LESTER TUBBS

THE COURT FINDS:
1. There is no evidence of domestic ... en the parties to the case.
2. Granting the parties the relief they ... nterests of any child in the case.
3. The parties have filed executed ... ey will not receive if their motion is granted.
4. Neither party receives public ...
5. No money is due the state ... months in this case.
6. No arrearage or custody ...
7. Neither party has reope... se be closed. (Note: This box should be
☒ 8. The parties do not wa...
   checked unless exception

IT IS ORDERED:
9. Subject to the provisio...
☒ 10. This case is not a t...
11. The friend of the court ... ting functions for custody, parenting
    time, or support in this c... arenting time, or support in this case.
12. The parties are responsib... paid directly by the payer to the payee,
13. Except as indicated below, ... s case become a friend of the court case,
    and the friend of the court shall ... e payer's source of income and any health
    the payer must keep the friend of ... t the payer maintains including the name of the
    care coverage that is available to the p... organization; the policy, certificate, or contract number,
    insurance company, health care org... sons for whose benefit the payer maintains the coverage.
    and the names and birth dates of ...
   ☐ a. Support shall be paid thro... the State Disbursement Unit (SDU). Support shall be paid by income withholding to the
       extent allowed by statutes and court rules, however, the friend of the court is not responsible for the income withholding.
       The friend of the court shall notify the employer that it is no longer involved in the case and that any further information
       concerning income withholding will be provided by the parties.
   ☐ b. Support shall be paid through the SDU.
    If support payments are to be made through the SDU by income withholding or otherwise, the friend of the court shall not close
    the friend of the court case until the SDU notifies the friend of the court that it has been provided with the information necessary
    to process the child support payments. There will be no accounting for support that is not paid through the SDU.
14. The friend of the court shall open a friend of the court case if a party applies for public assistance relating to a child of the parties
    or either party submits to the friend of the court a written request to reopen the friend of the court case. If this case becomes
    a friend of the court case for any reason, the provisions on the other side of this order shall apply.

1-2-99
Date
See provisions on back.

Judge

CERTIFICATE OF MAILING

I certify that on this date I mailed a copy of this order to the other party by first class mail addressed to the last known address as
defined in MCR 3.203.
1-2-99
Date
Signature

MCL 552.505, MCL 552.505a

FOC 102 (10/04) **ORDER EXEMPTING CASE FROM FRIEND OF THE COURT SERVICES**

THIS ORDER IS FOR A TOTAL OPT-OUT.

CHECK THE BOX AT #13a FOR A PARTIAL OPT-OUT WITH SDU-PAYMENT BY IMMEDIATE INCOME WITHHOLDING; CHECK THE BOX AT #13b FOR A PARTIAL OPT-OUT WITH SDU-PAYMENT BUT WITHOUT IMMEDIATE INCOME WITHHOLDING.

Approved, SCAO

STATE OF MICHIGAN
JUDICIAL CIRCUIT
COUNTY

Friend of the Court address

AGREEMENT SUSPENDING
IMMEDIATE INCOME WITHHOLDING

Original - Court
2nd copy - Friend of the Court
3rd copy - Plaintiff
4th copy - Defendant

CASE NO.

Plaintiff's name and address

v

Defendant's name and address

Court telephone no.

NOTE: MCL 552.604(3) requires that all new and modified support orders after December 31, 1990 include a provision for immediate income withholding and that income withholding take effect immediately unless the parties enter into a written agreement that the income withholding order shall not take effect immediately.

We understand that by law an order of income withholding in a support order shall take effect, agree to the following:

1. The order of income withholding shall not take effect immediately.

2. An alternative payment arrangement shall be made as follows:

DEFENDANT SHALL PAY THE SUPPORT DIRECTLY TO THE SDU.

DESCRIBE OTHER METHOD OF PAYMENT

3. Both the payer and the recipient of support shall keep the friend of the court informed of the following:
   a. the name, address, and telephone number of his/her current source of income;
   b. any health care coverage that is available to him/her as a benefit of employment or that is maintained by him/her; the name of the insurance company, health care organization, or health maintenance organization; the policy, certificate or contract number; and the name(s) and birth date(s) of the person(s) for whose benefit s/he maintains health care coverage under the policy, certificate, or contract; and
   c. his/her current residence, mailing address, and telephone number.

4. We further understand that proceedings to implement income withholding shall commence if the payer of support fails one month behind in his/her support payments.

5. We recognize that the court may order withholding of income to take effect immediately for cause or at the request of the payer.

1-1-99
Date
Darlene Lovelace
Plaintiff's signature

1-1-99
Date
Dudley Lovelace
Defendant's signature

FOC 63 (10/04) **AGREEMENT SUSPENDING IMMEDIATE INCOME WITHHOLDING**

MCL 552.604

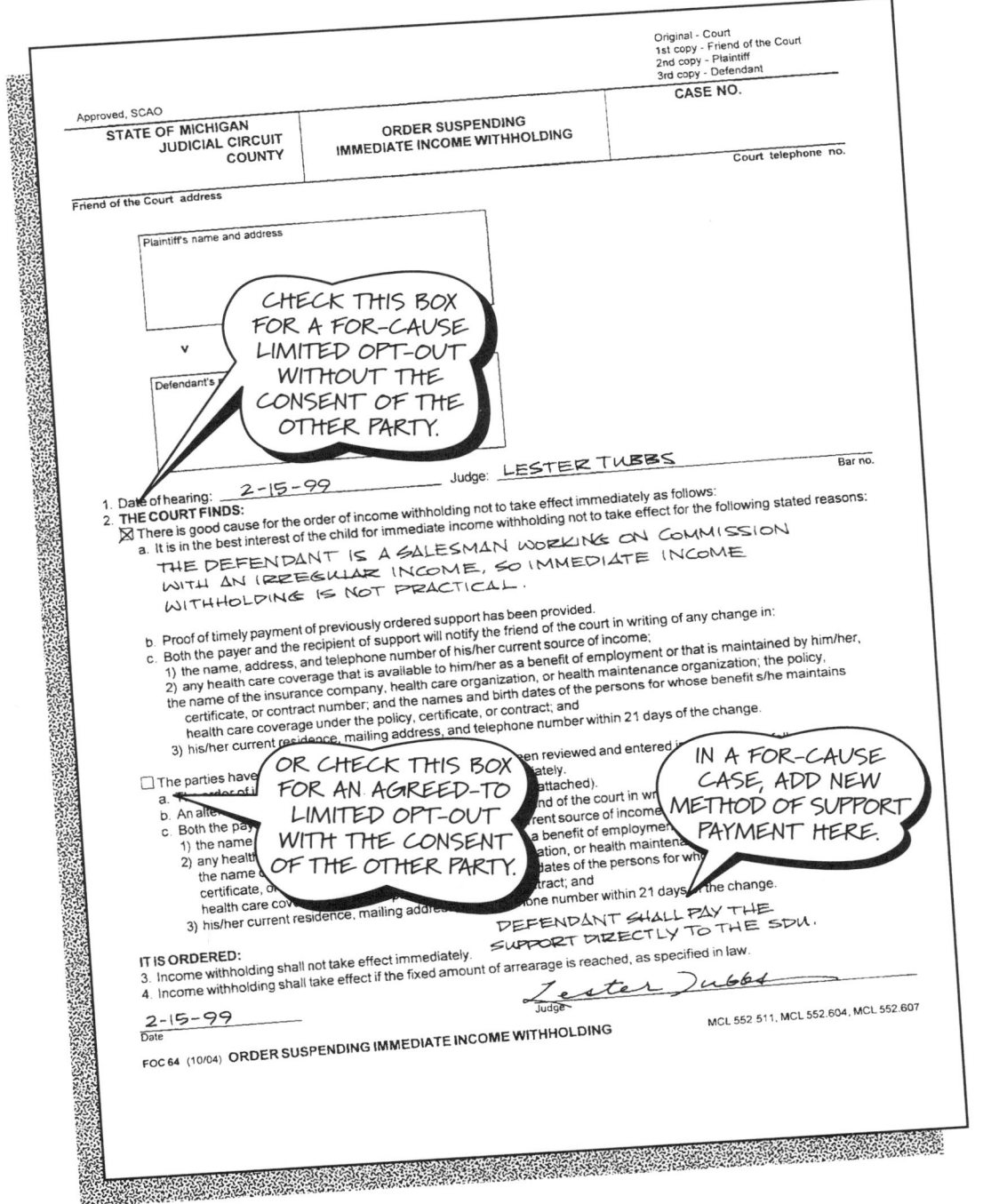

Approved, SCAO

STATE OF MICHIGAN JUDICIAL CIRCUIT COUNTY	Original - Court 1st copy - Friend of the Court	2nd copy - Plaintiff 3rd copy - Defendant
Friend of the Court address	**REQUEST TO REOPEN FRIEND OF THE COURT CASE**	**CASE NO.**

Plaintiff's name and address		Telephone no.
	v	
Attorney:	Defendant's name and address Attorney:	

1. On ___1-2-99___ an order was entered exempting this case from friend of the court services.
   Date

I REQUEST that the friend of the court case be reopened upon filing of this request with the friend of the court office. Attached is a completed Verified Statement and Application for IV-D Services.

___6-2-99___
Date

Signature *Darlene Lovelace*

CERTIFICATE OF MAILING

I certify that on this date I mailed a copy of this request to the friend of the court and to other party by first class mail addressed to his/her last known address as defined in MCR 3.203.

___6-2-99___
Date

Signature *Darlene Lovelace*

FOC 104   (10/04)   **REQUEST TO REOPEN FRIEND OF THE COURT CASE**

MCL 552.505, MCL 552.505a

Appendix E: Subpoena

For an evidentiary motion hearing, you may need the testimony of witnesses and/or portable items (documents, photographs, etc.) which witnesses have in their control. If they won't provide these to you voluntarily, you may have to get them by subpoena.

Who Can Be Subpoenaed?

Not everyone can be subpoenaed. The Michigan court rules say that subpoenas may only be issued to people who are present inside the state of Michigan; out-of-state individuals are immune from Michigan subpoenas.

Subpoena Costs

Courts issue subpoenas without charge. But to encourage attendance, a subpoenaed witness is entitled to a daily court attendance fee of the greater of: a) $12 (for a full day) or $6 (for a half-day), or b) the witness' daily lost wages or salary up to a maximum of $15 per day (unless unemployed, most witnesses will qualify for an attendance fee of $15 per day). The witness must also receive a mileage allowance at the state government rate for unclassified employees for travel to and from the courthouse for each day spent at court. In most cases, these court attendance fees (daily court attendance fee and mileage allowance) must be offered to the subpoenaed witness, in the form of cash, money order or cashier's check, when the subpoena is served on the witness. There may also be costs for serving subpoenas, which are described in "Serving Subpoenas" below.

Time for Subpoena

You must obtain subpoenas in advance of a motion hearing and have them served before the hearing. The extra time allows the subpoenaed witness to make arrangements to attend court and/or obtain requested items. According to the court rules, subpoenaed witnesses are entitled to a minimum of two days' notice. As a result, make sure your subpoenas are served on the witnesses more than two days before the hearing. See "Time" on page 30 for information about figuring time periods of days.

Obtaining a Subpoena

Lawyers, who are officers of the court, can issue their own subpoenas. As a nonlawyer, you will have to get your subpoenas from the clerk.

Some clerks have automated systems for issuing subpoenas and will make them for you at their office. But in most counties, you must prepare a Subpoena (MC 11) and then submit the form to the clerk for issuing.

Complete the MC 11 as shown in the sample form at the end of this section. Make four copies. Go to the clerk and have the clerk issue the subpoena by signing and sealing the original and all copies.

Set aside one copy of the Subpoena (MC 11) for proof of service. After service, you must have proof that the MC 11 was served on the witness. You prove service on the reverse of the extra copy of the MC 11, which will be referred to as the proof of service copy of the Subpoena (MC 11).

Serving Subpoenas

There are special rules for serving subpoenas, which are a little different from the service rules for motions. The court rules provide three ways to serve subpoenas: acknowledgment, mail and delivery. Service by acknowledgment is easiest and cheapest, followed by mail and then delivery.

Service by Acknowledgment

Service by acknowledgment is by far the simplest method of service. There are actually two ways to acknowledge service: personally and by mail. Both are easy to use.

Personal Acknowledgment

For personal acknowledgment, you simply hand the Subpoena (MC 11) and the court attendance fees to the witness. If the witness is in another Michigan county, you can arrange to have someone give the MC 11 and fees to the witness there. Service-by-personal acknowledgment is complete when the witness receives the Subpoena (MC 11) from you or your helper.

Proving Service by Personal Acknowledgment

Immediately after service, you or your helper should have the witness date (with both time and day) and sign the Acknowledgment of Service, which is at the bottom of the reverse of your proof of service copy of the Subpoena (MC 11). Afterward, make three copies of this paper and earmark one "FOC." File the original proof of service copy of the MC 11 and the friend of the court's copy with the clerk as the proof of service.

Acknowledgment by Mail

A subpoenaed witness can also acknowledge service through the mail. You simply send the Subpoena (MC 11), your proof of service copy of the MC 11 and the court attendance fees to the witness by ordinary first-class mail. Service by acknowledgment by mail is complete when the subpoenaed witness receives the mailing.

Proving Service by Acknowledgment by Mail

Right after service, the witness should date (with both time and day) and sign the Acknowledgment of Service, which is at the bottom of the reverse of your proof of service copy of the Subpoena (MC 11). The witness must then give or mail back the proof of service copy of the MC 11 to you. Afterward, make three copies of this paper and earmark one "FOC." File the original proof of service copy of the MC 11 and the friend of the court's copy with the clerk as the proof of service.

Service by Mail

Service by mail is a little more expensive than service by acknowledgment. But it's a very effective method of service because it goes anywhere U.S. mail is delivered. The court rules permit service by mail through either registered or certified mail. Use certified mail because it's cheaper than registered mail.

Cheaper (and easier) yet is service by acknowledgment by mail, since you can obtain acknowledgment by ordinary mail. Thus, you will probably want to use the acknowledgment method for witnesses who are friendly and willing to acknowledge service by mail. Service by mail, on the other hand, is better suited for witnesses you don't know or whom you believe are uncooperative.

To prove service, you need several special services available with certified mail: 1) restricted delivery 2) return receipt service showing the person receiving the papers and the date and address of delivery. By restricting delivery, the Subpoena (MC 11) is delivered only to the witness personally or someone s/he has designated in writing to receive mail. The return receipt provides proof of who received the MC 11 and the date and address of delivery. This receipt is a key part of the proof of service.

Prepare the mailing by placing the Subpoena (MC 11) and the court attendance fees in an envelope addressed to the witness. In addition, you must prepare two certified mail forms: Certified Mail Receipt (PS Form 3800) and Domestic Return Receipt (PS Form 3811), which are available at any post office.

On the PS Form 3800, fill in the witness' name and address at the bottom of the form. For the PS Form 3811, write your name and address on the front of the form, and on the reverse complete sections #1-4. In section #2, transfer the article number from the PS Form 3800. In section #3, check the certified mail box and ask for restricted delivery in #4.

After you complete the postal forms, peel off the plastic strips on the ends of the PS Form 3811 and attach the card to the envelope (there probably won't be room on the front of the envelope, so attach it to the reverse side). On the front of the envelope, to the left of the witness' address and below your return address, write "Restricted Delivery" and "Return Receipt Requested" on the envelope. By making these notations (the PS Form 3800 calls this "endorsement"), you will remind the letter carrier to restrict delivery and get a receipt.

Take the envelope containing the Subpoena (MC 11) and court attendance fees, with the Domestic Return Receipt (PS Form 3811) attached, the Certified Mail Receipt (PS Form 3800) and money to pay for the mailing to a post office window. Ask the postal clerk to mail the envelope by certified mail with the special services you have checked on the PS Form 3811. The clerk will prepare the certified mailing and return a postmarked PS Form 3800 to you. Keep this receipt for your records.

Later, a letter carrier will deliver the mailing to the witness, get his/her name (printed), signature and other delivery information on the reverse of the Domestic Return Receipt (PS Form 3811). Within a few days, you should get the PS Form 3811 back in the mail. You can then prove the service as described below. Service by mail is complete when the witness receives the mailing from the letter carrier.

If you get the whole envelope back, instead of the Domestic Return Receipt (PS Form 3811) alone, service by mail has failed. The witness may have refused to accept the mailing, wasn't home or moved without leaving a current forwarding order. Whatever went wrong, you will have to abandon service by mail because it only works when the witness is ready and willing to take the certified mailing from the letter carrier. If service by mail fails, try service by delivery instead.

Proving Service by Mail

After you get the Domestic Return Receipt (PS Form 3811) back in the mail, prove service on the reverse of your proof of service copy of the Subpoena (MC 11). Complete the information about the service by mail under the Affidavit of Process Server, and sign the form before a notary public. As proof of the witness' receipt of the mailing, staple the Domestic Return Receipt (PS Form 3811) to the reverse of your proof of service copy of the Subpoena (MC 11). Make three copies of this paper and earmark one "FOC." File the original proof of service copy of the MC 11 and the friend of the court's copy with the clerk as the proof of service.

Service by Delivery

You can also serve a Subpoena (MC 11) by delivering it to the witness. You or any mentally competent adult can deliver a Subpoena (MC 11).

If the witness is friendly and cooperative, consider service by personal acknowledgment instead of service by delivery.* Therefore, it's likely that you will serve by delivery when the witness is unfriendly, lives faraway or is otherwise difficult to serve. Moreover, service by delivery will probably be carried out by a professional process server, such as a commercial process server or a sheriff.

In cities, there are commercial process servers specializing in serving legal papers, for a fee. Small towns and rural areas seldom have access to these services. But wherever you are, the county sheriff department will serve subpoenas for you. Sheriff departments often have a separate division or deputy in charge of service.

Both types of servers charge fees for service. By law, sheriffs charge a basic service fee, currently $19, plus mileage at 1½ times the state government rate for classified civil service employees, for travel to and from the place of service. However, a sheriff's service fee can be suspended if you get a fee exemption (see Appendix A on page 195 for the details). Even if you have to pay, sheriffs' service fees are normally cheaper than those of commercial process servers, who often charge around $30-40 for service. On the other hand, commercial process servers may be more persistent in finding and serving witnesses.

Whomever you choose, you can often reduce the service fees by having the witness pick up the Subpoena (MC 11) at the server's office. This saves the server's mileage fee. It also spares the witness the possible embarrassment of being served with legal papers at home or work. If the witness is willing, tell the server that the witness will pick up the MC 11 and then have the witness call the server to arrange a time for the pick-up.

To obtain service by delivery in your area, take the Subpoena (MC 11), the court attendance fees and your proof of service copy of the MC 11 to the server and ask for service on the witness. The server will serve the witness at the witness' address just below the caption of the MC 11. If the witness can be found at another place, tell the server about the other address.

When the witness lives in another county, you must find a server nearby. After you find one, mail the Subpoena (MC 11), the court attendance fees

More Information

To find sheriffs, look under the county government section for the sheriff department in a telephone directory. For commercial process servers, use a telephone directory for the witness' area and look under "Process Servers" in the yellow pages.

Or you can find both kinds of process servers through process server trade associations, which provide referrals:

Court Officers, Deputy Sheriffs & Process Servers of Michigan (CODSA) at (989) 831-7644 or www.codsa.com

National Association of Professional Process Servers (NAPPS) at (800) 477-8211 or www.napps.com

United States Process Servers Association (USPSA) at (217) 787-5966 or www.usprocessservers.com

---

* Service by personal acknowledgment and delivery are similar. The only difference is the proof of service. With an acknowledgment, the witness assists in proving service; for delivery, the server proves service without help from the witness.

and your proof of service copy of the MC 11 to the server. Enclose a note asking for service and return of a proof of service. You may also want to prepay the service fee by estimating the fee and enclosing a check or money order for this amount. Instruct the server to apply your payment to the service fee, and refund or charge you for the difference between your estimate and the actual service fee.

If all goes as planned, the server will find the witness and deliver the Subpoena (MC 11) to him/her. Service by delivery is complete when the server delivers the MC 11 to the witness.

Proving Service by Delivery

After service, the server will prove service on the reverse of the proof of service copy of the Subpoena (MC 11) that you gave the server. For service by Michigan court officers, such as sheriff deputies, the proof of service will appear in the Officer Certificate. All other servers must use the Affidavit of Process Server.

After service is proved, the server will return the proof of service copy of the Subpoena (MC 11) to you. Make three copies of this paper and earmark one "FOC." File the original proof of service copy of the MC 11 and the friend of the court's copy with the clerk as the proof of service.

Witness in Court

If the witness obeys the subpoena, s/he will appear at the motion hearing and give the testimony or produce the things you seek. But if the witness doesn't show up, you can ask for adjournment of the hearing. The court should grant your request for more time. The court can also force the uncooperative witness to appear at the next hearing by threatening to hold him/her in contempt of court.

Approved, SCAO

Original - Return
1st copy - Witness
2nd copy - File
3rd copy - Extra

STATE OF MICHIGAN JUDICIAL DISTRICT JUDICIAL CIRCUIT COUNTY PROBATE	SUBPOENA Order to Appear and/or Produce	CASE NO.

Court address

Court telephone no.

Police Report No. (if applicable)

Plaintiff(s)/Petitioner(s) ☐ People of the State of Michigan ☒ DARLENE LOVELACE	v	Defendant(s)/Respondent(s) DUDLEY LOVELACE
☒ Civil ☐ Criminal		Charge

☐ Probate   In the matter of _____

In the Name of the People of the State of Michigan. TO: JOHN QUICK, LAKESIDE FAMILY COUNSELING CENTER, 100 S. FRONT, LAKE CITY, MI 48800

If you require special accommodations to use the court because of disabilities, please contact the court immediately to make arrangements.

YOU ARE ORDERED:

☒ 1. to appear personally at the time and place stated below: You may be required to appear from time to time and day to day until excused.

☒ The court address above   ☐ Other:

Day TUESDAY	Date 2-15-99	Time 9:00 AM

☒ 2. Testify at trial / examination / hearing.

☒ 3. Produce/permit inspection or copying of the following items: ALL DOCUMENTS, RECORDS AND FILES REGARDING PSYCHOLOGICAL TESTING AND/OR EVALUATION OF DUANE W. LOVELACE AND DARRYL W. LOVELACE

☐ 4. Testify as to your assets, and bring with you the items listed in line 3 above.

☐ 5. Testify at deposition.

☐ 6. MCL 600.6104(2), 600.6116, or 600.6119 prohibition against transferring or disposing of property is attached.

☐ 7. Other: _____

☒ 8.

Person requesting subpoena DUDLEY LOVELACE	Telephone no. 773-0011
Address 900 S. MAPLE	
City LAKE CITY	State MI	Zip 48800

NOTE: If requesting a debtor's examination under MCL 600.6110, or an injunction under item 6, this subpoena must be issued by a judge. For a debtor examination, the affidavit of debtor examination on the other side of this form must also be completed. Debtor's assets can also be discovered through MCR 2.305 without the need for an affidavit of debtor examination or issuance of this subpoena by a judge.

FAILURE TO OBEY THE COMMANDS OF THE SUBPOENA OR APPEAR AT THE STATED TIME AND PLACE MAY SUBJECT YOU TO PENALTY FOR CONTEMPT OF COURT.

2-1-99   Martha Gee
Date   Judge/Clerk/Attorney   Bar no

Court use only
☐ Served   ☐ Not served

MC 11 (6/04) SUBPOENA, Order to Appear and/or Produce

MCL 600.1455, 600.1701, 600.6110, 600.6119, MCR 2.506

CHECK BOX #2 TO OBTAIN WITNESS' TESTIMONY AND/OR BOX #3 TO OBTAIN DOCUMENTS OR OTHER THINGS THE WITNESS HAS.

USE OFFICER CERTIFICATE OR AFFIDAVIT OF PROCESS SERVER TO PROVE SERVICE BY DELIVERY OR SERVICE BY MAIL.

PROOF OF SERVICE	SUBPOENA
	Case No. 89-00501-DM

...S SERVER: You must make and file your return with the court clerk. If you are unable to complete service, you must ...original and all copies to the court clerk.

CERTIFICATE / AFFIDAVIT OF SERVICE / NON-SERVICE

☐ **OFFICER CERTIFICATE**
I certify that I am a sheriff, deputy sheriff, bailiff, appointed court officer, or attorney for a party [MCR 2.104(A)(2)], and that: (notarization not required)

OR

☐ **AFFIDAVIT OF PROCESS SERVER**
Being first duly sworn, I state that I am a legally competent adult who is not a party or an officer of a corporate party, and that: (notarization required)

☐ I served a copy of the subpoena, together with _____ Attachment _____ (including any required fees) by

☐ personal service ☐ registered or certified mail (copy of return receipt attached) on:

Name(s)	Complete address(es) of service	Day, date, time

☐ I have personally attempted to serve the subpoena and required fees, if any, together with _____ Attachment on the following person and have been unable to complete service.

Name(s)	Complete address(es) of service	Day, date, time

Service fee $	Miles traveled	Mileage fee $	Total fee $	Signature

Title _____

Subscribed and sworn to before me on _____ Date

My commission expires: _____ Date _____ , _____ County, Michigan.

Signature: _____

Notary public, State of Michigan, County of _____ Deputy court clerk/Notary public

ACKNOWLEDGMENT OF SERVICE

I acknowledge that I have received service of the subpoena and required fees, if any, together with _____ Attachment

on MON. 2-7-99 9:00 AM
Day, date, time

Signature *John Quick*

on behalf of AT: 100 S. FRONT
LAKE CITY, MI 48800

THIS IS A PROOF OF SERVICE BY ACKNOWLEDGMENT.

AFFIDAVIT FOR JUDGMENT DEBTOR EXAMINATION

I request that the court issue a subpoena which orders the party named on this form to be examined under oath before a judge concerning the money or property of: for the following reasons:

Subscribed and sworn to before me on _____ Date

Signature _____

My commission expires: _____ Date _____ , _____ County, Michigan.

Signature: _____

Notary public, State of Michigan, County of _____ Deputy court clerk/Notary public

MCR 2.105

Appendix F:
Michigan Child Support
Formula Manual

2004 Michigan Child Support Formula Manual

Effective: October 1, 2004

Friend of the Court Bureau
State Court Administrative Office
Michigan Hall of Justice
P.O. Box 30048
Lansing, Michigan 48909

TABLE OF CONTENTS

Changes to the Child Support Formula Manual

	2004 Formula Manual Changes
MCSF Section	**Change**
all	Manual contents reorganized into the new citation format.
all	Values converted to reflect changes from weekly to monthly amounts.
1.01	New section on citation of the formula manual added.
1.03	New section on the definition of support added.
1.04(D)	New subsection on deviation criteria added.
1.07	Minimum threshold for modification updated to $25 per month.
1.08	Minimum base support amount updated to $25 per month.
2.01(F)(29) 2.12(A)(1)	Alimony or Spousal Support between parties in the case no longer counted as income nor allowed as a deduction from income.
2.05(C)	Amended to clarify that noncustodial parent Social Security benefits received by children are to be counted as that parent's income.
2.11	Special considerations in determining income clarified to include others.
2.12(E)	Health insurance premiums paid for parent's other children are to be deducted from net income
3.0	Support obligation includes amounts calculated for base support, ordinary medical expenses, and child care expenses.
3.01	General Support Tables updated with February 2004 CPI-U figure.
3.02(A)	Updated with the 2004 DHHS Poverty Guideline.
3.07	Health care and medical expense section significantly changed and expanded. Includes new definition of health care, remedial care, ordinary expenses, and extraordinary expenses. Requirements added regarding determination of the responsibility to insure. Changed how reasonable cost of healthcare coverage is determined. Added payment of ordinary expenses to obligation.
3.08(B)	Child care expense apportionment percentage made uniform with health care percentages
4.03(B)(2)	Arrearage Guideline updated to 4.35% but not less than $80 per month.
4.04	Added reference to statutory deviation requirement to agreements related to property section.
4.05	Added SCAO policy on prorating and converting orders.
Supplement	Added Percentage of Income Schedules. Updated Support Schedules based on economic and monthly order changes. Separated to be published as a supplement to the manual.

PREFACE

The Michigan Friend of the Court Act of 1982 and the Federal Child Support Enforcement Amendments of 1984 require the State Court Administrative Office's (SCAO) Friend of the Court Bureau to develop "a formula to be used in establishing and modifying as a guideline in recommending a child support amount. The formula shall be based upon the needs of the child and the actual resources of each parent." MCL 552.519(3)(a)(vi); 42 USC 667(467)(a). "The child support formula developed by the bureau . . . shall be used as a guideline in recommending child support" by the friend of the court offices. MCL 552.505(h). In 1998, the Friend of the Court Act was amended to also provide "the formula shall include guidelines for setting and administratively adjusting the amount of periodic payments on overdue support..."

A committee began work on this Guideline in 1983. It extensively reviewed methodologies in use, held public hearings, conducted original research, and received input from professional economists and other researchers.

The SCAO adopted the first Guideline, which became effective May 1987. The Child Support Formula Subcommittee reviews comments and makes recommendations for the periodic update of this manual.

The Michigan Child Support Formula is reviewed as required by federal legislation, more commonly referred to as the Family Support Act of 1988. Comments regarding suggested changes to the formula should be made in writing to MCSF@courts.mi.gov or mailed to:

Michigan Child Support Formula
c/o State Court Administrative Office
P.O. Box 30048
Lansing, MI 48909

This document is available at: http://www.courts.mi.gov/scao/services/mcsf/mcsf.htm and at depository libraries for the State of Michigan (see a list on the Library of Michigan web page at: http://www.michigan.gov/hal).

1. Background

1.01 Citation

This manual is the "Michigan Child Support Formula of 2004," which may be abbreviated as "2004 MCSF." References to provisions in this manual should include the year of the manual cited and section number being referenced. For example, this section could be cited as "Michigan Child Support Formula of 2004 Section 1.01," or "2004 MCSF 1.01."

1.02 Purpose of this Formula

The formula is based on common factors which are appropriate for use in the determination of child support obligations. Based on the estimated costs of raising children and factors like parental income, family size, and ages of children, the formula provides for appropriate support amounts in orders involving the support of children.

The formula will assure greater uniformity by those who make recommendations and increase predictability for those who require child support orders.

There may be special cases where the formula cannot be relied on exclusively. For these cases, the formula will provide the court and friend of the court with points of reference from which a support determination can be made.

The formula will also assist parents in reaching agreements on the appropriate level of child support at the time of a divorce or other domestic relations proceeding, or upon modification of a previous order.

1.03 Support Defined

1.03 (A)   Support refers to the payment of money for a child or a spouse ordered by the court, and may include payment of the expenses of medical, dental, and other health care, child care expenses, and educational expenses. MCL 552.602(ee) contains a statutory definition of support.

1.03 (B)   For the purposes of this manual, a child support obligation includes payment for the general care and needs of a child, medical support, health care coverage, and child care.

1.03 (C)   A support obligation includes separately calculated figures for the base support (calculated in Sections 3.01 - 3.05), ordinary and extraordinary health care expenses, provision of health care coverage (Section 3.07), and child care expenses (Section 3.08).

1

1.04   **Application of and Deviation from the Formula**

1.04 (A)   Required Application.

(1)   All child support recommendations and orders must follow the formula, whether or not the parties agree on the amount of support, except where a court determines that the formula produces an "unjust or inappropriate" result. Except as otherwise provided in MCL 552.605, the court must order child support in an amount determined by application of the child support formula.

(2)   All support orders must be stated in monthly amounts. MCL 552.605c(1).

1.04 (B)   Agreements to Deviate.

MCL 552.605(3) states that subsection (2) (i.e., MCL 552.605(2)) does not prohibit the court from entering a support order that is agreed to by the parties and that deviates from the child support formula, if the requirements of that subsection are met and deviation factors (a) - (d) are recorded.

1.04 (C)   Deviation Requirements.

(1)   The court may enter an order that deviates from the formula if the court determines from the facts of the case that application of the child support formula would be unjust or inappropriate, and it includes all of the following:

(a)   The child support amount determined by application of the child support formula.

(b)   How the child support order deviates from the child support formula.

(c)   The value of property or other support awarded instead of the payment of child support, if applicable.

(d)   The reasons why application of the child support formula would be unjust or inappropriate in the case. MCL 552.605(2).

See: MCL 552.605, *Ghidotti v Barber* 459 Mich 189 (1998), and *Burba v Burba* 461 Mich 637 (2000).

(2)   The Michigan Supreme Court has held that the statutory deviation factors must be recorded. "While a trial court may enter an order of support that deviates from the formula, it may not do so without setting forth in writing or on the record why following the formula would be unjust or inappropriate." *Ghidotti v Barber*, 459 Mich 189 (1998). The criteria for deviating from the formula are mandatory and, to fulfill its statutory duty, a court must carefully

articulate these factors to memorialize and explain its decision. *Burba v Burba*, 461 Mich 637, 644-45 (2000).

1.04 (D)   Deviation Criteria.

(1)   The Michigan Supreme Court has clarified that deviations cannot be based simply on disagreement with the policies embodied in the statutes or the manual. In *Burba v Burba*, 461 Mich 637 (2000), the Court held that disagreement with the policies implicit in the formula cannot be the basis for a deviation.

(2)   In exercising the discretion set forth in this section, to the extent possible, the court should follow the formula's principles and algorithms, with the exception of those particular provisions that create an unjust or inappropriate result.

(3)   The only basis for deviation from the formula is a finding that application of its provisions would be unjust or inappropriate in a specific case.

(4)   Given the common factors considered, the law presumes that the Michigan Child Support Formula sets appropriate levels of support. However, in a limited number of individual cases, the amounts derived from application of the formula may have an unjust or inappropriate result. In those cases, the law anticipates that the court may exercise discretion in the best interests of the child to determine a just and appropriate amount of support.

(5)   In exercising the discretion set forth in this section, the court may consider any or all of the following factors, as well as any additional factor that it determines to be relevant to the best interests of the child:

(a)   The child has special needs.
(b)   The child has extraordinary educational expenses.
(c)   One or both of the parents are minors.
(d)   The child's residence income is below the threshold to qualify for public assistance, and at least one parent has sufficient income to pay additional support to raise the child's standard of living above the public assistance threshold.
(e)   A reduction of income available to support a child has occurred due to extraordinary levels of jointly accumulated debt.
(f)   The court awards property in lieu of support for the benefit of the child.
(g)   One or both parents are incarcerated without income or assets.
(h)   One or both parents have incurred, or are likely to incur, extraordinary medical expenses either for themselves or a dependent.

3

(i)   One or both parents earn incomes of a magnitude not fully taken into consideration by the formula.

(j)   One or both parents have varying amounts of irregular bonus income.

(k)   Someone other than the parent can supply reasonable and appropriate health care coverage.

1.05   Requirements to Investigate and Petition for Modification

1.05 (A)   The Friend of the Court Act states that after a final judgment or order has been entered, the friend of the court office is required to periodically review support orders under the criteria outlined in the Act. The friend of the court office must petition the court if there is a determination that a modification is necessary, unless: (a) the difference between the existing support order and the proposed support amount is within the minimum threshold amount (see Section 1.07) or (b) the court had previously determined that application of the formula was unjust or inappropriate, and the office determines that the facts of the case, the reason for the deviation, and amount of the prior ordered deviation all remain unchanged. MCL 552.517.

1.05 (B)   If ordered by the court, the friend of the court office must investigate all relevant facts and make a written report and recommendation to the parties, their attorneys, and the court regarding child support. MCL 552.505(1)(h).

1.05 (C)   Orders Lacking Health Care Provisions

                If an order lacks health care coverage provisions, the office must petition for modification to require one or both parents to maintain coverage for the child according to the terms of MCL 552.517(7).

1.06   Cases Involving Imputation

                When a friend of the court investigation shows voluntary reduction of income or where there is voluntary unexercised ability to earn, the office must make two recommendations: one is based on actual income and the other, an alternative recommendation, based on actual income plus imputed income. The alternative recommendation must include all factual assumptions that form the basis for imputation, the reasons for imputation, and all evidence known to the friend of the court that the individual is or is not able to earn the imputed income. MCL 552.517(3).

1.07   **Minimum Threshold for Modification**

1.07 (A)   Following review of child support by the friend of the court office, if the difference between the recommended amount and the current order exceeds the minimum threshold, the friend of the court office is required to petition to modify the order. For the actual language and requirements of the Friend of the Court Act on the child support review and modification process, please see MCL 552.517.

1.07 (B)   The "minimum threshold for modification" is ten-percent (10%) or more of the existing order or $25 per month, whichever is less.

Examples:

The friend of the court office conducts a support review as required by statute and the current support order is $270 per month. The proposed change is to $296. The friend of the court office must petition the court to modify the order, since the change is greater than the $25.00 threshold.

The friend of the court office conducts a support review as required by statute and the current support order is $120 per month. The proposed change is to $107. The friend of the court office must petition the court to modify the order, since the $13.00 change is greater than the ten-percent threshold.

The friend of the court office conducts a support review as required by statute and the current support order is $330 per month. The proposed change is to $352. The office is not required to petition to modify the order since the change is less than the ten-percent threshold and less than the $25 threshold.

1.08   **Minimum Order Amounts**

Support should not be recommended in amounts of less than $25 per month (plus that parent's share health care and child care), unless the court deviates from the formula.

1.09   **Orders with Multiple Children**

1.09 (A)   To comply with MCR 3.211(E)(1), and to avoid recalculating support each time the number of children for whom support is paid changes, all support orders for multiple children must include tiered amounts for the appropriate number of children.

Examples:

The order for this family of four children would state:

$984 base support per month for 4 children,
$866 base support per month for 3 children,
$668 base support per month for 2 children, and
$439 base support per month for 1 child.

1.09 (B)   Unless designated as owing for a particular child, amounts ordered for multiple children under MCR 3.211(E)(1) may be administratively allocated into equal per child amounts for record keeping purposes.

2. DETERMINING NET INCOME

The first step in determining each parent's support obligation is to ascertain each parent's net income.

2.01   **Sources and Variations in Income**

2.01 (A)   The objective of determining income for purposes of this formula is to establish, as accurately as possible, the monies available to support the children.

2.01 (B)   "Income" means any of the following:

         (i)   Commissions, earnings, salaries, wages, and other income due or to be due in the future to an individual from his or her employer and successor employers.

         (ii)   A payment due or to be due in the future to an individual from a profit-sharing plan, a pension plan, an insurance contract, an annuity, social security, unemployment compensation, supplemental unemployment benefits, or worker's compensation.

         (iii)   An amount of money that is due to an individual as a debt of another individual, partnership, association, or private or public corporation, the United States or a federal agency, this state or a political subdivision of this state, another state or a political subdivision of another state, or another legal entity that is indebted to the individual. MCL 552.602(n).

2.01 (C)   Where there is evidence of considerable variation in income due to seasonal employment, overtime, second jobs, bonuses, or profit sharing, etc., information from at least the preceding twelve months should be used in calculating net income. Certain occupations and self-employed persons may have considerable variation in income from year to year. The use of three years' income information is recommended where such variation exists.

2.01 (D)   "Source of income" means an employer or successor employer or any other individual or entity that owes or will owe income to the payer. MCL 552.602(bb).

2.01 (E)   The term "net income" refers to gross income minus all of the deductions allowed for the purpose of calculating child support. "Net income," many times, will not be equivalent to an individual's net pay, net taxable income, or other similar terms used by other governmental agencies.

2.01 (F)   The following list outlines types of income from which parents' incomes should be determined. Although the list includes common forms of income, it is not exhaustive and other sources may be considered. These types of income are for the purpose of establishing child support and may not correspond to the sources of taxable income as set forth by the Internal Revenue Service (IRS).

(1)   Salaries and Wages
(2)   Cost of Living Allowance (COLA)
(3)   Shift Premium
(4)   Overtime (Section 2.04)
(5)   Second Job (Section 2.04)
(6)   Commissions
(7)   All Bonuses
(8)   Profit Sharing
(9)   Interest
(10)   Dividends
(11)   Annuities
(12)   Pensions/Longevity
(13)   Deferred Compensation/Individual Retirement Account (IRA) (Section 2.06)
(14)   Trust Fund Payments
(15)   Unemployment Benefits
(16)   Strike Pay
(17)   Supplemental Unemployment Benefits (SUB) Pay
(18)   Sick Benefits
(19)   Worker's Compensation
(20)   Social Security Retirement/Disability Benefits (Subsections 2.05(A)-(C))
(21)   Veteran Administration Benefits
(22)   Disability Insurance
(23)   G.I. Benefits - excluding education allotment
(24)   National Guard and Reserves Drill Pay
(25)   Armed Services - base pay plus allowance for quarters, rations and specialty pay
(26)   Dividends Earned from Life Insurance Policies
(27)   Allowance for Rent (when provided by the employer as a fringe benefit)
(28)   Rental Income
(29)   Alimony/Spousal Support paid by someone other than the other parent in the case under consideration
(30)   Net Gambling and Lottery Winnings
(31)   Tax-exempt income, such as the interest and dividends paid on municipal bonds and other government securities.
(32)   Insurance or other similar payments received as compensation for lost earnings (but not payments to compensate for medical bills or for property loss or damage).
(33)   Adoption Subsidy - standard/basic needs portion for child(ren) in case under consideration. (The medical needs and intensive rate portion of the Adoption Subsidy and all of the Family Support Subsidy must not be considered as income. These subsidies are excluded for meeting special emotional and physical needs.)

See Section 2.11 for special considerations to keep in mind when determining the income of self-employed persons, business owners, business executives, and others.

2.02   **Identifying Net Income**

2.02 (A)   Net income should be determined from actual tax returns whenever possible. When determining the parties' net incomes for the purpose of modifying an existing child support order, it is beneficial for both parents to produce their actual tax returns because it will provide more accuracy in the determination of actual taxes paid and identify many types of income.

2.02 (B)   If a parent and that parent's new spouse file a joint tax return <u>and that return is made available</u>, deduct the new spouse's income from the total joint income and prorate joint taxes between the spouses. <u>When prorating, use the fraction obtained by dividing the employment income (salary, wages, tips, commissions, bonuses, profit sharing, etc.) of the parent by the total employment income of the parent and the new spouse.</u>

         Example:

<u>Step 1</u>:	Parent's employment income:		$20,000
	New spouse's employment income:	+	$40,000
	Total employment income:		$60,000
<u>Step 2</u>:	Parent's employment income divided by total employment income:		$20,000/$60,000
	Resulting fraction/percentage:		1/3 or 33.3%
<u>Step 3</u>:	Total joint tax obligation* (as stated on the tax return)		$15,000
	*Including taxes on non-employment income such as interest, dividends, capital gains, etc.		
	Multiply fraction/percentage by total joint tax obligation:		1/3 x $15,000
	Parent's share of joint tax obligation:		$5,000

2.02 (C)   If parents and their new spouses file joint tax returns and the entire return is <u>not</u> made available, assume that the parent's income is the total family income. Also assume that the parent is entitled to each dependency tax exemption claimed by the parent and the new spouse. *Note:* This approach may have the effect of understating the parent's tax liability and, therefore, overstating the parent's net income.

2.03	**Children's Income**

2.03 (A)   A child's income ***should not*** ordinarily be considered in calculating child support as long as a child is eligible to receive support.

2.03 (B)   A child's Supplemental Security Income (SSI) benefits ***should not*** be considered as income.

2.03 (C)   In cases where a child is a professional or is involved in some activity and earns a large income, discretion must be exercised.

2.04	**Overtime and Second Jobs**

2.04 (A)   All overtime and second job income should be considered income when setting support.

2.04 (B)   Evidence produced that overtime or second job hours will be changed in the future may be considered.

2.05	**Social Security Benefits**

2.05 (A)   Supplemental Security Income (SSI) benefits are a means tested source of income and may not be counted as income. (Section 2.09)

2.05 (B)   All Social Security Retirement, Survivor's, or Disability Insurance benefits received by the children in the case under consideration, other than those based on the earnings record of the noncustodial parent, must be considered custodial parent income.

2.05 (C)   Social Security Retirement, Survivor's, or Disability Insurance Program dependent benefits for the children in the case under consideration based on the earnings record of the noncustodial parent should be considered as noncustodial parent income, and ***not*** considered as custodial parent income.

2.05 (D)   However, benefits for the children based on the noncustodial parent's earnings record should be credited against the support obligation according to the following instructions:

Step 1:   Determine both parents' net incomes. (Remember to include the children's benefits according to Sections 2.05(B) and 2.05(C)).

Step 2:   Determine the total support amount (Chapter 3).

Step 3:   Determine the monthly amount of Social Security benefits attributable to the noncustodial parent received for the child(ren).

Step 4:   Subtract the attributable children's benefit amount from the total support amount calculated.

Step 5:   (1)   If the noncustodial benefits received by the child(ren) exceeds the total support amount calculated, no additional support should be paid.

           (2)   If the noncustodial benefits received by the child(ren) are <u>less than</u> the total support calculated, the difference between the benefits received and the total support calculated should be paid.

Example: Adjust support for noncustodial social security benefits paid for minor children.

Step 1:   Determine the noncustodial and the custodial parents' net incomes.

        The noncustodial parent earns $1,550 net per month (including children's benefits according Section 2.05(C)).

        The custodial parent earns $1,050 net per month.

Step 2:   Determine the total support amount (Chapter 3).

        Support is $689 per month for three children.

Step 3:   Determine the monthly amount of Social Security benefits attributable to the noncustodial parent received for the child(ren).

        $625 children's monthly benefit attributable to the noncustodial parent.

Step 4:   Subtract the attributable children's benefit amount from the total support amount calculated.

        $689 (total support) - $625 (monthly benefit) = $64 (per month)

Step 5:   Since the remaining benefit does not exceed the support amount, the payer must pay $64 per month

2.05 (E)   The following cases may offer information regarding consideration of Social Security benefits: *Frens v Frens*, 191 MichApp 654 (1990); *Jenerou v Jenerou*, 200 MichApp 265 (1993); *Paulson v Paulson*, 254 MichApp 568 (2002).

2.06   Deferred Compensation/Individual Retirement Account (IRA)

2.06 (A)   If a payer retires and receives payment from an IRA, defined contribution, or deferred compensation plan, income from contributions to the plan which were previously assessed for child support should be excluded on a prorated basis.

Example:

A payer's IRA account totals $200,000 at the time of retirement, but $15,000 in contributions to the account were made while the payer was under an obligation to pay child support, and were included as income at that time. Therefore, 15/200 of the benefit payments should be excluded from consideration as income.

2.07   Inheritances and One-Time Gifts

2.07 (A)   Property and principal should <u>not</u> be considered as income.

2.07 (B)   Interest earned from inheritances and gifts should be considered as income.

2.08   Non-Income and Low Income Producing Assets

2.08 (A)   Non-income or low-income producing assets should be evaluated to establish a reasonable rate of expected return depending on the type and nature of the asset. The expected income should be used when determining child support.

2.08 (B)   At a minimum, a reasonable rate of expected income may be attributed to those assets by using current average interest rates for passbook savings accounts, treasury bills, treasury bonds, certificates of deposit, etc.

2.08 (C)   Non-income producing assets that are owned by custodial and noncustodial parents, after the property is distributed pursuant to the judgment of divorce or at the time child support recommendations are made, may be used to determine expected income.

(1)   Non-income or low-income producing assets may include but are not limited to: cash, cash surrender value of insurance policies, loans to or stock in a controlled or family owned corporation, loans to third parties, real estate,

jewelry, antiques, collections, inventories, vehicles, pension and profit sharing plans, etc.

(2)   Certain non-income producing assets such as a home and its reasonable furnishings, an automobile, and other small non-income assets should be excluded from consideration.

2.09   Means Tested Income

Income from means tested sources, such as Temporary Assistance to Needy Families (TANF), Family Independence Payments (FIP) (formerly AFDC), Food Stamps, Earned Income Credit (Federal Taxes), Supplemental Security Income (SSI), etc. must not be considered income when determining child support.

2.10   Imputation of Income

2.10 (A)   Imputation of income is treating a party as having income or resources that the individual does not actually have. This usually occurs in cases where there is a voluntarily reduction of income or a voluntary unexercised ability to earn.

2.10 (B)   The final determination as to the appropriateness of imputation in a particular case is a judicial one.

2.10 (C)   Imputation should also take into account the possible inclusion of child care where imputation would make that issue relevant.

2.10 (D)   Include the basis for imputation and the amount imputed.

2.10 (E)   When determining what income, if any, consider among other equitable factors the following criteria:

(1)   Prior employment experience;
(2)   Educational level;
(3)   Physical and mental disabilities;
(4)   The presence of the parties' children in the individual's home and its impact on the earnings;
(5)   Availability of employment in the local geographical area;
(6)   The prevailing wage rates in the local geographical area;
(7)   Special skills and training; or
(8)   Whether there is any evidence that the individual in question is able to earn the imputed income.

2.10 (F)   Imputation must be applied equally to payers and payees, and to men and women. Imputation is not appropriate where:

(1)   A parent's source of income is a means tested income such as Temporary Assistance to Needy Families (TANF), Family Independence Payments (FIP) (formerly AFDC), Food Stamps, Supplemental Security Income (SSI), etc.;

(2)   There has not been a significant reduction in income compared to the period preceding the filing of the complaint (or the motion for modification, in a modification proceeding); or

(3)   The individual is employed full time (35 or more hours per week), but is in a situation where employment income has been reduced through reduced hours (such as leaving a second job or refusing overtime).

2.10 (G)   In cases in which income is imputed, the amount imputed should be sufficient to bring total income up to the level it would have been if there had been no reduction in income, provided that the imputation computation shall not be based on any hours beyond 40 per week nor any overtime or shift premiums.

2.10 (H)   The following cases offer guidance in determining whether imputation of income is appropriate; *Travis v Travis*, 19 Mich App 128 (1969); *Moncada v Moncada*, 81 Mich App 26 (1978); *Dunn v Dunn*, 105 Mich App 793 (1981); *Heilman v Heilman*, 95 Mich App 728 (1980); *Joslin v LaVance*, 154 Mich App 501 (1986); *Rohloff v Rohloff*, 161 Mich App 766 (1987); *Daniels v Daniels*, 165 Mich App 726 (1988); *Olson v Olson*, 189 Mich App 620 (1991) (aff'd in lieu of lv gtd, 439 Mich 986); and *Ghidotti v Barber* 459 Mich 189 (1998).

2.11   Special Considerations in Determining Income (Including Self-Employed Persons, Business Owners, Executives, and Others)

2.11 (A)   There are special difficulties in determining the income of certain individuals. This is due to at least four related causes. First, self-employed persons, business owners, and others often have types of income and expenses not frequently encountered in determining the income of most people. Second, the tax rules and tax forms associated with self-employment income are not only quite different from those associated with ordinary income from employment, but are designed with many additional purposes unrelated to child support determination and may therefore be difficult to translate into child support terms. Third, business balance sheets and other records also have purposes unrelated to child support determination, and are similarly difficult to translate into child support terms. Finally, there are potential difficulties because persons who have significant control over the form and manner of their own compensation may be able to arrange that compensation so as to be able to minimize the amount visible to friends of the court and others. To a somewhat lesser extent, all these considerations also apply to business executives who may have little or no ownership interest in the business.

2.11 (B)   The objective of determining income for purposes of this formula is to estimate as accurately as possible the monies available for support of children. Because tax rules and forms, and business balance sheets, as noted above, have quite different purposes, it is necessary to examine such documents carefully, with an emphasis on what is not available from those documents and what needs translation into child support terms.

2.11 (C)   These considerations apply to **all** forms of self-employment and business ownership, regardless of whether the business is organized as a corporation, a partnership, a sole proprietorship, or is a completely informal operation (of course, the form of organization will make a major difference in the sort of tax documents and business records available). As noted, many of these considerations will also apply to business executives, again without regard to the form of legal organization of the business.

2.11 (D)   Special attention should be given to the following factors:

    (1)   Unusual forms of income. Income may come in many forms other than wages and salaries. These might include distributed profits of the business (including under a profit-sharing plan), officers' fees and other compensation, management or consulting fees, commissions, and bonuses.

    (2)   In-kind income. Income might be received in a form other than cash. Among the most common forms of such income are use of a company car, free admission to entertainment provided by the business to its clients, and purchases of stock or other goods and services. All such in-kind income should be priced at its market value (the price that a person not affiliated with the business would have had to pay); the amount (if any) that was paid by the individual for the goods or services out of his or her pocket should be subtracted; and the remaining amount counted as income (note that part or all of the items added to income in this section may be allowable as deductions under Subsection (7).

    (3)   Re-directed income. In some cases, income to the owner or executive might be treated by the company as if it were something else. One example would be personal loans to the owner or executive which will not be paid back. These can later be "forgiven" by the company, or otherwise converted into income to the individual, once the time of child support determination is past. Although it should be presumed that such loans are in fact income, the presumption may be overcome if there is a history of such past loans being made and being repaid in a timely manner with market interest rates, and the current loan is at market interest rates and is fully paid up in accordance with a commercially reasonable time schedule. The amount by which a commercially reasonable repayment amount exceeds the amount actually repaid should be treated as income.

    (4)   Other forms of redirected income are payments by the business (in the form of wages, salaries, or payments for services) made to friends or relatives of

the individual. If the individual cannot demonstrate that there is a history of such payments preceding the separation (or motion for redetermination of child support) by several months or that the payments are a fair market value payment for services actually performed, then the payments shall be treated as income to the individual.

(5)   Deferred income. It is possible for business owners and executives to reduce their income for the period of a child support determination by temporarily lowering their own salaries, fees, distributed profits, etc. Past practices should be examined with care to determine whether the most recent information on such incomes is in line with historical patterns. For example, if it has been normal for a business to distribute a certain percentage of profits to owners, but the most recent year's distribution was substantially below that percentage, income for child support determination should be based on the historical average. Recent reductions in salary, bonuses, management fees, etc., as a percentage of gross income of the business should be treated the same manner.

(6)   Fringe Benefits. Certain fringe benefits paid by the business should be counted as income to the individual for child support determination purposes, even though such payments are not considered income for tax purposes. These include contributions to pension or other retirement plans, except for the employer share of Social Security and Medicare (FICA) taxes and contributions to qualified private retirement plans of up to 5.5 percent of the individual's gross income. Contributions in excess of these exceptions are to be counted as income.

(7)   Deductions. For a wide variety of historical and policy reasons, there are a considerable number of deductions allowed for taxation of business and individuals that are irrelevant to, and therefore **not** allowed as deductions from income for purposes of, child support determination, unless the expenses are consistent with the nature of the business. These include the following:

(a)   Rent paid by the business to the individual (unless the rent is otherwise counted as income to the individual);

(b)   Certain depreciation allowances. (Depreciation is an allowance for the presumed declining market value of assets used by the business. For tax purposes, depreciation allowances serve the function of spreading the deduction that would be associated with the expense of a purchase over several tax years; because the depreciation periods typically understate the useful life of many assets, depreciation allowances also provide some incentive to purchase new assets.) The **only** depreciation allowances that are permitted to be used as deductions from income for child support purposes are those that: 1) involve the property of the individual (not a corporation or partnership); **and** 2) involve tangible personal property (thus not financial assets or realty) other than automobiles or home offices; **and** 3) are based on straight-line (and not accelerated) tax depreciation. (Straight-line depreciation is when equal dollar amounts are claimed as depreciation allowances on a given asset in each of several tax years. Individuals who used accelerated depreciation on their tax returns can claim a deduction for the straight-line amount, provided the deduction meets the other criteria, if they can prove through an affidavit from an independent CPA what the straight-line amounts would have been).

(c)   Home office expenses, including rent, hazard insurance, utilities, repairs, and maintenance;

(d)   Business entertainment expenses spent on the parent (expenses on customers are allowable as deductions);

(e)   Travel expenses, except where such expenses are inherent in the nature of the business or occupation (e.g., a traveling salesperson), and in no case in excess of rates allowed by the state of Michigan for travel by its employees (such as automobile mileage rates, airplane coach rates, etc.); and

(f)   Automobile repair and maintenance expenses.

Note: Some items listed above appear in more than one section. This is because the items may appear on both individual and employer tax returns, in somewhat different guises.

2.12   Allowable Deductions from Gross Income

2.12 (A)   Alimony/Spousal Support

(1)   Any alimony/spousal support order <u>paid to someone other than the other parent of the case under consideration</u> should be deducted prior to the calculation and deduction of federal, state, and local income taxes. (Note: Alimony paid to the other parent may no longer be deducted).

(2)   The calculation of Social Security taxes (FICA) is based on gross income before deduction of the alimony/spousal support order.

2.12 (B)   Federal, State, and Local Income Taxes

(1)   In the absence of an explicit written agreement or judicial order to the contrary, the person with whom the child resides the greater number of days

17

during the calendar year must be presumed to be entitled to the dependent exemption for that child.

(2)   In determining filing status (Single or Married), presume the status that is most consistent with the situation of the parents as of the date of the order based on this recommendation.

(3)   When determining parents' net incomes for the purpose of establishing temporary child support recommendations, use each parent's current filing status.

(4)   In the event that tax returns are not made available, taxes should be estimated based on the best available information such as W-2 forms, employer statements, employer tax guides, pay vouchers, testimony, etc.

(5)   When tax returns cannot be obtained, utilize Employer Tax Guides for federal, state, and local taxes to determine net income by subtracting the deductions from gross earnings for the appropriate number of exemptions, rather than on the number claimed on the parent's W-4.

Example:

If an individual is currently single, presume that person will stay single and continue utilizing a single filing status. A parent may request a modification based on changed circumstances when that parent's filing status actually changes.

2.12 (C)   F.I.C.A.

2.12 (D)   Any mandatory withholdings required as a condition of employment (e.g., most union dues and some retirement plans).

2.12 (E)   The determinable portion of health insurance premiums for other children the parent is obligated to support.

(1)   The determinable portion of health insurance premiums paid by parents for any other child that parent is legally obligated to support (excluding children in case being evaluated) should be subtracted dollar for dollar from gross income.

(2)   If the children in the case under consideration, the parent, or others are included on the coverage, the other children's portion of the premium is represented in the difference in cost between single and family coverage, divided by the number covered by the family coverage (excluding the parent), and multiplied by the number of other children that the parent is obligated to support.

(3)   If the cost of single coverage cannot be determined or if the parent is not included, the children's portion of the premium is represented in the entire premium divided by the number of individuals covered, and multiplied by the number of other children that the parent is obligated to support.

2.12 (F)   Premiums for term equivalent insurance policies when the child(ren) are the beneficiaries by order or judgment.

(1)   When term life insurance premiums are being paid by either parent as ordered, that premium should be deducted dollar for dollar from gross income.

(2)   When whole life insurance policies are maintained as ordered, a premium amount should be calculated for the term insurance equivalent and subtracted from gross income.

2.12 (G)   Employer contributions to private qualified pension plans, to the extent that such contributions are less than 5.5 percent of the employee's gross income.

2.13   Existing Support Orders

2.13 (A)   *Existing* support orders are prior or subsequent support obligations for children other than those in the case specifically under consideration.

2.13 (B)   The actual amount of any existing order, including child care and ordinary medical expenses, must be subtracted from a parent's net income in order to determine the net income upon which child support for the case under consideration should be based. Arrearage payments should not be deducted.

2.13 (C)   If there is reliable information that the existing order has not been complied with for a significant period of time, two recommendations shall be prepared, one with and one without the existing order adjustment.

Example:

A noncustodial parent earns $1,450 net per month and pays child support of $299 per month for one child in another case.

$1,450 - $299 = $1,151

The noncustodial parent's support obligation for the case under consideration would be based on a monthly net income of $1,151.

2.14   **Ex Parte and Temporary Orders**

For the purpose of determining that parent's child support obligation, if a parent is ordered to pay taxes, mortgage, home insurance, telephone, or utilities in an ex parte or temporary order, those expenses should be subtracted from that parent's net income.

2.15   **Other Minor Children**

2.15 (A)   Parents should receive an adjustment to their net income for (other) biological or legally adopted minor children from other relationships living in their household before determining the income upon which child support for the case under consideration should be based.

2.15 (B)   After determining the parent's net income and subtracting existing support orders, multiply that income by the percentage for the appropriate number of "other" children found in Other Minor Children Percentages Table, and calculate the support based on the result.

Other Minor Children Percentages
Applied to Net Income

Number of Children	Adjustment Percentage
1	89.6%
2	84.1%
3	79.8%
4	77.3%
5 or more	75.2%

Example:

The noncustodial parent earns $1,750 net per month, and the custodial parent requests a modification of the support order for the three children. In considering this modification request, two additional biological children currently living in the noncustodial parent's household should be taken into account.

$1,750 x .841 = $1,472

The amount of support for the three children in the case under consideration should be determined based on a noncustodial parent income of $1,472.

2.16 **Stepchildren**

2.16 (A) In most circumstances, stepchildren should not be considered when determining the child support for a stepparent. In Michigan, children are the responsibility of their natural/adoptive parents. However, there may be cases in which support is unavailable from both natural/adoptive parents, and stepparents are required to make substantial contributions to their stepchildren's support.

2.16 (B) A parent in the case under consideration supporting stepchildren should receive a stepchild adjustment to net income when the stepchild's parents earn no income and do not have the ability to earn income.

2.16 (C) After determining that the parent in the case under consideration supports stepchildren and that the stepchildren are unsupported by their parents, multiply that parent's net income after all other preceding sections are applied by the percentage for the appropriate number of stepchildren found in the Stepchild Percentages Table, and calculate the support based on the result.

Stepchild Percentages
Applied to Net Income

Number of Children	Adjustment Percentage
1	94.8%
2	92.1%
3	89.9%
4	88.6%
5 or more	87.6%

3. CALCULATING CHILD SUPPORT AMOUNTS

The second step in determining each parent's child support obligation is calculation of the appropriate amount. This section describes the methods of calculating support obligations. Sections 3.01 through 3.05 outline the calculation of the portion of a support obligation that excludes amounts for medical and child care (i.e., base support). Section 3.07 outlines healthcare coverage determinations, the payment of extraordinary expenses, as well as calculation of the monthly medical support obligation to be paid toward ordinary health care expenses. Section 3.08 outlines the calculation of the child care support obligation.

Calculating child support obligations includes applying the appropriate base support calculations in Section 3.01 through 3.05 to both parents' monthly net incomes (calculated using Chapter 2) and the results of Section 3.07 and 3.08.

3.01 General Support Obligations

Various percentages of net income, which are based on the estimated costs of raising children, are used to determine child support in this formula. The percentages are based on the number of children and the total net family income displayed in the General Care Support Tables shown below and do not include medical or child care expenses. The total net family income levels against which the percentages are applied are annually adjusted using the Consumer Price Index for Metropolitan Detroit, with 1985 as the base.

General Support Tables

General Care Support Table: One Child						
Income Amount	Base Percentage	Base Support	&	Marginal Percentage		
$1,013	25.5%	$258.32	+	24.17%	over	$1,013
$1,627	25.0%	$406.75	+	17.49%	over	$1,627
$2,218	23.0%	$510.04	+	16.66%	over	$2,218
$2,847	21.6%	$614.95	+	14.64%	over	$2,847
$3,697	20.0%	$739.40	+	13.92%	over	$3,697
$5,250	18.2%	$955.50	+	12.37%	over	$5,250
$6,470	17.1%	$1,106.37	+	11.23%	over	$6,470
$8,133	15.9%	$1,293.15	+	10.00%	over	$8,133

General Care Support Table: Two Children

Monthly Family Net Income	Percentage Allocated	Base Support	+	Marginal Percentage	over	Income Level
$1,013	39.4%	$399.12	+	36.22%	over	$1,013
$1,627	38.2%	$621.51	+	26.19%	over	$1,627
$2,218	35.0%	$776.30	+	23.69%	over	$2,218
$2,847	32.5%	$925.28	+	22.50%	over	$2,847
$3,697	30.2%	$1,116.49	+	21.75%	over	$3,697
$5,250	27.7%	$1,454.25	+	20.28%	over	$5,250
$6,470	26.3%	$1,701.61	+	17.01%	over	$6,470
$8,133	24.4%	$1,984.45	+	15.00%	over	$8,133

General Care Support Table: Three Children

Monthly Family Net Income	Percentage Allocated	Base Support	+	Marginal Percentage	over	Income Level
$1,013	49.4%	$500.42	+	47.28%	over	$1,013
$1,627	48.6%	$790.72	+	35.09%	over	$1,627
$2,218	45.0%	$998.10	+	30.52%	over	$2,218
$2,847	41.8%	$1,190.05	+	28.75%	over	$2,847
$3,697	38.8%	$1,434.44	+	27.98%	over	$3,697
$5,250	35.6%	$1,869.00	+	23.40%	over	$5,250
$6,470	33.3%	$2,154.51	+	19.61%	over	$6,470
$8,133	30.5%	$2,480.57	+	19.00%	over	$8,133

General Care Support Table: Four Children

Monthly Family Net Income	Percentage Allocated	Base Support	+	Marginal Percentage	over	Income Level
$1,013	55.6%	$563.23	+	52.68%	over	$1,013
$1,627	54.5%	$886.72	+	39.86%	over	$1,627
$2,218	50.6%	$1,122.31	+	34.31%	over	$2,218
$2,847	47.0%	$1,338.09	+	33.08%	over	$2,847
$3,697	43.8%	$1,619.29	+	31.97%	over	$3,697
$5,250	40.3%	$2,115.75	+	24.92%	over	$5,250
$6,470	37.4%	$2,419.78	+	23.22%	over	$6,470
$8,133	34.5%	$2,805.89	+	22.00%	over	$8,133

General Care Support Table: Five or More Children						
Monthly Family Net Income	**Percentage Allocated**	**Base Support**	**+**	**Marginal Percentage**	**over**	**Income Level**
$1,013	60.8%	$615.90	+	57.36%	over	$1,013
$1,627	59.5%	$968.07	+	42.61%	over	$1,627
$2,218	55.0%	$1,219.90	+	37.80%	over	$2,218
$2,847	51.2%	$1,457.66	+	37.28%	over	$2,847
$3,697	48.0%	$1,774.56	+	35.83%	over	$3,697
$5,250	44.4%	$2,331.00	+	24.78%	over	$5,250
$6,470	40.7%	$2,633.29	+	24.07%	over	$6,470
$8,133	37.3%	$3,033.61	+	23.00%	over	$8,133

3.01 (A)   General Care Support Formula

To calculate a base support obligation, apply the total monthly net family income to the appropriate General Care Support Table and income level, and apportion the family support amount between both parents based on each parent's percentage of family income.

The noncustodial parent's <u>general care support obligation calculation formula</u> is:

$\{A + [B \times (C - D)]\} \times (E \div C) = G$

[Note: if E > P and C < I then support is calculated $(C \times J) (E \div C) = G$]

For the purposes of this formula:

A	=	Base Support for Family Income (General Care Support table, column 3)
B	=	Marginal Percentage (General Care Support table, column 4)
C	=	Actual Total Net Family Income (add net incomes of parties, rounded to nearest whole dollar)
D	=	Income Level (General Care Support table, last column)
E	=	Noncustodial Parent Allowable Net Income (round to nearest whole dollar)
G	=	Noncustodial Base Support-using table calculation (round to nearest whole dollar)
P	=	Poverty Level Income (Section 3.02(A))
I	=	Table Family Income Amount lowest level
J	=	Percentage Allocated (General Care Support table, column 2)

***Example*:**   Using General Care Support Formula, calculate the base support amount for the five children in this family.

25

Step 1:   Calculate monthly family net income.

Noncustodial parent earns $2,200 net per month, and the custodial parent earns $1,600. Add the parents' net incomes to determine the total net family income: $2,200 + $1,600 = $3,800

Step 2:   Calculate noncustodial parent's share of the base support obligation

{$1,774.56 + [35.83% x ($3,800 -$3,697)]} x ($2,200 ÷ $3,800) = G

{$1,774.56 + [.3583 x ($103)]} x (.5789) = G

{$1,774.56 + [$36.90]} x (.5789) = G

{1,822.46} x (.5789) = $1,049 Base Support per month.

3.02   Calculation of Child Support in Low/No Income Cases

3.02 (A)   For the purpose of this formula, poverty level income is defined as $776 or less per month (2004 United States HHS Poverty Guideline).

3.02 (B)   When custodial parents have a poverty level income or less, their incomes are not used in calculating the base support amount. In this way, those parents retain some income toward meeting their basic necessities, while contributing as much as possible to the support of their children.

3.02 (C)   The formula described in Section 3.01 does not apply when the payer earns income below the poverty level. In cases where a noncustodial parent has a poverty level income or lower, that parent's base support payment should be 10% of income.

(1)   The percentage adjustment (10%) should be decreased by 1% for every additional $450 per month that the custodial parent earns, as stated in the Poverty Level Income Percentage Adjustment Table.

(2)   The noncustodial parent poverty level income calculation formula is:

(E x K (or $25 whichever is more, see Section 1.08)) = L

For the purposes of this formula:

E =   Noncustodial Parent Net Income of poverty level or less (round to nearest whole dollar)
K =   Percentage Adjustment from Poverty Level Income Percentage Adjustment Table based on Custodial Parent Income
L =   Noncustodial Parent Monthly Base Support Amount (round to nearest whole dollar amount)

Poverty Level Income Percentage Adjustment Table			
Custodial Net Income	% Adjust	Custodial Net Income	% Adjust
$0 - $776	10%	$2,250 - $2,699	5%
$777 - $899	9%	$2,700 - $3,149	4%
$900 - $1,349	8%	$3,150 - $3,599	3%
$1,350 - $1,799	7%	$3,600 - $4,049	2%
$1,800 - $2,249	6%	$4,050 or more	1%

Example:

Using the noncustodial parent poverty level income calculation, figure the total monthly base support amount for three children in this family.

Step 1:   Calculate monthly net incomes.

Noncustodial parent earns $600 net per month, and the custodial parent earns $1400.

Step 2:   Calculate the monthly base support amount using the poverty level income calculation.

($600 x 7% (or $25 whichever is more, see Section 1.08)) =L
$42.00 = L

3.02 (D)   In low income cases where noncustodial parents earn more than a poverty level income, **the base support amount is** the apportioned support amount (calculated using the formula in Section 3.01), **or** is the difference between the noncustodial parent's net monthly income and the poverty level plus the support amount that the parent would pay at poverty level (using the noncustodial parent poverty level income calculation, above), **whichever is less.** The noncustodial parent low income calculation formula is:

(P x K (or $25 whichever is more see Section 1.08)) + (E -P) = M
if M < G then M = **L**
if M ≥ G then G = **L**

For the purposes of this formula:

P	=	Poverty Level Income (Section 3.02(A))
K	=	Percentage from the Poverty Level Income Percentage Adjustment Table
E	=	Noncustodial Parent Net Income (round to nearest whole dollar)
M	=	Noncustodial Support-using Low Income Adjustment calculation
G	=	Noncustodial Support-using Section 3.01 calculation
L	=	Base Support Amount (round to nearest whole dollar amount)

Example:

Using the noncustodial parent low income calculation, figure the base support amount for four children in this family.

Step 1:   Calculate net monthly incomes.

Noncustodial parent earns $950 net per month, and the custodial parent earns $1,300.

Step 2:   Calculate the total monthly support amount

$[\$776 \times 8\% \text{ (or } \$25 \text{)}] + (950-776) = M$

$[\$62.08] + (\$174) = M$

$\$236 = M$

Step 3:   The base support amount is the lesser of the results from the low income calculation formula and from the General Care Support calculation formula:

$M = \$236$
$G = \$478 = \{\$1,122.31 + [34.31\% \times (\$2,250 - \$2,218)]\} \times (\$950 \div \$2,250)$

Therefore, the base support amount for this example is $236.

3.03   Calculating Child Support Using Support Schedules

3.03 (A)   The monthly support schedules included in the Schedules Supplement provide approximate base support amounts at different incomes, and **incorporate the appropriate calculation formula** (Sections 3.01 and 3.02).

3.03 (B)   **The schedules do not include the required average ordinary health care expense amount** (Section 3.07(c)), **or child care** (Section 3.08), and do not factor in any costs or savings associated with parenting time or shared custody .

3.03 (C)   The percentage of income schedules included in the Schedules Supplement provide noncustodial parent's percentage of family income at specified income levels with 10% minimum and 90% maximum percentages.

(1)   To calculate the other parent's percentage of family income, subtract the noncustodial parent's percentage from 100%.

(2)   These percentages are used to apportion all medical support and health care support amounts, and child care expenses. The noncustodial percentage may be used to replace the apportionment part of the general support formula calculation.

3.03 (D)   To use the schedules, apply the following steps:

Step 1:   Determine each parent's net monthly income and round to the nearest increment of $50.

Step 2:   Find the schedule for the appropriate number of children.

Step 3:   Find the noncustodial parent's net income on the vertical column and the custodial parent's net income on the horizontal row. The noncustodial parent's monthly base support obligation is found where the noncustodial income line and the custodial income column intersect. (Note: The ordinary health care expense average amount from Section 3.07(C) is not included.)

Step 4:   Calculate and add the health care expenses average amount and child care expenses pursuant to Sections 3.07 and 3.08.

3.04   Calculation of Child Support in High Income Cases

In high income cases, where total family income exceeds the income categories listed in the Support Schedules Supplement, the base support amount should be calculated according to Section 3.01.

Example: Using Section 3.01, calculate the monthly support amount for the two children in this high income family.

Step 1:   Calculate monthly family net income.

Noncustodial parent earns $6,600 net per month, and the custodial parent earns $2,500.

Add the parents' net incomes to determine the monthly family net income:

$6,600 + $2,500 =$9,100

Step 2:   Calculate noncustodial parent's share of the base support obligation.

{$1,984.45 + [15.00% x ($9,100 - $8,133]} x ($6,600 ÷ $9,100) = G

{$1,984.45 + [.1500 x $967]} x .7253 = G

{$1,984.45 + [$145.05]} x .7253= G

{$2,129.50} x .7253 = $1,544.52 Base Support per month

3.05   Shared Economic Responsibility

When children share substantial amounts of time with both parents, child support should consider the costs and savings associated with parenting/custodial time. When a parent cares for a child overnight, that parent will cover many of the child's unduplicated costs. Conversely, the other parent will not be expending food or utility costs for the child. This calculation presumes that as parents spend more time with their children they directly contribute toward a greater share of all expenses.

3.05 (A)   Each parent must annually care for the children in the case under consideration a minimum of 128 overnights to meet the threshold for application of the shared economic responsibility formula.

3.05 (B)   The shared economic responsibility formula is:

$$\frac{(P^A_d)^2 (P^B_s) - (P^B_d)^2 (P^A_s)}{(P^A_d)^2 + (P^B_d)^2} = \text{Base Support}$$

P^A_d	=	The number of overnights the children will annually spend with Parent A.
P^B_d	=	The number of overnights the children will annually spend with Parent B.
P^A_s	=	Parent A's base support obligation calculated in Section 3.01 - 3.02.
P^B_s	=	Parent B's base support obligation calculated in Section 3.01 - 3.02.

3.05 (C)   The shared economic responsibility formula should only be used if an approximate annual number of overnights that the support payer will likely provide care for the children can be determined from the terms of the custody/parenting time order.

3.05 (D)   The shared economic responsibility formula should be applied to initial determinations and modifications based upon changed circumstances at the time of modification. It cannot be retroactively applied to existing support orders in a manner inconsistent with MCL 552.603(2).

3.05 (E)   In order to allow proper application of the formula, every child support order using this shared economic calculation should state that support was set using the shared economic responsibility formula.

Example:

Parent[A] has the child 235 overnights. Parent[A] earns $2,200 net per month. Parent[B] has the child 130 overnights. Parent[B] earns $1,800 net per month.

$$\frac{(\ 235 \ )^2 \ x \ (\ \$352 \ ) - (\ 130 \ )^2 \ x \ (\ \$430 \ )}{(\ 235 \ )^2 + (\ 130 \ )^2} \qquad = \qquad \text{Monthly Support}$$

$$\frac{\$19,439,200 \quad - \quad \$2,267,000}{55,225 + 16,900} \qquad = \qquad \text{Monthly Support}$$

$$\frac{\$12,172,200}{72,125} \qquad = \qquad \$168.76$$

Parent[B] should pay $169 each month for base support, plus medical support and child care.

3.06   Parenting Time Support Abatement

3.06 (A)   The payer's base support obligation for a child should be abated by 50% for periods of six or more consecutive overnights the child stays with that parent.

3.06 (B)   Every child support order not calculated using the shared economic responsibility formula should include a parenting time abatement provision that allows for abatement of the base support obligation following the conclusion of parenting time according to the terms of this section.

3.06 (C)   If the support order does not contain a parenting time support abatement provision, no abatement should occur except by written agreement of the parties.

3.06 (D)   Parenting time abatements must not be used in conjunction with the shared economic responsibility formula (Section 3.05, above) since it already considers parenting time.

3.06 (E)   The 50% abatement must be calculated based only on the base support obligation (Section 3.01 - 3.02), and not adjust medical (Section 3.07) or child care support amounts (Section 3.08). Medical and child care support obligations accommodate both parents' costs and account for the time the child is in the support payer's care.
Example:

The support payer picks up three children at 9:00 p.m. June 14, and returns one child at 11:00 a.m. June 24, and the other children at 3:00 p.m. June 30. One child spent

31

ten(10) consecutive overnights in the support payer's household, while the other two were there for seventeen (17) consecutive overnights. This entitles the support payer to ten (10) days parenting time abatement for one child and seventeen (17) days parenting time abatement for two children. If the child support order was $745 per month ($701 base support and $44 ordinary medical expense), the ordered 50% abatement would be determined as follows:

Step 1: Determine the daily support amount per child (see 4.05(B) for daily proration factor)

$701.00 x .033 month = $23.13 per day
$23.13 ÷ 3 children = $7.71 per child per day

Step 2: Based on the number of overnights, daily support, and participating children, figure the support for each period of parenting time.

($7.71 x 1 child) x 10 days = $77.11
($7.71 x 2 children) x 17 days = $262.17

Step 3: Figure the 50% abatement.

$ 77.11 x 50% =	$ 38 .56	For the 10 days with one child
$262.17 x 50% =	$131.09	For the 17 days with two children
Total abatement for period	$169.64	

3.07 Health Care and Medical Support

3.07 (A) Health Care / Medical Support Obligations

(1) Support includes provision of health care coverage, and the payment of medical, dental, and other health care-related expenses for children eligible for support. MCL 552.602(ee). A health care support obligation defines who will provide insurance coverage and what coverage should be provided, as well as the division of premiums and ordinary and extraordinary costs between the parents.

(2) Health care includes treatments, services, equipment, medicines, preventative care, etc. associated with oral, visual, psychological, medical, and other related needs, provided or prescribed by health care professionals.

(3) Routine remedial care costs (e.g., first-aid supplies, cough syrup, vitamins, etc.) are included in the base support amounts calculated in Section 3.01 -

3.05 and, for the purposes of this section, should not be considered as ordinary or extraordinary health care expenses.

(4)   As part of a total child support obligation, support orders must provide for health care coverage and payment of ordinary and extraordinary health care expenses.

(5)   Health care obligations should be apportioned between parents based on each parent's share of family income, provided that the proportion paid by either party shall not be less than 10.0% nor more than 90.0%. Proportions should be rounded to the nearest tenth percent. The Percentage of Income Schedule contains the noncustodial parent percentages for certain income levels. To calculate the other parent's percentage, subtract the non-custodial parent's percentage from 100%.

(6)   Every support order should set the percentage of costs for which each parent is responsible according to the terms of Subsection 3.07(A)(5). The percentage continues until further order of the court.

3.07 (B)   Health Care Coverage

(1)   Responsibility to Insure

(a)   The law directs that, if a child support order is entered, the court must make **one or both** parents responsible to obtain or maintain health care coverage for the benefit of the parents' children that is available at a reasonable cost as a benefit of employment. Further, if a parent is self-employed and maintains health care coverage, the court must order the parent to obtain or maintain dependent coverage for the benefit of the children. MCL 552.605a(2).

(b)   Many factors may be used in determining whether one or both parents should maintain employer, group, or private insurance coverage for minor children. When comparing plans, consider factors like: accessibility and comprehensiveness of included services, likely continuation of coverage, affordability of deductibles and co-payments (split as ordinary expenses, Subsection 3.07(C)), and reasonableness of the cost of coverage (Subsection 3.07(B)(3)).

(c)   Michigan law requires that orders of dependent health care coverage contain qualified medical child support order information. MCL 552.626b. Qualified medical child support orders must clearly specify: the name and the last known mailing address of the participant (providing parent), the name and mailing address of each child covered by the order, the name and mailing address of each child's custodial parent (except the order may provide that the name

33

and mailing address of an official substituted for the address of any child or custodian), a reasonable description of the type of coverage to be provided to each child or the manner in which the types of coverage is to be determined, and the period to which such order applies. 29 USC 1169.

(2) Reasonable Cost of Coverage

   (a) A reasonable cost for providing private health care coverage does not exceed five percent of the gross income of the providing parent.

   (b) Parents with a net income below 133 percent of the federal poverty level ($1,032) or whose resident child is covered by Medicaid based on that parent's income should not be ordered to contribute toward or provide private coverage, unless private coverage is obtainable without employee contribution.

   (c) A providing parent's costs for private health care coverage are unreasonable if the parent's total share of child support, child care, ordinary health care expenses, and net share of health care insurance (not including arrearage payments) exceed 50% of the parent's net income as defined in the Michigan Child Support Formula Manual.

(3) Allocation of Premiums

   (a) The net determinable portion of health insurance premiums paid by the parents for children eligible for support in this case should be apportioned between the parents according to their incomes.

   (b) The net premium amount should be included as part of the support payment.

   (c) Calculate the allocation of premiums according to the following steps.

   Step 1: Determine the portion of each parent's net health care premium attributable to the children.

      a. If the parent is included on the coverage, use the children's portion of the premium as represented in the difference in cost between single and family coverage. If the policy does not include single coverage or if the parent is not included, use the entire premium.

      b. Divide the children's portion of the premium by the number of individuals covered (excluding the parent

34

if single coverage was subtracted in Step 1 a), and multiply by the number of children covered in this case.

Step 2:   Determine the children's monthly premium that each parent pays, by dividing each parent's annual premium costs by 12.

Step 3   Offset the two amounts. Record the support payee's premium payment as a positive number and the other parent's premium payment as a negative number; then add the two amounts together. (Note: A positive result means an additional amount will be paid to cover the custodian's premium and a negative result means less money will be paid as support to offset the payee's portion of the premium).

Step 4:   Determine the payer's portion of the premium payment amount by multiplying the offset amount by the payer's percentage of family income (according to Subsection 3.07(A)(5) and rounding to the nearest cent.

Step 5:   Add the payer's portion of the premium amount, whether positive or negative, to the base support obligation calculated in Sections 3.01 - 3.05.

3.07 (C)   Ordinary Health Care Expenses

(1)   Ordinary health care and medical expenses include the payee's co-payments, deductibles, uninsured, and other health care-related costs for children eligible for support in this case. Routine remedial care items are not "ordinary" expenses and are covered in Subsection 3.07(A)(3).

(2)   Every support order should set an annual ordinary health care expense amount to cover the qualifying payee expenditures within a calendar year. The payment amount should be apportioned according to the terms of Subsection 3.07(A)(5). The payer's share of ordinary expenses (rounded to the nearest cent) payment should normally be ordered paid as part of the regular support payment. The recipient's share of ordinary expenses should be directly contributed by the recipient.

(3)   Ordinary Health Care Expense Amounts

(a)   On average, families routinely spend $289[1] per year per child on ordinary medical expenses.

(b)   The annual ordinary health care expense amount restarts every calendar year and continues with the support obligation or until further order of the court.

(c)   For the purpose of setting medical child support obligations, the amount corresponding to the appropriate number of children listed in the Ordinary Health Care Expense Average Table is presumed to be the amount that will be spent. However, amounts may be added to compensate for higher uninsured known or predictable expenses (e.g., orthodontia, special medical need, ongoing treatment, uninsured children, etc.).

Ordinary Health Care Expense Averages		
Number of Children	Annual Ordinary Expenses	Monthly Payment to Apportion (Annual/ 12)
1	$289.00	$24.08
2	$578.00	$48.17
3	$867.00	$72.25
4	$1,156.00	$96.33
5 or more	$1,445.00	$120.42

(4)   Ordinary Expense Accounting

(a)   The support recipient maintains the annual ordinary health care expense amounts (Subsection 3.07(C)(2) and (3)) to reimburse the children's eligible expenditures (Subsection 3.07(C)(1)).

(b)   All expenditures are considered made in proportion to each parent's percentage of income as established in the order.

(c)   It is presumed that the set amount for ordinary health care expenses will be spent and the recipient will not have to routinely provide proof

---

[1] *Annual Report on Access to and Utilization of Health Care for Children and Youth in the United States – 2000* in Ambulatory Pediatrics. 2001;8-9. Amount was updated using Detroit CPI-U Medical Index to Feb 2004.

of expenditure for ordinary medical expense amounts. (Note: An accounting showing that the established annual ordinary health care expense amount was exceeded is needed to seek reimbursement of extraordinary expenses.)

(d)   Amounts may be prorated for periods during which they are in effect. To prorate amounts for partial months, see section 4.05(C).

(e)   All qualifying payer health care expenses should be divided as extraordinary expenses.

3.07 (D)   Extraordinary Health Care Expenses

(1)   Extraordinary expenses include uninsured medical and health care-related expenditures that exceed the annual ordinary health care expense amount set in Subsection 3.07(C) and a payer's qualifying expenditures.

(2)   Net Extraordinary Health Care Expenses should be apportioned between the parents according to the percentages established in the support order.

3.07 (E)   Abatements and Adjustments

(1)   Medical support obligations are based on set costs allocated between both parents. Amounts of support designated for ordinary health care expenses should not be included in parenting time abatements or shared economic adjustments.

(2)   Health care child support figures should be added to the support obligation calculated by shared economic child support equation, rather than being used as part of each parent's support obligation in the shared economic calculation.

3.08   Child Care Support

3.08 (A)   When the custodian and/or noncustodial parent incurs work-related child care expenses, a child care support payment is required. Work-related child care expenses include those net expenses which allow the parent to look for employment, retain paid employment, or to enroll in and attend an educational program which will improve employment opportunities.

3.08 (B)   When custodians or parents have an established pattern of child care and can verify that they have actual, predictable and reasonable child care expenses on behalf of the children in the case under consideration, the total net expenses to each parent should be apportioned between parents according to their share of family income, provided that the proportion paid by either party shall not be less than 10% nor more than 90%. Proportions should be rounded to the nearest tenth percent. The Percentage of Income

Schedule contains the non-custodial parent percentages for certain income levels. To calculate the other parent's percentage, subtract the non-custodial parent's percentage from 100%.

3.08 (C)   In calculating child care expenses to be apportioned between the parents, the net cost to the parent or custodian must be used. Figure the net cost of child care by deducting any child care subsidies, credits (including federal tax credit), or reimbursements from any public or private source from the gross cost of child care.

3.08 (D)   The noncustodial parent's portion of the custodian's net costs minus the custodian's portion of the noncustodial parent's net child care must be added to the support calculated in Section 3.01 - 3.05 and the ordinary medical expense support payment.

3.08 (E)   When custodians do not have an established pattern of child care expenses, they may request a contingent child care provision. The order shall provide a specific amount for child support and a projected amount for child care. The projected determination should be based on information regarding average child care costs in the community as provided by the local friend of the court or on three written quotations for child care as provided to the friend of the court by the custodial parent. The net cost of child care shall be computed in the same manner as when there is an established pattern of child care. This contingent provision will become effective upon the following:

Step 1:   Proof provided by the custodian of employment or enrollment in an educational or training program which will improve employment opportunities.

Step 2:   Proof provided by the custodian of actual out-of-pocket child care expenses.

Step 3:   The friend of the court notifying the noncustodial parent of the activation of the contingent recommendation and providing that parent with a copy of the verifying documents.

Note: The implementation of the contingent provision may constitute a change of circumstances which would warrant a review or modification.

3.08 (F)   Child care shall be recommended up to the start of the school year immediately following the 12th birthday of the child but only to the extent thereafter that the health and safety needs of the child require continued child care.

3.08 (G)   In calculating annual child care costs, it shall be assumed that the court's specific parenting time and custody orders are followed.

3.08 (H) If a child care provider requires payment to retain an available slot for a child without regard to whether the child attends during parenting times, vacations, illness or other temporary absences, the required payment shall be used in computing child care costs.

3.08 (I) Prior to making a recommendation, documentation of a parent's child care costs shall be provided by the custodian to the friend of the court on the State Court Administrative Office Approved Child Care Verification Form, or its equivalent.

Example:

The parents have two minor children. The custodian has a monthly income of $1800 with gross child care costs of $350 per month and pays even when the child is absent. The noncustodial parent has a monthly income of $2400 with gross child care costs of $400 during extended summer parenting time specified in the court order.

Step	Custodian	Noncustodial Parent
Step I: Calculate each parent's gross annual child care costs.	12 months multiplied by $350 per month equals $4,200 annually.	$400 annually
Step II: Subtract the appropriate subsidy, credit, or reimbursement deductions.	$4,200 annual costs minus $966 credit equals $3,234.	$400 annual costs minus $0 credit equals $400.
Step III: Divide annual net child care costs by 12 to obtain average monthly child care costs.	$ 3,234 divided by 12 equals $270 per month.	$400 divided by 12 equals $33 per month.
Step IV: Prorate each parent's share of the other parent's average net monthly child care cost based on the net income of the parents per the Child Support Formula.	Noncustodial parent's prorated share of the parties' net income is 57.1% (Total net income of parties divided by the noncustodial parent's net income) $270 multiplied by 57.1% equals $154 per month.	Custodian's prorated share of the parties' net income is 42.9% (Total net income of parties divided by the custodian's net income) $33 multiplied by 42.9% equals $14 per month
Step V: Subtract the higher child care prorated share from the lower child care prorated share.	$154 noncustodial share of custodian's child care minus $14 custodian share of noncustodial child care equals net child care of $140 per month.	
Step VI: Add the net child care amount if noncustodial prorated share is higher. Subtract the net child care amount if the custodian's share is higher.	Add the $140 in child care to other child support amounts to determine the total support amount.	

4. OTHER FACTORS

4.01   Third Party Custodians

4.01 (A)   When a child is in the physical custody of a third party, <u>both</u> of the parents should be required to pay support. The level of support should be determined and apportioned according to the incomes of the parents.

4.01 (B)   Use this method when the parents of the child(ren) live in the same household:

<u>Step 1:</u>   Determine the combined family net income.

<u>Step 2:</u>   Calculate the base support, ordinary medical, and child care expense amount based on family net income.

<u>Step 3:</u>   Calculate each parent's individual support obligation by apportioning the combined family support between the incomes of both parents based on a each parent's share of the total family income.

4.01 (C)   Use this method when the parents of the child(ren) live in separate households.

<u>Step 1:</u>   Determine each parent's and the total family net income.

<u>Step 2:</u>   Calculate each parent's support obligation separately by using a custodian income of zero. Apportion the ordinary medical expense amount based on a each parent's share of the total family income.

<u>Step 3:</u>   Add a parent's base support obligation, respective share of ordinary medical, and child care expenses to determine that parent's support obligation.

4.02   Different Custody Arrangements For Different Children

It is not unusual for the court to order different custody arrangements for different children. The most obvious arrangement is for one parent to have sole custody of some children and the other parent to have sole custody of other children; this type of arrangement is usually called "split custody." However, it is also possible for some children to be in the sole custody of a parent and other children to be part of a shared custody arrangement, or for shared custody arrangements to vary from child to child. All this real-life complexity can make child support computations equally complex. The following method of computation is intended to apply in all such complex arrangements:

Step 1: Determine **each custody arrangement** involved in the present case (e.g., sole custody of one child with Parent A and sole custody of a second child with Parent B; shared custody of two children 60-40 with Parent A and B respectively and sole custody of a third child with Parent B; etc.).

Step 2: For **each custody arrangement** involved, compute what the child support including ordinary medical expenses, would be for **the child(ren) in that custody arrangement** as if there were no other children.

(**Note**: In order to keep distinct the amounts that would be paid from one parent to the other, record the computed support payments from Parent B to Parent A as positive numbers and those from Parent A to Parent B as negative numbers.)

Step 3: **Add** the amounts obtained in Step 2. The sum of all amounts is the support payment. (Note: If it is negative, it is a payment from Parent A to Parent B; if it is positive, it is a payment from Parent B to Parent A.).

Example 1:

Step 1: There are two children, one each in sole custody of Parent A and Parent B. Parent B has net income of $1300 per month and Parent A has net income of $1,050.

Step 2: A) Custody Arrangement #1: Parent A has sole custody of one child, the support amount would be $294 per month. This is recorded as +$294 since it is the amount to be a paid from Parent B to Parent A.

B) Custody Arrangement #2: If Parent B had sole custody of one child, the support amount would be $238 per month. This is recorded as -$258 since it is the amount to be a paid from Parent A to Parent B.

Step 3: Add +$294 and -$238 for a support payment of +$54. (Note: The positive number indicates the payment is to be made by Parent B to Parent A.

Example 2:

Step 1: There are three children. Two are in the sole custody of Parent A, but the third is in a shared custody arrangement with 60% of the time spent with Parent B and 40% spent with Parent A. Parent B has net income of $2,200 per month and Parent A has net income of $1,800.

Step 2: Custody Arrangement #1: Two children are in the sole custody of Parent A, the support amount is $663 per month. This is recorded as +$663 since it is the amount to be paid from Parent B to Parent A.

Custody Arrangement #2: One child is in a shared custody arrangement, the support would be $111. The payment should be recorded as -$111 per month from Parent A to Parent B.

Step 3:   Add +$663 and -$111 for a for a total support payment of +$552 from Parent B to Parent A.

4.03   **Arrearage Guidelines**

4.03 (A)   The Arrearage Guideline is for use by friends of the court, referees, and judges in making arrearage payment determinations and adjustments to ensure statewide consistency by trial courts and friend of the court offices when current support for a child terminates or the payer owes past due support.

(1)   Federal law requires states to have procedures to increase the amount of payments to include amounts for arrearages. 42 U.S.C. 666(c)(1)(H).

(2)   State law requires that the formula contain guidelines for setting and adjusting payments for overdue support when support for a child terminates. MCL 552.519(3)(a)(vi).

(3)   Statute requires the friend of the court office to use the Arrearage Guideline in setting or adjusting arrearage payments. MCL 552.517e.

(4)   When making administrative adjustments to arrearage payment amounts, the friend of the court office must follow procedures "to afford the payer due process including at least notice, an opportunity for an administrative hearing, and an opportunity for an appeal on the record to an independent administrative or judicial tribunal." MCL 552.517e.

(5)   This Guideline is not intended to interfere with the enforcement of past-due support and its collection through concurrent means and as quickly as is allowed by law, and does not apply to payments set for writs of garnishment and other lump sum collections.

(6)   The Arrearage Guideline is not intended to interfere with judicial discretion in setting fair and equitable payment amounts that deviate from the Guideline. Each case is decided on its own merits.

4.03 (B)   Arrearage Payment Calculation

(1)   Support arrearages should be repaid as quickly as possible.

If all or a substantial portion of the arrearage cannot be paid immediately, the Arrearage Guideline should be used when setting arrearage payment amounts where support or fees are owed.

(2)   The monthly arrearage payment is 4.35 percent of the total support arrearage at the time of the review, but not less than $80 nor more than the current support amount (if no current support charge, use the last ordered charge amount). 4.35 percent will eliminate most arrearages and surcharge within two years.

   (a)   The percentage, 0.6667%, approximates the minimum monthly amount needed to stay current with surcharge.

   (b)   When applying the Guideline, any monies held or retained by the friend of the court office or the State Disbursement Unit as payment of past due child support should be subtracted from the amount of arrearage used to calculate the repayment amount.

(3)   Payments set by this Guideline should be rounded to the nearest whole dollar amount.

(4)   Figure the confinement by applying the calculation (i.e. 4.35%, $80, or current order amount) to a support arrearage that includes the total confinement expenses and other support arrearages owed at the time of the review. The confinement expense repayment amount should not be less than $25.00, nor more than the confinement expenses pro-rata share of the total amount owed. Laws, regulations, and other policy determine how these amounts will be distributed on a specific case.

(5)   In order to repay arrearages as quickly as possible, the total-payment-amount used for determining the arrearage payment amount for collection must be the higher of: the most recent total-payment-amount, or the total-payment-amount presently figured using the arrearage payment calculation and current support charge.

(6)   If the support charge has been reduced since the most recent total-payment-amount was set for reasons other than a reduction in payer's income, add that reduction to the arrearage payment to automatically become a new arrearage payment amount. The total-payment-amount remains the same, and more monies are applied to arrears.

(7)   If the most recent total-payment-amount is the payment amount chosen, the aggregate amount remains the same, but consists of a reduced support and an increased arrearage payment amount, the total-payment-amount collected remains in effect until the arrearage has been paid in full, or until modified or adjusted by the court or friend of the court.

(8)   Adjustment of Payments When Current Support Obligations Terminate

    (a)   If arrearages exist when a current support obligation terminates or is reduced for reasons other than a reduction in the payer's income, there shall be no automatic reduction in the total-payment-amount unless ordered by the court.

    (b)   The reductions in the current support amount are added to the current arrearage payment amount and automatically becomes the new arrearage payment amount.

    (c)   The total-payment-amount collected remains in effect until the arrearage has been paid in full or until modified or adjusted by the court or friend of the court.

Example:

If a payer is required to pay $690 per month, $430 as current support plus $260 toward arrears, and the current support order terminates, the payer would continue to pay $690 per month, all to be applied on the arrearage.

4.03 (C)   Guideline Deviation and Exceptions

(1)   When application of this Guideline creates an unjust or inappropriate result, deviation may occur and an alternate arrearage payment amount may be established.

(2)   The friend of the court office may utilize its discretion and deviate from the Guideline to increase the arrearage repayment amount:

    (a)   if there has been no other significant change in circumstances (e.g., different source of income, higher income, etc.), **and**

    (b)   if the payer has made all of the payments for the entire period since the repayment amount was set, **and**

    (c)   arrearages have increased by an amount greater than one month's support solely because of accumulation of child support surcharge.

(3)   The friend of the court should not routinely apply the Guideline to administratively change repayment amounts in cases where:

    (a)   the court has set a specific periodic arrearage payment amount in an order, and since entry of that order the arrearages have not increased by an amount equivalent to one month's support based on the current support amount (if no current support charge use the last ordered charge amount) and the payer's support obligation has not decreased;

(b)   the total amount of arrearage has been reduced, but has not been paid in full since the repayment amount was set (because applying the Guideline when arrears have decreased since the repayment amount was set results in adjustments that extend the repayment period);

(c)   the court previously ordered or the friend of the court implemented a repayment amount that deviates from the Guideline based either upon an unjust or inappropriate result or a formal agreement between the parties, and circumstances have not significantly changed since entry of that order or implementation of the repayment amount; or

(d)   in interstate cases where Michigan and another state's tribunal have entered an order regarding the same payer and child, and the support order and arrears accumulated under the Michigan order are being enforced by another jurisdiction.

4.03 (D)   Administrative Adjustment Records

Information should be maintained to record: administrative adjustments by offices, arrearage repayment amounts deviating from the Arrearage Guideline, and the reasons for deviation.

4.03 (E)   Definitions for the purpose of the Arrearage Guideline:

(1)   Administrative Adjustment means a change in an amount not ordered by the court.

(2)   Arrearage Payment Amount means periodic amounts in addition to current support which are specifically designated to reduce the arrearage owed, but are not arrearage payments set for writs of garnishment and lump sum orders.

(3)   Confinement Expense means an amount of money ordered by the circuit court under the paternity act for the necessary expenses incurred by or for the mother in connection with her confinement or of other expenses incurred in connection with the pregnancy of the mother.

(4)   One Month's Support means an amount of support equivalent to the periodic charges that would occur in one month under the current support order, or absent a current support charge, the last ordered periodic amount.

(5)   Total-payment-amount means the sum of regular periodic current and past-due support, fees, and other amounts set by court order (support, enforcement,

repayment, etc.) or by administrative adjustment by the friend of the court office to collect support by income withholding or other means.

4.04   Agreements Related to Property

When parents connect property settlement with child support provisions, the provisions must be clearly stated in the judgment of divorce to be given continued effect. MCL 552.605 requires that any property awarded in lieu of support required under the formula must be recorded as a deviation.

4.05   Order Conversion, Proration, and Rounding

4.05 (A)   The SCAO has adopted the following factors to convert to monthly amounts. MCL 552.605c.

Multiply weekly amounts by 4.35.
Multiply bi-weekly amounts by 2.175.
Multiply semi-monthly amounts by 2.
Divide bi-monthly amounts by 2
Divide quarterly amounts by 3.
Divide semi-annual amounts by 6
Divide annual amounts by 12.

4.05 (B)   To convert monthly support obligations into daily amounts, multiply by .033.

4.05 (C)   Charges for orders that begin or change after the beginning of a month, or that terminate before the end of the month, must be prorated for the portion of the month they are effective. Prorate monthly support amounts by applying the following equation:

$$C_b - ((C_b - C_n) \times .033 \times D_n)$$

C_b	=	Beginning Monthly Charge
.033	=	Daily Adjustment (Section 4.05(B))
D_n	=	Number of Days New Amount Effective
C_n	=	New Monthly Charge Amount

Examples:

A new support order for $468 becomes effective on September 30.
$0 - (($0 - $468) x .033 x 1) = $15 is owed for September.

An existing order for $320 terminates on August 12.
$320 - (($320 - $0) x .033 x 20) = $109 is owed for August.

An existing order for $784 reduces to $590 on June 7 because the oldest child graduates.
$784 - (($784 - $590) x .033 x 24) = $630 is owed for June.

4.05 (D)   Support amounts should be rounded to the nearest whole dollar.

2004 Michigan Child Support Formula Schedules Supplement

NOTE: When using the schedules in this supplement, ONLY use net income amounts calculated according to the terms of the Formula Manual. Using other income calculations will produce inaccurate results.

The figures in this schedule only include monthly base support amounts. The amounts do not make any adjustment for parenting time, and do not include child care expenses.

2004 MICHIGAN CHILD SUPPORT FORMULA SCHEDULES
PERCENTAGE OF INCOME

Non-Custodial Parent Percentage of Income

CUSTODIAL PARENT MONTHLY INCOME

	0	250	300	350	400	450	500	550	600	650	700	750	800	850	900	950	1000
250]	90.0%	50.0%	45.5%	41.7%	38.5%	35.7%	33.3%	31.3%	29.4%	27.8%	26.3%	25.0%	23.8%	22.7%	21.7%	20.8%	20.0%
300]	90.0%	54.5%	50.0%	46.2%	42.9%	40.0%	37.5%	35.3%	33.3%	31.6%	30.0%	28.6%	27.3%	26.1%	25.0%	24.0%	23.1%
350]	90.0%	58.3%	53.8%	50.0%	46.7%	43.8%	41.2%	38.9%	36.8%	35.0%	33.3%	31.8%	30.4%	29.2%	28.0%	26.9%	25.9%
400]	90.0%	61.5%	57.1%	53.3%	50.0%	47.1%	44.4%	42.1%	40.0%	38.1%	36.4%	34.8%	33.3%	32.0%	30.8%	29.6%	28.6%
450]	90.0%	64.3%	60.0%	56.3%	52.9%	50.0%	47.4%	45.0%	42.9%	40.9%	39.1%	37.5%	36.0%	34.6%	33.3%	32.1%	31.0%
500]	90.0%	66.7%	62.5%	58.8%	55.6%	52.6%	50.0%	47.6%	45.5%	43.5%	41.7%	40.0%	38.5%	37.0%	35.7%	34.5%	33.3%
550]	90.0%	68.8%	64.7%	61.1%	57.9%	55.0%	52.4%	50.0%	47.8%	45.8%	44.0%	42.3%	40.7%	39.3%	37.9%	36.7%	35.5%
600]	90.0%	70.6%	66.7%	63.2%	60.0%	57.1%	54.5%	52.2%	50.0%	48.0%	46.2%	44.4%	42.9%	41.4%	40.0%	38.7%	37.5%
650]	90.0%	72.2%	68.4%	65.0%	61.9%	59.1%	56.5%	54.2%	52.0%	50.0%	48.1%	46.4%	44.8%	43.3%	41.9%	40.6%	39.4%
700]	90.0%	73.7%	70.0%	66.7%	63.6%	60.9%	58.3%	56.0%	53.8%	51.9%	50.0%	48.3%	46.7%	45.2%	43.8%	42.4%	41.2%
750]	90.0%	75.0%	71.4%	68.2%	65.2%	62.5%	60.0%	57.7%	55.6%	53.6%	51.7%	50.0%	48.4%	46.9%	45.5%	44.1%	42.9%
800]	90.0%	76.2%	72.7%	69.6%	66.7%	64.0%	61.5%	59.3%	57.1%	55.2%	53.3%	51.6%	50.0%	48.5%	47.1%	45.7%	44.4%
850]	90.0%	77.3%	73.9%	70.8%	68.0%	65.4%	63.0%	60.7%	58.6%	56.7%	54.8%	53.1%	51.5%	50.0%	48.6%	47.2%	45.9%
900]	90.0%	78.3%	75.0%	72.0%	69.2%	66.7%	64.3%	62.1%	60.0%	58.1%	56.3%	54.5%	52.9%	51.4%	50.0%	48.6%	47.4%
950]	90.0%	79.2%	76.0%	73.1%	70.4%	67.9%	65.5%	63.3%	61.3%	59.4%	57.6%	55.9%	54.3%	52.8%	51.4%	50.0%	48.7%
1000]	90.0%	80.0%	76.9%	74.1%	71.4%	69.0%	66.7%	64.5%	62.5%	60.6%	58.8%	57.1%	55.6%	54.1%	52.6%	51.3%	50.0%
1050]	90.0%	80.8%	77.8%	75.0%	72.4%	70.0%	67.7%	65.6%	63.6%	61.8%	60.0%	58.3%	56.8%	55.3%	53.8%	52.5%	51.2%
1100]	90.0%	81.5%	78.6%	75.9%	73.3%	71.0%	68.8%	66.7%	64.7%	62.9%	61.1%	59.5%	57.9%	56.4%	55.0%	53.7%	52.4%
1150]	90.0%	82.1%	79.3%	76.7%	74.2%	71.9%	69.7%	67.6%	65.7%	63.9%	62.2%	60.5%	59.0%	57.5%	56.1%	54.8%	53.5%
1200]	90.0%	82.8%	80.0%	77.4%	75.0%	72.7%	70.6%	68.6%	66.7%	64.9%	63.2%	61.5%	60.0%	58.5%	57.1%	55.8%	54.5%
1250]	90.0%	83.3%	80.6%	78.1%	75.8%	73.5%	71.4%	69.4%	67.6%	65.8%	64.1%	62.5%	61.0%	59.5%	58.1%	56.8%	55.6%
1300]	90.0%	83.9%	81.3%	78.8%	76.5%	74.3%	72.2%	70.3%	68.4%	66.7%	65.0%	63.4%	61.9%	60.5%	59.1%	57.8%	56.5%
1350]	90.0%	84.4%	81.8%	79.4%	77.1%	75.0%	73.0%	71.1%	69.2%	67.5%	65.9%	64.3%	62.8%	61.4%	60.0%	58.7%	57.4%
1400]	90.0%	84.8%	82.4%	80.0%	77.8%	75.7%	73.7%	71.8%	70.0%	68.3%	66.7%	65.1%	63.6%	62.2%	60.9%	59.6%	58.3%
1450]	90.0%	85.3%	82.9%	80.6%	78.4%	76.3%	74.4%	72.5%	70.7%	69.0%	67.4%	65.9%	64.4%	63.0%	61.7%	60.4%	59.2%
1500]	90.0%	85.7%	83.3%	81.1%	78.9%	76.9%	75.0%	73.2%	71.4%	69.8%	68.2%	66.7%	65.2%	63.8%	62.5%	61.2%	60.0%
1550]	90.0%	86.1%	83.8%	81.6%	79.5%	77.5%	75.6%	73.8%	72.1%	70.5%	68.9%	67.4%	66.0%	64.6%	63.3%	62.0%	60.8%
1600]	90.0%	86.5%	84.2%	82.1%	80.0%	78.0%	76.2%	74.4%	72.7%	71.1%	69.6%	68.1%	66.7%	65.3%	64.0%	62.7%	61.5%
1650]	90.0%	86.8%	84.6%	82.5%	80.5%	78.6%	76.7%	75.0%	73.3%	71.7%	70.2%	68.8%	67.3%	66.0%	64.7%	63.5%	62.3%
1700]	90.0%	87.2%	85.0%	82.9%	81.0%	79.1%	77.3%	75.6%	73.9%	72.3%	70.8%	69.4%	68.0%	66.7%	65.4%	64.2%	63.0%
1750]	90.0%	87.5%	85.4%	83.3%	81.4%	79.5%	77.8%	76.1%	74.5%	72.9%	71.4%	70.0%	68.6%	67.3%	66.0%	64.8%	63.6%
1800]	90.0%	87.8%	85.7%	83.7%	81.8%	80.0%	78.3%	76.6%	75.0%	73.5%	72.0%	70.6%	69.2%	67.9%	66.7%	65.5%	64.3%
1850]	90.0%	88.1%	86.0%	84.1%	82.2%	80.4%	78.7%	77.1%	75.5%	74.0%	72.5%	71.2%	69.8%	68.5%	67.3%	66.1%	64.9%
1900]	90.0%	88.4%	86.4%	84.4%	82.6%	80.9%	79.2%	77.6%	76.0%	74.5%	73.1%	71.7%	70.4%	69.1%	67.9%	66.7%	65.5%
1950]	90.0%	88.6%	86.7%	84.8%	83.0%	81.3%	79.6%	78.0%	76.5%	75.0%	73.6%	72.2%	70.9%	69.6%	68.4%	67.2%	66.1%
2000]	90.0%	88.9%	87.0%	85.1%	83.3%	81.6%	80.0%	78.4%	76.9%	75.5%	74.1%	72.7%	71.4%	70.2%	69.0%	67.8%	66.7%
2050]	90.0%	89.1%	87.2%	85.4%	83.7%	82.0%	80.4%	78.8%	77.4%	75.9%	74.5%	73.2%	71.9%	70.7%	69.5%	68.3%	67.2%
2100]	90.0%	89.4%	87.5%	85.7%	84.0%	82.4%	80.8%	79.2%	77.8%	76.4%	75.0%	73.7%	72.4%	71.2%	70.0%	68.9%	67.7%
2150]	90.0%	89.6%	87.8%	86.0%	84.3%	82.7%	81.1%	79.6%	78.2%	76.8%	75.4%	74.1%	72.9%	71.7%	70.5%	69.4%	68.3%
2200]	90.0%	89.8%	88.0%	86.3%	84.6%	83.0%	81.5%	80.0%	78.6%	77.2%	75.9%	74.6%	73.3%	72.1%	71.0%	69.8%	68.8%
2250]	90.0%	90.0%	88.2%	86.5%	84.9%	83.3%	81.8%	80.4%	78.9%	77.6%	76.3%	75.0%	73.8%	72.6%	71.4%	70.3%	69.2%
2300]	90.0%	90.0%	88.5%	86.8%	85.2%	83.6%	82.1%	80.7%	79.3%	78.0%	76.7%	75.4%	74.2%	73.0%	71.9%	70.8%	69.7%
2350]	90.0%	90.0%	88.7%	87.0%	85.5%	83.9%	82.5%	81.0%	79.7%	78.3%	77.0%	75.8%	74.6%	73.4%	72.3%	71.2%	70.1%
2400]	90.0%	90.0%	88.9%	87.3%	85.7%	84.2%	82.8%	81.4%	80.0%	78.7%	77.4%	76.2%	75.0%	73.8%	72.7%	71.6%	70.6%
2450]	90.0%	90.0%	89.1%	87.5%	86.0%	84.5%	83.1%	81.7%	80.3%	79.0%	77.8%	76.6%	75.4%	74.2%	73.1%	72.1%	71.0%
2500]	90.0%	90.0%	89.3%	87.7%	86.2%	84.7%	83.3%	82.0%	80.6%	79.4%	78.1%	76.9%	75.8%	74.6%	73.5%	72.5%	71.4%

NON-CUSTODIAL PARENT MONTHLY INCOME

2004 MICHIGAN CHILD SUPPORT FORMULA SCHEDULES
PERCENTAGE OF INCOME

Non-Custodial Parent Percentage of Income

CUSTODIAL PARENT MONTHLY INCOME

NCP Income	0	250	300	350	400	450	500	550	600	650	700	750	800	850	900	950	1000
2550]	90.0%	90.0%	89.5%	87.9%	86.4%	85.0%	83.6%	82.3%	81.0%	79.7%	78.5%	77.3%	76.1%	75.0%	73.9%	72.9%	71.8%
2600]	90.0%	90.0%	89.7%	88.1%	86.7%	85.2%	83.9%	82.5%	81.3%	80.0%	78.8%	77.6%	76.5%	75.4%	74.3%	73.2%	72.2%
2650]	90.0%	90.0%	89.8%	88.3%	86.9%	85.5%	84.1%	82.8%	81.5%	80.3%	79.1%	77.9%	76.8%	75.7%	74.6%	73.6%	72.6%
2700]	90.0%	90.0%	90.0%	88.5%	87.1%	85.7%	84.4%	83.1%	81.8%	80.6%	79.4%	78.3%	77.1%	76.1%	75.0%	74.0%	73.0%
2750]	90.0%	90.0%	90.0%	88.7%	87.3%	85.9%	84.6%	83.3%	82.1%	80.9%	79.7%	78.6%	77.5%	76.4%	75.3%	74.3%	73.3%
2800]	90.0%	90.0%	90.0%	88.9%	87.5%	86.2%	84.8%	83.6%	82.4%	81.2%	80.0%	78.9%	77.8%	76.7%	75.7%	74.7%	73.7%
2850]	90.0%	90.0%	90.0%	89.1%	87.7%	86.4%	85.1%	83.8%	82.6%	81.4%	80.3%	79.2%	78.1%	77.0%	76.0%	75.0%	74.0%
2900]	90.0%	90.0%	90.0%	89.2%	87.9%	86.6%	85.3%	84.1%	82.9%	81.7%	80.6%	79.5%	78.4%	77.3%	76.3%	75.3%	74.4%
2950]	90.0%	90.0%	90.0%	89.4%	88.1%	86.8%	85.5%	84.3%	83.1%	81.9%	80.8%	79.7%	78.7%	77.6%	76.6%	75.6%	74.7%
3000]	90.0%	90.0%	90.0%	89.6%	88.2%	87.0%	85.7%	84.5%	83.3%	82.2%	81.1%	80.0%	78.9%	77.9%	76.9%	75.9%	75.0%
3050]	90.0%	90.0%	90.0%	89.7%	88.4%	87.1%	85.9%	84.7%	83.6%	82.4%	81.3%	80.3%	79.2%	78.2%	77.2%	76.3%	75.3%
3100]	90.0%	90.0%	90.0%	89.9%	88.6%	87.3%	86.1%	84.9%	83.8%	82.7%	81.6%	80.5%	79.5%	78.5%	77.5%	76.5%	75.6%
3150]	90.0%	90.0%	90.0%	90.0%	88.7%	87.5%	86.3%	85.1%	84.0%	82.9%	81.8%	80.8%	79.7%	78.8%	77.8%	76.8%	75.9%
3200]	90.0%	90.0%	90.0%	90.0%	88.9%	87.7%	86.5%	85.3%	84.2%	83.1%	82.1%	81.0%	80.0%	79.0%	78.0%	77.1%	76.2%
3250]	90.0%	90.0%	90.0%	90.0%	89.0%	87.8%	86.7%	85.5%	84.4%	83.3%	82.3%	81.3%	80.2%	79.3%	78.3%	77.4%	76.5%
3300]	90.0%	90.0%	90.0%	90.0%	89.2%	88.0%	86.8%	85.7%	84.6%	83.5%	82.5%	81.5%	80.5%	79.5%	78.6%	77.6%	76.7%
3350]	90.0%	90.0%	90.0%	90.0%	89.3%	88.2%	87.0%	85.9%	84.8%	83.8%	82.7%	81.7%	80.7%	79.8%	78.8%	77.9%	77.0%
3400]	90.0%	90.0%	90.0%	90.0%	89.5%	88.3%	87.2%	86.1%	85.0%	84.0%	82.9%	81.9%	81.0%	80.0%	79.1%	78.2%	77.3%
3450]	90.0%	90.0%	90.0%	90.0%	89.6%	88.5%	87.3%	86.3%	85.2%	84.1%	83.1%	82.1%	81.2%	80.2%	79.3%	78.4%	77.5%
3500]	90.0%	90.0%	90.0%	90.0%	89.7%	88.6%	87.5%	86.4%	85.4%	84.3%	83.3%	82.4%	81.4%	80.5%	79.5%	78.7%	77.8%
3550]	90.0%	90.0%	90.0%	90.0%	89.9%	88.8%	87.7%	86.6%	85.5%	84.5%	83.5%	82.6%	81.6%	80.7%	79.8%	78.9%	78.0%
3600]	90.0%	90.0%	90.0%	90.0%	90.0%	88.9%	87.8%	86.7%	85.7%	84.7%	83.7%	82.8%	81.8%	80.9%	80.0%	79.1%	78.3%
3650]	90.0%	90.0%	90.0%	90.0%	90.0%	89.0%	88.0%	86.9%	85.9%	84.9%	83.9%	83.0%	82.0%	81.1%	80.2%	79.3%	78.5%
3700]	90.0%	90.0%	90.0%	90.0%	90.0%	89.2%	88.1%	87.1%	86.0%	85.1%	84.1%	83.1%	82.2%	81.3%	80.4%	79.6%	78.7%
3750]	90.0%	90.0%	90.0%	90.0%	90.0%	89.3%	88.2%	87.2%	86.2%	85.2%	84.3%	83.3%	82.4%	81.5%	80.6%	79.8%	78.9%
3800]	90.0%	90.0%	90.0%	90.0%	90.0%	89.4%	88.4%	87.4%	86.4%	85.4%	84.4%	83.5%	82.6%	81.7%	80.9%	80.0%	79.2%
3850]	90.0%	90.0%	90.0%	90.0%	90.0%	89.5%	88.5%	87.5%	86.5%	85.6%	84.6%	83.7%	82.8%	81.9%	81.1%	80.2%	79.4%
3900]	90.0%	90.0%	90.0%	90.0%	90.0%	89.7%	88.6%	87.6%	86.7%	85.7%	84.8%	83.9%	83.0%	82.1%	81.3%	80.4%	79.6%
3950]	90.0%	90.0%	90.0%	90.0%	90.0%	89.8%	88.8%	87.8%	86.8%	85.9%	84.9%	84.0%	83.2%	82.3%	81.4%	80.6%	79.8%
4000]	90.0%	90.0%	90.0%	90.0%	90.0%	89.9%	88.9%	87.9%	87.0%	86.0%	85.1%	84.2%	83.3%	82.5%	81.6%	80.8%	80.0%
4050]	90.0%	90.0%	90.0%	90.0%	90.0%	90.0%	89.0%	88.0%	87.1%	86.2%	85.3%	84.4%	83.5%	82.7%	81.8%	81.0%	80.2%
4100]	90.0%	90.0%	90.0%	90.0%	90.0%	90.0%	89.1%	88.2%	87.2%	86.3%	85.4%	84.5%	83.7%	82.8%	82.0%	81.2%	80.4%
4150]	90.0%	90.0%	90.0%	90.0%	90.0%	90.0%	89.2%	88.3%	87.4%	86.5%	85.6%	84.7%	83.8%	83.0%	82.2%	81.4%	80.6%
4200]	90.0%	90.0%	90.0%	90.0%	90.0%	90.0%	89.4%	88.4%	87.5%	86.6%	85.7%	84.8%	84.0%	83.2%	82.4%	81.6%	80.8%
4250]	90.0%	90.0%	90.0%	90.0%	90.0%	90.0%	89.5%	88.5%	87.6%	86.7%	85.9%	85.0%	84.2%	83.3%	82.5%	81.7%	81.0%
4300]	90.0%	90.0%	90.0%	90.0%	90.0%	90.0%	89.6%	88.7%	87.8%	86.9%	86.0%	85.1%	84.3%	83.5%	82.7%	81.9%	81.1%
4350]	90.0%	90.0%	90.0%	90.0%	90.0%	90.0%	89.7%	88.8%	87.9%	87.0%	86.1%	85.3%	84.5%	83.7%	82.9%	82.1%	81.3%
4400]	90.0%	90.0%	90.0%	90.0%	90.0%	90.0%	89.8%	88.9%	88.0%	87.1%	86.3%	85.4%	84.6%	83.8%	83.0%	82.2%	81.5%
4450]	90.0%	90.0%	90.0%	90.0%	90.0%	90.0%	89.9%	89.0%	88.1%	87.3%	86.4%	85.6%	84.8%	84.0%	83.2%	82.4%	81.7%
4500]	90.0%	90.0%	90.0%	90.0%	90.0%	90.0%	90.0%	89.1%	88.2%	87.4%	86.5%	85.7%	84.9%	84.1%	83.3%	82.6%	81.8%
4550]	90.0%	90.0%	90.0%	90.0%	90.0%	90.0%	90.0%	89.2%	88.3%	87.5%	86.7%	85.8%	85.0%	84.3%	83.5%	82.7%	82.0%
4600]	90.0%	90.0%	90.0%	90.0%	90.0%	90.0%	90.0%	89.3%	88.5%	87.6%	86.8%	86.0%	85.2%	84.4%	83.6%	82.9%	82.1%
4650]	90.0%	90.0%	90.0%	90.0%	90.0%	90.0%	90.0%	89.4%	88.6%	87.7%	86.9%	86.1%	85.3%	84.5%	83.8%	83.0%	82.3%
4700]	90.0%	90.0%	90.0%	90.0%	90.0%	90.0%	90.0%	89.5%	88.7%	87.9%	87.0%	86.2%	85.5%	84.7%	83.9%	83.2%	82.5%
4750]	90.0%	90.0%	90.0%	90.0%	90.0%	90.0%	90.0%	89.6%	88.8%	88.0%	87.2%	86.4%	85.6%	84.8%	84.1%	83.3%	82.6%
4800]	90.0%	90.0%	90.0%	90.0%	90.0%	90.0%	90.0%	89.7%	88.9%	88.1%	87.3%	86.5%	85.7%	85.0%	84.2%	83.5%	82.8%
4850]	90.0%	90.0%	90.0%	90.0%	90.0%	90.0%	90.0%	89.8%	89.0%	88.2%	87.4%	86.6%	85.8%	85.1%	84.3%	83.6%	82.9%
4900]	90.0%	90.0%	90.0%	90.0%	90.0%	90.0%	90.0%	89.9%	89.1%	88.3%	87.5%	86.7%	86.0%	85.2%	84.5%	83.8%	83.1%
4950]	90.0%	90.0%	90.0%	90.0%	90.0%	90.0%	90.0%	90.0%	89.2%	88.4%	87.6%	86.8%	86.1%	85.3%	84.6%	83.9%	83.2%
5000]	90.0%	90.0%	90.0%	90.0%	90.0%	90.0%	90.0%	90.0%	89.3%	88.5%	87.7%	87.0%	86.2%	85.5%	84.7%	84.0%	83.3%

(Left margin label: NON-CUSTODIAL PARENT MONTHLY INCOME)

2004 MICHIGAN CHILD SUPPORT FORMULA SCHEDULES
PERCENTAGE OF INCOME

Non-Custodial Parent Percentage of Income

CUSTODIAL PARENT MONTHLY INCOME

	1050	1100	1150	1200	1250	1300	1350	1400	1450	1500	1550	1600	1650	1700	1750	1800
250]	19.2%	18.5%	17.9%	17.2%	16.7%	16.1%	15.6%	15.2%	14.7%	14.3%	13.9%	13.5%	13.2%	12.8%	12.5%	12.2%
300]	22.2%	21.4%	20.7%	20.0%	19.4%	18.8%	18.2%	17.6%	17.1%	16.7%	16.2%	15.8%	15.4%	15.0%	14.6%	14.3%
350]	25.0%	24.1%	23.3%	22.6%	21.9%	21.2%	20.6%	20.0%	19.4%	18.9%	18.4%	17.9%	17.5%	17.1%	16.7%	16.3%
400]	27.6%	26.7%	25.8%	25.0%	24.2%	23.5%	22.9%	22.2%	21.6%	21.1%	20.5%	20.0%	19.5%	19.0%	18.6%	18.2%
450]	30.0%	29.0%	28.1%	27.3%	26.5%	25.7%	25.0%	24.3%	23.7%	23.1%	22.5%	22.0%	21.4%	20.9%	20.5%	20.0%
500]	32.3%	31.3%	30.3%	29.4%	28.6%	27.8%	27.0%	26.3%	25.6%	25.0%	24.4%	23.8%	23.3%	22.7%	22.2%	21.7%
550]	34.4%	33.3%	32.4%	31.4%	30.6%	29.7%	28.9%	28.2%	27.5%	26.8%	26.2%	25.6%	25.0%	24.4%	23.9%	23.4%
600]	36.4%	35.3%	34.3%	33.3%	32.4%	31.6%	30.8%	30.0%	29.3%	28.6%	27.9%	27.3%	26.7%	26.1%	25.5%	25.0%
650]	38.2%	37.1%	36.1%	35.1%	34.2%	33.3%	32.5%	31.7%	31.0%	30.2%	29.5%	28.9%	28.3%	27.7%	27.1%	26.5%
700]	40.0%	38.9%	37.8%	36.8%	35.9%	35.0%	34.1%	33.3%	32.6%	31.8%	31.1%	30.4%	29.8%	29.2%	28.6%	28.0%
750]	41.7%	40.5%	39.5%	38.5%	37.5%	36.6%	35.7%	34.9%	34.1%	33.3%	32.6%	31.9%	31.3%	30.6%	30.0%	29.4%
800]	43.2%	42.1%	41.0%	40.0%	39.0%	38.1%	37.2%	36.4%	35.6%	34.8%	34.0%	33.3%	32.7%	32.0%	31.4%	30.8%
850]	44.7%	43.6%	42.5%	41.5%	40.5%	39.5%	38.6%	37.8%	37.0%	36.2%	35.4%	34.7%	34.0%	33.3%	32.7%	32.1%
900]	46.2%	45.0%	43.9%	42.9%	41.9%	40.9%	40.0%	39.1%	38.3%	37.5%	36.7%	36.0%	35.3%	34.6%	34.0%	33.3%
950]	47.5%	46.3%	45.2%	44.2%	43.2%	42.2%	41.3%	40.4%	39.6%	38.8%	38.0%	37.3%	36.5%	35.8%	35.2%	34.5%
1000]	48.8%	47.6%	46.5%	45.5%	44.4%	43.5%	42.6%	41.7%	40.8%	40.0%	39.2%	38.5%	37.7%	37.0%	36.4%	35.7%
1050]	50.0%	48.8%	47.7%	46.7%	45.7%	44.7%	43.8%	42.9%	42.0%	41.2%	40.4%	39.6%	38.9%	38.2%	37.5%	36.8%
1100]	51.2%	50.0%	48.9%	47.8%	46.8%	45.8%	44.9%	44.0%	43.1%	42.3%	41.5%	40.7%	40.0%	39.3%	38.6%	37.9%
1150]	52.3%	51.1%	50.0%	48.9%	47.9%	46.9%	46.0%	45.1%	44.2%	43.4%	42.6%	41.8%	41.1%	40.4%	39.7%	39.0%
1200]	53.3%	52.2%	51.1%	50.0%	49.0%	48.0%	47.1%	46.2%	45.3%	44.4%	43.6%	42.9%	42.1%	41.4%	40.7%	40.0%
1250]	54.3%	53.2%	52.1%	51.0%	50.0%	49.0%	48.1%	47.2%	46.3%	45.5%	44.6%	43.9%	43.1%	42.4%	41.7%	41.0%
1300]	55.3%	54.2%	53.1%	52.0%	51.0%	50.0%	49.1%	48.1%	47.3%	46.4%	45.6%	44.8%	44.1%	43.3%	42.6%	41.9%
1350]	56.3%	55.1%	54.0%	52.9%	51.9%	50.9%	50.0%	49.1%	48.2%	47.4%	46.6%	45.8%	45.0%	44.3%	43.5%	42.9%
1400]	57.1%	56.0%	54.9%	53.8%	52.8%	51.9%	50.9%	50.0%	49.1%	48.3%	47.5%	46.7%	45.9%	45.2%	44.4%	43.8%
1450]	58.0%	56.9%	55.8%	54.7%	53.7%	52.7%	51.8%	50.9%	50.0%	49.2%	48.3%	47.5%	46.8%	46.0%	45.3%	44.6%
1500]	58.8%	57.7%	56.6%	55.6%	54.5%	53.6%	52.6%	51.7%	50.8%	50.0%	49.2%	48.4%	47.6%	46.9%	46.2%	45.5%
1550]	59.6%	58.5%	57.4%	56.4%	55.4%	54.4%	53.4%	52.5%	51.7%	50.8%	50.0%	49.2%	48.4%	47.7%	47.0%	46.3%
1600]	60.4%	59.3%	58.2%	57.1%	56.1%	55.2%	54.2%	53.3%	52.5%	51.6%	50.8%	50.0%	49.2%	48.5%	47.8%	47.1%
1650]	61.1%	60.0%	58.9%	57.9%	56.9%	55.9%	55.0%	54.1%	53.2%	52.4%	51.6%	50.8%	50.0%	49.3%	48.5%	47.8%
1700]	61.8%	60.7%	59.6%	58.6%	57.6%	56.7%	55.7%	54.8%	54.0%	53.1%	52.3%	51.5%	50.7%	50.0%	49.3%	48.6%
1750]	62.5%	61.4%	60.3%	59.3%	58.3%	57.4%	56.5%	55.6%	54.7%	53.8%	53.0%	52.2%	51.5%	50.7%	50.0%	49.3%
1800]	63.2%	62.1%	61.0%	60.0%	59.0%	58.1%	57.1%	56.3%	55.4%	54.5%	53.7%	52.9%	52.2%	51.4%	50.7%	50.0%
1850]	63.8%	62.7%	61.7%	60.7%	59.7%	58.7%	57.8%	56.9%	56.1%	55.2%	54.4%	53.6%	52.9%	52.1%	51.4%	50.7%
1900]	64.4%	63.3%	62.3%	61.3%	60.3%	59.4%	58.5%	57.6%	56.7%	55.9%	55.1%	54.3%	53.5%	52.8%	52.1%	51.4%
1950]	65.0%	63.9%	62.9%	61.9%	60.9%	60.0%	59.1%	58.2%	57.4%	56.5%	55.7%	54.9%	54.2%	53.4%	52.7%	52.0%
2000]	65.6%	64.5%	63.5%	62.5%	61.5%	60.6%	59.7%	58.8%	58.0%	57.1%	56.3%	55.6%	54.8%	54.1%	53.3%	52.6%
2050]	66.1%	65.1%	64.1%	63.1%	62.1%	61.2%	60.3%	59.4%	58.6%	57.7%	56.9%	56.2%	55.4%	54.7%	53.9%	53.2%
2100]	66.7%	65.6%	64.6%	63.6%	62.7%	61.8%	60.9%	60.0%	59.2%	58.3%	57.5%	56.8%	56.0%	55.3%	54.5%	53.8%
2150]	67.2%	66.2%	65.2%	64.2%	63.2%	62.3%	61.4%	60.6%	59.7%	58.9%	58.1%	57.3%	56.6%	55.8%	55.1%	54.4%
2200]	67.7%	66.7%	65.7%	64.7%	63.8%	62.9%	62.0%	61.1%	60.3%	59.5%	58.7%	57.9%	57.1%	56.4%	55.7%	55.0%
2250]	68.2%	67.2%	66.2%	65.2%	64.3%	63.4%	62.5%	61.6%	60.8%	60.0%	59.2%	58.4%	57.7%	57.0%	56.3%	55.6%
2300]	68.7%	67.6%	66.7%	65.7%	64.8%	63.9%	63.0%	62.2%	61.3%	60.5%	59.7%	59.0%	58.2%	57.5%	56.8%	56.1%
2350]	69.1%	68.1%	67.1%	66.2%	65.3%	64.4%	63.5%	62.7%	61.8%	61.0%	60.3%	59.5%	58.8%	58.0%	57.3%	56.6%
2400]	69.6%	68.6%	67.6%	66.7%	65.8%	64.9%	64.0%	63.2%	62.3%	61.5%	60.8%	60.0%	59.3%	58.5%	57.8%	57.1%
2450]	70.0%	69.0%	68.1%	67.1%	66.2%	65.3%	64.5%	63.6%	62.8%	62.0%	61.3%	60.5%	59.8%	59.0%	58.3%	57.6%
2500]	70.4%	69.4%	68.5%	67.6%	66.7%	65.8%	64.9%	64.1%	63.3%	62.5%	61.7%	61.0%	60.2%	59.5%	58.8%	58.1%

NONCUSTODIAL PARENT MONTHLY INCOME

2004 Michigan Child Support Formula Schedules
Percentage of Income

Non-Custodial Parent Percentage of Income

CUSTODIAL PARENT MONTHLY INCOME

NONCUSTODIAL PARENT MONTHLY INCOME

	1050	1100	1150	1200	1250	1300	1350	1400	1450	1500	1550	1600	1650	1700	1750	1800
2550]	70.8%	69.9%	68.9%	68.0%	67.1%	66.2%	65.4%	64.6%	63.8%	63.0%	62.2%	61.4%	60.7%	60.0%	59.3%	58.6%
2600]	71.2%	70.3%	69.3%	68.4%	67.5%	66.7%	65.8%	65.0%	64.2%	63.4%	62.7%	61.9%	61.2%	60.5%	59.8%	59.1%
2650]	71.6%	70.7%	69.7%	68.8%	67.9%	67.1%	66.3%	65.4%	64.6%	63.9%	63.1%	62.4%	61.6%	60.9%	60.2%	59.6%
2700]	72.0%	71.1%	70.1%	69.2%	68.4%	67.5%	66.7%	65.9%	65.1%	64.3%	63.5%	62.8%	62.1%	61.4%	60.7%	60.0%
2750]	72.4%	71.4%	70.5%	69.6%	68.8%	67.9%	67.1%	66.3%	65.5%	64.7%	64.0%	63.2%	62.5%	61.8%	61.1%	60.4%
2800]	72.7%	71.8%	70.9%	70.0%	69.1%	68.3%	67.5%	66.7%	65.9%	65.1%	64.4%	63.6%	62.9%	62.2%	61.5%	60.9%
2850]	73.1%	72.2%	71.3%	70.4%	69.5%	68.7%	67.9%	67.1%	66.3%	65.5%	64.8%	64.0%	63.3%	62.6%	62.0%	61.3%
2900]	73.4%	72.5%	71.6%	70.7%	69.9%	69.0%	68.2%	67.4%	66.7%	65.9%	65.2%	64.4%	63.7%	63.0%	62.4%	61.7%
2950]	73.8%	72.8%	72.0%	71.1%	70.2%	69.4%	68.6%	67.8%	67.0%	66.3%	65.6%	64.8%	64.1%	63.4%	62.8%	62.1%
3000]	74.1%	73.2%	72.3%	71.4%	70.6%	69.8%	69.0%	68.2%	67.4%	66.7%	65.9%	65.2%	64.5%	63.8%	63.2%	62.5%
3050]	74.4%	73.5%	72.6%	71.8%	70.9%	70.1%	69.3%	68.5%	67.8%	67.0%	66.3%	65.6%	64.9%	64.2%	63.5%	62.9%
3100]	74.7%	73.8%	72.9%	72.1%	71.3%	70.5%	69.7%	68.9%	68.1%	67.4%	66.7%	66.0%	65.3%	64.6%	63.9%	63.3%
3150]	75.0%	74.1%	73.3%	72.4%	71.6%	70.8%	70.0%	69.2%	68.5%	67.7%	67.0%	66.3%	65.6%	64.9%	64.3%	63.6%
3200]	75.3%	74.4%	73.6%	72.7%	71.9%	71.1%	70.3%	69.6%	68.8%	68.1%	67.4%	66.7%	66.0%	65.3%	64.6%	64.0%
3250]	75.6%	74.7%	73.9%	73.0%	72.2%	71.4%	70.7%	69.9%	69.1%	68.4%	67.7%	67.0%	66.3%	65.7%	65.0%	64.4%
3300]	75.9%	75.0%	74.2%	73.3%	72.5%	71.7%	71.0%	70.2%	69.5%	68.8%	68.0%	67.3%	66.7%	66.0%	65.3%	64.7%
3350]	76.1%	75.3%	74.4%	73.6%	72.8%	72.0%	71.3%	70.5%	69.8%	69.1%	68.4%	67.7%	67.0%	66.3%	65.7%	65.0%
3400]	76.4%	75.6%	74.7%	73.9%	73.1%	72.3%	71.6%	70.8%	70.1%	69.4%	68.7%	68.0%	67.3%	66.7%	66.0%	65.4%
3450]	76.7%	75.8%	75.0%	74.2%	73.4%	72.6%	71.9%	71.1%	70.4%	69.7%	69.0%	68.3%	67.6%	67.0%	66.3%	65.7%
3500]	76.9%	76.1%	75.3%	74.5%	73.7%	72.9%	72.2%	71.4%	70.7%	70.0%	69.3%	68.6%	68.0%	67.3%	66.7%	66.0%
3550]	77.2%	76.3%	75.5%	74.7%	74.0%	73.2%	72.4%	71.7%	71.0%	70.3%	69.6%	68.9%	68.3%	67.6%	67.0%	66.4%
3600]	77.4%	76.6%	75.8%	75.0%	74.2%	73.5%	72.7%	72.0%	71.3%	70.6%	69.9%	69.2%	68.6%	67.9%	67.3%	66.7%
3650]	77.7%	76.8%	76.0%	75.3%	74.5%	73.7%	73.0%	72.3%	71.6%	70.9%	70.2%	69.5%	68.9%	68.2%	67.6%	67.0%
3700]	77.9%	77.1%	76.3%	75.5%	74.7%	74.0%	73.3%	72.5%	71.8%	71.2%	70.5%	69.8%	69.2%	68.5%	67.9%	67.3%
3750]	78.1%	77.3%	76.5%	75.8%	75.0%	74.3%	73.5%	72.8%	72.1%	71.4%	70.8%	70.1%	69.4%	68.8%	68.2%	67.6%
3800]	78.4%	77.6%	76.8%	76.0%	75.2%	74.5%	73.8%	73.1%	72.4%	71.7%	71.0%	70.4%	69.7%	69.1%	68.5%	67.9%
3850]	78.6%	77.8%	77.0%	76.2%	75.5%	74.8%	74.0%	73.3%	72.6%	72.0%	71.3%	70.6%	70.0%	69.4%	68.8%	68.1%
3900]	78.8%	78.0%	77.2%	76.5%	75.7%	75.0%	74.3%	73.6%	72.9%	72.2%	71.6%	70.9%	70.3%	69.6%	69.0%	68.4%
3950]	79.0%	78.2%	77.5%	76.7%	76.0%	75.2%	74.5%	73.8%	73.1%	72.5%	71.8%	71.2%	70.5%	69.9%	69.3%	68.7%
4000]	79.2%	78.4%	77.7%	76.9%	76.2%	75.5%	74.8%	74.1%	73.4%	72.7%	72.1%	71.4%	70.8%	70.2%	69.6%	69.0%
4050]	79.4%	78.6%	77.9%	77.1%	76.4%	75.7%	75.0%	74.3%	73.6%	73.0%	72.3%	71.7%	71.1%	70.4%	69.8%	69.2%
4100]	79.6%	78.8%	78.1%	77.4%	76.6%	75.9%	75.2%	74.5%	73.9%	73.2%	72.6%	71.9%	71.3%	70.7%	70.1%	69.5%
4150]	79.8%	79.0%	78.3%	77.6%	76.9%	76.1%	75.5%	74.8%	74.1%	73.5%	72.8%	72.2%	71.6%	70.9%	70.3%	69.7%
4200]	80.0%	79.2%	78.5%	77.8%	77.1%	76.4%	75.7%	75.0%	74.3%	73.7%	73.0%	72.4%	71.8%	71.2%	70.6%	70.0%
4250]	80.2%	79.4%	78.7%	78.0%	77.3%	76.6%	75.9%	75.2%	74.6%	73.9%	73.3%	72.6%	72.0%	71.4%	70.8%	70.2%
4300]	80.4%	79.6%	78.9%	78.2%	77.5%	76.8%	76.1%	75.4%	74.8%	74.1%	73.5%	72.9%	72.3%	71.7%	71.1%	70.5%
4350]	80.6%	79.8%	79.1%	78.4%	77.7%	77.0%	76.3%	75.7%	75.0%	74.4%	73.7%	73.1%	72.5%	71.9%	71.3%	70.7%
4400]	80.7%	80.0%	79.3%	78.6%	77.9%	77.2%	76.5%	75.9%	75.2%	74.6%	73.9%	73.3%	72.7%	72.1%	71.5%	71.0%
4450]	80.9%	80.2%	79.5%	78.8%	78.1%	77.4%	76.7%	76.1%	75.4%	74.8%	74.2%	73.6%	73.0%	72.4%	71.8%	71.2%
4500]	81.1%	80.4%	79.6%	78.9%	78.3%	77.6%	76.9%	76.3%	75.6%	75.0%	74.4%	73.8%	73.2%	72.6%	72.0%	71.4%
4550]	81.3%	80.5%	79.8%	79.1%	78.4%	77.8%	77.1%	76.5%	75.8%	75.2%	74.6%	74.0%	73.4%	72.8%	72.2%	71.7%
4600]	81.4%	80.7%	80.0%	79.3%	78.6%	78.0%	77.3%	76.7%	76.0%	75.4%	74.8%	74.2%	73.6%	73.0%	72.4%	71.9%
4650]	81.6%	80.9%	80.2%	79.5%	78.8%	78.2%	77.5%	76.9%	76.2%	75.6%	75.0%	74.4%	73.8%	73.2%	72.7%	72.1%
4700]	81.7%	81.0%	80.3%	79.7%	79.0%	78.3%	77.7%	77.0%	76.4%	75.8%	75.2%	74.6%	74.0%	73.4%	72.9%	72.3%
4750]	81.9%	81.2%	80.5%	79.8%	79.2%	78.5%	77.9%	77.2%	76.6%	76.0%	75.4%	74.8%	74.2%	73.6%	73.1%	72.5%
4800]	82.1%	81.4%	80.7%	80.0%	79.3%	78.7%	78.0%	77.4%	76.8%	76.2%	75.6%	75.0%	74.4%	73.8%	73.3%	72.7%
4850]	82.2%	81.5%	80.8%	80.2%	79.5%	78.9%	78.2%	77.6%	77.0%	76.4%	75.8%	75.2%	74.6%	74.0%	73.5%	72.9%
4900]	82.4%	81.7%	81.0%	80.3%	79.7%	79.0%	78.4%	77.8%	77.2%	76.6%	76.0%	75.4%	74.8%	74.2%	73.7%	73.1%
4950]	82.5%	81.8%	81.1%	80.5%	79.8%	79.2%	78.6%	78.0%	77.3%	76.7%	76.2%	75.6%	75.0%	74.4%	73.9%	73.3%
5000]	82.6%	82.0%	81.3%	80.6%	80.0%	79.4%	78.7%	78.1%	77.5%	76.9%	76.3%	75.8%	75.2%	74.6%	74.1%	73.5%

2004 MICHIGAN CHILD SUPPORT FORMULA SCHEDULES
PERCENTAGE OF INCOME

Non-Custodial Parent Percentage of Income

CUSTODIAL PARENT MONTHLY INCOME

	1850	1900	1950	2000	2050	2100	2150	2200	2250	2300	2350	2400	2450	2500	2550	2600
250]	11.9%	11.6%	11.4%	11.1%	10.9%	10.6%	10.4%	10.2%	10.0%	10.0%	10.0%	10.0%	10.0%	10.0%	10.0%	10.0%
300]	14.0%	13.6%	13.3%	13.0%	12.8%	12.5%	12.2%	12.0%	11.8%	11.5%	11.3%	11.1%	10.9%	10.7%	10.5%	10.3%
350]	15.9%	15.6%	15.2%	14.9%	14.6%	14.3%	14.0%	13.7%	13.5%	13.2%	13.0%	12.7%	12.5%	12.3%	12.1%	11.9%
400]	17.8%	17.4%	17.0%	16.7%	16.3%	16.0%	15.7%	15.4%	15.1%	14.8%	14.5%	14.3%	14.0%	13.8%	13.6%	13.3%
450]	19.6%	19.1%	18.8%	18.4%	18.0%	17.6%	17.3%	17.0%	16.7%	16.4%	16.1%	15.8%	15.5%	15.3%	15.0%	14.8%
500]	21.3%	20.8%	20.4%	20.0%	19.6%	19.2%	18.9%	18.5%	18.2%	17.9%	17.5%	17.2%	16.9%	16.7%	16.4%	16.1%
550]	22.9%	22.4%	22.0%	21.6%	21.2%	20.8%	20.4%	20.0%	19.6%	19.3%	19.0%	18.6%	18.3%	18.0%	17.7%	17.5%
600]	24.5%	24.0%	23.5%	23.1%	22.6%	22.2%	21.8%	21.4%	21.1%	20.7%	20.3%	20.0%	19.7%	19.4%	19.0%	18.8%
650]	26.0%	25.5%	25.0%	24.5%	24.1%	23.6%	23.2%	22.8%	22.4%	22.0%	21.7%	21.3%	21.0%	20.6%	20.3%	20.0%
700]	27.5%	26.9%	26.4%	25.9%	25.5%	25.0%	24.6%	24.1%	23.7%	23.3%	23.0%	22.6%	22.2%	21.9%	21.5%	21.2%
750]	28.8%	28.3%	27.8%	27.3%	26.8%	26.3%	25.9%	25.4%	25.0%	24.6%	24.2%	23.8%	23.4%	23.1%	22.7%	22.4%
800]	30.2%	29.6%	29.1%	28.6%	28.1%	27.6%	27.1%	26.7%	26.2%	25.8%	25.4%	25.0%	24.6%	24.2%	23.9%	23.5%
850]	31.5%	30.9%	30.4%	29.8%	29.3%	28.8%	28.3%	27.9%	27.4%	27.0%	26.6%	26.2%	25.8%	25.4%	25.0%	24.6%
900]	32.7%	32.1%	31.6%	31.0%	30.5%	30.0%	29.5%	29.0%	28.6%	28.1%	27.7%	27.3%	26.9%	26.5%	26.1%	25.7%
950]	33.9%	33.3%	32.8%	32.2%	31.7%	31.1%	30.6%	30.2%	29.7%	29.2%	28.8%	28.4%	27.9%	27.5%	27.1%	26.8%
1000]	35.1%	34.5%	33.9%	33.3%	32.8%	32.3%	31.7%	31.3%	30.8%	30.3%	29.9%	29.4%	29.0%	28.6%	28.2%	27.8%
1050]	36.2%	35.6%	35.0%	34.4%	33.9%	33.3%	32.8%	32.3%	31.8%	31.3%	30.9%	30.4%	30.0%	29.6%	29.2%	28.8%
1100]	37.3%	36.7%	36.1%	35.5%	34.9%	34.4%	33.8%	33.3%	32.8%	32.4%	31.9%	31.4%	31.0%	30.6%	30.1%	29.7%
1150]	38.3%	37.7%	37.1%	36.5%	35.9%	35.4%	34.8%	34.3%	33.8%	33.3%	32.9%	32.4%	31.9%	31.5%	31.1%	30.7%
1200]	39.3%	38.7%	38.1%	37.5%	36.9%	36.4%	35.8%	35.3%	34.8%	34.3%	33.8%	33.3%	32.9%	32.4%	32.0%	31.6%
1250]	40.3%	39.7%	39.1%	38.5%	37.9%	37.3%	36.8%	36.2%	35.7%	35.2%	34.7%	34.2%	33.8%	33.3%	32.9%	32.5%
1300]	41.3%	40.6%	40.0%	39.4%	38.8%	38.2%	37.7%	37.1%	36.6%	36.1%	35.6%	35.1%	34.7%	34.2%	33.8%	33.3%
1350]	42.2%	41.5%	40.9%	40.3%	39.7%	39.1%	38.6%	38.0%	37.5%	37.0%	36.5%	36.0%	35.5%	35.1%	34.6%	34.2%
1400]	43.1%	42.4%	41.8%	41.2%	40.6%	40.0%	39.4%	38.9%	38.4%	37.8%	37.3%	36.8%	36.4%	35.9%	35.4%	35.0%
1450]	43.9%	43.3%	42.6%	42.0%	41.4%	40.8%	40.3%	39.7%	39.2%	38.7%	38.2%	37.7%	37.2%	36.7%	36.3%	35.8%
1500]	44.8%	44.1%	43.5%	42.9%	42.3%	41.7%	41.1%	40.5%	40.0%	39.5%	39.0%	38.5%	38.0%	37.5%	37.0%	36.6%
1550]	45.6%	44.9%	44.3%	43.7%	43.1%	42.5%	41.9%	41.3%	40.8%	40.3%	39.7%	39.2%	38.8%	38.3%	37.8%	37.3%
1600]	46.4%	45.7%	45.1%	44.4%	43.8%	43.2%	42.7%	42.1%	41.6%	41.0%	40.5%	40.0%	39.5%	39.0%	38.6%	38.1%
1650]	47.1%	46.5%	45.8%	45.2%	44.6%	44.0%	43.4%	42.9%	42.3%	41.8%	41.3%	40.7%	40.2%	39.8%	39.3%	38.8%
1700]	47.9%	47.2%	46.6%	45.9%	45.3%	44.7%	44.2%	43.6%	43.0%	42.5%	42.0%	41.5%	41.0%	40.5%	40.0%	39.5%
1750]	48.6%	47.9%	47.3%	46.7%	46.1%	45.5%	44.9%	44.3%	43.8%	43.2%	42.7%	42.2%	41.7%	41.2%	40.7%	40.2%
1800]	49.3%	48.6%	48.0%	47.4%	46.8%	46.2%	45.6%	45.0%	44.4%	43.9%	43.4%	42.9%	42.4%	41.9%	41.4%	40.9%
1850]	50.0%	49.3%	48.7%	48.1%	47.4%	46.8%	46.3%	45.7%	45.1%	44.6%	44.0%	43.5%	43.0%	42.5%	42.0%	41.6%
1900]	50.7%	50.0%	49.4%	48.7%	48.1%	47.5%	46.9%	46.3%	45.8%	45.2%	44.7%	44.2%	43.7%	43.2%	42.7%	42.2%
1950]	51.3%	50.6%	50.0%	49.4%	48.8%	48.1%	47.6%	47.0%	46.4%	45.9%	45.3%	44.8%	44.3%	43.8%	43.3%	42.9%
2000]	51.9%	51.3%	50.6%	50.0%	49.4%	48.8%	48.2%	47.6%	47.1%	46.5%	46.0%	45.5%	44.9%	44.4%	44.0%	43.5%
2050]	52.6%	51.9%	51.3%	50.6%	50.0%	49.4%	48.8%	48.2%	47.7%	47.1%	46.6%	46.1%	45.6%	45.1%	44.6%	44.1%
2100]	53.2%	52.5%	51.9%	51.2%	50.6%	50.0%	49.4%	48.8%	48.3%	47.7%	47.2%	46.7%	46.2%	45.7%	45.2%	44.7%
2150]	53.8%	53.1%	52.4%	51.8%	51.2%	50.6%	50.0%	49.4%	48.9%	48.3%	47.8%	47.3%	46.7%	46.2%	45.7%	45.3%
2200]	54.3%	53.7%	53.0%	52.4%	51.8%	51.2%	50.6%	50.0%	49.4%	48.9%	48.4%	47.8%	47.3%	46.8%	46.3%	45.8%
2250]	54.9%	54.2%	53.6%	52.9%	52.3%	51.7%	51.1%	50.6%	50.0%	49.5%	48.9%	48.4%	47.9%	47.4%	46.9%	46.4%
2300]	55.4%	54.8%	54.1%	53.5%	52.9%	52.3%	51.7%	51.1%	50.5%	50.0%	49.5%	48.9%	48.4%	47.9%	47.4%	46.9%
2350]	56.0%	55.3%	54.7%	54.0%	53.4%	52.8%	52.2%	51.6%	51.1%	50.5%	50.0%	49.5%	49.0%	48.5%	48.0%	47.5%
2400]	56.5%	55.8%	55.2%	54.5%	53.9%	53.3%	52.7%	52.2%	51.6%	51.1%	50.5%	50.0%	49.5%	49.0%	48.5%	48.0%
2450]	57.0%	56.3%	55.7%	55.1%	54.4%	53.8%	53.3%	52.7%	52.1%	51.6%	51.0%	50.5%	50.0%	49.5%	49.0%	48.5%
2500]	57.5%	56.8%	56.2%	55.6%	54.9%	54.3%	53.8%	53.2%	52.6%	52.1%	51.5%	51.0%	50.5%	50.0%	49.5%	49.0%

Left margin vertical label: NONCUSTODIAL PARENT MONTHLY INCOME

Non-Custodial Parent Percentage of Income

CUSTODIAL PARENT MONTHLY INCOME

		1850	1900	1950	2000	2050	2100	2150	2200	2250	2300	2350	2400	2450	2500	2550	2600
	2550]	58.0%	57.3%	56.7%	56.0%	55.4%	54.8%	54.3%	53.7%	53.1%	52.6%	52.0%	51.5%	51.0%	50.5%	50.0%	49.5%
	2600]	58.4%	57.8%	57.1%	56.5%	55.9%	55.3%	54.7%	54.2%	53.6%	53.1%	52.5%	52.0%	51.5%	51.0%	50.5%	50.0%
	2650]	58.9%	58.2%	57.6%	57.0%	56.4%	55.8%	55.2%	54.6%	54.1%	53.5%	53.0%	52.5%	52.0%	51.5%	51.0%	50.5%
	2700]	59.3%	58.7%	58.1%	57.4%	56.8%	56.3%	55.7%	55.1%	54.5%	54.0%	53.5%	52.9%	52.4%	51.9%	51.4%	50.9%
	2750]	59.8%	59.1%	58.5%	57.9%	57.3%	56.7%	56.1%	55.6%	55.0%	54.5%	53.9%	53.4%	52.9%	52.4%	51.9%	51.4%
	2800]	60.2%	59.6%	58.9%	58.3%	57.7%	57.1%	56.6%	56.0%	55.4%	54.9%	54.4%	53.8%	53.3%	52.8%	52.3%	51.9%
	2850]	60.6%	60.0%	59.4%	58.8%	58.2%	57.6%	57.0%	56.4%	55.9%	55.3%	54.8%	54.3%	53.8%	53.3%	52.8%	52.3%
N	2900]	61.1%	60.4%	59.8%	59.2%	58.6%	58.0%	57.4%	56.9%	56.3%	55.8%	55.2%	54.7%	54.2%	53.7%	53.2%	52.7%
O	2950]	61.5%	60.8%	60.2%	59.6%	59.0%	58.4%	57.8%	57.3%	56.7%	56.2%	55.7%	55.1%	54.6%	54.1%	53.6%	53.2%
N	3000]	61.9%	61.2%	60.6%	60.0%	59.4%	58.8%	58.3%	57.7%	57.1%	56.6%	56.1%	55.6%	55.0%	54.5%	54.1%	53.6%
C																	
U	3050]	62.2%	61.6%	61.0%	60.4%	59.8%	59.2%	58.7%	58.1%	57.5%	57.0%	56.5%	56.0%	55.5%	55.0%	54.5%	54.0%
S	3100]	62.6%	62.0%	61.4%	60.8%	60.2%	59.6%	59.0%	58.5%	57.9%	57.4%	56.9%	56.4%	55.9%	55.4%	54.9%	54.4%
T	3150]	63.0%	62.4%	61.8%	61.2%	60.6%	60.0%	59.4%	58.9%	58.3%	57.8%	57.3%	56.8%	56.3%	55.8%	55.3%	54.8%
O	3200]	63.4%	62.7%	62.1%	61.5%	61.0%	60.4%	59.8%	59.3%	58.7%	58.2%	57.7%	57.1%	56.6%	56.1%	55.7%	55.2%
D	3250]	63.7%	63.1%	62.5%	61.9%	61.3%	60.7%	60.2%	59.6%	59.1%	58.6%	58.0%	57.5%	57.0%	56.5%	56.0%	55.6%
I	3300]	64.1%	63.5%	62.9%	62.3%	61.7%	61.1%	60.6%	60.0%	59.5%	58.9%	58.4%	57.9%	57.4%	56.9%	56.4%	55.9%
A	3350]	64.4%	63.8%	63.2%	62.6%	62.0%	61.5%	60.9%	60.4%	59.8%	59.3%	58.8%	58.3%	57.8%	57.3%	56.8%	56.3%
L	3400]	64.8%	64.2%	63.6%	63.0%	62.4%	61.8%	61.3%	60.7%	60.2%	59.6%	59.1%	58.6%	58.1%	57.6%	57.1%	56.7%
	3450]	65.1%	64.5%	63.9%	63.3%	62.7%	62.2%	61.6%	61.1%	60.5%	60.0%	59.5%	59.0%	58.5%	58.0%	57.5%	57.0%
P																	
A	3500]	65.4%	64.8%	64.2%	63.6%	63.1%	62.5%	61.9%	61.4%	60.9%	60.3%	59.8%	59.3%	58.8%	58.3%	57.9%	57.4%
R	3550]	65.7%	65.1%	64.5%	64.0%	63.4%	62.8%	62.3%	61.7%	61.2%	60.7%	60.2%	59.7%	59.2%	58.7%	58.2%	57.7%
E	3600]	66.1%	65.5%	64.9%	64.3%	63.7%	63.2%	62.6%	62.1%	61.5%	61.0%	60.5%	60.0%	59.5%	59.0%	58.5%	58.1%
N	3650]	66.4%	65.8%	65.2%	64.6%	64.0%	63.5%	62.9%	62.4%	61.9%	61.3%	60.8%	60.3%	59.8%	59.3%	58.9%	58.4%
T	3700]	66.7%	66.1%	65.5%	64.9%	64.3%	63.8%	63.2%	62.7%	62.2%	61.7%	61.2%	60.7%	60.2%	59.7%	59.2%	58.7%
	3750]	67.0%	66.4%	65.8%	65.2%	64.7%	64.1%	63.6%	63.0%	62.5%	62.0%	61.5%	61.0%	60.5%	60.0%	59.5%	59.1%
M	3800]	67.3%	66.7%	66.1%	65.5%	65.0%	64.4%	63.9%	63.3%	62.8%	62.3%	61.8%	61.3%	60.8%	60.3%	59.8%	59.4%
O	3850]	67.5%	67.0%	66.4%	65.8%	65.3%	64.7%	64.2%	63.6%	63.1%	62.6%	62.1%	61.6%	61.1%	60.6%	60.2%	59.7%
N	3900]	67.8%	67.2%	66.7%	66.1%	65.5%	65.0%	64.5%	63.9%	63.4%	62.9%	62.4%	61.9%	61.4%	60.9%	60.5%	60.0%
T	3950]	68.1%	67.5%	66.9%	66.4%	65.8%	65.3%	64.8%	64.2%	63.7%	63.2%	62.7%	62.2%	61.7%	61.2%	60.8%	60.3%
H																	
L	4000]	68.4%	67.8%	67.2%	66.7%	66.1%	65.6%	65.0%	64.5%	64.0%	63.5%	63.0%	62.5%	62.0%	61.5%	61.1%	60.6%
Y	4050]	68.6%	68.1%	67.5%	66.9%	66.4%	65.9%	65.3%	64.8%	64.3%	63.8%	63.3%	62.8%	62.3%	61.8%	61.4%	60.9%
	4100]	68.9%	68.3%	67.8%	67.2%	66.7%	66.1%	65.6%	65.1%	64.6%	64.1%	63.6%	63.1%	62.6%	62.1%	61.7%	61.2%
I	4150]	69.2%	68.6%	68.0%	67.5%	66.9%	66.4%	65.9%	65.4%	64.8%	64.3%	63.8%	63.4%	62.9%	62.4%	61.9%	61.5%
N	4200]	69.4%	68.9%	68.3%	67.7%	67.2%	66.7%	66.1%	65.6%	65.1%	64.6%	64.1%	63.6%	63.2%	62.7%	62.2%	61.8%
C	4250]	69.7%	69.1%	68.5%	68.0%	67.5%	66.9%	66.4%	65.9%	65.4%	64.9%	64.4%	63.9%	63.4%	63.0%	62.5%	62.0%
O	4300]	69.9%	69.4%	68.8%	68.3%	67.7%	67.2%	66.7%	66.2%	65.6%	65.2%	64.7%	64.2%	63.7%	63.2%	62.8%	62.3%
M	4350]	70.2%	69.6%	69.0%	68.5%	68.0%	67.4%	66.9%	66.4%	65.9%	65.4%	64.9%	64.4%	64.0%	63.5%	63.0%	62.6%
E	4400]	70.4%	69.8%	69.3%	68.8%	68.2%	67.7%	67.2%	66.7%	66.2%	65.7%	65.2%	64.7%	64.2%	63.8%	63.3%	62.9%
	4450]	70.6%	70.1%	69.5%	69.0%	68.5%	67.9%	67.4%	66.9%	66.4%	65.9%	65.4%	65.0%	64.5%	64.0%	63.6%	63.1%
	4500]	70.9%	70.3%	69.8%	69.2%	68.7%	68.2%	67.7%	67.2%	66.7%	66.2%	65.7%	65.2%	64.7%	64.3%	63.8%	63.4%
	4550]	71.1%	70.5%	70.0%	69.5%	68.9%	68.4%	67.9%	67.4%	66.9%	66.4%	65.9%	65.5%	65.0%	64.5%	64.1%	63.6%
	4600]	71.3%	70.8%	70.2%	69.7%	69.2%	68.7%	68.1%	67.6%	67.2%	66.7%	66.2%	65.7%	65.2%	64.8%	64.3%	63.9%
	4650]	71.5%	71.0%	70.5%	69.9%	69.4%	68.9%	68.4%	67.9%	67.4%	66.9%	66.4%	66.0%	65.5%	65.0%	64.6%	64.1%
	4700]	71.8%	71.2%	70.7%	70.1%	69.6%	69.1%	68.6%	68.1%	67.6%	67.1%	66.7%	66.2%	65.7%	65.3%	64.8%	64.4%
	4750]	72.0%	71.4%	70.9%	70.4%	69.9%	69.3%	68.8%	68.3%	67.9%	67.4%	66.9%	66.4%	66.0%	65.5%	65.1%	64.6%
	4800]	72.2%	71.6%	71.1%	70.6%	70.1%	69.6%	69.1%	68.6%	68.1%	67.6%	67.1%	66.7%	66.2%	65.8%	65.3%	64.9%
	4850]	72.4%	71.9%	71.3%	70.8%	70.3%	69.8%	69.3%	68.8%	68.3%	67.8%	67.4%	66.9%	66.4%	66.0%	65.5%	65.1%
	4900]	72.6%	72.1%	71.5%	71.0%	70.5%	70.0%	69.5%	69.0%	68.5%	68.1%	67.6%	67.1%	66.7%	66.2%	65.8%	65.3%
	4950]	72.8%	72.3%	71.7%	71.2%	70.7%	70.2%	69.7%	69.2%	68.8%	68.3%	67.8%	67.3%	66.9%	66.4%	66.0%	65.6%
	5000]	73.0%	72.5%	71.9%	71.4%	70.9%	70.4%	69.9%	69.4%	69.0%	68.5%	68.0%	67.6%	67.1%	66.7%	66.2%	65.8%

Non-Custodial Parent Percentage of Income

CUSTODIAL PARENT MONTHLY INCOME

NON CUSTODIAL PARENT MONTHLY INCOME

	2650	2700	2750	2800	2850	2900	2950	3000	3050	3100	3150	3200	3250	3300	3350	3400
250]	10.0%	10.0%	10.0%	10.0%	10.0%	10.0%	10.0%	10.0%	10.0%	10.0%	10.0%	10.0%	10.0%	10.0%	10.0%	10.0%
300]	10.2%	10.0%	10.0%	10.0%	10.0%	10.0%	10.0%	10.0%	10.0%	10.0%	10.0%	10.0%	10.0%	10.0%	10.0%	10.0%
350]	11.7%	11.5%	11.3%	11.1%	10.9%	10.8%	10.6%	10.4%	10.3%	10.1%	10.0%	10.0%	10.0%	10.0%	10.0%	10.0%
400]	13.1%	12.9%	12.7%	12.5%	12.3%	12.1%	11.9%	11.8%	11.6%	11.4%	11.3%	11.1%	11.0%	10.8%	10.7%	10.5%
450]	14.5%	14.3%	14.1%	13.8%	13.6%	13.4%	13.2%	13.0%	12.9%	12.7%	12.5%	12.3%	12.2%	12.0%	11.8%	11.7%
500]	15.9%	15.6%	15.4%	15.2%	14.9%	14.7%	14.5%	14.3%	14.1%	13.9%	13.7%	13.5%	13.3%	13.2%	13.0%	12.8%
550]	17.2%	16.9%	16.7%	16.4%	16.2%	15.9%	15.7%	15.5%	15.3%	15.1%	14.9%	14.7%	14.5%	14.3%	14.1%	13.9%
600]	18.5%	18.2%	17.9%	17.6%	17.4%	17.1%	16.9%	16.7%	16.4%	16.2%	16.0%	15.8%	15.6%	15.4%	15.2%	15.0%
650]	19.7%	19.4%	19.1%	18.8%	18.6%	18.3%	18.1%	17.8%	17.6%	17.3%	17.1%	16.9%	16.7%	16.5%	16.3%	16.0%
700]	20.9%	20.6%	20.3%	20.0%	19.7%	19.4%	19.2%	18.9%	18.7%	18.4%	18.2%	17.9%	17.7%	17.5%	17.3%	17.1%
750]	22.1%	21.7%	21.4%	21.1%	20.8%	20.5%	20.3%	20.0%	19.7%	19.5%	19.2%	19.0%	18.8%	18.5%	18.3%	18.1%
800]	23.2%	22.9%	22.5%	22.2%	21.9%	21.6%	21.3%	21.1%	20.8%	20.5%	20.3%	20.0%	19.8%	19.5%	19.3%	19.0%
850]	24.3%	23.9%	23.6%	23.3%	23.0%	22.7%	22.4%	22.1%	21.8%	21.5%	21.3%	21.0%	20.7%	20.5%	20.2%	20.0%
900]	25.4%	25.0%	24.7%	24.3%	24.0%	23.7%	23.4%	23.1%	22.8%	22.5%	22.2%	22.0%	21.7%	21.4%	21.2%	20.9%
950]	26.4%	26.0%	25.7%	25.3%	25.0%	24.7%	24.4%	24.1%	23.8%	23.5%	23.2%	22.9%	22.6%	22.4%	22.1%	21.8%
1000]	27.4%	27.0%	26.7%	26.3%	26.0%	25.6%	25.3%	25.0%	24.7%	24.4%	24.1%	23.8%	23.5%	23.3%	23.0%	22.7%
1050]	28.4%	28.0%	27.6%	27.3%	26.9%	26.6%	26.3%	25.9%	25.6%	25.3%	25.0%	24.7%	24.4%	24.1%	23.9%	23.6%
1100]	29.3%	28.9%	28.6%	28.2%	27.8%	27.5%	27.2%	26.8%	26.5%	26.2%	25.9%	25.6%	25.3%	25.0%	24.7%	24.4%
1150]	30.3%	29.9%	29.5%	29.1%	28.8%	28.4%	28.0%	27.7%	27.4%	27.1%	26.7%	26.4%	26.1%	25.8%	25.6%	25.3%
1200]	31.2%	30.8%	30.4%	30.0%	29.6%	29.3%	28.9%	28.6%	28.2%	27.9%	27.6%	27.3%	27.0%	26.7%	26.4%	26.1%
1250]	32.1%	31.6%	31.3%	30.9%	30.5%	30.1%	29.8%	29.4%	29.1%	28.7%	28.4%	28.1%	27.8%	27.5%	27.2%	26.9%
1300]	32.9%	32.5%	32.1%	31.7%	31.3%	31.0%	30.6%	30.2%	29.9%	29.5%	29.2%	28.9%	28.6%	28.3%	28.0%	27.7%
1350]	33.8%	33.3%	32.9%	32.5%	32.1%	31.8%	31.4%	31.0%	30.7%	30.3%	30.0%	29.7%	29.3%	29.0%	28.7%	28.4%
1400]	34.6%	34.1%	33.7%	33.3%	32.9%	32.6%	32.2%	31.8%	31.5%	31.1%	30.8%	30.4%	30.1%	29.8%	29.5%	29.2%
1450]	35.4%	34.9%	34.5%	34.1%	33.7%	33.3%	33.0%	32.6%	32.2%	31.9%	31.5%	31.2%	30.9%	30.5%	30.2%	29.9%
1500]	36.1%	35.7%	35.3%	34.9%	34.5%	34.1%	33.7%	33.3%	33.0%	32.6%	32.3%	31.9%	31.6%	31.3%	30.9%	30.6%
1550]	36.9%	36.5%	36.0%	35.6%	35.2%	34.8%	34.4%	34.1%	33.7%	33.3%	33.0%	32.6%	32.3%	32.0%	31.6%	31.3%
1600]	37.6%	37.2%	36.8%	36.4%	36.0%	35.6%	35.2%	34.8%	34.4%	34.0%	33.7%	33.3%	33.0%	32.7%	32.3%	32.0%
1650]	38.4%	37.9%	37.5%	37.1%	36.7%	36.3%	35.9%	35.5%	35.1%	34.7%	34.4%	34.0%	33.7%	33.3%	33.0%	32.7%
1700]	39.1%	38.6%	38.2%	37.8%	37.4%	37.0%	36.6%	36.2%	35.8%	35.4%	35.1%	34.7%	34.3%	34.0%	33.7%	33.3%
1750]	39.8%	39.3%	38.9%	38.5%	38.0%	37.6%	37.2%	36.8%	36.5%	36.1%	35.7%	35.4%	35.0%	34.7%	34.3%	34.0%
1800]	40.4%	40.0%	39.6%	39.1%	38.7%	38.3%	37.9%	37.5%	37.1%	36.7%	36.4%	36.0%	35.6%	35.3%	35.0%	34.6%
1850]	41.1%	40.7%	40.2%	39.8%	39.4%	38.9%	38.5%	38.1%	37.8%	37.4%	37.0%	36.6%	36.3%	35.9%	35.6%	35.2%
1900]	41.8%	41.3%	40.9%	40.4%	40.0%	39.6%	39.2%	38.8%	38.4%	38.0%	37.6%	37.3%	36.9%	36.5%	36.2%	35.8%
1950]	42.4%	41.9%	41.5%	41.1%	40.6%	40.2%	39.8%	39.4%	39.0%	38.6%	38.2%	37.9%	37.5%	37.1%	36.8%	36.4%
2000]	43.0%	42.6%	42.1%	41.7%	41.2%	40.8%	40.4%	40.0%	39.6%	39.2%	38.8%	38.5%	38.1%	37.7%	37.4%	37.0%
2050]	43.6%	43.2%	42.7%	42.3%	41.8%	41.4%	41.0%	40.6%	40.2%	39.8%	39.4%	39.0%	38.7%	38.3%	38.0%	37.6%
2100]	44.2%	43.8%	43.3%	42.9%	42.4%	42.0%	41.6%	41.2%	40.8%	40.4%	40.0%	39.6%	39.3%	38.9%	38.5%	38.2%
2150]	44.8%	44.3%	43.9%	43.4%	43.0%	42.6%	42.2%	41.7%	41.3%	41.0%	40.6%	40.2%	39.8%	39.4%	39.1%	38.7%
2200]	45.4%	44.9%	44.4%	44.0%	43.6%	43.1%	42.7%	42.3%	41.9%	41.5%	41.1%	40.7%	40.4%	40.0%	39.6%	39.3%
2250]	45.9%	45.5%	45.0%	44.6%	44.1%	43.7%	43.3%	42.9%	42.5%	42.1%	41.7%	41.3%	40.9%	40.5%	40.2%	39.8%
2300]	46.5%	46.0%	45.5%	45.1%	44.7%	44.2%	43.8%	43.4%	43.0%	42.6%	42.2%	41.8%	41.4%	41.1%	40.7%	40.4%
2350]	47.0%	46.5%	46.1%	45.6%	45.2%	44.8%	44.3%	43.9%	43.5%	43.1%	42.7%	42.3%	42.0%	41.6%	41.2%	40.9%
2400]	47.5%	47.1%	46.6%	46.2%	45.7%	45.3%	44.9%	44.4%	44.0%	43.6%	43.2%	42.9%	42.5%	42.1%	41.7%	41.4%
2450]	48.0%	47.6%	47.1%	46.7%	46.2%	45.8%	45.4%	45.0%	44.5%	44.1%	43.8%	43.4%	43.0%	42.6%	42.2%	41.9%
2500]	48.5%	48.1%	47.6%	47.2%	46.7%	46.3%	45.9%	45.5%	45.0%	44.6%	44.2%	43.9%	43.5%	43.1%	42.7%	42.4%

2004 MICHIGAN CHILD SUPPORT FORMULA SCHEDULES
PERCENTAGE OF INCOME

Non-Custodial Parent Percentage of Income

CUSTODIAL PARENT MONTHLY INCOME

NONCUSTODIAL PARENT MONTHLY INCOME

	2650	2700	2750	2800	2850	2900	2950	3000	3050	3100	3150	3200	3250	3300	3350	3400
2550]	49.0%	48.6%	48.1%	47.7%	47.2%	46.8%	46.4%	45.9%	45.5%	45.1%	44.7%	44.3%	44.0%	43.6%	43.2%	42.9%
2600]	49.5%	49.1%	48.6%	48.1%	47.7%	47.3%	46.8%	46.4%	46.0%	45.6%	45.2%	44.8%	44.4%	44.1%	43.7%	43.3%
2650]	50.0%	49.5%	49.1%	48.6%	48.2%	47.7%	47.3%	46.9%	46.5%	46.1%	45.7%	45.3%	44.9%	44.5%	44.2%	43.8%
2700]	50.5%	50.0%	49.5%	49.1%	48.6%	48.2%	47.8%	47.4%	47.0%	46.6%	46.2%	45.8%	45.4%	45.0%	44.6%	44.3%
2750]	50.9%	50.5%	50.0%	49.5%	49.1%	48.7%	48.2%	47.8%	47.4%	47.0%	46.6%	46.2%	45.8%	45.5%	45.1%	44.7%
2800]	51.4%	50.9%	50.5%	50.0%	49.6%	49.1%	48.7%	48.3%	47.9%	47.5%	47.1%	46.7%	46.3%	45.9%	45.5%	45.2%
2850]	51.8%	51.4%	50.9%	50.4%	50.0%	49.6%	49.1%	48.7%	48.3%	47.9%	47.5%	47.1%	46.7%	46.3%	46.0%	45.6%
2900]	52.3%	51.8%	51.3%	50.9%	50.4%	50.0%	49.6%	49.2%	48.7%	48.3%	47.9%	47.5%	47.2%	46.8%	46.4%	46.0%
2950]	52.7%	52.2%	51.8%	51.3%	50.9%	50.4%	50.0%	49.6%	49.2%	48.8%	48.4%	48.0%	47.6%	47.2%	46.8%	46.5%
3000]	53.1%	52.6%	52.2%	51.7%	51.3%	50.8%	50.4%	50.0%	49.6%	49.2%	48.8%	48.4%	48.0%	47.6%	47.2%	46.9%
3050]	53.5%	53.0%	52.6%	52.1%	51.7%	51.3%	50.8%	50.4%	50.0%	49.6%	49.2%	48.8%	48.4%	48.0%	47.7%	47.3%
3100]	53.9%	53.4%	53.0%	52.5%	52.1%	51.7%	51.2%	50.8%	50.4%	50.0%	49.6%	49.2%	48.8%	48.4%	48.1%	47.7%
3150]	54.3%	53.8%	53.4%	52.9%	52.5%	52.1%	51.6%	51.2%	50.8%	50.4%	50.0%	49.6%	49.2%	48.8%	48.5%	48.1%
3200]	54.7%	54.2%	53.8%	53.3%	52.9%	52.5%	52.0%	51.6%	51.2%	50.8%	50.4%	50.0%	49.6%	49.2%	48.9%	48.5%
3250]	55.1%	54.6%	54.2%	53.7%	53.3%	52.8%	52.4%	52.0%	51.6%	51.2%	50.8%	50.4%	50.0%	49.6%	49.2%	48.9%
3300]	55.5%	55.0%	54.5%	54.1%	53.7%	53.2%	52.8%	52.4%	52.0%	51.6%	51.2%	50.8%	50.4%	50.0%	49.6%	49.3%
3350]	55.8%	55.4%	54.9%	54.5%	54.0%	53.6%	53.2%	52.8%	52.3%	51.9%	51.5%	51.1%	50.8%	50.4%	50.0%	49.6%
3400]	56.2%	55.7%	55.3%	54.8%	54.4%	54.0%	53.5%	53.1%	52.7%	52.3%	51.9%	51.5%	51.1%	50.7%	50.4%	50.0%
3450]	56.6%	56.1%	55.6%	55.2%	54.8%	54.3%	53.9%	53.5%	53.1%	52.7%	52.3%	51.9%	51.5%	51.1%	50.7%	50.4%
3500]	56.9%	56.5%	56.0%	55.6%	55.1%	54.7%	54.3%	53.8%	53.4%	53.0%	52.6%	52.2%	51.9%	51.5%	51.1%	50.7%
3550]	57.3%	56.8%	56.3%	55.9%	55.5%	55.0%	54.6%	54.2%	53.8%	53.4%	53.0%	52.6%	52.2%	51.8%	51.4%	51.1%
3600]	57.6%	57.1%	56.7%	56.3%	55.8%	55.4%	55.0%	54.5%	54.1%	53.7%	53.3%	52.9%	52.6%	52.2%	51.8%	51.4%
3650]	57.9%	57.5%	57.0%	56.6%	56.2%	55.7%	55.3%	54.9%	54.5%	54.1%	53.7%	53.3%	52.9%	52.5%	52.1%	51.8%
3700]	58.3%	57.8%	57.4%	56.9%	56.5%	56.1%	55.6%	55.2%	54.8%	54.4%	54.0%	53.6%	53.2%	52.9%	52.5%	52.1%
3750]	58.6%	58.1%	57.7%	57.3%	56.8%	56.4%	56.0%	55.6%	55.1%	54.7%	54.3%	54.0%	53.6%	53.2%	52.8%	52.4%
3800]	58.9%	58.5%	58.0%	57.6%	57.1%	56.7%	56.3%	55.9%	55.5%	55.1%	54.7%	54.3%	53.9%	53.5%	53.1%	52.8%
3850]	59.2%	58.8%	58.3%	57.9%	57.5%	57.0%	56.6%	56.2%	55.8%	55.4%	55.0%	54.6%	54.2%	53.8%	53.5%	53.1%
3900]	59.5%	59.1%	58.6%	58.2%	57.8%	57.4%	56.9%	56.5%	56.1%	55.7%	55.3%	54.9%	54.5%	54.2%	53.8%	53.4%
3950]	59.8%	59.4%	59.0%	58.5%	58.1%	57.7%	57.2%	56.8%	56.4%	56.0%	55.6%	55.2%	54.9%	54.5%	54.1%	53.7%
4000]	60.2%	59.7%	59.3%	58.8%	58.4%	58.0%	57.6%	57.1%	56.7%	56.3%	55.9%	55.6%	55.2%	54.8%	54.4%	54.1%
4050]	60.4%	60.0%	59.6%	59.1%	58.7%	58.3%	57.9%	57.4%	57.0%	56.6%	56.3%	55.9%	55.5%	55.1%	54.7%	54.4%
4100]	60.7%	60.3%	59.9%	59.4%	59.0%	58.6%	58.2%	57.7%	57.3%	56.9%	56.6%	56.2%	55.8%	55.4%	55.0%	54.7%
4150]	61.0%	60.6%	60.1%	59.7%	59.3%	58.9%	58.5%	58.0%	57.6%	57.2%	56.8%	56.5%	56.1%	55.7%	55.3%	55.0%
4200]	61.3%	60.9%	60.4%	60.0%	59.6%	59.2%	58.7%	58.3%	57.9%	57.5%	57.1%	56.8%	56.4%	56.0%	55.6%	55.3%
4250]	61.6%	61.2%	60.7%	60.3%	59.9%	59.4%	59.0%	58.6%	58.2%	57.8%	57.4%	57.0%	56.7%	56.3%	55.9%	55.6%
4300]	61.9%	61.4%	61.0%	60.6%	60.1%	59.7%	59.3%	58.9%	58.5%	58.1%	57.7%	57.3%	57.0%	56.6%	56.2%	55.8%
4350]	62.1%	61.7%	61.3%	60.8%	60.4%	60.0%	59.6%	59.2%	58.8%	58.4%	58.0%	57.6%	57.2%	56.9%	56.5%	56.1%
4400]	62.4%	62.0%	61.5%	61.1%	60.7%	60.3%	59.9%	59.5%	59.1%	58.7%	58.3%	57.9%	57.5%	57.1%	56.8%	56.4%
4450]	62.7%	62.2%	61.8%	61.4%	61.0%	60.5%	60.1%	59.7%	59.3%	58.9%	58.6%	58.2%	57.8%	57.4%	57.1%	56.7%
4500]	62.9%	62.5%	62.1%	61.6%	61.2%	60.8%	60.4%	60.0%	59.6%	59.2%	58.8%	58.4%	58.1%	57.7%	57.3%	57.0%
4550]	63.2%	62.8%	62.3%	61.9%	61.5%	61.1%	60.7%	60.3%	59.9%	59.5%	59.1%	58.7%	58.3%	58.0%	57.6%	57.2%
4600]	63.4%	63.0%	62.6%	62.2%	61.7%	61.3%	60.9%	60.5%	60.1%	59.7%	59.4%	59.0%	58.6%	58.2%	57.9%	57.5%
4650]	63.7%	63.3%	62.8%	62.4%	62.0%	61.6%	61.2%	60.8%	60.4%	60.0%	59.6%	59.2%	58.9%	58.5%	58.1%	57.8%
4700]	63.9%	63.5%	63.1%	62.7%	62.3%	61.8%	61.4%	61.0%	60.6%	60.3%	59.9%	59.5%	59.1%	58.8%	58.4%	58.0%
4750]	64.2%	63.8%	63.3%	62.9%	62.5%	62.1%	61.7%	61.3%	60.9%	60.5%	60.1%	59.7%	59.4%	59.0%	58.6%	58.3%
4800]	64.4%	64.0%	63.6%	63.2%	62.7%	62.3%	61.9%	61.5%	61.1%	60.8%	60.4%	60.0%	59.6%	59.3%	58.9%	58.5%
4850]	64.7%	64.2%	63.8%	63.4%	63.0%	62.6%	62.2%	61.8%	61.4%	61.0%	60.6%	60.2%	59.9%	59.5%	59.1%	58.8%
4900]	64.9%	64.5%	64.1%	63.6%	63.2%	62.8%	62.4%	62.0%	61.6%	61.3%	60.9%	60.5%	60.1%	59.8%	59.4%	59.0%
4950]	65.1%	64.7%	64.3%	63.9%	63.5%	63.1%	62.7%	62.3%	61.9%	61.5%	61.1%	60.7%	60.4%	60.0%	59.6%	59.3%
5000]	65.4%	64.9%	64.5%	64.1%	63.7%	63.3%	62.9%	62.5%	62.1%	61.7%	61.3%	61.0%	60.6%	60.2%	59.9%	59.5%

2004 MICHIGAN CHILD SUPPORT FORMULA SCHEDULES
PERCENTAGE OF INCOME

Non-Custodial Parent Percentage of Income

CUSTODIAL PARENT MONTHLY INCOME

	3450	3500	3550	3600	3650	3700	3750	3800	3850	3900	3950	4000	4050	4100	4150	4200
250]	10.0%	10.0%	10.0%	10.0%	10.0%	10.0%	10.0%	10.0%	10.0%	10.0%	10.0%	10.0%	10.0%	10.0%	10.0%	10.0%
300]	10.0%	10.0%	10.0%	10.0%	10.0%	10.0%	10.0%	10.0%	10.0%	10.0%	10.0%	10.0%	10.0%	10.0%	10.0%	10.0%
350]	10.0%	10.0%	10.0%	10.0%	10.0%	10.0%	10.0%	10.0%	10.0%	10.0%	10.0%	10.0%	10.0%	10.0%	10.0%	10.0%
400]	10.4%	10.3%	10.1%	10.0%	10.0%	10.0%	10.0%	10.0%	10.0%	10.0%	10.0%	10.0%	10.0%	10.0%	10.0%	10.0%
450]	11.5%	11.4%	11.3%	11.1%	11.0%	10.8%	10.7%	10.6%	10.5%	10.3%	10.2%	10.1%	10.0%	10.0%	10.0%	10.0%
500]	12.7%	12.5%	12.3%	12.2%	12.0%	11.9%	11.8%	11.6%	11.5%	11.4%	11.2%	11.1%	11.0%	10.9%	10.8%	10.6%
550]	13.8%	13.6%	13.4%	13.3%	13.1%	12.9%	12.8%	12.6%	12.5%	12.4%	12.2%	12.1%	12.0%	11.8%	11.7%	11.6%
600]	14.8%	14.6%	14.5%	14.3%	14.1%	14.0%	13.8%	13.6%	13.5%	13.3%	13.2%	13.0%	12.9%	12.8%	12.6%	12.5%
650]	15.9%	15.7%	15.5%	15.3%	15.1%	14.9%	14.8%	14.6%	14.4%	14.3%	14.1%	14.0%	13.8%	13.7%	13.5%	13.4%
700]	16.9%	16.7%	16.5%	16.3%	16.1%	15.9%	15.7%	15.6%	15.4%	15.2%	15.1%	14.9%	14.7%	14.6%	14.4%	14.3%
750]	17.9%	17.6%	17.4%	17.2%	17.0%	16.9%	16.7%	16.5%	16.3%	16.1%	16.0%	15.8%	15.6%	15.5%	15.3%	15.2%
800]	18.8%	18.6%	18.4%	18.2%	18.0%	17.8%	17.6%	17.4%	17.2%	17.0%	16.8%	16.7%	16.5%	16.3%	16.2%	16.0%
850]	19.8%	19.5%	19.3%	19.1%	18.9%	18.7%	18.5%	18.3%	18.1%	17.9%	17.7%	17.5%	17.3%	17.2%	17.0%	16.8%
900]	20.7%	20.5%	20.2%	20.0%	19.8%	19.6%	19.4%	19.1%	18.9%	18.8%	18.6%	18.4%	18.2%	18.0%	17.8%	17.6%
950]	21.6%	21.3%	21.1%	20.9%	20.7%	20.4%	20.2%	20.0%	19.8%	19.6%	19.4%	19.2%	19.0%	18.8%	18.6%	18.4%
1000]	22.5%	22.2%	22.0%	21.7%	21.5%	21.3%	21.1%	20.8%	20.6%	20.4%	20.2%	20.0%	19.8%	19.6%	19.4%	19.2%
1050]	23.3%	23.1%	22.8%	22.6%	22.3%	22.1%	21.9%	21.6%	21.4%	21.2%	21.0%	20.8%	20.6%	20.4%	20.2%	20.0%
1100]	24.2%	23.9%	23.7%	23.4%	23.2%	22.9%	22.7%	22.4%	22.2%	22.0%	21.8%	21.6%	21.4%	21.2%	21.0%	20.8%
1150]	25.0%	24.7%	24.5%	24.2%	24.0%	23.7%	23.5%	23.2%	23.0%	22.8%	22.5%	22.3%	22.1%	21.9%	21.7%	21.5%
1200]	25.8%	25.5%	25.3%	25.0%	24.7%	24.5%	24.2%	24.0%	23.8%	23.5%	23.3%	23.1%	22.9%	22.6%	22.4%	22.2%
1250]	26.6%	26.3%	26.0%	25.8%	25.5%	25.3%	25.0%	24.8%	24.5%	24.3%	24.0%	23.8%	23.6%	23.4%	23.1%	22.9%
1300]	27.4%	27.1%	26.8%	26.5%	26.3%	26.0%	25.7%	25.5%	25.2%	25.0%	24.8%	24.5%	24.3%	24.1%	23.9%	23.6%
1350]	28.1%	27.8%	27.6%	27.3%	27.0%	26.7%	26.5%	26.2%	26.0%	25.7%	25.5%	25.2%	25.0%	24.8%	24.5%	24.3%
1400]	28.9%	28.6%	28.3%	28.0%	27.7%	27.5%	27.2%	26.9%	26.7%	26.4%	26.2%	25.9%	25.7%	25.5%	25.2%	25.0%
1450]	29.6%	29.3%	29.0%	28.7%	28.4%	28.2%	27.9%	27.6%	27.4%	27.1%	26.9%	26.6%	26.4%	26.1%	25.9%	25.7%
1500]	30.3%	30.0%	29.7%	29.4%	29.1%	28.8%	28.6%	28.3%	28.0%	27.8%	27.5%	27.3%	27.0%	26.8%	26.5%	26.3%
1550]	31.0%	30.7%	30.4%	30.1%	29.8%	29.5%	29.2%	29.0%	28.7%	28.4%	28.2%	27.9%	27.7%	27.4%	27.2%	27.0%
1600]	31.7%	31.4%	31.1%	30.8%	30.5%	30.2%	29.9%	29.6%	29.4%	29.1%	28.8%	28.6%	28.3%	28.1%	27.8%	27.6%
1650]	32.4%	32.0%	31.7%	31.4%	31.1%	30.8%	30.6%	30.3%	30.0%	29.7%	29.5%	29.2%	28.9%	28.7%	28.4%	28.2%
1700]	33.0%	32.7%	32.4%	32.1%	31.8%	31.5%	31.2%	30.9%	30.6%	30.4%	30.1%	29.8%	29.6%	29.3%	29.1%	28.8%
1750]	33.7%	33.3%	33.0%	32.7%	32.4%	32.1%	31.8%	31.5%	31.3%	31.0%	30.7%	30.4%	30.2%	29.9%	29.7%	29.4%
1800]	34.3%	34.0%	33.6%	33.3%	33.0%	32.7%	32.4%	32.1%	31.9%	31.6%	31.3%	31.0%	30.8%	30.5%	30.3%	30.0%
1850]	34.9%	34.6%	34.3%	33.9%	33.6%	33.3%	33.0%	32.7%	32.5%	32.2%	31.9%	31.6%	31.4%	31.1%	30.8%	30.6%
1900]	35.5%	35.2%	34.9%	34.5%	34.2%	33.9%	33.6%	33.3%	33.0%	32.8%	32.5%	32.2%	31.9%	31.7%	31.4%	31.1%
1950]	36.1%	35.8%	35.5%	35.1%	34.8%	34.5%	34.2%	33.9%	33.6%	33.3%	33.1%	32.8%	32.5%	32.2%	32.0%	31.7%
2000]	36.7%	36.4%	36.0%	35.7%	35.4%	35.1%	34.8%	34.5%	34.2%	33.9%	33.6%	33.3%	33.1%	32.8%	32.5%	32.3%
2050]	37.3%	36.9%	36.6%	36.3%	36.0%	35.7%	35.3%	35.0%	34.7%	34.5%	34.2%	33.9%	33.6%	33.3%	33.1%	32.8%
2100]	37.8%	37.5%	37.2%	36.8%	36.5%	36.2%	35.9%	35.6%	35.3%	35.0%	34.7%	34.4%	34.1%	33.9%	33.6%	33.3%
2150]	38.4%	38.1%	37.7%	37.4%	37.1%	36.8%	36.4%	36.1%	35.8%	35.5%	35.2%	35.0%	34.7%	34.4%	34.1%	33.9%
2200]	38.9%	38.6%	38.3%	37.9%	37.6%	37.3%	37.0%	36.7%	36.4%	36.1%	35.8%	35.5%	35.2%	34.9%	34.6%	34.4%
2250]	39.5%	39.1%	38.8%	38.5%	38.1%	37.8%	37.5%	37.2%	36.9%	36.6%	36.3%	36.0%	35.7%	35.4%	35.2%	34.9%
2300]	40.0%	39.7%	39.3%	39.0%	38.7%	38.3%	38.0%	37.7%	37.4%	37.1%	36.8%	36.5%	36.2%	35.9%	35.7%	35.4%
2350]	40.5%	40.2%	39.8%	39.5%	39.2%	38.8%	38.5%	38.2%	37.9%	37.6%	37.3%	37.0%	36.7%	36.4%	36.2%	35.9%
2400]	41.0%	40.7%	40.3%	40.0%	39.7%	39.3%	39.0%	38.7%	38.4%	38.1%	37.8%	37.5%	37.2%	36.9%	36.6%	36.4%
2450]	41.5%	41.2%	40.8%	40.5%	40.2%	39.8%	39.5%	39.2%	38.9%	38.6%	38.3%	38.0%	37.7%	37.4%	37.1%	36.8%
2500]	42.0%	41.7%	41.3%	41.0%	40.7%	40.3%	40.0%	39.7%	39.4%	39.1%	38.8%	38.5%	38.2%	37.9%	37.6%	37.3%

NONCUSTODIAL PARENT MONTHLY INCOME

Non-Custodial Parent Percentage of Income

CUSTODIAL PARENT MONTHLY INCOME

(Left axis: NON-CUSTODIAL PARENT MONTHLY INCOME)

	3450	3500	3550	3600	3650	3700	3750	3800	3850	3900	3950	4000	4050	4100	4150	4200
2550]	42.5%	42.1%	41.8%	41.5%	41.1%	40.8%	40.5%	40.2%	39.8%	39.5%	39.2%	38.9%	38.6%	38.3%	38.1%	37.8%
2600]	43.0%	42.6%	42.3%	41.9%	41.6%	41.3%	40.9%	40.6%	40.3%	40.0%	39.7%	39.4%	39.1%	38.8%	38.5%	38.2%
2650]	43.4%	43.1%	42.7%	42.4%	42.1%	41.7%	41.4%	41.1%	40.8%	40.5%	40.2%	39.8%	39.6%	39.3%	39.0%	38.7%
2700]	43.9%	43.5%	43.2%	42.9%	42.5%	42.2%	41.9%	41.5%	41.2%	40.9%	40.6%	40.3%	40.0%	39.7%	39.4%	39.1%
2750]	44.4%	44.0%	43.7%	43.3%	43.0%	42.6%	42.3%	42.0%	41.7%	41.4%	41.0%	40.7%	40.4%	40.1%	39.9%	39.6%
2800]	44.8%	44.4%	44.1%	43.8%	43.4%	43.1%	42.7%	42.4%	42.1%	41.8%	41.5%	41.2%	40.9%	40.6%	40.3%	40.0%
2850]	45.2%	44.9%	44.5%	44.2%	43.8%	43.5%	43.2%	42.9%	42.5%	42.2%	41.9%	41.6%	41.3%	41.0%	40.7%	40.4%
2900]	45.7%	45.3%	45.0%	44.6%	44.3%	43.9%	43.6%	43.3%	43.0%	42.6%	42.3%	42.0%	41.7%	41.4%	41.1%	40.8%
2950]	46.1%	45.7%	45.4%	45.0%	44.7%	44.4%	44.0%	43.7%	43.4%	43.1%	42.8%	42.4%	42.1%	41.8%	41.5%	41.3%
3000]	46.5%	46.2%	45.8%	45.5%	45.1%	44.8%	44.4%	44.1%	43.8%	43.5%	43.2%	42.9%	42.6%	42.3%	42.0%	41.7%
3050]	46.9%	46.6%	46.2%	45.9%	45.5%	45.2%	44.9%	44.5%	44.2%	43.9%	43.6%	43.3%	43.0%	42.7%	42.4%	42.1%
3100]	47.3%	47.0%	46.6%	46.3%	45.9%	45.6%	45.3%	44.9%	44.6%	44.3%	44.0%	43.7%	43.4%	43.1%	42.8%	42.5%
3150]	47.7%	47.4%	47.0%	46.7%	46.3%	46.0%	45.7%	45.3%	45.0%	44.7%	44.4%	44.1%	43.8%	43.4%	43.2%	42.9%
3200]	48.1%	47.8%	47.4%	47.1%	46.7%	46.4%	46.0%	45.7%	45.4%	45.1%	44.8%	44.4%	44.1%	43.8%	43.5%	43.2%
3250]	48.5%	48.1%	47.8%	47.4%	47.1%	46.8%	46.4%	46.1%	45.8%	45.5%	45.1%	44.8%	44.5%	44.2%	43.9%	43.6%
3300]	48.9%	48.5%	48.2%	47.8%	47.5%	47.1%	46.8%	46.5%	46.2%	45.8%	45.5%	45.2%	44.9%	44.6%	44.3%	44.0%
3350]	49.3%	48.9%	48.6%	48.2%	47.9%	47.5%	47.2%	46.9%	46.5%	46.2%	45.9%	45.6%	45.3%	45.0%	44.7%	44.4%
3400]	49.6%	49.3%	48.9%	48.6%	48.2%	47.9%	47.6%	47.2%	46.9%	46.6%	46.3%	45.9%	45.6%	45.3%	45.0%	44.7%
3450]	50.0%	49.6%	49.3%	48.9%	48.6%	48.3%	47.9%	47.6%	47.3%	46.9%	46.6%	46.3%	46.0%	45.7%	45.4%	45.1%
3500]	50.4%	50.0%	49.6%	49.3%	49.0%	48.6%	48.3%	47.9%	47.6%	47.3%	47.0%	46.7%	46.4%	46.1%	45.8%	45.5%
3550]	50.7%	50.4%	50.0%	49.7%	49.3%	49.0%	48.6%	48.3%	48.0%	47.7%	47.3%	47.0%	46.7%	46.4%	46.1%	45.8%
3600]	51.1%	50.7%	50.3%	50.0%	49.7%	49.3%	49.0%	48.6%	48.3%	48.0%	47.7%	47.4%	47.1%	46.8%	46.5%	46.2%
3650]	51.4%	51.0%	50.7%	50.3%	50.0%	49.7%	49.3%	49.0%	48.7%	48.3%	48.0%	47.7%	47.4%	47.1%	46.8%	46.5%
3700]	51.7%	51.4%	51.0%	50.7%	50.3%	50.0%	49.7%	49.3%	49.0%	48.7%	48.4%	48.1%	47.7%	47.4%	47.1%	46.8%
3750]	52.1%	51.7%	51.4%	51.0%	50.7%	50.3%	50.0%	49.7%	49.3%	49.0%	48.7%	48.4%	48.1%	47.8%	47.5%	47.2%
3800]	52.4%	52.1%	51.7%	51.4%	51.0%	50.7%	50.3%	50.0%	49.7%	49.4%	49.0%	48.7%	48.4%	48.1%	47.8%	47.5%
3850]	52.7%	52.4%	52.0%	51.7%	51.3%	51.0%	50.7%	50.3%	50.0%	49.7%	49.4%	49.0%	48.7%	48.4%	48.1%	47.8%
3900]	53.1%	52.7%	52.3%	52.0%	51.7%	51.3%	51.0%	50.6%	50.3%	50.0%	49.7%	49.4%	49.1%	48.8%	48.4%	48.1%
3950]	53.4%	53.0%	52.7%	52.3%	52.0%	51.6%	51.3%	51.0%	50.6%	50.3%	50.0%	49.7%	49.4%	49.1%	48.8%	48.5%
4000]	53.7%	53.3%	53.0%	52.6%	52.3%	51.9%	51.6%	51.3%	51.0%	50.6%	50.3%	50.0%	49.7%	49.4%	49.1%	48.8%
4050]	54.0%	53.6%	53.3%	52.9%	52.6%	52.3%	51.9%	51.6%	51.3%	50.9%	50.6%	50.3%	50.0%	49.7%	49.4%	49.1%
4100]	54.3%	53.9%	53.6%	53.2%	52.9%	52.6%	52.2%	51.9%	51.6%	51.3%	50.9%	50.6%	50.3%	50.0%	49.7%	49.4%
4150]	54.6%	54.2%	53.9%	53.5%	53.2%	52.9%	52.5%	52.2%	51.9%	51.6%	51.2%	50.9%	50.6%	50.3%	50.0%	49.7%
4200]	54.9%	54.5%	54.2%	53.8%	53.5%	53.2%	52.8%	52.5%	52.2%	51.9%	51.5%	51.2%	50.9%	50.6%	50.3%	50.0%
4250]	55.2%	54.8%	54.5%	54.1%	53.8%	53.5%	53.1%	52.8%	52.5%	52.1%	51.8%	51.5%	51.2%	50.9%	50.6%	50.3%
4300]	55.5%	55.1%	54.8%	54.4%	54.1%	53.8%	53.4%	53.1%	52.8%	52.4%	52.1%	51.8%	51.5%	51.2%	50.9%	50.6%
4350]	55.8%	55.4%	55.1%	54.7%	54.4%	54.0%	53.7%	53.4%	53.0%	52.7%	52.4%	52.1%	51.8%	51.5%	51.2%	50.9%
4400]	56.1%	55.7%	55.3%	55.0%	54.7%	54.3%	54.0%	53.7%	53.3%	53.0%	52.7%	52.4%	52.1%	51.8%	51.5%	51.2%
4450]	56.3%	56.0%	55.6%	55.3%	54.9%	54.6%	54.3%	53.9%	53.6%	53.3%	53.0%	52.7%	52.4%	52.0%	51.7%	51.4%
4500]	56.6%	56.3%	55.9%	55.6%	55.2%	54.9%	54.5%	54.2%	53.9%	53.6%	53.3%	52.9%	52.6%	52.3%	52.0%	51.7%
4550]	56.9%	56.5%	56.2%	55.8%	55.5%	55.2%	54.8%	54.5%	54.2%	53.8%	53.5%	53.2%	52.9%	52.6%	52.3%	52.0%
4600]	57.1%	56.8%	56.4%	56.1%	55.8%	55.4%	55.1%	54.8%	54.4%	54.1%	53.8%	53.5%	53.2%	52.9%	52.6%	52.3%
4650]	57.4%	57.1%	56.7%	56.4%	56.0%	55.7%	55.4%	55.0%	54.7%	54.4%	54.1%	53.8%	53.4%	53.1%	52.8%	52.5%
4700]	57.7%	57.3%	57.0%	56.6%	56.3%	56.0%	55.6%	55.3%	55.0%	54.7%	54.3%	54.0%	53.7%	53.4%	53.1%	52.8%
4750]	57.9%	57.6%	57.2%	56.9%	56.5%	56.2%	55.9%	55.6%	55.2%	54.9%	54.6%	54.3%	54.0%	53.7%	53.4%	53.1%
4800]	58.2%	57.8%	57.5%	57.1%	56.8%	56.5%	56.1%	55.8%	55.5%	55.2%	54.9%	54.5%	54.2%	53.9%	53.6%	53.3%
4850]	58.4%	58.1%	57.7%	57.4%	57.1%	56.7%	56.4%	56.1%	55.7%	55.4%	55.1%	54.8%	54.5%	54.2%	53.9%	53.6%
4900]	58.7%	58.3%	58.0%	57.6%	57.3%	57.0%	56.6%	56.3%	56.0%	55.7%	55.4%	55.1%	54.7%	54.4%	54.1%	53.8%
4950]	58.9%	58.6%	58.2%	57.9%	57.6%	57.2%	56.9%	56.6%	56.3%	55.9%	55.6%	55.3%	55.0%	54.7%	54.4%	54.1%
5000]	59.2%	58.8%	58.5%	58.1%	57.8%	57.5%	57.1%	56.8%	56.5%	56.2%	55.9%	55.6%	55.2%	54.9%	54.6%	54.3%

2004 MICHIGAN CHILD SUPPORT FORMULA SCHEDULES
PERCENTAGE OF INCOME

Non-Custodial Parent Percentage of Income

CUSTODIAL PARENT MONTHLY INCOME

	4250	4300	4350	4400	4450	4500	4550	4600	4650	4700	4750	4800	4850	4900	4950	5000
250]	10.0%	10.0%	10.0%	10.0%	10.0%	10.0%	10.0%	10.0%	10.0%	10.0%	10.0%	10.0%	10.0%	10.0%	10.0%	10.0%
300]	10.0%	10.0%	10.0%	10.0%	10.0%	10.0%	10.0%	10.0%	10.0%	10.0%	10.0%	10.0%	10.0%	10.0%	10.0%	10.0%
350]	10.0%	10.0%	10.0%	10.0%	10.0%	10.0%	10.0%	10.0%	10.0%	10.0%	10.0%	10.0%	10.0%	10.0%	10.0%	10.0%
400]	10.0%	10.0%	10.0%	10.0%	10.0%	10.0%	10.0%	10.0%	10.0%	10.0%	10.0%	10.0%	10.0%	10.0%	10.0%	10.0%
450]	10.0%	10.0%	10.0%	10.0%	10.0%	10.0%	10.0%	10.0%	10.0%	10.0%	10.0%	10.0%	10.0%	10.0%	10.0%	10.0%
500]	10.5%	10.4%	10.3%	10.2%	10.1%	10.0%	10.0%	10.0%	10.0%	10.0%	10.0%	10.0%	10.0%	10.0%	10.0%	10.0%
550]	11.5%	11.3%	11.2%	11.1%	11.0%	10.9%	10.8%	10.7%	10.6%	10.5%	10.4%	10.3%	10.2%	10.1%	10.0%	10.0%
600]	12.4%	12.2%	12.1%	12.0%	11.9%	11.8%	11.7%	11.5%	11.4%	11.3%	11.2%	11.1%	11.0%	10.9%	10.8%	10.7%
650]	13.3%	13.1%	13.0%	12.9%	12.7%	12.6%	12.5%	12.4%	12.3%	12.1%	12.0%	11.9%	11.8%	11.7%	11.6%	11.5%
700]	14.1%	14.0%	13.9%	13.7%	13.6%	13.5%	13.3%	13.2%	13.1%	13.0%	12.8%	12.7%	12.6%	12.5%	12.4%	12.3%
750]	15.0%	14.9%	14.7%	14.6%	14.4%	14.3%	14.2%	14.0%	13.9%	13.8%	13.6%	13.5%	13.4%	13.3%	13.2%	13.0%
800]	15.8%	15.7%	15.5%	15.4%	15.2%	15.1%	15.0%	14.8%	14.7%	14.5%	14.4%	14.3%	14.2%	14.0%	13.9%	13.8%
850]	16.7%	16.5%	16.3%	16.2%	16.0%	15.9%	15.7%	15.6%	15.5%	15.3%	15.2%	15.0%	14.9%	14.8%	14.7%	14.5%
900]	17.5%	17.3%	17.1%	17.0%	16.8%	16.7%	16.5%	16.4%	16.2%	16.1%	15.9%	15.8%	15.7%	15.5%	15.4%	15.3%
950]	18.3%	18.1%	17.9%	17.8%	17.6%	17.4%	17.3%	17.1%	17.0%	16.8%	16.7%	16.5%	16.4%	16.2%	16.1%	16.0%
1000]	19.0%	18.9%	18.7%	18.5%	18.3%	18.2%	18.0%	17.9%	17.7%	17.5%	17.4%	17.2%	17.1%	16.9%	16.8%	16.7%
1050]	19.8%	19.6%	19.4%	19.3%	19.1%	18.9%	18.8%	18.6%	18.4%	18.3%	18.1%	17.9%	17.8%	17.6%	17.5%	17.4%
1100]	20.6%	20.4%	20.2%	20.0%	19.8%	19.6%	19.5%	19.3%	19.1%	19.0%	18.8%	18.6%	18.5%	18.3%	18.2%	18.0%
1150]	21.3%	21.1%	20.9%	20.7%	20.5%	20.4%	20.2%	20.0%	19.8%	19.7%	19.5%	19.3%	19.2%	19.0%	18.9%	18.7%
1200]	22.0%	21.8%	21.6%	21.4%	21.2%	21.1%	20.9%	20.7%	20.5%	20.3%	20.2%	20.0%	19.8%	19.7%	19.5%	19.4%
1250]	22.7%	22.5%	22.3%	22.1%	21.9%	21.7%	21.6%	21.4%	21.2%	21.0%	20.8%	20.7%	20.5%	20.3%	20.2%	20.0%
1300]	23.4%	23.2%	23.0%	22.8%	22.6%	22.4%	22.2%	22.0%	21.8%	21.7%	21.5%	21.3%	21.1%	21.0%	20.8%	20.6%
1350]	24.1%	23.9%	23.7%	23.5%	23.3%	23.1%	22.9%	22.7%	22.5%	22.3%	22.1%	22.0%	21.8%	21.6%	21.4%	21.3%
1400]	24.8%	24.6%	24.3%	24.1%	23.9%	23.7%	23.5%	23.3%	23.1%	23.0%	22.8%	22.6%	22.4%	22.2%	22.0%	21.9%
1450]	25.4%	25.2%	25.0%	24.8%	24.6%	24.4%	24.2%	24.0%	23.8%	23.6%	23.4%	23.2%	23.0%	22.8%	22.7%	22.5%
1500]	26.1%	25.9%	25.6%	25.4%	25.2%	25.0%	24.8%	24.6%	24.4%	24.2%	24.0%	23.8%	23.6%	23.4%	23.3%	23.1%
1550]	26.7%	26.5%	26.3%	26.1%	25.8%	25.6%	25.4%	25.2%	25.0%	24.8%	24.6%	24.4%	24.2%	24.0%	23.8%	23.7%
1600]	27.4%	27.1%	26.9%	26.7%	26.4%	26.2%	26.0%	25.8%	25.6%	25.4%	25.2%	25.0%	24.8%	24.6%	24.4%	24.2%
1650]	28.0%	27.7%	27.5%	27.3%	27.0%	26.8%	26.6%	26.4%	26.2%	26.0%	25.8%	25.6%	25.4%	25.2%	25.0%	24.8%
1700]	28.6%	28.3%	28.1%	27.9%	27.6%	27.4%	27.2%	27.0%	26.8%	26.6%	26.4%	26.2%	26.0%	25.8%	25.6%	25.4%
1750]	29.2%	28.9%	28.7%	28.5%	28.2%	28.0%	27.8%	27.6%	27.3%	27.1%	26.9%	26.7%	26.5%	26.3%	26.1%	25.9%
1800]	29.8%	29.5%	29.3%	29.0%	28.8%	28.6%	28.3%	28.1%	27.9%	27.7%	27.5%	27.3%	27.1%	26.9%	26.7%	26.5%
1850]	30.3%	30.1%	29.8%	29.6%	29.4%	29.1%	28.9%	28.7%	28.5%	28.2%	28.0%	27.8%	27.6%	27.4%	27.2%	27.0%
1900]	30.9%	30.6%	30.4%	30.2%	29.9%	29.7%	29.5%	29.2%	29.0%	28.8%	28.6%	28.4%	28.1%	27.9%	27.7%	27.5%
1950]	31.5%	31.2%	31.0%	30.7%	30.5%	30.2%	30.0%	29.8%	29.5%	29.3%	29.1%	28.9%	28.7%	28.5%	28.3%	28.1%
2000]	32.0%	31.7%	31.5%	31.3%	31.0%	30.8%	30.5%	30.3%	30.1%	29.9%	29.6%	29.4%	29.2%	29.0%	28.8%	28.6%
2050]	32.5%	32.3%	32.0%	31.8%	31.5%	31.3%	31.1%	30.8%	30.6%	30.4%	30.1%	29.9%	29.7%	29.5%	29.3%	29.1%
2100]	33.1%	32.8%	32.6%	32.3%	32.1%	31.8%	31.6%	31.3%	31.1%	30.9%	30.7%	30.4%	30.2%	30.0%	29.8%	29.6%
2150]	33.6%	33.3%	33.1%	32.8%	32.6%	32.3%	32.1%	31.9%	31.6%	31.4%	31.2%	30.9%	30.7%	30.5%	30.3%	30.1%
2200]	34.1%	33.8%	33.6%	33.3%	33.1%	32.8%	32.6%	32.4%	32.1%	31.9%	31.7%	31.4%	31.2%	31.0%	30.8%	30.6%
2250]	34.6%	34.4%	34.1%	33.8%	33.6%	33.3%	33.1%	32.8%	32.6%	32.4%	32.1%	31.9%	31.7%	31.5%	31.3%	31.0%
2300]	35.1%	34.8%	34.6%	34.3%	34.1%	33.8%	33.6%	33.3%	33.1%	32.9%	32.6%	32.4%	32.2%	31.9%	31.7%	31.5%
2350]	35.6%	35.3%	35.1%	34.8%	34.6%	34.3%	34.1%	33.8%	33.6%	33.3%	33.1%	32.9%	32.6%	32.4%	32.2%	32.0%
2400]	36.1%	35.8%	35.6%	35.3%	35.0%	34.8%	34.5%	34.3%	34.0%	33.8%	33.6%	33.3%	33.1%	32.9%	32.7%	32.4%
2450]	36.6%	36.3%	36.0%	35.8%	35.5%	35.3%	35.0%	34.8%	34.5%	34.3%	34.0%	33.8%	33.6%	33.3%	33.1%	32.9%
2500]	37.0%	36.8%	36.5%	36.2%	36.0%	35.7%	35.5%	35.2%	35.0%	34.7%	34.5%	34.2%	34.0%	33.8%	33.6%	33.3%

NONCUSTODIAL PARENT MONTHLY INCOME

Non-Custodial Parent Percentage of Income

CUSTODIAL PARENT MONTHLY INCOME

(Left axis: NON-CUSTODIAL PARENT MONTHLY INCOME)

	4250	4300	4350	4400	4450	4500	4550	4600	4650	4700	4750	4800	4850	4900	4950	5000
2550]	37.5%	37.2%	37.0%	36.7%	36.4%	36.2%	35.9%	35.7%	35.4%	35.2%	34.9%	34.7%	34.5%	34.2%	34.0%	33.8%
2600]	38.0%	37.7%	37.4%	37.1%	36.9%	36.6%	36.4%	36.1%	35.9%	35.6%	35.4%	35.1%	34.9%	34.7%	34.4%	34.2%
2650]	38.4%	38.1%	37.9%	37.6%	37.3%	37.1%	36.8%	36.6%	36.3%	36.1%	35.8%	35.6%	35.3%	35.1%	34.9%	34.6%
2700]	38.8%	38.6%	38.3%	38.0%	37.8%	37.5%	37.2%	37.0%	36.7%	36.5%	36.2%	36.0%	35.8%	35.5%	35.3%	35.1%
2750]	39.3%	39.0%	38.7%	38.5%	38.2%	37.9%	37.7%	37.4%	37.2%	36.9%	36.7%	36.4%	36.2%	35.9%	35.7%	35.5%
2800]	39.7%	39.4%	39.2%	38.9%	38.6%	38.4%	38.1%	37.8%	37.6%	37.3%	37.1%	36.8%	36.6%	36.4%	36.1%	35.9%
2850]	40.1%	39.9%	39.6%	39.3%	39.0%	38.8%	38.5%	38.3%	38.0%	37.7%	37.5%	37.3%	37.0%	36.8%	36.5%	36.3%
2900]	40.6%	40.3%	40.0%	39.7%	39.5%	39.2%	38.9%	38.7%	38.4%	38.2%	37.9%	37.7%	37.4%	37.2%	36.9%	36.7%
2950]	41.0%	40.7%	40.4%	40.1%	39.9%	39.6%	39.3%	39.1%	38.8%	38.6%	38.3%	38.1%	37.8%	37.6%	37.3%	37.1%
3000]	41.4%	41.1%	40.8%	40.5%	40.3%	40.0%	39.7%	39.5%	39.2%	39.0%	38.7%	38.5%	38.2%	38.0%	37.7%	37.5%
3050]	41.8%	41.5%	41.2%	40.9%	40.7%	40.4%	40.1%	39.9%	39.6%	39.4%	39.1%	38.9%	38.6%	38.4%	38.1%	37.9%
3100]	42.2%	41.9%	41.6%	41.3%	41.1%	40.8%	40.5%	40.3%	40.0%	39.7%	39.5%	39.2%	39.0%	38.8%	38.5%	38.3%
3150]	42.6%	42.3%	42.0%	41.7%	41.4%	41.2%	40.9%	40.6%	40.4%	40.1%	39.9%	39.6%	39.4%	39.1%	38.9%	38.7%
3200]	43.0%	42.7%	42.4%	42.1%	41.8%	41.6%	41.3%	41.0%	40.8%	40.5%	40.3%	40.0%	39.8%	39.5%	39.3%	39.0%
3250]	43.3%	43.0%	42.8%	42.5%	42.2%	41.9%	41.7%	41.4%	41.1%	40.9%	40.6%	40.4%	40.1%	39.9%	39.6%	39.4%
3300]	43.7%	43.4%	43.1%	42.9%	42.6%	42.3%	42.0%	41.8%	41.5%	41.3%	41.0%	40.7%	40.5%	40.2%	40.0%	39.8%
3350]	44.1%	43.8%	43.5%	43.2%	42.9%	42.7%	42.4%	42.1%	41.9%	41.6%	41.4%	41.1%	40.9%	40.6%	40.4%	40.1%
3400]	44.4%	44.2%	43.9%	43.6%	43.3%	43.0%	42.8%	42.5%	42.2%	42.0%	41.7%	41.5%	41.2%	41.0%	40.7%	40.5%
3450]	44.8%	44.5%	44.2%	43.9%	43.7%	43.4%	43.1%	42.9%	42.6%	42.3%	42.1%	41.8%	41.6%	41.3%	41.1%	40.8%
3500]	45.2%	44.9%	44.6%	44.3%	44.0%	43.8%	43.5%	43.2%	42.9%	42.7%	42.4%	42.2%	41.9%	41.7%	41.4%	41.2%
3550]	45.5%	45.2%	44.9%	44.7%	44.4%	44.1%	43.8%	43.6%	43.3%	43.0%	42.8%	42.5%	42.3%	42.0%	41.8%	41.5%
3600]	45.9%	45.6%	45.3%	45.0%	44.7%	44.4%	44.2%	43.9%	43.6%	43.4%	43.1%	42.9%	42.6%	42.4%	42.1%	41.9%
3650]	46.2%	45.9%	45.6%	45.3%	45.1%	44.8%	44.5%	44.2%	44.0%	43.7%	43.5%	43.2%	42.9%	42.7%	42.4%	42.2%
3700]	46.5%	46.3%	46.0%	45.7%	45.4%	45.1%	44.8%	44.6%	44.3%	44.0%	43.8%	43.5%	43.3%	43.0%	42.8%	42.5%
3750]	46.9%	46.6%	46.3%	46.0%	45.7%	45.5%	45.2%	44.9%	44.6%	44.4%	44.1%	43.9%	43.6%	43.4%	43.1%	42.9%
3800]	47.2%	46.9%	46.6%	46.3%	46.1%	45.8%	45.5%	45.2%	45.0%	44.7%	44.4%	44.2%	43.9%	43.7%	43.4%	43.2%
3850]	47.5%	47.2%	47.0%	46.7%	46.4%	46.1%	45.8%	45.6%	45.3%	45.0%	44.8%	44.5%	44.3%	44.0%	43.8%	43.5%
3900]	47.9%	47.6%	47.3%	47.0%	46.7%	46.4%	46.2%	45.9%	45.6%	45.3%	45.1%	44.8%	44.6%	44.3%	44.1%	43.8%
3950]	48.2%	47.9%	47.6%	47.3%	47.0%	46.7%	46.5%	46.2%	45.9%	45.7%	45.4%	45.1%	44.9%	44.6%	44.4%	44.1%
4000]	48.5%	48.2%	47.9%	47.6%	47.3%	47.1%	46.8%	46.5%	46.2%	46.0%	45.7%	45.5%	45.2%	44.9%	44.7%	44.4%
4050]	48.8%	48.5%	48.2%	47.9%	47.6%	47.4%	47.1%	46.8%	46.6%	46.3%	46.0%	45.8%	45.5%	45.3%	45.0%	44.8%
4100]	49.1%	48.8%	48.5%	48.2%	48.0%	47.7%	47.4%	47.1%	46.9%	46.6%	46.3%	46.1%	45.8%	45.6%	45.3%	45.1%
4150]	49.4%	49.1%	48.8%	48.5%	48.3%	48.0%	47.7%	47.4%	47.2%	46.9%	46.6%	46.4%	46.1%	45.9%	45.6%	45.4%
4200]	49.7%	49.4%	49.1%	48.8%	48.6%	48.3%	48.0%	47.7%	47.5%	47.2%	46.9%	46.7%	46.4%	46.2%	45.9%	45.7%
4250]	50.0%	49.7%	49.4%	49.1%	48.9%	48.6%	48.3%	48.0%	47.8%	47.5%	47.2%	47.0%	46.7%	46.4%	46.2%	45.9%
4300]	50.3%	50.0%	49.7%	49.4%	49.1%	48.9%	48.6%	48.3%	48.0%	47.8%	47.5%	47.3%	47.0%	46.7%	46.5%	46.2%
4350]	50.6%	50.3%	50.0%	49.7%	49.4%	49.2%	48.9%	48.6%	48.3%	48.1%	47.8%	47.5%	47.3%	47.0%	46.8%	46.5%
4400]	50.9%	50.6%	50.3%	50.0%	49.7%	49.4%	49.2%	48.9%	48.6%	48.4%	48.1%	47.8%	47.6%	47.3%	47.1%	46.8%
4450]	51.1%	50.9%	50.6%	50.3%	50.0%	49.7%	49.4%	49.2%	48.9%	48.6%	48.4%	48.1%	47.8%	47.6%	47.3%	47.1%
4500]	51.4%	51.1%	50.8%	50.6%	50.3%	50.0%	49.7%	49.5%	49.2%	48.9%	48.6%	48.4%	48.1%	47.9%	47.6%	47.4%
4550]	51.7%	51.4%	51.1%	50.8%	50.6%	50.3%	50.0%	49.7%	49.5%	49.2%	48.9%	48.7%	48.4%	48.1%	47.9%	47.6%
4600]	52.0%	51.7%	51.4%	51.1%	50.8%	50.5%	50.3%	50.0%	49.7%	49.5%	49.2%	48.9%	48.7%	48.4%	48.2%	47.9%
4650]	52.2%	52.0%	51.7%	51.4%	51.1%	50.8%	50.5%	50.3%	50.0%	49.7%	49.5%	49.2%	48.9%	48.7%	48.4%	48.2%
4700]	52.5%	52.2%	51.9%	51.6%	51.4%	51.1%	50.8%	50.5%	50.3%	50.0%	49.7%	49.5%	49.2%	49.0%	48.7%	48.5%
4750]	52.8%	52.5%	52.2%	51.9%	51.6%	51.4%	51.1%	50.8%	50.5%	50.3%	50.0%	49.7%	49.5%	49.2%	49.0%	48.7%
4800]	53.0%	52.7%	52.5%	52.2%	51.9%	51.6%	51.3%	51.1%	50.8%	50.5%	50.3%	50.0%	49.7%	49.5%	49.2%	49.0%
4850]	53.3%	53.0%	52.7%	52.4%	52.2%	51.9%	51.6%	51.3%	51.1%	50.8%	50.5%	50.3%	50.0%	49.7%	49.5%	49.2%
4900]	53.6%	53.3%	53.0%	52.7%	52.4%	52.1%	51.9%	51.6%	51.3%	51.0%	50.8%	50.5%	50.3%	50.0%	49.7%	49.5%
4950]	53.8%	53.5%	53.2%	52.9%	52.7%	52.4%	52.1%	51.8%	51.6%	51.3%	51.0%	50.8%	50.5%	50.3%	50.0%	49.7%
5000]	54.1%	53.8%	53.5%	53.2%	52.9%	52.6%	52.4%	52.1%	51.8%	51.5%	51.3%	51.0%	50.8%	50.5%	50.3%	50.0%

2004 MICHIGAN CHILD SUPPORT FORMULA SCHEDULES
MONTHLY BASE SUPPORT

One Child - Monthly Support

CUSTODIAL PARENT MONTHLY INCOME

NONCUSTODIAL PARENT MONTHLY INCOME	0	250	300	350	400	450	500	550	600	650	700	750	800	850	900	950	1000
250]	25	25	25	25	25	25	25	25	25	25	25	25	25	25	25	25	25
300]	30	30	30	30	30	30	30	30	30	30	30	30	27	27	25	25	25
350]	35	35	35	35	35	35	35	35	35	35	35	35	32	32	28	28	28
400]	40	40	40	40	40	40	40	40	40	40	40	40	36	36	32	32	32
450]	45	45	45	45	45	45	45	45	45	45	45	45	41	41	36	36	36
500]	50	50	50	50	50	50	50	50	50	50	50	50	45	45	40	40	40
550]	55	55	55	55	55	55	55	55	55	55	55	55	50	50	44	44	44
600]	60	60	60	60	60	60	60	60	60	60	60	60	54	54	48	48	48
650]	65	65	65	65	65	65	65	65	65	65	65	65	59	59	52	52	52
700]	70	70	70	70	70	70	70	70	70	70	70	70	63	63	56	56	56
750]	75	75	75	75	75	75	75	75	75	75	75	75	68	68	60	60	60
800]	102	102	102	102	102	102	102	102	102	102	102	102	94	94	86	86	86
850]	152	152	152	152	152	152	152	152	152	152	152	152	144	144	136	136	136
900]	202	202	202	202	202	202	202	202	202	202	202	202	194	194	186	186	186
950]	242	242	242	242	242	242	242	242	242	242	242	242	232	231	229	227	226
1000]	255	255	255	255	255	255	255	255	255	255	255	255	243	241	239	238	236
1050]	267	267	267	267	267	267	267	267	267	267	267	267	253	251	249	248	246
1100]	279	279	279	279	279	279	279	279	279	279	279	279	263	261	260	258	256
1150]	291	291	291	291	291	291	291	291	291	291	291	291	273	271	270	268	266
1200]	304	304	304	304	304	304	304	304	304	304	304	304	283	281	280	278	277
1250]	316	316	316	316	316	316	316	316	316	316	316	316	293	291	290	288	286
1300]	328	328	328	328	328	328	328	328	328	328	328	328	303	301	300	298	296
1350]	340	340	340	340	340	340	340	340	340	340	340	340	313	311	309	307	306
1400]	352	352	352	352	352	352	352	352	352	352	352	352	323	321	319	317	315
1450]	364	364	364	364	364	364	364	364	364	364	364	364	332	330	328	327	325
1500]	376	376	376	376	376	376	376	376	376	376	376	376	342	340	338	336	334
1550]	388	388	388	388	388	388	388	388	388	388	388	388	351	349	347	345	344
1600]	400	400	400	400	400	400	400	400	400	400	400	400	360	358	357	355	353
1650]	411	411	411	411	411	411	411	411	411	411	411	411	370	368	366	364	362
1700]	420	420	420	420	420	420	420	420	420	420	420	420	379	377	375	373	372
1750]	428	428	428	428	428	428	428	428	428	428	428	428	388	386	384	383	381
1800]	437	437	437	437	437	437	437	437	437	437	437	437	397	395	394	392	390
1850]	446	446	446	446	446	446	446	446	446	446	446	446	406	405	403	401	399
1900]	454	454	454	454	454	454	454	454	454	454	454	454	415	414	412	410	408
1950]	463	463	463	463	463	463	463	463	463	463	463	463	425	423	421	419	416
2000]	472	472	472	472	472	472	472	472	472	472	472	472	434	432	429	427	425
2050]	481	481	481	481	481	481	481	481	481	481	481	481	443	440	438	436	433
2100]	489	489	489	489	489	489	489	489	489	489	489	489	451	448	446	444	442
2150]	498	498	498	498	498	498	498	498	498	498	498	498	459	457	454	452	450
2200]	507	507	507	507	507	507	507	507	507	507	507	507	467	465	463	460	458
2250]	515	515	515	515	515	515	515	515	515	515	515	515	476	473	471	469	467
2300]	524	524	524	524	524	524	524	524	524	524	524	524	484	481	479	477	475
2350]	532	532	532	532	532	532	532	532	532	532	532	532	492	490	487	485	483
2400]	540	540	540	540	540	540	540	540	540	540	540	540	500	498	495	493	491
2450]	549	549	549	549	549	549	549	549	549	549	549	549	508	506	504	501	499
2500]	557	557	557	557	557	557	557	557	557	557	557	557	516	514	512	510	508

2004 MICHIGAN CHILD SUPPORT FORMULA SCHEDULES
MONTHLY BASE SUPPORT

One Child - Monthly Support

CUSTODIAL PARENT MONTHLY INCOME

	0	250	300	350	400	450	500	550	600	650	700	750	800	850	900	950	1000
2550]	565	565	565	565	565	565	565	565	565	565	565	565	524	522	520	518	516
2600]	574	574	574	574	574	574	574	574	574	574	574	574	532	530	528	526	524
2650]	582	582	582	582	582	582	582	582	582	582	582	582	540	538	536	534	532
2700]	590	590	590	590	590	590	590	590	590	590	590	590	548	546	544	542	540
2750]	599	599	599	599	599	599	599	599	599	599	599	599	556	554	552	550	548
2800]	607	607	607	607	607	607	607	607	607	607	607	607	564	562	560	558	555
2850]	615	615	615	615	615	615	615	615	615	615	615	615	572	570	568	565	563
2900]	623	623	623	623	623	623	623	623	623	623	623	623	580	578	575	573	571
2950]	630	630	630	630	630	630	630	630	630	630	630	630	587	585	583	581	579
3000]	637	637	637	637	637	637	637	637	637	637	637	637	595	593	591	588	586
3050]	645	645	645	645	645	645	645	645	645	645	645	645	603	600	598	596	594
3100]	652	652	652	652	652	652	652	652	652	652	652	652	610	608	606	604	601
3150]	659	659	659	659	659	659	659	659	659	659	659	659	618	615	613	611	609
3200]	667	667	667	667	667	667	667	667	667	667	667	667	625	623	621	619	617
3250]	674	674	674	674	674	674	674	674	674	674	674	674	633	631	628	626	624
3300]	681	681	681	681	681	681	681	681	681	681	681	681	640	638	636	634	632
3350]	689	689	689	689	689	689	689	689	689	689	689	689	648	646	643	641	639
3400]	696	696	696	696	696	696	696	696	696	696	696	696	655	653	651	649	647
3450]	703	703	703	703	703	703	703	703	703	703	703	703	663	661	659	656	655
3500]	711	711	711	711	711	711	711	711	711	711	711	711	670	668	666	664	662
3550]	718	718	718	718	718	718	718	718	718	718	718	718	678	676	673	671	670
3600]	725	725	725	725	725	725	725	725	725	725	725	725	685	683	681	679	677
3650]	733	733	733	733	733	733	733	733	733	733	733	733	692	690	688	686	685
3700]	740	740	740	740	740	740	740	740	740	740	740	740	700	698	696	694	692
3750]	747	747	747	747	747	747	747	747	747	747	747	747	707	705	703	701	699
3800]	754	754	754	754	754	754	754	754	754	754	754	754	715	713	711	709	707
3850]	761	761	761	761	761	761	761	761	761	761	761	761	722	720	718	716	714
3900]	768	768	768	768	768	768	768	768	768	768	768	768	729	727	726	724	722
3950]	775	775	775	775	775	775	775	775	775	775	775	775	737	735	733	731	729
4000]	782	782	782	782	782	782	782	782	782	782	782	782	744	742	740	738	737
4050]	789	789	789	789	789	789	789	789	789	789	789	789	751	750	748	746	744
4100]	795	795	795	795	795	795	795	795	795	795	795	795	759	757	755	753	751
4150]	802	802	802	802	802	802	802	802	802	802	802	802	766	764	762	761	759
4200]	809	809	809	809	809	809	809	809	809	809	809	809	773	772	770	768	766
4250]	816	816	816	816	816	816	816	816	816	816	816	816	781	779	777	775	774
4300]	823	823	823	823	823	823	823	823	823	823	823	823	788	786	784	783	780
4350]	830	830	830	830	830	830	830	830	830	830	830	830	795	794	792	789	787
4400]	837	837	837	837	837	837	837	837	837	837	837	837	803	801	798	796	794
4450]	844	844	844	844	844	844	844	844	844	844	844	844	810	807	805	803	800
4500]	851	851	851	851	851	851	851	851	851	851	851	851	817	814	812	809	807
4550]	858	858	858	858	858	858	858	858	858	858	858	858	823	821	818	816	814
4600]	865	865	865	865	865	865	865	865	865	865	865	865	830	827	825	823	820
4650]	872	872	872	872	872	872	872	872	872	872	872	872	836	834	832	829	827
4700]	879	879	879	879	879	879	879	879	879	879	879	879	843	841	838	836	834
4750]	886	886	886	886	886	886	886	886	886	886	886	886	850	847	845	843	840
4800]	893	893	893	893	893	893	893	893	893	893	893	893	856	854	852	849	847
4850]	900	900	900	900	900	900	900	900	900	900	900	900	863	860	858	856	854
4900]	907	907	907	907	907	907	907	907	907	907	907	907	869	867	865	863	860
4950]	914	914	914	914	914	914	914	914	914	914	914	914	876	874	871	869	867
5000]	921	921	921	921	921	921	921	921	921	921	921	921	882	880	878	876	874

(Left margin, vertical: NONCUSTODIAL PARENT MONTHLY INCOME)

Effective October 1, 2004

2004 MICHIGAN CHILD SUPPORT FORMULA SCHEDULES
MONTHLY BASE SUPPORT

One Child - Monthly Support

CUSTODIAL PARENT MONTHLY INCOME

NONCUSTODIAL PARENT MONTHLY INCOME	1050	1100	1150	1200	1250	1300	1350	1400	1450	1500	1550	1600	1650	1700	1750	1800
250]	25	25	25	25	25	25	25	25	25	25	25	25	25	25	25	25
300]	25	25	25	25	25	25	25	25	25	25	25	25	25	25	25	25
350]	28	28	28	28	28	28	25	25	25	25	25	25	25	25	25	25
400]	32	32	32	32	32	32	28	28	28	28	28	28	28	28	28	25
450]	36	36	36	36	36	36	32	32	32	32	32	32	32	32	32	27
500]	40	40	40	40	40	40	35	35	35	35	35	35	35	35	35	30
550]	44	44	44	44	44	44	39	39	39	39	39	39	39	39	39	33
600]	48	48	48	48	48	48	42	42	42	42	42	42	42	42	42	36
650]	52	52	52	52	52	52	46	46	46	46	46	46	46	46	46	39
700]	56	56	56	56	56	56	49	49	49	49	49	49	49	49	49	42
750]	60	60	60	60	60	60	53	53	53	53	53	53	53	53	53	45
800]	86	86	86	86	86	86	78	78	78	78	78	78	78	78	78	71
850]	136	136	136	136	136	136	128	128	128	128	128	128	128	128	128	121
900]	186	186	186	186	186	186	178	178	178	178	178	178	178	178	178	171
950]	224	223	221	220	219	218	216	215	214	213	212	211	210	209	208	207
1000]	235	233	232	230	229	228	226	225	224	223	222	221	220	219	218	217
1050]	245	243	242	241	239	238	236	235	234	233	232	231	230	229	228	227
1100]	255	253	252	251	249	248	246	245	244	243	242	241	240	239	238	236
1150]	265	263	262	260	259	258	256	255	254	253	251	250	249	248	247	246
1200]	275	273	272	270	269	267	266	265	264	262	261	260	259	258	256	255
1250]	285	283	281	280	279	277	276	275	273	272	271	270	268	267	266	264
1300]	294	293	291	290	288	287	286	284	283	282	281	279	278	276	275	273
1350]	304	302	301	299	298	297	295	294	293	292	290	288	287	285	284	283
1400]	314	312	310	309	308	306	305	304	302	301	299	297	296	294	293	292
1450]	323	322	320	319	317	316	314	313	311	310	308	306	305	303	302	301
1500]	333	331	329	328	327	325	324	322	320	319	317	315	314	312	311	310
1550]	342	340	339	337	336	335	333	331	329	328	326	324	323	321	320	319
1600]	351	350	348	347	345	344	342	340	338	337	335	333	332	330	329	327
1650]	361	359	358	356	354	352	351	349	347	345	344	342	341	339	338	336
1700]	370	369	367	365	363	361	359	358	356	354	353	351	349	348	347	345
1750]	379	378	376	374	372	370	368	366	365	363	361	360	358	357	355	354
1800]	389	387	384	382	380	379	377	375	373	372	370	368	367	365	364	363
1850]	397	395	393	391	389	387	385	384	382	380	379	377	376	374	373	371
1900]	406	404	402	400	398	396	394	392	391	389	387	386	384	383	381	380
1950]	414	412	410	408	406	404	403	401	399	397	396	394	393	391	390	388
2000]	423	421	419	417	415	413	411	409	408	406	404	403	401	400	398	397
2050]	431	429	427	425	423	421	420	418	416	415	413	411	410	408	407	405
2100]	440	437	435	434	432	430	428	426	425	423	421	420	418	417	415	413
2150]	448	446	444	442	440	438	436	435	433	431	430	428	426	425	423	422
2200]	456	454	452	450	448	447	445	443	442	440	438	436	435	433	431	430
2250]	465	462	461	459	457	455	453	452	450	448	446	445	443	441	440	438
2300]	473	471	469	467	465	463	462	460	458	456	454	453	451	449	448	446
2350]	481	479	477	475	473	472	470	468	466	464	463	461	459	458	456	454
2400]	489	487	485	483	482	480	478	476	474	472	471	469	467	466	464	463
2450]	497	495	494	492	490	488	486	484	482	480	479	477	475	474	472	471
2500]	506	504	502	500	498	496	494	492	490	488	487	485	483	482	480	479

Effective October 1, 2004

2004 Michigan Child Support Formula Schedules
Monthly Base support

One Child - Monthly Support

CUSTODIAL PARENT MONTHLY INCOME

	1050	1100	1150	1200	1250	1300	1350	1400	1450	1500	1550	1600	1650	1700	1750	1800
2550]	514	512	510	508	506	504	502	500	498	496	495	493	491	490	488	487
2600]	522	520	518	516	514	512	510	508	506	504	503	501	499	498	496	495
2650]	530	528	526	524	522	520	518	516	514	512	511	509	507	506	504	503
2700]	538	536	533	531	529	528	526	524	522	520	519	517	515	514	512	511
2750]	545	543	541	539	537	535	534	532	530	528	527	525	523	522	520	519
2800]	553	551	549	547	545	543	541	540	538	536	534	533	531	530	528	527
2850]	561	559	557	555	553	551	549	547	546	544	542	541	539	538	536	534
2900]	569	567	565	563	561	559	557	555	554	552	550	549	547	545	544	542
2950]	576	574	572	570	569	567	565	563	561	560	558	556	555	553	552	550
3000]	584	582	580	578	576	574	573	571	569	567	566	564	563	561	560	558
3050]	592	590	588	586	584	582	580	579	577	575	574	572	570	569	567	566
3100]	599	597	595	594	592	590	588	586	585	583	581	580	578	577	575	574
3150]	607	605	603	601	599	598	596	594	592	591	589	588	586	584	583	582
3200]	615	613	611	609	607	605	604	602	600	598	597	595	594	592	591	589
3250]	622	620	618	617	615	613	611	610	608	606	605	603	601	600	599	597
3300]	630	628	626	624	622	621	619	617	616	614	612	611	609	608	606	605
3350]	637	636	634	632	630	628	627	625	623	622	620	618	617	615	614	613
3400]	645	643	641	639	638	636	634	632	631	629	628	626	625	623	622	620
3450]	653	651	649	647	645	643	642	640	639	637	635	634	632	631	629	628
3500]	660	658	656	655	653	651	649	648	646	645	643	641	640	638	637	635
3550]	668	666	664	662	660	659	657	655	654	652	651	649	648	646	644	642
3600]	675	673	671	670	668	666	665	663	661	660	658	657	655	653	651	649
3650]	683	681	679	677	676	674	672	671	669	667	666	664	662	660	658	656
3700]	690	688	687	685	683	681	680	678	677	675	673	671	669	667	665	664
3750]	698	696	694	692	691	689	687	686	684	683	680	678	676	674	673	671
3800]	705	703	702	700	698	696	695	693	692	690	687	685	683	682	680	678
3850]	713	711	709	707	706	704	702	701	699	697	694	692	690	689	687	685
3900]	720	718	716	715	713	711	710	708	706	703	701	699	698	696	694	692
3950]	727	726	724	722	721	719	717	715	713	710	708	706	705	703	701	699
4000]	735	733	731	730	728	726	724	722	719	717	715	713	711	710	708	706
4050]	742	741	739	737	735	733	731	728	726	724	722	720	718	717	715	713
4100]	750	748	746	744	742	740	737	735	733	731	729	727	725	724	722	720
4150]	757	755	753	751	749	746	744	742	740	738	736	734	732	730	729	727
4200]	764	762	760	758	755	753	751	749	747	745	743	741	739	737	736	734
4250]	771	769	767	764	762	760	758	756	754	752	750	748	746	744	743	741
4300]	778	776	773	771	769	767	765	763	761	759	757	755	753	751	749	748
4350]	785	782	780	778	776	774	772	770	768	766	764	762	760	758	756	755
4400]	791	789	787	785	783	781	778	776	774	773	771	769	767	765	763	761
4450]	798	796	794	792	789	787	785	783	781	779	777	776	774	772	770	768
4500]	805	803	800	798	796	794	792	790	788	786	784	782	781	779	777	775
4550]	812	809	807	805	803	801	799	797	795	793	791	789	787	786	784	782
4600]	818	816	814	812	810	808	806	804	802	800	798	796	794	793	791	789
4650]	825	823	821	818	816	814	812	810	809	807	805	803	801	799	798	796
4700]	832	829	827	825	823	821	819	817	815	813	812	810	808	806	804	802
4750]	838	836	834	832	830	828	826	824	822	820	818	817	815	813	811	809
4800]	845	843	841	839	837	835	833	831	829	827	825	823	822	819	817	815
4850]	852	849	847	845	843	841	839	837	836	834	832	830	828	826	824	822
4900]	858	856	854	852	850	848	846	844	842	840	839	837	834	832	830	828
4950]	865	863	861	859	857	855	853	851	849	847	845	843	841	839	836	834
5000]	871	869	867	865	863	861	860	858	856	854	851	849	847	845	843	841

NONCUSTODIAL PARENT MONTHLY INCOME

Effective October 1, 2004

2004 MICHIGAN CHILD SUPPORT FORMULA SCHEDULES
MONTHLY BASE SUPPORT

One Child - Monthly Support

CUSTODIAL PARENT MONTHLY INCOME

		1850	1900	1950	2000	2050	2100	2150	2200	2250	2300	2350	2400	2450	2500	2550	2600
	250]	25	25	25	25	25	25	25	25	25	25	25	25	25	25	25	25
	300]	25	25	25	25	25	25	25	25	25	25	25	25	25	25	25	25
	350]	25	25	25	25	25	25	25	25	25	25	25	25	25	25	25	25
	400]	25	25	25	25	25	25	25	25	25	25	25	25	25	25	25	25
	450]	27	27	27	27	27	27	27	27	25	25	25	25	25	25	25	25
	500]	30	30	30	30	30	30	30	30	25	25	25	25	25	25	25	25
N	550]	33	33	33	33	33	33	33	33	28	28	28	28	28	28	28	28
O	600]	36	36	36	36	36	36	36	36	30	30	30	30	30	30	30	30
N	650]	39	39	39	39	39	39	39	39	33	33	33	33	33	33	33	33
C	700]	42	42	42	42	42	42	42	42	35	35	35	35	35	35	35	35
U	750]	45	45	45	45	45	45	45	45	38	38	38	38	38	38	38	38
S	800]	71	71	71	71	71	71	71	71	63	63	63	63	63	63	63	63
T	850]	121	121	121	121	121	121	121	121	113	113	113	113	113	113	113	113
O	900]	171	171	171	171	171	171	171	171	163	163	163	163	163	163	163	163
D	950]	206	205	204	203	202	201	200	199	198	197	196	195	194	194	193	192
I																	
A	1000]	216	215	214	212	211	210	209	208	207	206	206	205	204	203	202	201
L	1050]	225	224	223	222	221	220	219	218	217	216	215	214	213	212	212	211
	1100]	235	234	233	231	230	229	228	227	226	225	224	223	222	222	221	220
P	1150]	244	243	242	241	240	238	237	236	235	234	233	233	232	231	230	229
A	1200]	254	252	251	250	249	248	247	246	245	244	243	242	241	240	239	238
R	1250]	263	262	260	259	258	257	256	255	254	253	252	251	250	249	248	247
E	1300]	272	271	270	268	267	266	265	264	263	262	261	260	259	258	257	256
N	1350]	281	280	279	277	276	275	274	273	272	271	270	269	268	267	266	265
T	1400]	290	289	288	287	285	284	283	282	281	280	279	278	277	276	275	274
	1450]	299	298	297	296	294	293	292	291	290	289	288	286	285	284	283	282
M																	
O	1500]	308	307	306	305	303	302	301	300	299	298	296	295	294	293	292	291
N	1550]	317	316	315	313	312	311	310	309	307	306	305	304	303	302	301	300
T	1600]	326	325	324	322	321	320	319	317	316	315	314	313	312	310	309	308
H	1650]	335	334	332	331	330	329	327	326	325	324	322	321	320	319	318	317
L	1700]	344	342	341	340	339	337	336	335	333	332	331	330	329	328	327	326
Y	1750]	353	351	350	348	347	346	344	343	342	341	340	338	337	336	335	334
	1800]	361	360	358	357	356	354	353	352	350	349	348	347	346	345	344	343
I	1850]	370	368	367	366	364	363	361	360	359	358	357	355	354	353	352	351
N	1900]	378	377	375	374	373	371	370	369	367	366	365	364	363	362	360	359
C	1950]	387	385	384	382	381	380	378	377	376	375	373	372	371	370	369	368
O																	
M	2000]	395	394	392	391	389	388	387	385	384	383	382	381	379	378	377	376
E	2050]	404	402	401	399	398	396	395	394	393	391	390	389	388	387	386	384
	2100]	412	410	409	407	406	405	403	402	401	400	398	397	396	395	394	393
	2150]	420	419	417	416	414	413	412	410	409	408	407	405	404	403	402	401
	2200]	428	427	425	424	423	421	420	419	417	416	415	414	413	411	410	409
	2250]	437	435	434	432	431	429	428	427	426	424	423	422	421	420	419	417
	2300]	445	443	442	440	439	438	436	435	434	433	431	430	429	428	427	426
	2350]	453	451	450	449	447	446	445	443	442	441	440	438	437	436	435	434
	2400]	461	460	458	457	455	454	453	451	450	449	448	446	445	444	443	442
	2450]	469	468	466	465	463	462	461	459	458	457	456	455	453	452	451	450
	2500]	477	476	474	473	472	470	469	468	466	465	464	463	462	460	459	458

2004 MICHIGAN CHILD SUPPORT FORMULA SCHEDULES
MONTHLY BASE SUPPORT

One Child - Monthly Support

CUSTODIAL PARENT MONTHLY INCOME

	1850	1900	1950	2000	2050	2100	2150	2200	2250	2300	2350	2400	2450	2500	2550	2600
2550]	485	484	482	481	480	478	477	476	474	473	472	471	470	468	467	466
2600]	493	492	490	489	488	486	485	484	482	481	480	479	478	477	475	474
2650]	501	500	498	497	496	494	493	492	490	489	488	487	486	485	483	482
2700]	509	508	506	505	504	502	501	500	498	497	496	495	494	493	491	490
2750]	517	516	514	513	512	510	509	508	506	505	504	503	502	501	499	498
2800]	525	524	522	521	520	518	517	516	514	513	512	511	510	508	507	505
2850]	533	532	530	529	527	526	525	524	522	521	520	519	517	516	514	513
2900]	541	539	538	537	535	534	533	531	530	529	528	526	525	523	522	520
2950]	549	547	546	545	543	542	541	539	538	537	535	534	532	531	529	528
3000]	557	555	554	552	551	550	549	547	546	544	543	541	540	538	537	535
3050]	564	563	562	560	559	558	556	555	553	552	550	549	547	545	544	543
3100]	572	571	570	568	567	566	564	562	561	559	558	556	554	553	551	550
3150]	580	579	577	576	575	573	572	570	568	567	565	563	562	560	559	557
3200]	588	586	585	584	582	581	579	577	576	574	572	571	569	568	566	565
3250]	596	594	593	592	590	588	586	585	583	581	580	578	577	575	574	572
3300]	603	602	601	599	597	595	594	592	590	589	587	585	584	582	581	579
3350]	611	610	608	606	604	603	601	599	597	596	594	593	591	590	588	587
3400]	619	617	615	613	612	610	608	606	605	603	602	600	598	597	595	594
3450]	626	624	622	621	619	617	615	614	612	610	609	607	606	604	603	601
3500]	633	631	630	628	626	624	623	621	619	618	616	615	613	611	610	609
3550]	640	639	637	635	633	631	630	628	626	625	623	622	620	619	617	616
3600]	647	646	644	642	640	639	637	635	634	632	631	629	627	626	624	623
3650]	655	653	651	649	648	646	644	642	641	639	638	636	635	633	632	630
3700]	662	660	658	656	655	653	651	650	648	646	645	643	642	640	639	637
3750]	669	667	665	663	662	660	658	657	655	654	652	651	649	648	646	645
3800]	676	674	672	671	669	667	666	664	662	661	659	658	656	655	653	652
3850]	683	681	679	678	676	674	673	671	669	668	666	665	663	662	660	659
3900]	690	688	686	685	683	681	680	678	677	675	673	672	670	669	667	666
3950]	697	695	694	692	690	688	687	685	684	682	681	679	678	676	674	673
4000]	704	702	701	699	697	696	694	692	691	689	688	686	685	683	681	679
4050]	711	709	708	706	704	703	701	699	698	696	695	693	691	690	688	686
4100]	718	716	715	713	711	710	708	706	705	703	702	700	698	696	695	693
4150]	725	723	722	720	718	717	715	713	712	710	709	707	705	703	701	700
4200]	732	730	729	727	725	724	722	720	719	717	715	713	712	710	708	706
4250]	739	737	736	734	732	731	729	727	726	724	722	720	718	716	715	713
4300]	746	744	742	741	739	738	736	734	732	730	728	727	725	723	721	720
4350]	753	751	749	748	746	745	743	741	739	737	735	733	731	730	728	726
4400]	760	758	756	755	753	751	749	747	745	744	742	740	738	736	735	733
4450]	767	765	763	762	760	758	756	754	752	750	748	746	745	743	741	739
4500]	774	772	770	768	766	764	762	760	759	757	755	753	751	750	748	746
4550]	780	779	777	775	773	771	769	767	765	763	761	760	758	756	754	753
4600]	787	785	783	781	779	777	775	773	772	770	768	766	764	763	761	759
4650]	794	792	790	788	786	784	782	780	778	776	774	773	771	769	767	766
4700]	800	798	796	794	792	790	788	787	785	783	781	779	777	776	774	772
4750]	807	805	803	801	799	797	795	793	791	789	788	786	784	782	781	779
4800]	813	811	809	807	805	803	801	799	798	796	794	792	790	789	787	785
4850]	820	818	816	814	812	810	808	806	804	802	800	799	797	795	794	792
4900]	826	824	822	820	818	816	814	812	811	809	807	805	803	802	800	798
4950]	832	830	828	826	824	823	821	819	817	815	813	812	810	808	807	805
5000]	839	837	835	833	831	829	827	825	823	822	820	818	816	815	813	811

(Left vertical label: NONCUSTODIAL PARENT MONTHLY INCOME)

Effective October 1, 2004

2004 MICHIGAN CHILD SUPPORT FORMULA SCHEDULES
MONTHLY BASE SUPPORT

One Child - Monthly Support

CUSTODIAL PARENT MONTHLY INCOME

NONCUSTODIAL PARENT MONTHLY INCOME

	2650	2700	2750	2800	2850	2900	2950	3000	3050	3100	3150	3200	3250	3300	3350	3400
250]	25	25	25	25	25	25	25	25	25	25	25	25	25	25	25	25
300]	25	25	25	25	25	25	25	25	25	25	25	25	25	25	25	25
350]	25	25	25	25	25	25	25	25	25	25	25	25	25	25	25	25
400]	25	25	25	25	25	25	25	25	25	25	25	25	25	25	25	25
450]	25	25	25	25	25	25	25	25	25	25	25	25	25	25	25	25
500]	25	25	25	25	25	25	25	25	25	25	25	25	25	25	25	25
550]	28	25	25	25	25	25	25	25	25	25	25	25	25	25	25	25
600]	30	25	25	25	25	25	25	25	25	25	25	25	25	25	25	25
650]	33	26	26	26	26	26	26	26	26	26	25	25	25	25	25	25
700]	35	28	28	28	28	28	28	28	28	28	25	25	25	25	25	25
750]	38	30	30	30	30	30	30	30	30	30	25	25	25	25	25	25
800]	63	55	55	55	55	55	55	55	55	55	49	49	49	49	49	49
850]	113	105	105	105	105	105	105	105	105	105	99	99	99	99	99	99
900]	163	155	155	155	155	155	155	155	155	155	149	149	149	149	149	149
950]	191	191	190	189	188	188	187	186	186	185	184	184	183	182	182	181
1000]	201	200	199	198	198	197	196	195	195	194	193	193	192	191	191	190
1050]	210	209	208	207	207	206	205	204	204	203	202	202	201	200	200	199
1100]	219	218	217	217	216	215	214	213	213	212	211	211	210	209	209	208
1150]	228	227	226	226	225	224	223	222	222	221	220	220	219	218	218	217
1200]	237	236	235	234	234	233	232	231	231	230	229	228	228	227	226	226
1250]	246	245	244	243	243	242	241	240	239	239	238	237	236	236	235	234
1300]	255	254	253	252	251	251	250	249	248	247	247	246	245	244	244	243
1350]	264	263	262	261	260	259	258	258	257	256	255	255	254	253	252	252
1400]	273	272	271	270	269	268	267	266	266	265	264	263	263	262	261	260
1450]	281	280	279	279	278	277	276	275	274	273	273	272	271	270	270	269
1500]	290	289	288	287	286	285	285	284	283	282	281	281	280	279	278	278
1550]	299	298	297	296	295	294	293	292	292	291	290	289	288	288	287	286
1600]	307	306	305	304	304	303	302	301	300	299	298	298	297	296	295	295
1650]	316	315	314	313	312	311	310	309	309	308	307	306	305	305	304	303
1700]	324	323	323	322	321	320	319	318	317	316	315	315	314	313	312	312
1750]	333	332	331	330	329	328	327	326	326	325	324	323	322	321	321	320
1800]	341	340	339	339	338	337	336	335	334	333	332	331	331	330	329	328
1850]	350	349	348	347	346	345	344	343	342	342	341	340	339	338	337	337
1900]	358	357	356	355	354	353	353	352	351	350	349	348	347	347	346	345
1950]	367	366	365	364	363	362	361	360	359	358	357	357	356	355	354	353
2000]	375	374	373	372	371	370	369	368	367	367	366	365	364	363	362	361
2050]	383	382	381	380	379	378	378	377	376	375	374	373	372	371	370	369
2100]	392	391	390	389	388	387	386	385	384	383	382	381	380	379	378	377
2150]	400	399	398	397	396	395	394	393	392	391	390	389	388	387	386	385
2200]	408	407	406	405	404	403	402	401	400	399	398	397	396	395	393	392
2250]	416	415	414	413	412	411	410	410	408	407	406	405	404	402	401	400
2300]	425	424	423	422	421	420	419	417	416	415	414	413	411	410	409	408
2350]	433	432	431	430	429	428	426	425	424	423	421	420	419	418	417	416
2400]	441	440	439	438	437	435	434	433	432	430	429	428	427	426	425	424
2450]	449	448	447	446	445	443	442	441	439	438	437	436	435	433	432	431
2500]	457	456	455	454	452	451	450	448	447	446	445	443	442	441	440	439

Effective October 1, 2004

One Child - Monthly Support

CUSTODIAL PARENT MONTHLY INCOME

		2650	2700	2750	2800	2850	2900	2950	3000	3050	3100	3150	3200	3250	3300	3350	3400
	2550]	465	464	463	461	460	459	457	456	455	454	452	451	450	449	448	447
	2600]	473	472	470	469	468	466	465	464	462	461	460	459	458	457	455	454
	2650]	481	479	478	477	475	474	473	471	470	469	468	466	465	464	463	462
	2700]	488	487	486	484	483	482	480	479	478	476	475	474	473	472	471	469
	2750]	496	495	493	492	490	489	488	487	485	484	483	482	480	479	478	477
	2800]	504	502	501	499	498	497	495	494	493	492	490	489	488	487	486	485
	2850]	511	510	508	507	506	504	503	502	500	499	498	497	496	494	493	492
N	2900]	519	517	516	514	513	512	510	509	508	507	505	504	503	502	501	500
O	2950]	526	525	523	522	521	519	518	517	515	514	513	512	511	509	508	507
N																	
C	3000]	534	532	531	529	528	527	525	524	523	522	520	519	518	517	516	515
U	3050]	541	540	538	537	536	534	533	532	530	529	528	527	525	524	523	522
S	3100]	548	547	546	544	543	542	540	539	538	537	535	534	533	532	531	529
T	3150]	556	554	553	552	550	549	548	546	545	544	543	541	540	539	538	536
O	3200]	563	562	560	559	558	556	555	554	553	551	550	549	548	546	545	544
D	3250]	571	569	568	566	565	564	562	561	560	559	557	556	555	553	552	551
I	3300]	578	577	575	574	572	571	570	569	567	566	565	563	562	560	559	558
A	3350]	585	584	582	581	580	578	577	576	575	573	572	570	569	568	566	565
L	3400]	593	591	590	588	587	586	584	583	582	580	579	577	576	575	573	572
	3450]	600	598	597	596	594	593	592	590	589	587	586	584	583	582	580	579
P																	
A	3500]	607	606	604	603	602	600	599	598	596	594	593	591	590	589	587	586
R	3550]	614	613	612	610	609	608	606	605	603	601	600	598	597	595	594	593
E	3600]	622	620	619	617	616	615	613	611	610	608	607	605	604	602	601	600
N	3650]	629	627	626	625	623	622	620	618	617	615	614	612	611	609	608	607
T	3700]	636	635	633	632	630	628	627	625	624	622	621	619	618	616	615	613
	3750]	643	642	640	639	637	635	634	632	631	629	628	626	625	623	622	620
M	3800]	650	649	647	645	644	642	641	639	637	636	634	633	631	630	629	627
O	3850]	657	656	654	652	651	649	647	646	644	643	641	640	638	637	635	634
N	3900]	664	662	661	659	657	656	654	653	651	650	648	647	645	644	642	641
T	3950]	671	669	667	666	664	663	661	659	658	656	655	653	652	651	649	648
H																	
L	4000]	678	676	674	673	671	669	668	666	665	663	662	660	659	657	656	654
Y	4050]	684	683	681	679	678	676	675	673	671	670	668	667	666	664	663	661
	4100]	691	689	688	686	684	683	681	680	678	677	675	674	672	671	669	668
I	4150]	698	696	694	693	691	690	688	686	685	683	682	680	679	678	676	675
N	4200]	705	703	701	700	698	696	695	693	692	690	689	687	686	684	683	682
C	4250]	711	710	708	706	705	703	701	700	698	697	695	694	692	691	690	688
O	4300]	718	716	715	713	711	710	708	707	705	704	702	701	699	698	696	695
M	4350]	725	723	721	720	718	716	715	713	712	710	709	707	706	704	703	702
E	4400]	731	729	728	726	725	723	721	720	718	717	715	714	713	711	710	708
	4450]	738	736	734	733	731	730	728	727	725	724	722	721	719	718	716	715
	4500]	744	743	741	739	738	736	735	733	732	730	729	727	726	724	723	722
	4550]	751	749	748	746	744	743	741	740	738	737	735	734	733	731	730	728
	4600]	758	756	754	753	751	750	748	746	745	743	742	741	739	738	736	735
	4650]	764	762	761	759	758	756	755	753	752	750	749	747	746	744	743	742
	4700]	771	769	767	766	764	763	761	760	758	757	755	754	752	751	750	748
	4750]	777	776	774	772	771	769	768	766	765	763	762	760	759	758	756	755
	4800]	784	782	780	779	777	776	774	773	771	770	768	767	765	764	763	761
	4850]	790	789	787	785	784	782	781	779	778	776	775	773	772	771	769	767
	4900]	797	795	794	792	790	789	787	786	784	783	781	780	778	777	775	773
	4950]	803	802	800	798	797	795	794	792	791	789	788	786	785	783	781	779
	5000]	810	808	807	805	803	802	800	799	797	796	794	793	791	789	787	786

Effective October 1, 2004

One Child - Monthly Support

CUSTODIAL PARENT MONTHLY INCOME

	3450	3500	3550	3600	3650	3700	3750	3800	3850	3900	3950	4000	4050	4100	4150	4200
250]	25	25	25	25	25	25	25	25	25	25	25	25	25	25	25	25
300]	25	25	25	25	25	25	25	25	25	25	25	25	25	25	25	25
350]	25	25	25	25	25	25	25	25	25	25	25	25	25	25	25	25
400]	25	25	25	25	25	25	25	25	25	25	25	25	25	25	25	25
450]	25	25	25	25	25	25	25	25	25	25	25	25	25	25	25	25
500]	25	25	25	25	25	25	25	25	25	25	25	25	25	25	25	25
550]	25	25	25	25	25	25	25	25	25	25	25	25	25	25	25	25
600]	25	25	25	25	25	25	25	25	25	25	25	25	25	25	25	25
650]	25	25	25	25	25	25	25	25	25	25	25	25	25	25	25	25
700]	25	25	25	25	25	25	25	25	25	25	25	25	25	25	25	25
750]	25	25	25	25	25	25	25	25	25	25	25	25	25	25	25	25
800]	49	49	49	49	49	49	49	49	49	49	49	49	49	49	49	49
850]	99	99	99	99	99	99	99	99	99	99	99	99	99	99	99	99
900]	149	149	149	149	149	149	149	149	149	149	149	149	149	149	149	149
950]	181	180	180	179	179	178	178	177	177	176	176	175	175	175	174	174
1000]	190	189	189	188	188	187	187	186	186	185	185	184	184	183	183	182
1050]	199	198	197	197	196	196	195	195	194	194	193	193	192	192	192	191
1100]	207	207	206	206	205	205	204	204	203	203	202	202	201	201	200	200
1150]	216	216	215	214	214	213	213	212	212	211	211	210	210	209	209	208
1200]	225	224	224	223	223	222	222	221	220	220	219	219	218	218	217	216
1250]	234	233	233	232	231	231	230	230	229	229	228	228	227	226	225	225
1300]	242	242	241	241	240	239	239	238	238	237	237	236	235	234	234	233
1350]	251	250	250	249	249	248	247	247	246	246	245	244	244	243	242	241
1400]	260	259	258	258	257	257	256	255	255	254	253	253	252	251	250	250
1450]	268	268	267	266	266	265	265	264	263	262	262	261	260	259	259	258
1500]	277	276	276	275	274	274	273	272	271	271	270	269	268	268	267	266
1550]	285	285	284	283	283	282	281	280	280	279	278	277	276	276	275	274
1600]	294	293	293	292	291	290	289	289	288	287	286	285	285	284	283	282
1650]	302	302	301	300	299	299	298	297	296	295	294	293	293	292	291	290
1700]	311	310	309	308	308	307	306	305	304	303	302	302	301	300	299	298
1750]	319	319	318	317	316	315	314	313	312	311	310	310	309	308	307	306
1800]	328	327	326	325	324	323	322	321	320	319	318	318	317	316	315	314
1850]	336	335	334	333	332	331	330	329	328	327	326	326	325	324	323	322
1900]	344	343	342	341	340	339	338	337	336	335	334	334	333	332	331	330
1950]	352	351	350	349	348	347	346	345	344	343	342	342	341	340	339	338
2000]	360	359	358	357	356	355	354	353	352	351	350	349	349	348	347	346
2050]	368	367	366	365	364	363	362	361	360	359	358	357	356	356	355	354
2100]	376	375	374	373	372	371	370	369	368	367	366	365	364	363	363	362
2150]	383	382	381	380	379	378	377	377	376	375	374	373	372	371	370	370
2200]	391	390	389	388	387	386	385	384	383	383	382	381	380	379	378	377
2250]	399	398	397	396	395	394	393	392	391	390	389	389	388	387	386	385
2300]	407	406	405	404	403	402	401	400	399	398	397	396	395	395	394	393
2350]	415	414	413	412	411	410	409	408	407	406	405	404	403	402	401	400
2400]	422	421	420	419	418	417	416	415	414	413	413	412	411	410	409	408
2450]	430	429	428	427	426	425	424	423	422	421	420	419	418	417	416	415
2500]	438	437	436	435	434	433	432	431	430	429	428	427	426	425	424	422

(Left vertical label: NONCUSTODIAL PARENT MONTHLY INCOME)

Effective October 1, 2004

2004 MICHIGAN CHILD SUPPORT FORMULA SCHEDULES
MONTHLY BASE SUPPORT

One Child - Monthly Support

CUSTODIAL PARENT MONTHLY INCOME

		3450	3500	3550	3600	3650	3700	3750	3800	3850	3900	3950	4000	4050	4100	4150	4200
	2550]	446	444	443	442	441	440	439	438	437	436	435	434	433	432	431	430
	2600]	453	452	451	450	449	448	447	446	445	444	443	442	440	439	438	437
	2650]	461	460	459	458	457	456	455	454	452	451	450	449	448	447	446	445
	2700]	468	467	466	465	464	463	462	461	460	459	457	456	455	454	453	452
	2750]	476	475	474	473	472	471	470	468	467	466	465	464	462	461	460	459
	2800]	483	482	481	480	479	478	477	476	474	473	472	471	470	469	467	466
	2850]	491	490	489	488	487	485	484	483	482	480	479	478	477	476	475	474
N	2900]	499	497	496	495	494	493	491	490	489	488	486	485	484	483	482	481
O	2950]	506	505	504	502	501	500	499	497	496	495	494	492	491	490	489	488
N																	
C	3000]	513	512	511	510	508	507	506	504	503	502	501	500	499	497	496	495
U	3050]	521	519	518	517	515	514	513	512	510	509	508	507	506	505	503	502
S	3100]	528	527	525	524	523	521	520	519	518	516	515	514	513	512	511	509
T	3150]	535	534	532	531	530	528	527	526	525	523	522	521	520	519	518	517
O	3200]	542	541	539	538	537	535	534	533	532	531	529	528	527	526	525	524
D	3250]	549	548	546	545	544	543	541	540	539	538	536	535	534	533	532	531
I	3300]	556	555	554	552	551	550	548	547	546	545	543	542	541	540	539	538
A	3350]	563	562	561	559	558	557	555	554	553	552	550	549	548	547	546	545
L	3400]	570	569	568	566	565	564	562	561	560	559	558	556	555	554	553	552
	3450]	577	576	575	573	572	571	569	568	567	566	564	563	562	561	560	559
P																	
A	3500]	584	583	582	580	579	578	576	575	574	573	571	570	569	568	567	566
R	3550]	591	590	589	587	586	585	583	582	581	580	578	577	576	575	574	573
E	3600]	598	597	596	594	593	592	590	589	588	587	585	584	583	582	581	580
N	3650]	605	604	602	601	600	598	597	596	595	594	592	591	590	589	588	586
T	3700]	612	611	609	608	607	605	604	603	602	600	599	598	597	596	595	593
	3750]	619	618	616	615	614	612	611	610	609	607	606	605	604	603	601	600
M	3800]	626	624	623	622	620	619	618	617	615	614	613	612	611	609	608	607
O	3850]	633	631	630	629	627	626	625	623	622	621	620	619	617	616	615	614
N	3900]	639	638	637	635	634	633	632	630	629	628	627	625	624	623	622	621
T	3950]	646	645	644	642	641	640	638	637	636	635	633	632	631	630	629	628
H																	
L	4000]	653	652	650	649	648	646	645	644	643	641	640	639	638	637	636	634
Y	4050]	660	659	657	656	655	653	652	651	650	648	647	646	645	643	642	641
	4100]	667	665	664	663	661	660	659	658	656	655	654	653	651	650	648	647
I	4150]	673	672	671	669	668	667	666	664	663	662	661	659	658	656	655	653
N	4200]	680	679	677	676	675	674	672	671	670	669	667	666	664	663	661	660
C	4250]	687	686	684	683	682	680	679	678	677	675	674	672	671	669	668	666
O	4300]	694	692	691	690	688	687	686	685	683	682	680	679	677	676	674	673
M	4350]	700	699	698	696	695	694	692	691	690	688	686	685	683	682	681	679
E	4400]	707	706	704	703	702	700	699	697	696	694	693	691	690	688	687	686
	4450]	714	712	711	710	708	707	705	704	702	701	699	698	696	695	693	692
	4500]	720	719	718	716	715	713	712	710	709	707	706	704	703	701	700	698
	4550]	727	726	724	723	721	720	718	716	715	713	712	710	709	707	706	705
	4600]	734	732	731	729	728	726	724	723	721	720	718	717	715	714	712	711
	4650]	740	739	737	735	734	732	731	729	728	726	724	723	721	720	719	717
	4700]	747	745	743	742	740	738	737	735	734	732	731	729	728	726	725	723
	4750]	753	751	750	748	746	745	743	742	740	739	737	735	734	733	731	730
	4800]	759	758	756	754	753	751	749	748	746	745	743	742	740	739	737	736
	4850]	765	764	762	760	759	757	756	754	753	751	749	748	746	745	744	742
	4900]	772	770	768	767	765	763	762	760	759	757	756	754	753	751	750	748
	4950]	778	776	774	773	771	770	768	766	765	763	762	760	759	757	756	755
	5000]	784	782	781	779	777	776	774	773	771	770	768	767	765	764	762	761

Effective October 1, 2004.

One Child - Monthly Support

CUSTODIAL PARENT MONTHLY INCOME

	4250	4300	4350	4400	4450	4500	4550	4600	4650	4700	4750	4800	4850	4900	4950	5000
250]	25	25	25	25	25	25	25	25	25	25	25	25	25	25	25	25
300]	25	25	25	25	25	25	25	25	25	25	25	25	25	25	25	25
350]	25	25	25	25	25	25	25	25	25	25	25	25	25	25	25	25
400]	25	25	25	25	25	25	25	25	25	25	25	25	25	25	25	25
450]	25	25	25	25	25	25	25	25	25	25	25	25	25	25	25	25
500]	25	25	25	25	25	25	25	25	25	25	25	25	25	25	25	25
550]	25	25	25	25	25	25	25	25	25	25	25	25	25	25	25	25
600]	25	25	25	25	25	25	25	25	25	25	25	25	25	25	25	25
650]	25	25	25	25	25	25	25	25	25	25	25	25	25	25	25	25
700]	25	25	25	25	25	25	25	25	25	25	25	25	25	25	25	25
750]	25	25	25	25	25	25	25	25	25	25	25	25	25	25	25	25
800]	49	49	49	49	49	49	49	49	49	49	49	49	49	49	49	49
850]	99	99	99	99	99	99	99	99	99	99	99	99	99	99	99	99
900]	149	149	149	149	149	149	149	149	149	149	149	149	149	149	149	149
950]	173	173	172	172	171	171	170	170	169	169	169	168	168	167	167	166
1000]	182	181	181	180	180	179	179	178	178	177	177	176	176	176	175	175
1050]	191	190	189	189	188	188	187	187	186	186	185	185	184	184	183	183
1100]	199	198	198	197	197	196	196	195	195	194	194	193	193	192	192	191
1150]	207	207	206	206	205	205	204	203	203	202	202	201	201	200	200	199
1200]	216	215	215	214	213	213	212	212	211	211	210	210	209	209	208	208
1250]	224	224	223	222	222	221	221	220	219	219	218	218	217	217	216	216
1300]	233	232	231	231	230	229	229	228	228	227	227	226	226	225	224	224
1350]	241	240	239	239	238	238	237	236	236	235	235	234	234	233	233	232
1400]	249	248	248	247	246	246	245	245	244	243	243	242	242	241	241	240
1450]	257	257	256	255	255	254	253	253	252	252	251	250	250	249	249	248
1500]	265	265	264	263	263	262	261	261	260	260	259	258	258	257	257	256
1550]	274	273	272	271	271	270	270	269	268	268	267	266	266	265	265	264
1600]	282	281	280	280	279	278	278	277	276	276	275	274	274	273	272	272
1650]	290	289	288	288	287	286	286	285	284	284	283	282	282	281	280	280
1700]	298	297	296	296	295	294	294	293	292	292	291	290	289	289	288	287
1750]	306	305	304	304	303	302	301	301	300	300	299	298	297	296	296	295
1800]	314	313	312	312	311	310	309	309	308	307	307	306	305	304	303	303
1850]	322	321	320	319	319	318	317	317	316	315	314	313	313	312	311	310
1900]	330	329	328	327	327	326	325	324	324	323	322	321	320	319	319	318
1950]	337	337	336	335	334	334	333	332	331	330	330	329	328	327	326	326
2000]	345	345	344	343	342	341	341	340	339	338	337	336	335	335	334	333
2050]	353	352	352	351	350	349	348	347	346	346	345	344	343	342	341	341
2100]	361	360	359	359	358	357	356	355	354	353	352	351	351	350	349	348
2150]	369	368	367	366	365	364	363	362	362	361	360	359	358	357	356	356
2200]	377	376	375	374	373	372	371	370	369	368	367	366	366	365	364	363
2250]	384	383	382	381	380	379	378	377	377	376	375	374	373	372	371	371
2300]	392	391	390	389	388	387	386	385	384	383	382	381	380	380	379	378
2350]	399	398	397	396	395	394	393	392	391	391	390	389	388	387	386	385
2400]	407	406	405	404	403	402	401	400	399	398	397	396	395	394	394	393
2450]	414	413	412	411	410	409	408	407	406	405	404	403	403	402	401	400
2500]	421	420	419	418	417	416	415	414	414	413	412	411	410	409	408	407

(Row labels at left: NONCUSTODIAL PARENT MONTHLY INCOME)

Effective October 1, 2004

2004 MICHIGAN CHILD SUPPORT FORMULA SCHEDULES
MONTHLY BASE SUPPORT

One Child - Monthly Support

CUSTODIAL PARENT MONTHLY INCOME

	4250	4300	4350	4400	4450	4500	4550	4600	4650	4700	4750	4800	4850	4900	4950	5000
2550]	429	428	427	426	425	424	423	422	421	420	419	418	417	416	415	415
2600]	436	435	434	433	432	431	430	429	428	427	426	425	425	424	423	422
2650]	443	442	441	440	439	438	437	436	435	435	434	433	432	431	430	429
2700]	451	450	449	448	447	446	445	444	443	442	441	440	439	438	437	436
2750]	458	457	456	455	454	453	452	451	450	449	448	447	446	445	444	444
2800]	465	464	463	462	461	460	459	458	457	456	455	454	453	453	452	451
2850]	473	471	470	469	468	467	466	465	464	463	462	462	461	460	459	458
2900]	480	479	478	477	476	475	474	473	472	471	470	469	468	467	466	465
2950]	487	486	485	484	483	482	481	480	479	478	477	476	475	474	473	472
3000]	494	493	492	491	490	489	488	487	486	485	484	483	482	481	480	479
3050]	501	500	499	498	497	496	495	494	493	492	491	490	489	488	487	486
3100]	508	507	506	505	504	503	502	501	500	499	498	497	496	495	494	493
3150]	515	514	513	512	511	510	509	508	507	506	505	504	503	502	501	500
3200]	522	521	520	519	518	517	516	515	514	513	512	511	510	509	508	507
3250]	530	528	527	526	525	524	523	522	521	520	519	518	517	516	515	514
3300]	537	535	534	533	532	531	530	529	528	527	526	525	524	523	522	521
3350]	544	543	541	540	539	538	537	536	535	534	533	532	531	530	529	528
3400]	551	550	548	547	546	545	544	543	542	541	540	539	538	537	535	534
3450]	558	557	555	554	553	552	551	550	549	548	547	546	544	543	542	541
3500]	565	563	562	561	560	559	558	557	556	555	554	552	551	550	549	548
3550]	572	570	569	568	567	566	565	564	563	561	560	559	558	557	555	554
3600]	578	577	576	575	574	573	572	571	569	568	567	566	564	563	562	561
3650]	585	584	583	582	581	580	579	577	576	575	574	572	571	570	569	567
3700]	592	591	590	589	588	587	585	584	583	581	580	579	578	576	575	574
3750]	599	598	597	596	594	593	592	591	589	588	587	585	584	583	582	581
3800]	606	605	604	602	601	600	598	597	596	595	593	592	591	590	588	587
3850]	613	612	610	609	608	606	605	604	602	601	600	599	597	596	595	594
3900]	620	618	617	615	614	613	611	610	609	608	606	605	604	603	601	600
3950]	626	625	623	622	621	619	618	617	615	614	613	612	610	609	608	607
4000]	633	631	630	629	627	626	624	623	622	621	619	618	617	616	614	613
4050]	639	638	636	635	634	632	631	630	628	627	626	625	623	622	621	620
4100]	646	644	643	641	640	639	637	636	635	634	632	631	630	629	627	626
4150]	652	651	649	648	647	645	644	643	641	640	639	638	636	635	634	633
4200]	659	657	656	654	653	652	650	649	648	646	645	644	643	641	640	639
4250]	665	664	662	661	659	658	657	655	654	653	652	650	649	648	647	645
4300]	671	670	669	667	666	664	663	662	661	659	658	657	656	654	653	652
4350]	678	676	675	674	672	671	670	668	667	666	664	663	662	661	659	658
4400]	684	683	681	680	679	677	676	675	673	672	671	669	668	667	666	665
4450]	690	689	688	686	685	684	682	681	680	678	677	676	675	673	672	671
4500]	697	695	694	693	691	690	689	687	686	685	683	682	681	680	679	677
4550]	703	702	700	699	698	696	695	694	692	691	690	689	687	686	685	684
4600]	709	708	707	705	704	703	701	700	699	697	696	695	694	692	691	690
4650]	716	714	713	712	710	709	708	706	705	704	702	701	700	699	697	696
4700]	722	721	719	718	716	715	714	713	711	710	709	707	706	705	704	703
4750]	728	727	725	724	723	721	720	719	717	716	715	714	712	711	710	709
4800]	735	733	732	730	729	728	726	725	724	722	721	720	719	717	716	715
4850]	741	739	738	737	735	734	733	731	730	729	727	726	725	724	722	721
4900]	747	746	744	743	741	740	739	738	736	735	734	732	731	730	729	728
4950]	753	752	750	749	748	746	745	744	742	741	740	739	737	736	735	734
5000]	759	758	757	755	754	753	751	750	749	747	746	745	744	742	741	740

NONCUSTODIAL PARENT MONTHLY INCOME

Effective October 1, 2004

2004 MICHIGAN CHILD SUPPORT FORMULA SCHEDULES
MONTHLY BASE SUPPORT

Two Children - Monthly Support

CUSTODIAL PARENT MONTHLY INCOME

	0	250	300	350	400	450	500	550	600	650	700	750	800	850	900	950	1000
250]	25	25	25	25	25	25	25	25	25	25	25	25	25	25	25	25	25
300]	30	30	30	30	30	30	30	30	30	30	30	30	27	27	25	25	25
350]	35	35	35	35	35	35	35	35	35	35	35	35	32	32	28	28	28
400]	40	40	40	40	40	40	40	40	40	40	40	40	36	36	32	32	32
450]	45	45	45	45	45	45	45	45	45	45	45	45	41	41	36	36	36
500]	50	50	50	50	50	50	50	50	50	50	50	50	45	45	40	40	40
550]	55	55	55	55	55	55	55	55	55	55	55	55	50	50	44	44	44
600]	60	60	60	60	60	60	60	60	60	60	60	60	54	54	48	48	48
650]	65	65	65	65	65	65	65	65	65	65	65	65	59	59	52	52	52
700]	70	70	70	70	70	70	70	70	70	70	70	70	63	63	56	56	56
750]	75	75	75	75	75	75	75	75	75	75	75	75	68	68	60	60	60
800]	102	102	102	102	102	102	102	102	102	102	102	102	94	94	86	86	86
850]	152	152	152	152	152	152	152	152	152	152	152	152	144	144	136	136	136
900]	202	202	202	202	202	202	202	202	202	202	202	202	194	194	186	186	186
950]	252	252	252	252	252	252	252	252	252	252	252	252	244	244	236	236	236
1000]	302	302	302	302	302	302	302	302	302	302	302	302	294	294	286	286	286
1050]	352	352	352	352	352	352	352	352	352	352	352	352	344	344	336	336	336
1100]	402	402	402	402	402	402	402	402	402	402	402	402	394	394	386	386	386
1150]	449	449	449	449	449	449	449	449	449	449	449	449	416	414	411	408	406
1200]	467	467	467	467	467	467	467	467	467	467	467	467	432	429	426	423	421
1250]	485	485	485	485	485	485	485	485	485	485	485	485	447	444	441	438	435
1300]	503	503	503	503	503	503	503	503	503	503	503	503	461	459	456	453	450
1350]	521	521	521	521	521	521	521	521	521	521	521	521	476	473	470	467	464
1400]	539	539	539	539	539	539	539	539	539	539	539	539	491	488	484	481	478
1450]	557	557	557	557	557	557	557	557	557	557	557	557	505	502	498	495	492
1500]	576	576	576	576	576	576	576	576	576	576	576	576	519	515	512	509	506
1550]	594	594	594	594	594	594	594	594	594	594	594	594	533	529	526	523	520
1600]	612	612	612	612	612	612	612	612	612	612	612	612	546	543	540	536	533
1650]	628	628	628	628	628	628	628	628	628	628	628	628	560	556	553	550	547
1700]	641	641	641	641	641	641	641	641	641	641	641	641	573	570	567	564	561
1750]	654	654	654	654	654	654	654	654	654	654	654	654	587	583	580	577	574
1800]	667	667	667	667	667	667	667	667	667	667	667	667	600	597	594	591	588
1850]	680	680	680	680	680	680	680	680	680	680	680	680	613	610	607	604	601
1900]	693	693	693	693	693	693	693	693	693	693	693	693	627	623	620	617	614
1950]	706	706	706	706	706	706	706	706	706	706	706	706	640	637	634	630	627
2000]	719	719	719	719	719	719	719	719	719	719	719	719	653	650	646	643	640
2050]	732	732	732	732	732	732	732	732	732	732	732	732	666	663	659	656	653
2100]	745	745	745	745	745	745	745	745	745	745	745	745	679	675	672	669	665
2150]	758	758	758	758	758	758	758	758	758	758	758	758	691	688	684	681	678
2200]	772	772	772	772	772	772	772	772	772	772	772	772	704	700	697	694	691
2250]	784	784	784	784	784	784	784	784	784	784	784	784	716	713	710	706	703
2300]	796	796	796	796	796	796	796	796	796	796	796	796	729	725	722	719	716
2350]	808	808	808	808	808	808	808	808	808	808	808	808	741	738	735	731	728
2400]	819	819	819	819	819	819	819	819	819	819	819	819	754	750	747	744	741
2450]	831	831	831	831	831	831	831	831	831	831	831	831	766	763	759	756	753
2500]	843	843	843	843	843	843	843	843	843	843	843	843	778	775	772	769	766

(Row label axis: NONCUSTODIAL PARENT MONTHLY INCOME)

Effective October 1, 2004

Two Children - Monthly Support

CUSTODIAL PARENT MONTHLY INCOME

		0	250	300	350	400	450	500	550	600	650	700	750	800	850	900	950	1000
	2550]	855	855	855	855	855	855	855	855	855	855	855	855	790	787	784	781	778
	2600]	867	867	867	867	867	867	867	867	867	867	867	867	803	800	796	794	791
	2650]	879	879	879	879	879	879	879	879	879	879	879	879	815	812	809	806	803
	2700]	890	890	890	890	890	890	890	890	890	890	890	890	827	824	821	818	815
	2750]	902	902	902	902	902	902	902	902	902	902	902	902	839	836	833	830	827
	2800]	914	914	914	914	914	914	914	914	914	914	914	914	851	848	845	842	839
	2850]	926	926	926	926	926	926	926	926	926	926	926	926	864	861	857	854	851
N	2900]	937	937	937	937	937	937	937	937	937	937	937	937	876	872	869	866	863
O	2950]	948	948	948	948	948	948	948	948	948	948	948	948	887	884	881	878	875
N																		
C	3000]	960	960	960	960	960	960	960	960	960	960	960	960	899	896	893	890	887
U	3050]	971	971	971	971	971	971	971	971	971	971	971	971	911	908	905	902	899
S	3100]	982	982	982	982	982	982	982	982	982	982	982	982	923	919	916	913	910
T	3150]	993	993	993	993	993	993	993	993	993	993	993	993	934	931	928	925	922
O	3200]	1005	1005	1005	1005	1005	1005	1005	1005	1005	1005	1005	1005	946	943	940	937	934
D	3250]	1016	1016	1016	1016	1016	1016	1016	1016	1016	1016	1016	1016	958	955	952	949	946
I	3300]	1027	1027	1027	1027	1027	1027	1027	1027	1027	1027	1027	1027	969	966	963	960	957
A	3350]	1038	1038	1038	1038	1038	1038	1038	1038	1038	1038	1038	1038	981	978	975	972	969
L	3400]	1050	1050	1050	1050	1050	1050	1050	1050	1050	1050	1050	1050	992	989	987	984	981
	3450]	1061	1061	1061	1061	1061	1061	1061	1061	1061	1061	1061	1061	1004	1001	998	995	993
P																		
A	3500]	1072	1072	1072	1072	1072	1072	1072	1072	1072	1072	1072	1072	1016	1013	1010	1007	1004
R	3550]	1083	1083	1083	1083	1083	1083	1083	1083	1083	1083	1083	1083	1027	1024	1021	1019	1016
E	3600]	1095	1095	1095	1095	1095	1095	1095	1095	1095	1095	1095	1095	1039	1036	1033	1030	1027
N	3650]	1106	1106	1106	1106	1106	1106	1106	1106	1106	1106	1106	1106	1050	1047	1044	1042	1039
T	3700]	1117	1117	1117	1117	1117	1117	1117	1117	1117	1117	1117	1117	1062	1059	1056	1053	1051
	3750]	1128	1128	1128	1128	1128	1128	1128	1128	1128	1128	1128	1128	1073	1070	1068	1065	1062
M	3800]	1139	1139	1139	1139	1139	1139	1139	1139	1139	1139	1139	1139	1085	1082	1079	1076	1074
O	3850]	1150	1150	1150	1150	1150	1150	1150	1150	1150	1150	1150	1150	1096	1093	1091	1088	1085
N	3900]	1161	1161	1161	1161	1161	1161	1161	1161	1161	1161	1161	1161	1107	1105	1102	1099	1097
T	3950]	1172	1172	1172	1172	1172	1172	1172	1172	1172	1172	1172	1172	1119	1116	1114	1111	1108
H																		
L	4000]	1182	1182	1182	1182	1182	1182	1182	1182	1182	1182	1182	1182	1130	1128	1125	1122	1120
Y	4050]	1193	1193	1193	1193	1193	1193	1193	1193	1193	1193	1193	1193	1142	1139	1136	1134	1131
	4100]	1204	1204	1204	1204	1204	1204	1204	1204	1204	1204	1204	1204	1153	1150	1148	1145	1143
I	4150]	1215	1215	1215	1215	1215	1215	1215	1215	1215	1215	1215	1215	1165	1162	1159	1157	1154
N	4200]	1226	1226	1226	1226	1226	1226	1226	1226	1226	1226	1226	1226	1176	1173	1171	1168	1166
C	4250]	1237	1237	1237	1237	1237	1237	1237	1237	1237	1237	1237	1237	1187	1185	1182	1180	1177
O	4300]	1248	1248	1248	1248	1248	1248	1248	1248	1248	1248	1248	1248	1199	1196	1194	1191	1188
M	4350]	1259	1259	1259	1259	1259	1259	1259	1259	1259	1259	1259	1259	1210	1207	1205	1202	1199
E	4400]	1269	1269	1269	1269	1269	1269	1269	1269	1269	1269	1269	1269	1221	1219	1216	1213	1210
	4450]	1280	1280	1280	1280	1280	1280	1280	1280	1280	1280	1280	1280	1233	1230	1226	1223	1221
	4500]	1291	1291	1291	1291	1291	1291	1291	1291	1291	1291	1291	1291	1243	1240	1237	1234	1231
	4550]	1302	1302	1302	1302	1302	1302	1302	1302	1302	1302	1302	1302	1254	1251	1248	1245	1242
	4600]	1313	1313	1313	1313	1313	1313	1313	1313	1313	1313	1313	1313	1265	1262	1259	1256	1253
	4650]	1324	1324	1324	1324	1324	1324	1324	1324	1324	1324	1324	1324	1275	1272	1269	1266	1264
	4700]	1335	1335	1335	1335	1335	1335	1335	1335	1335	1335	1335	1335	1286	1283	1280	1277	1274
	4750]	1346	1346	1346	1346	1346	1346	1346	1346	1346	1346	1346	1346	1297	1294	1291	1288	1285
	4800]	1356	1356	1356	1356	1356	1356	1356	1356	1356	1356	1356	1356	1307	1304	1301	1299	1296
	4850]	1367	1367	1367	1367	1367	1367	1367	1367	1367	1367	1367	1367	1318	1315	1312	1309	1307
	4900]	1378	1378	1378	1378	1378	1378	1378	1378	1378	1378	1378	1378	1329	1326	1323	1320	1317
	4950]	1389	1389	1389	1389	1389	1389	1389	1389	1389	1389	1389	1389	1339	1336	1333	1331	1328
	5000]	1400	1400	1400	1400	1400	1400	1400	1400	1400	1400	1400	1400	1350	1347	1344	1341	1339

2004 MICHIGAN CHILD SUPPORT FORMULA SCHEDULES
MONTHLY BASE SUPPORT

Two Children - Monthly Support

CUSTODIAL PARENT MONTHLY INCOME

	1050	1100	1150	1200	1250	1300	1350	1400	1450	1500	1550	1600	1650	1700	1750	1800
250]	25	25	25	25	25	25	25	25	25	25	25	25	25	25	25	25
300]	25	25	25	25	25	25	25	25	25	25	25	25	25	25	25	25
350]	28	28	28	28	28	28	25	25	25	25	25	25	25	25	25	25
400]	32	32	32	32	32	32	28	28	28	28	28	28	28	28	28	25
450]	36	36	36	36	36	36	32	32	32	32	32	32	32	32	32	27
500]	40	40	40	40	40	40	35	35	35	35	35	35	35	35	35	30
550]	44	44	44	44	44	44	39	39	39	39	39	39	39	39	39	33
600]	48	48	48	48	48	48	42	42	42	42	42	42	42	42	42	36
650]	52	52	52	52	52	52	46	46	46	46	46	46	46	46	46	39
700]	56	56	56	56	56	56	49	49	49	49	49	49	49	49	49	42
750]	60	60	60	60	60	60	53	53	53	53	53	53	53	53	53	45
800]	86	86	86	86	86	86	78	78	78	78	78	78	78	78	78	71
850]	136	136	136	136	136	136	128	128	128	128	128	128	128	128	128	121
900]	186	186	186	186	186	186	178	178	178	178	178	178	178	178	178	171
950]	236	236	236	236	236	236	228	228	228	228	228	228	228	228	228	221
1000]	286	286	286	286	286	286	278	278	278	278	278	278	278	278	278	271
1050]	336	336	336	336	336	336	328	328	328	328	328	328	328	328	328	321
1100]	386	386	383	381	378	376	373	371	369	367	365	363	361	359	357	355
1150]	403	401	398	395	393	390	388	386	383	381	379	377	375	374	372	370
1200]	418	415	412	410	407	405	402	400	398	396	394	392	390	388	386	384
1250]	432	430	427	424	422	419	417	414	412	410	408	406	404	402	400	398
1300]	447	444	441	438	436	433	431	429	427	424	422	420	418	416	414	412
1350]	461	458	455	453	450	448	445	443	441	439	436	434	432	430	428	426
1400]	475	472	469	467	464	462	459	457	455	452	450	448	446	444	442	440
1450]	489	486	483	481	478	476	473	471	469	466	464	462	459	457	455	453
1500]	503	500	497	495	492	490	487	485	482	480	478	475	473	471	469	467
1550]	517	514	511	509	506	504	501	498	496	493	491	489	487	485	482	480
1600]	531	528	525	522	520	517	514	512	509	507	505	502	500	498	496	494
1650]	544	541	539	536	533	530	528	525	523	520	518	516	514	511	509	507
1700]	558	555	552	549	547	544	541	539	536	534	531	529	527	525	523	521
1750]	571	569	566	563	560	557	554	552	549	547	545	542	540	538	536	534
1800]	585	582	579	576	573	570	568	565	563	560	558	556	554	551	549	547
1850]	598	595	592	589	586	583	581	578	576	573	571	569	567	565	563	561
1900]	611	608	605	602	599	597	594	591	589	587	584	582	580	578	576	574
1950]	624	621	618	615	612	610	607	604	602	600	597	595	593	591	589	587
2000]	637	634	631	628	625	623	620	617	615	613	610	608	606	604	602	599
2050]	650	647	644	641	638	635	633	630	628	626	623	621	619	617	614	612
2100]	662	659	656	654	651	648	646	643	641	639	636	634	632	629	627	625
2150]	675	672	669	666	664	661	659	656	654	651	649	647	644	642	640	638
2200]	688	685	682	679	677	674	671	669	667	664	662	659	657	655	652	650
2250]	700	697	695	692	689	687	684	682	679	677	674	672	670	667	665	663
2300]	713	710	707	705	702	699	697	694	692	689	687	684	682	680	678	675
2350]	726	723	720	717	715	712	710	707	704	702	699	697	695	692	690	688
2400]	738	735	732	730	727	725	722	719	717	714	712	709	707	705	703	701
2450]	751	748	745	742	740	737	734	732	729	727	724	722	720	717	715	713
2500]	763	760	758	755	752	749	747	744	741	739	737	734	732	730	728	725

NONCUSTODIAL PARENT MONTHLY INCOME

Effective October 1, 2004

Two Children - Monthly Support

CUSTODIAL PARENT MONTHLY INCOME

	1050	1100	1150	1200	1250	1300	1350	1400	1450	1500	1550	1600	1650	1700	1750	1800
2550]	775	773	770	767	764	762	759	756	754	751	749	747	744	742	740	738
2600]	788	785	782	779	776	774	771	769	766	764	761	759	757	754	752	750
2650]	800	797	794	791	789	786	783	781	778	776	773	771	769	767	765	762
2700]	812	809	806	804	801	798	796	793	790	788	786	783	781	779	777	775
2750]	824	821	818	816	813	810	808	805	803	800	798	796	793	791	789	787
2800]	836	833	830	828	825	822	820	817	815	812	810	808	806	803	801	799
2850]	848	845	842	840	837	834	832	829	827	825	822	820	818	816	813	811
2900]	860	857	854	852	849	846	844	841	839	837	834	832	830	828	826	824
2950]	872	869	866	864	861	858	856	853	851	849	846	844	842	840	838	836
3000]	884	881	878	876	873	870	868	865	863	861	858	856	854	852	850	848
3050]	896	893	890	888	885	882	880	877	875	873	871	868	866	864	862	860
3100]	908	905	902	899	897	894	892	889	887	885	883	880	878	876	874	872
3150]	919	917	914	911	909	906	904	901	899	897	894	892	890	888	886	884
3200]	931	928	926	923	921	918	916	913	911	909	906	904	902	900	898	896
3250]	943	940	938	935	932	930	928	925	923	921	918	916	914	912	910	908
3300]	955	952	949	947	944	942	939	937	935	933	930	928	926	924	922	920
3350]	966	964	961	959	956	954	951	949	947	944	942	940	938	936	934	932
3400]	978	976	973	970	968	965	963	961	958	956	954	952	950	948	946	944
3450]	990	987	985	982	980	977	975	973	970	968	966	964	962	960	958	956
3500]	1002	999	996	994	991	989	987	984	982	980	978	976	974	972	970	967
3550]	1013	1011	1008	1006	1003	1001	998	996	994	992	990	987	985	983	981	978
3600]	1025	1022	1020	1017	1015	1013	1010	1008	1006	1004	1001	999	997	995	992	990
3650]	1036	1034	1031	1029	1027	1024	1022	1020	1017	1015	1013	1011	1008	1006	1004	1001
3700]	1048	1046	1043	1041	1038	1036	1034	1031	1029	1027	1025	1022	1020	1017	1015	1012
3750]	1060	1057	1055	1052	1050	1048	1045	1043	1041	1039	1036	1034	1031	1029	1026	1024
3800]	1071	1069	1066	1064	1062	1059	1057	1055	1053	1050	1047	1045	1042	1040	1037	1035
3850]	1083	1080	1078	1076	1073	1071	1069	1066	1064	1061	1059	1056	1053	1051	1049	1046
3900]	1094	1092	1090	1087	1085	1083	1080	1078	1075	1072	1070	1067	1065	1062	1060	1057
3950]	1106	1103	1101	1099	1096	1094	1091	1089	1086	1083	1081	1078	1076	1073	1071	1069
4000]	1117	1115	1113	1110	1108	1105	1102	1100	1097	1095	1092	1089	1087	1085	1082	1080
4050]	1129	1127	1124	1122	1119	1116	1114	1111	1108	1106	1103	1101	1098	1096	1093	1091
4100]	1140	1138	1136	1133	1130	1127	1125	1122	1119	1117	1114	1112	1109	1107	1104	1102
4150]	1152	1150	1147	1144	1141	1138	1136	1133	1130	1128	1125	1123	1120	1118	1116	1113
4200]	1163	1160	1158	1155	1152	1149	1147	1144	1141	1139	1136	1134	1131	1129	1127	1124
4250]	1174	1171	1168	1166	1163	1160	1158	1155	1152	1150	1147	1145	1143	1140	1138	1136
4300]	1185	1182	1179	1177	1174	1171	1169	1166	1163	1161	1158	1156	1154	1151	1149	1147
4350]	1196	1193	1190	1188	1185	1182	1179	1177	1174	1172	1169	1167	1165	1162	1160	1158
4400]	1207	1204	1201	1198	1196	1193	1190	1188	1185	1183	1180	1178	1176	1173	1171	1169
4450]	1218	1215	1212	1209	1207	1204	1201	1199	1196	1194	1191	1189	1187	1184	1182	1180
4500]	1228	1226	1223	1220	1217	1215	1212	1210	1207	1205	1202	1200	1198	1195	1193	1191
4550]	1239	1236	1234	1231	1228	1226	1223	1221	1218	1216	1213	1211	1209	1206	1204	1202
4600]	1250	1247	1245	1242	1239	1237	1234	1232	1229	1227	1224	1222	1220	1217	1215	1213
4650]	1261	1258	1255	1253	1250	1247	1245	1242	1240	1238	1235	1233	1231	1228	1226	1224
4700]	1272	1269	1266	1263	1261	1258	1256	1253	1251	1248	1246	1244	1241	1239	1237	1234
4750]	1282	1280	1277	1274	1272	1269	1267	1264	1262	1259	1257	1255	1252	1250	1247	1244
4800]	1293	1290	1288	1285	1283	1280	1277	1275	1273	1270	1268	1266	1263	1260	1257	1254
4850]	1304	1301	1298	1296	1293	1291	1288	1286	1283	1281	1279	1276	1273	1270	1267	1263
4900]	1315	1312	1309	1307	1304	1302	1299	1297	1294	1292	1290	1287	1283	1280	1276	1273
4950]	1325	1323	1320	1317	1315	1312	1310	1308	1305	1303	1300	1296	1293	1289	1286	1283
5000]	1336	1333	1331	1328	1326	1323	1321	1318	1316	1313	1309	1306	1302	1299	1296	1292

(Row labels at left, read vertically: NONCUSTODIAL PARENT MONTHLY INCOME)

Effective October 1, 2004

2004 MICHIGAN CHILD SUPPORT FORMULA SCHEDULES
MONTHLY BASE SUPPORT

Two Children - Monthly Support

CUSTODIAL PARENT MONTHLY INCOME

NONCUSTODIAL PARENT MONTHLY INCOME	1850	1900	1950	2000	2050	2100	2150	2200	2250	2300	2350	2400	2450	2500	2550	2600
250]	25	25	25	25	25	25	25	25	25	25	25	25	25	25	25	25
300]	25	25	25	25	25	25	25	25	25	25	25	25	25	25	25	25
350]	25	25	25	25	25	25	25	25	25	25	25	25	25	25	25	25
400]	25	25	25	25	25	25	25	25	25	25	25	25	25	25	25	25
450]	27	27	27	27	27	27	27	27	25	25	25	25	25	25	25	25
500]	30	30	30	30	30	30	30	30	25	25	25	25	25	25	25	25
550]	33	33	33	33	33	33	33	33	28	28	28	28	28	28	28	28
600]	36	36	36	36	36	36	36	36	30	30	30	30	30	30	30	30
650]	39	39	39	39	39	39	39	39	33	33	33	33	33	33	33	33
700]	42	42	42	42	42	42	42	42	35	35	35	35	35	35	35	35
750]	45	45	45	45	45	45	45	45	38	38	38	38	38	38	38	38
800]	71	71	71	71	71	71	71	71	63	63	63	63	63	63	63	63
850]	121	121	121	121	121	121	121	121	113	113	113	113	113	113	113	113
900]	171	171	171	171	171	171	171	171	163	163	163	163	163	163	163	163
950]	221	221	221	221	221	221	221	221	213	213	213	213	213	213	213	213
1000]	271	271	271	271	271	271	271	271	263	263	263	263	263	263	263	263
1050]	321	321	321	321	321	321	321	321	313	313	313	313	313	313	313	313
1100]	354	352	350	349	347	345	344	342	341	340	338	337	336	334	333	332
1150]	368	366	364	363	361	359	358	356	355	354	352	351	350	348	347	346
1200]	382	380	378	377	375	374	372	370	369	368	366	365	364	362	361	360
1250]	396	394	392	391	389	387	386	384	383	381	380	379	377	376	375	373
1300]	410	408	406	405	403	401	400	398	397	395	394	393	391	390	388	387
1350]	424	422	420	418	417	415	414	412	411	409	408	406	405	403	402	400
1400]	438	436	434	432	431	429	427	426	424	423	421	420	418	417	415	414
1450]	451	449	448	446	444	443	441	439	438	436	435	433	432	430	429	427
1500]	465	463	461	460	458	456	455	453	451	450	448	446	445	443	442	441
1550]	479	477	475	473	471	470	468	466	465	463	461	460	458	457	455	454
1600]	492	490	488	487	485	483	481	480	478	476	475	473	471	470	468	467
1650]	505	504	502	500	498	496	495	493	491	489	488	486	485	483	482	480
1700]	519	517	515	513	511	510	508	506	504	503	501	499	498	496	495	493
1750]	532	530	528	526	524	523	521	519	517	516	514	512	511	509	508	506
1800]	545	543	541	539	538	536	534	532	530	529	527	525	524	522	521	519
1850]	559	556	554	552	551	549	547	545	543	542	540	538	537	535	534	532
1900]	572	569	567	565	564	562	560	558	556	555	553	551	550	548	547	545
1950]	584	582	580	578	576	575	573	571	569	567	566	564	563	561	559	558
2000]	597	595	593	591	589	587	586	584	582	580	579	577	575	574	572	571
2050]	610	608	606	604	602	600	598	597	595	593	591	590	588	587	585	584
2100]	623	621	619	617	615	613	611	609	608	606	604	603	601	599	598	596
2150]	636	633	631	629	628	626	624	622	620	619	617	615	614	612	611	609
2200]	648	646	644	642	640	638	636	635	633	631	630	628	626	625	623	622
2250]	661	659	657	655	653	651	649	647	646	644	642	641	639	637	636	634
2300]	673	671	669	667	665	664	662	660	658	656	655	653	652	650	648	647
2350]	686	684	682	680	678	676	674	672	671	669	667	666	664	662	661	659
2400]	698	696	694	692	690	689	687	685	683	682	680	678	677	675	673	672
2450]	711	709	707	705	703	701	699	697	696	694	692	691	689	687	686	684
2500]	723	721	719	717	715	714	712	710	708	706	705	703	702	700	698	697

Effective October 1, 2004

Two Children - Monthly Support

CUSTODIAL PARENT MONTHLY INCOME

		1850	1900	1950	2000	2050	2100	2150	2200	2250	2300	2350	2400	2450	2500	2550	2600
	2550]	736	734	732	730	728	726	724	722	721	719	717	716	714	712	711	709
	2600]	748	746	744	742	740	738	736	735	733	731	730	728	726	725	723	722
	2650]	760	758	756	754	753	751	749	747	745	744	742	740	739	737	736	734
	2700]	773	771	769	767	765	763	761	759	758	756	754	753	751	749	748	746
	2750]	785	783	781	779	777	775	773	772	770	768	767	765	763	762	760	758
	2800]	797	795	793	791	789	788	786	784	782	781	779	777	776	774	772	770
	2850]	809	807	805	803	802	800	798	796	794	793	791	789	787	785	784	782
N	2900]	821	819	818	816	814	812	810	808	807	805	803	801	799	797	795	794
O	2950]	834	832	830	828	826	824	822	821	819	817	815	813	811	809	807	805
N	3000]	846	844	842	840	838	836	834	833	831	829	827	825	823	821	819	817
C																	
U	3050]	858	856	854	852	850	848	847	845	843	841	839	837	835	833	831	829
S	3100]	870	868	866	864	862	860	859	857	854	852	850	848	846	844	842	841
T	3150]	882	880	878	876	874	873	870	868	866	864	862	860	858	856	854	852
O	3200]	894	892	890	888	886	884	882	880	878	876	874	872	870	868	866	864
D	3250]	906	904	902	900	898	896	894	891	889	887	885	883	881	879	877	876
I	3300]	918	916	914	912	910	907	905	903	901	899	897	895	893	891	889	887
A	3350]	930	928	926	923	921	919	917	915	912	910	908	906	904	902	901	899
L	3400]	942	939	937	935	933	930	928	926	924	922	920	918	916	914	912	910
	3450]	953	951	949	946	944	942	940	938	935	933	931	929	927	926	924	922
P																	
A	3500]	965	962	960	958	955	953	951	949	947	945	943	941	939	937	935	933
R	3550]	976	974	971	969	967	965	963	960	958	956	954	952	950	949	947	945
E	3600]	987	985	983	981	978	976	974	972	970	968	966	964	962	960	958	956
N	3650]	999	996	994	992	990	987	985	983	981	979	977	975	973	971	970	968
T	3700]	1010	1008	1005	1003	1001	999	997	995	993	991	989	987	985	983	981	979
	3750]	1021	1019	1017	1015	1012	1010	1008	1006	1004	1002	1000	998	996	994	992	991
M	3800]	1033	1030	1028	1026	1024	1022	1019	1017	1015	1013	1011	1009	1007	1006	1004	1002
O	3850]	1044	1042	1039	1037	1035	1033	1031	1029	1027	1025	1023	1021	1019	1017	1015	1013
N	3900]	1055	1053	1051	1048	1046	1044	1042	1040	1038	1036	1034	1032	1030	1028	1026	1024
T	3950]	1066	1064	1062	1060	1058	1055	1053	1051	1049	1047	1045	1043	1041	1040	1037	1034
H																	
L	4000]	1078	1075	1073	1071	1069	1067	1065	1063	1061	1059	1057	1055	1053	1050	1047	1045
Y	4050]	1089	1086	1084	1082	1080	1078	1076	1074	1072	1070	1068	1066	1063	1061	1058	1055
	4100]	1100	1098	1095	1093	1091	1089	1087	1085	1083	1081	1079	1077	1074	1071	1068	1065
I	4150]	1111	1109	1107	1104	1102	1100	1098	1096	1094	1092	1090	1087	1084	1081	1078	1075
N	4200]	1122	1120	1118	1116	1114	1111	1109	1107	1105	1103	1100	1097	1094	1091	1088	1086
C	4250]	1133	1131	1129	1127	1125	1123	1121	1119	1116	1113	1110	1107	1104	1101	1099	1096
O	4300]	1144	1142	1140	1138	1136	1134	1132	1129	1126	1123	1120	1117	1114	1112	1109	1106
M	4350]	1155	1153	1151	1149	1147	1145	1142	1139	1136	1133	1130	1127	1124	1122	1119	1116
E	4400]	1167	1164	1162	1160	1158	1155	1152	1149	1146	1143	1140	1137	1135	1132	1129	1126
	4450]	1178	1175	1173	1171	1168	1165	1162	1159	1156	1153	1150	1147	1145	1142	1139	1136
	4500]	1189	1187	1184	1182	1178	1175	1172	1169	1166	1163	1160	1157	1155	1152	1149	1146
	4550]	1200	1198	1195	1191	1188	1185	1182	1179	1176	1173	1170	1167	1165	1162	1159	1156
	4600]	1211	1208	1205	1201	1198	1195	1192	1189	1186	1183	1180	1177	1175	1172	1169	1166
	4650]	1221	1218	1214	1211	1208	1205	1202	1199	1196	1193	1190	1187	1185	1182	1179	1176
	4700]	1231	1227	1224	1221	1218	1215	1212	1209	1206	1203	1200	1197	1195	1192	1189	1186
	4750]	1241	1237	1234	1231	1228	1225	1222	1219	1216	1213	1210	1207	1205	1202	1199	1196
	4800]	1250	1247	1244	1241	1238	1235	1232	1229	1226	1223	1220	1217	1214	1212	1209	1206
	4850]	1260	1257	1254	1251	1247	1244	1241	1238	1236	1233	1230	1227	1224	1222	1219	1216
	4900]	1270	1267	1263	1260	1257	1254	1251	1248	1245	1243	1240	1237	1234	1231	1229	1226
	4950]	1280	1276	1273	1270	1267	1264	1261	1258	1255	1252	1250	1247	1244	1241	1239	1236
	5000]	1289	1286	1283	1280	1277	1274	1271	1268	1265	1262	1259	1257	1254	1251	1249	1246

Effective October 1, 2004

Two Children - Monthly Support

CUSTODIAL PARENT MONTHLY INCOME

	2650	2700	2750	2800	2850	2900	2950	3000	3050	3100	3150	3200	3250	3300	3350	3400
250]	25	25	25	25	25	25	25	25	25	25	25	25	25	25	25	25
300]	25	25	25	25	25	25	25	25	25	25	25	25	25	25	25	25
350]	25	25	25	25	25	25	25	25	25	25	25	25	25	25	25	25
400]	25	25	25	25	25	25	25	25	25	25	25	25	25	25	25	25
450]	25	25	25	25	25	25	25	25	25	25	25	25	25	25	25	25
500]	25	25	25	25	25	25	25	25	25	25	25	25	25	25	25	25
550]	28	25	25	25	25	25	25	25	25	25	25	25	25	25	25	25
600]	30	25	25	25	25	25	25	25	25	25	25	25	25	25	25	25
650]	33	26	26	26	26	26	26	26	26	26	25	25	25	25	25	25
700]	35	28	28	28	28	28	28	28	28	28	25	25	25	25	25	25
750]	38	30	30	30	30	30	30	30	30	30	25	25	25	25	25	25
800]	63	55	55	55	55	55	55	55	55	55	49	49	49	49	49	49
850]	113	105	105	105	105	105	105	105	105	105	99	99	99	99	99	99
900]	163	155	155	155	155	155	155	155	155	155	149	149	149	149	149	149
950]	213	205	205	205	205	205	205	205	205	205	199	199	199	199	199	199
1000]	263	255	255	255	255	255	255	255	255	255	249	249	249	249	249	249
1050]	313	305	305	305	305	305	305	305	305	305	299	299	299	299	299	299
1100]	331	330	329	327	326	325	324	323	322	321	320	319	318	317	316	316
1150]	345	343	342	341	340	339	338	337	336	335	334	333	332	331	330	329
1200]	358	357	356	355	354	352	351	350	349	348	347	346	345	344	343	342
1250]	372	371	369	368	367	366	365	364	363	362	361	360	359	358	357	356
1300]	386	384	383	382	381	379	378	377	376	375	374	373	372	371	370	369
1350]	399	398	396	395	394	393	392	391	389	388	387	386	385	384	383	382
1400]	412	411	410	409	407	406	405	404	403	402	401	400	399	398	397	396
1450]	426	425	423	422	421	420	418	417	416	415	414	413	412	411	410	409
1500]	439	438	437	435	434	433	432	430	429	428	427	426	425	424	423	422
1550]	452	451	450	448	447	446	445	444	442	441	440	439	438	437	436	435
1600]	466	464	463	462	460	459	458	457	455	454	453	452	451	450	449	448
1650]	479	477	476	475	473	472	471	470	469	467	466	465	464	463	462	461
1700]	492	490	489	488	486	485	484	483	482	480	479	478	477	476	475	474
1750]	505	503	502	501	499	498	497	496	495	493	492	491	490	489	488	487
1800]	518	516	515	514	512	511	510	509	507	506	505	504	503	502	501	500
1850]	531	529	528	527	525	524	523	522	520	519	518	517	516	515	514	512
1900]	544	542	541	540	538	537	536	534	533	532	531	530	529	527	526	525
1950]	557	555	554	552	551	550	548	547	546	545	544	542	541	540	539	537
2000]	569	568	567	565	564	563	561	560	559	558	556	555	554	553	551	550
2050]	582	581	579	578	577	575	574	573	571	570	569	568	566	565	564	562
2100]	595	593	592	591	589	588	587	585	584	583	582	580	579	577	576	575
2150]	608	606	605	603	602	601	599	598	597	596	594	593	591	590	588	587
2200]	620	619	617	616	615	613	612	611	609	608	606	605	603	602	601	599
2250]	633	631	630	629	627	626	625	623	622	620	619	617	616	614	613	611
2300]	645	644	643	641	640	638	637	635	634	632	631	629	628	626	625	624
2350]	658	656	655	654	652	651	649	648	646	645	643	642	640	639	637	636
2400]	670	669	668	666	665	663	661	660	658	657	655	654	652	651	649	648
2450]	683	681	680	679	677	675	674	672	670	669	667	666	664	663	661	660
2500]	695	694	693	691	689	687	686	684	682	681	679	678	676	675	673	672

NONCUSTODIAL PARENT MONTHLY INCOME

Effective October 1, 2004

2004 MICHIGAN CHILD SUPPORT FORMULA SCHEDULES
MONTHLY BASE SUPPORT

Two Children - Monthly Support

CUSTODIAL PARENT MONTHLY INCOME

		2650	2700	2750	2800	2850	2900	2950	3000	3050	3100	3150	3200	3250	3300	3350	3400
	2550]	708	706	705	703	701	699	698	696	695	693	691	690	688	687	686	684
	2600]	720	718	717	715	713	711	710	708	707	705	703	702	700	699	698	696
	2650]	732	730	729	727	725	723	722	720	719	717	715	714	712	711	709	708
	2700]	744	742	741	739	737	735	734	732	730	729	727	726	724	723	721	720
	2750]	756	754	752	751	749	747	746	744	742	741	739	738	736	735	733	732
	2800]	768	766	764	763	761	759	758	756	754	753	751	750	748	747	745	744
	2850]	780	778	776	774	773	771	769	768	766	765	763	761	760	759	757	756
N	2900]	792	790	788	786	785	783	781	780	778	776	775	773	772	770	769	767
O	2950]	803	802	800	798	796	795	793	791	790	788	787	785	784	782	781	779
N																	
C	3000]	815	813	812	810	808	806	805	803	802	800	798	797	795	794	792	791
U	3050]	827	825	823	822	820	818	817	815	813	812	810	809	807	806	804	803
S	3100]	839	837	835	833	832	830	828	827	825	823	822	820	819	817	816	814
T	3150]	850	849	847	845	843	842	840	838	837	835	834	832	831	829	827	825
O	3200]	862	860	858	857	855	853	852	850	848	847	845	844	842	840	838	836
D	3250]	874	872	870	868	867	865	863	862	860	858	857	855	853	851	849	847
I	3300]	885	883	882	880	878	877	875	873	872	870	869	866	864	862	860	857
A	3350]	897	895	893	892	890	888	887	885	883	882	880	877	875	873	870	868
L	3400]	908	907	905	903	901	900	898	896	895	893	890	888	886	883	881	879
	3450]	920	918	916	915	913	911	910	908	906	903	901	899	896	894	892	890
P																	
A	3500]	931	930	928	926	925	923	921	919	917	914	912	909	907	905	902	900
R	3550]	943	941	939	938	936	934	932	930	927	925	922	920	918	915	913	911
E	3600]	954	953	951	949	948	945	943	940	938	935	933	931	928	926	924	921
N	3650]	966	964	962	961	958	956	953	951	948	946	943	941	939	937	934	932
T	3700]	977	976	974	972	969	966	964	961	959	956	954	952	949	947	945	943
	3750]	989	987	985	982	979	977	974	972	969	967	965	962	960	958	955	953
M	3800]	1000	998	995	992	990	987	985	982	980	977	975	973	970	968	966	964
O	3850]	1011	1008	1006	1003	1000	998	995	993	990	988	985	983	981	979	976	974
N	3900]	1021	1019	1016	1013	1011	1008	1006	1003	1001	998	996	994	991	989	987	985
T	3950]	1032	1029	1026	1024	1021	1018	1016	1014	1011	1009	1006	1004	1002	999	997	995
H																	
L	4000]	1042	1039	1037	1034	1031	1029	1026	1024	1021	1019	1017	1014	1012	1010	1008	1005
Y	4050]	1052	1050	1047	1044	1042	1039	1037	1034	1032	1029	1027	1025	1022	1020	1018	1016
	4100]	1063	1060	1057	1055	1052	1049	1047	1045	1042	1040	1037	1035	1033	1030	1028	1026
I	4150]	1073	1070	1067	1065	1062	1060	1057	1055	1052	1050	1048	1045	1043	1041	1039	1036
N	4200]	1083	1080	1078	1075	1073	1070	1067	1065	1063	1060	1058	1056	1053	1051	1049	1047
C	4250]	1093	1090	1088	1085	1083	1080	1078	1075	1073	1070	1068	1066	1064	1061	1059	1057
O	4300]	1103	1101	1098	1095	1093	1090	1088	1085	1083	1081	1078	1076	1074	1072	1069	1067
M	4350]	1113	1111	1108	1106	1103	1101	1098	1096	1093	1091	1089	1086	1084	1082	1079	1077
E	4400]	1124	1121	1118	1116	1113	1111	1108	1106	1103	1101	1099	1096	1094	1092	1090	1088
	4450]	1134	1131	1128	1126	1123	1121	1118	1116	1114	1111	1109	1107	1104	1102	1100	1098
	4500]	1144	1141	1139	1136	1133	1131	1129	1126	1124	1121	1119	1117	1114	1112	1110	1108
	4550]	1154	1151	1149	1146	1144	1141	1139	1136	1134	1131	1129	1127	1125	1122	1120	1118
	4600]	1164	1161	1159	1156	1154	1151	1149	1146	1144	1142	1139	1137	1135	1132	1130	1128
	4650]	1174	1171	1169	1166	1164	1161	1159	1156	1154	1152	1149	1147	1145	1143	1140	1138
	4700]	1184	1181	1179	1176	1174	1171	1169	1166	1164	1162	1159	1157	1155	1153	1150	1148
	4750]	1194	1191	1189	1186	1184	1181	1179	1176	1174	1172	1169	1167	1165	1163	1160	1158
	4800]	1204	1201	1199	1196	1194	1191	1189	1186	1184	1182	1179	1177	1175	1173	1170	1168
	4850]	1214	1211	1209	1206	1204	1201	1199	1196	1194	1192	1189	1187	1185	1182	1180	1177
	4900]	1224	1221	1218	1216	1214	1211	1209	1206	1204	1202	1199	1197	1195	1192	1189	1186
	4950]	1233	1231	1228	1226	1223	1221	1219	1216	1214	1212	1209	1207	1204	1201	1198	1196
	5000]	1243	1241	1238	1236	1233	1231	1229	1226	1224	1222	1219	1216	1213	1211	1208	1205

Effective October 1, 2004

Two Children - Monthly Support

CUSTODIAL PARENT MONTHLY INCOME

	3450	3500	3550	3600	3650	3700	3750	3800	3850	3900	3950	4000	4050	4100	4150	4200
250]	25	25	25	25	25	25	25	25	25	25	25	25	25	25	25	25
300]	25	25	25	25	25	25	25	25	25	25	25	25	25	25	25	25
350]	25	25	25	25	25	25	25	25	25	25	25	25	25	25	25	25
400]	25	25	25	25	25	25	25	25	25	25	25	25	25	25	25	25
450]	25	25	25	25	25	25	25	25	25	25	25	25	25	25	25	25
500]	25	25	25	25	25	25	25	25	25	25	25	25	25	25	25	25
550]	25	25	25	25	25	25	25	25	25	25	25	25	25	25	25	25
600]	25	25	25	25	25	25	25	25	25	25	25	25	25	25	25	25
650]	25	25	25	25	25	25	25	25	25	25	25	25	25	25	25	25
700]	25	25	25	25	25	25	25	25	25	25	25	25	25	25	25	25
750]	25	25	25	25	25	25	25	25	25	25	25	25	25	25	25	25
800]	49	49	49	49	49	49	49	49	49	49	49	49	49	49	49	49
850]	99	99	99	99	99	99	99	99	99	99	99	99	99	99	99	99
900]	149	149	149	149	149	149	149	149	149	149	149	149	149	149	149	149
950]	199	199	199	199	199	199	199	199	199	199	199	199	199	199	199	199
1000]	249	249	249	249	249	249	249	249	249	249	249	249	249	249	249	249
1050]	299	299	299	299	298	297	297	296	295	295	294	293	293	292	291	291
1100]	315	314	313	312	312	311	310	309	309	308	307	307	306	305	305	304
1150]	328	327	327	326	325	324	323	323	322	321	321	320	319	319	318	317
1200]	342	341	340	339	338	338	337	336	335	335	334	333	332	332	331	330
1250]	355	354	353	352	352	351	350	349	348	348	347	346	345	345	344	343
1300]	368	367	366	366	365	364	363	362	362	361	360	359	358	357	357	356
1350]	381	381	380	379	378	377	376	376	375	374	373	372	371	370	369	369
1400]	395	394	393	392	391	390	389	389	388	387	386	385	384	383	382	381
1450]	408	407	406	405	404	403	402	402	401	400	399	398	397	396	395	394
1500]	421	420	419	418	417	416	416	414	413	412	411	410	409	409	408	407
1550]	434	433	432	431	430	429	428	427	426	425	424	423	422	421	420	419
1600]	447	446	445	444	443	442	441	440	439	438	437	436	435	434	433	432
1650]	460	459	458	457	456	455	454	453	451	450	449	448	447	446	445	444
1700]	473	472	471	470	469	467	466	465	464	463	462	461	460	459	458	457
1750]	486	485	484	482	481	480	479	478	477	476	474	473	472	471	470	469
1800]	499	497	496	495	494	493	491	490	489	488	487	486	485	484	483	482
1850]	511	510	509	507	506	505	504	503	502	501	499	498	497	496	495	494
1900]	524	522	521	520	519	517	516	515	514	513	512	511	510	509	508	507
1950]	536	535	534	532	531	530	529	528	526	525	524	523	522	521	520	519
2000]	549	547	546	545	543	542	541	540	539	538	537	535	534	533	532	531
2050]	561	560	558	557	556	555	553	552	551	550	549	548	547	546	545	544
2100]	573	572	571	569	568	567	566	565	563	562	561	560	559	558	557	556
2150]	586	584	583	582	580	579	578	577	576	574	573	572	571	570	569	568
2200]	598	597	595	594	593	591	590	589	588	587	586	584	583	582	581	580
2250]	610	609	607	606	605	604	602	601	600	599	598	597	595	594	593	592
2300]	622	621	620	618	617	616	615	613	612	611	610	609	608	606	605	604
2350]	634	633	632	630	629	628	627	625	624	623	622	621	620	619	617	615
2400]	647	645	644	643	641	640	639	638	636	635	634	633	632	630	628	627
2450]	659	657	656	655	653	652	651	650	648	647	646	645	643	642	640	638
2500]	671	669	668	667	665	664	663	662	660	659	658	656	655	653	651	650

NONCUSTODIAL PARENT MONTHLY INCOME

Effective October 1, 2004

Two Children - Monthly Support

CUSTODIAL PARENT MONTHLY INCOME

	3450	3500	3550	3600	3650	3700	3750	3800	3850	3900	3950	4000	4050	4100	4150	4200
2550]	683	681	680	679	677	676	675	674	672	671	670	668	666	664	663	661
2600]	695	693	692	691	689	688	687	686	684	683	681	679	677	676	674	672
2650]	707	705	704	703	701	700	699	697	696	694	692	690	688	687	685	683
2700]	719	717	716	715	713	712	711	709	707	705	703	701	700	698	696	694
2750]	730	729	728	726	725	724	722	720	718	716	714	713	711	709	707	706
2800]	742	741	740	738	737	735	733	731	729	727	726	724	722	720	718	717
2850]	754	753	751	750	748	746	744	742	740	739	737	735	733	731	730	728
2900]	766	765	763	761	759	757	755	753	752	750	748	746	744	742	741	739
2950]	778	776	775	773	770	768	766	764	763	761	759	757	755	753	752	750
3000]	790	788	786	784	781	779	777	775	774	772	770	768	766	764	762	761
3050]	801	799	797	794	792	790	788	786	784	783	781	779	777	775	773	772
3100]	812	810	808	805	803	801	799	797	795	793	792	790	788	786	784	783
3150]	823	821	818	816	814	812	810	808	806	804	802	801	799	797	795	793
3200]	834	831	829	827	825	823	821	819	817	815	813	811	810	808	806	804
3250]	844	842	840	838	836	834	832	830	828	826	824	822	820	819	817	815
3300]	855	853	851	849	847	845	843	841	839	837	835	833	831	829	828	826
3350]	866	864	862	860	857	855	853	851	849	848	846	844	842	840	838	837
3400]	877	875	872	870	868	866	864	862	860	858	856	855	853	851	849	847
3450]	887	885	883	881	879	877	875	873	871	869	867	865	863	862	860	858
3500]	898	896	894	892	890	888	886	884	882	880	878	876	874	872	870	869
3550]	909	907	904	902	900	898	896	894	892	890	888	886	885	883	881	879
3600]	919	917	915	913	911	909	907	905	903	901	899	897	895	893	892	890
3650]	930	928	926	923	921	919	917	915	913	911	910	908	906	904	902	900
3700]	940	938	936	934	932	930	928	926	924	922	920	918	916	914	913	911
3750]	951	949	947	945	942	940	938	936	934	933	931	929	927	925	923	921
3800]	961	959	957	955	953	951	949	947	945	943	941	939	937	935	934	932
3850]	972	970	968	966	963	961	959	957	955	953	952	950	948	946	944	942
3900]	982	980	978	976	974	972	970	968	966	964	962	960	958	956	955	953
3950]	993	991	988	986	984	982	980	978	976	974	972	971	969	967	965	963
4000]	1003	1001	999	997	995	993	991	989	987	985	983	981	979	977	975	973
4050]	1013	1011	1009	1007	1005	1003	1001	999	997	995	993	991	989	987	985	983
4100]	1024	1022	1020	1017	1015	1013	1011	1009	1007	1005	1004	1002	1000	997	995	993
4150]	1034	1032	1030	1028	1026	1024	1022	1020	1018	1016	1014	1012	1009	1007	1005	1002
4200]	1044	1042	1040	1038	1036	1034	1032	1030	1028	1026	1024	1022	1019	1017	1015	1012
4250]	1055	1053	1050	1048	1046	1044	1042	1040	1038	1036	1034	1031	1029	1027	1024	1022
4300]	1065	1063	1061	1059	1057	1055	1052	1051	1048	1046	1043	1041	1039	1036	1034	1032
4350]	1075	1073	1071	1069	1067	1065	1063	1061	1058	1056	1053	1051	1048	1046	1044	1041
4400]	1085	1083	1081	1079	1077	1075	1073	1070	1068	1065	1063	1060	1058	1056	1053	1051
4450]	1096	1093	1091	1089	1087	1085	1082	1080	1077	1075	1073	1070	1068	1065	1063	1061
4500]	1106	1104	1101	1099	1097	1095	1092	1089	1087	1085	1082	1080	1077	1075	1073	1070
4550]	1116	1114	1112	1109	1107	1104	1102	1099	1097	1094	1092	1089	1087	1085	1082	1080
4600]	1126	1124	1121	1119	1116	1114	1111	1109	1106	1104	1101	1099	1097	1094	1092	1090
4650]	1136	1134	1131	1128	1126	1123	1121	1118	1116	1113	1111	1108	1106	1104	1101	1099
4700]	1146	1143	1141	1138	1135	1133	1130	1128	1125	1123	1120	1118	1116	1113	1111	1109
4750]	1155	1153	1150	1147	1145	1142	1140	1137	1135	1132	1130	1128	1125	1123	1121	1118
4800]	1165	1162	1159	1157	1154	1152	1149	1147	1144	1142	1139	1137	1135	1132	1130	1128
4850]	1174	1172	1169	1166	1164	1161	1159	1156	1154	1151	1149	1146	1144	1142	1139	1137
4900]	1184	1181	1178	1176	1173	1171	1168	1166	1163	1161	1158	1156	1154	1151	1149	1147
4950]	1193	1190	1188	1185	1183	1180	1177	1175	1173	1170	1168	1165	1163	1161	1158	1156
5000]	1202	1200	1197	1194	1192	1189	1187	1184	1182	1179	1177	1175	1172	1170	1168	1165

(Left vertical label: NONCUSTODIAL PARENT MONTHLY INCOME)

Effective October 1, 2004

Two Children - Monthly Support

CUSTODIAL PARENT MONTHLY INCOME

(Left margin, vertical: NONCUSTODIAL PARENT MONTHLY INCOME)

	4250	4300	4350	4400	4450	4500	4550	4600	4650	4700	4750	4800	4850	4900	4950	5000
250]	25	25	25	25	25	25	25	25	25	25	25	25	25	25	25	25
300]	25	25	25	25	25	25	25	25	25	25	25	25	25	25	25	25
350]	25	25	25	25	25	25	25	25	25	25	25	25	25	25	25	25
400]	25	25	25	25	25	25	25	25	25	25	25	25	25	25	25	25
450]	25	25	25	25	25	25	25	25	25	25	25	25	25	25	25	25
500]	25	25	25	25	25	25	25	25	25	25	25	25	25	25	25	25
550]	25	25	25	25	25	25	25	25	25	25	25	25	25	25	25	25
600]	25	25	25	25	25	25	25	25	25	25	25	25	25	25	25	25
650]	25	25	25	25	25	25	25	25	25	25	25	25	25	25	25	25
700]	25	25	25	25	25	25	25	25	25	25	25	25	25	25	25	25
750]	25	25	25	25	25	25	25	25	25	25	25	25	25	25	25	25
800]	49	49	49	49	49	49	49	49	49	49	49	49	49	49	49	49
850]	99	99	99	99	99	99	99	99	99	99	99	99	99	99	99	99
900]	149	149	149	149	149	149	149	149	149	149	149	149	149	149	149	149
950]	199	199	199	199	199	199	199	199	199	199	199	199	199	199	199	199
1000]	249	249	249	249	249	249	249	249	249	249	249	249	249	249	249	249
1050]	290	289	289	288	287	287	286	285	285	284	283	283	282	282	281	281
1100]	303	302	302	301	300	300	299	298	298	297	296	296	295	294	294	293
1150]	316	315	315	314	313	313	312	311	310	310	309	309	308	307	307	306
1200]	329	328	328	327	326	325	325	324	323	323	322	321	321	320	319	319
1250]	342	341	340	340	339	338	337	337	336	335	335	334	333	333	332	331
1300]	355	354	353	352	352	351	350	349	349	348	347	347	346	345	345	344
1350]	368	367	366	365	364	364	363	362	361	361	360	359	359	358	357	357
1400]	380	380	379	378	377	376	376	375	374	373	373	372	371	370	370	369
1450]	393	392	391	391	390	389	388	387	387	386	385	384	384	383	382	382
1500]	406	405	404	403	402	402	401	400	399	398	398	397	396	396	395	394
1550]	418	418	417	416	415	414	413	413	412	411	410	409	409	408	407	406
1600]	431	430	429	428	428	427	426	425	424	423	423	422	421	420	419	418
1650]	444	443	442	441	440	439	438	437	437	436	435	434	433	432	431	430
1700]	456	455	454	453	452	452	451	450	449	448	447	446	445	444	443	442
1750]	469	468	467	466	465	464	463	462	461	461	459	458	457	456	455	454
1800]	481	480	479	478	477	476	475	475	474	473	471	470	469	468	466	465
1850]	493	492	491	490	490	489	488	487	486	484	483	482	481	479	478	477
1900]	506	505	504	503	502	501	500	499	498	496	495	494	492	491	490	489
1950]	518	517	516	515	514	513	512	511	509	508	507	505	504	503	502	500
2000]	530	529	528	527	526	525	524	522	521	520	518	517	516	514	513	512
2050]	542	542	541	540	538	537	535	534	533	531	530	529	527	526	525	523
2100]	555	554	553	551	550	548	547	546	544	543	541	540	539	538	536	535
2150]	567	566	565	563	562	560	559	557	556	554	553	552	550	549	548	546
2200]	579	578	576	575	573	572	570	569	567	566	564	563	562	560	559	558
2250]	591	589	588	586	585	583	582	580	579	577	576	575	573	572	571	569
2300]	602	601	599	598	596	595	593	592	590	589	587	586	585	583	582	581
2350]	614	612	611	609	607	606	604	603	602	600	599	597	596	595	593	592
2400]	625	624	622	620	619	617	616	614	613	611	610	609	607	606	605	603
2450]	637	635	633	632	630	629	627	626	624	623	621	620	618	617	616	614
2500]	648	646	645	643	641	640	638	637	635	634	633	631	630	628	627	626

Effective October 1, 2004

Two Children - Monthly Support

CUSTODIAL PARENT MONTHLY INCOME

		4250	4300	4350	4400	4450	4500	4550	4600	4650	4700	4750	4800	4850	4900	4950	5000
	2550]	659	658	656	654	653	651	650	648	647	645	644	642	641	639	638	637
	2600]	670	669	667	666	664	662	661	659	658	656	655	653	652	651	649	648
	2650]	682	680	678	677	675	674	672	670	669	667	666	665	663	662	660	659
	2700]	693	691	689	688	686	685	683	682	680	679	677	676	674	673	671	670
	2750]	704	702	701	699	697	696	694	693	691	690	688	687	685	684	682	681
	2800]	715	713	712	710	708	707	705	704	702	701	699	698	696	695	693	692
	2850]	726	724	723	721	719	718	716	715	713	712	710	709	707	706	704	703
N	2900]	737	735	734	732	730	729	727	726	724	723	721	720	718	717	715	714
O	2950]	748	746	745	743	741	740	738	737	735	734	732	731	729	728	726	725
N																	
C	3000]	759	757	756	754	752	751	749	748	746	744	743	741	740	739	737	736
U	3050]	770	768	767	765	763	762	760	758	757	755	754	752	751	749	748	747
S	3100]	781	779	777	776	774	772	771	769	768	766	765	763	762	760	759	757
T	3150]	792	790	788	787	785	783	782	780	779	777	775	774	772	771	770	768
O	3200]	802	801	799	797	796	794	793	791	789	788	786	785	783	782	780	778
D	3250]	813	812	810	808	807	805	803	802	800	799	797	795	794	792	791	789
I	3300]	824	822	821	819	817	816	814	812	811	809	808	806	805	803	801	799
A	3350]	835	833	831	830	828	826	825	823	822	820	818	817	815	813	811	809
L	3400]	845	844	842	840	839	837	835	834	832	831	829	827	825	823	821	819
	3450]	856	854	853	851	849	848	846	844	843	841	839	837	835	833	831	830
P																	
A	3500]	867	865	863	862	860	858	857	855	853	851	849	847	845	844	842	840
R	3550]	877	876	874	872	871	869	867	866	863	861	859	858	856	854	852	850
E	3600]	888	886	885	883	881	879	878	876	874	872	870	868	866	864	862	860
N	3650]	899	897	895	893	892	890	888	886	884	882	880	878	876	874	872	870
T	3700]	909	907	906	904	902	900	898	896	894	892	890	888	886	884	882	880
	3750]	920	918	916	914	912	910	908	906	904	902	900	898	896	894	892	890
M	3800]	930	928	926	924	922	920	918	916	914	912	910	908	906	904	902	900
O	3850]	941	939	936	934	932	930	928	926	924	922	920	918	916	914	912	910
N	3900]	951	949	946	944	942	940	938	936	934	932	930	928	926	924	922	920
T	3950]	961	959	956	954	952	950	948	946	944	942	940	938	936	934	932	930
H																	
L	4000]	971	968	966	964	962	960	958	956	954	951	949	948	946	944	942	940
Y	4050]	981	978	976	974	972	970	968	965	963	961	959	957	955	953	952	950
	4100]	990	988	986	984	982	979	977	975	973	971	969	967	965	963	961	959
I	4150]	1000	998	996	994	991	989	987	985	983	981	979	977	975	973	971	969
N	4200]	1010	1008	1006	1003	1001	999	997	995	993	991	989	987	985	983	981	979
C	4250]	1020	1018	1015	1013	1011	1009	1007	1005	1003	1001	999	997	995	993	991	989
O	4300]	1029	1027	1025	1023	1021	1019	1016	1014	1012	1010	1008	1006	1004	1002	1000	998
M	4350]	1039	1037	1035	1033	1030	1028	1026	1024	1022	1020	1018	1016	1014	1012	1010	1008
E	4400]	1049	1047	1044	1042	1040	1038	1036	1034	1032	1030	1028	1026	1024	1022	1020	1018
	4450]	1059	1056	1054	1052	1050	1048	1046	1043	1041	1039	1037	1035	1033	1031	1029	1028
	4500]	1068	1066	1064	1062	1059	1057	1055	1053	1051	1049	1047	1045	1043	1041	1039	1037
	4550]	1078	1076	1073	1071	1069	1067	1065	1063	1061	1059	1057	1055	1053	1051	1049	1047
	4600]	1087	1085	1083	1081	1079	1076	1074	1072	1070	1068	1066	1064	1062	1060	1058	1056
	4650]	1097	1095	1092	1090	1088	1086	1084	1082	1080	1078	1076	1074	1072	1070	1068	1066
	4700]	1106	1104	1102	1100	1098	1096	1093	1091	1089	1087	1085	1083	1081	1079	1077	1075
	4750]	1116	1114	1112	1109	1107	1105	1103	1101	1099	1097	1095	1093	1091	1089	1087	1085
	4800]	1125	1123	1121	1119	1117	1115	1112	1110	1108	1106	1104	1102	1100	1098	1096	1094
	4850]	1135	1133	1131	1128	1126	1124	1122	1120	1118	1116	1114	1112	1110	1108	1106	1104
	4900]	1144	1142	1140	1138	1136	1134	1131	1129	1127	1125	1123	1121	1119	1117	1115	1113
	4950]	1154	1152	1149	1147	1145	1143	1141	1139	1137	1135	1133	1131	1129	1127	1125	1123
	5000]	1163	1161	1159	1157	1154	1152	1150	1148	1146	1144	1142	1140	1138	1136	1134	1132

2004 MICHIGAN CHILD SUPPORT FORMULA SCHEDULES
MONTHLY BASE SUPPORT

Three Children - Monthly Support

CUSTODIAL PARENT MONTHLY INCOME

	0	250	300	350	400	450	500	550	600	650	700	750	800	850	900	950	1000
250]	25	25	25	25	25	25	25	25	25	25	25	25	25	25	25	25	25
300]	30	30	30	30	30	30	30	30	30	30	30	30	27	27	25	25	25
350]	35	35	35	35	35	35	35	35	35	35	35	35	32	32	28	28	28
400]	40	40	40	40	40	40	40	40	40	40	40	40	36	36	32	32	32
450]	45	45	45	45	45	45	45	45	45	45	45	45	41	41	36	36	36
500]	50	50	50	50	50	50	50	50	50	50	50	50	45	45	40	40	40
550]	55	55	55	55	55	55	55	55	55	55	55	55	50	50	44	44	44
600]	60	60	60	60	60	60	60	60	60	60	60	60	54	54	48	48	48
650]	65	65	65	65	65	65	65	65	65	65	65	65	59	59	52	52	52
700]	70	70	70	70	70	70	70	70	70	70	70	70	63	63	56	56	56
750]	75	75	75	75	75	75	75	75	75	75	75	75	68	68	60	60	60
800]	102	102	102	102	102	102	102	102	102	102	102	102	94	94	86	86	86
850]	152	152	152	152	152	152	152	152	152	152	152	152	144	144	136	136	136
900]	202	202	202	202	202	202	202	202	202	202	202	202	194	194	186	186	186
950]	252	252	252	252	252	252	252	252	252	252	252	252	244	244	236	236	236
1000]	302	302	302	302	302	302	302	302	302	302	302	302	294	294	286	286	286
1050]	352	352	352	352	352	352	352	352	352	352	352	352	344	344	336	336	336
1100]	402	402	402	402	402	402	402	402	402	402	402	402	394	394	386	386	386
1150]	452	452	452	452	452	452	452	452	452	452	452	452	444	444	436	436	436
1200]	502	502	502	502	502	502	502	502	502	502	502	502	494	494	486	486	486
1250]	552	552	552	552	552	552	552	552	552	552	552	552	544	544	536	536	536
1300]	602	602	602	602	602	602	602	602	602	602	602	602	592	589	586	582	578
1350]	652	652	652	652	652	652	652	652	652	652	652	652	612	609	605	601	597
1400]	683	683	683	683	683	683	683	683	683	683	683	683	631	627	623	619	615
1450]	707	707	707	707	707	707	707	707	707	707	707	707	650	645	641	637	633
1500]	731	731	731	731	731	731	731	731	731	731	731	731	667	663	659	654	650
1550]	754	754	754	754	754	754	754	754	754	754	754	754	685	680	676	672	668
1600]	778	778	778	778	778	778	778	778	778	778	778	778	702	698	694	690	686
1650]	799	799	799	799	799	799	799	799	799	799	799	799	720	716	711	707	704
1700]	816	816	816	816	816	816	816	816	816	816	816	816	737	733	729	725	721
1750]	834	834	834	834	834	834	834	834	834	834	834	834	755	750	746	742	738
1800]	851	851	851	851	851	851	851	851	851	851	851	851	772	768	763	760	756
1850]	869	869	869	869	869	869	869	869	869	869	869	869	789	785	781	777	773
1900]	887	887	887	887	887	887	887	887	887	887	887	887	806	802	798	794	790
1950]	904	904	904	904	904	904	904	904	904	904	904	904	823	819	815	810	806
2000]	922	922	922	922	922	922	922	922	922	922	922	922	840	836	831	827	823
2050]	939	939	939	939	939	939	939	939	939	939	939	939	857	852	848	843	839
2100]	957	957	957	957	957	957	957	957	957	957	957	957	873	868	864	860	855
2150]	974	974	974	974	974	974	974	974	974	974	974	974	889	884	880	876	872
2200]	992	992	992	992	992	992	992	992	992	992	992	992	905	900	896	892	888
2250]	1008	1008	1008	1008	1008	1008	1008	1008	1008	1008	1008	1008	921	917	912	908	904
2300]	1023	1023	1023	1023	1023	1023	1023	1023	1023	1023	1023	1023	937	933	928	924	920
2350]	1038	1038	1038	1038	1038	1038	1038	1038	1038	1038	1038	1038	953	948	944	940	936
2400]	1054	1054	1054	1054	1054	1054	1054	1054	1054	1054	1054	1054	969	964	960	956	952
2450]	1069	1069	1069	1069	1069	1069	1069	1069	1069	1069	1069	1069	984	980	976	972	968
2500]	1084	1084	1084	1084	1084	1084	1084	1084	1084	1084	1084	1084	1000	996	992	988	984

(Row labels at left margin read vertically: NONCUSTODIAL PARENT MONTHLY INCOME)

2004 MICHIGAN CHILD SUPPORT FORMULA SCHEDULES
MONTHLY BASE SUPPORT

Three Children - Monthly Support

CUSTODIAL PARENT MONTHLY INCOME

	0	250	300	350	400	450	500	550	600	650	700	750	800	850	900	950	1000
2550]	1099	1099	1099	1099	1099	1099	1099	1099	1099	1099	1099	1099	1016	1012	1008	1004	1000
2600]	1115	1115	1115	1115	1115	1115	1115	1115	1115	1115	1115	1115	1032	1027	1023	1020	1016
2650]	1130	1130	1130	1130	1130	1130	1130	1130	1130	1130	1130	1130	1047	1043	1039	1035	1032
2700]	1145	1145	1145	1145	1145	1145	1145	1145	1145	1145	1145	1145	1063	1059	1055	1051	1047
2750]	1160	1160	1160	1160	1160	1160	1160	1160	1160	1160	1160	1160	1078	1074	1071	1067	1063
2800]	1176	1176	1176	1176	1176	1176	1176	1176	1176	1176	1176	1176	1094	1090	1086	1082	1078
2850]	1191	1191	1191	1191	1191	1191	1191	1191	1191	1191	1191	1191	1109	1106	1101	1097	1094
2900]	1205	1205	1205	1205	1205	1205	1205	1205	1205	1205	1205	1205	1125	1121	1117	1113	1109
2950]	1220	1220	1220	1220	1220	1220	1220	1220	1220	1220	1220	1220	1140	1136	1132	1128	1124
3000]	1234	1234	1234	1234	1234	1234	1234	1234	1234	1234	1234	1234	1155	1151	1147	1143	1139
3050]	1248	1248	1248	1248	1248	1248	1248	1248	1248	1248	1248	1248	1170	1166	1162	1158	1155
3100]	1263	1263	1263	1263	1263	1263	1263	1263	1263	1263	1263	1263	1185	1181	1177	1174	1170
3150]	1277	1277	1277	1277	1277	1277	1277	1277	1277	1277	1277	1277	1200	1196	1192	1189	1185
3200]	1292	1292	1292	1292	1292	1292	1292	1292	1292	1292	1292	1292	1215	1211	1208	1204	1200
3250]	1306	1306	1306	1306	1306	1306	1306	1306	1306	1306	1306	1306	1230	1226	1223	1219	1215
3300]	1320	1320	1320	1320	1320	1320	1320	1320	1320	1320	1320	1320	1245	1241	1238	1234	1230
3350]	1335	1335	1335	1335	1335	1335	1335	1335	1335	1335	1335	1335	1260	1256	1253	1249	1245
3400]	1349	1349	1349	1349	1349	1349	1349	1349	1349	1349	1349	1349	1275	1271	1268	1264	1260
3450]	1363	1363	1363	1363	1363	1363	1363	1363	1363	1363	1363	1363	1290	1286	1283	1279	1275
3500]	1378	1378	1378	1378	1378	1378	1378	1378	1378	1378	1378	1378	1305	1301	1297	1294	1290
3550]	1392	1392	1392	1392	1392	1392	1392	1392	1392	1392	1392	1392	1320	1316	1312	1309	1305
3600]	1407	1407	1407	1407	1407	1407	1407	1407	1407	1407	1407	1407	1335	1331	1327	1324	1320
3650]	1421	1421	1421	1421	1421	1421	1421	1421	1421	1421	1421	1421	1349	1346	1342	1339	1335
3700]	1435	1435	1435	1435	1435	1435	1435	1435	1435	1435	1435	1435	1364	1361	1357	1354	1350
3750]	1449	1449	1449	1449	1449	1449	1449	1449	1449	1449	1449	1449	1379	1375	1372	1368	1365
3800]	1463	1463	1463	1463	1463	1463	1463	1463	1463	1463	1463	1463	1394	1390	1387	1383	1380
3850]	1477	1477	1477	1477	1477	1477	1477	1477	1477	1477	1477	1477	1408	1405	1401	1398	1395
3900]	1491	1491	1491	1491	1491	1491	1491	1491	1491	1491	1491	1491	1423	1420	1416	1413	1410
3950]	1505	1505	1505	1505	1505	1505	1505	1505	1505	1505	1505	1505	1438	1434	1431	1428	1424
4000]	1519	1519	1519	1519	1519	1519	1519	1519	1519	1519	1519	1519	1453	1449	1446	1442	1439
4050]	1533	1533	1533	1533	1533	1533	1533	1533	1533	1533	1533	1533	1467	1464	1460	1457	1454
4100]	1547	1547	1547	1547	1547	1547	1547	1547	1547	1547	1547	1547	1482	1479	1475	1472	1469
4150]	1561	1561	1561	1561	1561	1561	1561	1561	1561	1561	1561	1561	1497	1493	1490	1487	1484
4200]	1575	1575	1575	1575	1575	1575	1575	1575	1575	1575	1575	1575	1511	1508	1505	1501	1498
4250]	1589	1589	1589	1589	1589	1589	1589	1589	1589	1589	1589	1589	1526	1522	1519	1516	1513
4300]	1603	1603	1603	1603	1603	1603	1603	1603	1603	1603	1603	1603	1540	1537	1534	1531	1526
4350]	1617	1617	1617	1617	1617	1617	1617	1617	1617	1617	1617	1617	1555	1552	1549	1544	1539
4400]	1631	1631	1631	1631	1631	1631	1631	1631	1631	1631	1631	1631	1570	1566	1561	1556	1551
4450]	1645	1645	1645	1645	1645	1645	1645	1645	1645	1645	1645	1645	1584	1579	1574	1569	1564
4500]	1659	1659	1659	1659	1659	1659	1659	1659	1659	1659	1659	1659	1597	1592	1587	1582	1577
4550]	1673	1673	1673	1673	1673	1673	1673	1673	1673	1673	1673	1673	1609	1604	1599	1595	1590
4600]	1687	1687	1687	1687	1687	1687	1687	1687	1687	1687	1687	1687	1622	1617	1612	1607	1603
4650]	1701	1701	1701	1701	1701	1701	1701	1701	1701	1701	1701	1701	1635	1630	1625	1620	1615
4700]	1715	1715	1715	1715	1715	1715	1715	1715	1715	1715	1715	1715	1647	1642	1637	1633	1628
4750]	1729	1729	1729	1729	1729	1729	1729	1729	1729	1729	1729	1729	1660	1655	1650	1645	1641
4800]	1743	1743	1743	1743	1743	1743	1743	1743	1743	1743	1743	1743	1672	1667	1663	1658	1653
4850]	1757	1757	1757	1757	1757	1757	1757	1757	1757	1757	1757	1757	1685	1680	1675	1670	1666
4900]	1771	1771	1771	1771	1771	1771	1771	1771	1771	1771	1771	1771	1697	1692	1688	1683	1679
4950]	1785	1785	1785	1785	1785	1785	1785	1785	1785	1785	1785	1785	1710	1705	1700	1696	1691
5000]	1799	1799	1799	1799	1799	1799	1799	1799	1799	1799	1799	1799	1722	1717	1713	1708	1704

(Left margin vertical label: NONCUSTODIAL PARENT MONTHLY INCOME)

Effective October 1, 2004

Three Children - Monthly Support

CUSTODIAL PARENT MONTHLY INCOME

	1050	1100	1150	1200	1250	1300	1350	1400	1450	1500	1550	1600	1650	1700	1750	1800
250]	25	25	25	25	25	25	25	25	25	25	25	25	25	25	25	25
300]	25	25	25	25	25	25	25	25	25	25	25	25	25	25	25	25
350]	28	28	28	28	28	28	25	25	25	25	25	25	25	25	25	25
400]	32	32	32	32	32	32	28	28	28	28	28	28	28	28	28	25
450]	36	36	36	36	36	36	32	32	32	32	32	32	32	32	32	27
500]	40	40	40	40	40	40	35	35	35	35	35	35	35	35	35	30
550]	44	44	44	44	44	44	39	39	39	39	39	39	39	39	39	33
600]	48	48	48	48	48	48	42	42	42	42	42	42	42	42	42	36
650]	52	52	52	52	52	52	46	46	46	46	46	46	46	46	46	39
700]	56	56	56	56	56	56	49	49	49	49	49	49	49	49	49	42
750]	60	60	60	60	60	60	53	53	53	53	53	53	53	53	53	45
800]	86	86	86	86	86	86	78	78	78	78	78	78	78	78	78	71
850]	136	136	136	136	136	136	128	128	128	128	128	128	128	128	128	121
900]	186	186	186	186	186	186	178	178	178	178	178	178	178	178	178	171
950]	236	236	236	236	236	236	228	228	228	228	228	228	228	228	228	221
1000]	286	286	286	286	286	286	278	278	278	278	278	278	278	278	278	271
1050]	336	336	336	336	336	336	328	328	328	328	328	328	328	328	328	321
1100]	386	386	386	386	386	386	378	378	378	378	378	378	378	378	378	371
1150]	436	436	436	436	436	436	428	428	428	428	428	428	428	428	428	421
1200]	486	486	486	486	486	486	478	478	478	478	478	478	478	478	478	471
1250]	536	536	536	536	536	536	528	528	528	527	525	522	520	517	514	512
1300]	574	571	567	564	560	557	554	551	549	546	543	540	537	535	532	530
1350]	593	589	585	582	579	576	573	570	567	564	561	558	555	553	550	547
1400]	611	607	604	600	597	594	591	588	585	582	579	576	573	570	568	565
1450]	629	625	622	618	615	612	609	606	603	599	596	594	591	588	585	583
1500]	647	643	640	636	633	630	627	623	620	617	614	611	608	605	603	600
1550]	665	661	657	654	651	648	644	641	638	634	631	628	626	623	620	618
1600]	682	679	675	672	669	665	662	658	655	652	649	646	643	640	637	635
1650]	700	696	693	689	686	682	679	675	672	669	666	663	660	657	655	652
1700]	717	714	710	707	703	699	696	692	689	686	683	680	677	675	672	669
1750]	735	731	727	724	720	716	713	710	706	703	700	697	694	692	689	686
1800]	752	748	744	740	737	733	730	726	723	720	717	714	711	709	706	703
1850]	769	765	761	757	754	750	747	743	740	737	734	731	728	725	723	720
1900]	786	782	778	774	770	767	763	760	757	754	751	748	745	742	740	737
1950]	802	798	794	791	787	784	780	777	774	771	768	765	762	759	756	754
2000]	819	815	811	807	804	800	797	794	790	787	784	781	779	776	773	770
2050]	835	831	827	824	820	817	813	810	807	804	801	798	795	792	789	787
2100]	851	848	844	840	837	833	830	827	824	820	818	815	812	809	806	803
2150]	868	864	860	857	853	850	846	843	840	837	834	831	828	825	822	819
2200]	884	880	876	873	869	866	863	860	856	853	850	847	844	841	838	836
2250]	900	896	893	889	886	882	879	876	873	870	866	863	860	857	855	852
2300]	916	913	909	905	902	899	895	892	889	886	883	879	876	874	871	868
2350]	932	929	925	922	918	915	912	908	905	902	899	896	893	890	887	884
2400]	948	945	941	938	934	931	928	924	921	918	915	912	909	906	903	900
2450]	964	961	957	954	950	947	943	940	937	934	931	927	925	922	919	916
2500]	980	977	973	970	966	963	959	956	953	950	946	943	940	938	935	932

(Left vertical label: NONCUSTODIAL PARENT MONTHLY INCOME)

Effective October 1, 2004

Three Children - Monthly Support

CUSTODIAL PARENT MONTHLY INCOME

	1050	1100	1150	1200	1250	1300	1350	1400	1450	1500	1550	1600	1650	1700	1750	1800
2550]	996	993	989	986	982	978	975	972	969	965	962	959	956	954	951	948
2600]	1012	1009	1005	1001	998	994	991	987	984	981	978	975	972	969	967	964
2650]	1028	1024	1020	1017	1013	1010	1006	1003	1000	997	994	991	988	985	982	980
2700]	1043	1040	1036	1032	1029	1025	1022	1019	1016	1013	1010	1007	1004	1001	998	995
2750]	1059	1055	1052	1048	1044	1041	1038	1035	1031	1028	1025	1022	1019	1017	1014	1011
2800]	1074	1071	1067	1063	1060	1057	1053	1050	1047	1044	1041	1038	1035	1032	1030	1027
2850]	1090	1086	1082	1079	1075	1072	1069	1066	1063	1060	1057	1054	1051	1048	1045	1043
2900]	1105	1101	1098	1094	1091	1088	1084	1081	1078	1075	1072	1069	1066	1064	1061	1058
2950]	1120	1117	1113	1110	1106	1103	1100	1097	1094	1091	1088	1085	1082	1079	1076	1074
3000]	1136	1132	1129	1125	1122	1118	1115	1112	1109	1106	1103	1100	1097	1095	1092	1089
3050]	1151	1147	1144	1140	1137	1134	1131	1128	1125	1122	1119	1116	1113	1110	1108	1105
3100]	1166	1163	1159	1156	1152	1149	1146	1143	1140	1137	1134	1131	1128	1126	1123	1120
3150]	1181	1178	1174	1171	1168	1165	1161	1158	1155	1152	1149	1147	1144	1141	1139	1136
3200]	1197	1193	1190	1186	1183	1180	1177	1174	1171	1168	1165	1162	1159	1157	1154	1151
3250]	1212	1208	1205	1201	1198	1195	1192	1189	1186	1183	1180	1177	1175	1172	1169	1167
3300]	1227	1223	1220	1217	1213	1210	1207	1204	1201	1198	1196	1193	1190	1187	1185	1182
3350]	1242	1238	1235	1232	1229	1226	1222	1219	1217	1214	1211	1208	1205	1203	1200	1198
3400]	1257	1254	1250	1247	1244	1241	1238	1235	1232	1229	1226	1223	1221	1218	1215	1213
3450]	1272	1269	1265	1262	1259	1256	1253	1250	1247	1244	1241	1239	1236	1233	1231	1228
3500]	1287	1284	1280	1277	1274	1271	1268	1265	1262	1259	1257	1254	1251	1249	1246	1242
3550]	1302	1299	1295	1292	1289	1286	1283	1280	1277	1274	1272	1269	1266	1264	1260	1256
3600]	1317	1314	1310	1307	1304	1301	1298	1295	1292	1290	1287	1284	1282	1277	1273	1269
3650]	1332	1329	1325	1322	1319	1316	1313	1310	1308	1305	1302	1299	1295	1291	1287	1283
3700]	1347	1344	1340	1337	1334	1331	1328	1325	1323	1320	1317	1313	1309	1305	1301	1297
3750]	1362	1359	1355	1352	1349	1346	1343	1341	1338	1335	1331	1326	1322	1318	1314	1310
3800]	1377	1373	1370	1367	1364	1361	1358	1356	1353	1348	1344	1340	1336	1332	1328	1324
3850]	1392	1388	1385	1382	1379	1376	1373	1371	1366	1362	1358	1353	1349	1345	1341	1337
3900]	1406	1403	1400	1397	1394	1391	1388	1384	1380	1375	1371	1367	1363	1359	1355	1351
3950]	1421	1418	1415	1412	1409	1406	1402	1397	1393	1389	1384	1380	1376	1372	1368	1364
4000]	1436	1433	1430	1427	1424	1419	1415	1410	1406	1402	1398	1394	1389	1385	1382	1378
4050]	1451	1448	1445	1442	1437	1433	1428	1424	1419	1415	1411	1407	1403	1399	1395	1391
4100]	1466	1463	1460	1455	1450	1446	1441	1437	1433	1428	1424	1420	1416	1412	1408	1404
4150]	1480	1477	1473	1468	1463	1459	1454	1450	1446	1442	1437	1433	1429	1425	1422	1418
4200]	1495	1490	1486	1481	1476	1472	1468	1463	1459	1455	1451	1447	1443	1439	1435	1431
4250]	1508	1503	1499	1494	1489	1485	1481	1476	1472	1468	1464	1460	1456	1452	1448	1444
4300]	1521	1516	1512	1507	1502	1498	1494	1489	1485	1481	1477	1473	1469	1465	1461	1458
4350]	1534	1529	1524	1520	1515	1511	1507	1502	1498	1494	1490	1486	1482	1478	1475	1471
4400]	1547	1542	1537	1533	1528	1524	1520	1515	1511	1507	1503	1499	1495	1492	1488	1484
4450]	1560	1555	1550	1546	1541	1537	1533	1529	1524	1520	1516	1512	1509	1505	1501	1497
4500]	1572	1568	1563	1559	1554	1550	1546	1542	1537	1533	1529	1526	1522	1518	1514	1511
4550]	1585	1581	1576	1572	1567	1563	1559	1554	1550	1546	1542	1539	1535	1531	1527	1524
4600]	1598	1593	1589	1584	1580	1576	1572	1567	1563	1559	1555	1552	1548	1544	1540	1537
4650]	1611	1606	1602	1597	1593	1589	1584	1580	1576	1572	1568	1565	1561	1557	1553	1550
4700]	1623	1619	1614	1610	1606	1602	1597	1593	1589	1585	1581	1578	1574	1570	1567	1562
4750]	1636	1632	1627	1623	1619	1614	1610	1606	1602	1598	1594	1591	1587	1583	1579	1574
4800]	1649	1644	1640	1636	1631	1627	1623	1619	1615	1611	1607	1604	1600	1595	1590	1585
4850]	1661	1657	1653	1648	1644	1640	1636	1632	1628	1624	1620	1617	1612	1607	1602	1597
4900]	1674	1670	1665	1661	1657	1653	1649	1645	1641	1637	1633	1629	1624	1618	1614	1609
4950]	1687	1682	1678	1674	1670	1666	1662	1658	1654	1650	1645	1640	1635	1630	1625	1620
5000]	1699	1695	1691	1687	1682	1678	1674	1670	1667	1662	1657	1652	1646	1642	1637	1632

(Left margin vertical label: NON CUSTODIAL PARENT MONTHLY INCOME)

2004 MICHIGAN CHILD SUPPORT FORMULA SCHEDULES
MONTHLY BASE SUPPORT

Three Children - Monthly Support

CUSTODIAL PARENT MONTHLY INCOME

	1850	1900	1950	2000	2050	2100	2150	2200	2250	2300	2350	2400	2450	2500	2550	2600
250]	25	25	25	25	25	25	25	25	25	25	25	25	25	25	25	25
300]	25	25	25	25	25	25	25	25	25	25	25	25	25	25	25	25
350]	25	25	25	25	25	25	25	25	25	25	25	25	25	25	25	25
400]	25	25	25	25	25	25	25	25	25	25	25	25	25	25	25	25
450]	27	27	27	27	27	27	27	27	25	25	25	25	25	25	25	25
500]	30	30	30	30	30	30	30	30	25	25	25	25	25	25	25	25
550]	33	33	33	33	33	33	33	33	28	28	28	28	28	28	28	28
600]	36	36	36	36	36	36	36	36	30	30	30	30	30	30	30	30
650]	39	39	39	39	39	39	39	39	33	33	33	33	33	33	33	33
700]	42	42	42	42	42	42	42	42	35	35	35	35	35	35	35	35
750]	45	45	45	45	45	45	45	45	38	38	38	38	38	38	38	38
800]	71	71	71	71	71	71	71	71	63	63	63	63	63	63	63	63
850]	121	121	121	121	121	121	121	121	113	113	113	113	113	113	113	113
900]	171	171	171	171	171	171	171	171	163	163	163	163	163	163	163	163
950]	221	221	221	221	221	221	221	221	213	213	213	213	213	213	213	213
1000]	271	271	271	271	271	271	271	271	263	263	263	263	263	263	263	263
1050]	321	321	321	321	321	321	321	321	313	313	313	313	313	313	313	313
1100]	371	371	371	371	371	371	371	371	363	363	363	363	363	363	363	363
1150]	421	421	421	421	421	421	421	421	413	413	413	413	413	413	413	413
1200]	471	471	471	471	471	471	471	471	463	463	463	463	463	463	463	462
1250]	509	507	505	502	500	498	496	494	492	490	488	487	485	483	481	480
1300]	527	525	522	520	518	516	514	512	510	508	506	504	502	501	499	497
1350]	545	542	540	538	536	534	531	529	527	526	524	522	520	518	516	514
1400]	563	560	558	555	553	551	549	547	545	543	541	539	537	535	533	532
1450]	580	578	575	573	571	569	567	564	562	560	558	556	554	553	551	549
1500]	598	595	593	590	588	586	584	582	580	578	576	574	572	570	568	566
1550]	615	613	610	608	606	603	601	599	597	595	593	591	589	587	585	583
1600]	632	630	627	625	623	621	618	616	614	612	610	608	606	604	602	600
1650]	650	647	645	642	640	638	635	633	631	629	627	625	623	621	619	617
1700]	667	664	662	659	657	655	652	650	648	646	644	642	640	638	636	634
1750]	684	681	679	676	674	671	669	667	665	662	660	658	656	654	652	651
1800]	701	698	696	693	691	688	686	684	681	679	677	675	673	671	669	667
1850]	718	715	712	710	707	705	703	700	698	696	694	692	690	688	686	684
1900]	734	732	729	727	724	722	719	717	715	713	710	708	706	704	702	701
1950]	751	748	746	743	741	738	736	734	731	729	727	725	723	721	719	717
2000]	767	765	762	760	757	755	752	750	748	746	744	741	739	737	735	734
2050]	784	781	779	776	774	771	769	767	764	762	760	758	756	754	752	750
2100]	800	798	795	792	790	788	785	783	781	778	776	774	772	770	768	766
2150]	817	814	811	809	806	804	802	799	797	795	793	791	789	787	785	783
2200]	833	830	828	825	823	820	818	816	813	811	809	807	805	803	801	799
2250]	849	846	844	841	839	836	834	832	830	827	825	823	821	819	817	815
2300]	865	863	860	858	855	853	850	848	846	844	841	839	837	835	833	831
2350]	881	879	876	874	871	869	866	864	862	860	858	855	853	851	849	847
2400]	897	895	892	890	887	885	883	880	878	876	874	872	869	867	865	864
2450]	913	911	908	906	903	901	899	896	894	892	890	888	886	883	882	880
2500]	929	927	924	922	919	917	915	912	910	908	906	904	902	900	898	896

NONCUSTODIAL PARENT MONTHLY INCOME

Effective October 1, 2004

Three Children - Monthly Support

CUSTODIAL PARENT MONTHLY INCOME

	1850	1900	1950	2000	2050	2100	2150	2200	2250	2300	2350	2400	2450	2500	2550	2600
2550]	945	943	940	938	935	933	931	928	926	924	922	920	917	915	913	912
2600]	961	959	956	954	951	949	946	944	942	940	938	935	933	931	929	927
2650]	977	974	972	969	967	965	962	960	958	956	953	951	949	947	945	943
2700]	993	990	988	985	983	980	978	976	974	971	969	967	965	963	961	958
2750]	1009	1006	1004	1001	999	996	994	992	989	987	985	983	981	979	976	973
2800]	1024	1022	1019	1017	1014	1012	1010	1007	1005	1003	1001	999	997	994	990	987
2850]	1040	1037	1035	1032	1030	1028	1025	1023	1021	1019	1017	1015	1011	1008	1005	1002
2900]	1056	1053	1051	1048	1046	1043	1041	1039	1037	1035	1032	1029	1026	1023	1019	1016
2950]	1071	1069	1066	1064	1061	1059	1057	1055	1052	1050	1047	1043	1040	1037	1034	1031
3000]	1087	1084	1082	1079	1077	1075	1072	1070	1068	1065	1061	1058	1055	1051	1048	1045
3050]	1102	1100	1097	1095	1093	1090	1088	1086	1082	1079	1075	1072	1069	1066	1063	1059
3100]	1118	1115	1113	1111	1108	1106	1104	1100	1097	1093	1090	1086	1083	1080	1077	1074
3150]	1133	1131	1128	1126	1124	1121	1118	1114	1111	1107	1104	1101	1097	1094	1091	1088
3200]	1149	1146	1144	1142	1139	1136	1132	1128	1125	1121	1118	1115	1112	1108	1105	1102
3250]	1164	1162	1159	1157	1153	1150	1146	1142	1139	1136	1132	1129	1126	1123	1119	1116
3300]	1180	1177	1175	1171	1167	1164	1160	1157	1153	1150	1146	1143	1140	1137	1134	1130
3350]	1195	1193	1189	1185	1181	1178	1174	1171	1167	1164	1160	1157	1154	1151	1148	1145
3400]	1210	1206	1203	1199	1195	1192	1188	1184	1181	1178	1174	1171	1168	1165	1162	1159
3450]	1224	1220	1217	1213	1209	1205	1202	1198	1195	1192	1188	1185	1182	1179	1176	1173
3500]	1238	1234	1230	1227	1223	1219	1216	1212	1209	1206	1202	1199	1196	1193	1190	1187
3550]	1252	1248	1244	1240	1237	1233	1230	1226	1223	1219	1216	1213	1210	1207	1203	1200
3600]	1265	1262	1258	1254	1251	1247	1243	1240	1237	1233	1230	1227	1224	1220	1217	1214
3650]	1279	1275	1272	1268	1264	1261	1257	1254	1250	1247	1244	1241	1237	1234	1231	1228
3700]	1293	1289	1285	1282	1278	1274	1271	1267	1264	1261	1258	1254	1251	1248	1245	1242
3750]	1306	1303	1299	1295	1292	1288	1285	1281	1278	1275	1271	1268	1265	1262	1259	1256
3800]	1320	1316	1312	1309	1305	1302	1298	1295	1291	1288	1285	1282	1279	1276	1272	1269
3850]	1334	1330	1326	1322	1319	1315	1312	1308	1305	1302	1299	1295	1292	1289	1286	1283
3900]	1347	1343	1340	1336	1332	1329	1325	1322	1319	1315	1312	1309	1306	1303	1300	1296
3950]	1361	1357	1353	1350	1346	1342	1339	1336	1332	1329	1326	1323	1320	1317	1313	1309
4000]	1374	1370	1367	1363	1359	1356	1353	1349	1346	1343	1339	1336	1333	1329	1325	1321
4050]	1387	1384	1380	1376	1373	1369	1366	1363	1359	1356	1353	1350	1346	1342	1338	1334
4100]	1401	1397	1393	1390	1386	1383	1380	1376	1373	1370	1367	1363	1358	1354	1350	1346
4150]	1414	1410	1407	1403	1400	1396	1393	1390	1386	1383	1379	1375	1371	1367	1362	1358
4200]	1427	1424	1420	1417	1413	1410	1406	1403	1400	1396	1392	1387	1383	1379	1375	1371
4250]	1441	1437	1434	1430	1427	1423	1420	1417	1413	1408	1404	1400	1395	1391	1387	1383
4300]	1454	1450	1447	1443	1440	1437	1433	1429	1425	1420	1416	1412	1407	1403	1399	1395
4350]	1467	1464	1460	1457	1453	1450	1446	1441	1437	1432	1428	1424	1420	1416	1411	1407
4400]	1481	1477	1473	1470	1467	1462	1458	1453	1449	1445	1440	1436	1432	1428	1424	1420
4450]	1494	1490	1487	1483	1479	1474	1470	1465	1461	1457	1452	1448	1444	1440	1436	1432
4500]	1507	1503	1500	1496	1491	1486	1482	1477	1473	1469	1464	1460	1456	1452	1448	1444
4550]	1520	1517	1512	1508	1503	1498	1494	1489	1485	1481	1476	1472	1468	1464	1460	1456
4600]	1533	1529	1524	1519	1515	1510	1506	1501	1497	1493	1488	1484	1480	1476	1472	1468
4650]	1546	1541	1536	1531	1527	1522	1518	1513	1509	1504	1500	1496	1492	1488	1484	1480
4700]	1557	1552	1548	1543	1538	1534	1529	1525	1521	1516	1512	1508	1504	1500	1496	1492
4750]	1569	1564	1559	1555	1550	1546	1541	1537	1533	1528	1524	1520	1516	1512	1508	1504
4800]	1581	1576	1571	1567	1562	1557	1553	1549	1544	1540	1536	1532	1528	1524	1520	1516
4850]	1592	1588	1583	1578	1574	1569	1565	1560	1556	1552	1548	1544	1540	1536	1532	1528
4900]	1604	1599	1594	1590	1585	1581	1577	1572	1568	1564	1560	1555	1551	1547	1543	1540
4950]	1615	1611	1606	1602	1597	1593	1588	1584	1580	1575	1571	1567	1563	1559	1555	1551
5000]	1627	1622	1618	1613	1609	1604	1600	1596	1591	1587	1583	1579	1575	1571	1567	1563

NONCUSTODIAL PARENT MONTHLY INCOME

Effective October 1, 2004

Three Children - Monthly Support

CUSTODIAL PARENT MONTHLY INCOME

	2650	2700	2750	2800	2850	2900	2950	3000	3050	3100	3150	3200	3250	3300	3350	3400
250]	25	25	25	25	25	25	25	25	25	25	25	25	25	25	25	25
300]	25	25	25	25	25	25	25	25	25	25	25	25	25	25	25	25
350]	25	25	25	25	25	25	25	25	25	25	25	25	25	25	25	25
400]	25	25	25	25	25	25	25	25	25	25	25	25	25	25	25	25
450]	25	25	25	25	25	25	25	25	25	25	25	25	25	25	25	25
500]	25	25	25	25	25	25	25	25	25	25	25	25	25	25	25	25
550]	28	25	25	25	25	25	25	25	25	25	25	25	25	25	25	25
600]	30	25	25	25	25	25	25	25	25	25	25	25	25	25	25	25
650]	33	26	26	26	26	26	26	26	26	26	25	25	25	25	25	25
700]	35	28	28	28	28	28	28	28	28	28	25	25	25	25	25	25
750]	38	30	30	30	30	30	30	30	30	30	25	25	25	25	25	25
800]	63	55	55	55	55	55	55	55	55	55	49	49	49	49	49	49
850]	113	105	105	105	105	105	105	105	105	105	99	99	99	99	99	99
900]	163	155	155	155	155	155	155	155	155	155	149	149	149	149	149	149
950]	213	205	205	205	205	205	205	205	205	205	199	199	199	199	199	199
1000]	263	255	255	255	255	255	255	255	255	255	249	249	249	249	249	249
1050]	313	305	305	305	305	305	305	305	305	305	299	299	299	299	299	299
1100]	363	355	355	355	355	355	355	355	355	355	349	349	349	349	349	349
1150]	413	405	405	405	405	405	405	405	405	405	399	399	399	399	399	399
1200]	460	455	455	455	454	453	451	450	449	447	446	445	444	442	441	440
1250]	478	476	475	473	472	470	469	467	466	465	463	462	461	460	458	457
1300]	495	494	492	491	489	488	486	485	483	482	481	479	478	477	476	474
1350]	513	511	509	508	506	505	503	502	500	499	498	496	495	494	493	491
1400]	530	528	527	525	523	522	520	519	518	516	515	513	512	511	510	508
1450]	547	545	544	542	541	539	538	536	535	533	532	530	529	528	527	525
1500]	564	563	561	559	558	556	555	553	552	550	549	547	546	545	543	542
1550]	581	580	578	576	575	573	571	570	568	567	566	564	563	562	560	559
1600]	598	597	595	593	592	590	588	587	585	584	582	581	580	578	577	576
1650]	615	613	612	610	608	607	605	604	602	601	599	598	596	595	594	592
1700]	632	630	628	627	625	623	622	620	619	617	616	614	613	612	610	609
1750]	649	647	645	644	642	640	639	637	635	634	633	631	630	628	627	626
1800]	665	664	662	660	658	657	655	654	652	651	649	648	646	645	643	642
1850]	682	680	679	677	675	673	672	670	669	667	666	664	663	661	660	659
1900]	699	697	695	693	692	690	688	687	685	684	682	681	679	678	676	674
1950]	715	713	712	710	708	706	705	703	702	700	699	697	696	694	692	690
2000]	732	730	728	726	725	723	721	720	718	716	715	713	712	710	707	705
2050]	748	746	744	743	741	739	738	736	734	733	731	730	727	725	723	721
2100]	764	763	761	759	757	756	754	752	751	749	748	745	743	740	738	736
2150]	781	779	777	775	774	772	770	769	767	765	763	760	758	756	753	751
2200]	797	795	793	792	790	788	786	785	783	781	778	776	773	771	769	766
2250]	813	811	810	808	806	804	803	801	798	796	793	791	789	786	784	782
2300]	829	828	826	824	822	820	819	816	814	811	809	806	804	801	799	797
2350]	846	844	842	840	838	837	834	831	829	826	824	821	819	816	814	812
2400]	862	860	858	856	854	852	849	846	844	841	839	836	834	831	829	827
2450]	878	876	874	872	869	867	864	861	859	856	854	851	849	846	844	842
2500]	894	892	890	887	884	882	879	876	874	871	868	866	863	861	859	856

NONCUSTODIAL PARENT MONTHLY INCOME

Three Children - Monthly Support

CUSTODIAL PARENT MONTHLY INCOME

NON-CUSTODIAL PARENT MONTHLY INCOME	2650	2700	2750	2800	2850	2900	2950	3000	3050	3100	3150	3200	3250	3300	3350	3400
2550]	910	908	905	902	899	896	894	891	888	886	883	881	878	876	874	871
2600]	926	923	920	917	914	911	908	906	903	901	898	896	893	891	888	886
2650]	940	937	934	932	929	926	923	921	918	915	913	910	908	905	903	901
2700]	955	952	949	946	943	941	938	935	933	930	927	925	922	920	918	915
2750]	970	967	964	961	958	955	953	950	947	945	942	940	937	935	932	930
2800]	984	981	978	975	973	970	967	964	962	959	957	954	952	949	947	944
2850]	999	996	993	990	987	984	982	979	976	974	971	969	966	964	961	959
2900]	1013	1010	1007	1004	1002	999	996	993	991	988	986	983	981	978	976	973
2950]	1028	1025	1022	1019	1016	1013	1011	1008	1005	1003	1000	998	995	993	990	988
3000]	1042	1039	1036	1033	1030	1028	1025	1022	1020	1017	1014	1012	1009	1007	1005	1002
3050]	1056	1053	1051	1048	1045	1042	1039	1037	1034	1031	1029	1026	1024	1021	1019	1017
3100]	1071	1068	1065	1062	1059	1056	1054	1051	1048	1046	1043	1041	1038	1036	1033	1030
3150]	1085	1082	1079	1076	1073	1071	1068	1065	1063	1060	1057	1055	1052	1050	1047	1044
3200]	1099	1096	1093	1090	1088	1085	1082	1079	1077	1074	1072	1069	1067	1064	1060	1057
3250]	1113	1110	1107	1105	1102	1099	1096	1094	1091	1088	1086	1083	1080	1077	1073	1070
3300]	1127	1124	1122	1119	1116	1113	1110	1108	1105	1102	1100	1097	1093	1090	1087	1083
3350]	1142	1139	1136	1133	1130	1127	1124	1122	1119	1117	1113	1110	1107	1103	1100	1097
3400]	1156	1153	1150	1147	1144	1141	1139	1136	1133	1130	1127	1123	1120	1116	1113	1110
3450]	1170	1167	1164	1161	1158	1155	1153	1150	1147	1143	1140	1136	1133	1129	1126	1123
3500]	1184	1181	1178	1175	1172	1169	1167	1163	1160	1156	1153	1149	1146	1142	1139	1136
3550]	1197	1195	1192	1189	1186	1183	1180	1176	1173	1169	1165	1162	1159	1155	1152	1149
3600]	1211	1208	1206	1203	1200	1197	1193	1189	1185	1182	1178	1175	1171	1168	1165	1161
3650]	1225	1222	1219	1217	1213	1209	1206	1202	1198	1195	1191	1188	1184	1181	1178	1174
3700]	1239	1236	1233	1230	1226	1222	1218	1215	1211	1208	1204	1201	1197	1194	1190	1187
3750]	1253	1250	1246	1242	1239	1235	1231	1227	1224	1220	1217	1213	1210	1207	1203	1200
3800]	1267	1263	1259	1255	1251	1248	1244	1240	1237	1233	1229	1226	1223	1219	1216	1213
3850]	1280	1276	1272	1268	1264	1260	1256	1253	1249	1246	1242	1239	1235	1232	1229	1225
3900]	1292	1288	1284	1280	1277	1273	1269	1265	1262	1258	1255	1251	1248	1245	1241	1238
3950]	1305	1301	1297	1293	1289	1285	1282	1278	1274	1271	1267	1264	1261	1257	1254	1251
4000]	1317	1313	1309	1305	1302	1298	1294	1291	1287	1283	1280	1276	1273	1270	1266	1263
4050]	1330	1326	1322	1318	1314	1310	1307	1303	1299	1296	1292	1289	1286	1282	1279	1276
4100]	1342	1338	1334	1330	1327	1323	1319	1315	1312	1308	1305	1301	1298	1295	1291	1288
4150]	1354	1350	1347	1343	1339	1335	1332	1328	1324	1321	1317	1314	1311	1307	1304	1301
4200]	1367	1363	1359	1355	1351	1348	1344	1340	1337	1333	1330	1326	1323	1320	1316	1313
4250]	1379	1375	1371	1367	1364	1360	1356	1353	1349	1346	1342	1339	1335	1332	1329	1326
4300]	1391	1387	1383	1380	1376	1372	1369	1365	1361	1358	1354	1351	1348	1344	1341	1338
4350]	1403	1400	1396	1392	1388	1384	1381	1377	1374	1370	1367	1363	1360	1357	1353	1350
4400]	1416	1412	1408	1404	1400	1397	1393	1389	1386	1382	1379	1376	1372	1369	1366	1362
4450]	1428	1424	1420	1416	1413	1409	1405	1402	1398	1395	1391	1388	1385	1381	1378	1375
4500]	1440	1436	1432	1428	1425	1421	1417	1414	1410	1407	1403	1400	1397	1393	1390	1387
4550]	1452	1448	1444	1441	1437	1433	1430	1426	1423	1419	1416	1412	1409	1406	1402	1399
4600]	1464	1460	1456	1453	1449	1445	1442	1438	1435	1431	1428	1424	1421	1418	1415	1411
4650]	1476	1472	1468	1465	1461	1457	1454	1450	1447	1443	1440	1437	1433	1430	1427	1424
4700]	1488	1484	1480	1477	1473	1469	1466	1462	1459	1455	1452	1449	1445	1442	1439	1436
4750]	1500	1496	1492	1489	1485	1481	1478	1474	1471	1467	1464	1461	1457	1454	1451	1448
4800]	1512	1508	1504	1501	1497	1493	1490	1486	1483	1479	1476	1473	1469	1466	1463	1459
4850]	1524	1520	1516	1513	1509	1505	1502	1498	1495	1491	1488	1485	1481	1478	1475	1471
4900]	1536	1532	1528	1525	1521	1517	1514	1510	1507	1503	1500	1497	1493	1490	1487	1483
4950]	1548	1544	1540	1536	1533	1529	1526	1522	1519	1515	1512	1509	1505	1502	1498	1495
5000]	1559	1556	1552	1548	1545	1541	1538	1534	1531	1527	1524	1520	1517	1513	1510	1507

2004 MICHIGAN CHILD SUPPORT FORMULA SCHEDULES
MONTHLY BASE SUPPORT

Three Children - Monthly Support

CUSTODIAL PARENT MONTHLY INCOME

		3450	3500	3550	3600	3650	3700	3750	3800	3850	3900	3950	4000	4050	4100	4150	4200
	250]	25	25	25	25	25	25	25	25	25	25	25	25	25	25	25	25
	300]	25	25	25	25	25	25	25	25	25	25	25	25	25	25	25	25
	350]	25	25	25	25	25	25	25	25	25	25	25	25	25	25	25	25
	400]	25	25	25	25	25	25	25	25	25	25	25	25	25	25	25	25
	450]	25	25	25	25	25	25	25	25	25	25	25	25	25	25	25	25
	500]	25	25	25	25	25	25	25	25	25	25	25	25	25	25	25	25
N	550]	25	25	25	25	25	25	25	25	25	25	25	25	25	25	25	25
O	600]	25	25	25	25	25	25	25	25	25	25	25	25	25	25	25	25
N	650]	25	25	25	25	25	25	25	25	25	25	25	25	25	25	25	25
C	700]	25	25	25	25	25	25	25	25	25	25	25	25	25	25	25	25
U	750]	25	25	25	25	25	25	25	25	25	25	25	25	25	25	25	25
S	800]	49	49	49	49	49	49	49	49	49	49	49	49	49	49	49	49
T	850]	99	99	99	99	99	99	99	99	99	99	99	99	99	99	99	99
O	900]	149	149	149	149	149	149	149	149	149	149	149	149	149	149	149	149
D	950]	199	199	199	199	199	199	199	199	199	199	199	199	199	199	199	199
I																	
A	1000]	249	249	249	249	249	249	249	249	249	249	249	249	249	249	249	249
L	1050]	299	299	299	299	299	299	299	299	299	299	299	299	299	299	299	299
	1100]	349	349	349	349	349	349	349	349	349	349	349	349	349	349	349	349
P	1150]	399	399	399	399	399	399	399	399	399	399	399	399	399	399	399	399
A	1200]	439	438	437	436	435	434	433	432	431	430	429	428	427	426	424	423
R	1250]	456	455	454	453	452	451	450	449	448	447	446	445	444	442	441	439
E	1300]	473	472	471	470	469	468	467	466	465	464	463	461	460	458	457	456
N	1350]	490	489	488	487	486	485	484	483	482	481	479	478	476	475	473	472
T	1400]	507	506	505	504	503	502	500	499	498	497	495	494	492	491	489	488
	1450]	524	523	522	521	519	518	517	516	515	513	511	510	508	507	505	504
M																	
O	1500]	541	540	539	537	536	535	534	532	531	529	527	526	524	523	521	520
N	1550]	558	556	555	554	553	552	550	548	547	545	543	542	540	538	537	535
T	1600]	574	573	572	571	570	568	566	564	562	561	559	557	556	554	553	551
H	1650]	591	590	589	587	586	584	582	580	578	577	575	573	572	570	568	567
L	1700]	608	606	605	603	601	599	598	596	594	592	591	589	587	586	584	582
Y	1750]	624	623	621	619	617	615	613	611	610	608	606	604	603	601	599	598
	1800]	641	639	637	635	633	631	629	627	625	623	622	620	618	617	615	613
I	1850]	656	654	652	650	648	646	644	643	641	639	637	635	634	632	630	629
N	1900]	672	670	668	666	664	662	660	658	656	654	653	651	649	647	646	644
C	1950]	688	685	683	681	679	677	675	674	672	670	668	666	664	663	661	659
O																	
M	2000]	703	701	699	697	695	693	691	689	687	685	683	682	680	678	676	675
E	2050]	718	716	714	712	710	708	706	704	702	700	699	697	695	693	691	690
	2100]	734	732	729	727	725	723	721	719	717	716	714	712	710	708	707	705
	2150]	749	747	745	743	741	738	737	735	733	731	729	727	725	723	722	720
	2200]	764	762	760	758	756	754	752	750	748	746	744	742	740	738	737	735
	2250]	779	777	775	773	771	769	767	765	763	761	759	757	755	753	752	750
	2300]	794	792	790	788	786	784	782	780	778	776	774	772	770	768	767	764
	2350]	809	807	805	803	801	799	797	795	793	791	789	787	785	783	781	779
	2400]	824	822	820	818	816	814	812	810	808	806	804	802	800	798	795	793
	2450]	839	837	835	833	831	828	826	824	822	820	818	817	814	812	809	807
	2500]	854	852	850	848	845	843	841	839	837	835	833	831	828	826	823	821

Effective October 1, 2004

Three Children - Monthly Support

CUSTODIAL PARENT MONTHLY INCOME

		3450	3500	3550	3600	3650	3700	3750	3800	3850	3900	3950	4000	4050	4100	4150	4200
	2550]	869	867	864	862	860	858	856	854	852	850	848	845	842	840	837	835
	2600]	884	881	879	877	875	873	871	869	867	864	861	859	856	854	851	849
	2650]	898	896	894	892	890	887	885	883	881	878	875	873	870	867	865	862
	2700]	913	911	908	906	904	902	900	897	895	892	889	886	884	881	879	876
	2750]	928	925	923	921	919	917	914	911	908	906	903	900	897	895	892	890
	2800]	942	940	938	935	933	931	928	925	922	919	916	914	911	909	906	903
	2850]	957	954	952	950	947	944	941	938	936	933	930	927	925	922	920	917
N	2900]	971	969	967	964	961	958	955	952	949	946	944	941	938	936	933	930
O	2950]	986	983	980	977	974	971	968	966	963	960	957	954	952	949	947	944
N																	
C	3000]	1000	997	994	991	988	985	982	979	976	973	971	968	965	963	960	957
U	3050]	1014	1011	1007	1004	1001	998	995	992	990	987	984	981	979	976	973	971
S	3100]	1027	1024	1021	1018	1015	1012	1009	1006	1003	1000	997	995	992	989	987	984
T	3150]	1040	1037	1034	1031	1028	1025	1022	1019	1016	1013	1011	1008	1005	1003	1000	997
O	3200]	1054	1051	1047	1044	1041	1038	1035	1032	1030	1027	1024	1021	1018	1016	1013	1011
D	3250]	1067	1064	1061	1058	1055	1052	1049	1046	1043	1040	1037	1034	1032	1029	1026	1024
I	3300]	1080	1077	1074	1071	1068	1065	1062	1059	1056	1053	1050	1048	1045	1042	1039	1037
A	3350]	1093	1090	1087	1084	1081	1078	1075	1072	1069	1066	1063	1061	1058	1055	1053	1050
L	3400]	1106	1103	1100	1097	1094	1091	1088	1085	1082	1079	1076	1074	1071	1068	1066	1063
	3450]	1119	1116	1113	1110	1107	1104	1101	1098	1095	1092	1089	1087	1084	1081	1079	1076
P																	
A	3500]	1132	1129	1126	1123	1120	1117	1114	1111	1108	1105	1102	1100	1097	1094	1092	1089
R	3550]	1145	1142	1139	1136	1133	1130	1127	1124	1121	1118	1115	1113	1110	1107	1105	1102
E	3600]	1158	1155	1152	1149	1146	1143	1140	1137	1134	1131	1128	1126	1123	1120	1117	1115
N	3650]	1171	1168	1165	1162	1159	1156	1153	1150	1147	1144	1141	1138	1136	1133	1130	1128
T	3700]	1184	1181	1178	1175	1171	1168	1165	1163	1160	1157	1154	1151	1148	1146	1143	1140
	3750]	1197	1194	1190	1187	1184	1181	1178	1175	1172	1170	1167	1164	1161	1159	1156	1153
M	3800]	1209	1206	1203	1200	1197	1194	1191	1188	1185	1182	1179	1177	1174	1171	1169	1166
O	3850]	1222	1219	1216	1213	1210	1207	1204	1201	1198	1195	1192	1189	1187	1184	1181	1179
N	3900]	1235	1232	1228	1225	1222	1219	1216	1213	1211	1208	1205	1202	1199	1197	1194	1191
T	3950]	1247	1244	1241	1238	1235	1232	1229	1226	1223	1220	1217	1215	1212	1209	1207	1204
H																	
L	4000]	1260	1257	1254	1251	1248	1245	1242	1239	1236	1233	1230	1227	1225	1222	1219	1216
Y	4050]	1273	1269	1266	1263	1260	1257	1254	1251	1248	1245	1243	1240	1237	1234	1231	1229
	4100]	1285	1282	1279	1276	1273	1270	1267	1264	1261	1258	1255	1252	1250	1247	1244	1241
I	4150]	1297	1294	1291	1288	1285	1282	1279	1276	1273	1270	1268	1265	1262	1259	1256	1253
N	4200]	1310	1307	1304	1301	1298	1295	1292	1289	1286	1283	1280	1277	1274	1271	1268	1266
C	4250]	1322	1319	1316	1313	1310	1307	1304	1301	1298	1295	1292	1289	1286	1284	1281	1278
O	4300]	1335	1332	1328	1325	1322	1319	1316	1313	1310	1307	1304	1302	1299	1296	1293	1290
M	4350]	1347	1344	1341	1338	1335	1332	1329	1326	1323	1320	1317	1314	1311	1308	1305	1302
E	4400]	1359	1356	1353	1350	1347	1344	1341	1338	1335	1332	1329	1326	1323	1320	1317	1315
	4450]	1372	1368	1365	1362	1359	1356	1353	1350	1347	1344	1341	1338	1335	1332	1329	1327
	4500]	1384	1381	1378	1375	1371	1368	1365	1362	1359	1356	1353	1350	1347	1344	1342	1339
	4550]	1396	1393	1390	1387	1383	1380	1377	1374	1371	1368	1365	1362	1359	1356	1354	1351
	4600]	1408	1405	1402	1399	1396	1392	1389	1386	1383	1380	1377	1374	1371	1369	1366	1363
	4650]	1420	1417	1414	1411	1407	1404	1401	1398	1395	1392	1389	1386	1383	1381	1378	1375
	4700]	1432	1429	1426	1423	1419	1416	1413	1410	1407	1404	1401	1398	1395	1393	1390	1387
	4750]	1444	1441	1438	1435	1431	1428	1425	1422	1419	1416	1413	1410	1407	1404	1402	1399
	4800]	1456	1453	1450	1446	1443	1440	1437	1434	1431	1428	1425	1422	1419	1416	1414	1411
	4850]	1468	1465	1462	1458	1455	1452	1449	1446	1443	1440	1437	1434	1431	1428	1426	1423
	4900]	1480	1477	1473	1470	1467	1464	1461	1458	1455	1452	1449	1446	1443	1440	1437	1435
	4950]	1492	1488	1485	1482	1479	1476	1473	1470	1467	1464	1461	1458	1455	1452	1449	1446
	5000]	1503	1500	1497	1494	1491	1488	1484	1481	1478	1475	1473	1470	1467	1464	1461	1458

Effective October 1, 2004

Three Children - Monthly Support

CUSTODIAL PARENT MONTHLY INCOME

	4250	4300	4350	4400	4450	4500	4550	4600	4650	4700	4750	4800	4850	4900	4950	5000
250]	25	25	25	25	25	25	25	25	25	25	25	25	25	25	25	25
300]	25	25	25	25	25	25	25	25	25	25	25	25	25	25	25	25
350]	25	25	25	25	25	25	25	25	25	25	25	25	25	25	25	25
400]	25	25	25	25	25	25	25	25	25	25	25	25	25	25	25	25
450]	25	25	25	25	25	25	25	25	25	25	25	25	25	25	25	25
500]	25	25	25	25	25	25	25	25	25	25	25	25	25	25	25	25
550]	25	25	25	25	25	25	25	25	25	25	25	25	25	25	25	25
600]	25	25	25	25	25	25	25	25	25	25	25	25	25	25	25	25
650]	25	25	25	25	25	25	25	25	25	25	25	25	25	25	25	25
700]	25	25	25	25	25	25	25	25	25	25	25	25	25	25	25	25
750]	25	25	25	25	25	25	25	25	25	25	25	25	25	25	25	25
800]	49	49	49	49	49	49	49	49	49	49	49	49	49	49	49	49
850]	99	99	99	99	99	99	99	99	99	99	99	99	99	99	99	99
900]	149	149	149	149	149	149	149	149	149	149	149	149	149	149	149	149
950]	199	199	199	199	199	199	199	199	199	199	199	199	199	199	199	199
1000]	249	249	249	249	249	249	249	249	249	249	249	249	249	249	249	249
1050]	299	299	299	299	299	299	299	299	299	299	299	299	299	299	299	299
1100]	349	349	349	349	349	349	349	349	349	349	349	349	349	349	349	349
1150]	399	399	399	399	399	399	398	397	396	395	394	393	392	391	390	389
1200]	422	421	419	418	417	416	414	413	412	411	410	409	408	407	406	405
1250]	438	437	435	434	433	432	431	429	428	427	426	425	424	423	422	421
1300]	454	453	452	450	449	448	447	445	444	443	442	441	440	438	437	436
1350]	470	469	468	466	465	464	462	461	460	459	458	456	455	454	453	452
1400]	486	485	484	482	481	480	478	477	476	475	473	472	471	470	469	468
1450]	502	501	499	498	497	495	494	493	492	490	489	488	487	486	484	483
1500]	518	517	515	514	512	511	510	509	507	506	505	504	502	501	500	499
1550]	534	532	531	530	528	527	525	524	523	522	520	519	518	517	515	514
1600]	550	548	547	545	544	542	541	540	538	537	536	535	533	532	530	528
1650]	565	564	562	561	559	558	557	555	554	553	551	550	548	547	545	543
1700]	581	579	578	576	575	573	572	571	569	568	567	565	563	562	560	558
1750]	596	595	593	592	590	589	587	586	585	583	582	580	578	576	575	573
1800]	612	610	609	607	606	604	603	601	600	598	596	595	593	591	589	587
1850]	627	626	624	622	621	620	618	617	615	613	611	609	607	606	604	602
1900]	642	641	639	638	636	635	633	631	630	628	626	624	622	620	618	616
1950]	658	656	655	653	651	650	648	646	644	642	640	638	636	635	633	631
2000]	673	671	670	668	667	665	663	661	659	657	655	653	651	649	647	645
2050]	688	686	685	683	681	679	677	675	673	671	669	667	665	663	661	660
2100]	703	702	700	698	696	694	692	689	687	685	683	681	679	678	676	674
2150]	718	717	715	712	710	708	706	704	702	700	698	696	694	692	690	688
2200]	733	731	729	727	724	722	720	718	716	714	712	710	708	706	704	702
2250]	748	745	743	741	739	736	734	732	730	728	726	724	722	720	718	716
2300]	762	760	757	755	753	751	748	746	744	742	740	738	736	734	732	730
2350]	776	774	772	769	767	765	763	760	758	756	754	752	750	748	746	744
2400]	790	788	786	783	781	779	777	774	772	770	768	766	764	762	760	758
2450]	804	802	800	797	795	793	790	788	786	784	782	780	778	776	774	772
2500]	818	816	814	811	809	807	804	802	800	798	796	794	792	789	787	785

NONCUSTODIAL PARENT MONTHLY INCOME

2004 MICHIGAN CHILD SUPPORT FORMULA SCHEDULES
MONTHLY BASE SUPPORT

Three Children - Monthly Support

CUSTODIAL PARENT MONTHLY INCOME

	4250	4300	4350	4400	4450	4500	4550	4600	4650	4700	4750	4800	4850	4900	4950	5000
2550]	832	830	827	825	823	820	818	816	814	812	809	807	805	803	801	799
2600]	846	844	841	839	837	834	832	830	828	825	823	821	819	817	815	813
2650]	860	857	855	853	850	848	846	843	841	839	837	835	833	831	829	826
2700]	874	871	869	866	864	862	859	857	855	853	850	848	846	844	842	840
2750]	887	885	882	880	878	875	873	871	868	866	864	862	860	858	856	854
2800]	901	898	896	894	891	889	887	884	882	880	878	875	873	871	869	867
2850]	914	912	909	907	905	902	900	898	895	893	891	889	887	885	883	880
2900]	928	925	923	921	918	916	913	911	909	907	904	902	900	898	896	894
2950]	941	939	936	934	932	929	927	925	922	920	918	916	913	911	909	907
3000]	955	952	950	947	945	943	940	938	936	933	931	929	927	925	923	920
3050]	968	966	963	961	958	956	954	951	949	947	944	942	940	938	936	934
3100]	981	979	976	974	972	969	967	965	962	960	958	955	953	951	949	947
3150]	995	992	990	987	985	982	980	978	975	973	971	969	966	964	962	960
3200]	1008	1005	1003	1000	998	996	993	991	989	986	984	982	980	977	975	973
3250]	1021	1019	1016	1014	1011	1009	1006	1004	1002	999	997	995	993	990	988	986
3300]	1034	1032	1029	1027	1024	1022	1019	1017	1015	1012	1010	1008	1006	1003	1001	999
3350]	1047	1045	1042	1040	1037	1035	1033	1030	1028	1026	1023	1021	1019	1016	1014	1012
3400]	1060	1058	1055	1053	1050	1048	1046	1043	1041	1039	1036	1034	1031	1029	1027	1025
3450]	1073	1071	1068	1066	1063	1061	1059	1056	1054	1051	1049	1047	1044	1042	1040	1037
3500]	1086	1084	1081	1079	1076	1074	1071	1069	1067	1064	1062	1059	1057	1055	1052	1050
3550]	1099	1097	1094	1092	1089	1087	1084	1082	1079	1077	1075	1072	1070	1067	1065	1063
3600]	1112	1110	1107	1105	1102	1100	1097	1095	1092	1090	1087	1085	1082	1080	1078	1076
3650]	1125	1122	1120	1117	1115	1112	1110	1107	1105	1102	1100	1098	1095	1093	1090	1088
3700]	1138	1135	1133	1130	1128	1125	1122	1120	1117	1115	1113	1110	1108	1105	1103	1101
3750]	1151	1148	1145	1143	1140	1138	1135	1133	1130	1128	1125	1123	1120	1118	1116	1113
3800]	1163	1161	1158	1155	1153	1150	1148	1145	1143	1140	1138	1135	1133	1131	1128	1126
3850]	1176	1173	1171	1168	1165	1163	1160	1158	1155	1153	1150	1148	1145	1143	1141	1138
3900]	1189	1186	1183	1180	1178	1175	1173	1170	1168	1165	1163	1160	1158	1156	1153	1151
3950]	1201	1198	1196	1193	1190	1188	1185	1183	1180	1178	1175	1173	1170	1168	1166	1163
4000]	1213	1211	1208	1205	1203	1200	1198	1195	1193	1190	1188	1185	1183	1180	1178	1176
4050]	1226	1223	1220	1218	1215	1213	1210	1207	1205	1202	1200	1198	1195	1193	1190	1188
4100]	1238	1236	1233	1230	1228	1225	1222	1220	1217	1215	1212	1210	1207	1205	1203	1200
4150]	1251	1248	1245	1242	1240	1237	1235	1232	1230	1227	1225	1222	1220	1217	1215	1213
4200]	1263	1260	1257	1255	1252	1250	1247	1244	1242	1239	1237	1234	1232	1230	1227	1225
4250]	1275	1272	1270	1267	1264	1262	1259	1257	1254	1252	1249	1247	1244	1242	1240	1237
4300]	1287	1285	1282	1279	1277	1274	1271	1269	1266	1264	1261	1259	1257	1254	1252	1249
4350]	1300	1297	1294	1291	1289	1286	1284	1281	1279	1276	1274	1271	1269	1266	1264	1262
4400]	1312	1309	1306	1304	1301	1298	1296	1293	1291	1288	1286	1283	1281	1279	1276	1274
4450]	1324	1321	1318	1316	1313	1311	1308	1305	1303	1300	1298	1295	1293	1291	1288	1286
4500]	1336	1333	1331	1328	1325	1323	1320	1318	1315	1312	1310	1308	1305	1303	1300	1298
4550]	1348	1345	1343	1340	1337	1335	1332	1330	1327	1325	1322	1320	1317	1315	1312	1310
4600]	1360	1357	1355	1352	1349	1347	1344	1342	1339	1337	1334	1332	1329	1327	1325	1322
4650]	1372	1369	1367	1364	1361	1359	1356	1354	1351	1349	1346	1344	1341	1339	1337	1334
4700]	1384	1381	1379	1376	1373	1371	1368	1366	1363	1361	1358	1356	1353	1351	1349	1346
4750]	1396	1393	1391	1388	1385	1383	1380	1378	1375	1373	1370	1368	1365	1363	1361	1358
4800]	1408	1405	1403	1400	1397	1395	1392	1390	1387	1385	1382	1380	1377	1375	1372	1370
4850]	1420	1417	1415	1412	1409	1407	1404	1402	1399	1396	1394	1392	1389	1387	1384	1382
4900]	1432	1429	1426	1424	1421	1419	1416	1413	1411	1408	1406	1403	1401	1399	1396	1394
4950]	1444	1441	1438	1436	1433	1430	1428	1425	1423	1420	1418	1415	1413	1411	1408	1406
5000]	1456	1453	1450	1448	1445	1442	1440	1437	1435	1432	1430	1427	1425	1422	1420	1418

NONCUSTODIAL PARENT MONTHLY INCOME

Effective October 1, 2004

2004 MICHIGAN CHILD SUPPORT FORMULA SCHEDULES
MONTHLY BASE SUPPORT

Four Children - Monthly Support

CUSTODIAL PARENT MONTHLY INCOME

		0	250	300	350	400	450	500	550	600	650	700	750	800	850	900	950	1000
	250]	25	25	25	25	25	25	25	25	25	25	25	25	25	25	25	25	25
	300]	30	30	30	30	30	30	30	30	30	30	30	30	27	27	25	25	25
	350]	35	35	35	35	35	35	35	35	35	35	35	35	32	32	28	28	28
	400]	40	40	40	40	40	40	40	40	40	40	40	40	36	36	32	32	32
	450]	45	45	45	45	45	45	45	45	45	45	45	45	41	41	36	36	36
	500]	50	50	50	50	50	50	50	50	50	50	50	50	45	45	40	40	40
N	550]	55	55	55	55	55	55	55	55	55	55	55	55	50	50	44	44	44
O	600]	60	60	60	60	60	60	60	60	60	60	60	60	54	54	48	48	48
N	650]	65	65	65	65	65	65	65	65	65	65	65	65	59	59	52	52	52
C	700]	70	70	70	70	70	70	70	70	70	70	70	70	63	63	56	56	56
U	750]	75	75	75	75	75	75	75	75	75	75	75	75	68	68	60	60	60
S	800]	102	102	102	102	102	102	102	102	102	102	102	102	94	94	86	86	86
T	850]	152	152	152	152	152	152	152	152	152	152	152	152	144	144	136	136	136
O	900]	202	202	202	202	202	202	202	202	202	202	202	202	194	194	186	186	186
D	950]	252	252	252	252	252	252	252	252	252	252	252	252	244	244	236	236	236
I																		
A	1000]	302	302	302	302	302	302	302	302	302	302	302	302	294	294	286	286	286
L	1050]	352	352	352	352	352	352	352	352	352	352	352	352	344	344	336	336	336
	1100]	402	402	402	402	402	402	402	402	402	402	402	402	394	394	386	386	386
P	1150]	452	452	452	452	452	452	452	452	452	452	452	452	444	444	436	436	436
A	1200]	502	502	502	502	502	502	502	502	502	502	502	502	494	494	486	486	486
R	1250]	552	552	552	552	552	552	552	552	552	552	552	552	544	544	536	536	536
E	1300]	602	602	602	602	602	602	602	602	602	602	602	602	594	594	586	586	586
N	1350]	652	652	652	652	652	652	652	652	652	652	652	652	644	644	636	636	636
T	1400]	702	702	702	702	702	702	702	702	702	702	702	702	694	694	686	686	686
	1450]	752	752	752	752	752	752	752	752	752	752	752	752	730	725	720	716	711
M																		
O	1500]	802	802	802	802	802	802	802	802	802	802	802	802	750	745	740	736	731
N	1550]	846	846	846	846	846	846	846	846	846	846	846	846	770	765	760	756	751
T	1600]	873	873	873	873	873	873	873	873	873	873	873	873	790	785	780	776	771
H	1650]	896	896	896	896	896	896	896	896	896	896	896	896	809	805	800	795	791
L	1700]	916	916	916	916	916	916	916	916	916	916	916	916	829	824	820	815	811
Y	1750]	936	936	936	936	936	936	936	936	936	936	936	936	848	844	839	835	830
	1800]	956	956	956	956	956	956	956	956	956	956	956	956	868	863	858	854	850
I	1850]	976	976	976	976	976	976	976	976	976	976	976	976	887	882	878	873	869
N	1900]	996	996	996	996	996	996	996	996	996	996	996	996	906	902	897	893	888
C	1950]	1015	1015	1015	1015	1015	1015	1015	1015	1015	1015	1015	1015	925	921	916	912	907
O																		
M	2000]	1035	1035	1035	1035	1035	1035	1035	1035	1035	1035	1035	1035	944	940	935	930	926
E	2050]	1055	1055	1055	1055	1055	1055	1055	1055	1055	1055	1055	1055	963	958	954	949	945
	2100]	1075	1075	1075	1075	1075	1075	1075	1075	1075	1075	1075	1075	982	977	972	968	963
	2150]	1095	1095	1095	1095	1095	1095	1095	1095	1095	1095	1095	1095	1000	995	991	986	982
	2200]	1115	1115	1115	1115	1115	1115	1115	1115	1115	1115	1115	1115	1018	1014	1009	1005	1000
	2250]	1133	1133	1133	1133	1133	1133	1133	1133	1133	1133	1133	1133	1037	1032	1027	1023	1019
	2300]	1150	1150	1150	1150	1150	1150	1150	1150	1150	1150	1150	1150	1055	1050	1046	1041	1037
	2350]	1168	1168	1168	1168	1168	1168	1168	1168	1168	1168	1168	1168	1073	1068	1064	1060	1055
	2400]	1185	1185	1185	1185	1185	1185	1185	1185	1185	1185	1185	1185	1091	1087	1082	1078	1074
	2450]	1202	1202	1202	1202	1202	1202	1202	1202	1202	1202	1202	1202	1109	1105	1100	1096	1092
	2500]	1219	1219	1219	1219	1219	1219	1219	1219	1219	1219	1219	1219	1127	1123	1118	1114	1110

(Left vertical label: NONCUSTODIAL PARENT MONTHLY INCOME)

Effective October 1, 2004

Four Children - Monthly Support

CUSTODIAL PARENT MONTHLY INCOME

	0	250	300	350	400	450	500	550	600	650	700	750	800	850	900	950	1000
2550]	1236	1236	1236	1236	1236	1236	1236	1236	1236	1236	1236	1236	1145	1141	1136	1132	1128
2600]	1253	1253	1253	1253	1253	1253	1253	1253	1253	1253	1253	1253	1163	1159	1154	1150	1146
2650]	1271	1271	1271	1271	1271	1271	1271	1271	1271	1271	1271	1271	1181	1177	1172	1168	1164
2700]	1288	1288	1288	1288	1288	1288	1288	1288	1288	1288	1288	1288	1199	1195	1190	1186	1182
2750]	1305	1305	1305	1305	1305	1305	1305	1305	1305	1305	1305	1305	1217	1212	1208	1204	1200
2800]	1322	1322	1322	1322	1322	1322	1322	1322	1322	1322	1322	1322	1234	1230	1226	1222	1217
2850]	1339	1339	1339	1339	1339	1339	1339	1339	1339	1339	1339	1339	1252	1248	1244	1239	1235
2900]	1356	1356	1356	1356	1356	1356	1356	1356	1356	1356	1356	1356	1270	1265	1261	1257	1252
2950]	1372	1372	1372	1372	1372	1372	1372	1372	1372	1372	1372	1372	1287	1283	1278	1274	1270
3000]	1389	1389	1389	1389	1389	1389	1389	1389	1389	1389	1389	1389	1304	1300	1296	1291	1287
3050]	1405	1405	1405	1405	1405	1405	1405	1405	1405	1405	1405	1405	1322	1317	1313	1309	1304
3100]	1422	1422	1422	1422	1422	1422	1422	1422	1422	1422	1422	1422	1339	1334	1330	1326	1322
3150]	1438	1438	1438	1438	1438	1438	1438	1438	1438	1438	1438	1438	1356	1351	1347	1343	1339
3200]	1455	1455	1455	1455	1455	1455	1455	1455	1455	1455	1455	1455	1373	1369	1364	1360	1356
3250]	1471	1471	1471	1471	1471	1471	1471	1471	1471	1471	1471	1471	1390	1386	1382	1377	1373
3300]	1488	1488	1488	1488	1488	1488	1488	1488	1488	1488	1488	1488	1407	1403	1399	1395	1391
3350]	1504	1504	1504	1504	1504	1504	1504	1504	1504	1504	1504	1504	1424	1420	1416	1412	1408
3400]	1521	1521	1521	1521	1521	1521	1521	1521	1521	1521	1521	1521	1441	1437	1433	1429	1425
3450]	1538	1538	1538	1538	1538	1538	1538	1538	1538	1538	1538	1538	1458	1454	1450	1446	1442
3500]	1554	1554	1554	1554	1554	1554	1554	1554	1554	1554	1554	1554	1475	1471	1467	1463	1459
3550]	1571	1571	1571	1571	1571	1571	1571	1571	1571	1571	1571	1571	1492	1488	1484	1480	1476
3600]	1587	1587	1587	1587	1587	1587	1587	1587	1587	1587	1587	1587	1509	1505	1501	1497	1493
3650]	1604	1604	1604	1604	1604	1604	1604	1604	1604	1604	1604	1604	1526	1522	1518	1514	1510
3700]	1620	1620	1620	1620	1620	1620	1620	1620	1620	1620	1620	1620	1542	1539	1535	1531	1527
3750]	1636	1636	1636	1636	1636	1636	1636	1636	1636	1636	1636	1636	1559	1555	1552	1548	1544
3800]	1652	1652	1652	1652	1652	1652	1652	1652	1652	1652	1652	1652	1576	1572	1568	1565	1561
3850]	1668	1668	1668	1668	1668	1668	1668	1668	1668	1668	1668	1668	1593	1589	1585	1582	1578
3900]	1684	1684	1684	1684	1684	1684	1684	1684	1684	1684	1684	1684	1610	1606	1602	1599	1595
3950]	1700	1700	1700	1700	1700	1700	1700	1700	1700	1700	1700	1700	1627	1623	1619	1615	1612
4000]	1716	1716	1716	1716	1716	1716	1716	1716	1716	1716	1716	1716	1643	1640	1636	1632	1629
4050]	1732	1732	1732	1732	1732	1732	1732	1732	1732	1732	1732	1732	1660	1656	1653	1649	1646
4100]	1748	1748	1748	1748	1748	1748	1748	1748	1748	1748	1748	1748	1677	1673	1669	1666	1662
4150]	1764	1764	1764	1764	1764	1764	1764	1764	1764	1764	1764	1764	1693	1690	1686	1683	1679
4200]	1780	1780	1780	1780	1780	1780	1780	1780	1780	1780	1780	1780	1710	1706	1703	1699	1696
4250]	1796	1796	1796	1796	1796	1796	1796	1796	1796	1796	1796	1796	1727	1723	1720	1716	1713
4300]	1812	1812	1812	1812	1812	1812	1812	1812	1812	1812	1812	1812	1743	1740	1736	1733	1727
4350]	1828	1828	1828	1828	1828	1828	1828	1828	1828	1828	1828	1828	1760	1757	1753	1747	1741
4400]	1844	1844	1844	1844	1844	1844	1844	1844	1844	1844	1844	1844	1777	1773	1767	1761	1754
4450]	1860	1860	1860	1860	1860	1860	1860	1860	1860	1860	1860	1860	1793	1787	1781	1774	1768
4500]	1876	1876	1876	1876	1876	1876	1876	1876	1876	1876	1876	1876	1807	1801	1794	1788	1782
4550]	1892	1892	1892	1892	1892	1892	1892	1892	1892	1892	1892	1892	1821	1814	1808	1802	1796
4600]	1908	1908	1908	1908	1908	1908	1908	1908	1908	1908	1908	1908	1834	1828	1822	1816	1810
4650]	1924	1924	1924	1924	1924	1924	1924	1924	1924	1924	1924	1924	1848	1841	1835	1829	1823
4700]	1940	1940	1940	1940	1940	1940	1940	1940	1940	1940	1940	1940	1861	1855	1849	1843	1837
4750]	1956	1956	1956	1956	1956	1956	1956	1956	1956	1956	1956	1956	1875	1869	1863	1857	1851
4800]	1972	1972	1972	1972	1972	1972	1972	1972	1972	1972	1972	1972	1888	1882	1876	1870	1864
4850]	1988	1988	1988	1988	1988	1988	1988	1988	1988	1988	1988	1988	1902	1896	1890	1884	1878
4900]	2004	2004	2004	2004	2004	2004	2004	2004	2004	2004	2004	2004	1915	1909	1903	1897	1892
4950]	2020	2020	2020	2020	2020	2020	2020	2020	2020	2020	2020	2020	1929	1923	1917	1911	1905
5000]	2036	2036	2036	2036	2036	2036	2036	2036	2036	2036	2036	2036	1942	1936	1930	1925	1919

(Row labels at left, reading vertically: NONCUSTODIAL PARENT MONTHLY INCOME)

Effective October 1, 2004

Four Children - Monthly Support

CUSTODIAL PARENT MONTHLY INCOME

	1050	1100	1150	1200	1250	1300	1350	1400	1450	1500	1550	1600	1650	1700	1750	1800
250]	25	25	25	25	25	25	25	25	25	25	25	25	25	25	25	25
300]	25	25	25	25	25	25	25	25	25	25	25	25	25	25	25	25
350]	28	28	28	28	28	28	25	25	25	25	25	25	25	25	25	25
400]	32	32	32	32	32	32	28	28	28	28	28	28	28	28	28	25
450]	36	36	36	36	36	36	32	32	32	32	32	32	32	32	32	27
500]	40	40	40	40	40	40	35	35	35	35	35	35	35	35	35	30
550]	44	44	44	44	44	44	39	39	39	39	39	39	39	39	39	33
600]	48	48	48	48	48	48	42	42	42	42	42	42	42	42	42	36
650]	52	52	52	52	52	52	46	46	46	46	46	46	46	46	46	39
700]	56	56	56	56	56	56	49	49	49	49	49	49	49	49	49	42
750]	60	60	60	60	60	60	53	53	53	53	53	53	53	53	53	45
800]	86	86	86	86	86	86	78	78	78	78	78	78	78	78	78	71
850]	136	136	136	136	136	136	128	128	128	128	128	128	128	128	128	121
900]	186	186	186	186	186	186	178	178	178	178	178	178	178	178	178	171
950]	236	236	236	236	236	236	228	228	228	228	228	228	228	228	228	221
1000]	286	286	286	286	286	286	278	278	278	278	278	278	278	278	278	271
1050]	336	336	336	336	336	336	328	328	328	328	328	328	328	328	328	321
1100]	386	386	386	386	386	386	378	378	378	378	378	378	378	378	378	371
1150]	436	436	436	436	436	436	428	428	428	428	428	428	428	428	428	421
1200]	486	486	486	486	486	486	478	478	478	478	478	478	478	478	478	471
1250]	536	536	536	536	536	536	528	528	528	528	528	528	528	528	528	521
1300]	586	586	586	586	586	586	578	578	578	578	578	578	578	578	578	571
1350]	636	636	636	636	636	636	628	628	628	628	628	628	625	622	619	616
1400]	686	683	679	675	671	668	664	661	658	654	651	648	645	642	639	637
1450]	707	703	699	695	692	688	685	681	678	674	671	668	665	662	659	656
1500]	727	723	719	715	712	708	705	701	698	694	691	688	685	682	679	676
1550]	747	743	739	735	732	728	725	721	717	714	711	708	705	702	699	696
1600]	767	763	759	755	752	748	744	741	737	734	731	727	724	721	719	716
1650]	787	783	779	775	771	767	764	760	757	753	750	747	744	741	738	735
1700]	807	803	799	795	791	787	783	780	776	773	770	767	763	761	758	755
1750]	826	822	818	814	810	806	803	799	796	792	789	786	783	780	777	774
1800]	846	841	837	833	829	826	822	818	815	812	808	805	802	799	796	794
1850]	865	861	856	852	848	845	841	838	834	831	828	824	821	819	816	813
1900]	884	880	875	871	868	864	860	857	853	850	847	844	841	838	835	832
1950]	903	898	894	890	887	883	879	876	872	869	866	863	860	857	854	851
2000]	921	917	913	909	905	902	898	895	891	888	885	882	879	876	873	870
2050]	940	936	932	928	924	921	917	914	910	907	904	901	898	894	891	888
2100]	959	955	951	947	943	939	936	932	929	926	923	920	916	913	910	907
2150]	977	973	969	966	962	958	955	951	948	945	941	938	935	932	928	925
2200]	996	992	988	984	980	977	973	970	967	963	960	957	953	950	947	944
2250]	1015	1010	1007	1003	999	995	992	989	985	982	978	975	972	968	965	962
2300]	1033	1029	1025	1021	1018	1014	1011	1007	1004	1000	997	993	990	987	984	981
2350]	1051	1047	1043	1040	1036	1033	1029	1025	1022	1018	1015	1011	1008	1005	1002	999
2400]	1070	1066	1062	1058	1055	1051	1047	1044	1040	1036	1033	1030	1026	1023	1020	1017
2450]	1088	1084	1080	1076	1073	1069	1065	1062	1058	1055	1051	1048	1045	1041	1038	1035
2500]	1106	1102	1098	1095	1091	1087	1083	1080	1076	1073	1069	1066	1063	1060	1057	1054

(Left margin vertical label: NONCUSTODIAL PARENT MONTHLY INCOME)

Effective October 1, 2004

Four Children - Monthly Support

CUSTODIAL PARENT MONTHLY INCOME

	1050	1100	1150	1200	1250	1300	1350	1400	1450	1500	1550	1600	1650	1700	1750	1800
2550]	1124	1120	1117	1113	1109	1105	1101	1098	1094	1091	1087	1084	1081	1078	1075	1072
2600]	1142	1139	1134	1130	1127	1123	1119	1116	1112	1109	1105	1102	1099	1096	1093	1090
2650]	1160	1156	1152	1148	1144	1141	1137	1133	1130	1126	1123	1120	1117	1114	1111	1108
2700]	1178	1174	1170	1166	1162	1158	1155	1151	1148	1144	1141	1138	1135	1132	1129	1126
2750]	1196	1192	1188	1184	1180	1176	1173	1169	1166	1162	1159	1156	1153	1149	1146	1144
2800]	1213	1209	1205	1201	1198	1194	1190	1187	1183	1180	1177	1173	1170	1167	1164	1161
2850]	1231	1227	1223	1219	1215	1212	1208	1204	1201	1198	1194	1191	1188	1185	1182	1179
2900]	1248	1244	1240	1236	1233	1229	1226	1222	1219	1215	1212	1209	1206	1203	1200	1197
2950]	1266	1262	1258	1254	1250	1247	1243	1240	1236	1233	1230	1227	1224	1221	1218	1215
3000]	1283	1279	1275	1271	1268	1264	1261	1257	1254	1251	1247	1244	1241	1238	1235	1232
3050]	1300	1297	1293	1289	1285	1282	1278	1275	1272	1268	1265	1262	1259	1256	1253	1250
3100]	1318	1314	1310	1306	1303	1299	1296	1292	1289	1286	1283	1280	1277	1274	1271	1268
3150]	1335	1331	1327	1324	1320	1317	1313	1310	1307	1303	1300	1297	1294	1291	1288	1285
3200]	1352	1349	1345	1341	1338	1334	1331	1327	1324	1321	1318	1315	1312	1309	1306	1303
3250]	1370	1366	1362	1358	1355	1351	1348	1345	1341	1338	1335	1332	1329	1326	1323	1320
3300]	1387	1383	1379	1376	1372	1369	1365	1362	1359	1356	1353	1350	1347	1344	1341	1338
3350]	1404	1400	1397	1393	1390	1386	1383	1379	1376	1373	1370	1367	1364	1361	1358	1355
3400]	1421	1417	1414	1410	1407	1403	1400	1397	1394	1390	1387	1384	1381	1379	1376	1373
3450]	1438	1435	1431	1427	1424	1421	1417	1414	1411	1408	1405	1402	1399	1396	1393	1390
3500]	1455	1452	1448	1445	1441	1438	1435	1431	1428	1425	1422	1419	1416	1413	1411	1405
3550]	1472	1469	1465	1462	1458	1455	1452	1449	1445	1442	1439	1436	1434	1431	1425	1420
3600]	1490	1486	1482	1479	1476	1472	1469	1466	1463	1460	1457	1454	1451	1446	1440	1435
3650]	1507	1503	1499	1496	1493	1489	1486	1483	1480	1477	1474	1471	1466	1460	1455	1450
3700]	1524	1520	1517	1513	1510	1507	1503	1500	1497	1494	1491	1486	1480	1475	1470	1465
3750]	1541	1537	1534	1530	1527	1524	1520	1517	1514	1511	1506	1500	1495	1490	1485	1480
3800]	1558	1554	1551	1547	1544	1541	1538	1534	1531	1526	1520	1515	1510	1505	1500	1495
3850]	1574	1571	1568	1564	1561	1558	1555	1552	1546	1540	1535	1530	1525	1520	1515	1510
3900]	1591	1588	1585	1581	1578	1575	1572	1566	1560	1555	1550	1544	1539	1534	1529	1524
3950]	1608	1605	1602	1598	1595	1592	1586	1580	1575	1570	1564	1559	1554	1549	1544	1539
4000]	1625	1622	1618	1615	1612	1606	1601	1595	1589	1584	1579	1574	1568	1563	1559	1554
4050]	1642	1639	1635	1632	1626	1621	1615	1609	1604	1598	1593	1588	1583	1578	1573	1568
4100]	1659	1656	1652	1646	1641	1635	1629	1624	1618	1613	1608	1603	1597	1593	1588	1583
4150]	1676	1672	1666	1661	1655	1649	1643	1638	1633	1627	1622	1617	1612	1607	1602	1597
4200]	1693	1687	1681	1675	1669	1663	1658	1652	1647	1642	1636	1631	1626	1621	1617	1612
4250]	1707	1701	1695	1689	1683	1677	1672	1666	1661	1656	1651	1646	1641	1636	1631	1626
4300]	1721	1715	1709	1703	1697	1692	1686	1681	1675	1670	1665	1660	1655	1650	1645	1641
4350]	1734	1728	1723	1717	1711	1706	1700	1695	1690	1684	1679	1674	1669	1665	1660	1655
4400]	1748	1742	1737	1731	1725	1720	1714	1709	1704	1699	1694	1689	1684	1679	1674	1670
4450]	1762	1756	1751	1745	1739	1734	1728	1723	1718	1713	1708	1703	1698	1693	1688	1684
4500]	1776	1770	1765	1759	1753	1748	1743	1737	1732	1727	1722	1717	1712	1707	1703	1698
4550]	1790	1784	1778	1773	1767	1762	1757	1751	1746	1741	1736	1731	1726	1722	1717	1712
4600]	1804	1798	1792	1787	1781	1776	1771	1765	1760	1755	1750	1745	1741	1736	1731	1727
4650]	1817	1812	1806	1801	1795	1790	1785	1779	1774	1769	1764	1760	1755	1750	1745	1741
4700]	1831	1826	1820	1814	1809	1804	1799	1793	1788	1783	1778	1774	1769	1764	1760	1755
4750]	1845	1839	1834	1828	1823	1818	1812	1807	1802	1797	1792	1788	1783	1778	1773	1768
4800]	1859	1853	1848	1842	1837	1832	1826	1821	1816	1811	1807	1802	1797	1792	1787	1782
4850]	1872	1867	1861	1856	1851	1845	1840	1835	1830	1825	1821	1816	1811	1806	1800	1795
4900]	1886	1880	1875	1870	1864	1859	1854	1849	1844	1839	1834	1829	1824	1819	1814	1809
4950]	1900	1894	1889	1883	1878	1873	1868	1863	1858	1853	1848	1843	1837	1832	1827	1822
5000]	1913	1908	1902	1897	1892	1887	1882	1877	1872	1867	1861	1856	1851	1846	1841	1836

NONCUSTODIAL PARENT MONTHLY INCOME

Effective October 1, 2004

2004 MICHIGAN CHILD SUPPORT FORMULA SCHEDULES
MONTHLY BASE SUPPORT

Four Children - Monthly Support

CUSTODIAL PARENT MONTHLY INCOME

	1850	1900	1950	2000	2050	2100	2150	2200	2250	2300	2350	2400	2450	2500	2550	2600
250]	25	25	25	25	25	25	25	25	25	25	25	25	25	25	25	25
300]	25	25	25	25	25	25	25	25	25	25	25	25	25	25	25	25
350]	25	25	25	25	25	25	25	25	25	25	25	25	25	25	25	25
400]	25	25	25	25	25	25	25	25	25	25	25	25	25	25	25	25
450]	27	27	27	27	27	27	27	27	25	25	25	25	25	25	25	25
500]	30	30	30	30	30	30	30	30	25	25	25	25	25	25	25	25
550]	33	33	33	33	33	33	33	33	28	28	28	28	28	28	28	28
600]	36	36	36	36	36	36	36	36	30	30	30	30	30	30	30	30
650]	39	39	39	39	39	39	39	39	33	33	33	33	33	33	33	33
700]	42	42	42	42	42	42	42	42	35	35	35	35	35	35	35	35
750]	45	45	45	45	45	45	45	45	38	38	38	38	38	38	38	38
800]	71	71	71	71	71	71	71	71	63	63	63	63	63	63	63	63
850]	121	121	121	121	121	121	121	121	113	113	113	113	113	113	113	113
900]	171	171	171	171	171	171	171	171	163	163	163	163	163	163	163	163
950]	221	221	221	221	221	221	221	221	213	213	213	213	213	213	213	213
1000]	271	271	271	271	271	271	271	271	263	263	263	263	263	263	263	263
1050]	321	321	321	321	321	321	321	321	313	313	313	313	313	313	313	313
1100]	371	371	371	371	371	371	371	371	363	363	363	363	363	363	363	363
1150]	421	421	421	421	421	421	421	421	413	413	413	413	413	413	413	413
1200]	471	471	471	471	471	471	471	471	463	463	463	463	463	463	463	463
1250]	521	521	521	521	521	521	521	521	513	513	513	513	513	513	513	513
1300]	571	571	571	571	571	571	571	571	563	563	563	563	563	563	563	561
1350]	614	611	609	606	604	602	599	597	595	593	591	589	587	585	583	581
1400]	634	631	629	626	624	622	619	617	615	613	611	609	607	605	603	601
1450]	654	651	649	646	644	642	639	637	635	633	630	628	626	624	622	620
1500]	674	671	669	666	664	661	659	657	654	652	650	648	646	644	642	640
1550]	693	691	688	686	683	681	679	676	674	672	669	667	665	663	661	659
1600]	713	710	708	705	703	701	698	696	693	691	689	686	684	682	680	678
1650]	733	730	727	725	723	720	717	715	713	710	708	706	704	701	699	697
1700]	752	750	747	744	742	739	737	734	732	729	727	725	723	721	718	716
1750]	772	769	766	764	761	758	756	753	751	748	746	744	742	740	737	735
1800]	791	788	785	783	780	777	775	772	770	767	765	763	761	759	756	754
1850]	810	807	804	802	799	796	794	791	789	786	784	782	780	777	775	773
1900]	829	826	823	821	818	815	813	810	808	805	803	801	798	796	794	792
1950]	848	845	842	839	837	834	831	829	826	824	822	819	817	815	813	811
2000]	867	864	861	858	855	853	850	848	845	843	840	838	836	834	832	830
2050]	885	882	880	877	874	871	869	866	864	861	859	857	855	852	850	848
2100]	904	901	898	895	893	890	887	885	883	880	878	875	873	871	869	867
2150]	922	920	917	914	911	909	906	904	901	899	896	894	892	890	887	885
2200]	941	938	935	932	930	927	925	922	920	917	915	913	910	908	906	904
2250]	959	956	954	951	948	946	943	940	938	936	933	931	929	926	924	922
2300]	978	975	972	969	967	964	961	959	956	954	952	949	947	945	943	941
2350]	996	993	990	988	985	982	980	977	975	972	970	968	965	963	961	959
2400]	1014	1011	1009	1006	1003	1001	998	995	993	991	988	986	984	981	979	977
2450]	1032	1030	1027	1024	1021	1019	1016	1014	1011	1009	1007	1004	1002	1000	998	995
2500]	1051	1048	1045	1042	1040	1037	1034	1032	1029	1027	1025	1022	1020	1018	1016	1014

NONCUSTODIAL PARENT MONTHLY INCOME

Effective October 1, 2004

Four Children - Monthly Support

CUSTODIAL PARENT MONTHLY INCOME

NONCUSTODIAL PARENT MONTHLY INCOME

	1850	1900	1950	2000	2050	2100	2150	2200	2250	2300	2350	2400	2450	2500	2550	2600
2550]	1069	1066	1063	1060	1058	1055	1053	1050	1048	1045	1043	1041	1038	1036	1034	1032
2600]	1087	1084	1081	1078	1076	1073	1071	1068	1066	1063	1061	1059	1056	1054	1052	1050
2650]	1105	1102	1099	1096	1094	1091	1089	1086	1084	1081	1079	1077	1074	1072	1070	1068
2700]	1123	1120	1117	1114	1112	1109	1107	1104	1102	1099	1097	1095	1092	1090	1088	1084
2750]	1141	1138	1135	1132	1130	1127	1125	1122	1120	1117	1115	1113	1110	1108	1104	1100
2800]	1159	1156	1153	1150	1148	1145	1143	1140	1138	1135	1133	1131	1128	1124	1120	1116
2850]	1176	1174	1171	1168	1166	1163	1160	1158	1156	1153	1151	1149	1144	1140	1136	1132
2900]	1194	1191	1189	1186	1183	1181	1178	1176	1173	1171	1169	1164	1160	1156	1152	1148
2950]	1212	1209	1206	1204	1201	1199	1196	1194	1191	1189	1185	1180	1176	1172	1168	1164
3000]	1230	1227	1224	1222	1219	1216	1214	1211	1209	1205	1200	1196	1192	1188	1184	1180
3050]	1247	1245	1242	1239	1237	1234	1232	1229	1225	1220	1216	1212	1208	1204	1200	1196
3100]	1265	1262	1260	1257	1254	1252	1249	1245	1240	1236	1232	1228	1224	1220	1216	1212
3150]	1283	1280	1277	1275	1272	1269	1265	1260	1256	1252	1247	1243	1239	1235	1231	1227
3200]	1300	1297	1295	1292	1290	1285	1280	1276	1272	1267	1263	1259	1255	1251	1247	1243
3250]	1318	1315	1312	1310	1305	1300	1296	1291	1287	1283	1279	1274	1270	1266	1262	1258
3300]	1335	1333	1330	1325	1320	1316	1311	1307	1302	1298	1294	1290	1286	1282	1278	1274
3350]	1353	1350	1345	1340	1336	1331	1327	1322	1318	1314	1309	1305	1301	1297	1293	1289
3400]	1370	1365	1360	1356	1351	1346	1342	1338	1333	1329	1325	1321	1317	1313	1309	1305
3450]	1385	1380	1376	1371	1366	1362	1357	1353	1348	1344	1340	1336	1332	1328	1324	1320
3500]	1400	1396	1391	1386	1381	1377	1372	1368	1364	1359	1355	1351	1347	1343	1339	1335
3550]	1415	1411	1406	1401	1397	1392	1388	1383	1379	1375	1370	1366	1362	1358	1355	1351
3600]	1430	1426	1421	1416	1412	1407	1403	1398	1394	1390	1386	1382	1378	1374	1370	1366
3650]	1445	1441	1436	1431	1427	1422	1418	1413	1409	1405	1401	1397	1393	1389	1385	1381
3700]	1460	1456	1451	1446	1442	1437	1433	1428	1424	1420	1416	1412	1408	1404	1400	1396
3750]	1475	1470	1466	1461	1457	1452	1448	1443	1439	1435	1431	1427	1423	1419	1415	1411
3800]	1490	1485	1481	1476	1471	1467	1463	1458	1454	1450	1446	1442	1438	1434	1430	1426
3850]	1505	1500	1495	1491	1486	1482	1478	1473	1469	1465	1461	1457	1453	1449	1445	1441
3900]	1520	1515	1510	1506	1501	1497	1492	1488	1484	1480	1476	1472	1468	1464	1460	1456
3950]	1534	1530	1525	1520	1516	1512	1507	1503	1499	1495	1491	1487	1483	1479	1475	1470
4000]	1549	1544	1540	1535	1531	1526	1522	1518	1514	1509	1505	1501	1498	1493	1489	1485
4050]	1564	1559	1554	1550	1545	1541	1537	1532	1528	1524	1520	1516	1512	1508	1503	1499
4100]	1578	1573	1569	1564	1560	1556	1551	1547	1543	1539	1535	1531	1526	1522	1518	1513
4150]	1593	1588	1584	1579	1575	1570	1566	1562	1558	1554	1549	1545	1541	1536	1532	1528
4200]	1607	1603	1598	1594	1589	1585	1581	1577	1572	1568	1564	1559	1555	1550	1546	1542
4250]	1622	1617	1613	1608	1604	1600	1595	1591	1587	1582	1578	1573	1569	1565	1560	1556
4300]	1636	1632	1627	1623	1618	1614	1610	1605	1601	1596	1592	1587	1583	1579	1574	1570
4350]	1651	1646	1642	1637	1633	1629	1624	1619	1615	1610	1606	1601	1597	1593	1588	1584
4400]	1665	1660	1656	1652	1647	1643	1638	1633	1629	1624	1620	1615	1611	1607	1603	1598
4450]	1679	1675	1670	1666	1661	1657	1652	1647	1643	1638	1634	1629	1625	1621	1617	1612
4500]	1694	1689	1685	1680	1675	1670	1666	1661	1657	1652	1648	1643	1639	1635	1631	1626
4550]	1708	1703	1699	1694	1689	1684	1680	1675	1670	1666	1661	1657	1653	1649	1644	1640
4600]	1722	1717	1712	1708	1703	1698	1693	1689	1684	1680	1675	1671	1667	1663	1658	1654
4650]	1736	1731	1726	1721	1716	1712	1707	1703	1698	1694	1689	1685	1681	1676	1672	1668
4700]	1750	1745	1740	1735	1730	1725	1721	1716	1712	1707	1703	1699	1694	1690	1686	1682
4750]	1763	1758	1753	1749	1744	1739	1735	1730	1726	1721	1717	1712	1708	1704	1700	1696
4800]	1777	1772	1767	1762	1757	1753	1748	1744	1739	1735	1730	1726	1722	1718	1714	1710
4850]	1790	1785	1781	1776	1771	1766	1762	1757	1753	1748	1744	1740	1736	1732	1727	1723
4900]	1804	1799	1794	1789	1785	1780	1775	1771	1767	1762	1758	1754	1749	1745	1741	1737
4950]	1817	1812	1808	1803	1798	1794	1789	1785	1780	1776	1771	1767	1763	1759	1755	1751
5000]	1831	1826	1821	1816	1812	1807	1803	1798	1794	1789	1785	1781	1777	1773	1769	1765

2004 MICHIGAN CHILD SUPPORT FORMULA SCHEDULES
MONTHLY BASE SUPPORT

Four Children - Monthly Support

CUSTODIAL PARENT MONTHLY INCOME

	2650	2700	2750	2800	2850	2900	2950	3000	3050	3100	3150	3200	3250	3300	3350	3400
250]	25	25	25	25	25	25	25	25	25	25	25	25	25	25	25	25
300]	25	25	25	25	25	25	25	25	25	25	25	25	25	25	25	25
350]	25	25	25	25	25	25	25	25	25	25	25	25	25	25	25	25
400]	25	25	25	25	25	25	25	25	25	25	25	25	25	25	25	25
450]	25	25	25	25	25	25	25	25	25	25	25	25	25	25	25	25
500]	25	25	25	25	25	25	25	25	25	25	25	25	25	25	25	25
550]	28	25	25	25	25	25	25	25	25	25	25	25	25	25	25	25
600]	30	25	25	25	25	25	25	25	25	25	25	25	25	25	25	25
650]	33	26	26	26	26	26	26	26	26	26	25	25	25	25	25	25
700]	35	28	28	28	28	28	28	28	28	28	25	25	25	25	25	25
750]	38	30	30	30	30	30	30	30	30	30	25	25	25	25	25	25
800]	63	55	55	55	55	55	55	55	55	55	49	49	49	49	49	49
850]	113	105	105	105	105	105	105	105	105	105	99	99	99	99	99	99
900]	163	155	155	155	155	155	155	155	155	155	149	149	149	149	149	149
950]	213	205	205	205	205	205	205	205	205	205	199	199	199	199	199	199
1000]	263	255	255	255	255	255	255	255	255	255	249	249	249	249	249	249
1050]	313	305	305	305	305	305	305	305	305	305	299	299	299	299	299	299
1100]	363	355	355	355	355	355	355	355	355	355	349	349	349	349	349	349
1150]	413	405	405	405	405	405	405	405	405	405	399	399	399	399	399	399
1200]	463	455	455	455	455	455	455	455	455	455	449	449	449	449	449	449
1250]	513	505	505	505	505	505	505	505	505	505	499	499	499	499	499	499
1300]	560	555	555	554	553	551	549	548	546	545	543	542	541	539	538	537
1350]	579	577	576	574	572	571	569	567	566	564	563	561	560	559	557	556
1400]	599	597	595	593	592	590	588	587	585	584	582	581	579	578	576	575
1450]	618	616	615	613	611	609	608	606	604	603	601	600	598	597	596	594
1500]	638	636	634	632	630	629	627	625	624	622	621	619	618	616	615	613
1550]	657	655	653	651	650	648	646	645	643	641	640	638	637	635	634	632
1600]	676	674	672	671	669	667	665	664	662	660	659	657	656	654	653	651
1650]	695	693	692	690	688	686	684	683	681	679	678	676	675	673	672	670
1700]	714	712	711	709	707	705	703	702	700	698	697	695	694	692	691	689
1750]	733	731	730	728	726	724	722	721	719	717	716	714	713	711	710	708
1800]	752	750	748	747	745	743	741	739	738	736	734	733	731	730	728	727
1850]	771	769	767	765	764	762	760	758	757	755	753	752	750	749	747	746
1900]	790	788	786	784	782	781	779	777	775	774	772	770	769	767	766	763
1950]	809	807	805	803	801	799	797	796	794	792	791	789	787	786	783	780
2000]	828	826	824	822	820	818	816	814	813	811	809	808	806	803	800	797
2050]	846	844	842	840	838	837	835	833	831	829	828	826	823	820	817	815
2100]	865	863	861	859	857	855	853	851	850	848	846	843	840	837	834	832
2150]	883	881	879	877	875	874	872	870	868	866	863	860	857	854	851	849
2200]	902	900	898	896	894	892	890	888	887	883	880	877	874	871	868	865
2250]	920	918	916	914	912	910	909	907	903	900	897	894	891	888	885	882
2300]	939	936	935	933	931	929	927	924	920	917	914	911	908	905	902	899
2350]	957	955	953	951	949	947	944	940	937	934	931	928	924	921	919	916
2400]	975	973	971	969	967	964	960	957	954	950	947	944	941	938	935	932
2450]	993	991	989	987	984	980	977	974	970	967	964	961	958	955	952	949
2500]	1012	1010	1008	1004	1000	997	993	990	987	983	980	977	974	971	968	965

NONCUSTODIAL PARENT MONTHLY INCOME

Effective October 1, 2004

Four Children - Monthly Support

CUSTODIAL PARENT MONTHLY INCOME

		2650	2700	2750	2800	2850	2900	2950	3000	3050	3100	3150	3200	3250	3300	3350	3400
	2550]	1030	1028	1024	1020	1017	1013	1010	1006	1003	1000	997	994	990	987	984	982
	2600]	1048	1044	1040	1037	1033	1030	1026	1023	1019	1016	1013	1010	1007	1004	1001	998
	2650]	1064	1060	1057	1053	1049	1046	1042	1039	1036	1033	1029	1026	1023	1020	1017	1014
	2700]	1080	1077	1073	1069	1066	1062	1059	1055	1052	1049	1046	1042	1039	1036	1033	1030
	2750]	1097	1093	1089	1085	1082	1078	1075	1071	1068	1065	1062	1058	1055	1052	1049	1046
	2800]	1113	1109	1105	1101	1098	1094	1091	1088	1084	1081	1078	1075	1071	1068	1065	1062
	2850]	1129	1125	1121	1118	1114	1110	1107	1104	1100	1097	1094	1091	1087	1084	1081	1078
N	2900]	1145	1141	1137	1133	1130	1126	1123	1120	1116	1113	1110	1107	1103	1100	1097	1094
O	2950]	1160	1157	1153	1149	1146	1142	1139	1135	1132	1129	1126	1122	1119	1116	1113	1110
N																	
C	3000]	1176	1173	1169	1165	1162	1158	1155	1151	1148	1145	1141	1138	1135	1132	1129	1126
U	3050]	1192	1188	1185	1181	1177	1174	1171	1167	1164	1161	1157	1154	1151	1148	1145	1142
S	3100]	1208	1204	1200	1197	1193	1190	1186	1183	1180	1176	1173	1170	1167	1164	1161	1157
T	3150]	1224	1220	1216	1212	1209	1205	1202	1199	1195	1192	1189	1186	1182	1179	1176	1173
O	3200]	1239	1235	1232	1228	1225	1221	1218	1214	1211	1208	1204	1201	1198	1195	1191	1188
D	3250]	1255	1251	1247	1244	1240	1237	1233	1230	1226	1223	1220	1217	1213	1210	1206	1203
I	3300]	1270	1266	1263	1259	1256	1252	1249	1245	1242	1239	1235	1232	1228	1225	1222	1218
A	3350]	1286	1282	1278	1275	1271	1268	1264	1261	1257	1254	1251	1247	1244	1240	1237	1233
L	3400]	1301	1297	1294	1290	1287	1283	1280	1276	1273	1269	1266	1262	1259	1255	1252	1248
	3450]	1316	1313	1309	1305	1302	1298	1295	1292	1288	1284	1281	1277	1274	1270	1267	1263
P																	
A	3500]	1332	1328	1324	1321	1317	1314	1310	1307	1303	1299	1296	1292	1288	1285	1281	1278
R	3550]	1347	1343	1340	1336	1333	1329	1325	1322	1318	1314	1310	1307	1303	1300	1296	1293
E	3600]	1362	1359	1355	1351	1348	1344	1340	1336	1333	1329	1325	1322	1318	1315	1311	1308
N	3650]	1377	1374	1370	1367	1363	1359	1355	1351	1347	1344	1340	1336	1333	1329	1326	1323
T	3700]	1393	1389	1385	1381	1377	1373	1370	1366	1362	1358	1355	1351	1348	1344	1341	1337
	3750]	1408	1404	1400	1396	1392	1388	1384	1380	1377	1373	1369	1366	1362	1359	1355	1352
M	3800]	1423	1419	1415	1411	1407	1403	1399	1395	1391	1388	1384	1380	1377	1373	1370	1367
O	3850]	1437	1433	1429	1425	1421	1417	1413	1410	1406	1402	1399	1395	1391	1388	1385	1381
N	3900]	1452	1448	1444	1440	1436	1432	1428	1424	1420	1417	1413	1410	1406	1403	1399	1396
T	3950]	1466	1462	1458	1454	1450	1446	1442	1439	1435	1431	1428	1424	1421	1417	1414	1410
H																	
L	4000]	1481	1477	1472	1468	1465	1461	1457	1453	1449	1446	1442	1438	1435	1432	1428	1425
Y	4050]	1495	1491	1487	1483	1479	1475	1471	1467	1464	1460	1456	1453	1449	1446	1443	1439
	4100]	1509	1505	1501	1497	1493	1489	1486	1482	1478	1474	1471	1467	1464	1460	1457	1454
I	4150]	1524	1519	1515	1511	1508	1504	1500	1496	1492	1489	1485	1482	1478	1475	1471	1468
N	4200]	1538	1534	1530	1526	1522	1518	1514	1510	1507	1503	1499	1496	1492	1489	1486	1482
C	4250]	1552	1548	1544	1540	1536	1532	1528	1525	1521	1517	1514	1510	1507	1503	1500	1497
O	4300]	1566	1562	1558	1554	1550	1546	1543	1539	1535	1532	1528	1524	1521	1518	1514	1511
M	4350]	1580	1576	1572	1568	1564	1561	1557	1553	1549	1546	1542	1539	1535	1532	1528	1525
E	4400]	1594	1590	1586	1582	1578	1575	1571	1567	1564	1560	1556	1553	1549	1546	1543	1539
	4450]	1608	1604	1600	1596	1593	1589	1585	1581	1578	1574	1570	1567	1564	1560	1557	1553
	4500]	1622	1618	1614	1610	1607	1603	1599	1595	1592	1588	1585	1581	1578	1574	1571	1567
	4550]	1636	1632	1628	1624	1621	1617	1613	1609	1606	1602	1599	1595	1592	1588	1585	1582
	4600]	1650	1646	1642	1638	1635	1631	1627	1623	1620	1616	1613	1609	1606	1602	1599	1596
	4650]	1664	1660	1656	1652	1649	1645	1641	1637	1634	1630	1627	1623	1620	1616	1613	1610
	4700]	1678	1674	1670	1666	1662	1659	1655	1651	1648	1644	1641	1637	1634	1630	1627	1624
	4750]	1692	1688	1684	1680	1676	1673	1669	1665	1662	1658	1655	1651	1648	1644	1641	1638
	4800]	1706	1702	1698	1694	1690	1686	1683	1679	1676	1672	1668	1665	1662	1658	1655	1651
	4850]	1719	1716	1712	1708	1704	1700	1697	1693	1689	1686	1682	1679	1676	1672	1668	1665
	4900]	1733	1729	1725	1722	1718	1714	1710	1707	1703	1700	1696	1693	1689	1685	1682	1678
	4950]	1747	1743	1739	1735	1732	1728	1724	1721	1717	1714	1710	1706	1703	1699	1695	1692
	5000]	1761	1757	1753	1749	1745	1742	1738	1734	1731	1727	1724	1720	1716	1712	1709	1705

Effective October 1, 2004

Four Children - Monthly Support

CUSTODIAL PARENT MONTHLY INCOME

		3450	3500	3550	3600	3650	3700	3750	3800	3850	3900	3950	4000	4050	4100	4150	4200
	250]	25	25	25	25	25	25	25	25	25	25	25	25	25	25	25	25
	300]	25	25	25	25	25	25	25	25	25	25	25	25	25	25	25	25
	350]	25	25	25	25	25	25	25	25	25	25	25	25	25	25	25	25
	400]	25	25	25	25	25	25	25	25	25	25	25	25	25	25	25	25
	450]	25	25	25	25	25	25	25	25	25	25	25	25	25	25	25	25
	500]	25	25	25	25	25	25	25	25	25	25	25	25	25	25	25	25
N	550]	25	25	25	25	25	25	25	25	25	25	25	25	25	25	25	25
O	600]	25	25	25	25	25	25	25	25	25	25	25	25	25	25	25	25
N	650]	25	25	25	25	25	25	25	25	25	25	25	25	25	25	25	25
C	700]	25	25	25	25	25	25	25	25	25	25	25	25	25	25	25	25
U	750]	25	25	25	25	25	25	25	25	25	25	25	25	25	25	25	25
S	800]	49	49	49	49	49	49	49	49	49	49	49	49	49	49	49	49
T	850]	99	99	99	99	99	99	99	99	99	99	99	99	99	99	99	99
O	900]	149	149	149	149	149	149	149	149	149	149	149	149	149	149	149	149
D	950]	199	199	199	199	199	199	199	199	199	199	199	199	199	199	199	199
I																	
A	1000]	249	249	249	249	249	249	249	249	249	249	249	249	249	249	249	249
L	1050]	299	299	299	299	299	299	299	299	299	299	299	299	299	299	299	299
	1100]	349	349	349	349	349	349	349	349	349	349	349	349	349	349	349	349
P	1150]	399	399	399	399	399	399	399	399	399	399	399	399	399	399	399	399
A	1200]	449	449	449	449	449	449	449	449	449	449	449	449	449	449	449	449
R	1250]	499	499	499	499	499	499	499	499	499	499	499	499	499	499	498	497
E	1300]	535	534	533	532	530	529	528	527	526	525	524	522	520	518	517	515
N	1350]	555	553	552	551	550	549	547	546	545	544	542	540	538	536	535	533
T	1400]	574	573	571	570	569	568	566	565	564	562	560	558	556	554	553	551
	1450]	593	592	590	589	588	587	586	584	582	580	578	576	574	572	570	569
M																	
O	1500]	612	611	609	608	607	606	605	602	600	598	596	594	592	590	588	586
N	1550]	631	630	628	627	626	625	622	620	618	616	614	612	610	608	606	604
T	1600]	650	649	647	646	645	642	640	638	636	634	631	629	627	625	623	621
H	1650]	669	668	666	665	663	660	658	656	653	651	649	647	645	643	641	639
L	1700]	688	686	685	683	680	678	676	673	671	669	667	664	662	660	658	656
Y	1750]	707	705	703	700	698	695	693	691	688	686	684	682	680	678	676	674
	1800]	725	723	720	718	715	713	710	708	706	704	701	699	697	695	693	691
I	1850]	743	740	738	735	733	730	728	725	723	721	719	716	714	712	710	708
N	1900]	760	758	755	752	750	747	745	743	740	738	736	734	731	729	727	725
C	1950]	778	775	772	770	767	765	762	760	757	755	753	751	748	746	744	742
O																	
M	2000]	795	792	789	787	784	782	779	777	774	772	770	768	765	763	761	759
E	2050]	812	809	806	804	801	799	796	794	791	789	787	784	782	780	778	776
	2100]	829	826	823	821	818	816	813	811	808	806	804	801	799	797	795	792
	2150]	846	843	840	838	835	833	830	828	825	823	820	818	816	814	811	809
	2200]	863	860	857	855	852	849	847	844	842	839	837	835	832	830	828	826
	2250]	879	877	874	871	869	866	863	861	859	856	854	851	849	847	845	842
	2300]	896	893	891	888	885	883	880	878	875	873	870	868	866	863	861	859
	2350]	913	910	907	905	902	899	897	894	892	889	887	884	882	880	877	875
	2400]	929	927	924	921	918	916	913	911	908	906	903	901	899	896	893	891
	2450]	946	943	940	938	935	932	930	927	925	922	920	917	915	912	909	907
	2500]	962	959	957	954	951	949	946	943	941	938	936	933	931	928	925	923

Effective October 1, 2004

2004 MICHIGAN CHILD SUPPORT FORMULA SCHEDULES
MONTHLY BASE SUPPORT

Four Children - Monthly Support

CUSTODIAL PARENT MONTHLY INCOME

	3450	3500	3550	3600	3650	3700	3750	3800	3850	3900	3950	4000	4050	4100	4150	4200
2550]	979	976	973	970	968	965	962	960	957	955	952	949	947	944	941	939
2600]	995	992	989	987	984	981	979	976	973	971	968	965	962	960	957	955
2650]	1011	1008	1005	1003	1000	997	995	992	989	987	984	981	978	976	973	970
2700]	1027	1024	1022	1019	1016	1013	1011	1008	1005	1002	999	997	994	991	989	986
2750]	1043	1041	1038	1035	1032	1030	1027	1024	1021	1018	1015	1012	1010	1007	1004	1002
2800]	1059	1057	1054	1051	1048	1045	1042	1039	1036	1034	1031	1028	1025	1022	1020	1017
2850]	1075	1073	1070	1067	1064	1061	1058	1055	1052	1049	1046	1043	1041	1038	1035	1033
2900]	1091	1089	1086	1083	1080	1077	1073	1070	1068	1065	1062	1059	1056	1053	1051	1048
2950]	1107	1104	1101	1098	1095	1092	1089	1086	1083	1080	1077	1074	1072	1069	1066	1064
3000]	1123	1120	1117	1114	1110	1107	1104	1101	1098	1095	1093	1090	1087	1084	1082	1079
3050]	1139	1135	1132	1129	1126	1123	1120	1117	1114	1111	1108	1105	1102	1100	1097	1094
3100]	1154	1151	1148	1144	1141	1138	1135	1132	1129	1126	1123	1120	1118	1115	1112	1109
3150]	1169	1166	1163	1160	1156	1153	1150	1147	1144	1141	1138	1136	1133	1130	1127	1125
3200]	1185	1181	1178	1175	1172	1169	1165	1162	1159	1157	1154	1151	1148	1145	1142	1140
3250]	1200	1196	1193	1190	1187	1184	1181	1178	1175	1172	1169	1166	1163	1160	1158	1155
3300]	1215	1211	1208	1205	1202	1199	1196	1193	1190	1187	1184	1181	1178	1175	1173	1170
3350]	1230	1227	1223	1220	1217	1214	1211	1208	1205	1202	1199	1196	1193	1190	1188	1185
3400]	1245	1242	1238	1235	1232	1229	1226	1223	1220	1217	1214	1211	1208	1205	1203	1200
3450]	1260	1257	1253	1250	1247	1244	1241	1238	1235	1232	1229	1226	1223	1220	1218	1215
3500]	1275	1271	1268	1265	1262	1259	1256	1253	1250	1247	1244	1241	1238	1235	1232	1230
3550]	1290	1286	1283	1280	1277	1274	1270	1267	1264	1261	1259	1256	1253	1250	1247	1245
3600]	1304	1301	1298	1295	1291	1288	1285	1282	1279	1276	1273	1270	1268	1265	1262	1259
3650]	1319	1316	1313	1309	1306	1303	1300	1297	1294	1291	1288	1285	1282	1280	1277	1274
3700]	1334	1331	1327	1324	1321	1318	1315	1312	1309	1306	1303	1300	1297	1294	1292	1289
3750]	1349	1345	1342	1339	1336	1333	1329	1326	1323	1320	1318	1315	1312	1309	1306	1304
3800]	1363	1360	1357	1353	1350	1347	1344	1341	1338	1335	1332	1329	1326	1324	1321	1318
3850]	1378	1375	1371	1368	1365	1362	1359	1356	1353	1350	1347	1344	1341	1338	1335	1333
3900]	1392	1389	1386	1383	1379	1376	1373	1370	1367	1364	1361	1358	1356	1353	1350	1347
3950]	1407	1404	1400	1397	1394	1391	1388	1385	1382	1379	1376	1373	1370	1367	1365	1362
4000]	1421	1418	1415	1412	1409	1405	1402	1399	1396	1393	1390	1388	1385	1382	1379	1376
4050]	1436	1433	1429	1426	1423	1420	1417	1414	1411	1408	1405	1402	1399	1396	1393	1390
4100]	1450	1447	1444	1441	1437	1434	1431	1428	1425	1422	1419	1416	1413	1410	1407	1404
4150]	1465	1461	1458	1455	1452	1449	1446	1443	1440	1437	1434	1431	1428	1424	1421	1418
4200]	1479	1476	1472	1469	1466	1463	1460	1457	1454	1451	1448	1445	1442	1438	1435	1432
4250]	1493	1490	1487	1484	1480	1477	1474	1471	1468	1465	1462	1459	1456	1452	1449	1446
4300]	1507	1504	1501	1498	1495	1492	1489	1485	1482	1479	1476	1473	1470	1466	1463	1460
4350]	1522	1518	1515	1512	1509	1506	1503	1500	1496	1493	1490	1487	1483	1480	1477	1474
4400]	1536	1533	1529	1526	1523	1520	1517	1514	1510	1507	1504	1501	1497	1494	1491	1488
4450]	1550	1547	1544	1540	1537	1534	1531	1527	1524	1521	1518	1514	1511	1508	1505	1502
4500]	1564	1561	1558	1555	1551	1548	1545	1541	1538	1535	1531	1528	1525	1522	1519	1516
4550]	1578	1575	1572	1569	1565	1562	1558	1555	1552	1548	1545	1542	1539	1536	1533	1530
4600]	1592	1589	1586	1582	1579	1575	1572	1569	1565	1562	1559	1556	1553	1550	1546	1543
4650]	1606	1603	1600	1596	1593	1589	1586	1582	1579	1576	1573	1570	1566	1563	1560	1557
4700]	1620	1617	1613	1610	1606	1603	1599	1596	1593	1590	1586	1583	1580	1577	1574	1571
4750]	1634	1630	1627	1623	1620	1616	1613	1610	1607	1603	1600	1597	1594	1591	1588	1585
4800]	1647	1644	1640	1637	1633	1630	1627	1623	1620	1617	1614	1611	1607	1604	1601	1598
4850]	1661	1657	1654	1651	1647	1644	1640	1637	1634	1631	1627	1624	1621	1618	1615	1612
4900]	1675	1671	1668	1664	1661	1657	1654	1651	1647	1644	1641	1638	1635	1631	1628	1625
4950]	1688	1685	1681	1678	1674	1671	1667	1664	1661	1658	1654	1651	1648	1645	1642	1639
5000]	1702	1698	1695	1691	1688	1684	1681	1678	1674	1671	1668	1665	1662	1659	1656	1653

NONCUSTODIAL PARENT MONTHLY INCOME (row labels, left margin)

Effective October 1, 2004

2004 MICHIGAN CHILD SUPPORT FORMULA SCHEDULES
MONTHLY BASE SUPPORT

Four Children - Monthly Support

CUSTODIAL PARENT MONTHLY INCOME

	4250	4300	4350	4400	4450	4500	4550	4600	4650	4700	4750	4800	4850	4900	4950	5000
250]	25	25	25	25	25	25	25	25	25	25	25	25	25	25	25	25
300]	25	25	25	25	25	25	25	25	25	25	25	25	25	25	25	25
350]	25	25	25	25	25	25	25	25	25	25	25	25	25	25	25	25
400]	25	25	25	25	25	25	25	25	25	25	25	25	25	25	25	25
450]	25	25	25	25	25	25	25	25	25	25	25	25	25	25	25	25
500]	25	25	25	25	25	25	25	25	25	25	25	25	25	25	25	25
550]	25	25	25	25	25	25	25	25	25	25	25	25	25	25	25	25
600]	25	25	25	25	25	25	25	25	25	25	25	25	25	25	25	25
650]	25	25	25	25	25	25	25	25	25	25	25	25	25	25	25	25
700]	25	25	25	25	25	25	25	25	25	25	25	25	25	25	25	25
750]	25	25	25	25	25	25	25	25	25	25	25	25	25	25	25	25
800]	49	49	49	49	49	49	49	49	49	49	49	49	49	49	49	49
850]	99	99	99	99	99	99	99	99	99	99	99	99	99	99	99	99
900]	149	149	149	149	149	149	149	149	149	149	149	149	149	149	149	149
950]	199	199	199	199	199	199	199	199	199	199	199	199	199	199	199	199
1000]	249	249	249	249	249	249	249	249	249	249	249	249	249	249	249	249
1050]	299	299	299	299	299	299	299	299	299	299	299	299	299	299	299	299
1100]	349	349	349	349	349	349	349	349	349	349	349	349	349	349	349	349
1150]	399	399	399	399	399	399	399	399	399	399	399	399	399	399	399	399
1200]	449	449	449	449	449	449	449	449	449	449	449	449	449	449	449	449
1250]	495	493	492	490	489	487	486	484	483	481	480	478	477	476	474	473
1300]	513	511	510	508	507	505	503	502	500	499	497	496	495	493	492	491
1350]	531	529	528	526	524	523	521	520	518	517	515	514	512	511	509	508
1400]	549	547	545	544	542	540	539	537	536	534	533	531	530	528	527	526
1450]	567	565	563	561	560	558	556	555	553	552	550	549	547	546	544	543
1500]	584	583	581	579	577	576	574	572	571	569	568	566	565	563	562	560
1550]	602	600	598	597	595	593	591	590	588	587	585	583	582	580	579	577
1600]	620	618	616	614	612	611	609	607	605	604	602	601	599	597	596	594
1650]	637	635	633	631	630	628	626	624	623	621	619	618	616	614	612	611
1700]	654	652	651	649	647	645	643	642	640	638	636	635	633	631	629	628
1750]	672	670	668	666	664	662	660	659	657	655	653	651	650	648	646	644
1800]	689	687	685	683	681	679	677	676	674	672	670	668	666	664	663	661
1850]	706	704	702	700	698	696	694	693	691	689	687	685	683	681	679	677
1900]	723	721	719	717	715	713	711	709	707	705	703	701	699	698	696	694
1950]	740	738	736	734	732	730	728	726	724	722	720	718	716	714	712	710
2000]	757	755	753	751	749	747	745	742	740	738	736	734	732	730	728	727
2050]	774	772	769	767	765	763	761	759	757	755	753	751	749	747	745	743
2100]	790	788	786	784	782	780	777	775	773	771	769	767	765	763	761	759
2150]	807	805	803	800	798	796	794	791	789	787	785	783	781	779	777	775
2200]	824	821	819	817	814	812	810	808	805	803	801	799	797	795	793	791
2250]	840	838	835	833	831	828	826	824	822	819	817	815	813	811	809	807
2300]	856	854	851	849	847	844	842	840	838	836	833	831	829	827	825	823
2350]	872	870	867	865	863	860	858	856	854	851	849	847	845	843	841	839
2400]	888	886	883	881	879	876	874	872	870	867	865	863	861	859	857	855
2450]	904	902	899	897	895	892	890	888	885	883	881	879	877	875	873	871
2500]	920	918	915	913	911	908	906	904	901	899	897	895	893	890	888	886

NONCUSTODIAL PARENT MONTHLY INCOME

Effective October 1, 2004

Four Children - Monthly Support

CUSTODIAL PARENT MONTHLY INCOME

		4250	4300	4350	4400	4450	4500	4550	4600	4650	4700	4750	4800	4850	4900	4950	5000
	2550]	936	934	931	929	926	924	922	919	917	915	913	910	908	906	904	902
	2600]	952	949	947	944	942	940	937	935	933	930	928	926	924	922	920	918
	2650]	968	965	963	960	958	955	953	951	948	946	944	942	939	937	935	933
	2700]	983	981	978	976	973	971	969	966	964	962	959	957	955	953	951	949
	2750]	999	996	994	991	989	987	984	982	979	977	975	973	971	968	966	964
	2800]	1015	1012	1009	1007	1004	1002	1000	997	995	993	990	988	986	984	982	979
	2850]	1030	1027	1025	1022	1020	1018	1015	1013	1010	1008	1006	1004	1001	999	997	995
N	2900]	1045	1043	1040	1038	1035	1033	1031	1028	1026	1023	1021	1019	1017	1014	1012	1010
O	2950]	1061	1058	1056	1053	1051	1048	1046	1043	1041	1039	1036	1034	1032	1030	1028	1025
N																	
C	3000]	1076	1074	1071	1069	1066	1064	1061	1059	1056	1054	1052	1049	1047	1045	1043	1041
U	3050]	1092	1089	1086	1084	1081	1079	1076	1074	1072	1069	1067	1065	1062	1060	1058	1056
S	3100]	1107	1104	1102	1099	1097	1094	1092	1089	1087	1084	1082	1080	1078	1075	1073	1071
T	3150]	1122	1119	1117	1114	1112	1109	1107	1104	1102	1100	1097	1095	1093	1090	1088	1086
O	3200]	1137	1134	1132	1129	1127	1124	1122	1119	1117	1115	1112	1110	1108	1105	1103	1101
D	3250]	1152	1150	1147	1144	1142	1139	1137	1134	1132	1130	1127	1125	1123	1120	1118	1115
I	3300]	1167	1165	1162	1159	1157	1154	1152	1149	1147	1145	1142	1140	1138	1135	1133	1130
A	3350]	1182	1180	1177	1174	1172	1169	1167	1164	1162	1160	1157	1155	1152	1150	1147	1145
L	3400]	1197	1195	1192	1189	1187	1184	1182	1179	1177	1175	1172	1170	1167	1164	1162	1159
	3450]	1212	1210	1207	1204	1202	1199	1197	1194	1192	1189	1187	1184	1182	1179	1177	1174
P																	
A	3500]	1227	1224	1222	1219	1217	1214	1212	1209	1207	1204	1201	1199	1196	1194	1191	1189
R	3550]	1242	1239	1237	1234	1231	1229	1226	1224	1221	1218	1216	1213	1211	1208	1206	1203
E	3600]	1257	1254	1251	1249	1246	1244	1241	1238	1236	1233	1230	1228	1225	1223	1220	1218
N	3650]	1271	1269	1266	1264	1261	1258	1256	1253	1250	1247	1245	1242	1240	1237	1234	1232
T	3700]	1286	1283	1281	1278	1276	1273	1270	1267	1264	1262	1259	1257	1254	1251	1249	1246
	3750]	1301	1298	1295	1293	1290	1287	1284	1282	1279	1276	1274	1271	1268	1266	1263	1261
M	3800]	1315	1313	1310	1307	1304	1301	1299	1296	1293	1290	1288	1285	1283	1280	1278	1275
O	3850]	1330	1327	1324	1321	1319	1316	1313	1310	1307	1305	1302	1299	1297	1294	1292	1289
N	3900]	1344	1342	1339	1336	1333	1330	1327	1324	1322	1319	1316	1314	1311	1309	1306	1303
T	3950]	1359	1356	1353	1350	1347	1344	1341	1339	1336	1333	1331	1328	1325	1323	1320	1318
H																	
L	4000]	1373	1370	1367	1364	1361	1358	1356	1353	1350	1347	1345	1342	1339	1337	1334	1332
Y	4050]	1387	1384	1381	1378	1375	1373	1370	1367	1364	1362	1359	1356	1354	1351	1348	1346
	4100]	1401	1398	1395	1392	1390	1387	1384	1381	1378	1376	1373	1370	1368	1365	1363	1360
I	4150]	1415	1412	1409	1406	1404	1401	1398	1395	1392	1390	1387	1384	1382	1379	1377	1374
N	4200]	1429	1426	1423	1420	1418	1415	1412	1409	1406	1404	1401	1398	1396	1393	1391	1388
C	4250]	1443	1440	1437	1435	1432	1429	1426	1423	1420	1418	1415	1412	1410	1407	1405	1402
O	4300]	1457	1454	1451	1448	1446	1443	1440	1437	1434	1432	1429	1426	1424	1421	1419	1416
M	4350]	1471	1468	1465	1462	1460	1457	1454	1451	1448	1446	1443	1440	1438	1435	1433	1430
E	4400]	1485	1482	1479	1476	1473	1471	1468	1465	1462	1460	1457	1454	1452	1449	1446	1444
	4450]	1499	1496	1493	1490	1487	1484	1482	1479	1476	1473	1471	1468	1465	1463	1460	1458
	4500]	1513	1510	1507	1504	1501	1498	1496	1493	1490	1487	1485	1482	1479	1477	1474	1472
	4550]	1527	1524	1521	1518	1515	1512	1509	1507	1504	1501	1498	1496	1493	1490	1488	1485
	4600]	1540	1537	1535	1532	1529	1526	1523	1520	1518	1515	1512	1509	1507	1504	1502	1499
	4650]	1554	1551	1548	1545	1542	1540	1537	1534	1531	1529	1526	1523	1521	1518	1515	1513
	4700]	1568	1565	1562	1559	1556	1553	1551	1548	1545	1542	1540	1537	1534	1532	1529	1527
	4750]	1582	1579	1576	1573	1570	1567	1564	1561	1559	1556	1553	1551	1548	1545	1543	1540
	4800]	1595	1592	1589	1586	1584	1581	1578	1575	1572	1570	1567	1564	1562	1559	1556	1554
	4850]	1609	1606	1603	1600	1597	1594	1592	1589	1586	1583	1581	1578	1575	1573	1570	1568
	4900]	1622	1619	1617	1614	1611	1608	1605	1602	1600	1597	1594	1592	1589	1586	1584	1581
	4950]	1636	1633	1630	1627	1624	1622	1619	1616	1613	1610	1608	1605	1603	1600	1597	1595
	5000]	1650	1647	1644	1641	1638	1635	1632	1629	1627	1624	1621	1619	1616	1613	1611	1608

Effective October 1, 2004

Five or More Children - Monthly Support

CUSTODIAL PARENT MONTHLY INCOME

	0	250	300	350	400	450	500	550	600	650	700	750	800	850	900	950	1000
250]	25	25	25	25	25	25	25	25	25	25	25	25	25	25	25	25	25
300]	30	30	30	30	30	30	30	30	30	30	30	30	27	27	25	25	25
350]	35	35	35	35	35	35	35	35	35	35	35	35	32	32	28	28	28
400]	40	40	40	40	40	40	40	40	40	40	40	40	36	36	32	32	32
450]	45	45	45	45	45	45	45	45	45	45	45	45	41	41	36	36	36
500]	50	50	50	50	50	50	50	50	50	50	50	50	45	45	40	40	40
550]	55	55	55	55	55	55	55	55	55	55	55	55	50	50	44	44	44
600]	60	60	60	60	60	60	60	60	60	60	60	60	54	54	48	48	48
650]	65	65	65	65	65	65	65	65	65	65	65	65	59	59	52	52	52
700]	70	70	70	70	70	70	70	70	70	70	70	70	63	63	56	56	56
750]	75	75	75	75	75	75	75	75	75	75	75	75	68	68	60	60	60
800]	102	102	102	102	102	102	102	102	102	102	102	102	94	94	86	86	86
850]	152	152	152	152	152	152	152	152	152	152	152	152	144	144	136	136	136
900]	202	202	202	202	202	202	202	202	202	202	202	202	194	194	186	186	186
950]	252	252	252	252	252	252	252	252	252	252	252	252	244	244	236	236	236
1000]	302	302	302	302	302	302	302	302	302	302	302	302	294	294	286	286	286
1050]	352	352	352	352	352	352	352	352	352	352	352	352	344	344	336	336	336
1100]	402	402	402	402	402	402	402	402	402	402	402	402	394	394	386	386	386
1150]	452	452	452	452	452	452	452	452	452	452	452	452	444	444	436	436	436
1200]	502	502	502	502	502	502	502	502	502	502	502	502	494	494	486	486	486
1250]	552	552	552	552	552	552	552	552	552	552	552	552	544	544	536	536	536
1300]	602	602	602	602	602	602	602	602	602	602	602	602	594	594	586	586	586
1350]	652	652	652	652	652	652	652	652	652	652	652	652	644	644	636	636	636
1400]	702	702	702	702	702	702	702	702	702	702	702	702	694	694	686	686	686
1450]	752	752	752	752	752	752	752	752	752	752	752	752	744	744	736	736	736
1500]	802	802	802	802	802	802	802	802	802	802	802	802	794	794	786	786	786
1550]	852	852	852	852	852	852	852	852	852	852	852	852	838	832	827	822	818
1600]	902	902	902	902	902	902	902	902	902	902	902	902	859	854	849	844	840
1650]	952	952	952	952	952	952	952	952	952	952	952	952	881	875	871	866	861
1700]	999	999	999	999	999	999	999	999	999	999	999	999	902	897	892	887	883
1750]	1020	1020	1020	1020	1020	1020	1020	1020	1020	1020	1020	1020	923	918	913	909	904
1800]	1042	1042	1042	1042	1042	1042	1042	1042	1042	1042	1042	1042	945	940	935	930	926
1850]	1063	1063	1063	1063	1063	1063	1063	1063	1063	1063	1063	1063	966	961	956	951	947
1900]	1084	1084	1084	1084	1084	1084	1084	1084	1084	1084	1084	1084	987	982	977	973	968
1950]	1106	1106	1106	1106	1106	1106	1106	1106	1106	1106	1106	1106	1008	1003	998	993	989
2000]	1127	1127	1127	1127	1127	1127	1127	1127	1127	1127	1127	1127	1028	1024	1019	1014	1010
2050]	1148	1148	1148	1148	1148	1148	1148	1148	1148	1148	1148	1148	1049	1044	1040	1035	1031
2100]	1170	1170	1170	1170	1170	1170	1170	1170	1170	1170	1170	1170	1070	1065	1060	1056	1051
2150]	1191	1191	1191	1191	1191	1191	1191	1191	1191	1191	1191	1191	1090	1086	1081	1076	1072
2200]	1212	1212	1212	1212	1212	1212	1212	1212	1212	1212	1212	1212	1111	1106	1101	1097	1093
2250]	1232	1232	1232	1232	1232	1232	1232	1232	1232	1232	1232	1232	1131	1126	1122	1117	1113
2300]	1251	1251	1251	1251	1251	1251	1251	1251	1251	1251	1251	1251	1151	1147	1142	1138	1134
2350]	1270	1270	1270	1270	1270	1270	1270	1270	1270	1270	1270	1270	1172	1167	1163	1158	1154
2400]	1289	1289	1289	1289	1289	1289	1289	1289	1289	1289	1289	1289	1192	1187	1183	1179	1174
2450]	1308	1308	1308	1308	1308	1308	1308	1308	1308	1308	1308	1308	1212	1208	1203	1199	1195
2500]	1326	1326	1326	1326	1326	1326	1326	1326	1326	1326	1326	1326	1232	1228	1223	1219	1215

(Left margin vertical label: NONCUSTODIAL PARENT MONTHLY INCOME)

Effective October 1, 2004

Five or More Children - Monthly Support

CUSTODIAL PARENT MONTHLY INCOME

	0	250	300	350	400	450	500	550	600	650	700	750	800	850	900	950	1000
2550]	1345	1345	1345	1345	1345	1345	1345	1345	1345	1345	1345	1345	1252	1248	1244	1239	1235
2600]	1364	1364	1364	1364	1364	1364	1364	1364	1364	1364	1364	1364	1272	1268	1264	1260	1255
2650]	1383	1383	1383	1383	1383	1383	1383	1383	1383	1383	1383	1383	1292	1288	1284	1280	1276
2700]	1402	1402	1402	1402	1402	1402	1402	1402	1402	1402	1402	1402	1312	1308	1304	1300	1296
2750]	1421	1421	1421	1421	1421	1421	1421	1421	1421	1421	1421	1421	1332	1328	1324	1320	1315
2800]	1440	1440	1440	1440	1440	1440	1440	1440	1440	1440	1440	1440	1352	1348	1344	1339	1335
2850]	1459	1459	1459	1459	1459	1459	1459	1459	1459	1459	1459	1459	1372	1368	1363	1359	1354
2900]	1477	1477	1477	1477	1477	1477	1477	1477	1477	1477	1477	1477	1392	1387	1382	1378	1374
2950]	1496	1496	1496	1496	1496	1496	1496	1496	1496	1496	1496	1496	1411	1406	1402	1397	1393
3000]	1515	1515	1515	1515	1515	1515	1515	1515	1515	1515	1515	1515	1430	1425	1421	1417	1412
3050]	1533	1533	1533	1533	1533	1533	1533	1533	1533	1533	1533	1533	1449	1445	1440	1436	1432
3100]	1552	1552	1552	1552	1552	1552	1552	1552	1552	1552	1552	1552	1468	1464	1459	1455	1451
3150]	1571	1571	1571	1571	1571	1571	1571	1571	1571	1571	1571	1571	1487	1483	1479	1474	1470
3200]	1589	1589	1589	1589	1589	1589	1589	1589	1589	1589	1589	1589	1506	1502	1498	1493	1489
3250]	1608	1608	1608	1608	1608	1608	1608	1608	1608	1608	1608	1608	1526	1521	1517	1513	1509
3300]	1627	1627	1627	1627	1627	1627	1627	1627	1627	1627	1627	1627	1545	1540	1536	1532	1528
3350]	1645	1645	1645	1645	1645	1645	1645	1645	1645	1645	1645	1645	1563	1559	1555	1551	1547
3400]	1664	1664	1664	1664	1664	1664	1664	1664	1664	1664	1664	1664	1582	1578	1574	1570	1566
3450]	1682	1682	1682	1682	1682	1682	1682	1682	1682	1682	1682	1682	1601	1597	1593	1589	1585
3500]	1701	1701	1701	1701	1701	1701	1701	1701	1701	1701	1701	1701	1620	1616	1612	1608	1604
3550]	1720	1720	1720	1720	1720	1720	1720	1720	1720	1720	1720	1720	1639	1635	1631	1627	1623
3600]	1738	1738	1738	1738	1738	1738	1738	1738	1738	1738	1738	1738	1658	1654	1650	1646	1642
3650]	1757	1757	1757	1757	1757	1757	1757	1757	1757	1757	1757	1757	1677	1673	1669	1665	1661
3700]	1776	1776	1776	1776	1776	1776	1776	1776	1776	1776	1776	1776	1696	1692	1688	1684	1680
3750]	1794	1794	1794	1794	1794	1794	1794	1794	1794	1794	1794	1794	1714	1710	1706	1703	1699
3800]	1811	1811	1811	1811	1811	1811	1811	1811	1811	1811	1811	1811	1733	1729	1725	1721	1718
3850]	1829	1829	1829	1829	1829	1829	1829	1829	1829	1829	1829	1829	1752	1748	1744	1740	1737
3900]	1847	1847	1847	1847	1847	1847	1847	1847	1847	1847	1847	1847	1771	1767	1763	1759	1755
3950]	1865	1865	1865	1865	1865	1865	1865	1865	1865	1865	1865	1865	1789	1786	1782	1778	1774
4000]	1883	1883	1883	1883	1883	1883	1883	1883	1883	1883	1883	1883	1808	1804	1800	1797	1793
4050]	1901	1901	1901	1901	1901	1901	1901	1901	1901	1901	1901	1901	1827	1823	1819	1816	1812
4100]	1919	1919	1919	1919	1919	1919	1919	1919	1919	1919	1919	1919	1845	1842	1838	1834	1831
4150]	1937	1937	1937	1937	1937	1937	1937	1937	1937	1937	1937	1937	1864	1860	1857	1853	1850
4200]	1955	1955	1955	1955	1955	1955	1955	1955	1955	1955	1955	1955	1883	1879	1875	1872	1868
4250]	1973	1973	1973	1973	1973	1973	1973	1973	1973	1973	1973	1973	1901	1898	1894	1891	1887
4300]	1991	1991	1991	1991	1991	1991	1991	1991	1991	1991	1991	1991	1920	1916	1913	1909	1901
4350]	2009	2009	2009	2009	2009	2009	2009	2009	2009	2009	2009	2009	1939	1935	1931	1923	1915
4400]	2026	2026	2026	2026	2026	2026	2026	2026	2026	2026	2026	2026	1957	1954	1945	1937	1930
4450]	2044	2044	2044	2044	2044	2044	2044	2044	2044	2044	2044	2044	1976	1968	1959	1952	1944
4500]	2062	2062	2062	2062	2062	2062	2062	2062	2062	2062	2062	2062	1990	1981	1973	1966	1958
4550]	2080	2080	2080	2080	2080	2080	2080	2080	2080	2080	2080	2080	2004	1995	1987	1980	1972
4600]	2098	2098	2098	2098	2098	2098	2098	2098	2098	2098	2098	2098	2017	2009	2001	1994	1986
4650]	2116	2116	2116	2116	2116	2116	2116	2116	2116	2116	2116	2116	2031	2023	2015	2008	2000
4700]	2134	2134	2134	2134	2134	2134	2134	2134	2134	2134	2134	2134	2045	2037	2029	2022	2014
4750]	2152	2152	2152	2152	2152	2152	2152	2152	2152	2152	2152	2152	2059	2051	2043	2035	2028
4800]	2170	2170	2170	2170	2170	2170	2170	2170	2170	2170	2170	2170	2072	2065	2057	2049	2042
4850]	2188	2188	2188	2188	2188	2188	2188	2188	2188	2188	2188	2188	2086	2078	2071	2063	2056
4900]	2206	2206	2206	2206	2206	2206	2206	2206	2206	2206	2206	2206	2100	2092	2084	2077	2070
4950]	2224	2224	2224	2224	2224	2224	2224	2224	2224	2224	2224	2224	2113	2106	2098	2091	2084
5000]	2241	2241	2241	2241	2241	2241	2241	2241	2241	2241	2241	2241	2127	2119	2112	2105	2097

N O N C U S T O D I A L   P A R E N T   M O N T H L Y   I N C O M E

Effective October 1, 2004

Five or More Children - Monthly Support

CUSTODIAL PARENT MONTHLY INCOME

		1050	1100	1150	1200	1250	1300	1350	1400	1450	1500	1550	1600	1650	1700	1750	1800
	250]	25	25	25	25	25	25	25	25	25	25	25	25	25	25	25	25
	300]	25	25	25	25	25	25	25	25	25	25	25	25	25	25	25	25
	350]	28	28	28	28	28	28	25	25	25	25	25	25	25	25	25	25
	400]	32	32	32	32	32	32	28	28	28	28	28	28	28	28	28	25
	450]	36	36	36	36	36	36	32	32	32	32	32	32	32	32	32	27
	500]	40	40	40	40	40	40	35	35	35	35	35	35	35	35	35	30
N	550]	44	44	44	44	44	44	39	39	39	39	39	39	39	39	39	33
O	600]	48	48	48	48	48	48	42	42	42	42	42	42	42	42	42	36
N	650]	52	52	52	52	52	52	46	46	46	46	46	46	46	46	46	39
C	700]	56	56	56	56	56	56	49	49	49	49	49	49	49	49	49	42
U	750]	60	60	60	60	60	60	53	53	53	53	53	53	53	53	53	45
S	800]	86	86	86	86	86	86	78	78	78	78	78	78	78	78	78	71
T	850]	136	136	136	136	136	136	128	128	128	128	128	128	128	128	128	121
O	900]	186	186	186	186	186	186	178	178	178	178	178	178	178	178	178	171
D	950]	236	236	236	236	236	236	228	228	228	228	228	228	228	228	228	221
I																	
A	1000]	286	286	286	286	286	286	278	278	278	278	278	278	278	278	278	271
L	1050]	336	336	336	336	336	336	328	328	328	328	328	328	328	328	328	321
	1100]	386	386	386	386	386	386	378	378	378	378	378	378	378	378	378	371
P	1150]	436	436	436	436	436	436	428	428	428	428	428	428	428	428	428	421
A	1200]	486	486	486	486	486	486	478	478	478	478	478	478	478	478	478	471
R	1250]	536	536	536	536	536	536	528	528	528	528	528	528	528	528	528	521
E	1300]	586	586	586	586	586	586	578	578	578	578	578	578	578	578	578	571
N	1350]	636	636	636	636	636	636	628	628	628	628	628	628	628	628	628	621
T	1400]	686	686	686	686	686	686	678	678	678	678	678	678	678	678	678	671
	1450]	736	736	736	736	736	736	728	728	728	728	728	728	726	723	720	717
M																	
O	1500]	786	786	783	779	775	771	768	764	761	757	754	751	748	745	742	739
N	1550]	813	809	805	801	797	793	790	786	783	779	776	773	770	767	764	761
T	1600]	835	831	827	823	819	815	811	808	804	801	798	795	792	789	786	783
H	1650]	857	853	849	845	841	837	833	830	826	823	819	816	813	810	807	805
L	1700]	878	874	870	866	862	858	855	851	848	844	841	838	835	832	829	826
Y	1750]	900	896	892	887	884	880	876	873	869	866	863	859	856	853	851	848
	1800]	921	917	913	909	905	901	897	894	891	887	884	881	878	875	872	869
I	1850]	942	938	934	930	926	922	919	915	912	909	905	902	899	896	893	891
N	1900]	964	959	955	951	947	944	940	936	933	930	927	923	920	917	915	912
C	1950]	985	980	976	972	968	965	961	958	954	951	948	945	942	939	936	933
O																	
M	2000]	1005	1001	997	993	989	986	982	979	975	972	969	966	963	960	957	953
E	2050]	1026	1022	1018	1014	1010	1007	1003	1000	996	993	990	987	984	980	977	974
	2100]	1047	1043	1039	1035	1031	1028	1024	1021	1017	1014	1011	1008	1004	1001	998	995
	2150]	1068	1064	1060	1056	1052	1048	1045	1042	1038	1035	1032	1028	1025	1022	1018	1015
	2200]	1088	1084	1080	1077	1073	1069	1066	1062	1059	1056	1052	1049	1045	1042	1039	1036
	2250]	1109	1105	1101	1097	1094	1090	1086	1083	1080	1076	1073	1069	1066	1062	1059	1056
	2300]	1130	1126	1122	1118	1114	1111	1107	1104	1100	1096	1093	1089	1086	1083	1080	1076
	2350]	1150	1146	1142	1138	1135	1131	1128	1124	1120	1117	1113	1110	1106	1103	1100	1097
	2400]	1170	1166	1163	1159	1155	1152	1148	1144	1140	1137	1133	1130	1127	1123	1120	1117
	2450]	1191	1187	1183	1179	1176	1172	1168	1164	1160	1157	1153	1150	1147	1143	1140	1137
	2500]	1211	1207	1203	1200	1196	1192	1188	1184	1181	1177	1173	1170	1167	1164	1160	1157

Effective October 1, 2004

Five or More Children - Monthly Support

CUSTODIAL PARENT MONTHLY INCOME

	1050	1100	1150	1200	1250	1300	1350	1400	1450	1500	1550	1600	1650	1700	1750	1800
2550]	1231	1228	1224	1220	1216	1212	1208	1204	1200	1197	1193	1190	1187	1184	1180	1177
2600]	1252	1248	1244	1239	1235	1232	1228	1224	1220	1217	1213	1210	1207	1204	1201	1197
2650]	1272	1267	1263	1259	1255	1251	1248	1244	1240	1237	1233	1230	1227	1224	1220	1217
2700]	1291	1287	1283	1279	1275	1271	1267	1264	1260	1257	1253	1250	1247	1244	1240	1237
2750]	1311	1307	1303	1299	1295	1291	1287	1283	1280	1276	1273	1270	1267	1263	1260	1257
2800]	1330	1326	1322	1318	1314	1311	1307	1303	1300	1296	1293	1290	1286	1283	1280	1277
2850]	1350	1346	1342	1338	1334	1330	1326	1323	1319	1316	1313	1309	1306	1303	1300	1297
2900]	1369	1365	1361	1357	1353	1350	1346	1343	1339	1336	1332	1329	1326	1323	1320	1317
2950]	1389	1385	1381	1377	1373	1369	1366	1362	1359	1355	1352	1349	1346	1342	1339	1336
3000]	1408	1404	1400	1396	1392	1389	1385	1382	1378	1375	1372	1368	1365	1362	1359	1356
3050]	1428	1423	1420	1416	1412	1408	1405	1401	1398	1394	1391	1388	1385	1382	1379	1376
3100]	1447	1443	1439	1435	1431	1428	1424	1421	1417	1414	1411	1407	1404	1401	1398	1395
3150]	1466	1462	1458	1454	1451	1447	1444	1440	1437	1433	1430	1427	1424	1421	1418	1415
3200]	1485	1481	1478	1474	1470	1467	1463	1460	1456	1453	1450	1447	1443	1440	1437	1435
3250]	1505	1501	1497	1493	1489	1486	1482	1479	1476	1472	1469	1466	1463	1460	1457	1454
3300]	1524	1520	1516	1512	1509	1505	1502	1498	1495	1492	1489	1485	1482	1479	1476	1474
3350]	1543	1539	1535	1532	1528	1524	1521	1518	1514	1511	1508	1505	1502	1499	1496	1493
3400]	1562	1558	1554	1551	1547	1544	1540	1537	1534	1530	1527	1524	1521	1518	1515	1512
3450]	1581	1577	1574	1570	1566	1563	1560	1556	1553	1550	1547	1544	1540	1538	1535	1532
3500]	1600	1596	1593	1589	1586	1582	1579	1575	1572	1569	1566	1563	1560	1557	1554	1548
3550]	1619	1615	1612	1608	1605	1601	1598	1595	1591	1588	1585	1582	1579	1576	1570	1563
3600]	1638	1635	1631	1627	1624	1620	1617	1614	1611	1607	1604	1601	1598	1592	1585	1579
3650]	1657	1654	1650	1646	1643	1640	1636	1633	1630	1627	1624	1621	1614	1607	1601	1594
3700]	1676	1673	1669	1665	1662	1659	1655	1652	1649	1646	1643	1636	1629	1623	1616	1610
3750]	1695	1692	1688	1684	1681	1678	1674	1671	1668	1665	1658	1651	1645	1638	1632	1625
3800]	1714	1710	1707	1703	1700	1697	1694	1690	1687	1680	1673	1666	1660	1653	1647	1641
3850]	1733	1729	1726	1722	1719	1716	1713	1709	1702	1695	1688	1682	1675	1669	1662	1656
3900]	1752	1748	1745	1741	1738	1735	1732	1724	1717	1710	1704	1697	1690	1684	1677	1671
3950]	1771	1767	1764	1760	1757	1754	1746	1739	1732	1725	1719	1712	1705	1699	1693	1686
4000]	1790	1786	1783	1779	1776	1769	1761	1754	1747	1740	1734	1727	1720	1714	1708	1702
4050]	1808	1805	1802	1798	1791	1783	1776	1769	1762	1755	1749	1742	1735	1729	1723	1717
4100]	1827	1824	1820	1813	1805	1798	1791	1784	1777	1770	1763	1757	1750	1744	1738	1732
4150]	1846	1843	1835	1827	1820	1813	1806	1799	1792	1785	1778	1772	1765	1759	1753	1747
4200]	1865	1857	1849	1842	1835	1827	1820	1813	1806	1800	1793	1787	1780	1774	1768	1762
4250]	1879	1871	1864	1856	1849	1842	1835	1828	1821	1814	1808	1801	1795	1789	1783	1777
4300]	1893	1886	1878	1871	1864	1856	1849	1843	1836	1829	1823	1816	1810	1804	1798	1792
4350]	1908	1900	1893	1885	1878	1871	1864	1857	1850	1844	1837	1831	1825	1819	1812	1807
4400]	1922	1914	1907	1900	1892	1885	1879	1872	1865	1858	1852	1846	1839	1833	1827	1821
4450]	1936	1929	1921	1914	1907	1900	1893	1886	1880	1873	1867	1860	1854	1848	1842	1836
4500]	1950	1943	1935	1928	1921	1914	1907	1901	1894	1888	1881	1875	1869	1863	1857	1851
4550]	1964	1957	1950	1943	1936	1929	1922	1915	1909	1902	1896	1890	1883	1877	1871	1866
4600]	1979	1971	1964	1957	1950	1943	1936	1930	1923	1917	1910	1904	1898	1892	1886	1880
4650]	1993	1985	1978	1971	1964	1957	1951	1944	1937	1931	1925	1919	1913	1907	1901	1895
4700]	2007	1999	1992	1985	1978	1972	1965	1958	1952	1946	1939	1933	1927	1921	1915	1909
4750]	2021	2013	2006	1999	1993	1986	1979	1973	1966	1960	1954	1948	1942	1936	1930	1924
4800]	2035	2027	2020	2013	2007	2000	1993	1987	1981	1974	1968	1962	1956	1950	1944	1938
4850]	2049	2041	2034	2028	2021	2014	2008	2001	1995	1989	1982	1976	1970	1964	1958	1952
4900]	2062	2055	2048	2042	2035	2028	2022	2015	2009	2003	1997	1991	1984	1978	1972	1966
4950]	2076	2069	2062	2056	2049	2042	2036	2030	2023	2017	2011	2005	1998	1992	1986	1981
5000]	2090	2083	2076	2070	2063	2057	2050	2044	2037	2031	2025	2019	2012	2006	2001	1995

NONCUSTODIAL PARENT MONTHLY INCOME

Effective October 1, 2004

2004 MICHIGAN CHILD SUPPORT FORMULA SCHEDULES
MONTHLY BASE SUPPORT

Five or More Children - Monthly Support

CUSTODIAL PARENT MONTHLY INCOME

	1850	1900	1950	2000	2050	2100	2150	2200	2250	2300	2350	2400	2450	2500	2550	2600
250]	25	25	25	25	25	25	25	25	25	25	25	25	25	25	25	25
300]	25	25	25	25	25	25	25	25	25	25	25	25	25	25	25	25
350]	25	25	25	25	25	25	25	25	25	25	25	25	25	25	25	25
400]	25	25	25	25	25	25	25	25	25	25	25	25	25	25	25	25
450]	27	27	27	27	27	27	27	27	25	25	25	25	25	25	25	25
500]	30	30	30	30	30	30	30	30	25	25	25	25	25	25	25	25
550]	33	33	33	33	33	33	33	33	28	28	28	28	28	28	28	28
600]	36	36	36	36	36	36	36	36	30	30	30	30	30	30	30	30
650]	39	39	39	39	39	39	39	39	33	33	33	33	33	33	33	33
700]	42	42	42	42	42	42	42	42	35	35	35	35	35	35	35	35
750]	45	45	45	45	45	45	45	45	38	38	38	38	38	38	38	38
800]	71	71	71	71	71	71	71	71	63	63	63	63	63	63	63	63
850]	121	121	121	121	121	121	121	121	113	113	113	113	113	113	113	113
900]	171	171	171	171	171	171	171	171	163	163	163	163	163	163	163	163
950]	221	221	221	221	221	221	221	221	213	213	213	213	213	213	213	213
1000]	271	271	271	271	271	271	271	271	263	263	263	263	263	263	263	263
1050]	321	321	321	321	321	321	321	321	313	313	313	313	313	313	313	313
1100]	371	371	371	371	371	371	371	371	363	363	363	363	363	363	363	363
1150]	421	421	421	421	421	421	421	421	413	413	413	413	413	413	413	413
1200]	471	471	471	471	471	471	471	471	463	463	463	463	463	463	463	463
1250]	521	521	521	521	521	521	521	521	513	513	513	513	513	513	513	513
1300]	571	571	571	571	571	571	571	571	563	563	563	563	563	563	563	563
1350]	621	621	621	621	621	621	621	621	613	613	613	613	613	613	613	613
1400]	671	671	671	671	671	671	671	671	663	663	663	663	663	663	661	659
1450]	715	712	710	707	705	702	700	698	696	694	691	689	687	685	683	681
1500]	737	734	732	729	727	724	722	720	717	715	713	710	708	706	704	702
1550]	759	756	753	751	748	746	744	741	739	737	734	732	730	728	725	723
1600]	780	778	775	773	770	768	765	763	760	758	756	753	751	749	747	745
1650]	802	799	797	794	792	789	787	784	782	779	777	774	772	770	768	766
1700]	824	821	818	816	813	810	808	805	803	800	798	796	793	791	789	787
1750]	845	842	840	837	834	832	829	826	824	821	819	817	814	812	810	808
1800]	866	864	861	858	855	853	850	847	845	842	840	838	835	833	831	829
1850]	888	885	882	879	876	874	871	868	866	863	861	859	856	854	852	850
1900]	909	906	903	900	897	894	892	889	887	884	882	880	877	875	873	871
1950]	930	927	924	921	918	915	913	910	908	905	903	900	898	896	894	892
2000]	950	947	944	942	939	936	933	931	928	926	923	921	919	917	914	912
2050]	971	968	965	962	959	957	954	952	949	947	944	942	939	937	935	933
2100]	992	989	986	983	980	977	975	972	970	967	965	962	960	958	956	953
2150]	1012	1009	1006	1003	1001	998	995	993	990	988	985	983	981	978	976	974
2200]	1033	1030	1027	1024	1021	1018	1016	1013	1011	1008	1006	1003	1001	999	997	994
2250]	1053	1050	1047	1044	1042	1039	1036	1034	1031	1029	1026	1024	1022	1019	1017	1015
2300]	1073	1070	1068	1065	1062	1059	1057	1054	1052	1049	1047	1044	1042	1040	1037	1035
2350]	1094	1091	1088	1085	1082	1080	1077	1074	1072	1069	1067	1065	1062	1060	1058	1056
2400]	1114	1111	1108	1105	1103	1100	1097	1095	1092	1090	1087	1085	1083	1080	1078	1076
2450]	1134	1131	1128	1126	1123	1120	1117	1115	1112	1110	1107	1105	1103	1101	1098	1096
2500]	1154	1151	1149	1146	1143	1140	1138	1135	1133	1130	1128	1125	1123	1121	1118	1116

(Left margin label: NONCUSTODIAL PARENT MONTHLY INCOME)

Effective October 1, 2004

2004 MICHIGAN CHILD SUPPORT FORMULA SCHEDULES
MONTHLY BASE SUPPORT

Five or More Children - Monthly Support

CUSTODIAL PARENT MONTHLY INCOME

	1850	1900	1950	2000	2050	2100	2150	2200	2250	2300	2350	2400	2450	2500	2550	2600
2550]	1174	1171	1169	1166	1163	1160	1158	1155	1153	1150	1148	1145	1143	1141	1139	1136
2600]	1194	1192	1189	1186	1183	1180	1178	1175	1173	1170	1168	1166	1163	1161	1159	1157
2650]	1214	1212	1209	1206	1203	1201	1198	1195	1193	1190	1188	1186	1183	1181	1179	1177
2700]	1234	1231	1229	1226	1223	1220	1218	1215	1213	1210	1208	1206	1203	1201	1199	1194
2750]	1254	1251	1249	1246	1243	1240	1238	1235	1233	1230	1228	1226	1223	1221	1216	1211
2800]	1274	1271	1268	1266	1263	1260	1258	1255	1253	1250	1248	1246	1243	1238	1233	1228
2850]	1294	1291	1288	1286	1283	1280	1278	1275	1273	1270	1268	1265	1260	1255	1250	1245
2900]	1314	1311	1308	1305	1303	1300	1297	1295	1292	1290	1288	1282	1277	1272	1267	1262
2950]	1334	1331	1328	1325	1322	1320	1317	1315	1312	1310	1304	1299	1294	1289	1283	1279
3000]	1353	1350	1348	1345	1342	1340	1337	1334	1332	1326	1321	1316	1310	1305	1300	1295
3050]	1373	1370	1367	1365	1362	1359	1357	1354	1349	1343	1338	1332	1327	1322	1317	1312
3100]	1393	1390	1387	1384	1382	1379	1376	1371	1365	1360	1354	1349	1344	1338	1333	1328
3150]	1412	1409	1407	1404	1401	1399	1393	1387	1381	1376	1371	1365	1360	1355	1350	1345
3200]	1432	1429	1426	1423	1421	1415	1409	1403	1398	1392	1387	1382	1376	1371	1366	1361
3250]	1451	1448	1446	1443	1437	1431	1425	1420	1414	1409	1403	1398	1393	1388	1383	1378
3300]	1471	1468	1465	1459	1453	1447	1441	1436	1430	1425	1419	1414	1409	1404	1399	1394
3350]	1490	1487	1481	1475	1469	1463	1458	1452	1446	1441	1436	1430	1425	1420	1415	1410
3400]	1510	1503	1497	1491	1485	1479	1474	1468	1462	1457	1452	1446	1441	1436	1431	1426
3450]	1525	1519	1513	1507	1501	1495	1489	1484	1478	1473	1468	1462	1457	1452	1447	1442
3500]	1541	1535	1529	1523	1517	1511	1505	1500	1494	1489	1484	1478	1473	1468	1463	1458
3550]	1557	1551	1545	1539	1533	1527	1521	1516	1510	1505	1499	1494	1489	1484	1479	1474
3600]	1572	1566	1560	1554	1548	1543	1537	1531	1526	1521	1515	1510	1505	1500	1495	1490
3650]	1588	1582	1576	1570	1564	1558	1553	1547	1542	1536	1531	1526	1521	1516	1511	1506
3700]	1604	1597	1591	1585	1580	1574	1568	1563	1557	1552	1547	1542	1537	1532	1527	1522
3750]	1619	1613	1607	1601	1595	1590	1584	1578	1573	1568	1562	1557	1552	1547	1542	1538
3800]	1634	1628	1622	1617	1611	1605	1599	1594	1589	1583	1578	1573	1568	1563	1558	1553
3850]	1650	1644	1638	1632	1626	1621	1615	1610	1604	1599	1594	1589	1584	1579	1574	1569
3900]	1665	1659	1653	1647	1642	1636	1630	1625	1620	1614	1609	1604	1599	1594	1589	1584
3950]	1680	1674	1668	1663	1657	1651	1646	1640	1635	1630	1625	1620	1615	1610	1605	1600
4000]	1696	1690	1684	1678	1672	1667	1661	1656	1650	1645	1640	1635	1630	1625	1620	1615
4050]	1711	1705	1699	1693	1687	1682	1676	1671	1666	1661	1655	1650	1645	1640	1635	1630
4100]	1726	1720	1714	1708	1703	1697	1692	1686	1681	1676	1671	1666	1660	1655	1650	1645
4150]	1741	1735	1729	1723	1718	1712	1707	1702	1696	1691	1686	1681	1675	1670	1665	1660
4200]	1756	1750	1744	1739	1733	1727	1722	1717	1711	1706	1701	1696	1690	1685	1680	1676
4250]	1771	1765	1759	1754	1748	1743	1737	1732	1726	1721	1716	1711	1705	1700	1695	1691
4300]	1786	1780	1774	1769	1763	1758	1752	1747	1741	1736	1731	1726	1720	1715	1710	1706
4350]	1801	1795	1789	1784	1778	1773	1767	1762	1756	1751	1746	1740	1735	1730	1725	1720
4400]	1815	1810	1804	1798	1793	1787	1782	1776	1771	1766	1760	1755	1750	1745	1740	1735
4450]	1830	1825	1819	1813	1808	1802	1797	1791	1786	1780	1775	1770	1765	1760	1755	1750
4500]	1845	1839	1834	1828	1822	1817	1811	1806	1800	1795	1790	1785	1780	1775	1770	1765
4550]	1860	1854	1848	1843	1837	1831	1826	1820	1815	1810	1805	1800	1795	1790	1785	1780
4600]	1874	1869	1863	1857	1851	1846	1840	1835	1830	1825	1819	1814	1809	1804	1799	1795
4650]	1889	1883	1877	1872	1866	1860	1855	1850	1844	1839	1834	1829	1824	1819	1814	1809
4700]	1903	1898	1892	1886	1880	1875	1870	1864	1859	1854	1849	1844	1839	1834	1829	1824
4750]	1918	1912	1906	1900	1895	1889	1884	1879	1873	1868	1863	1858	1853	1848	1843	1839
4800]	1932	1926	1920	1915	1909	1904	1898	1893	1888	1883	1878	1873	1868	1863	1858	1853
4850]	1946	1940	1935	1929	1924	1918	1913	1908	1902	1897	1892	1887	1882	1877	1873	1868
4900]	1960	1955	1949	1944	1938	1933	1927	1922	1917	1912	1907	1902	1897	1892	1887	1882
4950]	1975	1969	1963	1958	1952	1947	1942	1936	1931	1926	1921	1916	1911	1906	1902	1897
5000]	1989	1983	1978	1972	1967	1961	1956	1951	1946	1940	1935	1931	1926	1921	1916	1911

The left margin column reads vertically: NONCUSTODIAL PARENT MONTHLY INCOME

Five or More Children - Monthly Support

CUSTODIAL PARENT MONTHLY INCOME

	2650	2700	2750	2800	2850	2900	2950	3000	3050	3100	3150	3200	3250	3300	3350	3400
250]	25	25	25	25	25	25	25	25	25	25	25	25	25	25	25	25
300]	25	25	25	25	25	25	25	25	25	25	25	25	25	25	25	25
350]	25	25	25	25	25	25	25	25	25	25	25	25	25	25	25	25
400]	25	25	25	25	25	25	25	25	25	25	25	25	25	25	25	25
450]	25	25	25	25	25	25	25	25	25	25	25	25	25	25	25	25
500]	25	25	25	25	25	25	25	25	25	25	25	25	25	25	25	25
550]	28	25	25	25	25	25	25	25	25	25	25	25	25	25	25	25
600]	30	25	25	25	25	25	25	25	25	25	25	25	25	25	25	25
650]	33	26	26	26	26	26	26	26	26	26	25	25	25	25	25	25
700]	35	28	28	28	28	28	28	28	28	28	25	25	25	25	25	25
750]	38	30	30	30	30	30	30	30	30	30	25	25	25	25	25	25
800]	63	55	55	55	55	55	55	55	55	55	49	49	49	49	49	49
850]	113	105	105	105	105	105	105	105	105	105	99	99	99	99	99	99
900]	163	155	155	155	155	155	155	155	155	155	149	149	149	149	149	149
950]	213	205	205	205	205	205	205	205	205	205	199	199	199	199	199	199
1000]	263	255	255	255	255	255	255	255	255	255	249	249	249	249	249	249
1050]	313	305	305	305	305	305	305	305	305	305	299	299	299	299	299	299
1100]	363	355	355	355	355	355	355	355	355	355	349	349	349	349	349	349
1150]	413	405	405	405	405	405	405	405	405	405	399	399	399	399	399	399
1200]	463	455	455	455	455	455	455	455	455	455	449	449	449	449	449	449
1250]	513	505	505	505	505	505	505	505	505	505	499	499	499	499	499	499
1300]	563	555	555	555	555	555	555	555	555	555	549	549	549	549	549	549
1350]	613	605	605	605	605	605	605	605	605	605	599	599	599	599	599	599
1400]	657	655	653	652	650	648	646	645	643	642	640	639	637	636	634	633
1450]	679	677	675	673	671	670	668	666	665	663	661	660	658	657	655	654
1500]	700	698	696	694	693	691	689	687	686	684	683	681	680	678	677	675
1550]	721	719	718	716	714	712	710	709	707	705	704	702	701	699	698	696
1600]	743	741	739	737	735	733	731	730	728	726	725	723	722	720	719	717
1650]	764	762	760	758	756	754	753	751	749	747	746	744	743	741	740	738
1700]	785	783	781	779	777	775	774	772	770	768	767	765	764	762	761	759
1750]	806	804	802	800	798	796	795	793	791	789	788	786	784	783	781	780
1800]	827	825	823	821	819	817	815	814	812	810	809	807	805	804	802	801
1850]	848	846	844	842	840	838	836	834	833	831	829	828	826	824	823	821
1900]	869	867	865	863	861	859	857	855	853	852	850	848	847	845	844	840
1950]	889	887	885	883	881	880	878	876	874	872	871	869	867	866	862	859
2000]	910	908	906	904	902	900	898	897	895	893	891	890	888	884	881	877
2050]	931	929	927	925	923	921	919	917	915	914	912	910	906	903	899	895
2100]	951	949	947	945	943	941	940	938	936	934	932	929	925	921	917	914
2150]	972	970	968	966	964	962	960	958	956	955	951	947	943	939	935	932
2200]	992	990	988	986	984	982	980	979	977	973	969	965	961	957	953	950
2250]	1013	1011	1009	1007	1005	1003	1001	999	995	991	987	983	979	975	971	968
2300]	1033	1031	1029	1027	1025	1023	1021	1017	1013	1009	1005	1001	997	993	989	986
2350]	1053	1051	1049	1047	1045	1043	1039	1035	1031	1026	1022	1018	1015	1011	1007	1003
2400]	1074	1072	1070	1068	1066	1061	1057	1053	1048	1044	1040	1036	1032	1028	1025	1021
2450]	1094	1092	1090	1088	1083	1079	1074	1070	1066	1062	1058	1054	1050	1046	1042	1038
2500]	1114	1112	1110	1105	1101	1096	1092	1088	1083	1079	1075	1071	1067	1063	1060	1056

NONCUSTODIAL PARENT MONTHLY INCOME

Effective October 1, 2004

Five or More Children - Monthly Support

CUSTODIAL PARENT MONTHLY INCOME

		2650	2700	2750	2800	2850	2900	2950	3000	3050	3100	3150	3200	3250	3300	3350	3400
	2550]	1134	1132	1127	1123	1118	1114	1109	1105	1101	1097	1093	1089	1085	1081	1077	1073
	2600]	1154	1150	1145	1140	1136	1131	1127	1123	1118	1114	1110	1106	1102	1098	1094	1091
	2650]	1172	1167	1162	1158	1153	1148	1144	1140	1136	1131	1127	1123	1119	1115	1112	1108
	2700]	1189	1184	1179	1175	1170	1166	1161	1157	1153	1149	1144	1140	1136	1133	1129	1125
	2750]	1206	1201	1196	1192	1187	1183	1178	1174	1170	1166	1162	1158	1154	1150	1146	1142
	2800]	1223	1218	1214	1209	1204	1200	1195	1191	1187	1183	1179	1175	1171	1167	1163	1159
	2850]	1240	1235	1230	1226	1221	1217	1212	1208	1204	1200	1196	1191	1187	1184	1180	1176
N	2900]	1257	1252	1247	1243	1238	1234	1229	1225	1221	1216	1212	1208	1204	1200	1197	1193
O	2950]	1274	1269	1264	1259	1255	1250	1246	1242	1237	1233	1229	1225	1221	1217	1213	1210
N																	
C	3000]	1290	1286	1281	1276	1272	1267	1263	1258	1254	1250	1246	1242	1238	1234	1230	1226
U	3050]	1307	1302	1297	1293	1288	1284	1279	1275	1271	1267	1263	1258	1254	1251	1247	1243
S	3100]	1324	1319	1314	1309	1305	1300	1296	1292	1287	1283	1279	1275	1271	1267	1263	1259
T	3150]	1340	1335	1331	1326	1321	1317	1312	1308	1304	1300	1296	1292	1288	1284	1280	1276
O	3200]	1356	1352	1347	1342	1338	1333	1329	1325	1320	1316	1312	1308	1304	1300	1296	1292
D	3250]	1373	1368	1363	1359	1354	1350	1345	1341	1337	1333	1328	1324	1320	1316	1312	1308
I	3300]	1389	1384	1380	1375	1370	1366	1362	1357	1353	1349	1345	1341	1336	1332	1328	1324
A	3350]	1405	1400	1396	1391	1387	1382	1378	1374	1369	1365	1361	1357	1352	1348	1344	1340
L	3400]	1421	1417	1412	1407	1403	1398	1394	1390	1385	1381	1377	1373	1368	1364	1360	1356
	3450]	1437	1433	1428	1423	1419	1415	1410	1406	1402	1397	1393	1389	1384	1380	1376	1372
P																	
A	3500]	1454	1449	1444	1440	1435	1431	1426	1422	1417	1413	1409	1405	1400	1396	1392	1388
R	3550]	1469	1465	1460	1456	1451	1447	1442	1438	1433	1429	1425	1420	1416	1412	1408	1404
E	3600]	1485	1481	1476	1471	1467	1462	1458	1453	1449	1445	1440	1436	1432	1428	1424	1420
N	3650]	1501	1497	1492	1487	1483	1478	1474	1469	1465	1460	1456	1452	1448	1444	1440	1436
T	3700]	1517	1512	1508	1503	1498	1494	1489	1485	1480	1476	1472	1468	1463	1459	1455	1451
	3750]	1533	1528	1523	1519	1514	1509	1505	1500	1496	1492	1487	1483	1479	1475	1471	1467
M	3800]	1548	1544	1539	1534	1529	1525	1520	1516	1512	1507	1503	1499	1495	1491	1486	1483
O	3850]	1564	1559	1554	1550	1545	1540	1536	1531	1527	1523	1518	1514	1510	1506	1502	1498
N	3900]	1579	1575	1570	1565	1560	1556	1551	1547	1543	1538	1534	1530	1526	1522	1518	1514
T	3950]	1595	1590	1585	1580	1576	1571	1567	1562	1558	1554	1549	1545	1541	1537	1533	1529
H																	
L	4000]	1610	1605	1600	1596	1591	1587	1582	1578	1573	1569	1565	1561	1556	1552	1548	1544
Y	4050]	1625	1620	1616	1611	1606	1602	1597	1593	1589	1584	1580	1576	1572	1568	1564	1560
	4100]	1640	1636	1631	1626	1622	1617	1613	1608	1604	1600	1595	1591	1587	1583	1579	1575
I	4150]	1656	1651	1646	1641	1637	1632	1628	1623	1619	1615	1611	1606	1602	1598	1594	1590
N	4200]	1671	1666	1661	1657	1652	1647	1643	1639	1634	1630	1626	1622	1618	1613	1609	1606
C	4250]	1686	1681	1676	1672	1667	1663	1658	1654	1649	1645	1641	1637	1633	1629	1625	1621
O	4300]	1701	1696	1691	1687	1682	1678	1673	1669	1664	1660	1656	1652	1648	1644	1640	1636
M	4350]	1716	1711	1706	1702	1697	1693	1688	1684	1680	1675	1671	1667	1663	1659	1655	1651
E	4400]	1731	1726	1721	1717	1712	1708	1703	1699	1695	1690	1686	1682	1678	1674	1670	1666
	4450]	1745	1741	1736	1732	1727	1723	1718	1714	1710	1705	1701	1697	1693	1689	1685	1681
	4500]	1760	1756	1751	1746	1742	1737	1733	1729	1724	1720	1716	1712	1708	1704	1700	1696
	4550]	1775	1770	1766	1761	1757	1752	1748	1744	1739	1735	1731	1727	1723	1719	1715	1711
	4600]	1790	1785	1781	1776	1772	1767	1763	1758	1754	1750	1746	1742	1738	1734	1730	1726
	4650]	1805	1800	1795	1791	1786	1782	1778	1773	1769	1765	1761	1757	1753	1749	1745	1741
	4700]	1819	1815	1810	1806	1801	1797	1792	1788	1784	1780	1775	1771	1767	1763	1759	1756
	4750]	1834	1829	1825	1820	1816	1811	1807	1803	1799	1794	1790	1786	1782	1778	1774	1770
	4800]	1849	1844	1839	1835	1830	1826	1822	1817	1813	1809	1805	1801	1797	1793	1789	1785
	4850]	1863	1859	1854	1850	1845	1841	1836	1832	1828	1824	1820	1816	1812	1808	1803	1799
	4900]	1878	1873	1869	1864	1860	1855	1851	1847	1843	1838	1834	1830	1826	1822	1818	1814
	4950]	1892	1888	1883	1879	1874	1870	1866	1861	1857	1853	1849	1845	1841	1836	1832	1828
	5000]	1907	1902	1898	1893	1889	1884	1880	1876	1872	1868	1864	1859	1855	1851	1846	1842

Effective October 1, 2004

Five or More Children - Monthly Support

CUSTODIAL PARENT MONTHLY INCOME

	3450	3500	3550	3600	3650	3700	3750	3800	3850	3900	3950	4000	4050	4100	4150	4200
250]	25	25	25	25	25	25	25	25	25	25	25	25	25	25	25	25
300]	25	25	25	25	25	25	25	25	25	25	25	25	25	25	25	25
350]	25	25	25	25	25	25	25	25	25	25	25	25	25	25	25	25
400]	25	25	25	25	25	25	25	25	25	25	25	25	25	25	25	25
450]	25	25	25	25	25	25	25	25	25	25	25	25	25	25	25	25
500]	25	25	25	25	25	25	25	25	25	25	25	25	25	25	25	25
550]	25	25	25	25	25	25	25	25	25	25	25	25	25	25	25	25
600]	25	25	25	25	25	25	25	25	25	25	25	25	25	25	25	25
650]	25	25	25	25	25	25	25	25	25	25	25	25	25	25	25	25
700]	25	25	25	25	25	25	25	25	25	25	25	25	25	25	25	25
750]	25	25	25	25	25	25	25	25	25	25	25	25	25	25	25	25
800]	49	49	49	49	49	49	49	49	49	49	49	49	49	49	49	49
850]	99	99	99	99	99	99	99	99	99	99	99	99	99	99	99	99
900]	149	149	149	149	149	149	149	149	149	149	149	149	149	149	149	149
950]	199	199	199	199	199	199	199	199	199	199	199	199	199	199	199	199
1000]	249	249	249	249	249	249	249	249	249	249	249	249	249	249	249	249
1050]	299	299	299	299	299	299	299	299	299	299	299	299	299	299	299	299
1100]	349	349	349	349	349	349	349	349	349	349	349	349	349	349	349	349
1150]	399	399	399	399	399	399	399	399	399	399	399	399	399	399	399	399
1200]	449	449	449	449	449	449	449	449	449	449	449	449	449	449	449	449
1250]	499	499	499	499	499	499	499	499	499	499	499	499	499	499	499	499
1300]	549	549	549	549	549	549	549	549	549	549	549	549	549	549	549	549
1350]	599	599	599	599	599	599	599	599	599	599	597	594	592	590	587	585
1400]	631	630	629	628	626	625	624	623	622	619	616	614	612	609	607	604
1450]	653	651	650	649	647	646	645	644	641	638	636	633	631	628	626	624
1500]	674	672	671	670	668	667	666	663	660	658	655	653	650	648	645	643
1550]	695	693	692	691	689	688	685	683	680	677	674	672	669	667	664	662
1600]	716	714	713	712	710	707	705	702	699	696	693	691	688	686	683	681
1650]	737	735	734	733	730	727	724	721	718	715	712	710	707	704	702	699
1700]	758	756	755	752	749	746	743	740	737	734	731	728	726	723	721	718
1750]	778	777	774	771	767	764	761	758	756	753	750	747	744	742	739	737
1800]	799	796	793	789	786	783	780	777	774	771	768	766	763	760	758	755
1850]	818	815	811	808	805	802	799	796	793	790	787	784	781	779	776	773
1900]	837	833	830	827	823	820	817	814	811	808	805	803	800	797	794	792
1950]	855	852	848	845	842	839	836	833	830	827	824	821	818	815	812	810
2000]	874	870	867	863	860	857	854	851	848	845	842	839	836	833	831	828
2050]	892	888	885	882	878	875	872	869	866	863	860	857	854	851	849	846
2100]	910	907	903	900	897	893	890	887	884	881	878	875	872	869	866	864
2150]	928	925	921	918	915	911	908	905	902	899	896	893	890	887	884	882
2200]	946	943	939	936	933	929	926	923	920	917	914	911	908	905	902	899
2250]	964	961	957	954	950	947	944	941	937	934	931	928	925	923	920	917
2300]	982	978	975	971	968	965	962	958	955	952	949	946	943	940	937	934
2350]	1000	996	993	989	986	982	979	976	973	970	967	964	961	958	955	952
2400]	1017	1014	1010	1007	1003	1000	997	993	990	987	984	981	978	975	972	969
2450]	1035	1031	1028	1024	1021	1017	1014	1011	1008	1005	1001	998	995	992	989	986
2500]	1052	1049	1045	1042	1038	1035	1032	1028	1025	1022	1019	1016	1012	1009	1006	1003

NONCUSTODIAL PARENT MONTHLY INCOME

Effective October 1, 2004

Five or More Children - Monthly Support

CUSTODIAL PARENT MONTHLY INCOME

		3450	3500	3550	3600	3650	3700	3750	3800	3850	3900	3950	4000	4050	4100	4150	4200
	2550]	1070	1066	1062	1059	1056	1052	1049	1046	1042	1039	1036	1033	1029	1026	1023	1020
	2600]	1087	1083	1080	1076	1073	1069	1066	1063	1059	1056	1053	1050	1046	1043	1040	1037
	2650]	1104	1101	1097	1093	1090	1087	1083	1080	1077	1073	1070	1067	1063	1060	1057	1054
	2700]	1121	1118	1114	1111	1107	1104	1100	1097	1093	1090	1087	1083	1080	1077	1074	1071
	2750]	1138	1135	1131	1128	1124	1121	1117	1114	1110	1107	1104	1100	1097	1094	1091	1088
	2800]	1155	1152	1148	1144	1141	1137	1134	1130	1127	1124	1120	1117	1114	1111	1107	1104
	2850]	1172	1169	1165	1161	1158	1154	1151	1147	1144	1140	1137	1134	1130	1127	1124	1121
N	2900]	1189	1185	1182	1178	1174	1171	1167	1164	1160	1157	1154	1150	1147	1144	1141	1138
O	2950]	1206	1202	1198	1195	1191	1187	1184	1180	1177	1173	1170	1167	1164	1160	1157	1154
N																	
C	3000]	1222	1219	1215	1211	1207	1204	1200	1197	1193	1190	1187	1183	1180	1177	1174	1170
U	3050]	1239	1235	1231	1228	1224	1220	1217	1213	1210	1206	1203	1200	1196	1193	1190	1187
S	3100]	1255	1252	1248	1244	1240	1237	1233	1230	1226	1223	1219	1216	1213	1209	1206	1203
T	3150]	1272	1268	1264	1260	1257	1253	1249	1246	1242	1239	1236	1232	1229	1226	1222	1219
O	3200]	1288	1284	1280	1277	1273	1269	1266	1262	1259	1255	1252	1248	1245	1242	1239	1236
D	3250]	1304	1300	1297	1293	1289	1285	1282	1278	1275	1271	1268	1265	1261	1258	1255	1252
I	3300]	1320	1316	1313	1309	1305	1302	1298	1294	1291	1287	1284	1281	1277	1274	1271	1268
A	3350]	1336	1333	1329	1325	1321	1318	1314	1310	1307	1304	1300	1297	1293	1290	1287	1284
L	3400]	1352	1349	1345	1341	1337	1334	1330	1326	1323	1320	1316	1313	1309	1306	1303	1300
	3450]	1368	1365	1361	1357	1353	1350	1346	1342	1339	1335	1332	1329	1325	1322	1319	1316
P																	
A	3500]	1384	1380	1377	1373	1369	1365	1362	1358	1355	1351	1348	1345	1341	1338	1335	1332
R	3550]	1400	1396	1392	1389	1385	1381	1378	1374	1371	1367	1364	1360	1357	1354	1351	1347
E	3600]	1416	1412	1408	1405	1401	1397	1394	1390	1386	1383	1380	1376	1373	1370	1366	1363
N	3650]	1432	1428	1424	1420	1417	1413	1409	1406	1402	1399	1395	1392	1389	1385	1382	1379
T	3700]	1447	1444	1440	1436	1432	1429	1425	1421	1418	1414	1411	1408	1404	1401	1398	1395
	3750]	1463	1459	1455	1452	1448	1444	1441	1437	1434	1430	1427	1423	1420	1417	1413	1410
M	3800]	1479	1475	1471	1467	1463	1460	1456	1453	1449	1446	1442	1439	1436	1432	1429	1426
O	3850]	1494	1490	1486	1483	1479	1475	1472	1468	1465	1461	1458	1454	1451	1448	1445	1441
N	3900]	1510	1506	1502	1498	1495	1491	1487	1484	1480	1477	1473	1470	1467	1463	1460	1457
T	3950]	1525	1521	1517	1514	1510	1506	1503	1499	1496	1492	1489	1485	1482	1479	1475	1472
H																	
L	4000]	1540	1537	1533	1529	1525	1522	1518	1515	1511	1508	1504	1501	1497	1494	1491	1487
Y	4050]	1556	1552	1548	1544	1541	1537	1534	1530	1526	1523	1520	1516	1513	1509	1506	1502
	4100]	1571	1567	1564	1560	1556	1552	1549	1545	1542	1538	1535	1531	1528	1525	1521	1518
I	4150]	1586	1583	1579	1575	1571	1568	1564	1561	1557	1554	1550	1547	1543	1540	1536	1533
N	4200]	1602	1598	1594	1590	1587	1583	1579	1576	1572	1569	1565	1562	1558	1555	1551	1548
C	4250]	1617	1613	1609	1606	1602	1598	1595	1591	1588	1584	1580	1577	1573	1569	1566	1562
O	4300]	1632	1628	1624	1621	1617	1613	1610	1606	1603	1599	1595	1592	1588	1584	1581	1577
M	4350]	1647	1643	1640	1636	1632	1628	1625	1621	1617	1614	1610	1606	1603	1599	1596	1592
E	4400]	1662	1658	1655	1651	1647	1644	1640	1636	1632	1629	1625	1621	1618	1614	1611	1607
	4450]	1677	1673	1670	1666	1662	1659	1655	1651	1647	1643	1640	1636	1632	1629	1625	1622
	4500]	1692	1688	1685	1681	1677	1673	1669	1666	1662	1658	1654	1651	1647	1644	1640	1637
	4550]	1707	1703	1700	1696	1692	1688	1684	1680	1676	1673	1669	1665	1662	1658	1655	1651
	4600]	1722	1718	1714	1710	1706	1703	1699	1695	1691	1687	1684	1680	1676	1673	1669	1666
	4650]	1737	1733	1729	1725	1721	1717	1713	1710	1706	1702	1698	1695	1691	1688	1684	1681
	4700]	1752	1748	1744	1740	1736	1732	1728	1724	1720	1717	1713	1709	1706	1702	1699	1695
	4750]	1766	1762	1758	1754	1750	1746	1742	1739	1735	1731	1727	1724	1720	1717	1713	1710
	4800]	1781	1777	1773	1769	1765	1761	1757	1753	1749	1746	1742	1738	1735	1731	1728	1724
	4850]	1795	1791	1787	1783	1779	1775	1771	1768	1764	1760	1756	1753	1749	1746	1742	1739
	4900]	1809	1805	1801	1797	1794	1790	1786	1782	1778	1775	1771	1767	1764	1760	1757	1753
	4950]	1824	1820	1816	1812	1808	1804	1800	1796	1793	1789	1785	1782	1778	1775	1771	1768
	5000]	1838	1834	1830	1826	1822	1818	1815	1811	1807	1803	1800	1796	1793	1789	1786	1782

Effective October 1, 2004

2004 MICHIGAN CHILD SUPPORT FORMULA SCHEDULES
MONTHLY BASE SUPPORT

Five or More Children - Monthly Support

CUSTODIAL PARENT MONTHLY INCOME

		4250	4300	4350	4400	4450	4500	4550	4600	4650	4700	4750	4800	4850	4900	4950	5000
	250]	25	25	25	25	25	25	25	25	25	25	25	25	25	25	25	25
	300]	25	25	25	25	25	25	25	25	25	25	25	25	25	25	25	25
	350]	25	25	25	25	25	25	25	25	25	25	25	25	25	25	25	25
	400]	25	25	25	25	25	25	25	25	25	25	25	25	25	25	25	25
	450]	25	25	25	25	25	25	25	25	25	25	25	25	25	25	25	25
	500]	25	25	25	25	25	25	25	25	25	25	25	25	25	25	25	25
N	550]	25	25	25	25	25	25	25	25	25	25	25	25	25	25	25	25
O	600]	25	25	25	25	25	25	25	25	25	25	25	25	25	25	25	25
N	650]	25	25	25	25	25	25	25	25	25	25	25	25	25	25	25	25
C	700]	25	25	25	25	25	25	25	25	25	25	25	25	25	25	25	25
U	750]	25	25	25	25	25	25	25	25	25	25	25	25	25	25	25	25
S	800]	49	49	49	49	49	49	49	49	49	49	49	49	49	49	49	49
T	850]	99	99	99	99	99	99	99	99	99	99	99	99	99	99	99	99
O	900]	149	149	149	149	149	149	149	149	149	149	149	149	149	149	149	149
D	950]	199	199	199	199	199	199	199	199	199	199	199	199	199	199	199	199
I																	
A	1000]	249	249	249	249	249	249	249	249	249	249	249	249	249	249	249	249
L	1050]	299	299	299	299	299	299	299	299	299	299	299	299	299	299	299	299
	1100]	349	349	349	349	349	349	349	349	349	349	349	349	349	349	349	349
P	1150]	399	399	399	399	399	399	399	399	399	399	399	399	399	399	399	399
A	1200]	449	449	449	449	449	449	449	449	449	449	449	449	449	449	449	449
R	1250]	499	499	499	499	499	499	499	499	499	499	499	499	499	499	499	499
E	1300]	549	549	549	549	549	549	549	549	547	545	543	542	540	538	536	535
N	1350]	583	581	578	576	574	572	570	568	566	564	562	561	559	557	555	554
T	1400]	602	600	598	596	593	591	589	587	585	583	581	580	578	576	574	572
	1450]	621	619	617	615	612	610	608	606	604	602	600	598	596	595	593	591
M																	
O	1500]	640	638	636	634	631	629	627	625	623	621	619	617	615	613	611	609
N	1550]	659	657	655	652	650	648	646	644	642	640	638	636	634	632	630	628
T	1600]	678	676	673	671	669	667	664	662	660	658	656	654	652	650	648	646
H	1650]	697	695	692	690	687	685	683	681	679	677	674	672	670	668	666	664
L	1700]	716	713	711	708	706	704	701	699	697	695	693	691	688	686	684	682
Y	1750]	734	732	729	727	724	722	720	718	715	713	711	709	707	704	702	700
	1800]	753	750	748	745	743	740	738	736	733	731	729	727	724	722	720	718
I	1850]	771	768	766	763	761	759	756	754	752	749	747	745	742	740	738	736
N	1900]	789	786	784	781	779	777	774	772	769	767	765	762	760	758	756	754
C	1950]	807	805	802	800	797	795	792	790	787	785	783	780	778	776	773	771
O																	
M	2000]	825	823	820	817	815	812	810	807	805	803	800	798	796	793	791	789
E	2050]	843	841	838	835	833	830	828	825	823	820	818	815	813	811	809	806
	2100]	861	858	856	853	850	848	845	843	840	838	835	833	831	828	826	824
	2150]	879	876	873	871	868	865	863	860	858	855	853	850	848	846	843	841
	2200]	896	894	891	888	885	883	880	878	875	873	870	868	865	863	861	858
	2250]	914	911	908	906	903	900	898	895	892	890	887	885	883	880	878	875
	2300]	931	929	926	923	920	918	915	912	910	907	905	902	900	897	895	893
	2350]	949	946	943	940	937	935	932	929	927	924	922	919	917	914	912	910
	2400]	966	963	960	957	955	952	949	947	944	941	939	936	934	931	929	927
	2450]	983	980	977	975	972	969	966	964	961	958	956	953	951	948	946	944
	2500]	1000	997	994	992	989	986	983	981	978	975	973	970	968	965	963	960

(Left vertical label: NONCUSTODIAL PARENT MONTHLY INCOME)

Effective October 1, 2004

Five or More Children - Monthly Support

CUSTODIAL PARENT MONTHLY INCOME

NON CUSTODIAL PARENT MONTHLY INCOME	4250	4300	4350	4400	4450	4500	4550	4600	4650	4700	4750	4800	4850	4900	4950	5000
2550]	1017	1014	1011	1009	1006	1003	1000	998	995	992	990	987	985	982	980	977
2600]	1034	1031	1028	1025	1023	1020	1017	1014	1012	1009	1006	1004	1001	999	996	994
2650]	1051	1048	1045	1042	1039	1037	1034	1031	1028	1026	1023	1021	1018	1016	1013	1011
2700]	1068	1065	1062	1059	1056	1053	1051	1048	1045	1042	1040	1037	1035	1032	1030	1027
2750]	1085	1082	1079	1076	1073	1070	1067	1064	1062	1059	1056	1054	1051	1049	1046	1044
2800]	1101	1098	1095	1092	1090	1087	1084	1081	1078	1076	1073	1070	1068	1065	1063	1060
2850]	1118	1115	1112	1109	1106	1103	1100	1098	1095	1092	1089	1087	1084	1082	1079	1077
2900]	1134	1131	1128	1125	1123	1120	1117	1114	1111	1109	1106	1103	1101	1098	1096	1093
2950]	1151	1148	1145	1142	1139	1136	1133	1130	1128	1125	1122	1120	1117	1114	1112	1109
3000]	1167	1164	1161	1158	1155	1152	1150	1147	1144	1141	1139	1136	1133	1131	1128	1126
3050]	1184	1181	1178	1175	1172	1169	1166	1163	1160	1158	1155	1152	1150	1147	1144	1142
3100]	1200	1197	1194	1191	1188	1185	1182	1179	1177	1174	1171	1168	1166	1163	1161	1158
3150]	1216	1213	1210	1207	1204	1201	1198	1196	1193	1190	1187	1185	1182	1179	1177	1174
3200]	1232	1229	1226	1223	1220	1217	1215	1212	1209	1206	1203	1201	1198	1195	1193	1190
3250]	1249	1245	1242	1239	1236	1233	1231	1228	1225	1222	1219	1217	1214	1211	1208	1206
3300]	1265	1262	1258	1255	1252	1250	1247	1244	1241	1238	1235	1233	1230	1227	1224	1221
3350]	1281	1278	1274	1271	1268	1266	1263	1260	1257	1254	1251	1249	1246	1243	1240	1237
3400]	1297	1293	1290	1287	1284	1281	1279	1276	1273	1270	1267	1264	1261	1258	1256	1253
3450]	1313	1309	1306	1303	1300	1297	1294	1292	1289	1286	1283	1280	1277	1274	1271	1268
3500]	1328	1325	1322	1319	1316	1313	1310	1307	1304	1301	1298	1295	1292	1290	1287	1284
3550]	1344	1341	1338	1335	1332	1329	1326	1323	1320	1317	1314	1311	1308	1305	1302	1299
3600]	1360	1357	1354	1351	1348	1345	1342	1339	1335	1332	1329	1326	1323	1321	1318	1315
3650]	1376	1373	1369	1366	1363	1360	1357	1354	1351	1348	1345	1342	1339	1336	1333	1330
3700]	1391	1388	1385	1382	1379	1376	1373	1369	1366	1363	1360	1357	1354	1351	1348	1346
3750]	1407	1404	1401	1398	1394	1391	1388	1385	1382	1379	1376	1373	1370	1367	1364	1361
3800]	1423	1419	1416	1413	1410	1406	1403	1400	1397	1394	1391	1388	1385	1382	1379	1376
3850]	1438	1435	1432	1428	1425	1422	1419	1415	1412	1409	1406	1403	1400	1397	1394	1391
3900]	1454	1450	1447	1443	1440	1437	1434	1431	1428	1424	1421	1418	1415	1412	1410	1407
3950]	1469	1465	1462	1459	1455	1452	1449	1446	1443	1440	1437	1434	1431	1428	1425	1422
4000]	1484	1480	1477	1474	1471	1467	1464	1461	1458	1455	1452	1449	1446	1443	1440	1437
4050]	1499	1496	1492	1489	1486	1482	1479	1476	1473	1470	1467	1464	1461	1458	1455	1452
4100]	1514	1511	1507	1504	1501	1497	1494	1491	1488	1485	1482	1479	1476	1473	1470	1467
4150]	1529	1526	1522	1519	1516	1512	1509	1506	1503	1500	1497	1494	1491	1488	1485	1482
4200]	1544	1541	1537	1534	1531	1527	1524	1521	1518	1515	1512	1509	1506	1503	1500	1497
4250]	1559	1556	1552	1549	1546	1542	1539	1536	1533	1530	1527	1524	1521	1518	1515	1512
4300]	1574	1571	1567	1564	1561	1557	1554	1551	1548	1545	1542	1539	1536	1533	1530	1527
4350]	1589	1585	1582	1579	1575	1572	1569	1566	1563	1560	1556	1553	1550	1547	1544	1542
4400]	1604	1600	1597	1594	1590	1587	1584	1581	1577	1574	1571	1568	1565	1562	1559	1556
4450]	1618	1615	1612	1608	1605	1602	1599	1595	1592	1589	1586	1583	1580	1577	1574	1571
4500]	1633	1630	1626	1623	1620	1617	1613	1610	1607	1604	1601	1598	1595	1592	1589	1586
4550]	1648	1644	1641	1638	1634	1631	1628	1625	1622	1619	1616	1612	1609	1606	1604	1601
4600]	1663	1659	1656	1652	1649	1646	1643	1640	1636	1633	1630	1627	1624	1621	1618	1615
4650]	1677	1674	1670	1667	1664	1661	1657	1654	1651	1648	1645	1642	1639	1636	1633	1630
4700]	1692	1688	1685	1682	1678	1675	1672	1669	1666	1663	1659	1656	1653	1650	1647	1645
4750]	1706	1703	1700	1696	1693	1690	1687	1683	1680	1677	1674	1671	1668	1665	1662	1659
4800]	1721	1717	1714	1711	1708	1704	1701	1698	1695	1692	1689	1686	1682	1680	1677	1674
4850]	1735	1732	1729	1725	1722	1719	1716	1712	1709	1706	1703	1700	1697	1694	1691	1688
4900]	1750	1746	1743	1740	1736	1733	1730	1727	1724	1721	1718	1715	1711	1709	1706	1703
4950]	1764	1761	1758	1754	1751	1748	1744	1741	1738	1735	1732	1729	1726	1723	1720	1717
5000]	1779	1775	1772	1769	1765	1762	1759	1756	1753	1749	1746	1743	1740	1737	1734	1732

Effective October 1, 2004

Forms

Note: To remove the forms cleanly from the book, follow these steps: 1) keep the back of the book as flat as possible on a table or other hard surface 2) open the front of the book at the form you want to remove and pull gently on the form, keeping the back of the book flat.

Original - Friend of the court/Chief judge/
Citizen Advisory Committee
1st copy - Grieving party (with response)
2nd copy - SCAO (with response)
3rd copy - Grieving party (on filing)

| STATE OF MICHIGAN
JUDICIAL CIRCUIT
COUNTY | FRIEND OF THE COURT GRIEVANCE
☐ Friend of the Court ☐ Chief Judge
☐ Citizen Advisory Committee | THIS SPACE FOR COURT USE ONLY
CASE NO.:
GRIEVANCE NO.:
DATE RECEIVED: |

Friend of the Court address   **Telephone no.**

| Plaintiff's name and address | v | Defendant's name and address |

County: _____   This grievance is about

☐ employee(s).
☐ office operations.
☐ a decision based on gender rather than the best interests of the child.

STATEMENT OF GRIEVANCE:

Date _____ Your telephone no. _____ Signature _____

SEE INSTRUCTONS ON BACK OF FORM

FOC 1a (4/01) **FRIEND OF THE COURT GRIEVANCE**   MCL 552.526; MSA 25.176(26)

INSTRUCTIONS FOR GRIEVANCE FORM

The friend of the court grievance procedure is to be used if you have a complaint regarding the actions of an employee or office operations of the friend of the court office. **A judge's or referee's decision and an order of the court are not issues to be handled through the grievance procedure.**

A grievance shall first be filed in writing with the friend of the court. If you are not satisfied with the decision of the friend of the court, you may file a further grievance, in writing, with the chief judge.

The friend of the court/chief judge will investigate and respond to your grievance in a reasonable period of time. If the response cannot be given within 30 days, you will be given a reason why the response is not possible within that time.

You may also file a grievance regarding friend of the court office operations with your local Citizen Advisory Committee at any time during the proceedings. The Citizen Advisory Committee cannot consider grievances about office employees or a court or office decision or recommendation regarding a specific case. The Citizen Advisory Committee cannot correct problems it discovers. Instead, it will advise the friend of the court, the court, or the county board of the problems in its discretion.

When filling out this grievance form, you should type or press firmly to assure all copies are readable. In the alternative, you may photocopy the appropriate number of copies of the completed form. You must also:

1. Provide the names and addresses of the parties in the court case. This will assist the friend of the court, chief judge, or Citizen Advisory Committee in identifying your case.

2. Name of the county where your domestic relations case is located.

3. Check the appropriate box for the type of complaint (grievance).

4. State your complaint, providing specific details, dates, names, and other important information.

5. Mail or deliver the completed form to the friend of the court, the chief judge's office, or the Citizen Advisory Committee office, whichever is appropriate. Keep the last copy (third copy) for your records.

Release of Information:

MCR 3.218(B) states: A party, third-party custodian, guardian, guardian ad litem or counsel for a minor, lawyer-guardian ad litem, and an attorney of record must be given access to friend of the court records related to the case, other than confidential information.

MCR 3.218(C) states: A citizen advisory committee established under the friend of the court act, MCL 552.501 et seq.; MSA 25.176(1) et seq.: 1) shall be given access to a grievance filed with the friend of the court, and to information related to the case, other than confidential information; 2) may be given access to confidential information related to a grievance if the court so orders, upon clear demonstration by the committee that the information is necessary to the performance of its duties and that the release will not impair the rights of a party or the well-being of a child involved in the case.

"Confidential information" means any of the following: staff notes from investigations, mediation sessions, and settlement conferences; Family Independence Agency protective service reports; formal mediaton records; communications from minors; friend of the court grievances filed by the opposing party and the responses; a party's address or any other information if release is prohibited by a court order; except as provided in MCR 3.219, any information for which a privilege could be claimed, or that was provided by a governmental agency, subject to the express written condition that it remain confidential; and all information classifed as confidential by the laws and regulations of title IV, part D of the Social Security Act, 42 USC 651 et seq.

REQUEST FOR ACCOMMODATIONS	Court name and location

Today's date	***Instructions for completing form:*** *Provide your name, address, and telephone number. Check the boxes which apply to you and provide any necessary details. When you have completed this request, please return it to the court at the above address.*

1.

Name			
Address			
City	State	Zip	Telephone no.

2. Court activity you need accommodations for:

☐ Hearing _____
             Date

☐ Mediation meeting _____
                        Date

☐ Jury duty _____
            Date(s)

☐ Other (specify): _____
                    include dates if relevant

3. What is the nature of your disability?

☐ Physical mobility impairment (wheelchair, walker, crutches, etc.)

☐ Speech impairment (specify): _____

☐ Visual impairment

☐ Hearing impairment (specify)   ☐ deaf   ☐ hard of hearing

☐ Other (specify): _____

4. What type of accommodation are you requesting?

☐ Interpreter for deaf (specify whether ASL, tactile, oral, etc.) _____

☐ Assistive listening device (specify type of device) _____

☐ Physical location accessible for persons with a physical mobility concern.

☐ Other (specify)_____

_____
For court use only

Original - Court file
1st copy - Assignment Clerk/Extra
2nd copy - Friend of the Court/Extra
3rd copy - Opposing party
4th copy - Moving party

STATE OF MICHIGAN JUDICIAL DISTRICT JUDICIAL CIRCUIT COUNTY	MOTION AND ORDER FOR APPOINTMENT OF FOREIGN LANGUAGE INTERPRETER	CASE NO.

Court address   Court telephone no.

Plaintiff name(s) ☐ moving party Plaintiff's attorney, bar no., address, and telephone no.	v	Defendant name(s) ☐ moving party Defendant's attorney, bar no., address, and telephone no.

MOTION

1. I state that I am unable to speak English sufficiently to understand and participate in the proceedings in this case.

2. ☐ I am represented by an attorney.   ☐ I am not represented by an attorney.

3. I request the court to appoint a foreign language interpreter to interpret for me.

4. I request an interpreter who speaks the _____ language.

5. If required, place my request on the motion calendar.

_____
Date

_____
Signature

To be completed only if the court
requires a hearing on the motion

NOTICE OF HEARING

You are notified that a hearing has been scheduled on this matter for:

Judge	Bar no.	Date	Time
Hearing location			
☐ Court address above ☐			

If you require special accommodations to use the court because of disabilities, please contact the court immediately to make arrangements.

_____
Date

_____
Signature

CERTIFICATE OF MAILING

I certify that on this date I mailed a copy of this motion and notice of hearing (if applicable) to the other party at the last known address.

_____
Date

_____
Signature

ORDER

IT IS ORDERED the above motion is   ☐ granted.   ☐ denied.

_____
Date

_____
Judge

MC 81 (10/01) **MOTION AND ORDER FOR APPOINTMENT OF FOREIGN LANGUAGE INTERPRETER**

Original - Court
1st copy - Moving Party
2nd copy - Objecting Party

3rd copy - Friend of the Court
4th copy - Proof of Service
5th copy - Proof of Service

STATE OF MICHIGAN JUDICIAL CIRCUIT COUNTY	OBJECTION TO REFEREE'S RECOMMENDED ORDER	CASE NO.

Court address   **Court telephone no.**

Plaintiff's name, address, and telephone no. ☐ Moving party		Defendant's name, address, and telephone no. ☐ Moving party
	v	
Third party's name, address, and telephone no. ☐ Moving party		

I object to the entry of the referee's recommended order dated _____ and request a de novo hearing by the court. My objection is based on the following reason(s):

I declare that the statements above are true to the best of my information, knowledge, and belief.

_____
Date

_____
Signature of objecting party

_____
Name (type or print)

NOTICE OF HEARING

A hearing will be held on this objection before Hon. _____
Name of judge

on _____ at _____ at _____.
Date   Time   Place

If you require special accommodations to use the court because of a disability, please contact the court immediately to make arrangements.

CERTIFICATE OF MAILING

I certify that on this date I mailed a copy of this objection and notice of hearing on the other party(ies) by ordinary mail at the above address(es).

_____
Date

_____
Signature of objecting party

FOC 68   (6/98)   **OBJECTION TO REFEREE'S RECOMMENDED ORDER**   MCR 3.215(E)

Original - Court
1st copy - Other Party
2nd copy - Moving Party

3rd copy - Friend of the Court
4th copy - Proof of Service
5th copy - Proof of Service

Approved, SCAO

| STATE OF MICHIGAN JUDICIAL CIRCUIT COUNTY | NOTICE TO ENTER ORDER WITHOUT HEARING | CASE NO. |

Court address

Court telephone no.

| Plaintiff's name ☐ moving party | v | Defendant's name ☐ moving party |

| Third party's name ☐ moving party | | |

1. On _____ a hearing was held on a motion regarding _____
   Date   Type of order
   and a decision was made.

2. The attached proposed order states what the judge or referee said at the hearing.

3. This is your notice that the proposed order will be given to the judge to sign. If you don't think that the order accurately states what was ordered in court, you must file your written objections with the court within 7 days of the date this notice was mailed. A form to use for filing objections is available at the friend of the court office. Contact the friend of the court and ask for form FOC 78.

4. If you do not file written objections to the proposed order within 7 days of the date of this notice, the judge may sign the proposed order without a hearing. If the judge decides that a hearing is needed, you will be notified of the hearing date.

5. If you file written objections to the proposed order, a hearing will be scheduled. You will be notified of the hearing date.

6. Parties may be represented by their attorneys in this matter.

_____
Date

_____
Signature of moving party

CERTIFICATE OF MAILING

I certify that on this date I mailed a copy of this notice proposed order on the other party(ies) by ordinary mail at the above address(es).

_____
Date

_____
Signature of moving party

FOC 54 (12/96) **NOTICE TO ENTER ORDER WITHOUT HEARING**   MCR 2.602(B)

Original - Court
1st copy - Moving Party
2nd copy - Objecting Party

3rd copy - Friend of the Court
4th copy - Proof of Service
5th copy - Proof of Service

STATE OF MICHIGAN JUDICIAL CIRCUIT COUNTY	OBJECTION TO PROPOSED ORDER	CASE NO.

Court address

Court telephone no.

Plaintiff's name, address, and telephone no. ☐ Moving party		Defendant's name, address, and telephone no. ☐ Moving party
	v	
Third party's name, address, and telephone no. ☐ Moving party		

I received a notice to enter a proposed order without a hearing dated _____

I object to the entry of the proposed order and request a hearing by the court. My objection is based on the following reason(s):

I declare that the statements above are true to the best of my information, knowledge, and belief.

_____
Date

_____
Signature of objecting party

_____
Name (type or print)

CERTIFICATE OF MAILING

I certify that on this date I mailed a copy of this objection on the other party(ies) by ordinary mail at the above address(es).

_____
Date

_____
Signature of objecting party

FOC 78 (12/96) **OBJECTION TO PROPOSED ORDER**   MCR 2.602(B)

Original - Court
1st copy - Other Party
2nd copy - Moving Party

3rd copy - Friend of the Court
4th copy - Proof of Service
5th copy - Proof of Service

STATE OF MICHIGAN **JUDICIAL CIRCUIT COUNTY**	**NOTICE OF HEARING TO ENTER ORDER**	**CASE NO.**

Court address   **Court telephone no.**

Plaintiff's name, address, and telephone no. ☐ moving party		Defendant's name, address, and telephone no. ☐ moving party
	v	
Third party's name, address, and telephone no. ☐ moving party		

1. On_____ a hearing was held on a motion regarding _____
   Date   Type of order

   and a decision was made.

2. The attached proposed order states what the judge or referee said at the hearing.

3. This is your notice that a hearing will be held before _____ on
   Name of judge or referee

   _____ at _____ at _____
   Date   Time   Place

   to have the proposed order signed.   If you don't think that the order accurately states what was ordered in court, attend

   the scheduled hearing.

4. Parties may be represented by their attorneys in this matter.

_____   _____
Date   Signature of moving party

If you require special accommodations to use the court because of a disability, or if you require a foreign language interpreter to help you fully participate in court proceedings, please contact the court immediately to make arrangements. When contacting the court, provide your case number(s).

CERTIFICATE OF MAILING

I certify that on this date I mailed a copy of this notice of hearing and proposed order on the other party(ies) by ordinary mail at the above address(es).

_____   _____
Date   Signature of moving party

STATE OF MICHIGAN THIRD JUDICIAL CIRCUIT WAYNE COUNTY	CERTIFICATE OF CONFORMITY FOR DOMESTIC RELATIONS ORDER OR JUDGMENT	CASE NO.

Penobscot Bldg. 645 Griswold Ave. Detroit, MI 48226   *313-224-5372*

PLAINTIFF'S NAME		DEFENDANT'S NAME
	V.	

I certify the attached Order or Judgment as presented for entry to be in full conformity with the requirements set forth by statute, INCLUDING A PROVISION FOR IMMEDIATE INCOME WITHHOLDING (WHICH SHALL BE IMPLEMENTED BY THE FRIEND OF THE COURT), THE PAYER'S SOCIAL SECURITY NUMBER AND THE NAME AND ADDRESS OF HIS/HER SOURCE OF INCOME IF KNOWN , UNLESS OTHERWISE ORDERED BY THE COURT, and with Michigan Court Rules 3.201 and following, and if applicable, includes all provisions of the Friend of the Court recommendation or is in conformity with the decision of

_____ rendered on the _____ day of

_____ , 19 _____ .

_____   _____
Date   Attorney / Bar No.

Instructions :   Please sign and present this Certificate to the Court Clerk when the Order or Judgment is presented
for entry. If an ex parte interim order is being presented to the Judge, please complete the "Certificate
on Behalf of Plaintiff regarding Ex Parte Interim Support Order" and follow Local Court Rule 3.206.

#1225 (7/95) CERTIFICATE OF CONFORMITY FOR DOMESTIC RELATIONS ORDER OR JUDGMENT

Approved, SCAO

Original - Court
1st copy - Other Party
2nd copy - Moving Party

3rd copy - Friend of the Court
4th copy - Proof of Service
5th copy - Proof of Service

STATE OF MICHIGAN JUDICIAL CIRCUIT COUNTY	MOTION REGARDING CUSTODY	CASE NO.

Friend of the Court address   **Telephone no.**

Plaintiff's name, address, and telephone no. ☐ moving party		Defendant's name, address, and telephone no. ☐ moving party
	v	
Third party name, address, and telephone no. ☐ moving party		

1. ☐ a. On _____ a judgment
   Date
   or order was entered regarding custody.
   ☐ b. There is currently no order regarding custody.

☐ 2. The   ☐ plaintiff   ☐ defendant   ☐ third party   was ordered to have custody of the following child(ren):

3. The child(ren) have been living with _____ at
   Name(s)

_____ since _____ .
Complete address   Date

4. Circumstances have changed as follows that require custody or a change in custody:
   Use a separate sheet to explain in detail what has happened and attach. Include all necessary facts.

5. Proper cause exists as follows that require custody or a change in custody: Use a separate sheet to explain in detail which
   factors of the Child Custody Act for determining best interests of the child(ren) are affected by the circumstances in 4. above. Include all necessary
   facts.

☐ 6. _____ and I agree to custody, support, and parenting time as follows:
   Name
   Use a separate sheet to explain in detail what you have agreed on and attach. Include all necessary facts.

7. **I ask the court to order that custody, parenting time, and support be** as follows:
   Use a separate sheet to explain in detail what you want the court to order and attach.

I declare that the above statements are true to the best of my information, knowledge, and belief.

_____
Date

_____
Moving party's signature

NOTICE OF HEARING

A hearing will be held on this motion before _____
                                              Name of judge or referee

on _____ at _____ at _____ .
   Date   Time   Place

NOTE: If you are the person receiving this motion, you may file a response. Contact the friend of the court office and request form FOC 88.

CERTIFICATE OF MAILING

I certify that on this date I mailed a copy of this motion and notice of hearing on the other party(ies) by ordinary mail at the above address(es).

_____
Date

_____
Moving party's signature

Approved, SCAO

Original - Court
1st copy - Moving Party
2nd copy - Responding Party

3rd copy - Friend of the Court
4th copy - Proof of Service
5th copy - Proof of Service

STATE OF MICHIGAN JUDICIAL CIRCUIT COUNTY	RESPONSE TO MOTION REGARDING CUSTODY	CASE NO.

Friend of the Court address   **Telephone no.**

Plaintiff's name, address, and telephone no.   ☐ moving party

v

Defendant's name, address, and telephone no.   ☐ moving party

Third party name, address, and telephone no.   ☐ moving party

1. ☐ a. On _____ a judgment
Date
or order was entered regarding custody.
☐ b. There is currently no order regarding custody.

☐ 2. The   ☐ plaintiff   ☐ defendant   ☐ third party   was ordered to have custody of the following child(ren):

3. The child(ren) have been living with _____ at
Name(s)

_____ since _____ .
Complete address   Date

4. I   ☐ agree   ☐ do not agree   that circumstances have changed as stated in the motion.
Explain in detail what you do not agree with and why. Include all necessary facts. Use a separate sheet of paper if needed.

5. I   ☐ agree   ☐ do not agree   that proper cause exists as stated in the motion.
Explain in detail what you do not agree with and why. Include all necessary facts. Use a separate sheet of paper if needed.

☐ 6. I agreed with the other party to custody, parenting time, and support:
☐ a. exactly as stated in the motion.
☐ b. but not as stated in the motion.
If b. is checked, explain in detail what you did agree on. Include all necessary facts. Use a separate sheet of paper if needed.

7. ☐ a. I agree with what is being asked for in the motion.
☐ b. I do not agree with what is being asked for in the motion and ask the court to order custody, parenting time, and support as follows: If b. is checked, explain in detail why and what you want the court to order. Use a separate sheet of paper if needed.

I declare that the above statements are true to the best of my information, knowledge, and belief.

Date _____   Responding party's signature _____

CERTIFICATE OF MAILING

I certify that on this date I mailed a copy of this response on the other party by ordinary mail at the above address.

Date _____   Responding party's signature _____

FOC 88   (6/03)   **RESPONSE TO MOTION REGARDING CUSTODY**   MCL 722.21 et seq., MCR 2.119

Approved, SCAO

Original - Court
1st copy - Other Party
2nd copy - Moving Party

3rd copy - Friend of the Court
4th copy - Proof of Service
5th copy - Proof of Service

STATE OF MICHIGAN JUDICIAL CIRCUIT COUNTY	ORDER REGARDING CUSTODY AND PARENTING TIME	CASE NO.

Friend of the Court address   **Telephone no.**

Plaintiff's name, address, and telephone no.		Defendant's name, address, and telephone no.
	v	

Third party's name, address, and telephone no.

Date: _____

Judge: _____

Bar no.

1. This order is entered ☐ after hearing.   ☐ on consent of the parties.   ☐ on stipulation of the parties.

THE COURT FINDS:

☐2. A motion requesting custody, parenting time, and support or a change to custody, parenting time, and support was filed.

☐3. A response to the motion was filed.

☐4. A change of circumstances ☐does ☐does not   exist which warrants a custody order or change in custody.

☐5. Proper cause ☐does ☐does not   exist which warrants a custody order or a change in custody.

☐6. It ☐is ☐is not   in the best interests of the child(ren) to ☐establish ☐change   parenting time.

☐7. A material change of circumstances exists which warrants a change in the support order.

☐8. It is in the best interests of the child(ren) to dismiss the motion.

IT IS ORDERED:

☐ 9. The motion regarding custody, parenting time, and support is dismissed. The prior order remains in effect.

☐ 10.   Custody is granted as follows:

Name(s) of child(ren): _____

☐ Joint legal to   ☐ plaintiff   ☐ defendant   ☐ third party

Unless otherwise agreed, a parent whose custody or parenting time of a child is governed by this order shall not change the legal residence of the child except in compliance with section 11 of the Child Custody Act of 1970, 1970 PA 91, MCL 722.31.

☐ Joint physical to   ☐ plaintiff   ☐ defendant   ☐ third party

☐ Sole legal to   ☐ plaintiff   ☐ defendant   ☐ third party

☐ Sole physical to   ☐ plaintiff   ☐ defendant   ☐ third party

11.   Parenting time is   ☐ established   ☐ changed   as follows:

Explain in detail what the court has ordered.

12.   The parents shall cooperate with respect to a child so as, in a maximum degree, to advance a child's health, emotional, and physical well-being and to give and afford a child the affection of both parents and a sense of security. Neither parent will, directly or indirectly, influence a child so as to prejudice a child against the other parent. The parents will endeavor to guide a child so as to promote the affectionate relationship between a child and the mother and a child and the father. The parties will cooperate with each other in carrying out the provisions of this order for a child' best interests. Whenever it seems necessary to adjust, vary or increase the time allotted to either party, or otherwise take action regarding a child, each of the parties shall act in the best interests of the child. Neither party shall do anything which may estrange the other from the child, injure the child's opinion of the other party, or which will hamper the free and natural development of the child for the other party.

13.   The parent with primary physical custody shall notify the friend of the court in writing whenever the address of a minor child changes.

_____   _____
Date   Judge

Support provisions ordered on form FOC 10 / 52.

MCL 552.14, MCL 552.517b(3), MCL 722.21 et seq., MCR 2.119

FOC 89   (6/03)   ORDER REGARDING CUSTODY AND PARENTING TIME

STATE OF MICHIGAN JUDICIAL CIRCUIT COUNTY	MOTION REGARDING PARENTING TIME	CASE NO.

Court address

Court telephone no.

Plaintiff's name, address, and telephone no. ☐ moving party

v

Defendant's name, address, and telephone no. ☐ moving party

Third party name, address, and telephone no. ☐ moving party

1. ☐ a. On _____ a judgment
   Date
   or order was entered regarding parenting time.
   ☐ b. There is currently no order regarding parenting time.

☐ 2. _____ has disobeyed the parenting time order as follows:
Name

☐ a. he/she has denied me parenting time with the child(ren) as follows:
☐ b. he/she has not had parenting time with the child(ren) as follows:
☐ c. he/she has made changes in parenting time without court order as follows:
☐ d. he/she has not followed the specific conditions of parenting time as follows:
Use a separate sheet to explain in detail what has happened and attach. Include all necessary facts.

☐ 3. _____ and I have agreed to parenting time as follows:
Name
Use a separate sheet to explain in detail what you have agreed on and attach. Include all necessary facts.

4. It is in the best interests of the child(ren) to ☐ establish parenting time ☐ change parenting time because:
Use a separate sheet to explain why it is in the best interests of the child(ren) and attach.

5. **I ask the court to order that parenting time be** ☐ established ☐ changed ☐ made up as follows:
Use a separate sheet to explain in detail what you want the court to order and attach.

I declare that the above statements are true to the best of my information, knowledge, and belief.

_____
Date

_____
Moving party's signature

NOTICE OF HEARING

A hearing will be held on this motion before _____
Name of judge or referee

on _____ at _____ at _____ .
Date   Time   Place

NOTE: If you are the person receiving this motion, you may file a response. Contact the friend of the court office and request form FOC 66.

CERTIFICATE OF MAILING

I certify that on this date I mailed a copy of this motion and notice of hearing on the other party(ies) by ordinary mail at the above address(es).

_____
Date

_____
Moving party's signature

Original - Court
1st copy - Moving Party
2nd copy - Responding Party

3rd copy - Friend of the Court
4th copy - Proof of Service
5th copy - Proof of Service

Approved, SCAO

STATE OF MICHIGAN JUDICIAL CIRCUIT COUNTY	RESPONSE TO MOTION REGARDING PARENTING TIME	CASE NO.

Court address

Court telephone no.

Plaintiff's name, address, and telephone no. ☐ moving party

v

Defendant's name, address, and telephone no. ☐ moving party

Third party name, address, and telephone no. ☐ moving party

1. ☐ a. On _____ a judgment
       Date
       or order was entered regarding parenting time.
   ☐ b. There is currently no order regarding parenting time.

☐ 2. I ☐ have ☐ have not disobeyed the parenting time order as stated in the motion.
   Explain in detail what you do not agree with in item 2. of the motion and why. Include all necessary facts. Use a separate sheet of paper if needed.

☐ 3. ☐ a. I agreed with the other party to start or make changes in parenting time as stated in the motion.
   ☐ b. I agreed with the other party to start or make changes in parenting time. They were not what was stated in the motion.
   ☐ c. I did not agree with the other party to start or make changes in parenting time.
   If b. is checked, explain in detail what you did agree on. Include all necessary facts. Use a separate sheet of paper if needed.

4. I ☐ agree ☐ do not agree that it is in the best interests of the child(ren) to ☐ establish ☐ change parenting time as stated in the motion.
   If you do not agree with the motion, explain why it is in the best interests of the child(ren). Use a separate sheet of paper if needed.

5. **I ask the court to order that parenting time** ☐ be ☐ not be ☐ established ☐ changed ☐ made up
   as stated in the motion.
   If you do not agree with the request in the motion, explain in detail what you want the court to order. Use a separate sheet of paper if needed.

I declare that the above statements are true to the best of my information, knowledge, and belief.

_____
Date

_____
Responding party's signature

CERTIFICATE OF MAILING

I certify that on this date I mailed a copy of this response on the other party(ies) by ordinary mail at the above address(es).

_____
Date

_____
Responding party's signature

FOC 66 (12/96) **RESPONSE TO MOTION REGARDING PARENTING TIME**

MCL 552.14; MSA 25.94, MCR 2.119

Original - Court   3rd copy - Friend of the Court
1st copy - Other Party   4th copy - Proof of Service
2nd copy - Moving Party   5th copy - Proof of Service

STATE OF MICHIGAN JUDICIAL CIRCUIT COUNTY	ORDER REGARDING PARENTING TIME	CASE NO.

Court address   **Court telephone no.**

Plaintiff's name, address, and telephone no.

v

Defendant's name, address, and telephone no.

Third party's name, address, and telephone no.

Date: _____

Judge: _____

1. This order is entered ☐ after hearing. ☐ on consent of the parties. ☐ on stipulation of the parties.

THE COURT FINDS:

☐ 2. A motion requesting parenting time/change to parenting time was filed.

☐ 3. A response to the motion was filed.

☐ 4. It ☐ is ☐ is not   in the best interests of the child(ren) to ☐ establish ☐ change   parenting time.

☐ 5. It is in the best interests of the child(ren) to dismiss the motion.

IT IS ORDERED:

☐ 6. The motion is dismissed. Parenting time is unchanged and the existing order remains in effect.

☐ 7. Parenting time is ☐ established ☐ changed ☐ to be made up   as follows:
    Explain in detail what the court has ordered.

8. Except as changed in this order, the prior order (if one) remains in effect.

_____
Plaintiff's signature (consent/stipulation)

_____
Defendant's signature (consent/stipulation)

_____
Third party's signature (consent/stipulation)

Approved as to form:_____
      Friend of the court signature (only if required)

_____
Date

_____
Circuit court judge

PROOF OF SERVICE

I certify that on this date I mailed a copy of this order on the other party(ies) by ordinary mail at the above address(es).

_____
Date

_____
Signature

STATE OF MICHIGAN Circuit Court - Family Division COUNTY	MOTION REGARDING RESIDENCE OF CHILDREN	CASE NO.

Plaintiff: ☐ moving party

Defendant: ☐ moving party

v

1. (Names) _____

after the parties' divorce on _____ , currently have legal residences with:

plaintiff at _____

defendant at _____

third party (named) at _____

2. I want to change these minor children's legal residence with me:

☐ inside the state of Michigan but the move isn't permitted by MCL 722.31 without a court order;

☐ outside the state of Michigan;

to _____

on _____

3. Circumstances have changed as follows that require a change of residence as proposed above:

4. Proper cause exists as follows that requires a change of residence:

☐ 5. _____ and I agree to a change of residence and parenting time as follows:

6. **I ask the court to order a change of residence and parenting time** as follows:

I declare that the above statements are true to the best of my information, knowledge and belief.

Date _____   Moving party _____

NOTICE OF HEARING

A hearing will be held on this motion before (judge or referee) _____

on _____ at (time) _____ at (place) _____

Note: If you are the person receiving this motion, you may file a response.

CERTIFICATE OF MAILING

I certify that on this date I mailed a copy of this motion and notice of hearing to the other party(ies) by ordinary mail at the above address(es).

Date _____   Moving party _____

GRP 20 (9/04)   **MOTION REGARDING RESIDENCE OF CHILDREN**

STATE OF MICHIGAN Circuit Court - Family Division COUNTY	RESPONSE TO MOTION REGARDING RESIDENCE OF CHILDREN	CASE NO.

Plaintiff: ☐ moving party   **Defendant**: ☐ moving party

v

1. A motion has been filed to change the legal residence of these minor children:
(names) _____

    ☐ inside the state of Michigan.

    ☐ outside the state of Michigan.

2. I   ☐ agree   ☐ do not agree   that circumstances have changed as stated in the motion.

3. I   ☐ agree   ☐ do not agree   that proper cause exists as stated in the motion.

☐ 4. I agreed with the other party to a change of residence and parenting time:

    ☐ a. exactly as stated in the motion.

    ☐ b. but not as stated in the motion. (Describe agreement)

5. ☐ a. I agree with what is being asked for in the motion.

    ☐ b. I do not agree with what is being asked for in the motion and ask the court to make an order regarding residence of children and parenting time as follows:

I declare that the above statements are true to the best of my information, knowledge and belief.

Date _____   Responding party _____

CERTIFICATE OF MAILING

I certify that on this date I mailed a copy of this response to the other party(ies) by ordinary mail at the above address(es).

Date _____   Responding party _____

GRP 21   (9/04)   **RESPONSE TO MOTION REGARDING RESIDENCE OF CHILDREN**

STATE OF MICHIGAN **Circuit Court - Family Division** COUNTY	**ORDER REGARDING RESIDENCE OF CHILDREN**	**CASE NO.**

Plaintiff:

Defendant:

v

Date of hearing _____   Judge _____

1. This order is entered ☐ after hearing. ☐ on consent. ☐ on stipulation.

THE COURT FINDS:

☐ 2. A motion to change the legal residence of the parties' minor children was filed.

☐ 3. A response to the motion was filed.

☐ 4. A change of circumstances ☐ does ☐ does not exist warranting a change of residence.

☐ 5. Proper cause ☐ does ☐ does not exist which warrants a change of residence.

☐ 6. The parties have agreed to the change of the children's residence.

IT IS ORDERED:

☐ 7. The motion to change the legal residence of the minor children is dismissed, leaving the current residences intact.

☐ 8. a. Starting _____, the legal residence of the following minor children:

(names) _____

shall be changed from their current residence with:

☐ plaintiff ☐ defendant ☐ third party (named):

at _____

to _____

b. Except as permitted above, the minor children's residence (domicile) shall not be moved from the state of Michigan without the prior approval of the court.

c. The person awarded custody shall promptly notify the friend of the court in writing when the minor is moved to another address.

9. The parenting time order dated _____ is modified to provide that ☐ plaintiff ☐ defendant ☐ third party   shall have parenting time with the minor children as follows:

Date/plaintiff _____   Date/defendant _____

Date _____   Judge _____

PROOF OF SERVICE

I certify that on this date I mailed a copy of this order to the other party(ies) by ordinary mail at the above address(es).

Date _____   Signature _____

GRP 22 (9/04)   ORDER REGARDING RESIDENCE OF CHILDREN

STATE OF MICHIGAN JUDICIAL CIRCUIT COUNTY	CHANGE IN PERSONAL INFORMATION	CASE NO.

Friend of the Court address

Please type or print information. Complete only those sections that apply. You can only file changes for yourself or those minor children of whom you have physical custody. Use another form when making changes for more than one person. **YOU MUST SIGN THIS FORM.**

1. New Address and/or Telephone Number   ☐ for party and minor child(ren)   ☐ for party only
☐ for minor child _____ no longer living with custodial parent
Name

Street address			
City	State	Zip	Area code and telephone number

I understand that by filing this change of address, it will be used to automatically update address information on any other child support cases I have in Michigan. This change is effective for (check all that apply)

☐ all addresses you have listed for me   ☐ mailing address only (where I receive mail)
☐ residence address only (where I live)   ☐ legal address only (where I want legal notices to be sent)
☐ an address that is confidential by court order and which remains confidential with this change

2. Alternate Address

The court has entered an order making my address confidential under Michigan Court Rule 3.203(F). The following is an alternate address for the court, the friend of the court office, and the other party to use in serving me with notice and other court papers. I will retrieve all my mail regarding this case from this alternate address.

Street address	City	State	Zip

3. Name Change (attach order changing name or certificate of marriage)

New name

4. New Employer   ☐ employer information is confidential by court order

Employer name	Street address		
City	State	Zip	Area code and telephone number

5. New Driver License

Issuing state	License number	Expiration date

6. New Occupational License

Issuing state	Type of occupation	License number	Expiration date

7. New Social Security Number   ☐ for you   ☐ for minor child _____
Name

Social security number

8. Health Care Insurance Provider

Name	Type	Contract number

9. Other Information: (to be provided as ordered by the court) (attach separate sheet)

Name of party filing the change (type or print)	Social security number	Date of filing
Signature of party filing the change	Name of other party (type or print)	

FOC 108 (10/04) **CHANGE IN PERSONAL INFORMATION**

Original - Court   3rd copy - Friend of the Court
1st copy - Other Party   4th copy - Proof of Service
2nd copy - Moving Party   5th copy - Proof of Service

Approved, SCAO

STATE OF MICHIGAN JUDICIAL CIRCUIT COUNTY	MOTION REGARDING SUPPORT	CASE NO.

Court address   Court telephone no.

Plaintiff's name, address, and telephone no.   ☐ moving party

v

Defendant's name, address, and telephone no.   ☐ moving party

Third party name, address, and telephone no.   ☐ moving party

1. ☐ a. On _____ a judgment
     Date
or order was entered regarding support.
   ☐ b. There is currently no order regarding support.

☐ 2. The ☐ plaintiff ☐ defendant   is ordered to pay support of $_____ each _____ .
                                                                       week, month, etc.

☐ 3. The ☐ plaintiff ☐ defendant   is ordered to pay child care of $_____ each _____ .
                                                                        week, month, etc.

☐ 4. The ☐ plaintiff ☐ defendant   is ordered to pay health care of $_____ each _____ .
                                                                        week, month, etc.

☐ 5. Conditions regarding support have changed as follows:
     Use a separate sheet to explain in detail what has happened and attach. Include all necessary facts.

☐ 6. _____ and I have agreed to support as follows:
     Name
     Use a separate sheet to explain in detail what you have agreed on and attach. Include all necessary facts.

7. **I ask the court to order that support be** paid as follows: ☐ See 6. above for details.
     Use a separate sheet to explain in detail what you want the court to order and attach.

I declare that the above statements are true to the best of my information, knowledge, and belief.

_____   _____
Date   Moving party's signature

NOTICE OF HEARING

A hearing will be held on this motion before _____
                                         Name of judge or referee

on _____ at _____ at _____ .
   Date   Time   Place

NOTE: If you are the person receiving this motion, you may file a response. Contact the friend of the court office and request form FOC 51.

CERTIFICATE OF MAILING

I certify that on this date I mailed a copy of this motion and notice of hearing on the other party(ies) by ordinary mail at the above address(es).

_____   _____
Date   Moving party's signature

FOC 50   (12/96)   **MOTION REGARDING SUPPORT**   MCL 552.14; MSA 25.94, MCR 2.119, MCR 3.213

Approved, SCAO

Original - Court
1st copy - Moving Party
2nd copy - Responding Party

3rd copy - Friend of the Court
4th copy - Proof of Service
5th copy - Proof of Service

STATE OF MICHIGAN JUDICIAL CIRCUIT COUNTY	RESPONSE TO MOTION REGARDING SUPPORT	CASE NO.

Court address

Court telephone no.

Plaintiff's name, address, and telephone no. ☐ moving party

v

Defendant's name, address, and telephone no. ☐ moving party

Third party name, address, and telephone no. ☐ moving party

1. ☐ a. On _____ a judgment
   Date
   or order was entered regarding support.
   ☐ b. There is currently no order regarding support.

☐ 2. The ☐ plaintiff ☐ defendant   is ordered to pay support of $ _____ each _____ .
week, month, etc.

☐ 3. The ☐ plaintiff ☐ defendant   is ordered to pay child care of $ _____ each _____ .
week, month, etc.

☐ 4. The ☐ plaintiff ☐ defendant   is ordered to pay health care of $ _____ each _____ .
week, month, etc.

☐ 5. I ☐ agree ☐ do not agree   that conditions regarding support have changed as stated in the motion.
Explain in detail what you do not agree with and why. Include all necessary facts. Use a separate sheet of paper if needed.

☐ 6. I agreed with the other party to start/change support:
   ☐ a. exactly as stated in the motion.
   ☐ b. but not as stated in the motion.
   If b. is checked, explain in detail what you did agree on. Include all necessary facts. Use a separate sheet of paper if needed.

7. ☐ a. I agree with what is being asked for in the motion.
   ☐ b. I do not agree with what is being asked for in the motion and ask the court to order that support be paid as follows:
   If you do not agree with the request in the motion, explain in detail why and what you want the court to order. Use a separate sheet of paper if needed.

I declare that the above statements are true to the best of my information, knowledge, and belief.

_____
Date

_____
Responding party's signature

CERTIFICATE OF MAILING

I certify that on this date I mailed a copy of this response on the other party(ies) by ordinary mail at the above address(es).

_____
Date

_____
Responding party's signature

FOC 51 (12/96) **RESPONSE TO MOTION REGARDING SUPPORT**

MCL 552.14; MSA 25.94, MCR 2.119

	Original - Court 1st copy - Plaintiff	2nd copy - Defendant 3rd copy - Friend of the Court
STATE OF MICHIGAN **JUDICIAL CIRCUIT** **COUNTY**	**UNIFORM CHILD SUPPORT ORDER** **(PAGE 1)** ☐ **MODIFICATION**	**CASE NO.**

Court address | FAX no. | Court telephone no.

Plaintiff's name, address, and telephone no.		Defendant's name, address, and telephone no.
	v	
Plaintiff's attorney name, address, telephone no., and bar no.		Defendant's atttorney name, address, telephone no., and bar no.
Plaintiff's source of income name, address, and telephone no.		Defendant's source of income name, address, and telephone no.

Unless otherwise ordered:

1. This order continues until each child is age 18 or graduates from high school, as provided by MCL 552.605b, whichever is later, but no longer than age 19 1/2. Child care for each child terminates effective September 1 following each child's 12th birthday.

2. Income withholding shall take immediate effect. All payments shall be made through the friend of the court or State Disbursement Unit.

3. **Support.** The payer has a monthly support obligation as follows:

Payer:	Payee:	Effective date:

Children's names and birth dates:

Children supported:	1 child	2 children	3 children	4 children	5 or more children
Base support:	$	$	$	$	$
Ordinary medical:	$	$	$	$	$
Child care:	$	$	$	$	$
Other:	$	$	$	$	$
Total:	$	$	$	$	$

☐ Base support shall abate 50% after 6 consecutive overnights with the payer
☐ Support was set based on the shared economic responsibility formula using _____ overnights of parenting time.
☐ Base support considers health care premiums of $_____ paid by plaintiff and $_____ paid by defendant.
The above ordered support provisions ☐ do ☐ do not follow the child support formula.

4. **Insurance.** For the benefit of the children, ☐ plaintiff ☐ defendant shall maintain health care coverage through an insurer [as defined in MCL 552.602(o)] that includes payment for hospital, dental, optical, and other medical expenses when that coverage is available through an employer or under an existing individual policy at the following reasonable cost:
☐ up to a maximum of $_____ for plaintiff. ☐ up to a maximum of $_____ for defendant.
☐ not to exceed 5% of the plaintiff's/defendant's gross income.

(see Page 2 for remainder of order)

STATE OF MICHIGAN JUDICIAL CIRCUIT COUNTY	UNIFORM CHILD SUPPORT ORDER (PAGE 2) ☐ MODIFICATION	CASE NO.

Court address

FAX no.   Court telephone no.

Plaintiff's name	v	Defendant's name

5. **Uninsured Medical Expenses.** All uninsured health care expenses exceeding the ordinary medical amount will be paid _____% by the plaintiff and _____% by the defendant. Uninsured expenses exceeding the ordinary medical amount for the year they are incurred that are not paid within 28 days of a written payment request may be enforced by the friend of the court. The ordinary medical amount is $ _____ year.

6. **Qualified Medical Support Order.** This order is a qualified medical support order under 29 USC 1169. To qualify this order, the friend of the court shall issue a notice to enroll under MCL 552.626b. A parent may contest the notice by requesting a review or hearing concerning availability of health care at a reasonable cost.

7. **Retroactive Modification, Surcharge for Past Due Support, and Liens for Unpaid Support.** Support is a judgment the date it is due and is not modifiable retroactively. A surcharge will be added to past due support. Unpaid support is a lien by operation of law and the payer's property can be encumbered or seized if an arrearage accrues for more than the periodic support payments payable for two months under the payer's support order.

8. **Change of Address, Employment Status, Health Insurance.** Both parties shall notify the friend of the court in writing, within 21 days of any change in: a) their mailing or residence address and telephone number; b) the name, address, and telephone number of their sources of income; c) their health maintenance or insurance company, insurance coverage, persons insured, or contract number; d) their occupational or driver licenses; and e) their social security number unless exempt by law under MCL 552.603.

9. **Redirection and Abatement:** Subject to statutory procedures, the friend of the court : 1) may redirect support paid for a child to the person who is legally responsible for that child; 2) shall abate support charges for a child who resides on a full-time basis with the payer of support; or 3) shall redirect support to the Family Independence Agency for a child placed in foster care.

10. **Fees.** The payer of support shall pay statutory and service fees as required by law.

11. **Prior Orders.** Except as changed in this order, prior provisions remain in effect. Support payable under any prior order is preserved.

12. **Other: (attach separate sheets as needed)**

IT IS SO ORDERED:

_____   _____   _____   _____
Plaintiff (if consent/stipulation)   Date   Defendant (if consent/stipulation)   Date

_____   _____   _____
Date   Judge   Bar no.

CERTIFICATE OF MAILING

I certify that on this date I served a copy of this order on the parties by first class mail addressed to their last known addresses as defined in MCR 3.203.

_____   _____
Date   Signature

Original - Obligor
1st copy - Requesting party
2nd copy - for court as needed

STATE OF MICHIGAN JUDICIAL CIRCUIT COUNTY	REQUEST FOR HEALTH CARE EXPENSE PAYMENT	CASE NO.

Friend of the Court address   Telephone no.

Plaintiff	v	Defendant

INSTRUCTIONS FOR REQUESTING PARTY:

The following is important information should you later seek to obtain the friend of the court's help to enforce payment of health care expenses (medical, dental, and other health care expenses).

1. Your court order must require the other party to pay a portion of health care expenses.
2. The expense must exceed any amounts your child support order requires as a prerequisite for enforcement.
3. You must submit your request for payment to the other party within 28 days of either the date insurance has paid on the expenses or the date insurance denies payment.
4. If you and the other party reach an agreement concerning the expenses, the agreement must be in writing, list the expenses to be paid, state the total amount to be paid, and provide a schedule for payment. Both parties must sign the agreement.
5. The bills must be presented to the friend of the court on or before the following: 1 year after the expense was incurred; or 6 months after the insurer's final denial of coverage for the expense (as long as all measures necessary to submit the claim to insurance were completed within 2 months after the expense was incurred); or 6 months after a default in a repayment agreement as set forth above. You will need to fill out a second form to request enforcement.
6. In the event it is necessary for the friend of the court to enforce payment of the expenses, you must have supporting bills and receipts for the expenses you list. You will be responsible for establishing the expenses and their necessity. Please bring your documentation to all court hearings where medical expenses may be discussed.
7. Attach a copy of all bills and insurance notifications to this form.
8. **You must keep a copy of this form and all attachments for the friend of the court to use in the event enforcement action is necessary.**

TO:

Obligor's name and address

Complete expenses incurred on the other side of this form.

The following expenses have been incurred for the health care of a minor child for whom you are obligated to provide health care support.

Name of Child Receiving Service	Name of Medical Provider	Date of Service	Type of Service	Total Medical Cost	Amt. Paid by Insurance	Balance Due*	Obligor's %	Amt. Owed by Obligor

I declare that the above statements are true to the best of my information, knowledge, and belief and that on this date I mailed a copy of this Request for Health Care Expense Payment to the obligor at his or her last known address.

_____
Signature

_____
Date

*Balance due means balance owed after payment by insurance and any adjustments to the total medical cost.

Approved, SCAO

Original - Court (A)
1st copy - Other Party (B)
2nd copy - Moving Party (C)

3rd copy - Friend of the Court (D)
4th copy - Proof of Service (E)

STATE OF MICHIGAN JUDICIAL CIRCUIT COUNTY	OBJECTION TO CHILD SUPPORT REVIEW	CASE NO.

Court address

FAX no.   Court telephone no.

Plaintiff's name, address, and telephone no. ☐ Moving party		Defendant's name, address, and telephone no. ☐ Moving party
	v	

I received a notice of child support review from the friend of the court dated _____
I object to the to the determination that no change in the child support/health care order should occur and request a hearing by the court. My objection is based on the following reason(s):

I declare that the statements above are true to the best of my information, knowledge, and belief.

Date _____

Signature of objecting party _____

Name (type or print) _____

CERTIFICATE OF MAILING

I certify that on this date I mailed a copy of this objection on the other party by ordinary mail at the above address.

Date _____

Signature of objecting party _____

FOC 79 (6/96) **OBJECTION TO CHILD SUPPORT REVIEW**   MCL 552.517; MSA 25.176(17), MCL 552.517b; MSA 25.176(17b)

THE CIRCUIT COURT
FOR THE THIRD JUDICIAL CIRCUIT OF MICHIGAN
FAMILY DIVISION – FRIEND OF THE COURT

ORDER DATA FORM-SUPPORT
FOR SUBMISSION OF DOMESTIC RELATIONS ORDER FOR ENTRY INTO
Michigan Child Support Enforcement System (MiCSES) BY FOC

NON-EX PARTE ORDERS:

1. Complete legibly and attach this form to the Friend of the Court (FOC) True Copy of the Order.

2. Please note that the FOC worker will not review the order. If required fields are not completed (noted by asterisk *), the Order Data Form and the Order will be returned to you.

3. Do not submit Orders with non-specific dates, such as orders that start support as of the date of sale of the marital home.

4. If an order provides for different support amounts for different periods of time, complete an Order Data Form for each period. Label each with "1 of 'n', …, 'n' of 'n', in the upper right corner.

5. The Judge's Circuit Court Clerk will forward the FOC copy of the Order, with attached Order Data Form, to FOC for entry into the MiCSES System.

EX PARTE ORDERS:

1. Attach the Proof of Service if the Order is an Ex Parte Order. (The Order will not be entered into the MiCSES System unless the Proof of Service is attached.)

2. Ex Parte Orders, with completed Order Data Form and Proof of Service, should be faxed or mailed to:

Order Entry Department
3rd Floor, Penobscot Building
645 Griswold   **or delivered to:**
Detroit, Michigan 48226
FAX: (313) 237-9290

Attorney Window
2nd Floor, Penobscot Building
645 Griswold
Detroit, Michigan 48226
FAX: (313) 237-9290

THE ORDER DATA FORM IS AVAILABLE FOR DOWNLOAD TO YOUR COMPUTER
OR FOR PRINTING
ON THE COURT WEBSITE AT http://3rdcc.org OR FAX LIBRARY: (313) 967-3662

Rev. 11/06/02

ABOUT THE NEW AND REQUIRED "ORDER DATA FORM-SUPPORT"

Friend of the Court, with the support of the Family Law Bench, has developed a data form, now called ORDER DATA FORM-SUPPORT (ODF-S), (formerly known as Fast Track Form) to assist the FOC in the task of loading the provisions of a support order into the Michigan Child Support Enforcement System. (MiCSES) It is now two pages.

A completed ODF-S must be attached to the FOC copy of any domestic relations order.

The old Fast Track form you have used was developed before and during the transition to the Michigan Child Support Enforcement System and is now obsolete.

Here are some features of the new form, as well as some practical considerations that should be noted when an order is being prepared for entry.

First, please note that it is the responsibility of the party submitting the order to the court for signature to enter all the relevant details of the new order into the ODF-S [ORDER DETAILS). The FOC worker will rely upon that information when loading the order and will not consult the attached order, nor any other previously entered order(s).

Second, the information required on page one, "ORDER DETAILS", of the ODF-S should be garnered only from the order attached. If the order results in a change in a certain element of the account, you check the relevant boxes and complete the relevant text areas. If the order does not impact a certain element of the account, then you do not check those boxes and no change would be noted on MiCSES for that aspect of the account.

For example: the order modifies child support but not childcare. You would check the relevant boxes and enter the ordered amounts and dates into the text fields in the child support section. You would not check any of the childcare boxes. The worker will load the new child support, with its commencement date, and leave the childcare portion of the account as is.

For example: an order might provide for a certain cycle for one period of time, then a different amount for a subsequent period of time [for example, $10/wk from 04-01-02 to 05-31-02, then $40/wk from 06-01-02 until further order of the court]. You will prepare a "1 of 2" ODF-S (ORDER DETAILS) sheet for the '04-01-02 to 05-31-02 period' and a "2 of 2" ODF-S (ORDER DETAILS) sheet for the '06-01-02 until further order of the court' period of time. Only one copy of page 2, ODF-S (DEMOGRAPHICS) would need to be attached.

The only time an arrearage amount would be entered would be when the order, by its specific terms, sets a specific amount of arrearage for a date certain.

Again, the first page of the form (ORDER DETAILS) should contain the specifics of only the attached order.

The second page, DEMOGRAPHICS is also attached to the new order being submitted for entry. FOC will check and correct/update the account for any changes or errors. The information required is standard information you obtain from your clients. Your client's and the other parties' information should be on the verified statement initially and updated in your client file as you interact with your client and opposing counsel. Family Independence Agency account #'s, children's dates of birth and social security numbers, etc. are known to your clients and should be in your client files.

MiCSES has an automated Income Withholding Notice feature. The worker, as a part of the order loading activity that day, reviews the Demographics page and updates the employer, if necessary. Upon entry into MiCSES of a new support order, the system generates an Income Withholding Notice (IWN) that night, in batch, to the active employer. If the order specifies a certain $ amount to be wage deducted, that amount is loaded into MiCSES and the IWN is generated in that amount. If the order does not specify a certain amount to be withheld, the system calculates the guideline amount and the IWN is generated in that amount.

I believe that, especially if you download the template version of this form from the Website, you will find that it is very straightforward and quick to complete. The boxes and text areas, which are impacted by the order, are checked and filled and the balance of the choices are left blank.

ORDER DETAILS

STATE OF MICHIGAN COUNTY OF WAYNE THIRD JUDICIAL CIRCUIT COURT FAMILY DIVISION	**ORDER DATA FORM-SUPPORT** Re: SUBMISSION FOR LOADING ATTACHED SUPPORT ORDER INTO MiCSES ON FOC COMPUTER SYSTEM THE ORDER WAS ENTERED ON: _____ (DATE ON ORDER STAMPED BY JUDGE'S CLERK)	(PLACE LABEL HERE) CASE #: _____ _____ JUDGE

*INDICATES REQUIRED INFORMATION

CHECK ONLY THE BOXES WHICH APPLY TO PROVISIONS IN THE SUBMITTED ORDER

* PLAINTIFF NAME:	* DEFENDANT NAME:

*THIS ORDER IS:
☐ EX PARTE (PROOF OF SERVICE REQUIRED)   ☐ TEMPORARY ☐ JUDGMENT   ☐ MODIFICATION

*WERE CHILD SUPPORT GUIDELINES FOLLOWED?   ☐ YES   ☐ NO

***THE CHILD SUPPORT PAYER IS   ☐ PLAINTIFF ☐ DEFENDANT   ☐ NOT APPLICABLE.**

☐ **CHILD SUPPORT.**   COMMENCEMENT DATE IS _____   ☐ **PAY DIRECT, NOT THROUGH FOC.**

* 5 CHILDREN PER WEEK	* 4 CHILDREN PER WEEK	* 3 CHILDREN PER WEEK	* 2 CHILDREN PER WEEK	* 1 CHILD PER WEEK
CHILD SUPPORT AMOUNT $	CHILD SUPPORT AMOUNT $	CHILD SUPPORT AMOUNT $	CHILD SUPPORT AMOUNT $	CHILD SUPPORT AMOUNT $

☐ **INCOME WITHHOLDING:**   ☐ PROCESS AT GUIDELINE AMOUNT   ☐ PROCESS AT $ _____ PER WEEK

☐ **CHILD SUPPORT ARREARAGE:**
☐ PRESERVED ☐ CANCELED AS OF DATE: _____   ☐ SET AT $ _____ AS OF DATE: _____

☐ **CHILD CARE EXPENSES:** $ _____ PER WEEK, COMMENCEMENT DATE IS _____ ;
END DATE IS ☐ GUIDELINE DATE **OR** ☐ DATE: _____

☐ **CHILD CARE ARREARAGE:**
☐ PRESERVED ☐ CANCELED AS OF DATE: _____   ☐ SET AT $ _____ AS OF DATE: _____

☐ **ARREARAGE ADJUSTMENT:**
☐ DIRECT CREDIT IN AMOUNT OF $ _____   ☐ ADD ADDITIONAL OBLIGATION IN AMOUNT OF $ _____

☐ **MEDICAL INSURANCE IN ORDER.**
☐ **CHILD SUPPORT PAYER RESPONSIBLE FOR** _____ **% OF UNINSURED MEDICAL EXPENSES.**

☐ **PARENTING TIME ABATEMENT:** ____ % PARENTING TIME CREDIT AFTER ___ CONSECUTIVE OVERNIGHTS.
☐ **PARENTING TIME ORDERED: (CHECK ONE):**
☐ REASONABLE   ☐ SPECIFIC   ☐ SUPERVISED   ☐ RESERVED   ☐ REFER TO FAMILY COUNSELING/OTHER

***THE SPOUSAL SUPPORT PAYER IS   ☐ PLAINTIFF ☐ DEFENDANT   ☐ NOT APPLICABLE.**

☐ **SPOUSAL SUPPORT:** ☐ $ _____ PER WEEK, COMMENCEMENT DATE: _____ .
☐ PERMANENT   ☐ END DATE _____   ☐ **PAY DIRECT, NOT THROUGH FOC**

☐ **SPOUSAL SUPPORT ARREARAGE:**
☐ PRESERVED ☐ CANCELED AS OF DATE: _____   ☐ SET AT $ _____ AS OF DATE: _____

☐ **ORDER REFERS MATTERS TO DIVORCE INVESTIGATION/MODIFICATION FOR FURTHER INVESTIGATION.**

I CERTIFY THAT THE ABOVE INFORMATION IS TRUE TO THE BEST OF MY KNOWLEDGE, INFORMATION AND BELIEF, AND IS IN FULL CONFORMITY WITH THE REQUIREMENTS SET FORTH BY STATUTE AND COURT RULE AND THE DECISION OF THE COURT. (NOTE: FOC WILL NOT READ THE ORDER WHEN ENTERING IT ON MiCSES.)

_____   _____   _____
DATE: SIGNATURE OF ATTORNEY   BAR NO.

PLEASE PRINT:
                                     _____
                                     ATTORNEY NAME

                                     _____
                                     ADDRESS

                                     _____   _____
                                     CITY/STATE/ZIP   TELEPHONE NO.

FD/FOC 4002 (11/06/02) **ORDER DATA FORM-SUPPORT**

DEMOGRAPHICS

| STATE OF MICHIGAN
COUNTY OF WAYNE
THIRD JUDICIAL CIRCUIT
COURT
FAMILY DIVISION | **ORDER DATA FORM-SUPPORT**
Re: SUBMISSION FOR LOADING
ATTACHED SUPPORT ORDER INTO
MiCSES ON FOC COMPUTER SYSTEM

THE ORDER WAS ENTERED ON:
_____
(DATE ON ORDER STAMPED BY JUDGE'S CLERK) | (PLACE LABEL HERE)

CASE #:
_____

_____
JUDGE |

*INDICATES REQUIRED INFORMATION

CHECK ONLY THE BOXES WHICH APPLY TO PROVISIONS IN THE SUBMITTED ORDER

* PLAINTIFF NAME:	* DEFENDANT NAME:

* NAME(S) OF CHILDREN (OLDEST TO YOUNGEST)	* DATE(S) OF BIRTH	* SOCIAL SECURITY NUMBER(S)

(ADD ADDITIONAL CHILDREN ON SEPARATE SHEET)

NON-CUSTODIAL PARENT (OR FATHER IF JOINT CUSTODY) ☐ PLAINTIFF ☐ DEFENDANT

* NAME:	* DATE OF BIRTH:	* SOC. SEC. NO.	HOME TELEPHONE NO:
* RESIDENTIAL ADDRESS:	* CITY, STATE, ZIP	OTHER TELEPHONE NUMBERS: ☐ WORK ☐ MOBILE	FIA/TANF N0.: NOW ACTIVE: ☐ YES ☐ NO
* EMPLOYER:	* EMPLOYER ADDRESS:	EMPLOYER TELEPHONE NO.:	EMPLOYER FED I.D. NO.:

CUSTODIAL PERSON (OR MOTHER IF JOINT CUSTODY) ☐ PLAINTIFF ☐ DEFENDANT

* NAME:	* DATE OF BIRTH:	* SOC. SEC. NO.	HOME TELEPHONE NO:
* RESIDENTIAL ADDRESS:	* CITY, STATE, ZIP	OTHER TELEPHONE NUMBERS: ☐ WORK ☐ MOBILE	FIA/TANF N0.: NOW ACTIVE: ☐ YES ☐ NO
* EMPLOYER:	* EMPLOYER ADDRESS:	EMPLOYER TELEPHONE NO.:	EMPLOYER FED I.D. NO.:

I CERTIFY THAT THE ABOVE INFORMATION IS TRUE TO THE BEST OF MY KNOWLEDGE, INFORMATION AND BELIEF, AND IS IN FULL CONFORMITY WITH THE REQUIREMENTS SET FORTH BY STATUTE AND COURT RULE AND THE DECISION OF THE COURT. (NOTE: FOC WILL NOT READ THE ORDER WHEN ENTERING IT ON MiCSES.)

DATE: _____   _____   BAR NO. _____
                            SIGNATURE OF ATTORNEY

PLEASE PRINT: _____
                   ATTORNEY NAME

FD/FOC 4002 (11/06/02) **ORDER DATA FORM-SUPPORT**

Original - Court
1st copy - Other Party
2nd copy - Moving Party

3rd copy - Friend of the Court
4th copy - Proof of Service
5th copy - Proof of Service

Approved, SCAO

STATE OF MICHIGAN JUDICIAL CIRCUIT COUNTY	MOTION REGARDING SUPPORT	CASE NO.

Court address

Court telephone no.

Plaintiff's name, address, and telephone no. ☐ moving party		Defendant's name, address, and telephone no. ☐ moving party

v

Third party name, address, and telephone no. ☐ moving party

1. ☐ a. On _____ a judgment
   Date

   or order was entered regarding support.
   ☐ b. There is currently no order regarding support.

☐ 2. The ☐ plaintiff ☐ defendant is ordered to pay support of $_____ each _____ .
week, month, etc.

☐ 3. The ☐ plaintiff ☐ defendant is ordered to pay child care of $_____ each _____ .
week, month, etc.

☐ 4. The ☐ plaintiff ☐ defendant is ordered to pay health care of $_____ each _____ .
week, month, etc.

☐ 5. Conditions regarding support have changed as follows:
Use a separate sheet to explain in detail what has happened and attach. Include all necessary facts.

☐ 6. _____ and I have agreed to support as follows:
Name
Use a separate sheet to explain in detail what you have agreed on and attach. Include all necessary facts.

7. **I ask the court to order that support be** paid as follows: ☐ See 6. above for details.
Use a separate sheet to explain in detail what you want the court to order and attach.

I declare that the above statements are true to the best of my information, knowledge, and belief.

_____
Date

_____
Moving party's signature

NOTICE OF HEARING

A hearing will be held on this motion before _____
Name of judge or referee

on _____ at _____ at _____ .
Date   Time   Place

NOTE: If you are the person receiving this motion, you may file a response. Contact the friend of the court office and request form FOC 51.

CERTIFICATE OF MAILING

I certify that on this date I mailed a copy of this motion and notice of hearing on the other party(ies) by ordinary mail at the above address(es).

_____
Date

_____
Moving party's signature

FOC 50 (12/96) **MOTION REGARDING SUPPORT**

MCL 552.14; MSA 25.94, MCR 2.119, MCR 3.213

Approved, SCAO

Original - Court
1st copy - Moving Party
2nd copy - Responding Party

3rd copy - Friend of the Court
4th copy - Proof of Service
5th copy - Proof of Service

STATE OF MICHIGAN JUDICIAL CIRCUIT COUNTY	RESPONSE TO MOTION REGARDING SUPPORT	CASE NO.

Court address   **Court telephone no.**

Plaintiff's name, address, and telephone no. ☐ moving party

v

Defendant's name, address, and telephone no. ☐ moving party

Third party name, address, and telephone no. ☐ moving party

1. ☐ a. On _____ a judgment
     Date
   or order was entered regarding support.
   ☐ b. There is currently no order regarding support.

☐ 2. The ☐ plaintiff ☐ defendant   is ordered to pay support of $ _____ each _____ .
                                                                                                week, month, etc.

☐ 3. The ☐ plaintiff ☐ defendant   is ordered to pay child care of $ _____ each _____ .
                                                                                                   week, month, etc.

☐ 4. The ☐ plaintiff ☐ defendant   is ordered to pay health care of $ _____ each _____ .
                                                                                                    week, month, etc.

☐ 5. I ☐ agree ☐ do not agree   that conditions regarding support have changed as stated in the motion.
      Explain in detail what you do not agree with and why. Include all necessary facts. Use a separate sheet of paper if needed.

☐ 6. I agreed with the other party to start/change support:
   ☐ a. exactly as stated in the motion.
   ☐ b. but not as stated in the motion.
      If b. is checked, explain in detail what you did agree on. Include all necessary facts. Use a separate sheet of paper if needed.

7. ☐ a. I agree with what is being asked for in the motion.
   ☐ b. I do not agree with what is being asked for in the motion and ask the court to order that support be paid as follows:
      If you do not agree with the request in the motion, explain in detail why and what you want the court to order. Use a separate sheet of paper if needed.

I declare that the above statements are true to the best of my information, knowledge, and belief.

_____   _____
Date   Responding party's signature

CERTIFICATE OF MAILING

I certify that on this date I mailed a copy of this response on the other party(ies) by ordinary mail at the above address(es).

_____   _____
Date   Responding party's signature

STATE OF MICHIGAN Circuit Court - Family Division COUNTY	ORDER REGARDING SPOUSAL SUPPORT	CASE NO.

Plaintiff:

Defendant:

v

Date of hearing _____   Judge _____

1. This order is entered ☐ after hearing. ☐ on consent. ☐ on stipulation.

THE COURT FINDS:

☐ 2. A motion requesting ☐ change of spousal support ☐ entry of an original spousal support order   was filed.

☐ 3. A response to the motion was filed.

☐ 4. A change of circumstances ☐ does ☐ does not   exist which warrants a change in the spousal support order.

☐ 5. Spousal support, previously reserved, is now granted for ☐ plaintiff ☐ defendant   below.

IT IS ORDERED:

☐ 6. The motion regarding spousal support is dismissed.

☐ 7. On _____ , this ☐ modified ☐ original   spousal support order shall take effect:

8. Income withholding shall continue or be implemented immediately upon entry of this order.

9. a. Spousal support is an order the date it is due and shall not be modified retroactively except as allowed by MCL 552.603 and 552.603b.

b. Unpaid spousal support is a lien on the payer's property by operation of law and the payer's property can be encumbered or seized if past-due support exceeds two times the monthly amount of periodic support payments. In a friend of the court case, a surcharge will be added to past-due support as provided by MCL 552.603a. Currently past-due spousal support is preserved and shall be paid as follows _____

10. While this case is a friend of the court case, the support payer shall pay friend of the court service fees and other statutory fees.

11. The parties have previously provided information about their addresses, telephone and social security nos., driver's and occupational licenses, sources of income and health care coverage. In a friend of the court case, the parties must inform the friend of the court of any changes in this information, reporting changes in their residence information in writing within 21 days of a change.

Date/plaintiff _____   Date/defendant _____

Date _____   Judge _____

PROOF OF SERVICE

I certify that on this date I mailed a copy of this order to the other party by ordinary mail at his/her address above.

Date _____   Signature _____

GRP 23 (9/04)   ORDER REGARDING SPOUSAL SUPPORT

SPECIAL INSTRUCTIONS FOR NAME CHANGE

Every person 22 years of age or older whose name appears on the Petition for Name change must follow these instructions before the court can act on the petition.

Under Michigan law, every person 22 years of age or older who is requesting a name change must have a complete set of fingerprints taken at a local police agency. Those fingerprints will be used by the Michigan State Police and Federal Bureau of Investigation to check criminal records. The Michigan State Police will send a report to the court regarding any criminal records.

If you have a criminal record, it will be presumed that you are seeking the name change with fraudulent intent. You must prove to the court that the name change is not being sought with fraudulent intent.

INSTRUCTIONS:

1. File Petition for Name Change with circuit court and pay filing fee.

2. Make 1 copy of the completed Petition for Name Change (Form PC 51).

3. Go to your local police agency for the fingerprint card and to have your fingerprints taken. They will advise you of the appropriate fee. Take a copy of the Petition for Name Change with you.

4. After you have had your fingerprints taken, mail or deliver the copy of the Petition for Name Change, the fingerprint card, and the appropriate fee to the Michigan State Police. The fee must be made payable to the State of Michigan. Mail or deliver to:

> Michigan State Police
> Criminal Justice Information Center
> 7150 Harris Drive
> Lansing, Michigan 48913

5. The Michigan State Police will review their criminal records and will forward the fingerprints to the Federal Bureau of Investigation. Once the Federal Bureau of Investigation has reviewed their records and reported the information to the Michigan State Police, the Michigan State Police will send a report to the court.

6. After the court receives the required report from the Michigan State Police, the court can schedule a hearing on your Petition for Name Change.

   ☐ The court will mail you a notice when the required report is received. You must give the court a pre-addressed, postage paid envelope for mailing this notice.

   ☐ Contact the court eight weeks after you mail or deliver your fingerprint card to the Michigan State Police to find out if the required report has been received.

rev. 9/03

STATE OF MICHIGAN **JUDICIAL CIRCUIT - FAMILY DIVISION** **COUNTY**	**PETITION TO CHANGE NAME**	**FILE NO.**

In the matter of the name change of _____

Present first name(s), middle name(s), and last name(s) (type or print)

to _____

Requested new first name(s), middle name(s), and last name(s) (type or print)

☐ 1. An action within the jurisdiction of the family division of circuit court involving the family or family members of the above named

person(s) has been previously filed in _____ Court, Case Number _____, was

assigned to Judge _____ , and   ☐ remains   ☐ is no longer   pending.

2. The name change is for:

    ☐ a. a married person who wishes to also include a name change for:

        ☐ his/her spouse.   ☐ his/her minor child(ren), of whom the petitioner has legal custody.

    ☐ b. an adult.

    ☐ c. a minor, whose natural or adopted parents are: _____ and

        Mother

_____ .

Father

        Both parents are deceased. The guardian is _____ . (attach letters of guardianship)

        Name

3. The name change is for the following reason: _____

4. The name change is not sought for any fraudulent intent.

5. The following person(s) seeking a name change have a criminal record: _____

_____

6. Each person for whom a name change is sought has been a resident of the county for at least one year.

[Complete item 7. only if the name change is for a minor. Please see other side for remainder of petition.]

☐ 7. I have legal custody of the minor.

    ☐ a. The noncustodial parent has had the ability to visit, contact, or communicate with the child and has regularly and

    substantially failed or neglected to do so for a period of two years or more before the filing of this petition **and either:**

        ☐ a support order has been entered, and the noncustodial parent has failed to substantially comply with the order for

        a period of two years or more before the filing of this petition; **or**

        ☐ a support order has not been entered and the noncustodial parent, having the ability to support or assist in supporting

        the child, has failed or neglected to provide regular and substantial support for two years or more before the filing of

        this petition.

    ☐ b. The noncustodial parent has been convicted of child abuse (MCL 750.136b), criminal sexual conduct (MCL 750.520b,

    MCL 750.520c, 750.520d, or 750.520e), or assault with intent to commit criminal sexual conduct (MCL 750.520g) and the child or

    a sibling of the child was the victim. (attach judgment of sentence)

    c. The last known address of the noncustodial parent is: _____

_____

    ☐ The noncustodial parent is not living at the above address, and I have taken the following steps to locate him/her:

_____

(PLEASE SEE OTHER SIDE)

Do not write below this line - For court use only

PC 51 (9/03) **PETITION TO CHANGE NAME**   MCL 333.2872, MCL 711.1, MCR 3.613

8. **I request** the following name change(s): (type or print first name, middle name, and last name)

FROM	TO	DATE OF BIRTH
Petitioner		month, day, year
Spouse		month, day, year
Minor child		
Minor child		
Minor child		
Minor child		

If you want a new live birth certificate, check item 9. A special order is not needed if you only want to add the changed name(s) to the original certificate(s).

☐ 9. **I request** the court to order the State Registrar to create a new live birth certificate that does not disclose the name of

_____ at birth and to seal the original certificate.
Name

I declare that this petition has been examined by me and that its contents are true to the best of my information, knowledge, and belief.

_____   _____
Date   Date

_____   _____
Petitioner signature   Petitioner signature

_____   _____
Name (type or print)   Name (type or print)

_____   _____
Address   Address

_____   _____
City, state, zip   Telephone no.   City, state, zip   Telephone no.

☐ 10. I am the spouse of the petitioner or the non-custodial parent of the minor and consent to the granting of this petition to change name.

_____   _____
Date   Signature

☐
11. I am a minor 14 years of age or older, and I consent to the granting of this petition to change my name.

_____   _____
Date   Minor's signature

_____   _____
Date   Minor's signature

☐
12. I am a minor under 14 years of age, and I state my preference to the name change above.

_____   _____
Date   Minor's signature

_____   _____
Date   Minor's signature

_____   _____
Attorney signature   Address

_____   _____
Attorney name (type or print)   Bar no. City, state, zip   Telephone no.

STATE OF MICHIGAN PROBATE COURT COUNTY CIRCUIT COURT - FAMILY DIVISION	NOTICE OF HEARING	FILE NO.

In the matter of _____

TAKE NOTICE: A hearing will be held on _____ at _____ m.,
Date   Time

at _____ before Judge_____
Location   Bar no.

for the following purpose(s): state the nature of the hearing

If you require special accommodations to use the court because of a disability, or if you require a foreign language interpreter to help you fully participate in court proceedings, please contact the court immediately to make arrangements.

_____
Date

_____   _____
Attorney name   Bar no.   Petitioner name

_____   _____
Address   Address

_____   _____
City, state, zip   Telephone no.   City, state, zip   Telephone no.

The law provides that you should be notified of this hearing. Unless the check box below is marked, you are not required to attend the hearing, but it is your privilege to do so.

☐ You are required to attend this hearing.

Do not write below this line - For court use only

STATE OF MICHIGAN PROBATE COURT _____ COUNTY CIRCUIT COURT - FAMILY DIVISION	PROOF OF SERVICE	FILE NO.

In the matter of _____

1. Titles of the papers served or mailed: _____

_____

☐ 2. I served by ☐ ordinary mail ☐ registered mail (copy of return receipt attached) ☐ certified mail (copy of return receipt attached) the papers described above on:

Name	Complete address of service	Date

☐ 3. I served by **personal service** the papers described above on:

Name	Complete address of service	Date and Time

☐ 4. After diligent search and inquiry, I have been unable to find and serve the following interested persons:

_____

_____

I have made the following efforts in attempting to serve process: _____

_____

I declare under the penalties of perjury that this proof of service has been examined by me and that its contents are true to the best of my information, knowledge, and belief.

Service fee	Miles traveled	Mileage fee	Total fee	Date
$		$	$	

Date

Signature

Do not write below this line - For court use only

STATE OF MICHIGAN PROBATE COURT COUNTY CIRCUIT COURT - FAMILY DIVISION	PUBLICATION OF NOTICE OF HEARING	FILE NO.

In the matter of _____

TO ALL INTERESTED PERSONS including:*

whose address(es) are unknown and whose interest in the matter may be barred or affected by the following:

TAKE NOTICE: A hearing will be held on _____ at _____ m.

                                        Date   Time

at _____ before Judge _____

   Location   Bar no.

for the following purpose:

_____

Date

_____	_____
Attorney name (type or print) Bar no.	Petitioner name (type or print)
_____	_____
Address	Address
_____	_____
City, state, zip Telephone no.	City, state, zip Telephone no.

PUBLISH ABOVE INFORMATION ONLY

Publish _____ time(s) in _____ in _____ County

                                       Name of publication

Furnish _____ copies to _____

Furnish affidavit of publication to the court.

Forward statement for publication charges to _____

*NOTE TO PREPARER: This notice may be combined with the Notice to Creditors (form PC 574) by adding the language from the Notice to Creditors.

Do not write below this line - For court use only

STATE OF MICHIGAN JUDICIAL CIRCUIT - FAMILY DIVISION COUNTY	ORDER FOLLOWING HEARING ON PETITION TO CHANGE NAME	FILE NO.

In the matter of the name change of _____
Present first name(s), middle name(s), and last name(s) (type or print)

to _____
Requested new first name(s), middle name(s), and last name(s) (type or print)

1. Date of Hearing: _____ Judge: _____

Bar no.

THE COURT FINDS:

2. A petition for name change has been filed.

3. Notice of hearing was given by publication.

4. Each person for whom a name change is sought has been a resident of the county for at least one year.

☐ 5. The court has received the required criminal record report(s) from the Michigan Department of State Police.

☐ 6. _____ has a criminal record.
Name(s) (type or print)

7. ☐ a. The request for name change of _____ is
made with fraudulent intent.   Name(s) (type or print)

   ☐ b. The request for name change of _____ is not
made with fraudulent intent.   Name(s) (type or print)

☐ 8. The petitioner, having legal custody, requests the name change of a minor. The noncustodial parent has consented to the change.

☐ 9. The petitioner requests the name change of a minor. The custodial parent has consented to the name change. The noncustodial parent was given notice of the hearing.

   ☐ a. The noncustodial parent has had the ability to visit, contact, or communicate with the minor but has regularly and substantially failed or neglected to do so for the past two years, **and**
   ☐ a support order has been entered, and the noncustodial parent has failed to substantially comply with the order for a period of two years or more before the filing of the petition for name change; **or**
   ☐ a support order has not been entered and the noncustodial parent, having the ability to support or assist in supporting the child, has failed or neglected to provide regular and substantial support for two years or more before the filing of the petition for name change.

   ☐ b. The noncustodial parent has been convicted of child abuse (MCL 750.136b), criminal sexual conduct (MCL 750.520b, 750.520c, 750.520d, or 750.520e), or assault with intent to commit criminal sexual conduct (MCL 750.520g) and the child or a sibling of the child was the victim.

☐ 10. The minor(s) under the age of 14 have stated their preference to a name change.

☐ 11. The minor(s) is/are not of sufficient age to express their preference to a name change.

(PLEASE SEE OTHER SIDE)

Do not write below this line - For court use only

MCL 333.2872; MSA 14.15(2872), MCL 711.1; MSA 27.3178(561), MCR 5.781

IT IS ORDERED:

12. The name(s) of the following person(s) are changed:

From: **To:**

_____   _____

_____   _____

_____   _____

_____   _____

_____   _____

_____   _____

☐ 13. The State Registrar shall create a new live birth certificate for _____

which does not disclose the name at birth and shall seal the original certificate.

☐ 14. The request to change the name of _____ is denied.

☐ 15. The request is denied and the petition is dismissed.

_____
Date

_____
Judge

_____
Attorney name (type or print)   Bar no.

_____
Address

_____
City, state, zip   Telephone no.

NOTE TO PETITIONER: You must provide this order to the State Registrar if you want to change your birth certificate.

Note to Clerk: Under MCL 711.1(3), if the court enters an order to change the name of a person who has a criminal record, the court shall forward the order to the central records division of the Michigan State Police and to 1 or more of the following:

- The Department of Corrections if the person named in the order is in prison or on parole or has been imprisoned or released from parole in the immediately preceding 2 years.

- The sheriff of the county in which the person named in the order was last convicted if the person was incarcerated in a county jail or released from a county jail within the immediately preceding 2 years.

- The court that has jurisdiction over the person named in the order if the person named in the order is under the jurisdiction of the family division of the circuit court, or until January 1, 1998, the probate court, or has been discharged from the jurisdiction of that court within the immediately preceding 2 years.

STATE OF MICHIGAN **Circuit Court - Family Division** **COUNTY**	ORDER REGARDING ASSIGNMENT OF DEPENDENCY EXEMPTIONS	CASE NO.

Plaintiff:

Defendant:

v

Date of hearing _____   Judge _____

1. This order is entered ☐ after hearing. ☐ on consent. ☐ on stipulation.

THE COURT FINDS:

☐ 2. A motion for assignment of dependency exemptions for the parties' children was filed.

☐ 3. A response to the motion was filed.

☐ 4. A change of circumstances ☐ does ☐ does not exist which warrants assignment of the dependency exemptions.

IT IS ORDERED:

☐ 5. The motion for assignment of dependency exemptions is dismissed.

☐ 6. Starting the tax year of _____ , the dependency exemptions for the parties' children shall be assigned to ☐ plaintiff ☐ defendant and the other party shall no longer claim these exemptions. The assigning party shall also sign and submit to the assignee-party IRS Form 8332 to carry out the assignment.

Date/plaintiff _____   Date/defendant _____

Date _____   Judge _____

PROOF OF SERVICE

I certify that on this date I mailed a copy of this order to the other party by ordinary mail at his/her address above.

Date _____   Signature _____

	Original - Court 1st copy - Applicant	2nd copy - Opposing party PROBATE OSM CODE: OSF

STATE OF MICHIGAN JUDICIAL DISTRICT JUDICIAL CIRCUIT COUNTY PROBATE	**AFFIDAVIT AND ORDER SUSPENSION OF FEES/COSTS**	**CASE NO.**

Court address   **Court telephone no.**

Plaintiff/Petitioner name, address, and telephone no.		Defendant/Respondent name, address, and telephone no.
	v	
Plaintiff's/Petitioner's attorney, bar no., address, and telephone no.		Defendant's/Respondent's attorney, bar no., address, and telephone no.

☐ Probate   In the matter of _____

NOTE: Requests for waiver/suspension of transcript costs must be made separately by motion.   **AFFIDAVIT**

1. The attached pleading is to be filed with the court by or on behalf of _____ ,
                                                                                                       Name

   applicant, who is   ☐ plaintiff/petitioner.   ☐ defendant/respondent.

2. The applicant is entitled to and asks the court for suspension of fees and costs in the action for the following reason:

   ☐ a. S/he is currently receiving public assistance: $ _____ per _____ Case No.: _____ .

   ☐ b. S/he is unable to pay those fees and costs because of indigency, based on the following facts:

   INCOME: _____
                 Employer name and address

   _____   _____   _____   per ☐ week.   ☐ month.   ☐ two weeks.
   Length of employment   Average gross pay   Average net pay

   ASSETS: State value of car, home, bank deposits, bonds, stocks, etc.

   OBLIGATIONS: Itemize monthly rent, installment payments, mortgage payments, child support, etc.

☐ 3. (in domestic relations cases only) The applicant is entitled to an order requiring his/her spouse to pay attorney fees.

REIMBURSEMENT: It is understood that the court may order the applicant to pay the fees and costs when the reason for their waiver or suspension no longer exists.

_____
Affiant signature

Subscribed and sworn to before me on _____ , _____County, Michigan.
                                                      Date

My commission expires: _____   Signature: _____
                              Date   Deputy clerk/Register/Notary public

Notary public, State of Michigan, County of _____

(SEE REVERSE SIDE FOR ORDER)

MC 20 (6/04) **AFFIDAVIT AND ORDER, SUSPENSION OF FEES/COSTS**   MCR 2.002

CERTIFICATION OF ATTORNEY

1. I have reviewed the affidavit of indigency, and I certify that its contents are true to the best of my information, knowledge, and belief.

2. I will bring to the court's attention the matter of suspended costs and fees and the availability of funds to pay them before any disposition is entered. I will report at that time any changes in the information contained in the affidavit of indigency or any other information regarding the affiant's financial status or alterations of the fee arrangement.

_____
Date

_____
Attorney signature

_____
Attorney name (type or print)   Bar no.

CERTIFICATION BY PERSON OTHER THAN PARTY

1. I have personal knowledge of the facts appearing in the affidavit.

2. The person in whose behalf the petition is filed is unable to sign it because of

☐ minority: _____   ☐ other disability: _____
        Date of birth   Nature of disability

Relationship: _____

_____
Date

_____
Affiant signature

_____
Affiant name (type or print)

_____
Address

_____
City, state, zip   Telephone no.

ORDER

IT IS ORDERED:

☐ 1. Fees and costs in this action required by law or court rule are waived/suspended until further order of the court. Before any final disposition or discontinuance is entered, the moving party shall bring the fee and costs suspension to the attention of the judge for final disposition.

☐ 2. The applicant's spouse shall pay the fees and costs required by law or court rule.

☐ 3. This application is denied.

_____
Date

_____
Judge   Bar no.

Original - Originating court
1st copy - Receiving court
2nd copy - Friend of the court

3rd copy - Plaintiff
4th copy - Defendant

Approved, SCAO

STATE OF MICHIGAN JUDICIAL CIRCUIT COUNTY	MOTION/STIPULATION FOR TRANSFERRING CASE (Post Judgment)	CASE NO.

Court address

Court telephone no.

Plaintiff's name, address, and telephone no.		Defendant's name, address, and telephone no.
	v	

☐ MOTION ☐ STIPULATION

☐ 1. I, ☐ the plaintiff, ☐ the defendant, ☐ the court-ordered custodian, request transfer of this case to

_____ County.

a. This transfer is requested on the basis of residence and for the convenience of the parties and is in the best interests of the minor child(ren).

b. All parties have resided in counties other than the county of current jurisdiction for more than six months.

c. _____ has resided in the county to which the transfer is
Name of plaintiff/defendant

requested for at least six months.

d. The county to which the transfer is requested is not adjacent to the county of current jurisdiction.

☐ We stipulate to the transfer of this case.

☐ 2. I, the friend of the court, request transfer of this case to _____ County for the following reasons:

I declare that the statements above are true to the best of my information, knowledge, and belief.

_____
Date

_____
Signature

_____
Name and title (type or print)

_____
Signature

_____
Signature

_____
Name and title (type or print)

_____
Name and title (type or print)

NOTICE OF HEARING

A hearing will be held on the above motion on _____ at _____ at the above court address.
Date   Time

If you require special accommodations to use the court because of a disability, please contact the court immediately to make arrangements.

CERTIFICATE OF MAILING

I certify that on this date I mailed a copy of this motion and notice of hearing on the other party by ordinary mail addressed to his/her last known address.

_____
Date

_____
Signature

FOC 24 (6/98) **MOTION/STIPULATION FOR TRANSFERRING CASE (Post Judgment)**   MCR 3.212

STATE OF MICHIGAN Circuit Court - Family Division COUNTY	RESPONSE TO MOTION FOR TRANSFERRING CASE	CASE NO.

Plaintiff: ☐ moving party

Defendant: ☐ moving party

v

1. A motion has been filed for transfer of this case to another county in Michigan.

2. I ☐ agree ☐ do not agree that this case is eligible for transfer.

3. I ☐ agree ☐ do not agree that proper cause exists for transfer.

☐ 4. I agreed with the other party for transfer of this case to another county.

    ☐ a. exactly as stated in the motion.

    ☐ b. but not as stated in the motion. (Describe agreement)

5. ☐ a. I agree with what is being asked for in the motion.

    ☐ b. I do not agree with what is being asked for in the motion and ask the court to make an order regarding case transfer as follows:

I declare that the above statements are true to the best of my information, knowledge and belief.

Date _____   Responding party _____

CERTIFICATE OF MAILING

I certify that on this date I mailed a copy of this reponse to the other party(ies) by ordinary mail at the above address(es).

Date _____   Responding party _____

GRP 25 (9/04)   RESPONSE TO MOTION FOR TRANSFERRING CASE

Original - Originating court
1st copy - Receiving court
2nd copy - Friend of the court

3rd copy - Plaintiff
4th copy - Defendant

Approved, SCAO

STATE OF MICHIGAN JUDICIAL CIRCUIT COUNTY	ORDER CHANGING VENUE AND TRANSFERRING CASE (Post Judgment)	CASE NO.

Court address

Court telephone no.

Plaintiff's name and address

v

Defendant's name and address

CERTIFICATE OF ARREARAGE

1. I certify that as of _____
   Date

   the arrears on the records of the friend of the court

   were $ _____ .

   _____
   Friend of the court

ORDER

2. Date of hearing: _____ Judge: _____
   Bar no.

3. **THE COURT FINDS** that there are arrearages in the amount of $ _____ as certified above by the friend of the court.

IT IS ORDERED:

4. Venue is changed and this case shall be transferred to _____

   by _____ .
      Date

☐ 5. Before the date of transfer _____ shall pay to the court of current
                                 Name

   jurisdiction all past due fees and costs in the amount of $ _____ .

6. ☐ a. ☐ Plaintiff ☐ Defendant ☐ Both parties equally   shall pay the statutory filing fee to the court of current
         jurisdiction before the date of transfer. The court of current jurisdiction shall submit the filing fee to the court to which
         the case is transferred. The case shall not be transferred until the fee is paid.

   ☐ b. The statutory filing fee is waived because ☐ the transfer was initiated by the court or friend of the court.
        ☐ the parties are indigent.

☐ 7. The transferring office of the friend of the court and/or the Michigan State Disbursement Unit shall continue to process support
     payments under the current support order until it receives notice that the case has been accepted for filing by the transferee
     office of the friend of the court. Any payments received during this interim period shall be credited to the payer's account.

_____   _____
Date   Judge

STATE OF MICHIGAN **Circuit Court - Family Division** COUNTY	WAIVER OF MILITARY RELIEF LAW RIGHTS	CASE NO.

Plaintiff: ☐ moving party

Defendant: ☐ moving party

v

1. On _____, the moving party filed a motion for _____

2. I am in active-duty military service currently assigned to:

3. I waive the following military relief law rights and protections available to me during the motion cited above:

☐ a. judgment-stay protections provided by sec. 524 of the federal Servicemembers Civil Relief Act (50 USC App. 501 et seq.).

☐ b. general lawsuit relief provided by Michigan's military relief law (MCL 32.517) or a similar military relief law from another state.

Date _____   Nonmoving party _____

GRP 27 (9/04)   **WAIVER OF MILITARY RELIEF LAW RIGHTS**

STATE OF MICHIGAN Circuit Court - Family Division COUNTY	REQUEST FOR STAY UNDER THE SERVICEMEMBERS CIVIL RELIEF ACT	CASE NO.

Plaintiff: ☐ moving party   **Defendant:** ☐ moving party

	v	

1. Following the parties' divorce, the moving party has filed a motion for_____

and a hearing before a judge/referee has been scheduled for _____

2. I am in active-duty military service and am currently assigned to_____

at _____

I expect to remain at that duty station until _____, followed by reassignment to this unit and

and unit location (if known) _____

My current enlistment expires on _____

3. My military service has materially affected my ability to comply with post-judgment motion requirements, particularly attendance at the motion hearing, for these reasons:

☐ A. Geographical distance:
   1. My current duty station is distant from the court in this case preventing my attendance at the
   hearing without leave.
   2. I have tried to obtain ordinary or emergency leave to attend the hearing but:

☐ B. Financial hardship:
   1. My pre-enlistment annual income was _____ and my in-service annual income is _____
   and the loss of income makes it difficult to afford a local nonmilitary lawyer in Michigan to represent me in this matter.

4. **I request a stay of the motion** under sec. 524 of the Servicemembers Civil Relief Act until:

☐ date: _____   ☐ duration of my military service.   ☐ duration of my military service
plus 90 days.

I declare that the above statements are true to the best of my information, knowledge and belief.

Date _____   Nonmoving party _____

CERTIFICATE OF MAILING

I certify that on this date I mailed a copy of this request to the other party(ies) by ordinary mail at the
above address(es).

Date _____   Nonmoving party _____

TO THE CLERK OF THE COURT:

Please notify me about whether this request is granted or denied.

GRP 28 (9/04)   **REQUEST FOR STAY UNDER THE SERVICEMEMBERS CIVIL RELIEF ACT**

<table>
<tr><td>STATE OF MICHIGAN
Circuit Court - Family Division
COUNTY</td><td>MOTION/STIPULATION
TO OPT OUT OF THE
FRIEND OF THE COURT SYSTEM</td><td>CASE NO.</td></tr>
</table>

Plaintiff: ☐ moving party

Defendant: ☐ moving party

v

☐ **MOTION** ☐ **STIPULATION**

1. I request to opt this post-judgment divorce case out of these friend of the court services:
☐ a. all friend of the court services.
☐ b. all friend of the court services except payment of support through the state disbursement unit (SDU) by: ☐ immediate income withholding. ☐ payment directly from payer.
☐ c. immediate income withholding only, with support payment directly to: ☐ SDU. ☐ recipient.

☐ 2. For an opt-out under 1a. or 1b., this case is eligible for opt-out because:

a. neither party receives public assistance for a child in this case;

b. no money is due the state because of past public assistance for a child in this case;

c. no child support arrearage or custody or parenting time violation has occurred during the previous 12 months in this case;

d. neither party has reopened a friend of the court case during the previous 12 months;

e. there is no evidence: (1) of domestic violence or unequal bargaining position between the parties, or (2) that a party has chosen to opt out against the best interests of the party or the party's child;

f. the parties are filing a form signed by them advising about the friend of the court services they will lose if this motion is granted. (FOC 101 is attached)

g. the parties stipulate to the opt-out selected in 1a. or 1b by co-signing below.

☐ 3. For an opt-out under 1c., there is good cause for opt-out because:

a. it is in the best interests of the children for immediate income withholding to stop because:

b. the file in this case shows that previously ordered support has been paid on time;

c. in a friend of the court case, the payer of support agrees to keep the friend of the court informed of: 1) current sources of income 2) health care coverage.

I declare that the above statements are true to the best of my information, knowledge and belief.

Date/plaintiff _____   Date/defendant _____

NOTICE OF HEARING

A hearing will be held on this motion before (judge or referee) _____
on _____ at (time) _____ at (place) _____
Note: If you are the person receiving this motion, you may file a response.

CERTIFICATE OF MAILING

I certify that on this date I mailed a copy of this motion and notice of hearing to the other party(ies) by ordinary mail at the above address(es).
Date _____   Moving party _____

GRP 26 (9/04)   **MOTION/STIPULATION TO OPT OUT OF THE FRIEND OF THE COURT SYSTEM**

STATE OF MICHIGAN JUDICIAL CIRCUIT COUNTY	ADVICE OF RIGHTS REGARDING USE OF FRIEND OF THE COURT SERVICES	CASE NO.

Friend of the Court address

Telephone no.

1. Right to Refuse Friend of the Court Services

a. You have the right to refuse friend of the court services for custody, parenting time, and support. To decline friend of the court services, you must file with the court a motion requesting that friend of the court services not be required. You must attach a signed copy of this advice of rights to the motion. The court will grant the motion provided both parties agree and have signed this advice of rights and it determines that the following are true:

   1) Neither of you receives public assistance for the child(ren) or requests friend of the court services.
   2) There is no evidence of domestic violence or uneven bargaining position between you.
   3) The court finds that declining to receive friend of the court services is not against the best interests of a child.

b. If you already have a friend of the court case, you can file a motion to discontinue friend of the court services provided both parties agree and have signed this advice of rights and the court finds that the following are true:

   1) Neither of you receives public assistance for the child(ren) or requests friend of the court services.
   2) There is no evidence of domestic violence or uneven bargaining position between you.
   3) The court finds that declining to receive friend of the court services is not against the best interests of a child.
   4) No money is due the state because of past public assistance.
   5) No arrearage or a custody or parenting time order violation has occurred in the last 12 months.
   6) Neither of you has reopened a friend of the court case in the last 12 months.

2. Friend of the Court Services (you will not receive these services if you choose not to use the Friend of the Court)

The friend of the court must provide the following services for friend of the court cases. You are entitled to these services unless you choose to refuse the services and the court grants that choice.

a. Accounting Services

Friends of the court must collect support and disburse it within 48 hours. Friend of the court accounting services include: 1) friend of the court accounting for payments received and sent; 2) adjustments of support for parenting time or other credits; and 3) annual statements of accounts, if requested.

b. Support Enforcement Services

The friend of the court must begin to enforce support when one month of support is overdue. For friend of the court cases, child support enforcement services include:

- Paying support out of tax refunds.
- Asking the court to order the nonpaying party to come to court to explain the failure to pay.
- Having unpaid support paid out of property the payer owns.
- Reporting support arrearage to a consumer reporting agency or requesting that the payer's licenses be suspended.
- Collecting support by an income withholding order.

If you choose not to receive friend of the court services, any existing income withholding source will be notified that the friend of the court is no longer responsible for income withholding. **The parties will be solely responsible for stopping or changing income withholding as the law allows.** The friend of the court will stop any unfinished collection actions.

c. Medical Support Enforcement Services

The friend of the court is required to recommend how the parents divide health care expenses and to take action to collect the amounts that a parent fails or refuses to pay. When a parent is required to insure the children the friend of the court is authorized to instruct an employer to enroll the children in an insurance plan when the parent fails or refuses to do so.

d. Support Review and Modification Services

Once every two years persons with friend of the court cases may request the friend of the court to review the support amount. After completing the review, the friend of the court must file a motion to raise or lower support, or inform the parties that it recommends no change. It must also review support when changed circumstances lead it to believe that support should be modified.

See other side

e. Custody and Parenting Time Enforcement Services

For friend of the court cases, the friend of the court must enforce custody and parenting time when a party complains that it is violated. Child custody and parenting time enforcement services include:

- Asking the court to order the noncooperating party to come to the court to explain the failure to obey the parenting time order.
- Suspending the licenses of individuals who deny parenting time.
- Awarding makeup parenting time.
- Joint meetings to resolve complaints.

f. Custody and Parenting Time Investigation Services

For disputes about custody or parenting time in friend of the court cases, the friend of the court sometimes must investigate and provide reports to the parties and the court.

g. Mediation Services

Friend of the court offices must provide mediation services to help parties with friend of the court cases settle custody and parenting time disputes.

3. State Disbursement Unit and IV-D Services

a. State Disbursement Unit (SDU)

If you choose not to receive friend of the court services, you may continue to make payments to, and receive payments through, the state disbursement unit (SDU). The SDU will keep track of the amount paid and sent out. However, the SDU cannot provide you with all of the accounting functions the friend of the court provides.

All payments made through the SDU must be distributed to the amounts due as required by federal law. When a payer has more than one case, federal law determines how a payment is divided among the cases. **Even if you choose not to receive friend of the court services, payments through the SDU must be divided among all a payer's cases and distributed in the same manner as payments on FOC cases. You cannot discontinue friend of the court services if you want to use the SDU unless you first provide to the SDU all the information that the SDU needs to set up an account.**

b. Your Rights Under Title IV-D of the Social Security Act

Title IV-D of the Social Security Act provides federal government resources to collect child support and it allows certain funding to be used for parenting time and custody services. In Michigan, critical title IV-D services are delivered by the friend of the court. **If you choose not to receive friend of the court services, you cannot receive most IV-D services.**

ACKNOWLEDGMENT REGARDING SERVICES

Check below only if you do not want to receive friend of the court services. Then date, print name, and sign.

I have read this advice of rights and I understand the friend of the court services I am entitled to receive.

☐ I acknowledge that by signing below **I am choosing not to receive** any friend of the court services. I understand that before this choice can take effect, a motion requesting this choice and the other party's agreement must be filed with the court for approval. I also understand that the court may deny this choice if certain conditions are not met as stated in this advice of rights.

_____   _____
Name (type or print)   Name (type or print)

_____   _____
Signature   Date   Signature   Date

If you did not check the above, you are choosing to receive friend of the court services. **For the most effective friend of the court services,** you can request IV-D services by dating and signing below.

I request IV-D services through the friend of the court office.

_____   _____
Date   Signature

Original - Court
1st copy - Plaintiff

2nd copy - Defendant
3rd copy - Friend of the Court

STATE OF MICHIGAN JUDICIAL CIRCUIT COUNTY	ORDER EXEMPTING CASE FROM FRIEND OF THE COURT SERVICES	CASE NO.

Friend of the Court address   FAX no.   Telephone no.

Plaintiff's name and address

v

Defendant's name and address

Attorney:

Attorney:

Date of hearing: _____ Judge: _____

Bar no.

THE COURT FINDS:

1. There is no evidence of domestic violence or unequal bargaining position between the parties to the case.
2. Granting the parties the relief they have requested would not be against the best interests of any child in the case.
3. The parties have filed executed copies of a form advising them of the services they will not receive if their motion is granted.
4. Neither party receives public assistance for a child in the case.
5. No money is due the state because of past public assistance for a child in the case.
6. No arrearage or custody or parenting time order violation has occurred in the last 12 months in this case.
7. Neither party has reopened a friend of the court case in the last 12 months.
☐ 8. The parties do not want IV-D services and have requested that any existing IV-D case be closed. (Note: This box should be checked unless exceptional circumstances exist that entitle the IV-D case to remain open.)

IT IS ORDERED:

9. Subject to the provisions of item 14 below, this case is not a friend of the court case.
☐ 10. This case is not a title IV-D case. (Note: This box should be checked if item 8 has been checked.)
11. The friend of the court shall not be involved in the enforcement, investigation, or accounting functions for custody, parenting time, or support in this case.
12. The parties are responsible for all enforcement and accounting functions for custody, parenting time, or support in this case.
13. Except as indicated below, there is no income withholding in this case, support will be paid directly by the payer to the payee, and the friend of the court shall terminate any existing income withholding. Should this case become a friend of the court case, the payer must keep the friend of the court advised of the name and address of the payer's source of income and any health care coverage that is available to the payer as a benefit of employment or that the payer maintains including the name of the insurance company, health care organization, or health maintenance organization; the policy, certificate, or contract number; and the names and birth dates of the persons for whose benefit the payer maintains the coverage.
    ☐ a. Support shall be paid through the State Disbursement Unit (SDU). Support shall be paid by income withholding to the extent allowed by statutes and court rules, however, the friend of the court is not responsible for the income withholding. The friend of the court shall notify the employer that it is no longer involved in the case and that any further information concerning income withholding will be provided by the parties.
    ☐ b. Support shall be paid through the SDU.
If support payments are to be made through the SDU by income withholding or otherwise, the friend of the court shall not close the friend of the court case until the SDU notifies the friend of the court that it has been provided with the information necessary to process the child support payments. There will be no accounting for support that is not paid through the SDU.
14. The friend of the court shall open a friend of the court case if a party applies for public assistance relating to a child of the parties or either party submits to the friend of the court a written request to reopen the friend of the court case. If this case becomes a friend of the court case for any reason, the provisions on the other side of this order shall apply.

_____
Date

_____
Judge

See provisions on back.

CERTIFICATE OF MAILING

I certify that on this date I mailed a copy of this order to the other party by first class mail addressed to the last known address as defined in MCR 3.203.

_____
Date

_____
Signature

FOC 102 (10/04) **ORDER EXEMPTING CASE FROM FRIEND OF THE COURT SERVICES**   MCL 552.505, MCL 552.505a

If this case becomes a friend of the court case for any reason, the following provisions apply:

1. The parties must cooperate fully with the friend of the court in establishing the case as a friend of the court case.

2. The parties must provide copies of all orders in their case to the friend of the court.

3. The parties must supply any documents that a party to a friend of the court case is required to supply if they have not already done so.

4. The friend of the court is not responsible for determining any support arrearage that is not indicated by payment made through the SDU.

5. Support is payable through the friend of the court effective the date the case becomes a friend of the court case.

6. The friend of the court may prepare and submit, exparte, a uniform child support order that contains all the statutory requirements of a Michigan support order as long as the order does not contradict the existing support order.

7. At the request of the friend of the cuort, the parties shall complete a Verified Statement and Application for IV-D Services.

8. An order entry fee can be assessed.

Original - Court
2nd copy - Friend of the Court
3rd copy - Plaintiff
4th copy - Defendant

STATE OF MICHIGAN JUDICIAL CIRCUIT COUNTY	AGREEMENT SUSPENDING IMMEDIATE INCOME WITHHOLDING	CASE NO.

Friend of the Court address

Court telephone no.

Plaintiff's name and address

v

Defendant's name and address

NOTE: MCL 552.604(3) requires that all new and modified support orders after December 31, 1990 include a provision for immediate income withholding and that income withholding take effect immediately unless the parties enter into a written agreement that the income withholding order shall not take effect immediately.

We understand that by law an order of income withholding in a support order shall take effect immediately. However, we agree to the following:

1. The order of income withholding shall not take effect immediately.

2. An alternative payment arrangement shall be made as follows:

3. Both the payer and the recipient of support shall keep the friend of the court informed of the following:
   a. the name, address, and telephone number of his/her current source of income;
   b. any health care coverage that is available to him/her as a benefit of employment or that is maintained by him/her; the name of the insurance company, health care organization, or health maintenance organization; the policy, certificate or contract number; and the name(s) and birth date(s) of the person(s) for whose benefit s/he maintains health care coverage under the policy, certificate, or contract; and
   c. his/her current residence, mailing address, and telephone number.

4. We further understand that proceedings to implement income withholding shall commence if the payer of support falls one month behind in his/her support payments.

5. We recognize that the court may order withholding of income to take effect immediately for cause or at the request of the payer.

_____
Date

_____
Date

_____
Plaintiff's signature

_____
Defendant's signature

FOC 63 (10/04) **AGREEMENT SUSPENDING IMMEDIATE INCOME WITHHOLDING**

MCL 552.604

Approved, SCAO

STATE OF MICHIGAN JUDICIAL CIRCUIT COUNTY	ORDER SUSPENDING IMMEDIATE INCOME WITHHOLDING	CASE NO.

Friend of the Court address

Court telephone no.

Plaintiff's name and address

v

Defendant's name and address

1. Date of hearing: _____ Judge: _____

   Bar no.

2. **THE COURT FINDS:**

   ☐ There is good cause for the order of income withholding not to take effect immediately as follows:

   a. It is in the best interest of the child for immediate income withholding not to take effect for the following stated reasons:

   b. Proof of timely payment of previously ordered support has been provided.

   c. Both the payer and the recipient of support will notify the friend of the court in writing of any change in:
   1) the name, address, and telephone number of his/her current source of income;
   2) any health care coverage that is available to him/her as a benefit of employment or that is maintained by him/her, the name of the insurance company, health care organization, or health maintenance organization; the policy, certificate, or contract number; and the names and birth dates of the persons for whose benefit s/he maintains health care coverage under the policy, certificate, or contract; and
   3) his/her current residence, mailing address, and telephone number within 21 days of the change.

   ☐ The parties have entered into a written agreement that has been reviewed and entered in the record as follows:

   a. The order of income withholding shall not take effect immediately.

   b. An alternative payment arrangement has been agreed upon (attached).

   c. Both the payer and the recipient of support will notify the friend of the court in writing of any change in:
   1) the name, address, and telephone number of his/her current source of income;
   2) any health care coverage that is available to him/her as a benefit of employment or that is maintained by him/her, the name of the insurance company, health care organization, or health maintenance organization; the policy, certificate, or contract number; and the names and birth dates of the persons for whose benefit s/he maintains health care coverage under the policy, certificate, or contract; and
   3) his/her current residence, mailing address, and telephone number within 21 days of the change.

IT IS ORDERED:

3. Income withholding shall not take effect immediately.

4. Income withholding shall take effect if the fixed amount of arrearage is reached, as specified in law.

_____   _____
Date   Judge

FOC 64 (10/04) **ORDER SUSPENDING IMMEDIATE INCOME WITHHOLDING**   MCL 552.511, MCL 552.604, MCL 552.607

STATE OF MICHIGAN JUDICIAL CIRCUIT COUNTY	REQUEST TO REOPEN FRIEND OF THE COURT CASE	CASE NO.

Friend of the Court address   **Telephone no.**

Plaintiff's name and address		Defendant's name and address
	v	

Attorney: Attorney:

1. On _____ an order was entered exempting this case from friend of the court services.
   _{Date}

I REQUEST that the friend of the court case be reopened upon filing of this request with the friend of the court office. Attached is a completed Verified Statement and Application for IV-D Services.

_____   _____
Date   Signature

CERTIFICATE OF MAILING

I certify that on this date I mailed a copy of this request to the friend of the court and to other party by first class mail addressed to his/her last known address as defined in MCR 3.203.

_____   _____
Date   Signature

	Original - Court 1st copy - Plaintiff	2nd copy - Defendant 3rd copy - Friend of the Court

STATE OF MICHIGAN JUDICIAL CIRCUIT COUNTY	UNIFORM CHILD SUPPORT ORDER, NO FRIEND OF COURT SERVICES (PAGE 1) ☐ MODIFICATION	CASE NO.

Court address		FAX no.	Court telephone no.

Plaintiff's name, address, and telephone no.	v	Defendant's name, address, and telephone no.
Plaintiff's attorney name, address, telephone no., and bar no.		Defendant's atttorney name, address, telephone no., and bar no.
Plaintiff's source of income name, address, and telephone no.		Defendant's source of income name, address, and telephone no.

Unless otherwise ordered:

1. This order continues until each child is age 18 or graduates from high school, as provided by MCL 552.605b, whichever is later, but no longer than age 19 1/2. Child care for each child terminates effective September 1 following each child's 12th birthday.

2. **Support.** The payer has a monthly support obligation as follows:

Payer:	Payee:	Effective date:

Children's names and birth dates:

Children supported:	1 child	2 children	3 children	4 children	5 or more children
Base support:	$	$	$	$	$
Ordinary medical:	$	$	$	$	$
Child care:	$	$	$	$	$
Other:	$	$	$	$	$
Total:	$	$	$	$	$

☐ Base support shall abate 50% after 6 consecutive overnights with the payer
☐ Support was set based on the shared economic responsibility formula using _____ overnights of parenting time.
☐ Base support considers health care premiums of $_____ paid by plaintiff and $_____ paid by defendant.
The above ordered support provisions   ☐ do   ☐ do not   follow the child support formula.

4. **Insurance.** For the benefit of the children,   ☐ plaintiff   ☐ defendant   shall maintain health care coverage through an insurer [as defined in MCL 552.602(o)] that includes payment for hospital, dental, optical, and other medical expenses when that coverage is available through an employer or under an existing individual policy at the following reasonable cost:
☐ up to a maximum of $_____ for plaintiff.   ☐ up to a maximum of $_____ for defendant.
☐ not to exceed 5% of the plaintiff's/defendant's gross income.

5. **Uninsured Medical Expenses.** All uninsured health care expenses exceeding the ordinary medical amount will be paid _____% by the plaintiff and _____% by the defendant. Uninsured expenses exceeding the ordinary medical amount for the year they are incurred that are not paid within 28 days of a written payment request may be enforced by filing a motion with the court. The ordinary medical amount is $ _____ year.

(see Page 2 for remainder of order)

MCL 552.14, MCL 552.517, MCL 552.517b(3), MCR 3.211

FOC 10a / 52a   (9/04)   UNIFORM CHILD SUPPORT ORDER, NO FRIEND OF COURT SERVICES, PAGE 1

	Original - Court 1st copy - Plaintiff	2nd copy - Defendant 3rd copy - Friend of the Court

STATE OF MICHIGAN JUDICIAL CIRCUIT COUNTY	UNIFORM CHILD SUPPORT ORDER NO FRIEND OF COURT SERVICES (PAGE 2) ☐ MODIFICATION	CASE NO.

Court address		FAX no.	Court telephone no.

Plaintiff's name	v	Defendant's name

6. **Qualified Medical Support Order.** This order is a qualified medical support order under 29 USC 1169.

7. **Retroactive Modification, Surcharge for Past Due Support, and Liens for Unpaid Support.** Support is a judgment the date it is due and is not modifiable retroactively. Unpaid support is a lien by operation of law and the payer's property can be encumbered or seized if an arrearage accrues for more than the periodic support payments payable for two months under the payer's support order.

8. **Change of Address, Employment Status, Health Insurance.** Both parties shall notify each other in writing, within 21 days of any change in: a) their mailing or residence address and telephone number; b) the name, address, and telephone number of their sources of income; c) their health maintenance or insurance company, insurance coverage, persons insured, or contract number; d) their occupational or driver licenses; and e) their social security number unless exempt by law under MCL 552.603.

9. **Prior Orders.** Except as changed in this order, prior provisions remain in effect. Support payable under any prior order is preserved.

10. **Other: (attach separate sheets as needed)**

IT IS SO ORDERED.

_____   _____
Plaintiff (if consent/stipulation)   Date

_____   _____
Defendant (if consent/stipulation)   Date

_____   _____
Date

_____   _____
Judge   Bar no.

CERTIFICATE OF MAILING

I certify that on this date I served a copy of this order on the parties by first class mail addressed to their last known addresses as defined in MCR 3.203.

_____
Date

_____
Signature

MCL 552.14, MCL 552.517, MCL 552.517b(3), MCR 3.211

FOC 10a / 52a (9/04) **UNIFORM CHILD SUPPORT ORDER, NO FRIEND OF COURT SERVICES, PAGE 2**

Original - Return
1st copy - Witness
2nd copy - File
3rd copy - Extra

STATE OF MICHIGAN JUDICIAL DISTRICT JUDICIAL CIRCUIT COUNTY PROBATE	SUBPOENA Order to Appear and/or Produce	CASE NO.

Court address		Court telephone no.

Police Report No. (if applicable)

Plaintiff(s)/Petitioner(s) ☐ People of the State of Michigan ☐ _____	v	Defendant(s)/Respondent(s)
☐ Civil ☐ Criminal		Charge
☐ Probate In the matter of _____		

In the Name of the People of the State of Michigan.   TO:

If you require special accommodations to use the court because of disabilities, please contact the court immediately to make arrangements.

YOU ARE ORDERED:

☐ 1. to appear personally at the time and place stated below: You may be required to appear from time to time and day to day until excused.

☐ The court address above   ☐ Other:

Day	Date	Time

☐ 2. Testify at trial / examination / hearing.

☐ 3. Produce/permit inspection or copying of the following items:_____

_____

_____

☐ 4. Testify as to your assets, and bring with you the items listed in line 3 above.

☐ 5. Testify at deposition.

☐ 6. MCL 600.6104(2), 600.6116, or 600.6119 prohibition against transferring or disposing of property is attached.

☐ 7. Other: _____

☐ 8.

Person requesting subpoena	Telephone no.
Address	
City	State Zip

NOTE: If requesting a debtor's examination under MCL 600.6110, or an injunction under item 6. this subpoena must be issued by a judge. For a debtor examination, the affidavit of debtor examination on the other side of this form must also be completed. Debtor's assets can also be discovered through MCR 2.305 without the need for an affidavit of debtor examination or issuance of this subpoena by a judge.

FAILURE TO OBEY THE COMMANDS OF THE SUBPOENA OR APPEAR AT THE STATED TIME AND PLACE MAY SUBJECT YOU TO PENALTY FOR CONTEMPT OF COURT.

Court use only
☐ Served   ☐ Not served

_____   _____   _____
Date   Judge/Clerk/Attorney   Bar no.

MC 11 (6/04) **SUBPOENA, Order to Appear and/or Produce**   MCL 600.1455, 600.1701, 600.6110, 600.6119, MCR 2.506

TO PROCESS SERVER: You must make and file your return with the court clerk. If you are unable to complete service, you must return this original and all copies to the court clerk.

CERTIFICATE / AFFIDAVIT OF SERVICE / NON-SERVICE

☐ **OFFICER CERTIFICATE**	**OR**	☐ **AFFIDAVIT OF PROCESS SERVER**
I certify that I am a sheriff, deputy sheriff, bailiff, appointed court officer, or attorney for a party [MCR 2.104(A)(2)], and that: (notarization not required)		Being first duly sworn, I state that I am a legally competent adult who is not a party or an officer of a corporate party, and that: (notarization required)

☐ I served a copy of the subpoena, together with _____ (including any required fees) by
Attachment

☐ personal service ☐ registered or certified mail (copy of return receipt attached) on:

Name(s)	Complete address(es) of service	Day, date, time

☐ I have personally attempted to serve the subpoena and required fees, if any, together with _____
on the following person and have been unable to complete service.   Attachment

Name(s)	Complete address(es) of service	Day, date, time

Service fee	Miles traveled	Mileage fee	Total fee
$		$	$

Signature _____

Title _____

Subscribed and sworn to before me on _____ , _____ County, Michigan.
Date

My commission expires: _____ Signature: _____
Date   Deputy court clerk/Notary public

Notary public, State of Michigan, County of _____

ACKNOWLEDGMENT OF SERVICE

I acknowledge that I have received service of the subpoena and required fees, if any, together with _____
Attachment

_____ on _____
Day, date, time

_____ on behalf of _____ .

Signature

AFFIDAVIT FOR JUDGMENT DEBTOR EXAMINATION

I request that the court issue a subpoena which orders the party named on this form to be examined under oath before a judge concerning the money or property of:
for the following reasons:

_____

Signature

Subscribed and sworn to before me on _____ , _____ County, Michigan.
Date

My commission expires: _____ Signature: _____
Date   Deputy court clerk/Notary public

Notary public, State of Michigan, County of _____

MCR 2.105